Risk and protective factors in the development of psychopathology

Edited by
JON ROLF, ANN S. MASTEN,
DANTE CICCHETTI, KEITH H. NUECHTERLEIN,
and SHELDON WEINTRAUB

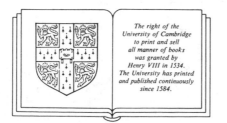

CAMBRIDGE UNIVERSITY PRESS

Cambridge
New York   Port Chester   Melbourne   Sydney

Published by the Press Syndicate of the University of Cambridge
The Pitt Building, Trumpington Street, Cambridge CB2 1RP
40 West 20th Street, New York, NY 10011, USA
10 Stamford Road, Oakleigh, Melbourne 3166, Australia

First published in 1990

Printed in the United States of America

Library of Congress Cataloging-in-Publication Data
Risk and protective factors in the development of psychopathology /
edited by Jon Rolf . . . [et al.].
p.   cm.
"This volume is a tribute to Norman Garmezy by students and
colleagues" – Pref.
Includes bibliographies and indexes.
ISBN 0-521-35099-9
1. Mental illness – Risk factors.   2. Child development
3. Adjustment (Psychology) in children.   4. Schizophrenia – Risk
factors.   I. Rolf, Jon E.   II. Garmezy, Norman.
[DNLM: 1. Adaptation, Psychological.   2. Child development
Disorders – psychology.   3. Psychopathology.   4. Risk Factors.
5. Schizophrenia – etiology.   WM 100 R595]
RC455.4.R56R57   1989
616.89′071 – dc20
DNLM/DLC
for Library of Congress   89-15807
                                                                  CIP

British Library Cataloguing in Publication Data
Risk and protective factors in the development of
psychopathology.
1. Medicine. Psychopathology
I. Rolf, Jon
616.89′07

ISBN 0-521-35099-9

Contents

v

Contributors

Thomas M. Achenbach
Department of Psychiatry
University of Vermont
Burlington, Vermont

Alfred L. Baldwin
Department of Psychology
University of Rochester
Rochester, New York

Clara Baldwin
Department of Psychology
University of Rochester
Rochester, New York

Jack Block
Board of Studies in Psychology
University of California, Berkeley
Berkeley, California

Deborah M. Capaldi
Oregon Social Learning Center
University of Oregon
Eugene, Oregon

Dante Cicchetti
Departments of Psychology and
    Psychiatry
Mt. Hope Family Center
University of Rochester
Rochester, New York

Robert E. Cole
Department of Psychology
University of Rochester
Rochester, New York

John J. Conger
School of Medicine
University of Colorado
Denver, Colorado

Regina Driscoll
Children's Hospital
St. Paul, Minnesota

Aaron T. Ebata
Department of Psychiatry and
    Behavioral Sciences
Stanford University School of
    Medicine
Stanford, California

Byron Egeland
Institute of Child Development
University of Minnesota
Minneapolis, Minnesota

Norman Garmezy
Department of Psychology
University of Minnesota
Minneapolis, Minnesota

Jane L. Gibbons
Department of Psychology
Harvard University
Cambridge, Massachusetts

Per F. Gjerde
Board of Studies in Psychology
University of California at Santa Cruz
Santa Cruz, California

Marion Glick
Department of Psychology
Yale University
New Haven, Connecticut

Michael J. Goldstein
Department of Psychology
University of California,
  Los Angeles
Los Angeles, California

Irving I. Gottesman
Department of Psychology
University of Virginia
Charlottesville, Virginia

Daniel R. Hanson
Department of Psychiatry
University of Minnesota
Minneapolis, Minnesota

Courtenay M. Harding
Department of Psychiatry
Yale University School of
  Medicine
New Haven, Connecticut

Leonard L. Heston
Department of Psychiatry
University of Minnesota
Minneapolis, Minnesota

Philip S. Holzman
Department of Psychology
Harvard University
Cambridge, Massachusettes

Debra M. Japzon
Department of Psychology
University of Denver
Denver, Colorado

Jeannette Johnson
Laboratory of Clinical Brain Studies
National Institute of Alcohol and Drug
  Abuse
Bethesda, Maryland

Maureen O. Johnson
Department of Psychology
Harvard University
Cambridge, Massachusettes

Jerome Kagan
Department of Psychology
Harvard University
Cambridge, Massachusettes

Gloria G. Keller
Department of Psychology
University of Denver
Denver, Colorado

Ann S. Masten
Institute of Child Development
University of Minnesota
Minneapolis, Minnesota

Olivia Moorehead-Slaughter
Judge Baker Children's Center
Children's Hospital
Harvard Medical School
Cambridge, Massachusetts

Patricia Morison
Department of Psychology
University of Minnesota
Minneapolis, Minnesota

Keith H. Nuechterlein
Department of Psychiatry and
  Biobehavioral Sciences
University of California,
  Los Angeles
Los Angeles, California

Margaret O'Dougherty
Department of Psychology
Ohio State University
Columbus, Ohio

Gerald R. Patterson
Oregon Social Learning Center
University of Oregon
Eugene, Oregon

David Pellegrini
Center for the Study of Youth
  Development
Catholic University
Washington, D.C.

Anne C. Petersen
Department of Human Development
  and Family Studies
Pennsylvania State University
University Park, Pennsylvania

Susan Phipps-Yonas
Minnesota Psychotherapy and
  Consultation Services
St. Paul, Minnesota

Robert C. Pianta
Curry Programs in Clinical and School
  Psychology
University of Virginia
Charlottesville, Virginia

Marian Radke-Yarrow
Laboratory of Developmental
  Psychology
National Institute of Mental Health
Bethesda, Maryland

J. Steven Reznick
Department of Psychology
Yale University
New Haven, Connecticut

John Richters
Child and Adolescent Disorders
  Research Branch
National Institute of Mental Health
Rockville, Maryland

Judith Rodin
Department of Psychology
Yale University
New Haven, Connecticut

Jon Rolf
Department of Maternal and Child
  Health
School of Hygiene and Public Health
Johns Hopkins University
Baltimore, Maryland

Michael Rutter
Department of Child and Adolescent
  Psychiatry
Institute of Psychiatry
Denmark Hill
London, England

Arnold J. Sameroff
Department of Psychiatry and Human
  Behavior
Brown University
E. P. Bradley Hospital
East Providence, Rhode Island

Ronald Seifer
Department of Psychiatry and Human
  Behavior
Brown University
E. P. Bradley Hospital
East Providence, Rhode Island

Tracy Sherman
Laboratory of Developmental
  Psychology
National Institute of Mental Health
Bethesda, Maryland

Lisa R. Silberstein
Department of Psychology
Yale University
New Haven, Connecticut

Nancy Snidman
Department of Psychology
Harvard University
Cambridge, Massachusetts

L. Alan Sroufe
Institute of Child Development
University of Minnesota
Minneapolis, Minnesota

John S. Strauss
Department of Psychiatry
Yale University School of
  Medicine
New Haven, Connecticut

Ruth H. Striegel-Moore
Department of Psychology
Wesleyan University
Middletown, Connecticut

Auke Tellegen
Department of Psychology
University of Minnesota
Minneapolis, Minnesota

Norman F. Watt
Department of Psychology
University of Denver
Denver, Colorado

Sheldon Weintraub
Department of Psychology
SUNY at Stony Brook
Stony Brook, New York

Francis S. Wright
Department of Pediatrics and Neurology
Ohio State University
Columbus, Ohio

Edward Zigler
Department of Psychology
Yale University
New Haven, Connecticut

Preface

This volume is a tribute to Norman Garmezy by students and colleagues he has influenced during four decades of research and teaching. Norm has been described as the Johnny Appleseed of American psychology, planting ideas around the world concerning risk, competence, and protective factors in the development of psychopathology. The fruits of his ideas and research are reflected in the diverse chapters of this volume, which span infancy to adult development.

Garmezy has had a profound influence on the direction of research in psychopathology, pioneering new areas of study throughout his career. One abiding interest has been understanding the roots of schizophrenia. Initially, he studied this serious disorder in adults (Garmezy, 1952a,b; Rodnick & Garmezy, 1957). The theme of competence, a hallmark of Norm's career, soon emerged as he and Elliott Rodnick studied the role of premorbid competence in schizophrenia (Garmezy, 1970a; Garmezy & Rodnick, 1959).

Norm's interest in the etiology of schizophrenia took a new turn in Minnesota as he, along with a cadre of students and other pioneering investigators, adopted the "risk" strategy for studying the development of schizophrenia (Garmezy, 1974a, 1976; Garmezy & Devine, 1984; Garmezy & Streitman, 1974). His influence in this area is evident in chapters in this volume written by students who trained with Norm during this period of focus, including Regina Driscoll, Keith H. Nuechterlein, Susan Phipps-Yonas, Jon Rolf, and Sheldon Weintraub, as well as chapters by colleagues in the risk consortium.

Once again the theme of competence quickly surfaced. Garmezy immediately recognized the significance of the large proportion of high-risk children who, often despite adverse rearing conditions, appeared to develop well. The ideas of invulnerability, stress resistance, and resilience soon took root in his thinking and research (Garmezy, 1970b, 1971, 1974b). Gradually, Garmezy and his students broadened their focus on successful adaptation despite risk to include psychosocially disadvantaged children (Garmezy & Nuechterlein, 1972), children exposed to stressful life events (Garmezy, 1981), and handicapped children (O'Dougherty, Wright, Garmezy, Loewenson, & Torres, 1983; Raison, 1982; Silverstein, 1982). Students from this later period of research who have contributed to this volume include Ann S. Masten, Patricia Morison, Margaret O'Dougherty, and David Pellegrini.

One legacy of the risk researchers, including Norm, is the boost they gave to the emergence of developmental psychopathology as an integrative, interdisciplinary framework for the study of psychopathology (Garmezy 1974c, 1977). The risk strategy inevitably yielded greater concern with longitudinal research designs, developmental patterns of behavior, and adaptation to stress, now viewed as fundamental to developmental psychopathology. Thomas M. Achenbach and Dante Cicchetti, both of whom were influenced by Garmezy in their training at Minnesota, set the stage in this volume by reviewing the history of this perspective and its potential for theory, research, and practice in psychology.

This volume is divided into five parts. Following the introductory chapters on developmental psychopathology, Part II focuses on early risks to development. The theme of Part III is competence under adversity, with emphasis on studies of school-aged children. The last two parts focus on adaptation in adolescence and adulthood, the latter part primarily dealing with the development of schizophrenia. In each part, the themes of Garmezy's career are evidenced: psychopathology and competence, risk and protective factors, vulnerability and resilience. To conclude the volume, we thought it most appropriate for Garmezy himself to close with his reflections on the future for research on risk and protective factors in developmental psychopathology.

Norman Garmezy's inspiration and generosity as a teacher and mentor led to this festschrift. His generativity as a colleague and catalyst for research in the field is honored by the contributions of his peers in the following pages.

The Editors

References

Garmezy, N. (1952a). Approach and avoidance behavior of schizophrenic and normal subjects as a function of reward and punishment. *American Psychologist, 7,* 334.

Garmezy, N. (1952b). Stimulus differentiation by schizophrenic and normal subjects under conditions of reward and punishment. *Journal of Personality, 20,* 253–76.

Garmezy, N. (1970a). Process and reactive schizophrenia: Some conceptions and issues. In M. Katz, J. Cole, & W. E. Barton (Eds.), *The role and methodology of classification in psychiatry and psychopathology* (pp. 419–66) (Department of Health, Education, and Welfare). Washington, DC: U.S. Government Printing Office. (Revised and reprinted in *Schizophrenia Bulletin, 1,* 30–74)

Garmezy, N. (1970b). Vulnerable children: Implications derived from studies on an internalizing–externalizing symptom dimension. In J. Zubin & Z. M. Freedman (Eds.), *Psychopathology of adolescence* (pp. 212–39). New York: Grune & Stratton.

Garmezy, N. (1971). Vulnerability research and the issue of primary prevention. *American Journal of Orthopsychiatry, 41,* 101–16.

Garmezy, N. (1974a). Children at risk: The search for the antecedents to schizophrenia: Part II. Ongoing research programs, issues and intervention. *Schizophrenia Bulletin, 9,* 55–125.

Garmezy, N. (1974b). The study of competence in children at risk for severe psychopathology. In E. J. Anthony & C. Koupernick (Eds.), *The child in his family: Children at psychiatric risk* (Vol. 3, pp. 77–98). New York: Wiley.

Garmezy, N. (1974c). *The study of children at risk: New perspectives for developmental psychopathology.* Distinguished Scientist Award Presentation, Section III, Division 12, APA.

Garmezy, N. (1976). The experimental study of children vulnerable to psychopathology. In A. Davids (Ed.), *Child personality and psychopathology* (Vol. 2, pp. 171–216). New York: Wiley.

Garmezy, N. (1977). The role of an emergent developmental psychopathology in the study of vulnerability to psychosis. In B. Brown (Ed.), *The study of vulnerability to psychosis.* Washington, DC: U.S. Government Printing Office.

Garmezy, N. (1981). Children under stress: Perspectives on antecedents and correlates of vulnerability and resistance to psychopathology. In A. I. Rabin, J. Aronoff, A. M. Barclay, & R. A. Zucker (Eds.), *Further explorations in personality* (pp. 196–269). New York: Wiley.

Garmezy, N., & Devine, V. T. (1984). Project Competence: The Minnesota studies of children vulnerable to psychopathology. In N. Watt, J. Rolf, L. C. Wynne, & E. J. Anthony (Eds.), *Children at risk for schizophrenia* (pp. 289–303). Cambridge University Press.

Garmezy, N., & Nuechterlein, K. (1972). Invulnerable children: The fact and fiction of competence and disadvantage. *American Journal of Orthopsychiatry, 42,* 328–9 (abstract).

Garmezy, N., & Rodnick, E. H. (1959). Premorbid adjustment and performance in schizophrenia: Implications of interpreting heterogeneity in schizophrenia. *Journal of Nervous and Mental Disease, 129,* 450–66.

Garmezy, N., & Streitman, S. (1974). Children at risk: The search for the antecedents of schizophrenia. Part I. Conceptual models and research methods. *Schizophrenia Bulletin, 8,* 14–90.

O'Dougherty, M., Wright, F. S., Garmezy, N., Loewenson, R. B., & Torres, F. (1983). Later competence and adaptation in infants who survive heart defects. *Child Development, 54,* 1129–42.

Raison, S. B. (1982). *Coping behavior of mainstreamed physically handicapped students.* Unpublished doctoral dissertation, University of Minnesota.

Rodnick, E. H., & Garmezy, N. (1957). An experimental approach to the study of motivation in schizophrenia. In M. R. Jones (Ed.), *Nebraska Symposium on Motivation* (pp. 109–84). Lincoln: University of Nebraska Press.

Silverstein, P. R. (1982). *Coping and adaptation in families of physically handicapped school children.* Unpublished doctoral dissertation, University of Minnesota.

Part I

Introduction: Historical and theoretical roots of developmental psychopathology

Dante Cicchetti and Thomas M. Achenbach set the stage for this volume in these first two chapters by examining the historical and theoretical underpinnings of developmental psychopathology. Cicchetti traces the roots of this new discipline in three theories of development, each of which was influenced by Western philosophy and embryology: Freudian psychoanalytic theory, Wernerian organismic theory, and Piagetian structural theory. Cicchetti illustrates how, in diverse disciplines, the study of atypical or pathological populations has served to enrich and confirm the understanding of normal development, particularly in regard to the hierarchically integrated and dynamic nature of development. More recently, a developmental approach to pathological or atypical populations is leading to exciting advances in our knowledge of normal development as well as abnormal development.

Achenbach examines in detail the potential of the developmental perspective as a framework for organizing research on psychopathology and stimulating integrative theory, as well as for improving our assessment and intervention efforts with children at risk for or already manifesting psychological problems. The implications of this perspective for training in different disciplines are also explored, with Achenbach suggesting core areas of training for professionals who share a common concern about psychopathology whether they are students of nursing, pediatrics, psychiatry, clinical psychology, human development, education, or social work.

1   A historical perspective on the discipline of developmental psychopathology

Dante Cicchetti

One way of measuring the success of a new scientific discipline is to examine its impact on the current literature. The recent increase in the number of books, articles, and journals dealing with developmental psychopathology reflects a growing recognition of the significance of this discipline within the behavioral sciences. For example, several journals, including the *American Journal of Psychiatry, The Journal of Consulting and Clinical Psychology,* and *The Journal of the American Academy of Child and Adolescent Psychiatry,* have published special sections on the topic. Moreover, three journals have devoted one or more special issues to the field of developmental psychopathology – *Child Development* (Cicchetti, 1984b), *The Journal of Child Psychology and Psychiatry* (Stevenson, 1985), and *New Directions for Child Development* (Cicchetti & Beeghly, 1987; Cicchetti & Schneider-Rosen, 1984a; Nannis & Cowan, 1988; Rizley & Cicchetti, 1981; Selman & Yando, 1980; Tronick & Field, 1986). Furthermore, the most recent edition of the *Handbook of Child Psychology* (Mussen, 1983) contained the first chapter on the topic of developmental psychopathology (Rutter & Garmezy, 1983) since the publication of its first edition over 40 years ago. In addition, textbooks, handbooks, and scholarly references are appearing increasingly in the literature (Achenbach, 1974/1982; Cicchetti & Beeghly, 1990; Cicchetti & Carlson, 1989; Gollin, 1984; Lewis & Miller, in press; Rutter, Izard, & Read, 1986; Santostefano, 1978; Trad, 1986, 1987; Wenar, 1982; Zigler & Glick, 1986). Moreover, there is now a journal devoted

The writing of this manuscript was supported by grants from the John D. and Catherine T. MacArthur Foundation Network on Early Childhood, the Foundation for Child Development Young Scholars Program, and the National Institute of Mental Health (R01-MH-37960). In addition, I would like to extend my appreciation to Jennifer White for providing me with important critical feedback on this manuscript. Moreover, I would like to thank Sara Campbell, Joia DiStefano, and Victoria Gill for typing it. Finally, I would like to dedicate this chapter to Norman Garmezy. As a teacher, mentor, and friend, he has been a continued source of inspiration to me. Without his guidance and example, I would not have chosen to become a developmental psychopathologist. For that, and for many other things known to him, I give my sincerest affection and gratitude.

2

exclusively to the discipline of developmental psychopathology, entitled *Development and Psychopathology.*

Although it has been only during the past two decades that developmental psychopathology has crystallized as a new interdisciplinary science with its own integrity, it nonetheless has historical roots within a variety of areas and disciplines. An exploration of the ways in which the study of psychopathology and the study of development have been intertwined historically is the focus of this chapter. Such an undertaking will yield valuable insights into the contemporary state of the developmental psychopathology discipline, as well as serve as a basis for further direction and guidance of its future.

Organismic theories of development: historical underpinnings

Whereas the concept of development as qualitative change over time was hardly fathomable in 1800, by midcentury it had blossomed into a major viewpoint (Hofstadter, 1955; Nisbet, 1969). In particular, Herbert Spencer's (1862/1900, 1864/1896) "developmental hypothesis" or "doctrine of evolution" had a predominant influence on the social and scientific ideologies of the late nineteenth and early twentieth centuries. Spencer depicted development as a uniform process that was governed by universal laws and principles.

Three major developmental theories predominated within the behavioral sciences before the 1970s. These included the Wernerian organismic developmental theory, the psychoanalytic developmental theory, and the Piagetian structural developmental theory. All of these theories are rooted in an "organismic," rather than a "mechanistic," conceptualization of development (Overton, 1984; Reese & Overton, 1970). An organismic model of development stresses the dynamic role of the individual and depicts the individual as an organized whole. Principles of behavior are seen in terms of the organization among parts and wholes and of the dynamic relationship between the individual and the environment. In contrast, a mechanistic model of development views the individual as a passive, reactive organism. All activity results from forces that act on the individual in predictable ways (Overton, 1976; Santostefano, 1978).

It is interesting to note that every one of these ideas that are central to the organismic model of development can be identified in the very beginnings of Western thought – in the writings of Plato and Aristotle (Kaplan, 1967). The notion of the role of integration of multiple domains of behavior for the harmonious functioning of the individual was anticipated by the Platonic conception of the triune character of the soul. In Plato, one also can find the idea of hierarchically integrated domains of functioning within his conceptualization of the dominance of reason (a higher function) over passion (a lower function). Moreover, in Plato's view of the dynamic role of the individual one discovers another historical root of the organismic perspective.

Likewise, Aristotle was one of the first to argue that individuation, differentiation, and self-actualization were the characteristic aspects of developmental transformations (Kaplan, 1967, 1983). Aristotle also stressed the interdependence between the environment and the individual. A believer in the concept of the multiple determination of behavior, Aristotle argued that different levels of behavioral organization existed in humans. Moreover, one also can find in Aristotle an emphasis on a holistic understanding of behavior – the part must be viewed in relation to the whole in order to understand its true meaning. Although neither Aristotle nor Plato focused on the interrelation between these ideas and the psychopathological condition, nonetheless they built a potent theoretical foundation for the discipline of developmental psychopathology.

The fact that the systematization of the organismic model of development was aided greatly by work within embryology (Cairns, 1983; Sameroff, 1983) underscores an important theme within the developmental psychopathology discipline – namely, the way that advances in our knowledge of development and within particular scientific disciplines can mutually inform each other. The work of embryologists since the nineteenth century has provided a rich empirical foundation for the emergence of organismic theories of development of great significance for understanding human behavior (Spemann, 1938; von Baer, 1828/1837; Waddington, 1957; Weiss, 1969b). From their efforts to learn about normal embryological functioning, early embryologists derived the principles of a dynamically active organism and of a hierarchically integrated system that were later used in investigations of the processes of abnormal development within the neurosciences, embryology, and experimental psychopathology.

For example, a key question for embryologists has been how to understand the way in which somatic cells with similar genetic codes develop toward increasing differentiation in functioning. The discovery by Hans Spemann (1938) that cellular tissues could be successfully transplanted from one functional area to another marked the development of an important contribution to an understanding of the dynamic aspects of the developmental process in general. In his research, Spemann was able to transplant the neural plate of amphibia into an area specialized for limb growth and found that the transplanted tissue took on the characteristics of skin and muscle, rather than the characteristics of neural tissue from which it had originated. From this, Spemann put forth the idea that contextual forces can serve to "organize" cellular development. In this view, biological development was seen as being directed by the interactions among the various elements of a developmental system. The basic elements of such systems depended on the whole system for their meaning, and at the same time their mutual regulation permitted self-regulation.

The work of Kuo (1939) further exemplifies the valuable theoretical contributions of embryologists to developmental psychopathology. For example, in studies of the embryological development of chicks, Kuo (1939) showed the

importance of the developing organism's behavioral feedback on its development, thereby underscoring the significance of acknowledging the dynamic
quality of behavior within development. In a later summary of his approach,
Kuo (1967, p. 25) wrote the following:

The study of behavior is a synthetic science. It includes comparative anatomy, comparative embryology, comparative physiology (in the biophysical and biochemical sense),
experimental morphology, and the qualitative and quantitative analysis of the dynamic
relationships between the organism and the external physical and social environment.

Kuo further states that one of the major goals to accomplish in this venture is
to obtain a comprehensive understanding of the behavioral repertoire of the
organism and to ascertain the causal factors that occur from stage to stage
during ontogenesis. Kuo's aims bear a striking resemblance to the goal of
developmental psychopathologists to achieve a multidomain, interdisciplinary
study of psychopathological and normal development.

A similar emphasis on a holistic, dynamically functioning entity defined by
its environmental interactions is found in the work of later organismic theorists such as Werner (1948) and Piaget (1952). In particular, the significance of
the work of the embryologist Paul Weiss (1969b) for the organismic developmental theorist Werner and that of the embryologist C. H. Waddington (1957)
for Piaget has been noted previously (Sameroff, 1983). In fact, it is possible to
see in the embryological studies the underlying basis for Werner's orthogenetic principle "that wherever development occurs it proceeds from a state
of relative globality and lack of differentiation to a state of increasing differentiation, integration, articulation, and hierarchic integration" (1957, p. 26).
There is no doubt that the study of embryology proved to be highly significant
for the demonstration and the emergence of the developmental principles of
differentiation, hierarchical organization, and dynamic environmental transac-
tion (Fishbein, 1976; Nowakowski, 1987).

Moreover, within the beginnings of the discipline of neuroembryology it is
possible to find the foundation for the principle of hierarchical integration
(Hamburger, 1980). The late 1880s were dominated by the reticular theory
that envisioned the nervous system as a syncytial network of nerve fibers that
were continuous with each other and in which the cell bodies were seen as
trophic elements, as points of intersection. Such a conceptualization of the
nervous system prevented delineation of specific pathways and connections,
which are the necessary prerequisites of integrated function. The demonstration by the Spanish neurologist Santiago Ramon y Cajal that the nerve fibers
have terminal structures that contact with other nerve cells but do not fuse
with them – that they are contiguous rather than continuous – provided the
empirical basis for a hierarchically integrated nervous system (Cajal, 1893,
1937). Moreover, this demonstration was made possible by Cajal's use of
embryos to study the developing nervous system, a method that Cajal (1937,

p. 324) defended in the following terms: "Since the full grown forest turns out to be impenetrable and indefinable, why not revert to the study of the young wood, in the nursery stage, as we might say?"

Cajal's work illustrates the importance of a developmental approach to the understanding of a system, in this case, the nervous system. Moreover, the structural discoveries made possible by such a method can be seen as contributing further to an understanding of the major developmental principle of hierarchical integration. The strong dynamic orientation of Cajal's neuronal theory also made him an important precursor of the organismic perspective.

Although the developmental theories of Freud, Werner, and Piaget all stem from a common organismic tradition, there are many important differences among them, and these have been well chronicled (Baldwin, 1980). Most important for our purposes here, psychoanalytic theory focused largely on the emotions, whereas the structural developmental theories of Piaget and Werner stressed cognition (Cicchetti & Hesse, 1983; Cicchetti & Pogge-Hesse, 1981). In part as a consequence of their relative emphasis, psychoanalytic theory was influential primarily among clinicians in psychology and psychiatry, while the Piagetian and Wernerian organismic developmental theories had a dramatic impact on researchers.

The interrelation between abnormal and normal functioning

The study of pathological populations enabled researchers working within all three developmental traditions to confirm and to expand the developmental principles on which their theories were based. For example, Werner (1948, p. 23) stated: "A whole series of mental diseases are important to developmental psychology in that they represent the regression, the dissolution, of the higher mental processes, or inhibitions of the genetically advanced levels." Furthermore, Werner (1948, pp. 33–4) believed that "psychopathology will shed light on the genetic data of other developmental fields . . . the results of psychopathology . . . become valuable in many ways for the general picture of mental development, just as psychopathology is itself enriched and its methods facilitated by the adoption of the genetic approach."

In their recognition of the importance of the abnormal for confirmation of the normal, these researchers were borrowing from a well-established tradition. Historically, numerous eminent scientists, theoreticians, and clinicians have adopted the premise that studies of normal development and abnormal development can be mutually informative. William James (1902, 1917, 1920) emphasized the significance that an understanding of abnormal mental functioning could have for our understanding of human nature. Goethe viewed psychopathology as resulting from "regressive metamorphoses" and stressed the intimate connection between abnormal and normal functioning. According to Goethe, the study of pathology allowed one to see, magnified, the normal processes of development and functioning. In the ideas of Goethe on the nature of psychopathology it is possible to find a primary influence on Freud, Werner, and Goldstein (Kaplan, 1967).

The principle of the interrelatedness of abnormal and normal functioning finds perhaps its clearest expression in the work of Sigmund Freud (1927/ 1955a, 1937/1955b, 1940/1955c, 1940/1955d), who indeed drew no sharp distinction between normal and abnormal functioning. Freud's emphasis on the prime importance of the irrational highlighted the close connection between the normal and the abnormal. As Freud's ideas gradually permeated the substance of psychology proper, his thesis that there was a normality–abnormality continuum met with increasingly wide acceptance.

Furthermore, prominent workers in the biological sciences also have long recognized the interrelations between the normal and abnormal. In *The Expression of the Emotions in Man and the Animals* (1872/1965), Darwin paid much attention to the facial expressions of the insane and the mentally retarded. Through his keen observations, Darwin raised many questions about the nature of the interrelations among cognition, affect, and biology. Many of his assertions were crystallized not only by his knowledge of people who were emotionally and/or cognitively disturbed but also by his work with people from different cultures. Indeed, research in the area of developmental psychopathology is necessary for the same reasons that cross-cultural research is essential. Both kinds of studies can tell us what development sequences are logically necessary and what alternate pathways of development are possible, as well as provide evidence on which factors accounting for normal growth are most important (e.g., biological, genetic/biochemical, socioemotional, cognitive, linguistic/representational).

The importance of studying atypical, pathological, and psychopathological populations for understanding normal development

Working within diverse disciplines, including embryology, the neurosciences, clinical and experimental psychology and psychiatry, researchers have utilized atypical, pathological, and psychopathological populations to elucidate, expand, and affirm further the basic underlying principles of their developmental theories. In the following sections, we provide illustrations of these efforts within a variety of different disciplines.

Embryology

Paul Weiss (1961, 1969a,b), an embryologist whose work greatly influenced Werner, defined development as a hierarchic systems operation and showed quite clearly that the study of pathological embryos could inform us greatly about normal embryogenesis. In an important paper entitled "Deformities as Cues to Understanding Development of Form," Weiss (1961, p. 50) stated his viewpoint on the interrelation between normality and pathology: "Pathology and developmental biology must be reintegrated so that our understanding of the 'abnormal' will become but an extension of our insight into the 'normal,' while . . . the study of the 'abnormal' will contribute to the deepening of that very insight." The similarities between Weiss's reasoning and that of contemporary developmental psychopathologists are striking. In addition, as Nowakowski (1987) has pointed out, there is considerable variability in neurogenesis. Furthermore, it is conceivable that this variability may be related to the emergence of several developmental psychopathologies, including schizophrenia (Kovelman & Scheibel, 1983) and dyslexia (Kemper, 1984; Sherman, Galaburda, & Geschwind, 1985).

Neurosciences

Although studies of pathological embryogenesis helped to confirm the significance of the principle of hierarchical integration, studies conducted in the neurosciences have provided even stronger evidence in support of the principle of hierarchical integration. In fact, workers within the field of the neurosciences have a long history of demonstrating the importance of pathology to the elucidation of the nature of normal developmental processes and principles.

John Hughlings Jackson's study (1884/1958) of neurological conditions (e.g., epilepsy and hemiplegia) advanced our understanding of developmental processes, in particular regarding the principle of hierarchical integration. By examining the way in which various disease processes interfered with the passage of information between higher nervous centers and consequently decreased the control over lower centers, Jackson (1884/1958) provided firm support for the idea of a nervous system that developed in accordance with the principle of hierarchical integration; see Sulkowski (1983) for a modern-day perspective on the implications for schizophrenia of a Jacksonian approach.

Based on his study of clinical neurological populations, Jackson formulated a conceptualization of development that entailed a change from levels of simplicity and automaticity toward levels characterized by greater complexity, flexibility, and voluntary control. Jackson argued that the more recent phylogenetic centers were more highly evolved than the older centers and that these more recent centers involved the greatest organizational complexity and were most subject to voluntary, rather than automatic, control.

Furthermore, Jackson's work with neurologically diseased patients provided the confirmation of the knowledge of a hierarchically organized model of normal nervous system functioning on which Bronson (1965) could further elaborate (Luria, 1966/1980). Bronson (1965) likewise proposed a hierarchically organized model of the central nervous system and speculated on the implications of such an organization for the ontogenesis of learning processes and critical periods in early development. Subsequently, Bronson (1974) proposed a similar model to account for the postnatal growth of human visual capacity. In both of these depictions, Bronson argued that the phylogenetically older brain structures matured first and were more differentiated at birth than the most recently evolved center and that their functions were subordinated to and inhibited by these new, higher centers during the course of normal ontogenesis. Moreover, a summary of the evidence integrating the data on patterns of myelinization during neural growth (Yakovlev & Lecours, 1967), histological developments within the neocortex (Conel, 1937–67), and the growth of evoked potentials (Desmedt, 1977) strongly suggests that Bronson's ideas are plausible.

In fact, virtually every prominent developmental theorist over the course of the twentieth century has espoused similar beliefs about the importance of hierarchical integration (Baldwin, 1894, 1906; Bruner, 1970; Fischer, 1980; Kaplan, 1966; Piaget, 1971; Spencer, 1862/1900, 1864/1896; Sroufe, 1979a,b; Waddington, 1957; Werner, 1948; White, 1965). For example, Spencer conceived of the developmental process as one of integration of successively higher stages that occurred in an invariant sequence. Spencer likewise considered these stages to be hierarchical while coexisting in time. Because an organism's early structures are not lost in development via hierarchical integration, the organism can maintain feelings of integrity and continuity in the face of change so rapid that it might otherwise cause problems for the sense of internal continuity (Spencer, 1862/1900, 1864/1896), an idea that has been pursued further by current developmental thinkers (Block & Block, 1980; Cicchetti & Schneider-Rosen, 1986; Kagan & Brim, 1980; Sackett, Sameroff, Cairns, & Suomi, 1981; Sroufe, 1979a) and that has figured significantly among developmental psychopathologists (Cicchetti & Schneider-Rosen, 1986; Garmezy, 1974b; Sroufe & Rutter, 1984).

Additional empirical contributions to knowledge of the developmental processes of differentiation and integration may be traced to the discipline of clinical neurology. In the late 1940s, Seyfarth and Denny-Brown (1948) and Denny-Brown, Twitchell, and Saenz-Arroyo (1949), while working with patients with a variety of neurological disorders, identified three discrete types of grasp responses. Twitchell (1951), in his investigations of hemiplegic patients, discovered these exact types of grasp responses and found that they always appeared in the same sequence in the course of complete recovery – from the more primitive undifferentiated response to the more advanced, differentiated response. In later work on motor skill acquisition in human infancy, Twitchell (1970) demonstrated the exact sequence in the voluntary control of grasping in infants that he had found in clinical neurology patients recovering from hemiplegia. Twitchell (1970) later theorized that these three different grasping responses were mediated at different levels of integration of the brain. Specifically, he hypothesized that the simplest motor response was integrated at the level of the brain stem, that the mechanisms of the intermediately complex motor responses were integrated at the subcortical level, and that the most advanced grasp reaction was integrated at the cortical level. Furthermore, Jolly (1972), in a review of the evolution of motoric grasping from the prosimians through the New and Old World monkeys to humans, found evidence for the same ontogenetic sequence as that noted by Twitchell in his study of neurologically impaired patients.

Moreover, the degenerative processes underlying dementia have provided another example of the importance of pathological processes for elucidating the hierarchically integrated nature of development. For example, when cortical layers of the brain are destroyed by disease during senescence, as in the case of senile dementia, the most primitive fetal and neonatal reflexes reappear (e.g., rooting, sucking, and grasping) (Paulson & Gottlieb, 1968).

Another example of the importance of developmental disturbances for confirming the hierarchically integrated nature of development comes from studies of disturbed fetal development. For example, during fetal development, anoxia or asphyxia will cause the more recently developed secondary reflexes to disappear, bringing about the reappearance of the earlier-developed primary reflexes (Humphrey, 1953). It appears that what occurs in this instance is that the more newly evolutionarily evolved higher motor centers are destroyed first. Consequently, the behavior of the fetus is reduced to an earlier stage of functioning in which only the phylogenetically older motor neurons are functional.

Likewise, the psychobiologists Teitelbaum, Cheng, and Rozin (1969) have demonstrated that we can learn about the functioning of the normal nervous system by observing how it puts itself back together after disturbances. For example, Teitelbaum and colleagues (1969; Teitelbaum, 1971) have demonstrated that the recovery of functions in rats, such as feeding and drinking, following lesions to the areas of the brain that play relevant roles in these activities (i.e., the lateral hypothalamus) display the same ordering as in the development of these functions in normal rats. The results of these studies provide strong empirical evidence in support of the principle of hierarchical integration in development.

Clinical and experimental psychology and psychiatry

Kurt Goldstein (1939, 1940, 1943, 1948) consistently stated that the study of pathological processes was essential to an understanding of normal ontogenesis and personality functioning. He strove to investigate the organism in its *entirety* and to uncover the transformations of the total personality following perturbations in normal functioning. Goldstein eschewed focusing on unitary aspects or domains of behavior in his experiments in the area of psychopathology (e.g., patients with organic brain lesions and schizophrenics). In his words, "the testing of single capacities, no matter how minutely examined, yields more or less piece-meal material of rather peripheral significance . . . to know the change of reaction time, attention span, or retention, etc., in itself does not help us gain an understanding of the essential personality change in the patient" (Goldstein, 1943, p. 262). By virtue of his emphasis on examining multiple aspects of functioning, Goldstein may be viewed as a forerunner of the "organizational" perspective on normal and abnormal development (Cicchetti & Pogge-Hesse, 1982; Cicchetti & Schneider-Rosen, 1984a, 1986; Cicchetti & Sroufe, 1978; Sroufe & Rutter, 1984; Sroufe & Waters, 1976).

One can see a similar approach in the work of David Shakow (1946, 1962, 1963, 1968, 1972). Through his brilliant experiments on attention, perception, audition, motor function, and aspiration level in schizophrenia, Shakow's work offered significant insights about the nature of normal psychological functioning – most notably on the interaction between affect and cognition in normal development. Moreover, Shakow contributed greatly to our understanding of schizophrenic disorganization. As Shakow contended, "in schizophrenia one sees a distinct weakening of the control center that serves the integrating, organizing function and provides the base for the establishment of . . . 'generalized' or 'major' sets in the normal person" (1968, p. 188). In his elucidation of normal developmental processes through careful study of schizophrenic disintegration, Shakow is an important precursor to developmental psychopathological thought.

What makes the results described in the previous sections so compelling is that similar phenomena were observed and drawn from diverse areas and disciplines (e.g., clinical neurology, embryology, neurosciences, psychology, and psychiatry). In addition to the support provided for the principle of hierarchical integration, the results of the foregoing studies illustrate other related developmental principles: (a) There are changes in structure–function relationships over time. (b) The changes that occur are both qualitative and quantitative. (c) The changes can best be characterized by Werner's orthogenetic principle (e.g., from globality and undifferentiation to increasing articulation, differentiation, organization, and hierarchical integration). (d) Those developmental changes may best be conceived as a move toward increasing cephalic control over the more diffuse, automatic behavior centers (cf. Sherrington, 1906 – a major forerunner of and influence on modern-day developmental psychobiology – and Stelzner, 1986). Furthermore, the examples presented in the last section have shown that work with a diversity of clinical populations conducted by scientists from a variety of disciplines can challenge, affirm, and expand on the regulative principles underlying organismic and biodevelopmental frameworks.

The importance of the developmental approach to atypical and psychopathological development

The theories and studies of the kind sketched in the last section provide developmental psychopathologists with clear models of scientific rigor worthy of emulation by contemporary researchers and theoreticians in their efforts to learn about normal development from abnormal development, while applying their improved knowledge about normal development to the study of psychopathology.

Concurrently, clinical theorists were using developmental theory to better understand psychopathology in children and adults. For the most part, these efforts were guided by the psychoanalytical theory of development. Previously, before the 1970s, very little interaction occurred between researchers and clinicians. Consequently, the Wernerian and Piagetian developmental theories that figured so importantly among researchers and academicians had minimal impact on clinicians (Anthony, 1956; Santostefano, 1978). Moreover, very few academics conducted clinical research, which perpetuated the split between the academic and the clinical branches of psychology. However, as the work reviewed in the following section illustrates, although the majority of developmental approaches to psychopathological and atypical populations were psychoanalytic, a few examples of developmental approaches also can be found within the structuralist and the organismic developmental traditions.

Illustrations of psychoanalytic developmental approaches to psychopathology

Bowlby (1951, 1961, 1969/1982, 1979) argued that maternal deprivation and problematic mother–child relationships during early childhood lie at the root of later psychopathology (Spitz, 1965). Bowlby (1961) traced the conception of the child's response to object loss, which proceeds through successive stages of protest, despair, and detachment. In his concept of "representational models," Bowlby (1969/1982) attempted to formulate a developmental mechanism to explain the connection between early life events and later behavior. In his search for earlier factors (such as maternal deprivation) in the onset of later psychopathology (such as juvenile delinquency), Bowlby (1944, 1979) can be seen as an important contributor to the roots of developmental psychopathology theory (Sroufe, 1986). Likewise, in his interest in connecting the work of ethologists such as Lorenz (1950) and experimental psychologists such as Harlow and Zimmerman (1959), Bowlby is a forerunner of the developmental psychopathologist's emphasis on a multidisciplinary, multidomain approach.

Mahler's well-known work (1952) on infantile psychopathology derives directly from analytical developmental theory. Mahler attributed infantile autism to a developmental arrest in ego functioning. For example, symbiotic infantile psychosis is marked by failure of the early mother–infant symbiotic relationship to progress to the stage of object-libidinal cathexis of the mother. According to Mahler (1952), the mental representation of the mother remains regressively fused with the self, leading to the delusion of omnipotence on the part of the child. Mahler (1952) noted that the developmental arrest can be seen as a fearful response provoked by the challenge to dependence on the mother inherent in the developmental transition in the third or fourth year toward ego differentiation and psychosexual development. Mahler argued that when separation anxiety overwhelms the fragile ego, the child creates the delusion of oneness with the primary caretaker that is further accompanied by somatic delusions and hallucinations of reunion.

In her classic work *Normality and Pathology in Childhood* (1965), Anna Freud outlined a developmental approach to child psychopathology based on psychoanalytic theory (A. Freud, 1974, 1976). Arguing against a symptomatological diagnostic system, she advocated instead an assessment of psychopathology in children based on their ability to perform age-appropriate tasks. "This implies redirecting . . . attention from the symptomatology of the patient to . . . whether the child under examination has reached developmental levels which are adequate for his age, whether and in what respects he has either gone beyond or remained behind them." To this end, Anna Freud called for a "scheme of average developmental norms" on which assessments of psychopathology could be more accurately made. She pointed out that a particular symptom such as a temper tantrum could have, in fact, many underlying causes and that it was more important to understand these mechanisms than to describe the symptom itself.

Based on psychoanalytic theory, Anna Freud (1965) set forth the notion of "developmental lines" along which children's development would be normally expected to proceed. By mastering tasks within the realms of object relations (e.g., the internalization of norms), children progressed from emotional dependency to emotional self-reliance and from egocentricity to companionship. A knowledge of normal development allowed distinctions to be made between normal, age-appropriate behavior and abnormal activity. For example, certain problems such as lying or stealing would not be regarded as symptoms in very young children who were not capable of distinguishing cognitively between lying and fantasy. In this developmental framework, deviations from the norm were due primarily to the processes of regression, arrest, or developmental delay.

Anna Freud also argued that there was not necessarily continuity between early and later psychopathology. In her words, "there is no certainty that a particular type of infantile neurosis will prove to be the forerunner of the same type of adult neurosis" (1965, p. 151). In addition, she observed that children's development within different spheres (e.g., emotional, cognitive, and motor) could progress at different rates.

Illustrations of organismic developmental approaches to psychopathology

Heinz Werner (1948, 1957; Werner & Kaplan, 1963) formulated a grand theoretical structure that called for a broad-band approach to the study of human behavior. By studying different cultures, diverse patient populations, and drug-induced and hypnagogic states, Werner magnificently illustrated the significance of general experimental and developmental psychology for understanding abnormal behavior and its treatment and prevention. In the context of an organismic developmental model, Kaplan (1966) examined language and symbolic functioning in psychiatric patients. In an important paper, Kaplan (1966) elucidated the parallels between earlier levels of symbolic functioning and those found in psychiatric patients. Kaplan (1966) argued that in various forms of psychopathology, typical patterns of symbolic and language functioning (e.g., loss of ideality, and the tendency to concretize the abstract and to confuse the symbol and the referent) could be explained by the principle of disintegration. In contrast to normal development, in which increasing differentiation and hierarchical integration of functioning are characteristic, in the symbolic and linguistic functioning of schizophrenics, disintegration and dedifferentiation occur. By applying the principles of organismic developmental theory (which themselves were affirmed by studies of pathological populations) to psychiatric patients, Kaplan (1966) was able to achieve insights into important cognitive aspects of schizophrenia that might not have been possible otherwise.

Over the course of the past several years, the Werner-Kaplan (1963) perspective on symbol formation has continued to exert a powerful impact on the understanding of developmental organization in atypical populations. Conversely, research conducted with these clinical populations provides continued corroborative evidence of the Werner-Kaplan (1963) framework; see the chapters in Cicchetti and Beeghly (1987) for examples.

Historically, the phenomena of dedifferentiation and disintegration have been noted as characteristic of psychopathology by a number of psychiatric researchers and clinicians embracing an organismic developmental perspective; see, for example, the work of Goldstein (1939, 1948) on abstract thinking in schizophrenic and brain-damaged patients, Shakow (1946, 1962) on the nature of deterioration in schizophrenic conditions, Rapaport (1951) on the organization and pathology of thought, Arieti (1955) on schizophrenic logic and thought, Searles (1959a,b) on depicting schizophrenia as a malfunctioning of integration-differentiation (Bleuler, 1911/1950; Kraepelin, 1919/1971; Sullivan, 1956), McGhie and Chapman (1961) on disorders of attention and perception in schizophrenia, and Arieti (1967) on the relation between emotion and cognition in normal and pathological development.

In *The Intrapsychic Self,* by Arieti (1967), one finds a compelling example of the way in which the conceptualization of pathology as a process of disintegration and dedifferentiation serves as a valuable tool for understanding the relationship between affect and cognition in psychopathology. Borrowing from Werner (1957), Arieti argues that in the process of normal development, primitive forms of emotions and cognitions become hierarchically integrated into increasingly more advanced affective and cognitive forms. The earlier affective forms, or "protoemotions," lose importance in development as they become gradually transformed into higher types of emotions through a process of evolution in interpersonal relations, in particular with the mother. In conditions of drug addiction, psychopathology, and creativity, these primitive forms can become available again to the psyche. The schizophrenic, argues Arieti, resorts to an earlier mode of emotional and cognitive development in order to reduce anxiety. However, this is considered to be a pathological or a maladaptive alternative because the patient originally operated on a higher level; therefore, it is not possible for the patient to adjust healthily to an earlier level of functioning.

Illustrations of Piagetian developmental approaches to psychopathological and atypical populations

Anthony (1956) discussed the significance of a Piagetian developmental framework for child psychiatry. According to Anthony, Piaget's conceptualization of cognitive development provides a valuable framework within which psychopathological functioning can be understood. As Anthony pointed out, the relevance of a Piagetian framework of development for psychopathology lies less in its ability to shed light on emotional functioning than in the way it can elucidate the underlying mental processes that lead up to psychopathological symptoms. Through the processes of developmental retardation, fixation, or retrogression, individuals can become out of synchronization with the developmental level appropriate for chronological age. For example, using Piaget's scale of object development, Anthony (1956) argued that the psychotic child shows evidence of disturbances in object and space–time development. Furthermore, Anthony stressed the importance of examining the interrelations between affective and cognitive processes in psychopathology, arguing that "it is not sufficient to understand the dynamics of feeling; we must also understand the genetics of thinking, after which we may claim with greater truth that we really understand our patients" (1956, p. 34). This emphasis on a multidomain approach has been echoed by developmental psychopathologists (Cicchetti & Sroufe, 1978).

Barbel Inhelder (1943/1968, 1966, 1976a,b), a close collaborator of Piaget, used developmental theory to diagnose the reasoning abilities of retarded persons. Inhelder found that mentally retarded children displayed difficulties of integration from one developmental level to the next. In particular, she discovered that the reasoning of retarded children often shows traces of previous levels of thinking, a phenomenon Inhelder labeled "viscosity." Inhelder observed this viscosity in retarded children who remained in a state of transition between two stages for a much longer duration than did nonretarded children, oscillating between levels of construction not only on different tasks but also on different times on the same task.

With a developmental perspective, Inhelder further elucidated the nature of mental retardation. She found that mentally retarded children frequently showed a false equilibrium, a phenomenon she called "closure" or "passive stability" of thought. In Inhelder's words, "a system is said to be completed once it has attained a level of structuration such that each of its elements has become consolidated with the others. It is thus capable of becoming integrated into larger systems" (1976a, p. 223). Thus, a completed system simultaneously constitutes an opening – it has the germ for additional development. Inhelder (1976a) found that for some mentally retarded children, access to certain structures seemed to be an end in itself, without hope for any subsequent ontogenetic changes.

One aspect of development closely related to the lack of hierarchical integration and consolidation of stage structures in mentally retarded children is the explanation of stage transitions. Inhelder discovered so-called oscillations – that is, fluctuations between various stage levels – in retarded children. Another way of putting this is that retarded children's stage transitions do not reflect a clear trend toward increasing integration, differentiation, and organization as postulated by Piaget and Werner. This demonstrates further how Inhelder's developmental perspective has proved to be a valuable tool in adding to our understanding of the nature of mental retardation.

Because developmentalists are interested in the mechanisms underlying change, not merely in describing these changes at the phenotypic level, Inhelder's work on the nature of stage transitions in retarded children was an important landmark for the field of developmental psychopathology. Clearly, further investigations of stage transitions in retarded children will be required in order to determine if the processes accounting for their development are different from those in the normal children studied by Piaget or if their oscillations are universal phenomena that become visible only in retarded children because of the slower nature of their development (Cicchetti & Sroufe, 1976). Regardless, the study of these transitions may enable us to come up with a more microscopic account for developmental changes.

Other related illustrations of developmental approaches to psychopathology

The discipline of developmental psychopathology likewise owes a great deal to the work of Adolf Meyer (1957). Meyer's psychobiological life history approach to psychiatry is perhaps his best known and most respected contribution to psychiatric theorizing (Rutter, 1986). Meyer stressed the importance of examining all the intricate details of patients' life histories as potential clues to their illnesses. Meyer believed that the most valuable determining feature of psychopathology was, as a rule, the symptom complex – both the time and duration and the circumstances of its development. A concern with why life stressors sometimes led only to transient problems and at other times led to lasting mental disorders underlay Meyer's psychobiological approach. Another important theme in Meyer's work was how life experiences impacted on individuals and why there were such individual differences in response to them. Meyer stressed the importance of using knowledge gained from psychology and biology in order to understand both how constitutional factors modified individuals' responses to life events and how the effects of events modified individuals. For Meyer, the somatic and mental were not separate, mutually exclusive entities, but components of an underlying process. Individuals were seen as active participants within and on their environments. Furthermore, individuals were viewed as being engaged in a dynamic interaction with their environment, as opposed to being passive recipients of external forces. Consequently, Meyer emphasized the way in which individuals interpreted and made meaning of life events, as well as how coping mechanisms were developed. Meyer particularly emphasized the importance of the extrafamilial environment and argued that development must be viewed within a social context. For example, he placed great emphasis on the impact of the school environment on children's development. Moreover, Meyer emphasized viewing the impact of an event on an individual not only at the time of the event but also during the individual's future development.

With his emphasis on the need to consider the multitude of factors and their interactions within the search for the causes of pathology, Meyer must be recognized as an important forerunner of the focus within developmental psychopathology on examining the interactions of multiple domains of behavior. Additionally, the emphasis in Meyer's work on individual differences and coping strategies in response to stressful life events is a concern that predominates in developmental psychopathology (Garmezy, 1983; chapter 9, this volume). Like Meyer, developmental psychopathologists are interested in understanding the effects of experiences on both current and future adaptation and in identifying those factors both within and beyond the individual that either promote or inhibit competence in individuals (Cicchetti & Rizley, 1981; Garmezy, 1974a,b, 1983; Garmezy, Masten, & Tellegen, 1984; Waddington, 1957; chapter 9, this volume).

Like Meyer, Lee Robins has not been strongly associated with any one developmental framework. However, Robins's efforts (1966) to follow up children with an early history of psychiatric clinic attendance into adulthood make her an important developmental psychopathological progenitor. Her classic work *Deviant Children Grown Up* (1966) serves as a prototypical example of how transformations may appear in studies of developmental psychopathology. She found that among children who attended psychiatric clinics and were followed up into their adulthood, there was a greater incidence of psychopathology than in a control group. In fact, some childhood difficulties actually predicted later adult outcome; however, Robins did not find evidence for symptomatic isomorphism over time. For example, shy, withdrawn children did not develop clinical schizophrenia as adults. Instead, it was the children who were characterized by externalizing behavior problems who were overrepresented in the adult schizophrenia group. Robins's research foreshadows the prospective longitudinal research on the pathways to adaptive and maladaptive outcomes conducted by "organizational" theorists (Cicchetti & Schneider-Rosen, 1986; Erickson, Egeland, & Pianta, 1989; Farber & Egeland, 1987; Garmezy, 1974a,b; Kohlberg, LaCrosse, & Ricks, 1972; Sroufe, 1979a, 1986; Sroufe & Rutter, 1984; chapter 9, this volume).

Reasons for the emergence of the discipline of developmental psychopathology

These illustrations taken from diverse disciplines underscore the long history of the developmental psychopathology perspective. Until the 1970s the basic and applied branches underwent increasing differentiation into separate subdisciplines. However, over the course of the last two decades, through a kind of hierarchical integration, these subdisciplines have been meeting together in increasingly interesting ways to bring about new interdisciplinary approaches, one of which is developmental psychopathology.

Before developmental psychopathology could emerge as a distinct discipline, the science of normal development needed to mature, and a broader basis of firm results had to be acquired. During the past two decades, researchers and theoreticians have paid increasing attention to the noncognitive domains of development. In particular, major advancements have been made in a number of areas, including emotional development (Cicchetti & Hesse, 1983; Izard, 1977; Lewis & Michalson, 1983; Sroufe, 1979b), social development (Ainsworth, Blehar, Waters, & Wall, 1978; Damon, 1977; Hartup, 1983), social cognition (Selman, 1980), self-development (Damon & Hart, 1982; Harter, 1983; Lewis & Brooks-Gunn, 1979), and symbolization (Bates, Benigni, Bretherton, Camaioni, & Volterra, 1979; Cicchetti & Beeghly, 1987; Rubin, Fein, & Vandenberg, 1983).

In addition to the empirical advances within developmental psychology, increasingly sophisticated theoretical contributions made the developmental approach more viable. One important example is the principle of equifinality, which refers to the observation that many paths are available to a given outcome within a particular system (Bertalanffy, 1968; Weiss, 1969a,b; Wilden, 1980). Consequently, the breakdown, as well as the maintenance, of a system's function can occur in a large variety of ways, especially when taking into account environment–organism interaction. To predict the pathology or health of a system based on any single component alone is not possible according to this formulation. Thus, the principle of equifinality offers a more complex and realistic approach to understanding the course of psychopathological disorders and anticipates the failure to identify unique predictors or correlates of psychopathology.

The principle of multifinality (Wilden, 1980) provides another important theoretical tool. This principle states that the effect on functioning of any one component's value may vary in different systems. Actual effects will depend on the conditions set by the values of additional components with which it is structurally linked. Thus, the pathology or health of a system must be identified in terms of how adequately its essential functions are maintained. In other words, a particular adverse event should not necessarily be seen as leading to the same psychopathological or nonpsychopathological outcome in every individual. Together, these principles exemplify significant theoretical progressions within developmental approaches to understanding psychopathology.

In conjunction with advancements in developmental knowledge, the 1970s witnessed an increasingly greater acceptance, among both researchers and clinicians, of the roles that a variety of factors (e.g., constitutional, genetic, biochemical, psychological, environmental, sociological) play in the etiology and sequelae of mental disorders. As a consequence, simplistic reductionistic notions of disease became increasingly less tenable (Cassell, 1986; Cicchetti & Schneider-Rosen, 1984b; Eisenberg, 1977; Engel, 1977; Marmor, 1983; Meehl, 1972, 1977; Sameroff & Chandler, 1975; Zubin & Spring, 1977). The increasing sophistication of the medical model employed by clinicians allowed for a more integrative understanding of disease than had "main-effect" (Overton & Reese, 1973) Virchowian conceptions of disease.

Among researchers, the discipline of ethology played a catalytic role in the emergence of an awareness of the importance of a multidomain, multidiscipline approach to psychopathology (Hinde, 1983a,b). As Charlesworth (1978) observed, the strength and appeal of ethology are derived from its fundamentally interdisciplinary approach, for its goal is an overall synthetic understanding of behavior. As such, ethology draws not only on evolutionary biology but also, when necessary, on biochemistry, neurophysiology, behavioral genetics, strict behaviorism, comparative biology, and ecology. The past two decades have witnessed two important advances: the application of ethological techniques to studies of human pathology, and the integration of a developmental framework with these ethological techniques.

Moreover, the incorporation of the developmental perspective into other disciplines such as the neurosciences, psychobiology, and behavioral and molecular genetics offers exciting prospects for constructing an empirically and theoretically sound integrative view of developmental psychopathology: For the neurosciences, see Crnic and Pennington (1987), Edelman (1978), Goldman-Rakic (1987), Goldman-Rakic, Isseroff, Schwartz, and Bugbee (1983), Hartlage and Telzrow (1985), Jacobson (1978), Mountcastle (1978), Puig-Antich et al. (1979, 1984), Rakic and Goldman-Rakic (1982), Rutter (1983), Sulkowski (1983), Weinberger (1987), Wiggins, McCandless, and Enna (1985), and Wilson (1983). For psychobiology, see Greenough, Black, and Wallace (1987), Greenough and Juraska (1986), Stelzner (1986), and Teitelbaum (1971, 1977). For behavioral and molecular genetics, see Brown (1973), Gottesman (1974), Hotta and Benzer (1972), Ohno (1972), Plomin (1983, 1986), and Scarr and Kidd (1983).

Conclusion

The impressive array of findings within the more recent developmental literature mentioned earlier, in concert with the concomitant progress made in the neurosciences and related disciplines, has led to increasing acknowledgment of the need to conduct collaborative, multidisciplinary, multidomain studies on normal, "high-risk," and psychopathological populations (Garmezy, 1974a,b, 1981; Watt, Anthony, Wynne, & Rolf, 1984). It has now become more widely accepted that research into pathological conditions must proceed hand-in-hand with so-called basic research into human functioning. As progress in ontogenetic approaches to the various subdisciplines of developmental psychopathology continues, the common theoretical and empirical threads running through this work will come together in a foundation on which an increasingly sophisticated developmental psychopathology discipline can grow. Such a science should bridge fields of study, span the life cycle, and aid in the discovery of important new truths about the processes underlying adaptation and maladaptation, as well as provide the best means of preventing or ameliorating psychopathology. Moreover, this discipline should contribute greatly to reducing the dualisms that exist between clinical study of and theoretical research into childhood and adult disorders, between the behavioral and biological sciences, between developmental psychology and psychopathology, and between basic and applied research.

References

Achenbach, T. (1982). *Developmental psychopathology.* New York: Wiley. (Original work published 1974)

Ainsworth, M., Blehar, M., Waters, E., & Wall, S. (1978). *Patterns of attachment.* Hillsdale, NJ: Erlbaum.

Anthony, E. J. (1956). The significance of Jean Piaget for child psychiatry. *British Journal of Medical Psychology, 29,* 20–34.

Arieti, S. (1955). *Interpretation of schizophrenia.* New York: Brunner.

Arieti, S. (1967). *The intrapsychic self: Feeling, cognition, and creativity in health and mental illness.* New York: Basic Books.

Baldwin, A. (1980). *Theories of child development* (2nd ed.). New York: Wiley.

Baldwin, J. M. (1894). *Mental development in the child and the race.* New York: Macmillan.

Baldwin, J. M. (1906). *Social and ethical interpretations in mental development.* New York: Macmillan.

Bates, E., Benigni, L., Bretherton, I., Camaioni, L., & Volterra, V. (1979). *The emergence of symbols.* Orlando, FL: Academic.

Bertalanffy, L. von. (1968). *General system theory.* New York: Braziller.

Bleuler, E. (1950). *Dementia praecox or the group of schizophrenias.* New York: International Universities Press. (Original work published 1911)

Block, J. H., & Block, J. (1980). The role of ego-control and ego resiliency in the organization of behavior. In W. A. Collins (Ed.), *Minnesota symposium on child psychology* (Vol. 13, pp. 39–101). Hillsdale, NJ: Erlbaum.

Bowlby, J. (1944). *Forty-four juvenile thieves.* London: Bailliere, Tindall & Cox.

Bowlby, J. (1951). *Maternal care and mental health* (WHO monograph 2). Geneva: World Health Organization.

Bowlby, J. (1961). Childhood mourning and its implications for psychiatry. *American Journal of Psychiatry, 118,* 481–98.

Bowlby, J. (1979). *The making and breaking of affectional bonds.* London: Tavistock Publications.

Bowlby, J. (1982). *Attachment and loss. Vol. 1: Attachment.* New York: Basic Books. (Original work published 1969)

Bronson, G. W. (1965). The hierarchical organization of the central nervous system: Implications for learning processes and critical periods in early development. *Behavioral Science, 10,* 7–25.

Bronson, G. W. (1974). The postnatal growth of visual capacity. *Child Development, 45,* 873–90.

Brown, D. D. (1973). The isolation of genes. *Scientific American, 229,* 20–9.

Bruner, J. S. (1970). The growth and structure of skill. In K. J. Connolly (Ed.), *Mechanisms of motor development* (pp. 63–94). London: Academic Press.

Cairns, R. B. (1983). The emergence of developmental psychology. In P. Mussen (Ed.), *Handbook of child psychology* (Vol. 1, pp. 41–102). New York: Wiley.

Cajal, S. Ramon y. (1893). New findings about the histological structure of the central nervous system. *Archiv für Anatomie und Physiologie (Anatomie),* pp. 319–428.

Cajal, S. Ramon y. (1937). *Recollections of my life.* Philadelphia: American Philosophical Society.

Cassell, E. J. (1986). Ideas in conflict: The rise and fall (and rise and fall) of new views of disease. *Daedalus, 115,* 19–41.

Charlesworth, W. R. (1978). Ethology: Its relevance for observational studies of human adaptation. In G. Sackett (Ed.), *Observing behavior* (Vol. 1, pp. 7–32). Baltimore: University Park Press.

Cicchetti, D. (1984a). The emergence of developmental psychopathology. *Child Development, 55,* 1–7.

Cicchetti, D. (Ed.). (1984b). Special issue: Developmental psychopathology. *Child Development, 55,* 1–314.

Cicchetti, D., & Aber, J. L. (1986). Early precursors to later depression: An organizational perspective. In L. Lipsitt & C. Rovee-Collier (Eds.), *Advances in infancy* (Vol. 4, pp. 87–137). Norwood, NJ: Ablex.

Cicchetti, D., & Beeghly, M. (1990). *Children with Down syndrome: A developmental perspective.* Cambridge University Press.

Cicchetti, D., & Beeghly, M. (Eds.). (1987). *Atypical symbolic development.* San Francisco: Jossey-Bass.

Cicchetti, D., & Carlson, V. (Eds.). (1989). *Child maltreatment: Theory and research on the causes and consequences of child abuse and neglect.* Cambridge University Press.

Cicchetti, D., & Hesse, P. (1983). Affect and intellect: Piaget's contributions to the study of infant emotional development. In R. Plutchik & H. Kellerman (Eds.), *Emotion: Research and theory* (Vol. 2, pp. 115–69). New York: Academic Press.

Cicchetti, D., & Pogge-Hesse, P. (1981). The relation between emotion and cognition in infant development: Past, present, and future perspectives. In M. Lamb & L. Sherrod (Eds.), *Infant social cognition: Empirical and theoretical considerations* (pp. 205–72). Hillsdale, NJ: Erlbaum.

Cicchetti, D., & Pogge-Hesse, P. (1982). Possible contributions of the study of organically retarded persons to developmental theory. In E. Zigler & D. Balla (Eds.), *Mental retardation: The developmental-difference controversy* (pp. 277–318). Hillsdale, NJ: Erlbaum.

Cicchetti, D., & Rizley, R. (1981). Developmental perspectives on the etiology, intergenerational transmission, and sequelae of child maltreatment. *New Directions for Child Development, 11,* 31–55.

Cicchetti, D., & Schneider-Rosen, K. (1984a). Theoretical and empirical considerations in the investigation of the relationship between affect and cognition in atypical populations of infants: Contributions to the formulation of an integrative theory of development. In C. Izard, J. Kagan, & R. Zajonc (Eds.), *Emotions, cognition, and behavior* (pp. 366–406). Cambridge University Press.

Cicchetti, D., & Schneider-Rosen, K. (1984b). Toward a developmental model of the depressive disorders. *New Directions for Child Development, 26,* 5–27.

Cicchetti, D., & Schneider-Rosen, K. (1986). An organizational approach to childhood depression. In M. Rutter, C. E. Izard, & P. B. Read (Eds.), *Depression in young people: Developmental and clinical perspectives* (pp. 71–134). New York: Guilford Press.

Cicchetti, D., & Sroufe, L. A. (1976). The relationship between affective and cognitive development in Down's syndrome infants. *Child Development, 47,* 920–9.

Cicchetti, D., & Sroufe, L. A. (1978). An organizational view of affect: Illustration from the study of Down's syndrome infants. In M. Lewis & L. Rosenblum (Eds.), *The development of affect* (pp. 309–50). New York: Plenum.

Conel, J. L. (1937–67). *The postnatal development of the human cerebral cortex* (Vols. I–VIII). Cambridge, MA: Harvard University Press.

Crnic, L., & Pennington, B. (Eds.). (1987). Developmental psychology and the neurosciences. *Child Development, 58,* 533–717.

Damon, W. (1977). *The social world of the child.* San Francisco: Jossey-Bass.

Damon, W., & Hart, D. (1982). The development of self-understanding from infancy through adolescence. *Child Development, 53,* 841–64.

Darwin, C. (1965). *The expression of the emotions in man and the animals.* University of Chicago Press. (Original work published 1872)

Denny-Brown, D., Twitchell, T. E., & Saenz-Arroyo, L. (1949). The nature of spasticity resulting from cerebral lesions. *Transactions of the American Neurological Association, 74,* 108–13.

Desmedt, J. E. (1977). *Visual evoked potentials in man: New developments.* Oxford: Clarendon Press.

Edelman, G. (1978). Group selection and phasic reentrant signaling: A theory of higher brain function. In G. Edelman (Ed.), *The mindful brain* (pp. 51–100). Cambridge, MA: MIT Press.

Eisenberg, L. (1977). Development as a unifying concept in psychiatry. *British Journal of Psychiatry, 131,* 225–37.

Engel, G. (1977). The need for a new medical model: A challenge for biomedicine. *Science, 196,* 129–35.

Erickson, M., Egeland, B., & Pianta, R. (1989). The effects of maltreatment on the development of young children. In D. Cicchetti & V. Carlson (Eds.), *Child maltreatment: Theory and research on the causes and consequences of child abuse and neglect* (pp. 647–84). Cambridge University Press.

Farber, E., & Egeland, B. (1987). Invulnerability among abused and neglected children. In E. J. Anthony & B. Cohler (Eds.), *The invulnerable child* (pp. 253–88). New York: Guilford Press.

Fischer, K. W. (1980). A theory of cognitive development: Control and construction of hierarchies of skills. *Psychological Review, 87,* 477–531.

Fishbein, H. (1976). *Evolution, development, and children's learning.* Pacific Palisades, CA: Goodyear Publishing Co.

Freud, A. (1965). *Normality and pathology in childhood.* New York: International Universities Press.

Freud, A. (1974). A psychoanalytic view of developmental psychopathology. *Journal of the Philadelphia Association for Psychoanalysis, 1,* 7–17.

Freud, A. (1976). Psychopathology seen against the background of normal development. *British Journal of Psychiatry, 129,* 401–6.

Freud, S. (1955a). Fetishism. In J. Strachey (Ed.), *The standard edition of the complete works of Sigmund Freud* (Vol. 21). London: Hogarth. (Original work published 1927)

Freud, S. (1955b). Analysis terminable and interminable. In J. Strachey (Ed.), *The standard edition of the complete works of Sigmund Freud* (Vol. 23). London: Hogarth. (Original work published 1937)

Freud, S. (1955c). An outline of psycho-analysis. In J. Strachey (Ed.), *The standard edition of the complete works of Sigmund Freud* (Vol. 23). London: Hogarth. (Original work published 1940)

Freud, S. (1955d). Splitting of the ego in the process of defense. In J. Strachey (Ed.), *The standard edition of the complete works of Sigmund Freud* (Vol. 23). London: Hogarth. (Original work published 1940)

Garmezy, N. (1974a). Children at risk: The search for the antecedents of schizophrenia. *Schizophrenia Bulletin, 8,* 14–90.

Garmezy, N. (1974b). Children at risk: Conceptual models and research methods. *Schizophrenia Bulletin, 9,* 55–125.

Garmezy, N. (1981). Children under stress: Perspectives on antecedents and correlates of vulnerability and resistance to psychopathology. In A. I. Rubin, J. Aronoff, A. M. Barclay, & R. A. Zucker (Eds.), *Further explorations in personality* (pp. 196–269). New York: Wiley.

Garmezy, N. (1983). Stressors of childhood. In N. Garmezy & M. Rutter (Eds.), *Stress, coping, and development in children* (pp. 43–84). New York: McGraw-Hill.

Garmezy, N., Masten, A., & Tellegen, A. (1984). The study of stress and competence in children: A building block for developmental psychopathology. *Child Development, 55,* 97–111.

Goldman-Rakic, P. (1987). Development of cortical circuitry and cognitive function. *Child Development, 58,* 601–22.

Goldman-Rakic, P., Isseroff, A., Schwartz, M., & Bugbee, N. (1983). The neurobiology of cognitive development. In M. Haith & J. Campos (Eds.), *Carmichael's manual of child psychology* (Vol. 2, pp. 281–344). New York: Wiley.

Goldstein, K. (1939). *The organism.* New York: American Book Company.

Goldstein, K. (1940). *Human nature in the light of psychopathology.* Cambridge, MA: Harvard University Press.

Goldstein, K. (1943). The significance of psychological research in schizophrenia. *Journal of Nervous and Mental Disease, 97,* 261–79.

Goldstein, K. (1948). *Language and language disturbances.* New York: Grune & Stratton.

Gollin, E. S. (Ed.). (1984). *Malformations of development.* Orlando, FL: Academic Press.

Gottesman, I. I. (1974). Developmental genetics and ontogenetic psychology: Overdue detente and propositions from a matchmaker. In A. Pick (Ed.), *Minnesota symposium on child psychology* (pp. 55–80). Minneapolis: University of Minnesota Press.

Greenough, W., Black, J., & Wallace, C. (1987). Experience and brain development. *Child Development, 58,* 539–59.

Greenough, W. T., & Juraska, J. M. (Eds.) (1986). *Developmental neuropsychobiology.* New York: Academic Press.

Hamburger, V. (1980). S. Ramon y Cajal, R. G. Harrison, and the beginnings of neuroembryology. *Perspectives in Biology and Medicine, 23,* 600–16.

Harlow, H., & Zimmerman, R. (1959). Affectional response in the infant monkey. *Science, 130,* 421–32.

Harter, S. (1983). Developmental perspectives on the self-system. In E. M. Hetherington (Ed.), *Carmichael's manual of child psychology. Vol. 4: Social and personality development* (pp. 275–386). New York: Wiley.

Hartlage, L. C., & Telzrow, C. F. (Eds.). (1985). *The neuropsychology of individual differences: A developmental perspective.* New York: Plenum.

Hartup, W. (1983). Peer relations. In P. Mussen (Ed.), *Handbook of child psychology.* New York: Wiley.

Hinde, R. A. (1983a). Ethology and child development. In M. Haith & J. Campos (Eds.), *Carmichael's manual of child psychology* (Vol. 2, pp. 27–94). New York: Wiley.

Hinde, R. A. (1983b). Ethology and psychiatry. In M. Shepard (Ed.), *The scientific foundations of psychiatry.* Cambridge University Press.

Hofstadter, R. (1955). *Social Darwinism in American thought.* Boston: Beacon Press.

Hotta, Y., & Benzer, S. (1972). Mapping of behavior in *Drosophila* mosaics. *Nature, 240,* 527–35.

Humphrey, T. (1953). The relation of oxygen deprivation to fetal reflex arcs and the development of behavior. *Journal of Psychology, 35,* 3–43.

Inhelder, B. (1966). Cognitive development and its contribution to the diagnosis of some phenomena of mental deficiency. *Merrill-Palmer Quarterly, 22,* 299–319.

Inhelder, B. (1968). *The diagnosis of reasoning in the mentally retarded.* New York: John Day Co. (Original work published 1943)

Inhelder, B. (1976a). Some pathologic phenomena analyzed in the perspective of developmental psychology. In B. Inhelder & H. Chipman (Eds.), *Piaget and his school* (pp. 221–7). New York: Springer.

Inhelder, B. (1976b). Operatory thought processes in psychotic children. In B. Inhelder & H. Chipman (Eds.), *Piaget and his school* (pp. 228–33). New York: Springer.

Izard, C. (1977). *Human emotions.* New York: Plenum.

Jackson, J. H. (1958). Evolution and dissolution of the nervous system. In J. Taylor (Ed.), *The selected writings of John Hughlings Jackson* (Vol. 2). New York: Basic Books. (Original work published 1884)

Jacobson, M. (1978). *Developmental neurobiology.* New York: Plenum.

James, W. (1902). *The varieties of religious experience.* London: Longmans, Green.

James, W. (1917). *Memories and studies.* New York: Longmans, Green.

James, W. (1920). *Collected essays and reviews.* New York: Longmans, Green.

Jolly, A. (1972). *The evolution of primate behavior.* New York: Macmillan.

Kagan, J., & Brim, O. G. (Eds.) (1980). *Constancy and change in human development.* Cambridge, MA: Harvard University Press.

Kaplan, B. (1966). The study of language in psychiatry: The comparative developmental approach and its application to symbolization and language in psychopathology. In S. Arieti (Ed.), *American handbook of psychiatry.* New York: Basic Books.

Kaplan, B. (1967). Meditations on genesis. *Human Development, 10,* 65–87.

Kaplan, B. (1983). Genetic-dramatism: Old wine in new bottles. In S. Wapner & B. Kaplan (Eds.), *Toward a holistic developmental psychology.* Hillsdale, NJ: Erlbaum.

Kemper, T. L. (1984). Asymmetrical lesions in dyslexia. In N. Geschwind & A. M. Galaburda (Eds.), *Cerebral dominance: The biological foundations* (pp. 75–89). Cambridge, MA: Harvard University Press.

Kohlberg, L., LaCrosse, J., & Ricks, D. (1972). The predictability of adult mental health from childhood behavior. In B. Wolman (Ed.), *Manual of child psychopathology* (pp. 1217–84). New York: Wiley.

Kovelman, J., & Scheibel, A. (1983). A neuroanatomical correlate of schizophrenia. *Society of Neuroscience Abstracts, 9,* 850.

Kraepelin, E. (1971). *Dementia praecox and paraphrenia.* New York: Robert E. Krieger Publishing Co. (Original work published 1919)

Kuo, Z.-Y. (1939). Studies in the physiology of the embryonic nervous system: IV. Development of acetylcholine in the chick embryo. *Journal of Neurophysiology, 2,* 488–93.

Kuo, Z.-Y. (1967). *The dynamics of behavior development.* New York: Random House.

Lewis, M., & Brooks-Gunn, J. (1979). *Social cognition and the acquisition of self.* New York: Plenum.

Lewis, M., & Michalson, L. (1983). *Children's emotions and moods: Developmental theory and measurement.* New York: Plenum.

Lewis, M., & Miller, S. (in press). *Handbook of developmental psychopathology*. New York: Plenum.

Lorenz, K. (1950). The comparative method in studying innate behaviour patterns. In J. F. Danielli & R. Brown (Eds.), *Physiological mechanisms in animal behaviour* (pp. 221–68). Cambridge University Press.

Luria, A. R. (1980). *Higher cortical functions in man*. New York: Basic Books. (Original work published 1966)

McGhie, A., & Chapman, J. (1961). Disorders of attention and perception in early schizophrenia. *British Journal of Medical Psychology, 34*, 103–15.

Mahler, M. (1952). On childhood psychosis and schizophrenia: Autistic and symbiotic infantile psychoses. *The psychoanalytic study of the child* (Vol. 7). New York: International Universities Press.

Marmor, J. (1983). Systems thinking in psychiatry: Some theoretical and clinical implications. *American Journal of Psychiatry, 140*, 833–8.

Meehl, P. E. (1972). Specific genetic etiology, psychodynamics, and therapeutic nihilism. *International Journal of Mental Health, 1*, 10–27.

Meehl, P. E. (1977). Specific etiology and other forms of strong influence: Some quantitative meanings. *Journal of Medicine and Philosophy, 2*, 33–53.

Meyer, A. (1957). *Psychobiology: A science of man*. Springfield, IL: Charles C Thomas.

Mountcastle, V. B. (1978). An organizing principle for cerebral function: The unit module and the distributed system. In G. Edelman (Ed.), *The mindful brain* (pp. 7–50). Cambridge, MA: MIT Press.

Mussen, P. (Ed.) (1983). *Handbook of child psychology* (Vol. 1). New York: Wiley.

Nannis, E., & Cowan, P. (Eds.) (1988). *Developmental psychopathology and its treatment*. San Francisco: Jossey-Bass.

Nisbet, R. A. (1969). *Social change and history*. London: Oxford University Press.

Nowakowski, R. S. (1987). Basic concepts of CNS development. *Child Development, 58*, 568–95.

Ohno, S. (1972). Gene duplication, mutation load, and mammalian genetic regulatory systems. *Journal of Medical Genetics, 9*, 254–63.

Overton, W. (1976). The active organism in structuralism. *Human Development, 19*, 71–86.

Overton, W. (1984). World views and their influence on psychological theory and research: Kuhn-Lakatos-Laudan. In H. Reese (Ed.), *Advances in child development and behavior* (Vol. 18, pp. 191–226). New York: Academic Press.

Overton, W., & Reese, H. (1973). Models of development: Methodological implications. In J. R. Nesselroade & H. Reese (Eds.), *Life-span developmental psychology: Methodological issues*. New York: Academic Press.

Paulson, G., & Gottlieb, G. (1968). Developmental reflexes in aged patients. *Brain, 91*, 37–52.

Piaget, J. (1952). *The origins of intelligence in children*. New York: International Universities Press.

Piaget, J. (1971). *Biology and knowledge*. University of Chicago Press.

Plomin, R. (Ed.). (1983). Developmental behavioral genetics. *Child Development, 54*.

Plomin, R. (1986). *Development, genetics and psychology*. Hillsdale, NJ: Erlbaum.

Puig-Antich, J., Novacenko, H., Davies, M., Chambers, W. J., Tabrizi, M. A., Krawiec, V., Ambrosini, P. J., & Sachar, E. J. (1984). Growth hormone secretion in prepubertal children with major depression. *Archives of General Psychiatry, 41*, 455–60.

Puig-Antich, J., Perel, J. M., Lupartkin, W., Chambers, W. J., Shea, C., Tabrizi, M., & Stiller, R. L. (1979). Plasma levels of imipramine (IMI) and desmethylimipramine (DMI) and clinical response to prepubertal major depressive disorder. *Journal of the American Academy of Child Psychiatry, 18*, 616–27.

Rakic, P. & Goldman-Rakic, P. S. (1982). Development and modifiability of the cerebral cortex. *Neurosciences Research Program Bulletin, 20*, 433–8.

Rapaport, D. (1951). *Organization and pathology of thought.* New York: Columbia University Press.

Reese, H., & Overton, W. (1970). Models of development and theories of development. In L. R. Goulet & P. Baltes (Eds.), *Life span developmental psychology: Research and theory* (pp. 115–45). New York: Academic Press.

Rizley, R., & Cicchetti, D. (Eds.). (1981). *Developmental perspectives on child maltreatment.* San Francisco: Jossey-Bass.

Robins, L. (1966). *Deviant children grown up.* Baltimore: Williams & Wilkins.

Rubin, K., Fein, G., & Vandenberg, B. (1983). Play. In E. M. Hetherington (Ed.), *Carmichael's manual of child psychology. Vol. 4: Social and personality development* (pp. 693–774). New York: Wiley.

Rutter, M. (Ed.). (1983). *Developmental neuropsychiatry.* New York: Guilford Press.

Rutter, M. (1986). Meyerian psychobiology, personality development, and the role of life experiences. *American Journal of Psychiatry, 143,* 1077–87.

Rutter, M., & Garmezy, N. (1983). Developmental psychopathology. In P. Mussen (Ed.), *Handbook of child psychology* (Vol. 4, pp. 775–911). New York: Wiley.

Rutter, M., Izard, C. E., & Read, P. B. (Eds.). (1986). *Depression in young people: Developmental and clinical perspectives.* New York: Guilford Press.

Sackett, G., Sameroff, A., Cairns, R., & Suomi, S. (1981). Continuity in behavioral development: Theoretical and empirical issues. In K. Immelman, G. Barlow, L. Petrinovich, & M. Main (Eds.), *Behavioral development* (pp. 23–57). Cambridge University Press.

Sameroff, A. J. (1983). Developmental systems: Contexts and evolution. In P. Mussen, (Ed.), *Handbook of child psychology.* (Vol. 1, pp. 237–94). New York: Wiley.

Sameroff, A., & Chandler, M. (1975). Reproductive risk and the continuum of caretaking casualty. In F. Horowitz, M. Hetherington, S. Scarr-Salapatek, & G. Siegel (Eds.), *Review of child development research* (Vol. 4, pp. 187–244). University of Chicago Press.

Santostefano, S. (1978). *A bio-developmental approach to clinical child psychology.* New York: Wiley.

Scarr, S., & Kidd, K. (1983). Developmental behavior genetics. In M. Haith & J. Campos (Eds.), *Carmichael's manual of child psychology* (Vol. 2, pp. 345–434). New York: Wiley.

Searles, H. F. (1959a). Integration and differentiation in schizophrenia: An overall view. *Journal of Nervous and Mental Diseases, 32,* 261–81.

Searles, H. F. (1959b). Integration and differentiation in schizophrenia. *British Journal of Medical Psychology, 129,* 542–50.

Selman, R. (1980). *The growth of interpersonal understanding: Developmental and clinical analyses.* New York: Academic Press.

Selman, R., & Yando, R. (1980). *Clinical-developmental psychology.* San Francisco: Jossey-Bass.

Seyfarth, H., & Denny-Brown, D. (1948). The grasp reflex and the instinctive grasp reaction. *Brain, 6,* 109–83.

Shakow, D. (1946). The nature of deterioration in schizophrenic conditions. *Journal of Nervous and Mental Diseases Monographs, 70,* 1–88.

Shakow, D. (1962). Segmental set: A theory of the formal psychological deficit in schizophrenia. *Archives of General Psychiatry, 6,* 1–17.

Shakow, D. (1963). Psychological deficit in schizophrenia. *Journal of Behavior Science, 8,* 275–305.

Shakow, D. (1968). Contributions from schizophrenia to the understanding of normal psychological function. In M. Simmel (Ed.), *The reach of mind: Essays in memory of Kurt Goldstein* (pp. 173–99). New York: Springer.

Shakow, D. (1972). The Worcester state hospital research on schizophrenia. *Journal of Abnormal Psychology, 80,* 67–110.

Sherman, G., Galaburda, A., & Geschwind, N. (1985). Cortical anomalies in brains of New Zealand mice: A neuropathologic model of dyslexia. *Proceedings of the National Academy of Sciences USA, 82,* 8072–4.

Sherrington, X. (1906). *The integrative action of the nervous system.* New York: Scribner's.

Spemann, H. (1938). *Embryonic development and induction.* New Haven: Yale University Press.

Spencer, H. (1896). *The principles of biology* (Vol. 2). New York: Appleton. (Original work published 1864)

Spencer, H. (1900). *First principles.* (6th ed.). New York: Appleton. (Original work published 1862)

Spitz (1965). *The first year of life.* New York: International Universities Press.

Sroufe, L. A. (1979a). The coherence of individual development: Early care, attachment, and subsequent developmental issues. *American Psychologist, 43,* 834–41.

Sroufe, L. A. (1979b). Socioemotional development. In J. Osofsy (Ed.), *Handbook of infant development* (pp. 462–516). New York: Wiley.

Sroufe, L. A. (1986). Appraisal: Bowlby's contribution to analytic theory and developmental psychopathology. *Journal of Child Psychology and Psychiatry, 27,* 841–9.

Sroufe, L. A., & Rutter, M. (1984). The domain of developmental psychopathology. *Child Development, 83,* 173–89.

Sroufe, L. A., & Waters, E. (1976). The ontogenesis of smiling and laughter: A perspective on the organization of development in infancy. *Psychological Review, 55,* 173–89.

Stelzner, D. J. (1986). Ontogeny of encephalization process. In W. T. Greenough & J. M. Juraska (Eds.), *Developmental neuropsychobiology* (pp. 242–70). New York: Academic Press.

Stevenson, J. E. (Ed.). (1985). *Recent research in developmental psychopathology.* Oxford: Pergamon Press.

Sulkowski, A. (1983). Psychobiology of schizophrenia: A neo-Jacksonian detour. *Perspectives in Biology and Medicine, 26,* 205–18.

Sullivan, H. S. (1956). *Clinical studies in psychiatry.* New York: W. W. Norton.

Teitelbaum, P. (1971). The encephalization of hunger. In E. Stellar & J. Sprague (Eds.), *Progress in physiological psychology* (Vol. 4). New York: Academic Press.

Teitelbaum, P. (1977). Levels of integration of the operant. In W. K. Honig & J. Staddon (Eds.), *Handbook of operant behavior.* Englewood Cliffs, NJ: Prentice-Hall.

Teitelbaum, P., Cheng, M. F., & Rozin, P. (1969). Development of feeding parallels its recovery after hypothalamic damage. *Journal of Comparative and Physiological Psychology, 67,* 430–41.

Trad, P. (1986). *Infant depression, paradigms, and paradoxes.* New York: Springer.

Trad, P. (1987). *Infant and childhood depression: Developmental factors.* New York: Wiley.

Tronick, E., & Field, T. (1986). *Maternal depression and infant disturbance.* San Francisco: Jossey-Bass.

Twitchell, T. E. (1951). The restoration of motor function following hemiplegia in man. *Brain, 74,* 443–80.

Twitchell, T. E. (1970). Reflex mechanisms and the development of prehension. In K. J. Connolly (Ed.), *Mechanisms of motor skill development.* New York: Academic Press.

von Baer, K. E. (1837). *Über Entwicklungsgeschichte der Thiere.* Konigsberg: Gebruder Borntrager. (Original work published 1828)

Waddington, C. H. (1957). *The strategy of the genes.* London: Allen & Unwin.

Watt, N., Anthony, J., Wynne, L., & Rolf, J. (Eds.). (1984). *Children at risk for schizophrenia: A longitudinal perspective.* Cambridge University Press.

Weinberger, D. R. (1987). Implications of normal brain development for the pathogenesis of schizophrenia. *Archives of General Psychiatry, 44,* 660–9.

Weiss, P. (1961). Deformities as cues to understanding development of form. *Perspectives in Biology and Medicine, 4,* 133–51.

Weiss, P. A. (1969a). The living system: Determinism stratified. In A. Koestler & J. Smythies (Eds.), *Beyond reductionism.* Boston: Beacon Press.

Weiss, P. A. (1969b). *Principles of development.* New York: Hafner.

Wenar, C. (1982). *Psychopathology from infancy through adolescence.* New York: Random House.

Werner, H. (1948). *Comparative psychology of mental development.* New York: International Universities Press.

Werner, H. (1957). The concept of development from a comparative and organismic point of view. In D. B. Harris (Ed.), *The concept of development* (pp. 125–48). Minneapolis: University of Minnesota Press.

Werner, H., & Kaplan, B. (1963). *Symbol formation: An organismic-developmental approach to language and the expression of thought.* New York: Wiley.

White, S. H. (1965). Evidence for a hierarchical arrangement of learning processes. In L. P. Lipsitt & C. C. Spiker (Eds.), *Advances in child development and behavior* (Vol. 2). New York: Academic Press.

Wiggins, R., McCandless, D., & Enna, S. (1985). *Developmental neurochemistry.* Austin: University of Texas Press.

Wilden, A. (1980). *System and structure.* London: Tavistock.

Wilson, B. (1983). An approach to the neuropsychological assessment of the preschool child with developmental deficits. In O. Spreen (Ed.), *Developmental neuropsychology.* Oxford University Press.

Yakovlev, P. I., & Lecours, A. (1967). The myelogenetic cycles of regional maturation of the brain. In A. Minkowski (Ed.), *Regional development of the brain in early life* (pp. 3–70). Oxford: Blackwell Scientific.

Zigler, E., & Glick, M. (1986). *A developmental approach to adult psychopathology.* New York: Wiley.

Zubin, J., & Spring, B. (1977). Vulnerability: A new view of schizophrenia. *Journal of Abnormal Psychology, 56,* 103–26.

2   What is "developmental" about developmental psychopathology?

Thomas M. Achenbach

As a graduate student at Minnesota in 1963, I naively thought it obvious that our understanding of psychopathology could be advanced by studying it in relation to developmental changes. This seemed most apparent with respect to disorders of childhood and adolescence. Yet it also seemed apparent with respect to the possible roots of adult disorders in earlier developmental periods and to the differences between disorders occurring at different periods of adult development.

The relevance of development to psychopathology seemed especially compelling in light of the major theories of the day. These theories emphasized the early history of the individual as a source of psychopathology and implied that early events had a marked impact on later development. They disagreed on what the most influential early determinants might be, whether psychodynamic, learning, genetic, or pathophysiological, but none had documented the form that childhood disorders actually took. In fact, anyone hoping to study the developmental course of child and adolescent disorders faced a nosology that until 1968 distinguished only between Adjustment Reaction of Childhood and Schizophrenic Reaction, Childhood Type (DSM-I, American Psychiatric Association, 1952).

Since that time, interest in childhood disorders has grown, spawning numerous distinctions among disorders that are thought to characterize children. DSM-II, DSM-III, and DSM-III-R all introduced diagnostic distinctions that had little prior history or research support (American Psychiatric Association, 1968, 1980, 1987). These distinctions reflect implicit assumptions about the nature of childhood disorders, largely extrapolated from concepts of adult disorders. Although research on adults undoubtedly offers useful concepts and data, it tends to portray childhood disorders as miniature versions of adult

This work was supported by grants from the William T. Grant Foundation and the Spencer Foundation. The author is indebted to Dr. Craig Edelbrock and Dr. Stephanie McConaughy for their helpful comments.

29

disorders, especially where we lack a clear picture of what constitutes the disorders actually occurring in children.

An example is the recent quest for childhood depression. Although it was essential to overcome the long neglect of depressive affect in children, the quest focused largely on inferred depressive illnesses for which there was little independent evidence. Instead of assessing the prevalence and patterning of depressive problems in children of different ages, clinical theorists equated a broad array of behavioral problems with depression (Cytryn & McKnew, 1979; Frommer, 1967; Weinberg, Rutman, Sullivan, Penick, & Dietz, 1973). As a result, many children were diagnosed as suffering from depressive illnesses in the absence of validated criteria for what constituted childhood depression and how it could be distinguished from other problems.

The preoccupation with childhood depression has been followed by a quest for childhood anxiety disorders, largely as a result of new interest in adult anxiety disorders (Achenbach, 1985b; Tuma & Maser, 1985). Because little is known about the relations between anxiety problems in children and adults, it is certainly important to study these relations. Yet it would be misleading to assume either that adult forms of anxiety disorders underlie children's problems or that childhood expressions of anxiety necessarily portend specific adult anxiety disorders. Some childhood anxiety problems at certain developmental periods may well be early manifestations of certain adult anxiety disorders, whereas others may be transient responses to situational or developmental stress. But we do not yet know how to tell which childhood problems, assessed in what manner, during which developmental periods, are precursors of which adult disorders. This is true for many conditions of childhood, where we need to consider both the current developmental context and the possibilities that current problems will interfere with subsequent development or that they are early manifestations of disorders that will crystallize at later developmental periods. How can we conceptualize the many possible relations between development and psychopathology?

A framework for studying relations between development and psychopathology

The term "developmental psychopathology" highlights the value of studying psychopathology in relation to the major changes that typically occur across the life cycle. It does not dictate a specific theoretical explanation for disorders, their causes, or their outcomes. Instead, it suggests a conceptual framework for organizing the study of psychopathology around milestones and sequences in areas such as physical, cognitive, social-emotional, and educational development. Its heuristic value is analogous to that of terms such as "learning," "cognition," "genetic," and "biological." The utility of such terms does not stem from prescriptive definitions of a field, but from focusing attention on connections among phenomena that otherwise seem haphazard and unrelated.

Prescriptive definitions for broad heuristic terms such as "developmental psychopathology" may limit rather than enhance their value. This is because such definitions may prematurely exclude ideas, variables, and methods that fail to conform to preconceived notions of what a field of study should include, but that are especially valuable in opening new lines of inquiry or forming links with other fields. Some discussions of developmental psychopathology, for example, imply a restriction to developmental explanations, theories, or research strategies, such as longitudinal designs; see the examples in the volume edited by Cicchetti (1984). If we impose a priori limitations of this sort, the heuristic value of the term "developmental psychopathology" may be diminished in the following ways:

1. It implies a dogmatic orthodoxy for determining what is and is not developmental.
2. It implies that research is relevant only if it yields developmental explanations, even though much useful research does not yield explanations, and some explanations may happen to be correct without being developmental.
3. It implies that there is or will be a unitary developmental theory, whereas development and psychopathology include such diverse phenomena that they have prompted numerous theories. These theories are likely to become further specialized rather than more unitary.

Developmental psychopathology as a macroparadigm

To capitalize on developmental psychopathology's potential for expanding rather than restricting our thinking, it is better viewed as a guide to studying important problems than as a source of ready-made answers. Accordingly, it can be thought of as a "macroparadigm" to distinguish it from paradigms and theories pertaining to more limited sets of variables, methods, or explanations. Figure 2.1 illustrates relations between developmental psychopathology viewed in this way and several more specific paradigms and theories relevant to development and psychopathology. The biomedical, behavioral, psychodynamic, and other paradigms are designated as "microparadigms" only in the sense of dealing with one facet of phenomena whose linkages are not apt to be adequately dealt with by any one of them alone. Most of them cover large domains, but each can be viewed as a subset of methods, constructs, and theories that may contribute to the developmental study of psychopathology.

The location of the developmental psychopathology box above the others in Figure 2.1 does not mean that they are subordinate to developmental psychopathology. On the contrary, each microparadigm and theory has a life of its own, apart from its relation to the macroparadigm of developmental psychopathology. In fact, several of the microparadigms would serve as macroparadigms in other hierarchical schemes. For purposes of studying psycho-

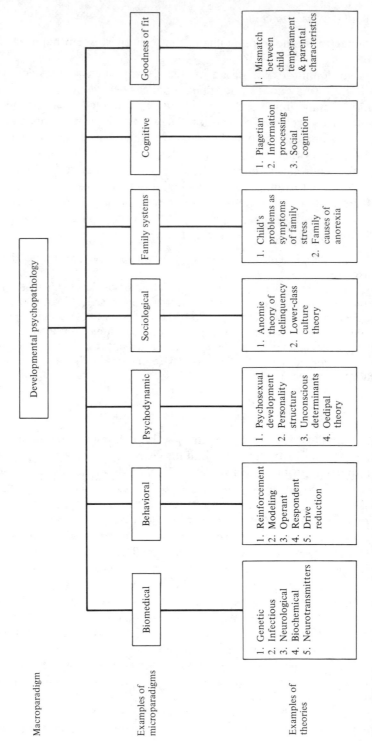

Figure 2.1. Schematic overview of developmental psychopathology as a macroparadigm in relation to other conceptual levels. (© Thomas M. Achenbach.)

pathology in relation to development, however, it is helpful to organize the many potentially relevant paradigms and theories around a central conceptual structure. This structure should provide a framework for integrating diverse ideas and findings that would otherwise appear unrelated. By highlighting interconnections and providing an overarching conceptual map, it should also stimulate hypotheses that will converge on common issues. Even though researchers inevitably specialize within particular microparadigms and theories of the sort listed in Figure 2.1, reference to a macroparadigm of developmental psychopathology can enhance the value of the more specialized contributions. Some examples follow.

Phenylketonuria

Phenylketonuria (PKU) provides a simple example. If a child inherits a particular Mendelian recessive gene from both parents, the child will be unable to metabolize phenylalanine, which is found in many foods. Under normal dietary conditions, unmetabolized phenylalanine will accumulate and be converted to phenylpyruvic acid. This condition causes brain damage, mental retardation, bleaching of the skin, and hyperactive behavior. Its etiology is well understood according to the biomedical paradigm. Because phenylpyruvic acid can be detected in infancy by routine blood and urine tests, organic damage can be prevented by providing a diet low in phenylalanine. Yet, special diets are difficult to enforce on children as they grow older, and low-phenylalanine diets can lead to malnutrition. It is therefore essential to monitor the children's cognitive, behavioral, and physical development in order to titrate the diet appropriately for successive developmental levels. Research on the developmental course of children receiving the diet and modifications of it made for individual cases can provide guidelines for optimizing it in relation to multiple developmental dimensions. This requires standardized procedures and data for comparing the development of PKU children with that of normative samples of age-mates. A full understanding of the disorder and how to treat it thus involves integrating several of the microparadigms and theories listed in Figure 2.1 within a developmental framework.

Goodness of fit

A more complex example is the relation between temperament and psychopathology. This has become a popular topic as a result of the New York Longitudinal Study (NYLS) (Chess & Thomas, 1984; Thomas, Chess, & Birch, 1968; Thomas & Chess, 1977). The NYLS focused on nine dimensions of temperament thought to represent constitutionally based individual differences in behavioral style. The dimensions were combined to classify infants as easy, difficult, or slow to warm up. During the preschool years, behavior problems were more common among children who had been previously classified as difficult than among those classified as easy. These findings suggested the concept of "goodness of fit" between the child and environment, which is listed as one of the microparadigms in Figure 2.1. According to this concept, many childhood disorders result from a poor fit between the child's temperament and environment, especially parental expectations and behavior.

The goodness-of-fit paradigm has broad appeal because it implies that crucial characteristics of the child can be identified early and then communicated to parents, enabling them to adjust their expectations accordingly. Unfortunately, the nine dimensions inferred by Chess and Thomas have not been supported by further research. Nor have the characteristics ascribed to temperament been found to remain stable over the infant and preschool years. Furthermore, efforts to assess the fit between temperament and expectations by parents and teachers have not produced more accurate predictions of problems than have ratings of temperament alone; see Buss and Plomin (1984) for a review of these issues.

This appealing paradigm for analyzing the development of behavior problems thus needs help from other paradigms to provide a more accurate picture of the relations between development and psychopathology. It is possible, for example, that goodness of fit accounts for different proportions of variance in different disorders. Some disorders may be caused by specific organic abnormalities that are not affected much by either the child's temperament or the parents' expectations. In such cases, contributions from the biomedical paradigm may be crucial. Other disorders may be affected more by characteristics of the larger social environment, such as the "culture of poverty," than by individual differences in either children's temperaments or their parents' expectations. Here, the sociological paradigm may be important. Even where both temperament and expectations are potentially influential, extremes of child temperament may overwhelm the effects of parental expectations, or vice versa. To determine how and when goodness-of-fit concepts are helpful, it is thus necessary to seek greater differentiation of development and psychopathology than is afforded by the goodness-of-fit paradigm alone. To do this requires linking concepts and procedures from multiple paradigms in ways that will tell us when and to what degree the goodness-of-fit paradigm is applicable. This is equally true for the other paradigms.

Applications of developmental psychopathology

The potential applications of developmental psychopathology are not limited to basic research. Instead, the products of research and the overarching conceptual framework should help us prevent childhood disorders whenever possible and, when that is not possible, should help to improve the development of troubled children. Figure 2.2 outlines some applications of developmental psychopathology to research, training, prevention, service, and planning. The areas listed under each general activity are based on cur-

Macroparadigm

Developmental psychopathology

Examples of
activities

| Research | Training | Prevention | Service | Planning |

Examples of
specific areas

Research
1. Assessment
2. Taxonomy
3. Epidemiology
4. Developmental course
5. Prognosis
6. Etiology
7. Treatment

Training
1. Goals
2. Common core
3. Professional models
4. Subject matter
5. Practical experience

Prevention
1. Identifying causes
2. Inventing preventive techniques
3. Evaluating outcomes

Service
1. Common core for assessment
2. Case identification
3. Prognostication
4. Intervention
5. Outcome
6. Follow-up

Planning
1. Needs assessment
2. Advocacy
3. Service development
4. Funding
5. Evaluation of services

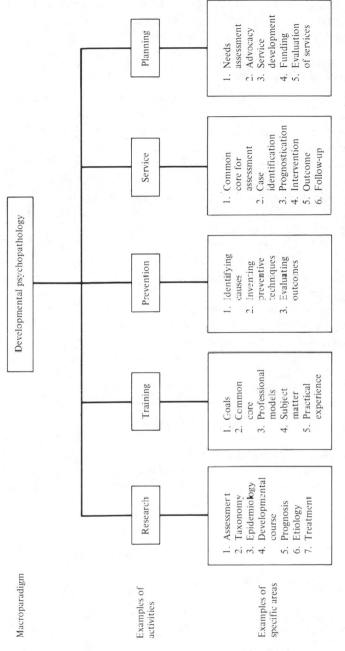

Figure 2.2. Diagram showing potential applications of developmental psychopathology. (© Thomas M. Achenbach.)

rent levels of knowledge and services. The following sections outline some
agendas suggested by the overview in Figure 2.2, but these agendas are subject to change as knowledge and services advance.

Applications to research

In contrast to the microparadigms and theories listed in Figure 2.1,
the research applications of developmental psychopathology in Figure 2.2
concern areas that cut across microparadigms and theories. Work in these
areas requires contributions from multiple microparadigms and, in turn, may
help to advance individual microparadigms. Because several of the areas are
interdependent, a lack of knowledge in one limits progress in others. Conversely, advances in one can facilitate advances in others.

As an example, specific research area 1 in Figure 2.2 – assessment – concerns the identification of the distinguishing features of individual cases or disorders. Procedures drawn from several paradigms are potentially relevant to
assessment, such as biomedical tests for physical abnormalities, behavioral assessment, interviews, tests of cognitive development, and so forth. If these
procedures are properly standardized and normed, they should be able to identify ways in which a particular child differs from normative reference groups.

To identify individual differences that validly discriminate between different
kinds of psychopathology, assessment must be linked to taxonomic constructs
(research area 2 in Figure 2.2). To be effective, taxonomic constructs require
population-based epidemiological data (research area 3) on the distribution of
problems in order to determine if a child's problems are clinically deviant.
This determination also requires developmental data (research area 4) to
indicate which problems typify particular developmental periods, as well as
prognostic data (research area 5) to distinguish between problems that are
transient and those that are more persistent.

Research on assessment, taxonomy, epidemiology, development, and prognosis can in turn facilitate research on etiology (research area 6) and treatment (research area 7) by providing more precise operational definitions of
disorders and better procedures for evaluating their outcomes. Conversely,
discovery of specific etiologies and optimal treatments can pinpoint characteristics that are the most crucial for assessment, taxonomy, and epidemiology.

Applications to training

Because multiple research and clinical specialties are involved in the
study and treatment of psychopathology, no single core training curriculum is
shared by all the relevant professionals. Even those who are especially interested in child and adolescent psychopathology seldom receive a thorough
grounding in normal development, the disorders occurring in different developmental periods, all relevant treatment modalities, and broad clinical experi-

ence. Instead, child-and-adolescent training is usually a supplement to adult training. Furthermore, much child training is shaped by a particular theoretical approach, such as psychodynamic, behavioral, biomedical, or family systems, and by the availability of particular clinical populations, such as retarded children, outpatient clients of psychological clinics, or children in residential care. Differences in the research aspects of training are even greater, with few professionals receiving systematic training in research on relations between development and psychopathology.

To advance the developmental study of psychopathology and its applications to helping children, it would be desirable to have a common core of concepts and goals to guide the training of professionals concerned with troubled children. Such a core need not consist of utopian requirements for all trainees. However, by specifying a model set of training components for the highest-level trainees, such as child psychiatrists and Ph.D. clinical child psychologists, we could reduce the fragmentation that now impedes communication and limits the supply of broadly trained professionals. If the model training components were used to set standards for the highest levels of training, trainees and programs could be evaluated in terms of their deviation from the standards. For child psychiatrists and psychologists, omissions of key training components would be considered deficiencies to be remedied. For workers not expected to have such comprehensive training, the omissions would be indicative of the differences between their qualifications and those of the people expected to be most broadly qualified in child clinical work. Some key components of training suggested by developmental psychopathology are discussed next.

Normal development. All professionals working with children should have a basic grounding in life-span development. This would include important milestones in physical development, language, cognition, skills, behavior problems, social-emotional issues, and adult development. The study of adult development is important even for child specialists, in order to highlight the adaptive challenges children need to be prepared for, as well as those that their parents are experiencing. Major theoretical constructs – such as the cognitive changes hypothesized by Piaget (1983) and the psychosocial conflicts hypothesized by Erikson (1980) – should be central components of training, without stipulating acceptance of these theoretical explanations for development.

Standardized assessment procedures. A second component of training would be standardized tests of ability, achievement, and perceptual motor development, as well as standardized assessment of behavior as reported by key informants, including parents, teachers, clinicians, trained observers, and children themselves (Achenbach & McConaughy, 1987). Although not all trainees need to master the methodological underpinnings or the administration of such procedures, they should be familiar with their theoretical and normative bases, their content, their relations to various aspects of development, and their general predictive power. They should also know where to obtain details regarding reliability and validity when needed. Depending on their special-ties, some trainees will need specific skills in administering infant develop-ment tests such as the Bayley Scales, ability tests such as the WISC-R, and neurological exams such as the PANESS (Mikkelsen, Brown, Minichiello, Millican, & Rapoport, 1982).

Disorders of childhood and adolescence. A third component of training con-cerns the disorders typical of childhood and adolescence. This would involve not only the prevailing nosology but also alternative conceptions of disorders, because official nosologies tend to be arbitrary and changeable. By consider-ing alternative conceptions, as well as data on age at onset and typical course, trainees should acquire a sophisticated perspective on the relations between development and psychopathology. This would entail recognition that most child and adolescent disorders involve quantitative variations on the normal course of development, rather than qualitatively distinct disease entities. It would also highlight the need to set therapeutic goals in terms of promoting further development, rather than restoring children to their premorbid status.

Organic development and abnormalities. Although organic treatments would be the responsibility of physicians, all trainees should learn about major or-ganic determinants and changes, such as physical maturation, changes in hor-mone levels, the course of puberty, and developmental aspects of pharmacoki-netics. Genetic factors in organic development and developmental behavior genetics (Plomin, 1986) are likely to become increasingly important in the study of relations between development and psychopathology. Trainees should also learn enough about symptoms of organic abnormalities and the psychological concomitants of physical illness to facilitate appropriate medical referrals and collaboration with medical personnel.

Interventions. Unlike adults, children seldom seek treatment for themselves. Nor are they the primary informants about their problems or history. Instead, help is sought by adults, such as parents and teachers, for problems reported mainly by the adults. Furthermore, the child's dependence on adults means that interventions usually focus as much on the adults as on the child. Multiple interventions are therefore needed in many cases, and the practitioner must be prepared to use a greater variety of techniques than when treating only adults, who often seek a practitioner specializing in one treatment approach.

Although practitioners cannot be experts in all techniques, trainees should receive didactic instruction and experience in behavioral, family, psychody-namic, cognitive, psychoeducational, and social skills techniques, as well as techniques for helping parents change their behavior toward their child. Group and milieu approaches are also desirable for work with certain populations. Pharmacologic training would be needed by child psychiatrists, but nonmedical trainees should learn about indications and contraindications for particular drugs, side effects, and ways of meshing other interventions with pharmacotherapy.

Clinical and research tracks. As disciplines become more differentiated, it becomes difficult for single individuals to master all their aspects. In earlier days, leaders of a field were idealized as simultaneously being great teachers, clinicians, researchers, and theoreticians. Although some people may, in fact, display exceptional talent in all these areas at some point in their careers, it is unrealistic to expect people to make significant contributions in all of them at once. Instead, training and career ladders need to help people maximize their contributions in the one or two areas where they are strongest. This argues for a differentiation between the advanced training of those who will be primarily clinicians and those who will be primarily researchers.

The small size and heterogeneity of most programs in clinical child psychology (Tuma, 1986) and child psychiatry would make it difficult for them to create a viable research track in addition to basic clinical training. It would certainly be desirable, however, for all such programs to teach trainees to evaluate current research literature in their field, including research design, standard measures, statistics, and the logic of drawing conclusions from data. The trainees would not necessarily be expected to generate their own research, but should become skilled consumers who can evaluate and communicate about the research reported in the literature of their field.

For more differentiated clinical and research training in developmental psychopathology, it is probably necessary to look to the postdoctoral level for psychologists and the postfellow level for child psychiatrists. Training at this level is, of course, common in many fields today. It is at this level that clinical and research specialization becomes more feasible. Those oriented toward clinical careers would learn more specialized skills and would be given greater supervised responsibility with a wider range of more difficult cases than would be feasible at the level of the psychological intern or psychiatric resident. Those oriented toward research careers would work closely with research mentors, collaborating on research, obtaining instruction in methodology, learning how to obtain grants, and initiating and reporting their own research. Considering the lagging supply of rigorously trained child clinicians and the gaps between the available research training and the field's potential for advancement, it may be worth investing in a few flagship programs to provide both clinical and research leadership.

Applications to prevention

Prevention is an appealing concept that has not yet produced many measurable results with respect to psychopathology. Although it is easy to agree on the desirability of eliminating general social evils such as racism, sexism, and violence, it is harder to show (a) how mental health professionals can eliminate them and (b) how their elimination would reduce psychopathology. It is also questionable that mental health professionals have any greater competence to remedy these larger social ills than do other concerned citizens.

In areas where mental health professionals may potentially know and accomplish more than other citizens, they are handicapped by a lack of firm evidence on causal relations between potentially manipulable independent variables and important outcome variables. Some phenomena, such as child abuse, are obviously harmful and should be stopped. Yet, despite the widespread publicity and efforts against child abuse, little is yet known about how to prevent it or how best to handle it when it does occur.

Research is under way on the characteristics of both the abusers and the victims, but the macroparadigm of developmental psychopathology may be helpful in linking research questions, findings, training, and services. For example, the stimuli for abuse, the form of abuse, its consequences, and the appropriate remedies are likely to depend on both the developmental history of the abuser and the developmental history and level of the victim. It is often reported that abusive adults were themselves abused as children (Webster-Stratton, 1985). It should thus not be surprising if a family culture of abuse is transmitted across generations, but it is unlikely that every abused child becomes an abusive adult or that every abusive adult was an abused child.

Standards for what constitutes abuse are relativistic, varying across generations and religious convictions. It is only recently that state agencies have become heavily involved in detecting and punishing long-standing practices that have even been considered virtuous, as in the biblical admonition, "spare the rod and spoil the child." In fact, church–state conflicts have arisen when child abuse laws have been applied to religious sects. In a recent Vermont case, for example, police raided a religious sect to take their children into protective custody because of alleged beatings. Although it appears that the sect beat children with thin wooden balloon sticks, the case was eventually thrown out of court amid confusion over what constitutes abuse, religious freedom, and the questionable benefits of state intervention.

Even when abuse is legally proved and intensive interventions are available for the abusive parents, they may be unwilling to accept help (Reid & Kavanagh, 1985). Constructing an appropriate conceptual schema that will generate effective preventive and therapeutic efforts thus remains a major challenge for mental health professionals.

Another challenging area for applications of developmental psychopathology to prevention is the longitudinal study of children who are at high risk for particular disorders. This reverses the traditional approach of trying to infer the antecedents of disorders by studying people who already manifest them. A prototype high-risk study was launched in the 1960s by Sarnoff Mednick, who sought to assess the developmental course of children who were at high risk for schizophrenia because they had schizophrenic mothers. By comparing the developmental courses of high risk children who eventually manifested schizophrenia, high-risk children who did not manifest it, and children whose parents were not schizophrenic, Mednick expected to pinpoint the etiology of schizophrenia.

The first follow-ups of the subjects indicated that perinatal abnormalities were the best predictors of schizophrenialike psychopathology in the high-risk group (Mednick & Schulsinger, 1972). Later follow-ups, however, showed that subjects initially thought to be schizophrenic no longer appeared so, whereas other subjects had begun to show symptoms of schizophrenia. Instead of perinatal problems as a common antecedent, the antecedents seemed to differ for males and females (John, Mednick, & Schulsinger, 1982). The developmental study of high-risk children thus revealed unexpected complexities in the course of the disorder itself, as well as in its possible antecedents. Long-term follow-ups of adult schizophrenics have also revealed unexpected diversity in the course of what had been viewed as a permanent and deteriorating condition (Ciompi & Müller, 1976; Clausen, 1984; Harding, Brooks, Ashikaga, Strauss, & Breier, 1987; Tsuang, Woolson, & Fleming, 1979). Furthermore, research comparing children at risk for affective disorders with those at risk for schizophrenia has shown that both groups have attention deficits previously considered specific to schizophrenia (Harvey, Winters, Weintraub, & Neale, 1981).

The developmental findings of marked variations in the courses of schizophrenialike symptoms cast doubt on assumptions based on nondevelopmental research. These findings underline the need for a clearer picture of the step-by-step progression of psychopathology over various developmental periods in order to devise effective preventive methods.

Applications to services

Services for troubled children date back to the beginning of the twentieth century. Improvements are needed, however, in the distribution, accessibility, coordination, and evaluation of services. Many communities lack specialized services geared to the needs of troubled children. Furthermore, local services may be fragmented according to different mandates (e.g., schools, mental health, court, welfare, foster care), treatment philosophies (e.g., psychoanalytic versus behavioral versus drug), service models (e.g., child guidance versus community mental health versus private practice), and the backgrounds of service providers. Few communities offer a clear-cut continuum of care whereby the initial identification of problems leads directly to the most appropriate type and level of help. Instead, a child manifesting problems may be seen at one point by a practitioner who favors one kind of assessment and intervention, but later by practitioners of other persuasions. Although extensive records may be compiled at each step, the differences in approach often preclude integrating data from one step to the next. This duplicates costly efforts and makes it hard to track changes in the child's functioning from one point to another.

To make better use of existing services and to provide a better focus for new ones, it would be helpful to have a common core of procedures and concepts analogous to that discussed earlier for training. Because no single treatment model is appropriate for all facets of all disorders, it would be desirable for the common core to comprise assessment procedures and concepts that are widely applicable, unrestricted by the philosophies of individual practitioners. This is already done to a large extent in the assessment of cognitive ability and school achievement, where certain standardized tests are widely used for individual assessments of learning problems. The assessment of behavioral and emotional problems, however, has been subject to much more variation, based largely on differences in practitioners' personal philosophies. Psychodynamically oriented workers, for example, tend to use projective tests to infer underlying conflicts and personality structures. Analogously, psychometricians use personality tests to tap traits, behaviorists use direct observations to identify target behaviors and environmental contingencies, and medically oriented workers use interviews and test data to make nosological diagnoses.

Without necessarily excluding any of these microparadigms, the developmental psychopathology macroparadigm implies a normative developmental approach to assessment that compares the problems and competencies of individual children with those of normative samples of age-mates. As discussed earlier, standardized assessment should be linked to taxonomic procedures that reflect syndromes or patterns of problems, population-based epidemiological data, and data on developmental differences in problems and competencies. Assessment should also take account of differences between a child's functioning in different contexts, as reported by different informants. To illustrate this approach, Table 2.1 lists five major axes relevant to assessment of most child and adolescent disorders. Axis I (parent reports), axis II (teacher reports), and axis V (direct assessment of the child) reflect the type of normative developmental assessment of problems and competencies implied by developmental psychopathology. Two other important facets of child assessment are represented by axis III (standardized cognitive assessment) and axis IV (biomedical assessment).

If all child services drew on a common set of assessment procedures, such as those listed in Table 2.1, different stages and types of services could be linked together more effectively. For example, if the same standardized instruments were used for case finding via screening, needs assessment, and referral procedures, they could yield common reference points for all the child services in a community. The same standardized data would thus be available, whatever the route by which a child was initially identified as needing help. If a child was seen by one practitioner and then referred to another, the assessment process would

Table 2.1. *Examples of multiaxial assessment*

Age range	Axis I Parent reports	Axis II Teacher reports	Axis III Cognitive assessment	Axis IV Biomedical assessment	Axis V Direct assessment of child
0–2	Developmental history; Minnesota Child Development Inventory (Ireton & Thwing, 1974)	—	Bayley (1969) Infant Scales	Height, weight, neurological and medical exam	Observations during developmental testing
2–5	Developmental history; Child Behavior Checklist (Achenbach & Edelbrock, 1983, 1986a); Louisville Behavior Checklist (Miller, 1981)	Kohn (1977) Symptom Checklist; Preschool Behavior Checklist (Behar & Stringfield, 1974)	McCarthy (1972) Scales	Height, weight, neurological and medical exam	Observations during play interview
6–11	Developmental history; Child Behavior Checklist; Louisville Behavior Checklist	CBCL–Teacher's Report Form (Achenbach & Edelbrock, 1986b); School Behavior Checklist (Miller, 1972)	Achievement tests; Kaufman & Kaufman (1983) Assessment Battery; Koppitz (1975) Bender Gestalt; WISC-R (Wechsler, 1974)	Height, weight, neurological and medical exam	Child Assessment Schedule (Hodges et al., 1982); Semistructured Clinical Interview for Children (Achenbach & McConaughy, 1985)
12–18	Developmental history; Child Behavior Checklist; Louisville Behavior Checklist	CBCL–Teacher's Report Form; School Behavior Checklist	Achievement tests; WISC-R, WAIS-R (Wechsler, 1981)	Height, weight, neurological and medical exam	DISC (Costello et al., 1984); Youth Self-Report (Achenbach & Edelbrock, 1983, 1987)

Note: Where multiple instruments are available, those with the most promising reliability, validity, and normative data are listed.
Source: Adapted from Achenbach (1985a, p. 173).

not have to be repeated each time. Instead, the standardized aspects of the initial assessment would be useful to subsequent practitioners, although they would also be free to add other components as they saw fit. Furthermore, even if a child is seen by only one practitioner, the use of standardized assessment procedures to obtain base-line data makes it easy to evaluate outcomes by repeating the same procedures at later points, such as after an intervention has had time to take effect and again at longer follow-up periods such as 6, 12, or 24 months. This enables the practitioner or agency to document outcomes for children having particular presenting problems and receiving particular interventions. If outcomes are consistently poor for particular kinds of problems, this would argue for changing the services offered for these problems or referring children to services specializing in such problems.

Applications to planning

Like the prevention of psychopathology, the planning of mental health services is an appealing concept that is honored more in the breach than in the observance. In most of the United States, the kinds and distributions of services for children reflect political vicissitudes, fads, and market forces more than systematic planning based on direct assessment of children's needs. At the state level, a long-standing impediment to effective planning for children is the orientation of state mental health systems toward chronic adult patients. This began with the establishment of state hospitals in the nineteenth century. It continued through the establishment of community mental health centers in the 1960s, which had no mandate to serve children at all until 1975. Even since this mandate, few centers have devoted much effort to children. The massive erosion of funding in the 1980s and the swelling ranks of homeless adult patients have further limited efforts on behalf of children.

Aside from the low priority and inadequate resources accorded children's needs, obstacles to planning also arise from fragmentation like that discussed earlier in relation to training and services. Various public agencies have responsibility for troubled children, including schools, welfare departments, protective services, and courts, as well as mental health agencies. The same children often fall under the aegis of several of these agencies. Yet there is seldom much coordination among agencies in identifying, assessing, and serving the children who are their joint responsibility. Instead, the different agencies resemble the proverbial blind men describing an elephant in terms of the different pieces they touch, unaware that all the pieces are parts of the same beast. Differences between agencies' ways of categorizing problems and the failure to identify cases that overlap between agencies hamper effective planning.

The developmental psychopathology macroparadigm could contribute to the aspects of planning listed in Figure 2.1 by providing different agencies with common focal points for identifying the children to be served. One obvious focal point would be the age of children, with welfare and protective services usually having the main responsibility for infants, joined thereafter by mental health, education, and juvenile courts. The agencies relevant to each major age period – such as infancy, preschool, elementary school, and adolescence – could then collaborate in obtaining population-based data using standardized assessment procedures. For school-aged populations, this can be done economically by taking random samples of one or two pupils from each classroom and obtaining standardized ratings of problems by people who know the pupils well, such as parents and teachers. For adolescents, standardized self-reports constitute an important additional source of data on the distribution of problems in a state or other area. Table 2.1 lists parent, teacher, and self-report instruments that have been used in this way in several cultures (Achenbach, Bird, Canino, Phares, Gould, & Rubio-Stipec, 1990). Obtaining data on representative general population samples of infants and preschoolers may be harder, although follow-ups of random samples from birth certificates would be relatively easy for state agencies having access to names and addresses in birth records. The primary data on preschoolers could include standardized parental reports on developmental and behavior problem inventories, such as those listed in Table 2.1. A more ambitious effort might include data from pediatricians on major disorders such as mental retardation and autism.

To document cases actually referred for mental health services, each agency could participate in a case register whereby they would obtain the same standardized assessment data on each referred child for entry in a central computer file. Over a designated period, such as a year, the distribution of problems seen by each agency and the overlap in caseloads could then be determined. The number of cases served could also be compared with the rates of problems found in the general population samples, in order to estimate unmet needs.

The types of data outlined here are important for accurate projections of needs and for planning appropriate services. They are also important for effective advocacy in government bureaucracies and legislatures, where it is otherwise difficult to make a strong case for children's mental health services. Furthermore, if agencies could collaborate in using a common set of normative developmental assessment procedures to ascertain the distributions of problems in the general population and in referred samples, this would provide them with a basis for coordinating their planning, seeking appropriate funding, evaluating existing services in light of data on empirically documented needs, and designing new services to fill unmet needs.

Conclusions

In this chapter, I have outlined a variety of endeavors relevant to the study of psychopathology from a developmental perspective. With an orientation toward future possibilities (Garmezy, 1982), I have advocated a broad, nonrestrictive view of developmental psychopathology intended to highlight the connections between diverse paradigms, theories, and activities, including research, training, prevention, services, and planning.

What is "developmental" about developmental psychopathology? In my view, the current value of the developmental study of psychopathology lies less in its capacity for supplanting existing theories than in its potential for bringing conceptual order out of a welter of contrasting concepts and activities. Its most compelling applications are in the period from birth to maturity, but it is potentially applicable to later periods as well.

The relevant phenomena are too diverse to be fully explained by any single theory. As knowledge advances, theory and services are likely to become more specialized rather than more general. A macroparadigm of developmental psychopathology is therefore needed to provide integrative concepts and common reference points in the face of inevitable specialization.

The centrality of developmental concepts stems from the massive biological, cognitive, and social-emotional changes that occur from birth to maturity. If we look at the dramatic differences between an infant, preschooler, fourth-grader, early adolescent, and college student, it is obvious that developmental changes have a tremendous impact on the challenges faced by the individual, the individual's self-concept, and other people's expectations. The extent to which the environment and people's expectations are geared to the typical capabilities of each age level gives normative developmental assessment a key role in identifying deviance and evaluating subsequent change. Research, training, prevention, service, planning, and communication can be improved by reference to the common denominator of developmental norms and by viewing specific forms of deviance in relation to the developmental sequences in which they are embedded. It is by integrating concepts of psychopathology around normative sequences and highlighting maladaptive deviations from such sequences that a macroparadigm of developmental psychopathology can make a major contribution.

References

Achenbach, T. M. (1985a). *Assessment and taxonomy of child and adolescent psychopathology.* Beverly Hills, CA: Sage.

Achenbach, T. M. (1985b). Assessment of anxiety in children. In A. H. Tuma & J. Maser (Eds.), *Anxiety and the anxiety disorders* (pp. 707–34). Hillsdale, NJ: Erlbaum.

Achenbach, T. M., & Edelbrock, C. S. (1983). *Manual for the Child Behavior Checklist and Revised Child Behavior Profile.* Burlington: University of Vermont Department of Psychiatry.

Achenbach, T. M., & Edelbrock, C. S. (1986a). *Child Behavior Checklist and Profile for ages 2–3.* Burlington: University of Vermont Department of Psychiatry.

Achenbach, T. M., & Edelbrock, C. S. (1986b). *Manual for the Teacher's Report Form and teacher version of the Child Behavior Profile.* Burlington: University of Vermont Department of Psychiatry.

Achenbach, T. M., & Edelbrock, C. S. (1987). *Manual for the Youth Self-Report and Profile.* Burlington: University of Vermont Department of Psychiatry.

Achenbach, T. M., & McConaughy, S. H. (1985). *Child Interview Checklist – Self-Report Form; Child Interview Checklist – Observation Form.* Burlington: University of Vermont Department of Psychiatry.

Achenbach, T. M., & McConaughy, S. H. (1987). *Empirically-based assessment of child and adolescent psychopathology: Practical applications.* Beverly Hills, CA: Sage.

Achenbach, T. M., Bird, H. R., Canino, G., Phares, V., Gould, M. S., Rubio-Stipec, M. (1990). Epidemiological comparisons of Puerto Rican and U.S. mainland children: parent, teacher, and self reports. *Journal of the American Academy of Child and Adolescent Psychiatry.*

American Psychiatric Association. (1st ed. 1952; 2nd ed. 1968; 3rd ed. 1980; 3rd rev. ed. 1987). *Diagnostic and statistical manual of mental disorders.* Washington, DC: APA.

Bayley, N. (1969). *Bayley Scales of Infant Development.* New York: New York Psychological Corp.

Behar, L. B., & Stringfield, S. (1974). A behavior rating scale for the preschool child. *Developmental Psychology, 10,* 601–10.

Buss, A. H., & Plomin, R. (1984). *Temperament: Early developing personality traits.* Hillsdale, NJ: Erlbaum.

Chess, S., & Thomas, A. (1984). *Origins and evolution of behavior disorders: From infancy to early adult life.* New York: Brunner/Mazel.

Cicchetti, D. (1984). Special issue: Developmental psychopathology. *Child Development, 55,* 1–316.

Ciompi, L., & Müller, C. (1976). *Lebensweg und alter Schizophrenen. Eine katamnestic Langzeitstudie bis ins Senum.* Berlin: Springer.

Clausen, J. A. (1984). Mental illness and life course. In P. B. Baltes & O. G. Brim (Eds.), *Life span development and behavior* (Vol. 6, pp. 203–42). New York: Academic Press.

Costello, A. J., Edelbrock, C., Dulcan, M. K., Kalas, R., & Klaric, S. H. (1984). *Report on the Diagnostic Interview Schedule for Children (DISC).* University of Pittsburgh Department of Psychiatry.

Cytryn, L., & McKnew, D. H. (1979). In J. Noshpitz (Ed.), *Basic handbook of child psychiatry* (Vol. 2). New York: Basic Books.

Erikson, E. H. (1980). Elements of a psychoanalytic theory of psychosocial development. In S. I. Greenspan & G. H. Pollock (Eds.), *The course of life: Psychoanalytic contributions toward understanding personality development. Vol. 1: Infancy and early childhood.* Adelphi, MD: NIMH Mental Health Study Center.

Frommer, E. A. (1967). Treatment of childhood depression with antidepressant drugs. *British Medical Journal, 1,* 729–32.

Garmezy, N. (1982). Research in clinical psychology: Serving the future hour. In P. C. Kendall & J. N. Butcher (Eds.), *Handbook of research methods in clinical psychology* (pp. 677–90). New York: Wiley.

Harding, C. M., Brooks, G. W., Ashikaga, T., Strauss, J. S., Breier, A. (1987). The Vermont Longitudinal Study: Long-term outcome for DSM-III schizophrenia. *American Journal of Psychiatry, 44,* 727–35.

Harvey, P., Winters, K., Weintraub, S., & Neale, J. M. (1981). Distractibility in children vulnerable to psychopathology. *Journal of Abnormal Psychology, 90,* 298–304.

Hodges, K., McKnew, D., Cytryn, L., Stern, L., & Kline, J. (1982). The Child Assessment Schedule (CAS) diagnostic interview: A report on reliability and validity. *Journal of the American Academy of Child Psychiatry, 21,* 468–73.

Ireton, H., & Thwing, E. J. (1974). *Minnesota Child Development Inventory.* Minneapolis: Behavior Science Systems.

John, R. S., Mednick, S. A., & Schulsinger, F. (1982). Teacher reports as a predictor of schizophrenia and borderline schizophrenia: A Bayesian decision analysis. *Journal of Abnormal Psychology, 91,* 399–413.

Kaufman, A. S., & Kaufman, N. L. (1983). *Kaufman Assessment Battery for Children*. Circle Pines, MN: American Guidance Service.

Kohn, M. (1977). *Social competence, symptoms, and underachievement in childhood: A longitudinal perspective*. New York: Wiley.

Koppitz, E. M. (1975). *The Bender Gestalt Test for young children*. (Vol. 2). New York: Grune & Stratton.

McCarthy, D. (1972). *McCarthy scales of children's abilities*. New York: Psychological Corporation.

Mednick, S. A., & Schulsinger, F. (1972). *Studies of children at high risk for schizophrenia*. Unpublished manuscript, New School for Social Research.

Mikkelsen, E. J., Brown, G. L., Minichiello, M. D., Millican, F. K., & Rapoport, J. L. (1982). Neurologic status in hyperactive, enuretic, encopretic, and normal boys. *Journal of the American Academy of Child Psychiatry, 21*, 75–81.

Miller, L. C. (1972). School Behavior Checklist: An inventory of deviant behavior for elementary school children. *Journal of Consulting & Clinical Psychology, 38*, 134–44.

Miller, L. C. (1981). *Louisville Behavior Checklist Manual* (rev. ed.). Los Angeles: Western Psychological Services.

Piaget, J. (1983). Piaget's theory. In P. H. Mussen (Ed.), *Handbook of child psychology. Vol. 1: History, theory, and methods* (4th ed.). New York: Wiley.

Plomin, R. (1986). *Development, genetics, and psychology*. Hillsdale, NJ: Erlbaum.

Reid, J. B., & Kavanagh, K. (1985). A social interactional approach to child abuse: Risk, prevention, and treatment. In M. Chesney & R. Rosman (Eds.), *Anger and hostility in behavioral and cardiovascular disorders* (pp. 241–57). New York: Hemisphere/ McGraw-Hill.

Thomas, A., & Chess, S. (1977). *Temperament and development*. New York: Brunner/Mazel.

Thomas, A., Chess, S., & Birch, H. G. (1968). *Temperament and behavior disorders in children*. New York University Press.

Tsuang, M. T., Woolson, R. F., & Fleming, J. A. (1979). Long-term outcome of major psychoses. I. Schizophrenia and affective disorders compared with psychiatrically symptom-free surgical conditions. *Archives of General Psychiatry, 36*, 1295–301.

Tuma, A. H., & Maser, J. (Eds.). (1985). *Anxiety and the anxiety disorders*. Hillsdale, NJ: Erlbaum.

Tuma, J. M. (1986). The Hilton Head Conference on Training Clinical Child Psychologists: History and background. *Clinical Psychologist, 39*, 4–7.

Webster-Stratton, C. (1985). Comparison of abusive and nonabusive families with conduct-disordered children. *American Journal of Orthopsychiatry, 55*, 59–69.

Wechsler, D. (1974). *Wechsler Intelligence Scale for Children – Revised*. New York: Psychological Corporation.

Wechsler, D. (1981). *Wechsler Adult Intelligence Scale – Revised*. New York: Psychological Corporation.

Weinberg, W. A., Rutman, J., Sullivan, L., Penick, E. C., & Dietz, S. G. (1973). Depression in children referred to an educational diagnostic center: Diagnosis and treatment. *Journal of Pediatrics, 83*, 1065–72.

Part II

Contributions of the high-risk child paradigm: continuities and changes in adaptation during development

In the first chapter in this part, Arnold J. Sameroff and Ronald Seifer begin by providing a historical overview of the traditional debates regarding the etiologies of mental disorders. They then discuss some of the successes and short-comings of the risk-research strategy focused on parental psychopathology as the prepotent risk factor for psychopathology. Using parental schizophrenia as an exemplary model, these authors outline the bases for the early etiologic reasoning of the risk-for-schizophrenia researchers and describe how the Rochester Risk Project failed to confirm all of the model's predictions. Of particular importance to these authors were the discoveries of the nonspecificity of effects of parental diagnosis on children's current adjustment, the more salient effects of chronicity and severity regardless of maternal diagnosis, and the powerful influences of socioeconomic status on children's early adaptations. Given these findings and those of their contemporaries in both risk research and more basic developmental research, these authors contend that the medical-illness model and the high-risk child model are flawed. This is because the models fail to include a transactive systems model of competence and vulnerability during development.

The next chapter is authored by John Richters and Sheldon Weintraub. It illustrates the promise of the developmental psychopathology perspective when applied to the rich body of prospective data from the Stony Brook Risk Project. This project is one of the largest and longest-running longitudinal studies from the Risk for Schizophrenia Research Consortium. Their data, gathered from children, parents, schools, and clinical records, provide evidence of the dynamic interplay between the parents' schizophrenic or affective disorder, rearing family environments, and the changing competencies of the at-risk offspring. Initially, Stony Brook project investigators sought only markers for predicting breakdowns. However, they subsequently became absorbed in solving the puzzle of understanding the reasons for some of the offspring's invulnerabilities. They found that to achieve this understanding required that they improve their conceptual clarity concerning the operational

49

definitions of risk, vulnerability, resilience, risk reducers, and protective factors. They also discuss how a test of a resilience model must be based on data from actually stressed versus nonstressed children. Obvious as this caution seems, presumptions of stress have been used as data in other high-risk group studies.

In their chapter, Marian Radke-Yarrow and Tracy Sherman report on findings from the NIMH prospective study of the adjustment of young children of depressed parents. In the view of these authors, developmental psychopathologists can also study processes that translate two often ignored protective constructs – love and nurturance – into successful adaptation among children who are constitutionally vulnerable to maladjustment. In similarity to the views espoused by Sameroff and Seifer, Radke-Yarrow and Sherman contend that research questions concerning vulnerability and resilience must be cast into testable developmental process models. They then show how they tackled the problem of determining resilience and invulnerability in children of affectively disturbed parents. They introduce the concept of "hard growing" for children reared in chaotic home environments where parent psychopathology is frequently modeled. To qualify as a survivor, a high-risk child will have to evidence no psychiatrically diagnosable disorder and no school failures or other indicators of serious maladaptation. Through vivid descriptions of case histories, Radke-Yarrow and Sherman illustrate how survival can be assisted by three protective qualities: (a) above-average IQ, (b) a quality that elicits positive responses from other persons, and (c) "parental match." The last results when some quality in the child at risk matches a core need in his or her disturbed parent. Such matching can result in positive parenting experiences and lead to enhancing the child's self-regard. By continuing this longitudinal study, the NIMH research team expects to be able to predict changes in adjustment problems during such stages of increased developmental challenge as adolescence.

The chapter by Margaret O'Dougherty and Francis Wright explores how certain processes, either internal or external to the developing child, can exacerbate or diminish risk expression. Because these authors' research is conducted in pediatric clinical settings, they are able to study how individual differences in biological deficits interact with other psychosocial factors during maturation to produce variations in competence. Therefore, the chapter explores the moderating potential of several external processes (rearing environment and parental stress responses to the child's medical problems) and several internal processes (the medical conditions of chronic hypoxia and open heart surgery). Similar to Richters and Weintraub's caution concerning the need for actually measuring versus assuming the experience of stress, O'Dougherty and Wright discuss how *dosage of risk* from presumed brain damage must be verified from multiple sources of assessment, including new brain-imaging techniques. These authors go on to demonstrate with their data how cumulative risk scores can be compiled and interpreted in a developmental psychopathology model incorporating multiple internal and external processes affecting successive adaptations of children at high risk.

The chapter by Gerald R. Patterson and Deborah M. Capaldi integrates clinical, epidemiological, and mathematical modeling research perspectives, providing a clear step-by-step presentation of how to move from theoretical inferences to construct development and validation in order to begin testing causal models relevant to developmental psychopathology. They point out how their research into the origins of antisocial behavior has taught them not to expect to find a single, simple path to any specific child behavior of concern to developmental psychopathologists. They review how their research experiences have led them to rely on multimethod, multisource assessment strategies and to use aggregated indicators to ensure adequate measurement of a latent construct hypothesized to underlie the expression of a behavioral outcome. To illustrate this point, the authors focus on how to study the determinants and concomitants of the construct of depressive mood. The models examined by Patterson and Capaldi stipulate that children's depressive mood is a frequent concomitant of the same process that produces antisocial behavior. They demonstrate how they tested theoretically acceptable but distinctly different models of association among affective, family functioning, peer social approval, self-esteem, and academic-achievement constructs. Patterson and Capaldi's cogent interpretations concerning the procedures to assess the inadequacy of the additive model and the usefulness of the alternate mediational model should be very instructive to other developmental psychopathologists who are trying to fit causal or associative models to their own complex longitudinal data sets.

The final chapter in this part by Jerome Kagan, Jane L. Gibbons, Maureen O. Johnson, J. Steven Reznick, and Nancy Snidman extends the discussion of various temperament and behavioral traits that may serve as risks for maladaptation during early development. Specifically, they focus on tendencies toward high levels of irritability and inhibited behavior in response to uncertainty, and they describe how these tendencies may be studied as indicators of general vulnerability to environmental stressors. These authors illustrate their discussions with data they have obtained from a prospective series of laboratory and social-setting experiments with inhibited (shy and timid) versus uninhibited (outgoing and bold) young children. Their longitudinal findings demonstrate greater stability in uninhibited behavioral tendencies and greater positive associations between inhibited behavioral tendencies and the experience of childhood fears. These authors also discuss the implications that tendencies involving behavioral inhibition have for testing the construct of vulnerability to stress. Clearly, developmental psychopathologists are well advised to consider how best to assess both constitutional and learned tendencies for behavioral inhibition in the face of challenging events in designing their future research programs.

3   Early contributors to developmental risk

Arnold J. Sameroff and Ronald Seifer

The emerging field of developmental psychopathology has begun to impact on a number of the traditional problem areas in child psychiatry by illuminating new possibilities for understanding the etiology, future course, and treatment of many childhood problems. Such new possibilities are contained in the dynamic models of development that are implicit in the new discipline. A redefinition of psychopathology in developmental terms was provided by Sroufe and Rutter (1984, p. 18), who saw the discipline as "the study of the origins and course of individual patterns of behavioral adaptation."

Rutter and Garmezy (1983) described the differences between developmental psychopathology and other disciplines. They argued that developmental psychologists assume an essential *continuity* in functioning such that severe symptoms (e.g., depression) are placed on the same dimension as normal behaviors (e.g., sadness or unhappiness). On the other hand, clinical psychiatrists use an implicit assumption of *discontinuity* such that disordered behavior is interpreted as different in kind from normal behavior. In contrast to both approaches, developmental psychopathologists make no prior assumptions about either continuity or discontinuity. They are concerned centrally with both the connections and lack of connections between normality and disorder.

The need for a new orientation to the etiology of psychopathology arises not solely out of academic interests but rather because of the failure of more customary models to explain how mental and behavioral disorders arise and are maintained. Within the health sciences, the traditional model of disorder is based on the presumption that there are identifiable somatic entities that underlie definable disease syndromes. The current dominant view of mental disorder within psychiatry is still strongly biomedical and disease-oriented, with little role allowed for social and psychological etiological factors (Engel, 1977). From the biomedical perspective, individuals are seen not as integrated

This project was supported by grants from the National Institutes of Health and the William T. Grant Foundation.

systems of biological, psychological, and social functioning, but rather as isolated units with strong unidirectional effects of biological events on behavioral expression. If the biology is impacted, through constitution, infection, or cure, then the behavior is affected. Another characteristic of this biomedical approach is the lack of attention to models that include the etiology of *competent* as well as incompetent behaviors.

Three principles emerge from such biomedical models that are frequently applied to the study of psychopathology:

1. The same entity will cause the same disorder in all affected individuals, whether they be children or adults.
2. The same symptoms at different ages should be caused by the same entity.
3. Specific disorders of children should lead to similar adult disorders.

The failure of this disease model to explain human behavior is evident in the fact that none of these three principles can be generalized, especially with respect to the study of psychopathology. In fact, this model is proving inadequate to explain many physiological disease processes, which often have varying developmental processes and modes of expression, depending on the age, general health status, and social context of individuals (Cassell, 1986). Yet much of the psychiatric research in the area of severe mental disorder still is directed at isolating specific biochemical or structural defects (or markers of them).

Models of competence

In contrast to models of illness, models of competence attempt to explain the nature and causes of successful developmental outcomes. Such models tend to be behavioral in nature, with little emphasis on underlying biological processes. Also, these models are increasingly evident in studies of early developmental processes, for example, in the areas of problem-solving ability (Matas, Arend, & Sroufe, 1978) and mastery motivation (Messer et al., 1986).

The importance of developmental models of competence is that they have become well articulated in terms of identifying the interplay among individual and social systems that may lead to successful outcomes. Multiple domains of competent functioning within individual children have been identified, as well as aspects of parent–child interaction and context that should explain individual variations in patterns of competence (Seifer, Vaughn, Lefever, & Smith, in press).

Another approach to competence seeks specific factors that will explain the successful development of individuals presumed to be at high risk for poor outcomes. This approach, which is the subject of this volume and has been well articulated by Garmezy and others, leads to the study of stress resistance, invulnerability, and resilience.

Vulnerability models and systems models of competence are superficially different, but there is no theoretical reason for them to be incompatible. Models that specifically examine populations at risk can (and we believe should) search for explanations for successful outcomes in terms of developing systems and contexts (Sameroff, 1983; Sameroff & Seifer, 1983). Conversely, such systems models must ultimately account for a variety of risk factors if they are to become comprehensive explanations of human development.

Developmental models of psychopathology

The developmental approach expands on traditional models of mental disease by incorporating biological and behavioral functioning into a general systems model of developmental regulation. Within this approach, underlying entities do not exist independent of developmental organization. The expression of biological vulnerabilities can occur only in relation to the balance between coping skills and stresses in each individual's life history (Zubin & Spring, 1977). Continuities in competence or incompetence from childhood into adulthood cannot be simply related to continuities in underlying pathology or health. The relations between earlier and later behavior have to be understood in terms of the continuity of ordered or disordered experience across time, interacting with an individual's unique biobehavioral characteristics. To the extent that experience becomes more organized, problems in adaptation will diminish. To the extent that experience becomes more chaotic, problems in adaptation will increase. What the developmental approach contributes is the identification of factors that influence the child's ability to organize experience and consequently the child's level of adaptive functioning.

Schizophrenia

The disease model has been most frequently applied in the study of severe mental illness. Among many investigators, the assumption is made (often implicitly) that a specific somatic disturbance leads to expression of psychiatric dysfunction. In terms of expression at different ages, the case for continuity has a strong face validity with respect to affective disorders because of the similarity of topology of emotional expression in children and adults (regardless of whether or not one accepts that children manifest true depressive disorders). Children, like adults, exhibit elation and sadness, experience sleep disorders, become agitated, and exhibit mood swings. However, for schizophrenia, continuities in the form of specific behaviors across ages have been difficult to identify; so the research focus has been on the search for continuity in underlying process. Investigators have sought consistent differences in basic processes (e.g., attention), or biochemical substances, in populations of children thought to be at risk for schizophrenia and adult populations diagnosed as having schizophrenia.

High-risk model

As noted earlier, it is difficult to identify research populations by characterizing a set of behaviors in children that directly and consistently lead to schizophrenia in adults. As a result, other strategies for examining developmental processes related to schizophrenia have been developed. Most popular among these are high-risk models, most often based on family characteristics (Garmezy, 1974).

Clear familial patterns were found in a study of schizophrenia that were interpreted as evidence supporting hereditary transmission (Kallmann, 1938, 1946). Large numbers of the offspring of schizophrenic parents had mental disturbances, and high concordance rates were found for twins (particularly monozygotic twins), siblings, and other relatives. Whereas the rate of schizophrenia in the general population is about 1%, close to 10% of children with a single schizophrenic parent themselves become schizophrenic (Hanson, Gottesman, & Mcehl, 1977).

In the context of such high familial risk, secular trends have acted to increase the number of children born to, and reared by, schizophrenic parents. Whereas schizophrenic patients formerly were kept in long-term institutional care, often lasting entire life spans, most are now medicated and returned to normal society after brief hospital stays. As a result, more chronic schizophrenics have the opportunity to become parents and to retain custody of their children.

At about the time that hospitalizations for schizophrenia were becoming dramatically shorter, many researchers became interested in the children of schizophrenics as a promising population in which to study the etiology of the disorder (Fish, 1963; Mednick & McNeil, 1968). This interest in pursuing a risk research model was a reaction to serious shortcomings associated with studying etiological factors in already diagnosed individuals: inaccurate or systematically distorted retrospective reports (Robins, 1966); low comparability of follow-back information from sources such as school records (Watt, Stolorow, Lubensky, & McClelland, 1970); and effects of psychiatric care, such as institutionalization, having a diagnostic label, medication, and diet.

In response to these types of problems, Mednick and McNeil (1968) proposed that finding a group of children, a significant portion of whom would later develop schizophrenia, would provide a population that would not suffer from such methodological defects. Stimulated by the work of Mednick and Schulsinger (1968), many researchers have studied samples of these high-risk children during the past 25 years (Garmezy, 1974; Watt, Anthony, Wynne, & Rolf, 1984) to address the age-old question regarding schizophrenia: Is it caused by heredity or environment or some combination of the two?

Two of the earliest high-risk studies took very different approaches to studying the etiology of schizophrenia. Mednick and Schulsinger (1968) examined a Danish sample of adolescents born to schizophrenic parents who were compared with a group of matched controls born to normal parents. These children were to be followed through adulthood, with the expectation that the entire risk period for schizophrenia (18–45 years of age) would be examined during the course of the study. In contrast, Fish and Alpert (1962) began their longitudinal study with a much smaller sample size, and they began at the time the children were born. In addition, their major risk index was a constitutional marker in the children (variability in neuromotor integration), as well as pathology in the parents. Finally, the study by Fish and Alpert was far more clinically oriented. Although there were striking differences in these two pioneering studies, important commonalities have served to define the field of high-risk research: identification of a constitutional marker (in either subjects or their families) and identification of subjects *before* any symptoms of schizophrenia were present.

These designs have merit if one assumes a primarily biological etiology for schizophrenia. The major factor to control is the presence or absence of the biological risk factor. However, there are many other confounding factors: Schizophrenia is found disproportionately among those of lower social status (Kohn, 1973); it is a severe mental illness, comparable to major affective disorders; and it is a chronic, long-term illness in many individuals. Therefore, well-designed studies must examine and appropriately control for these factors.

In addition to controls for various factors, the basic research strategy must also be considered in this very costly research. The most elegant design is to examine high-risk subjects until the entire 30-year risk period for schizophrenia is completed. Obviously the problems with this approach concern the time and expenditure involved; a more subtle problem is that during the period between assessment and final data analysis, measures that represented the state of the art at the beginning of the study may have become obsolete. The alternative is a cross-sectional or short-term longitudinal approach to examine differences in high-risk versus low-risk groups, with the assumption that such differences might indicate important factors in the etiology of schizophrenia. The obvious problem here is in not knowing who in the high-risk group will eventually become schizophrenic, preventing validation of the marker variable.

In the context of such major conceptual problems in determining causal factors specific to schizophrenia, the rich data bases from the high-risk studies conducted in the 1970s and 1980s have also been used to evaluate hypotheses that may not pertain specifically to the etiology of schizophrenia. One of the major alternate strategies has been in the development of competence models, as noted earlier. Given that most of the high-risk subjects in these studies will not become schizophrenic (about 90%) and that about half should not show any psychiatric disturbance, there are excellent opportunities to search for factors related to good outcomes for these children.

Rochester Longitudinal Study

We have been conducting a longitudinal study since 1970 to investigate the role of parental mental illness, social status, and other family cognitive and social variables that might be risk factors in the development of children. The target population comprised the offspring of schizophrenic women; such children have been shown to have more than ten times the risk for developing schizophrenia as offspring of nonschizophrenic women. The rationale for this study was not based on the possibility of determining which index subject would ultimately receive a diagnosis of schizophrenia, because of the long duration before the end of the risk period. The strategy of using young children was aimed at identifying risk factors that would be markers for later specific psychiatric diagnoses, because it was known that these children would later manifest increased incidences of those diagnoses.

We did not directly examine the ultimate schizophrenic diagnostic status for which this population was at risk. Rather, our study specifically measured levels of competence early in life that had relatively broad developmental implications. The rationale for such an approach was that early developmental incompetencies would increase the probability that later in life the children would continue to exhibit problems, some of them of an increasingly severe nature. As such, the child risk was expressed early in life in a *nonspecific* manner (e.g., as broad cognitive or social maladaptation) rather than as specific deficits observable in every risk child.

At the outset we considered three major hypotheses: (a) that deviant behavior would be attributable to variables associated with a specific maternal diagnosis (e.g., schizophrenia); (b) that deviant behavior would be attributable to variables associated with mental illness in general, but no diagnostic group in particular; (c) that deviant behavior would be associated with social status [i.e., minority or socioeconomic status (SES)] exclusive of maternal psychopathology. These hypotheses were not presumed to be independent or mutually exclusive; additive and interactive effects were considered likely.

The sample of 337 families used to address these questions was heterogeneous on many dimensions (Sameroff, Seifer, & Zax, 1982). Three diagnostic groups (as well as a no-mental-illness group, all matched on demographic factors of SES, race, family size, mother's education, marital status, and sex of child) were identified: schizophrenia ($n = 29$), depression ($n = 59$), and personality disorder ($n = 40$). Each mother was also assigned a score for severity of mental illness (the degree of overall pathology) and chronicity of illness (the frequency of psychiatric contacts and hospitalizations). All of the Hollingshead social classes were represented in the sample, and about one-third of those in the sample were black. Many of the mothers were unmarried at the time their children were born (either divorced or had never married).

The mothers were interviewed regarding psychiatric status and other personality factors during their pregnancies. Records of the delivery process were kept for all subjects, and each child was examined during the hospital lying-in period. Follow-up visits in the home and laboratory were completed at 4, 12, 30, and 48 months of age. A 13-year follow-up is currently in progress (see Chapter 12, this volume). A summary of results from the prenatal assessments through 48-month assessments in terms of diagnosis, general mental illness, and social status factors follows; see Sameroff et al. (1982) for details regarding the sample, procedures, and results.

Diagnosis

In general, the first hypothesis of diagnostic specificity received little support. Most of the significant differences found for the schizophrenic group were observed during the prenatal period, and these were differences in the mothers, not in the children. The schizophrenic mothers were the most anxious and the least socially competent, and they had the lowest scores on the prenatal obstetric scale.

After the births of their children, the schizophrenic group was nearly indistinguishable from the control group during evaluations of both mother and child behaviors. We found that children of schizophrenics had nonreliably lower birth weights than did those in the other diagnostic groups. At 4 months, the Bayley developmental quotient scores for children of schizophrenic women were slightly lower, and indices of mothers' behavior during home observations indicated less involvement with their children. No differences in infant behavior were noted in the home, nor were there any differences in temperament ratings. By 12 months the only differences found were on the Bayley scores for a subset of offspring who were living in foster homes. By 30 months, behavioral differences between the offspring of schizophrenic women and those of controls had disappeared.

In contrast to the paucity of differences between the schizophrenic group and the no-mental-illness control group, the depressive group showed many significant effects. At all ages both the mothers and children in the depression group showed a variety of differences from controls. The depressed mothers were more anxious and lower in social competence. Their newborns had by far the worst obstetric status and exhibited poor functioning on a number of behavioral measures during the newborn laboratory examination. At 4 months the mothers showed less involvement with their infants at home, and the infants, in turn, had poorer responsivity to people in the laboratory and were given lower activity and distractibility temperament ratings by their mothers. No differences were found between the depressive group and other groups at 12 months, but at 30 and 48 months these infants scored lower on a variety of adaptive behavior scales.

To summarize these diagnostic comparisons, if one were to choose a diagnostic group in which children were at most risk, it would be depression rather than schizophrenia. Further, the effect associated with a schizophrenic parent appears to decrease somewhat with age as the child moves from biological or simple motor functioning to more complex behavior, whereas the effect of maternal depression remains constant throughout the first few years. The personality disorder group showed few effects throughout.

General mental illness

The second hypothesis, that mental illness in general would produce substantial effects, was supported more strongly than was the hypothesis regarding specific diagnosis effects. In almost every instance where there was an effect due to one or another diagnostic group, there was a corresponding effect for severity and/or chronicity of illness. Further, there was a large number of variables that had severity and/or chronicity effects, but did not have corresponding specific diagnosis differences.

These general effects of maternal psychopathology (i.e., severity and chronicity) were ubiquitous throughout the study. Children of more severely ill or chronically ill mothers had poorer obstetric and newborn status. At 4 months they had more difficult temperaments, lower Bayley scores, and less-adaptive behavior in the laboratory. These mothers were less involved and more negative in affect during home observations. At 12 months their infants were less spontaneous and mobile when observed in the home and less responsive in the laboratory. The ill mothers remained less involved and less positive during home observations. At 30 and 48 months their children were again less responsive in the laboratory, had lower developmental test scores, and scored lower on adaptive behavior scales.

Social status

The third hypothesis regarding social status effects was also strongly supported. Like the general psychopathology findings, the social status effects were apparent throughout the first 4 years of life. The low-SES nonwhites in our sample exhibited the poorest development, the high-SES whites showed the best, and the low-SES whites were generally in between these two groups on measures taken at all age periods from birth to 4 years of age.

We compared the effects of mental illness dimensions and social status on the social and adaptive competence of the children in the study when the children were 30 and 48 months old (Seifer, Sameroff, & Jones, 1981). At 30 months children from families with mentally ill mothers differed from those whose families had no parental mental illness, and children from lower-social-status families differed from children in higher-social-status homes on most of the same dimensions. Both groups of risk children were less cooperative, more timid, more fearful, and more depressed and engaged in more bizarre behavior than their comparison groups. However, at 48 months there was a separation

between the risk group behaviors. The children of mentally ill mothers continued to show the same differences from children of healthy mothers as they had
at 30 months, but some of the differences among children in different social
status groups became less pronounced.

Integration of research findings

The effects on preschool children's social-emotional functioning of
having a parent with social-emotional problems may be more pervasive and
long-lasting than the effects of having a low-social-status parent, at least in
some domains at certain developmental periods. Alternatively, the risk for
early incompetence associated with social status and maternal psychopathology
may be different in kind. The effect of social status may be merely to delay the
common achievements of childhood. In contrast, mentally ill mothers may
provide a qualitatively different child-rearing environment that distorts their
children's development in kind, rather than in timing.

Of equal interest is the necessity for a developmental analysis in such areas.
If the children had been assessed at only one point in time, we would have
reached far different conclusions based on evaluations made only at 30
months or only at 48 months. A further caution is that although one can
attempt to separate the effects of social status and mental illness, they are
correlated in the real world. The prevalence rate for schizophrenia, for example, is eight times as high in the lowest-SES group as in the highest (Hollingshead & Redlich, 1958).

Our findings are not strikingly different from those in other high-risk research. The results presented here in the domain of general risk factors are
clear in documenting the deleterious effects of parental mental illness (in terms
of severity or chronicity) and low social status. In terms of the specifics of
schizophrenia, it is less clear that any marker or etiological factor has been
identified. Other studies of infant offspring of schizophrenic women also have
had difficulty in illuminating the issue, despite using methods heavily weighted
toward identifying unique qualities of offspring of schizophrenics (Marcus,
Auerbach, Wilkinson, & Burack, 1984). McNeil and Kaij (1987) have found
few factors specific to the offspring of schizophrenic women, with a larger
number of effects associated with their total group of index cases (which included several diagnoses in addition to schizophrenia).

In an alternative analysis strategy, McNeil and Kaij (1987) examined longitudinal relationships within the group of index cases and separately within the
group of control cases. The outcome measure was disturbance versus non-
disturbance on a global assessment measure when the child was 6 years of age
(note that all of the child disturbances were mild in nature). McNeil and Kaij
reported a series of relationships between childhood status at 6 years and
infant and toddler measures in their index group only; these developmental
relationships were not replicated in their control group. Again, the index

group contained many different diagnoses, and these relationships were not linked to schizophrenia in particular.

This general pattern of findings, where differences are related to mental illness in general rather than to schizophrenia in particular, extends to older children as well, including domains of cognition, social competence, academic achievement, teacher ratings, and parent ratings (Watt, 1984). The major exception is a series of tantalizing findings that implicate a variety of attentional measures in children of schizophrenics when compared with other-mental-illness controls (Nuechterlein, 1984; Harvey, Winters, Weintraub, & Neale, 1981). However, these positive findings result from different methodologies and do not represent a convergence on a single marker variable.

Sources of risk in early childhood

The crux of the matter is to define what, indeed, constitutes a high-risk sample. The risk for early problems (and ultimately for later mental illness) associated with maternal illness may be subdivided into two categories: schizophrenia in particular and mental disturbance in general. The data from the Rochester Longitudinal Study indicate that the offspring of schizophrenics indeed compose a high-risk sample of children, but no more so than samples of children of other severely ill mothers. Further, poor families and minority group families appear to be at even greater risk for general developmental problems than are families with maternal mental illness. Finally, the combined risk of illness and low social status appears to produce the worst child outcomes.

These childhood outcomes, however, are not schizophrenia, nor is there any evidence that they may lead to schizophrenia. To the extent that one of these poor intermediate outcomes is a function of a particular child's experience with a multirisk family and social environment, then a later poor outcome will also be a function of a currently incompetent child in a multirisk family and social environment. Moreover, children with early patterns of incompetence will be less well equipped to overcome later caretaking disturbances; they may have neither the skills nor the resilience to negotiate troubled times and emerge relatively unimpaired. Thus, children exposed to continuous family and cultural disruption become increasingly unable to develop in a healthy, competent direction and become more vulnerable to developing severe psychopathology.

Multiple risk analysis

In the course of conducting the Rochester Longitudinal Study, we have become convinced that etiological questions must be embedded in an analysis of the general risks to which young children are subject, as well as the range of outcomes associated with those risks. To this end we developed a multiple risk index composed of 10 individual risk factors that characterize individual children's familial and cultural contexts. These include maternal mental health (chronicity), anxiety, perspectives on child rearing, education, occupation, minority status, interaction style, family support, life events, and family size. These factors were chosen because they index (a) individual psychological functioning of the mother, (b) aspects of the status of the family, and (c) the broader cultural context in which the family operates.

The composite risk score predicted 4-year IQ far better than any single risk factor alone, with the extreme categories differing by over 30 IQ points (Sameroff, Seifer, Barocas, Zax, & Greenspan, 1987). Similar, though less dramatic, results were found for social-emotional competence at 4 years of age (Sameroff & Seifer, 1983). An especially interesting feature of these analyses was that no individual risk factor, or combination of risk factors, could account for the results. For example, when groups were formed based on cluster analyses of families with the same degree of overall risk, there were no differences among these groups on the outcomes even though there were different distinct patterns of risk factors present in the groups (Sameroff et al., 1987).

Conceptualization of risk and protective factors

In our conceptualization of risk, we have not differentiated between so-called risk factors and protective factors. Instead, we have concentrated on analyzing multiple factors and assigning them equivalent status. To a large extent this is the result of the conceptual difficulty in operationally defining the difference between risk and protective factors. If one assumes a disease model of illness, where there is a presumed constitutional difference, then the risk factor is clearly identified, and the protective factors will, by default, be the remaining physical, social, and cultural factors not associated with the constitutional deficit. However, if one assumes, as we do, that the etiology of schizophrenia is much less specific in constitutional terms, then the primary definition of risk is far more difficult.

One strategy is to define risk solely in terms of the population under study – in our case the children of schizophrenic mothers. However, this strategy only begs the question of what truly constitutes the developmental risk. Should one include all of the associated individual and cultural factors confounded with schizophrenia in the risk definition, such as low social status, periodic disruptions in family constellation, effects of chronic medication, high levels of anxiety, or disturbed social interaction? In the Kauai study of Werner and Smith (1982), small family size and a low number of life events were identified as protective factors, and low SES as a risk factor. However, when our sample of schizophrenics' offspring is considered, such a scheme presents conceptual problems: Family size is strongly associated with SES, which is related to the diagnosis of schizophrenia; the disruptions of family life associated with psychotic episodes and erratic behavior of schizophrenics will increase the number of negative life events impacting on a family. Should these factors of family size and life events, which were identified in the Werner and Smith study as protective factors, be classified as risk factors or as protective factors in subsequent research that may have a slightly different focus?

Systems of relationships in the development of pathology

From our theoretical perspective, we are less concerned with entering such a semantic debate over how to label each individual variable. We are more concerned with identifying the relevant systems that impact on the development of competence in individual children, whether or not they develop in the context of one or another type of family (defined through maternal diagnosis, social status, or other criterion). One approach to this type of solution is to focus attention on the development of *relationship disorders* with individual families (Sameroff & Emde, 1989).

Relationship disorders are defined as major disturbances in the process by which individual parents and children develop affective bonds, communication patterns, and social interaction patterns that impact on the child's development of generalized competent behavior. In the context of attachment theory, which covers the first 2 years of life, Sroufe and Waters (1977) have described a specific example of a developmental process that may lead to relationship disorders in cases where healthy parent–child relationships are not formed. The task of interest in such theories is to define the individual components of domain-specific systems that result in achieving a particular milestone. In the example of Sroufe and Waters, that milestone is a relationship involving security, independence, and a strong affective bond around the first year of life. This approach is by no means antithetical to the vulnerability and protective models identified by Garmezy and others. It merely involves examination of a set of variables as they impact on *competence* in children, without introducing conceptual difficulties associated with categorizing all measures into one of two categories (risk or protective).

In the Rochester Longitudinal Study data concerning multiple risk presented earlier, the focus was on the larger contextual factors associated with potential problems in the formation of strong family relationships. The next step in this research program is to focus more specifically on individual and dyadic measures that more microscopically define the development of healthy versus disordered parent–child relationships. This approach contrasts with a disease model in that it does not locate the source of pathology or risk in the individual child. Instead, the focus is on following the development of family relationships over time to examine (a) specific developmental periods and variables that lead to disturbances and (b) the means by which these disturbances are translated into individual patterns of incompetence. Conversely, the focus is simultaneously on social and cultural pressures that serve to promote the maintenance of strong family relationships through development and the means by which these strengths are manifest in child competence. It should be noted that an approach focusing on relationships during early child-hood is not fully compatible with the current dominant diagnostic scheme, DSM-III-R (American Psychiatric Association, 1987). The exclusive reliance of DSM-III-R on characterizing pathology as a property of individuals does not allow for the definition of relationship disorders.

Contributions of a developmental approach

High-risk studies of schizophrenia have evolved, to some extent, in their understanding of mental disorder in pace with the evolution of the field of developmental psychopathology. Before the introduction of developmental concepts, it was believed that each disorder had an underlying organic basis, with direct connections between cause and symptoms; regardless of age, a disorder should manifest itself in similar patterns of behavior. The problems that beset this model arose when it was admitted that children could have different diseases than adults, that children and adults with the same symp-toms could have different disorders, and, most pertinent to schizophrenia, that children and adults with the same presumed somatic deficit could have different symptoms.

To the extent that schizophrenia is viewed as a disease rooted in the biology of the individual, the task for etiologists is to discover manifestations of the biologi-cal substrate that occur earlier in time than the actual disease. The relatively unsuccessful search for marker variables that has consumed most of our efforts is in this tradition. To the extent that schizophrenia is viewed as a developmen-tal disorder, a different strategy may be necessary to identify the etiological course. From a developmental perspective, outcome is viewed as the product of a particular child and a particular experiential context. Because of the normaliz-ing effect of most human child-rearing environments, individual biological differences need not manifest themselves directly as later behavioral distur-bances. Children with a variety of handicaps, ranging from blindness to cere-bral palsy, emerge as intellectually and social-emotionally competent adults, even though they retain their biological differences; see Cassell (1986) for a similar discussion regarding physical illness. To the extent that children do not overcome biological risk, the sources of individual variations often can be found in the poor adaptability of the child-rearing context (Werner & Smith, 1982).

What we have demonstrated in the Rochester Longitudinal Study is that social status and parental psychopathology are general risk factors that pro-duce general incompetencies in young children. To understand the develop-ment of specific incompetencies, like schizophrenia, will require the analysis of specific features of the family and social experience of the child that may or may not interact with a yet-to-be-identified biological substrate. In any event, future studies will need to examine the characteristics of the child-rearing system in the same or greater detail than was devoted to the individual child in past studies.

References

American Psychiatric Association. (1987). *Diagnostic and statistical manual of mental disorders* (3rd rev. ed.). Washington, DC: APA.

Cassell, E. J. (1986). Ideas in conflict: The rise and fall (and rise and fall) of new views of disease. *Daedalus, 115,* 19–41.

Engel, G. L. (1977). The need for a new medical model: A challenge for biomedicine. *Science, 196,* 129–36.

Fish, B. (1963). The maturation of arousal and attention in the first months of life: A study of variations in ego development. *Journal of the American Academy of Child Psychiatry, 2,* 253–70.

Fish, B., & Alpert, M. S. (1962). Abnormal states of consciousness and muscle tone in infants born to schizophrenic mothers. *American Journal of Psychiatry, 119,* 439–45.

Garmezy, N. (1974). Children at risk: The search for antecedents of schizophrenia. I. Conceptual models and research methods. *Schizophrenia Bulletin, 8,* 14–90.

Hanson, D. R., Gottesman, I. I., & Meehl, P. (1977). Genetic theories and the validation of psychiatric diagnoses: Implications for the study of children of schizophrenics. *Journal of Abnormal Psychology, 86,* 575–88.

Harvey, P., Winters, K., Weintraub, S., & Neale, J. M. (1981). Distractibility in children vulnerable to psychopathology. *Journal of Abnormal Psychology, 90,* 298–304.

Hollingshead, A. B., & Redlich, F. C. (1958). *Social class and mental illness: A community study.* New York: Wiley.

Kallmann, F. J. (1938). *The genetics of schizophrenia.* New York: Augustin.

Kallmann, F. J. (1946). The genetic theory of schizophrenia: An analysis of 691 schizophrenic twin index families. *American Journal of Psychiatry, 103,* 309–22.

Kohn, M. L. (1973). Social class and schizophrenia: A critical review and a reformulation. *Schizophrenia Bulletin, 7,* 60–79.

McNeil, T. F., & Kaij, L. (1987). Swedish high-risk study: Sample characteristics at age 6. *Schizophrenia Bulletin, 13,* 373–81.

Marcus, J., Auerbach, J., Wilkinson, L., & Burack, C. M. (1984). Infants at risk for schizophrenia: The Jerusalem Infant Development Study. In N. F. Watt, E. J. Anthony, L. C. Wynne, & J. E. Rolf (Eds.), *Children at risk for schizophrenia: A longitudinal perspective* (pp. 440–64). Cambridge University Press.

Matas, L., Arend, R. A., & Sroufe, L. A. (1978). Continuity of adaptation in the second year: The relationship between quality of attachment and later competence. *Child Development, 49,* 547–56.

Mednick, S. A., & McNeil, T. F. (1968). Current methodology in research on the etiology of schizophrenia: Serious difficulties which suggest the use of the high-risk group method. *Psychological Bulletin, 70,* 681–93.

Mednick, S. A., & Schulsinger, F. (1968). Some premorbid characteristics related to breakdown in children with schizophrenic mothers. In D. Rosenthal & S. S. Kety (Eds.), *The transmission of schizophrenia* (pp. 267–91). Oxford: Pergamon Press.

Messer, D. J., McCarthy, M. E., McQuiston, S., MacTurk, R. H., Yarrow, L. J., & Vietze, P. M. (1986). Relation between mastery behavior in infancy and competence in early childhood. *Developmental Psychology, 22,* 366–72.

Nuechterlein, K. H. (1984). Sustained attention among children vulnerable to adult schizophrenia and among hyperactive children. In N. F. Watt, E. J. Anthony, L. C. Wynne, & J.

E. Rolf (Eds.), *Children at risk for schizophrenia: A longitudinal perspective* (pp. 304–11). Cambridge University Press.

Robins, L. N. (1966). *Deviant children grown up.* Baltimore: Williams & Wilkins.

Rutter, M. R., & Garmezy, N. (1983). Childhood psychopathology. In M. Hetherington (Ed.), *Socialization, personality, and social development.* Vol. 4 of P. H. Mussen (Ed.) *Handbook of child psychology* (pp. 775–911). New York: Wiley.

Sameroff, A. J. (1983). Developmental systems: Contexts and evolution. In W. Kessen (Ed.), *History, theory, and methods.* Vol. 1 of P. H. Mussen (Ed.), *Handbook of child psychology* (pp. 238–94). New York: Wiley.

Sameroff, A. J., & Emde, R. N. (Eds.). (1989). *Relationship disturbances in early childhood: A developmental approach.* New York: Basic Books.

Sameroff, A. J., & Seifer, R. (1983). Familial risk and child competence. *Child Development, 54,* 1254–68.

Sameroff, A. J., Seifer, R., Barocas, R., Zax, M., & Greenspan, S. (1987). IQ scores of 4-year-old children: Social environmental risk factors: *Pediatrics, 79,* 343–50.

Sameroff, A. J., Seifer, R., & Zax, M. (1982). *Early development of children at risk for emotional disorder.* Monographs of the Society for Research in Child Development, 47 (serial number 199).

Seifer, R., Sameroff, A. J., & Jones, F. (1981). Adaptive behavior in young children of emotionally disturbed women. *Journal of Applied Developmental Psychology, 1,* 251–76.

Seifer, R., Vaughn, B. E., Lefever, G., & Smith, C. (in press). Relationships among mastery motivation and attachment within a general model of competence. In P. M. Vietze & R. H. MacTurk (Eds.), *Perspectives on mastery motivation in infants and children.* Norwood, NJ: Ablex.

Sroufe, L. A., & Rutter, M. (1984). The domain of developmental psychopathology. *Child Development, 55,* 17–29.

Sroufe, L. A., & Waters, E. (1977). Attachment as an organizational construct. *Child Development, 48,* 1184–99.

Watt, N. F. (1984). In a nutshell: The first two decades of high-risk research in schizophrenia. In N. F. Watt, E. J. Anthony, L. C. Wynne, & J. E. Rolf (Eds.), *Children at risk for schizophrenia: A longitudinal perspective* (pp. 572–95). Cambridge University Press.

Watt, N. F., Anthony, E. J., Wynne, L. C., & Rolf, J. E. (1984). *Children at risk for schizophrenia: A longitudinal perspective.* Cambridge University Press.

Watt, N. F., Stolorow, R. D., Lubensky, A. W., & McClelland, D. C. (1970). School adjustment and behavior in children hospitalized for schizophrenia as adults. *American Journal of Orthopsychiatry, 40,* 637–57.

Werner, E. E., & Smith, R. S. (1982). *Vulnerable but invincible: A longitudinal study of resilient children and youth.* New York: McGraw-Hill.

Zubin, J., & Spring, B. (1977). Vulnerability – a new view of schizophrenia. *Journal of Abnormal Psychology, 86,* 103–26.

4 Beyond diathesis: toward an understanding of high-risk environments

John Richters and Sheldon Weintraub

During the formative years of the high-risk-for-schizophrenia movement, researchers devoted most of their attention to isolating early patterns of maladjustment and deviance among high-risk offspring. Their primary research agenda was to develop an understanding of those deficits, with an eye toward tracing them to later functioning and ultimately to diagnostic status. In more recent years there has been increased interest in and enthusiasm for examining protective factors: the environmental resources available to and the adaptive strengths characteristic of those high-risk children who do *not* show early signs of deviance. Whether this newer interest reflects a broadening of focus consistent with the seminal writings of Garmezy (1971, 1976, 1981, 1983) and others, or more accurately represents a displacement or misplacement of interest in factors responsible for early deviance, is a question with important implications for the future directions of high-risk research.

At the heart of this question is unsettling evidence throughout the high-risk literature of blurred distinctions between the concepts of risk, vulnerability, and maladjustment, and between risk reducers and protective factors. It is no less true in high-risk research than in other domains of inquiry that important answers often are obscured by the ways we frame our questions. And as we hope to demonstrate in this chapter, there is much to be gained through maintaining conceptual clarity in our thinking about and usage of these terms.

We begin by reviewing briefly the origins and current status of research concerning the etiology of schizophrenia and related disorders among the offspring of schizophrenic parents. Our goal is to highlight some of the methodological and conceptual issues that have shaped the nature and direction of this research. We then examine the concepts of risk, vulnerability, and protective factors, with an eye toward emphasizing some of the dangers inherent in not paying careful attention to important distinctions among them. Against

We gratefully acknowledge the thoughtful contributions of Jill Hooley and John Neale to an earlier draft of this manuscript.

this backdrop we present a rationale for exploring hypotheses of environmental influence to account for patterns of early deviance among high-risk offspring. And in the context of this discussion we summarize recent findings from the Stony Brook High-Risk Project that buttress our confidence in the usefulness of this pursuit.

Early etiological research

Prior to the late 1960s, efforts to understand the etiology of schizophrenia were based primarily on cross-sectional designs, and focused almost exclusively on the characteristics of adult schizophrenics. Many of these studies were successful at generating promising hypotheses concerning the etiology of schizophrenia. But most were incapable of answering the very questions they raised. Major obstacles to the interpretation and generalizability of many early findings have been detailed by Mednick and McNeil (1968), ranging from a widespread reliance on retrospective reports to the failure of researchers to employ appropriate control groups for comparison purposes. But even beyond these considerations, there is an inherent methodological weakness in the cross-sectional method itself that imposes boundaries on the interpretability of even the most rigorous of research designs: namely, its inability to determine whether observed differences between schizophrenics and nonschizophrenics are causes or consequences of the disorder.

High-risk research

In recognition of these shortcomings, Mednick and McNeil (1968) formalized a rationale for employing prospective, longitudinal designs to study the development of those who have not yet been diagnosed as schizophrenic. A chief advantage of this approach is that, because the subjects under study presumably are not yet manifesting schizophrenic symptoms, their responses on various measures are unlikely to be influenced by features of the disorder or its treatment. Similarly, information about them provided by others cannot be biased by knowledge of the disorder, because no one knows in advance who will be diagnosed as schizophrenic. In addition, the prospective method allows for theoretically anchored, systematic, and ongoing assessments of *current* subject information. It therefore tends to yield not only more complete data, but also data that are relatively free from the well-known inaccuracies of distal event recall (Yarrow, Campbell, & Burton, 1970). Although there are disadvantages to the prospective method as well (Moffitt, Mednick, & Cudeck, 1983), it is nonetheless far superior to traditional cross-sectional designs for pursuing questions of etiology.

The high-risk movement

On the basis of these considerations, Mednick (1965, 1966, 1967) and his colleagues in Copenhagen (Mednick & Schulsinger, 1968), and later a host of American investigators (Watt, Anthony, Wynne, & Rolf, 1984), turned from the cross-sectional study of schizophrenic patients to the prospective study of their offspring. There is nothing implicit in the prospective method that calls for a focus on children of schizophrenics to answer questions of etiology. But the majority of researchers employing this method have targeted the offspring of schizophrenics in an economical effort to exceed the population base rate of less than 1% for eventual diagnosis of schizophrenia. In contrast to children of nonschizophrenic parents, those with one schizophrenic parent are 10–15 times more likely to develop schizophrenia at some point in their lives. During the past two decades approximately 15 of these so-called high-risk projects have spent in excess of $11 million in their efforts to document ongoing patterns of development among the offspring of schizophrenics (Watt, 1984).

The initial ages at which high-risk offspring have been assessed, as well as the particular variables under study, have varied considerably across these projects. So also have their foci, which range from personal indices of cognitive, attentional, neurophysiological, social, emotional, and academic functioning, to environmental factors such as social class, marital discord, and family communication deviance. Most studies have assessed a fairly wide range of personal and environmental characteristics of their high-risk offspring. The variables emphasized in particular analyses, however, often reflect differences in theoretical and conceptual orientations of the investigators to the etiology of schizophrenia. Before turning to a discussion of these differences it will be useful to examine briefly the common conceptual framework within which much of the high-risk-for-schizophrenia research has been conducted.

Diathesis–stress

There is tremendous theoretical diversity among the high-risk projects. Nonetheless, most researchers view themselves as working within a diathesis–stress framework that acknowledges, in principle, the potential roles of both heredity and environment in the development of psychopathology. This diathesis-stress (Meehl, 1962; Rosenthal, 1970) or vulnerability (Zubin & Spring, 1977) model holds that individuals may inherit and/or acquire traitlike deviations or vulnerabilities that mediate their risk for eventual onset of schizophrenia. These vulnerabilities constitute an individual's diathesis, and are conceptualized broadly as characteristics of functioning that lower one's threshold of susceptibility to environmental stressors that may subsequently trigger the onset of maladjustment or psychopathology.

The vulnerability model thus assigns a dual role to stress. Certain environmental stressors may have a *formative* influence on individuals by increasing their vulnerability to a disorder. Others may have a *precipitating* influence by triggering the actual onset of an episode. As Spring and Coons (1982) have pointed out, it is possible for individuals to either inherit or acquire certain vulnerabilities to psychopathology, and yet still not succumb to an episode if they are not subjected to the eliciting stressors. Others, according to the general model, may possess no known vulnerability to a disorder, and yet may still succumb to an episode if the eliciting stressors are of sufficient magnitude.

Beyond these general postulates, the diathesis–stress model of psychopathology – which applies equally well to nondiagnosable forms of maladjustment – leaves open a host of questions concerning (a) the domains of functioning in which vulnerabilities to particular disorders are likely to be manifest, (b) the types of stressors that might (alone or in combination) influence one's vulnerability to a disorder and the eventual onset of disorder, (c) whether, and when, particular vulnerabilities should be conceptualized as dichotomous or continuous variables, (d) the processes through which distal environmental events might influence or translate into an increase in one's vulnerability, and (e) the processes through which vulnerabilities might interact with subsequent stressors to influence an episode of disorder. In short, the diathesis–stress model itself yields no conclusions about the development of maladjustment and psychopathology. Instead, it provides an important heuristic for the formulation of research questions, while at the same time providing a conceptual structure within which the meaning of research findings can be evaluated.

It is within the context of this diathesis–stress model that the potential significance of high-risk research becomes clear. If researchers are successful in isolating specific early functioning characteristics of high-risk offspring that are differentially related to subsequent onset of a disorder, these characteristics may be interpreted either as early manifestations of the disorder itself or as markers of vulnerability that influence the likelihood of later disorder. Either interpretation would require a fairly specific theory and convergent evidence for its justification. But the common goal of high-risk researchers to study the *development* of schizophrenia prospectively reveals a bias toward the vulnerability hypothesis. That is, the high-risk enterprise – at least in its early stages – is by nature an effort to document and understand early and ongoing manifestations of vulnerability or diathesis.

Understanding diathesis

Among the etiological questions raised by the diathesis–stress model, those pertaining to diathesis can be divided roughly into two overlapping categories. The first concerns fundamental questions about the basic nature of vulnerabilities: How should they be conceptualized and measured, and how and when are they likely to be manifested? The second class of questions concerns how particular types of vulnerabilities are acquired: How, in terms of actual processes, do they influence functioning? Obviously, the two categories are of equal importance to an understanding of the etiology of psychopathology. Most high-risk researchers to date, however, have concentrated their efforts primarily on the former. That is, the majority of findings published by the high-risk projects during the past two decades have been devoted to describing differences in various modes of functioning between high-risk offspring and comparison groups. Relatively little attention, in contrast, has been directed toward analyses of the precursors and/or concurrent correlates of these differences that might *explain* their development. Many published reports have defined their high-risk groups solely on the basis of parental diagnosis and have reported differences in the functioning of offspring without reference to factors other than parental diagnosis that might provide an explanation for the deviance found. As we shall argue in later discussion, there is reason to believe that this practice is in some measure the result of a failure of researchers to maintain a clear distinction between the concepts of risk and vulnerability. Before turning to an analysis of this issue, however, it will be useful to examine first the progress of the high-risk projects in their search for markers of vulnerability in high-risk offspring.

The search for markers of vulnerability

The first two decades of high-risk research have yielded a wealth of information about children with schizophrenic parents across a wide range of variables. These include measures of cognitive (Oltmanns, Weintraub, Stone, & Neale, 1978; Sameroff & Zax, 1978), attentional (Erlenmeyer-Kimling & Cornblatt, 1978; Neale, Winters, & Weintraub, 1984), academic (Rolf, 1972; Rolf & Garmezy, 1974), social (Weintraub & Neale, 1984; Weintraub, Prinz, & Neale, 1978), and neurological (Friedman, Erlenmeyer-Kimling, & Vaughn, 1984) functioning. In general, these studies have consistently demonstrated that children of schizophrenic parents tend to perform less well than the children of nonschizophrenic parents across many of the same dimensions of functioning that characterize adult schizophrenics. These between-group differences often are not striking, but they are reliable. Most of these successes have been limited, however; similar patterns of deviance have been found among the offspring of affectively disordered parents on many of these same measures (Lewine, 1984; Weintraub & Neale, 1984). Thus, most of the reported deviance among offspring of schizophrenics appears not to be specific to schizophrenia per se. Instead, it is more appropriately attributable to unknown factors associated with having a psychiatrically ill parent. The few measures on which high-risk-for-schizophrenia offspring have been distinguishable from offspring of psychiatric control parents await replication on new samples. Moreover, their significance as indices of vulnerability must be evaluated against the eventual diagnostic status of the high-risk-for-schizophrenia offspring.

This failure to isolate deficits in early functioning that are specific to the offspring of schizophrenics has been interpreted by some (Lewine, 1984) as evidence suggestive of a general vulnerability to psychopathology, rather than a diathesis for schizophrenia per se. Yet others have pointed to a number of factors that might render such a conclusion premature. Prominent among these is the fact that most of the high-risk offspring being studied by the major projects have not yet passed through the age period of highest risk. Obviously this is a limiting factor on any conclusions about etiology, because a number of these offspring may yet be diagnosed as schizophrenic or otherwise disordered. In addition, it remains possible that eventual diagnosis of schizophrenia may be differentially related to particular *patterns* of early deviance across more than one mode of functioning, to *changes* in functioning over time, and/ or to unknown functioning characteristics of the high-risk offspring.

Domains of assessment. As Neale (1984) has emphasized, most of the high-risk projects have based their measures of childhood functioning on the assumption that a continuity exists between the functioning of adult schizophrenics and that of preschizophrenic children. Accordingly, many of the measures employed in assessments of high-risk children have been downward extensions in age of variables assessed in adult schizophrenics. But many of these measures have failed in the past to discriminate reliably between adult schizophrenics and patients in other diagnostic categories. There was therefore little empirical basis for expectations that they would discriminate more successfully between the children of patients in these categories.

Neale has further proposed that other domains of disturbance in functioning that are more common among schizophrenics might provide fruitful avenues of exploration. Particular types of hallucinations and delusions, for example, although not pathognomonic of schizophrenia, are more closely linked to its symptom pattern than to those of affective disorders. Thus, variables such as irrational belief systems and tendencies to confuse internal and external realities – which plausibly may be related to subsequent hallucinations and delusions – might be explored as precursors of these symptoms.

Sensitivity of analyses. A number of researchers (Neale & Oltmanns, 1980; Erlenmeyer-Kimling et al., 1984; Watt, 1984) have also emphasized that comparisons of group means between high-risk offspring and children in control groups may be a relatively insensitive method for pursuing questions of vulnerability to schizophrenia. After all, only 10–15% of high-risk offspring are expected to be diagnosed as schizophrenics as adults. A complementary strategy for identifying vulnerable high-risk offspring consists in isolating the most deviant responders on two or more measures. This practice has already been employed by several investigators (Cornblatt &

Erlenmeyer-Kimling, 1984; Stone, Weintraub, & Neale, 1977) and appears to hold considerable promise.

An additional factor influencing the insensitivity of group comparisons might well lie in the relatively broad DSM-II criteria for the diagnosis of schizophrenia on which most of the high-risk-for-schizophrenia projects relied for sample selection. With the introduction of DSM-III and its more restrictive diagnostic criteria, substantial numbers of index patients previously classified as schizophrenic were reclassified by the major projects into other diagnostic groups. It is quite possible that comparisons of the newly defined high-risk offspring with newly defined nonschizophrenic contrast groups will yield more discriminating comparisons than did the original analyses. This possibility always exists when comparisons of subjects are made on the basis of tentative classification criteria.

In summary, it is clear that the high-risk projects have experienced only limited success in their search for early markers of vulnerability to schizophrenia. On a more positive note, the high-risk movement has made considerable progress in its recognition of the complexities inherent in the search for early markers of vulnerability. How well these insights are translated into more innovative and rigorous research designs will no doubt weigh heavily in the ultimate success of the high-risk approach to tracking the development of schizophrenia and other disorders.

Maladjustment and vulnerability

Before turning to what we know about the causes of early deviance in high-risk offspring, it is worth noting that early maladjustment is not necessarily synonymous with vulnerability to disorder – either inherited or acquired. We still have much to learn about the meaning and interpretability of childhood maladjustment – particularly within the domains of social and emotional functioning. Most indices of childhood adjustment are based on parent, teacher, peer, or interviewer ratings of a child's externalizing and internalizing behaviors, sociability, likability, and so forth. Children who deviate significantly from their peers along these dimensions are to that extent considered maladjusted. Obviously, early adjustment problems for some children may reflect relatively short-lived reactions to transient disturbances within the family and for that reason may not be predictive of subsequent maladjustment. It is also possible that, for some children at least, early maladjustment may reflect an overgeneralization of response patterns or styles that are actually *adaptive* – albeit in the short term – within the narrower context of the family. It is easy to imagine, for example, how a child's withdrawal from dependence and/or closeness with others might be an adaptive coping response to inconsistent, insensitive, and/or abusive parents. Similarly, an initial overgeneralization of this strategy in contexts beyond the family may be a prudent posture that gradually gives way to more discriminating response styles based on positive experiences with peers, teachers, and other adults. For other children, patterns of withdrawal may not be functional either within or outside the home; they may be due instead to a child's low threshold for stimulation and/or a well-consolidated response style, and for these reasons may be quite resistant to change.

Obviously, similar considerations may apply to other forms of early social-emotional maladjustment. The important point is that phenotypically similar behavior patterns may serve different functions for different children, and these differences no doubt have important implications for assessing, understanding, and predicting children's developmental trajectories. All children who suffer early adjustment problems are not vulnerable to later disorder, and many who suffer from disorder later in life show no signs of maladjustment in childhood.

None of this alters the importance of studying early maladjustment or functioning deficits in children. To the contrary, it underscores the fact that we have much to learn about the norms of social-emotional development and about which forms of deviation under which conditions should bear different substantive and theoretical interpretations. It also suggests that the common practice of indiscriminately predicting bad outcomes from bad beginnings is unlikely to yield more than the modest success rates it currently enjoys in most longitudinal studies.

The origins of early deviance

It is clear that empirical support for a specific vulnerability to schizophrenia has thus far eluded researchers. This is due in part to the likely complexity of the phenomenon itself, to limitations in our present methodologies, and to the fact that claims of specific etiology must await the eventual diagnostic status of the high-risk offspring under study, many of whom have not yet passed through the age period of highest risk.

Nonetheless, the high-risk projects have amassed an impressive body of data on the cognitive, social, and emotional functioning of at-risk children of psychiatrically ill parents across a wide range of diagnostic categories and age groups. Yet given the tremendous amount of energy devoted to accumulating these data, we still know relatively little about why elevated rates of early maladjustment are found in high-risk groups.

We know from our genetic models and related data that there is no basis for assuming that all or even most offspring of psychiatrically ill parents are genetically predisposed to maladjustment or psychopathology. There appears to be an undeniable though not well-understood genetic component to schizophrenia (Gottesman & Shields, 1972), and there is growing evidence of genetic involvement in affective disorders (Gershon, 1984), adult criminality (Crowe, 1983), and some forms of alcoholism (Cloninger, Bohman, & Sigvardsson, 1981) as well. But neither the nature and extent of genetic influences on these disorders nor the processes through which they take their toll are well enough understood at present to justify any assumptions about the role or pervasiveness of genetic vulnerability in high-risk offspring samples. Even less well understood is the role, if any, of genetic diathesis in accounting for more general forms of childhood maladjustment among high-risk offspring. This may be particularly true of childhood adjustment problems, which are less reliably assessed and less well understood.

We know also from existing data that there is no basis for the assumption that all offspring of diagnosed parents are exposed to particularly deviant or noxious environments. One need only consult the empirical reports published by the high-risk-for-schizophrenia projects during the past two decades to appreciate the degree of overlap between diagnostic and control groups on many measures of family environment (Watt et al., 1984). There is certainly evidence that families with a psychiatrically ill parent *tend* to have more negative characteristics than those with nondiagnosed parents, but this by no means holds for a majority of the high-risk families studied.

It is clear that our relative lack of progress in understanding the origins of early deviance in high-risk offspring may have less to do with the quality of data generated by the high-risk projects than it does with the questions that have been asked of those data. Some projects, to be sure, have emphasized environmental factors such as correlates of social class (Sameroff, Barocas, & Seifer, 1984), parental communication deviance (Wynne, Singer, Bartko, & Toohey, 1977), and family communication patterns (Goldstein & Rodnick, 1975) as primary causal candidates in high-risk offspring maladjustment. But many others have given little or no attention to factors other than parental diagnosis that might explain early deviance in high-risk offspring. Numerous examples of this inattention to environmental factors can be found in the recent volume *Children at Risk for Schizophrenia* (Watt et al., 1984), which is a compilation of progress reports from the high-risk-for-schizophrenia projects. This pattern of omission is particularly unsettling because most investigators have placed great emphasis on indices of early childhood functioning as markers of and/or causal agents in the etiology of schizophrenia and related disorders. Therefore, if links are established between early functioning and later maladjustment or disorder, the field may be at a considerable disadvantage in its efforts to explain their origins.

The assumption of inherited diathesis

It is difficult to escape the conclusion that the relative inattention to environmental correlates of parental psychiatric disorder stems in many cases from a tacit assumption that early maladjustment among high-risk children reflects *inherited* rather than acquired deficits. For some investigators, of course, the assumption of an inherited diathesis is made explicit within the framework of a particular theoretical model. Those with a strong genetic orientation, for example, have emphasized indices of neurophysiological and neurointegrative (Erlenmeyer-Kimling et al., 1984) functioning among high-risk offspring in the service of testing specific genetic models of etiology. Studies such as these posit that deficits in particular areas of functioning reflect vulnerabilities to schizophrenia that are related in theoretically important ways both to early deviance and to later onset of schizophrenia. In perhaps the clearest illustration of such a model, Erlenmeyer-Kimling and her colleagues (Erlenmeyer-Kimling et al., 1984) characterized the assumptions underlying the New York High-Risk Project as follows: "except for non-genetic phenocopies, schizophrenia occurs in persons with a genetic predisposition in interaction with probably nonspecific environmental factors" (p. 169).

Most of the American high-risk projects have not been guided by theories of etiology as specific as this. But many still seem to have embraced the assumption that high-risk children – or at least those who manifest early functioning and adjustment problems – possess an inherited diathesis for schizophrenia and/or related disorders. It is telling in this regard that Lewine, Watt, and Grubb (1984) have characterized the high-risk-for-schizophrenia projects as "genetic risk studies" (p. 559), even though there is no evidence that these offspring samples are at any more genetic than environmental risk. Similarly, Garmezy and Phipps-Yonas (1984) have described high-risk offspring as those who are "presumably predisposed to the disorder" (p. 6) and as "children at genetic risk for schizophrenia" (p. 16). Lewine, Watt, and Grubb (1984) have also characterized the high-risk-for-schizophrenia studies as employing the "genetic risk selection procedure" (p. 558). Even the authors of the Stony Brook study, which has been described as one of the more theoretically eclectic of the high-risk projects (Watt, 1984), have acknowledged that they based their choice of childhood measures on variables such as cognitive functioning and social withdrawal that might "reflect the high-risk genotype" (Weintraub & Neale, 1984, p. 243).

Risk versus vulnerability

The assumption that statistical risk for a disorder implies the presence of a genetic diathesis or vulnerability is surprisingly common in the high-risk literature and reflects either a misunderstanding or misrepresentation of what the at-risk designation means. Consider, for example, familial risk for schizophrenia. Descriptively, we know that between 10% and 15% of children with one schizophrenic parent will themselves be diagnosed as schizophrenic at some time during their lives. Hence their classification into a 10–15% risk category and their designation as high-risk offspring. Importantly, however, *this risk designation is conditional in the sense that having a schizophrenic parent is the only risk-relevant information one either has or chooses to use in the assessment of risk.*

As statistician Reichenbach (1938) once pointed out, there is no such thing as *the* probability of an event; there are as many probabilities of a given event as there are specifiable subclasses. Elaborating on this point, Meehl (1954) has emphasized that no probability estimate is any more or less true than the next. From the standpoint of prediction, of course, there is always a best class, and it is always defined as the smallest class (i.e., extensionally smallest and intentionally most complex) for which the *n* is large enough to generate stable relative frequencies. In the present case, this so-called best class is always the known class that most closely approximates a condition of perfect discrimination between those who will and those who will not be diagnosed as schizophrenic. Thus, it should be clear that risk classifications are by nature tentative; each member of a given class is potentially reclassifiable into an unlimited number of different classes associated with higher or lower risk rates on the basis of additional risk-related information.

Another fact easily overlooked when considering risk rates is that an individual's chances of succumbing to psychopathology or maladjustment are influenced by the patterns in the individual's life, not by the frequencies found in the population or its subclasses. As Allport (1942) once stated it, "psychological causation is always personal and never actuarial" (p. 156). This observation calls our attention to an apparently underappreciated fact concerning high-risk offspring: Namely, a child with a schizophrenic parent is not, by virtue of placement in this class, 10–15% of the way toward a diagnosis of schizophrenia; the child does not possess 10–15% of functioning deficits that lead to a diagnosis of schizophrenia. Nor does the at-risk designation imply anything about the families in which offspring are raised. In short, *the fact that someone has a schizophrenic parent implies nothing necessarily about that individual* beyond the fact that he or she has a schizophrenic parent. Obviously, this limitation applies not only to risk for schizophrenia but also to other forms of maladjustment and psychopathology.

Rutter and Quinton (1984) recently reviewed the possible explanations for the association between parental psychopathology and offspring maladjustment in terms of actual causal mechanisms. The first is genetic transmission – a suggestion based on genetic models of vulnerability and supported by evidence suggestive of a genetic component to schizophrenia (Gottesman & Shields, 1972), affective disorder (Gershon, 1984), adult criminality (Crowe, 1983), and some forms of alcoholism (Cloninger et al., 1981). It should be emphasized, however, that there is no basis for assuming that all individuals diagnosed with these disorders themselves suffer from a genetic diathesis. And there is even less of a basis for assuming that the majority of their offspring inherit such a diathesis.

A second possible mechanism, according to Rutter and Quinton, concerns the direct environmental impact of exposure to parental symptoms. Rutter

(1966), for example, found tentative support for this hypothesis on the basis of retrospective reports concerning children of psychiatrically ill parents. Children in Rutter's study were considered most at risk when they were the victims of hostile or aggressive behavior, when they were involved in the patient-parent's symptomatology, and/or when they were neglected for reasons connected with the parent's psychopathology. Anthony (1978) and others have also written extensively on the effects of a child's involvement in a parent's symptom pattern (e.g., folie à deux).

A third potential source of environmental influence on the child stems from indirect effects of the patient's psychopathology, such as family disruptions and interference with the patient's parental and housekeeping functioning. And finally, the patient's psychopathology may have an indirect influence on the child by engendering marital discord, which itself places children at a substantially increased risk for maladjustment and psychopathology (Emery, 1982). Clearly, there is something about having a psychiatrically ill parent that is causally related to elevated rates of negative outcomes among their offspring. And there is at least some evidence to implicate each of the domains of influence outlined by Rutter and Quinton. None, however, has yet emerged as clearly more important than the others; each remains an important area of empirical inquiry. And for each of these paths of influence, it remains the task of researchers to isolate specific processes that might explain exactly how and under what conditions being born to and/or living with a psychiatrically ill parent might exert an influence. To assume a priori that the at-risk designation implies the presence of a diathesis – genetic or otherwise – is to delude ourselves into believing that we already understand the origins of maladjustment in high-risk offspring. And this delusion, in turn, will virtually ensure premature closure of environmental avenues of inquiry.

Protective factors

The risk-as-vulnerability assumption is also evident in the growing literature concerning so-called protective factors in the lives of high-risk offspring. Garmezy, for example, has played a decisive role in focusing the attention of researchers on positive environmental and personal factors in childhood development. Yet among those who study the offspring of psychiatrically ill parents, the search for protective factors seems to stem from surprise at finding high-risk offspring who are doing well – so-called resilient children. The personal and environmental factors that characterize them are assumed to be protective factors. Presumably, children of nondiagnosed parents who are coping as well do *not* deserve the resilient label, nor are the personal and environmental factors that characterize them labeled protective. Why, then, are these concepts deemed so necessary to explain well-functioning children of psychiatrically ill parents? Or, perhaps more to the point, what is it from which we assume they are being protected?

Risk reducers versus protective factors

This is perhaps an appropriate juncture to highlight an important distinction between two uses of the protective factors concept in child development literature. In its weaker form, the term "protective factor" is a purely *descriptive* label; it is synonymous with "risk reducer" in that it refers to a high-risk child's personal and environmental characteristics that are associated with reduced rates of deviance on measures of cognitive, emotional and/or social functioning. In its more ambitious and common form, the protective factors concept carries with it both a descriptive claim and an *inferential* claim. That is, beyond mere description it also claims or implies an understanding of why these factors are associated with reduced probabilities of negative outcomes. Examples of this form of usage are found throughout the literature on childhood stress, which is rich with accounts of children who are functioning competently in the face of extremely stressful or noxious experiences (Despert, 1942; Moskovitz, 1983; Murphy & Moriarty, 1976; Werner & Smith, 1982), including natural disasters, war, and other traumatic events (Garmezy & Rutter, 1985).

The appeal of this literature derives from the fact that among children who are exposed to even the most harrowing experiences one can always find a subset who seem resilient – that is, who do not manifest subsequent maladjustment. And often these so-called resilient children have been found to have different preexisting personality characteristics, relationships, available resources, and background experiences than those who do succumb (Garmezy, 1983). Although often it is not clear which, if any, of these factors actually played a causal role in protecting the children from their stressful experiences, the general belief that *something* related to these factors served a protective function holds considerable appeal. It bears underscoring, however, that this appeal derives from the fact that the so-called resilient children are *known* to have experienced extremely stressful events or circumstances.

In the literature concerning offspring of psychiatrically ill parents, however, the protective factors concept is often invoked in the absence of known stressors to which the offspring have been exposed. That is, when personal and environmental factors are found to be associated with reduced rates of maladjustment among children who are at risk because of parental psychopathology, often it is not clear that these factors are in any meaningful sense *protecting* the children from anything. Descriptively, it is true that positive personality characteristics of the child, a supportive family milieu, and external support systems are associated with lower rates of maladjustment among high-risk offspring (Garmezy, 1986). But also it has been demonstrated that the opposites of these – namely, negative personality characteristics, hostile/impoverished family milieu, and deficient extrafamilial support systems – may be the very factors that give rise to the association between parental psychopathology and offspring maladjustment (Rutter & Quinton, 1984).

Therefore, high-risk offspring for whom there is no *direct* evidence of proximal environmental stressors may not truly be at risk; these offspring may have been misplaced in a high-risk category as a result of our relatively crude understanding of the parental psychopathology/offspring maladjustment link.

Unfortunately, this possibility seldom receives the attention it deserves. The reason in many cases seems to be that the offspring were expected to manifest adjustment problems as a result of their unspecified yet presumed inherited vulnerabilities. Therefore, when the presence of positive environmental factors is found to be associated with reduced rates of maladjustment in some high-risk offspring, the association is almost always interpreted as evidence for the buffering or protecting influence of those factors. There is a circularity in this de facto strategy that has at least two unfortunate consequences. First, it perpetuates a belief that there is something *inherently* bad about being the offspring of a psychiatrically ill parent – an empirically indefensible position with significant negative social consequences. Moreover, it is a strategy that draws attention away from the need to develop a process-level understanding of the factors responsible for maladjustment among the offspring who *are* somehow affected.

Importantly, our concern here is not with the protective factors concept itself but rather with the practice of automatically invoking it as a quasi explanation for virtually any factor associated with reduced rates of negative outcomes among high-risk offspring. Garmezy rendered an invaluable service to psychology by emphasizing the need to consider protective or buffering factors in any meaningful analysis of the influences of childhood stress. Progress beyond Garmezy's insights to an empirically based understanding of the processes through which protective factors work, however, will require a prior understanding of the processes through which stressors themselves exert an influence. Moreover, a necessary (though not sufficient) condition for invoking "protective factors" as an *explanation* for positive outcomes in high-risk offspring samples should be a demonstration of the proximal stressors to which the offspring are being subjected and from which they are being protected.

Isolating environmental sources of childhood deviance

The search for environmental factors associated with early maladjustment in high-risk offspring derives its impetus and rationale from several related observations. The most fundamental of these is that, beyond their risk for a genetic diathesis, high-risk offspring may be exposed to a host of adverse environmental factors associated with having a disturbed parent, such as marital discord, separations due to the ill parent's hospitalization, disruptions in family life, social stigma, strained relationships within and outside the immediate family, and so forth. Moreover, and equally salient to the present discussion, high-risk offspring are exposed to these factors in widely varying degrees. Therefore, variations in exposure to adverse environmental influences may be viewed as potential causal candidates in efforts to explain early signs of maladjustment in high-risk offspring. Importantly, variations in many of these same factors may also account for early signs of maladjustment in the offspring of nondiagnosed parents. Moreover, they ultimately may play an important role in subjecting the hypothesis of a genetic diathesis for all forms of schizophrenia to risk of refutation. Although traditional high-risk designs certainly are not capable of supporting or rejecting genetic hypotheses, they are capable of isolating environmental factors that might serve as a foundation for such tests.

At the same time, environmental variables may play a significant role in accounting for enough within-diagnostic-group and within-family variance to allow for more sensitive tests of specific vulnerability models. That is, they hold potential for reducing the proportion of unexplained variance in measures of childhood functioning within different parental diagnostic and control categories, thereby reducing the degree of overlap between schizophrenic and psychiatric control groups. Thus, even those with narrow interests in the onset of schizophrenia and those pursuing specific models of vulnerability to schizophrenia have much to gain from a consideration of environmental factors. Because only 10–15% of the offspring of schizophrenics will themselves be diagnosed as schizophrenic, it remains possible that much of the early deviance found in high-risk offspring samples is attributable to environmental factors associated with having a schizophrenic parent. Moreover, as we emphasized earlier, some forms of early maladjustment may reflect relatively short-lived responses to transient environmental disturbances.

Although these observations provide a very general rationale for the examination of environmental factors, neither they nor the diathesis-stress model itself point to specific factors that might serve as a starting point for analyses. The diathesis–stress model does, of course, emphasize the concept of environmental stress, but it makes no claims about which types of experiences might constitute important stressors in childhood. The fact that we are concerned here with childhood functioning, however, leads naturally to an emphasis on family environment. Not only does the influence of family occupy center stage in most theories of child development (Baldwin, 1980), but there is ample empirical evidence for effects of family influences on virtually all aspects of early cognitive and social development (Wachs & Gruen, 1982).

Selection criteria

The results of cross-sectional analyses of high-risk offspring suggest at least two criteria by which promising candidates may be chosen from among the vast domain of family variables. The first concerns between-group (diagnostic and control) variability; the second concerns within-group and within-family variability.

One of the most consistent findings of the high-risk studies to date has been that children of psychiatrically ill parents, as a group, are more deviant than children of normal parents across a variety of variables. Although the issues raised earlier call for caution in the interpretation of these findings, the reliability of this phenomenon highlights the importance of exploring variables that are likely inter alia to discriminate well between normal families and those with a psychiatrically ill parent.

It is also clear that there is considerable within-group variability as well as within-family variability across many of the child outcome measures employed. It is well known, for example, that among families containing a psychiatrically ill parent there are some whose children are all functioning at least at normal levels. Moreover, even within families with a psychiatrically ill parent, some children may be deviant across several modes of functioning while their siblings are indistinguishable from children of nondiagnosed parents on these same measures – and in some cases perform consistently better. We should therefore be looking for variables with potential for discriminating between groups of children (a) in target and control families, (b) among index families, and (c) within both index and control families as well. Obviously, this second criterion calls for the selection of variables beyond those that measure normative characteristics of family environment. This does not rule out an emphasis on traditional variables such as parenting, family cohesiveness, marital discord, and the like. It does, however, suggest that variables such as these may be optimally effective in shedding light on important influence processes when assessed with reference to individual children within a family. This strategy is also suggested by the general pattern of weak associations between family variables and child adjustment that is characteristic of the child development literature (Maccoby & Martin, 1983). And finally, there is convergent evidence from behavioral genetics studies suggesting that *nonshared* within-family factors are largely responsible for environmentally caused differences in adjustment between siblings raised in the same family (Plomin & Daniels, 1987).

Limitations of labeled environments

Our emphasis on an idiographic approach to early environmental influences also takes its lead from the more general research literature concerning "labeled environments" (Wachs & Gruen, 1982), such as social class, parenting style, home environment, and the like. The designation "schizophrenic family" shares much in common with variables such as these. Each is used as a grouping label to subsume environmental factors that are believed to be distinct sources of stimulation. Social class is perhaps the most popular of labeled environments, as indexed by its long history and widespread usage as an independent variable in the social sciences. It has long been prominent among variables assessed in major longitudinal studies of development (Kagan & Freeman, 1963; Bayley & Schaefer, 1964), in genetic twin studies

(Farber, 1981), in high-risk research (Sameroff, Bakow, McComb, & Collins, 1978), and more generally throughout the literature on factors influencing the socioemotional development of children (Vaughn, Gove, & Egeland, 1980). Despite its popularity and undeniable usefulness as a general index of environmental quality, social class is nonetheless inherently limited in its ability to inform the very questions it raises about environmental influence.

As Wachs and Gruen (1982) have pointed out in a thoughtful discussion of labeled environments, social class conveys no information about specific *proximal* experiences to which children within a given level of social class are exposed. In addition, there is considerable evidence indicating that specific measures of mother–child interaction (Ainsworth & Bell, 1974), parental disciplinary practices (Hoffman, 1970), marital disharmony (Emery, 1982), and other proximal environmental variables predict significantly more variance in child functioning than do more general measures of environment such as social class. The reason for this is obvious: Whereas there is a higher likelihood of finding negative environmental characteristics at lower levels of social class, the link between particular environmental factors and social class often is only moderate; factors such as inadequate child-rearing, parental insensitivity, marital distress, and the like are found at all levels of social class. Similarly, whereas there is a higher likelihood of childhood maladjustment at lower levels of social class, childhood maladjustment is found at all levels of social class. Finally, it is not social class per se that exerts an influence on children's adjustment. Rather, it is proximal environmental influences such as these that are nested – often broadly – within and across levels of social class. And because it is this diverse array of influences that gives rise to social class differences, the variables that constitute this matrix should be the ultimate focus of our efforts. Although social class variables have played an undeniable role in establishing the importance of environmental variables, it is only at the level of proximal influences that process-level models of cause and effect can be generated and tested.

The utility of proceeding from the level of labeled environments to successively more proximal environmental influences is nicely illustrated in the history of research concerning the link between parental divorce and children's adjustment. Over the span of two decades researchers have advanced from the once widely held belief that separation from parents per se has a direct, negative influence on children's adjustment (Bowlby, 1973) to the considerably more enlightened view that specific environmental factors surrounding divorce may better explain these child outcomes. Proximal variables such as parental discord (Lambert, Essen, & Head, 1977), disciplinary practices (Hetherington, 1989), modeling (Schwartz, 1979), and others (Wallerstein, 1983) have been implicated as important environmental mediators of children's responses to divorce. Moreover, in his review of this literature, Emery (1982) concluded that future research should concentrate on even more specific variables such as the timing of changes in parent–child interactions relative to changes in parent–parent interactions and the effects of different types and lengths of conflict on children's adjustment patterns.

It is clear that a reliance on labeled environment variables is necessary and even desirable in the initial stages of isolating sources of environmental influence. They often highlight the most promising directions and strategies for subsequent research. Efforts to understand and predict the causes of childhood maladjustment, however, invariably lead to questions of individual differences within those environments and to questions concerning how those differences interact with one another to influence patterns of adaptation and development.

The Stony Brook High-Risk Project

In the discussion that follows, we review briefly the results of some recent analyses based on data from the Stony Brook High-Risk Project, a prospective, longitudinal study of the offspring of schizophrenic parents and bipolar and unipolar depressed parents (Weintraub & Neale, 1984; Weintraub, 1987). These analyses extend beyond previously demonstrated associations between patient psychopathology and the functioning of family members and examine competing environmental models to account for these links. In the first analysis we consider the roles of timing and chronicity of patient-related stress in accounting for the association between parental psychopathology and offspring adjustment. In the second analysis, we explore the often replicated but poorly understood link between psychopathology and marital distress. Both analyses demonstrate the utility of examining dimensions of psychopathology beyond DSM-III classifications in an effort to understand the possible mechanisms of their impact on family members.

Stress and children's adjustment

Critical periods. A recurring theme in the literature of psychopathology has been an interest in the extent to which the timing and duration of exposure to certain environmental stressors influence the likely impact of those stressors on children's development. In the past, researchers have focused primarily on the role of timing, often reporting that children's early exposure to parental psychopathology and/or separation from parents are associated with an increased likelihood of maladjustment and psychopathology (Cohen-Sadler, Berman, & King, 1982; Friedman et al., 1984; Kokes et al., 1985; Rutter, 1966; Stanley & Barter, 1970; Walker, Hoppes, Mednick, Emory, & Schulsinger, 1981; Walton, 1958).

Initial analyses of our own data seemed to confirm these reports. Subsequent analyses, however, revealed that the association between early exposure to parental psychopathology and offspring maladjustment may have little to do with timing per se. The association may be due instead to a link between early exposure and overall levels of exposure (Richters & Weintraub, 1986). In particular, we found that children who were first exposed to parental psychopathology at earlier ages tended to have parents who were more severely ill on a number of dimensions of illness. Early exposure to parent hospitalizations in our sample was significantly related to more frequent exposures, to exposures of longer duration, and to exposures to more severe episodes of parental psychopathology. These data suggest that reports from other investigators suggesting a causal link between early exposure to parental psychopathology and offspring maladjustment should be read with extreme caution. They are essentially uninterpretable in the absence of information concerning characteristics of the patient-parents' disorders and their children's overall exposure levels.

Chronic versus episodic stress. Beyond the issue of timing per se, an equally important question concerns the types of stressors associated with parental illness that might be differentially predictive of offspring maladjustment. To examine this, we created separate composites representing (a) the patients' severity of symptoms and role functioning impairment within and across multiple hospitalizations and (b) their base-line levels of functioning prior to their first episodes of illness (premorbid functioning). Although we did not have available to us direct observations of patient functioning between hospitalizations, there is good reason to believe that standard measures of premorbid functioning provide a useful indirect index of interepisodic functioning. Stoffelmayr, Dillavou, and Hunter (1983), for example, recently reviewed the results of 40 independent follow-up studies of schizophrenic patients. The single most important finding to emerge from their cumulative analysis was an average correlation of .62 between premorbid functioning and level of functioning at follow-up.

We examined the association between these indices of chronic and episodic sources of patient-related stress and the social adjustment of their young adult offspring (Richters, 1987). The chronic stress index was significantly related to the independent assessments of the school-aged children by teachers and peers. Moreover, this association between chronic stress and offspring adjustment was still evident when the same offspring were assessed by our staff in early adulthood. In contrast, stressors associated with parental psychiatric hospitalizations were relatively weakly and inconsistently related to measures of offspring adjustment in childhood, and the association was no longer evident by young adulthood.

It should be noted that these associations are also consistent with a genetic model of maladjustment: Patient-parents with lower levels of base-line functioning, more chronic courses of illness, and earlier onset of diagnosed psychopathology may have a stronger genetic component to their illnesses. And this, of course, would increase the likelihood that their offspring would also possess predisposing genes. Although the prospect of genetic diathesis always looms large in studies such as this, there is simply no basis in the current data – or in the study design on which the data are based – to address this question. Nevertheless, it is worthy of note that both the premorbid functioning of patient-parents and their hospitalization histories in this sample have been demonstrated to have significant associations with independent assessments of the home environments provided by their children (Richters, 1987).

It is also worthy of note that the trend in this sample is toward a *negative* correlation between episodic patient severity and offspring adjustment. That is, patients with more severe impairment *during an episode* tend to have offspring with better levels of adjustment. Although this association may seem at first counterintuitive, it is quite coherent from the perspective of at least two different models of environmental influence. The first stems from the widely replicated relationships between premorbid functioning and the onset and the course of psychopathology. In brief, patients with relatively good levels of premorbid functioning tend to have more acute onsets of illness and often manifest florid (e.g., positive) symptom patterns. This pattern is also associated with an increased responsiveness to medication and with more rapid and complete recovery to base-line levels of functioning. Patients with poorer levels of premorbid functioning, in contrast, tend to have a more insidious pattern of illness onset, are less likely to manifest florid symptoms, and typically have less rapid recovery to base-line functioning. Thus, the relation between severity at time of illness and premorbid functioning is a negative one. Although the association is close to zero for the parents of our follow-up offspring sample, it is negative and significant for our full patient sample. It is possible, therefore, that severity at time of episode may be interpretable as an inverse measure of premorbid functioning. This interpretation would buttress a general argument that patient premorbid functioning, because of its correlation with interepisodic functioning, indexes an enduring source of stress to which the offspring are exposed.

An alternative, attributional model for the trend toward a negative association between patient functioning during episode and offspring adjustment, as well as the overall positive association between offspring adjustment and patient premorbid functioning, can easily be imagined. It may be easier for children, spouses, and friends to classify and discount as disturbed and/or not responsible for their actions those patients who manifest florid symptoms. Such an attribution would provide the developing child with a basis for discounting certain patterns of parental behavior as inevitable and unreconcilable within a rational framework. Moreover, similar attributions by family members and friends might actually engender supportiveness within and toward the family and children. More chronically ill patient-parents with less florid symptom patterns, in contrast, might be less likely to engender such attributions. Their more chronic patterns of poorer functioning may exact a toll on family members in a manner not easily attributable to an illness.

We turn now to another recent report from our project in which we found support for a similar attributional model to account for the relation between psychopathology and marital distress in the same sample (Hooley, Richters, Weintraub, & Neale, 1987).

Psychopathology and marital distress

Despite the consistency with which associations among psychopathology, marital distress, and offspring adjustment have been reported in the literature, the processes through which they are linked remain poorly understood. As Rutter and Quinton (1984) have pointed out, psychopathology may have a direct influence on offspring through a patient-parent's symptomatic behavior and/or role functioning impairment. It may also have an indirect influence through the toll it takes on the marital relationship.

Similarly, there are numerous mechanisms through which a patient's psychopathology may influence the spouse's level of marital satisfaction. Again, its influence may be a direct result of the patient's symptoms, and/or it may have a more indirect influence through frictions associated with the patient's lessened ability to perform in the roles of parent and spouse. Whatever the specific processes giving rise to these links, it is likely that gains in our knowledge on any one front will yield insights in tracking the others. Thus, the advantages to be gained from an understanding of the processes underlying the psychopathology–marital-distress link are clear.

As in the case of offspring maladjustment, there is currently no consistent evidence to suggest that any particular DSM diagnostic category is any more closely associated with marital distress than any other. Levels of marital distress higher than normal have been reported in marriages in which one or both partners have been diagnosed as depressed (Gotlib & Hooley, 1988), schizophrenic (Erlenmeyer-Kimling, Wunsch-Hitzig, & Deutsch, 1980), antisocial (Briscoe, Smith, Robins, Marten, & Gaskin, 1973), or bipolar (Brodie & Leff, 1971).

Yet there are other ways of dimensionalizing psychopathology that might prove more valuable in understanding marital distress. Despite the obvious usefulness of DSM in the classification and treatment of psychiatric disorders, it is important to bear in mind that its criteria were not developed with regard to the possible impact that patients' symptoms might have on their relationships. It should therefore not surprise us to learn that symptom patterns most relevant to diagnosis and treatment are not more closely related to phenomena such as marital distress. This, however, does not preclude the possibility that certain symptoms or non-DSM symptom constellations may provide a more fruitful avenue for understanding marital distress.

Recent reports in the marital literature (Berley & Jacobson, 1984; Doherty, 1981; Fincham & O'Leary, 1983; Holtzworth-Munroe & Jacobson, 1985; Jacobson, McDonald, Follette, & Berley, 1985; Weiss, 1980) suggest that the attributions spouses make about the causes of deviant behavior in their patient-partners may be very important in understanding the quality of the marital relationship. Particularly worthy of consideration in this regard are those behaviors that reflect the distinction between positive and negative symptoms (Andreasen, 1982; Andreasen & Olsen, 1982; Crow, 1980). Negative symptoms (e.g., self-neglect, alogia, apathy) have been described by Strauss and his colleagues as involving primarily an absence of normal functions (Strauss, Carpenter, & Bartko, 1974). These symptoms share the common thread of not involving any apparent physical inability to speak, move, or engage in appropriate self-care. Most patients with negative symptoms, particularly those who are married, have been able to exhibit relatively normal levels of such behavior in the past. A spouse may therefore easily attribute behavioral deficits to an unwillingness of the patient to engage in appropriate behaviors. That is, rather than attributing the cause of negative symptoms to the "illness," the spouse may instead attribute them to the patient's volition.

In contrast, the florid and unusual nature of positive symptoms (e.g., hallucinations, delusions) is such that they may be more readily perceived as unintentional and involuntary. Consequently, these symptoms may be more easily attributed to genuine illness. Thus, despite their highly disruptive nature, positive symptoms are predicted by the symptom-controllability model to be associated with higher levels of marital satisfaction than are negative symptoms: The spouse is more likely to blame the illness rather than the patient for any interpersonal difficulties that may develop from the symptomatic behavior. Finally, symptoms that involve deficits in impulse control (e.g., alcohol abuse, antisocial behavior) are also, from a symptom-controllability perspective, unlikely to be viewed as reflecting true illness behavior. Although they share with positive symptoms the characteristic of behavioral excess, they differ importantly along a dimension of apparent intention. The model assumes that this is a decisive factor in spouses' attributions of controllability.

By collapsing across formal DSM-III diagnosis and examining these dimensions of patient psychopathology, we found that spouse ratings of marital satisfaction were significantly related to the symptom profiles of their patient-partners when those profiles were ordered along a continuum of perceived controllability. Consistent with predictions derived from our controllability model, spouses of positive-symptom patients reported significantly higher levels of marital satisfaction than did spouses of both negative-symptom and impulse-control-deficit patients. We view this finding as particularly noteworthy in light of the fact that positive-symptom patients were independently rated as having significantly lower levels of overall functioning *at time of episode* than were patients in the other symptom profile groups. The model was further supported by our finding that the marital ratings of the spouses of negative-symptom and impulse-control-deficit patients were not significantly different.

Although these data are consistent with our symptom-controllability hypothesis, several alternative explanations for the results also deserve consideration. By choosing to classify patients' symptom profiles within the positive–negative framework, we were able to take advantage of an existing rationale for classification that is largely consistent with differences in symptom controllability. One drawback of this indirect approach, however, is that the resulting symptom clusters may be somewhat different from those that would have been obtained using spouses' ratings of symptom controllability. In view of this unavailability of attributional data from spouses in our sample, therefore, our analyses must be interpreted as an indirect test of the model.

In addition, the possibility exists that observed differences in spouse-rated marital satisfaction result less from the perceived controllability of the symptom profiles than from other dimensions on which the symptom groupings differ. One dimension particularly worthy of consideration is symptom stability. Negative or deficit symptoms are generally considered to be more chronic and traitlike than positive symptoms (Crow, 1980; Strauss et al., 1974). They are also associated with poorer levels of premorbid adjustment (Andreasen & Olsen, 1982). These characteristics of negative-symptom patients often have been viewed as indirect evidence for a stronger biological load to their illnesses. Our data suggest the possibility that psychosocial factors may also play a role in the causal chain. That is, if negative symptoms engender nonsupportiveness from others, then the resulting lack of social support may serve to perpetuate or exacerbate a patient's symptoms. In its most ambitious form, this model might ultimately account for both the poor premorbid functioning and symptom stability of negative-symptom patients. In its weaker form, the model holds that negative-symptom patients may simply be in double jeopardy; their symptoms may have a stronger biological substrate as well as an aversive quality that engenders nonsupportiveness from others.

Conclusion

We have reviewed briefly the origins of the high-risk movement, its current status in the search for markers of vulnerability, and its relative lack of progress in understanding the origins of early deviance among high-risk children. We highlighted several patterns in the high-risk literature that reflect a bias toward the assumption of genetic diathesis in high-risk offspring samples. The most obvious and pervasive of these is the widespread reliance on cross-sectional comparisons of high-risk offspring with the offspring of nondiagnosed parents on early outcome measures, without an adequate consideration of factors associated with parental diagnosis that might explain observed group differences. There are also numerous characterizations of high-risk offspring samples as "genetic risk" samples, even though there is no compelling evidence that these offspring are at any more genetic risk than environmental risk.

We also devoted considerable discussion to the concepts of risk, vulnerability, maladjustment, and protective factors. These have proved to be indispensable concepts to contemporary thinking and research on the functioning of high-risk offspring. But there is also unsettling evidence that a failure to maintain conceptual clarity and consistency in how these terms are employed may be working against us. Current usage to the contrary notwithstanding, the concepts of risk and vulnerability are not synonymous. Moreover, childhood maladjustment does not necessarily reflect either genetic or environmentally induced vulnerability, and the absence of childhood maladjustment does not necessarily signal the absence of vulnerability. Finally, factors that are associated with reduced probabilities of negative outcomes among high-risk offspring are not necessarily protective factors in any meaningful (scientifically productive) sense of the word. They may instead be signaling an absence of the proximal stressors that are causally related to negative outcomes in other high-risk offspring. As we have tried to emphasize, these distinctions and issues are not merely semantic; they have and will continue to have important consequences for our ability to refine our risk classifications and progress toward a process-level understanding of the origins of deviance in affected high-risk offspring.

In our own analyses we have begun to pursue sources of environmental influence on several related fronts. The findings we have summarized share a common strategy of examining dimensions of patient psychopathology that cut across formal DSM diagnoses, in an effort to track particular types of proximal stressors that may be giving rise to adjustment problems in our offspring sample. In the first set of analyses, we were able to demonstrate that the timing per se of a child's exposure to parental psychopathology may have little to do with the child's development. Children who are first exposed at younger ages to parental illness tend to have more seriously ill parents in terms of functioning impairment during an episode, age of first hospitalization, and total number of hospitalizations. Not surprisingly, then, a child's early first exposure to parental psychopathology is associated with more frequent exposure to higher levels of patient-related stress, thereby providing support for a cumulative stress model rather than a critical period model of maladjustment. At a minimum, these results suggest that effects of negative experiences attributable to timing alone may be exceedingly difficult to document.

Continuing with this exposure theme, we also examined links between two distinct dimensions of parental psychopathology and offspring adjustment: patient functioning during (episodic stress) and between (chronic stress) episodes of illness and hospitalization. Overall, we found that our indices of chronic stress were more strongly and enduringly related to offspring adjustment from early childhood to young adulthood. These data provide initial support for our hypothesis that it is the base-line levels of patient functioning between episodes of hospitalization, rather than episodic bouts of illness and hospitalization, that impact on their children's adjustment.

Finally, in our efforts to understand the links among psychopathology, marital distress, and offspring adjustment, we found support for an attributional model of marital distress. In particular, we found that spouse ratings of marital satisfaction were significantly related to the symptom profiles of their patient-partners when those profiles were ordered along a continuum of perceived controllability. We are currently extending this model to analyses of offspring adjustment as well.

Isolating proximal sources of environmental influence to account for the link between parental psychopathology and offspring maladjustment is very much a stepwise task. And each of the strategies we are employing holds potential for bringing us closer to a process-level understanding of what are no doubt the multidetermined origins of deviance in high-risk offspring. There is by definition something about having a psychiatrically ill parent that is causally related to higher rates of psychopathology and maladjustment among their offspring. And there is at least some evidence to support a role for the influence of a host of environmental factors, both directly and indirectly linked to parental psychopathology (Rutter & Quinton, 1984). None, however, has yet emerged as clearly more important than the others; each remains an important focus for empirical inquiry. The most important questions about why the offspring of psychiatrically ill parents suffer rates of maladjustment and psychopathology higher than average are unanswerable on the basis of what we now know. And to assume a priori that high-risk offspring share a common diathesis – genetic or otherwise – is to risk constraining or bringing premature closure to each of these lines of inquiry.

References

Ainsworth, M. D. S., & Bell, S. M. (1974). Mother–infant interaction and the development of competence. In K. J. Connolly & J. S. Bruner (Eds.), *The growth of competence* (pp. 97–118). New York: Academic Press.

Allport, G. W. (1942). The use of psychological documents in psychological science. *S.S.R.C. Bulletin, 49.*

Andreasen, N. C. (1982). Negative symptoms in schizophrenia: Definition and reliability. *Archives of General Psychiatry, 39,* 784–8.

Andreasen, N. C., & Olsen, S. (1982). Negative vs. positive schizophrenia: Definition and validation. *Archives of General Psychiatry, 39,* 789–94.

Anthony, E. J. (1978). From birth to breakdown: A prospective study of vulnerability. In E. J. Anthony, C. Koupernik, & C. Chiland (Eds.), *The child in his family: Vulnerable children* (pp. 273–85). New York: Wiley.

Baldwin, A. L. (1980). *Theories of child development* (2nd ed.). New York: Wiley.

Bayley, N., & Schaefer, E. (1964). Correlations of maternal and child behaviors with the development of mental abilities: Data from the Berkeley Growth Study. *Monographs of the Society for Research in Child Development, 29.*

Beardslee, W. R. (1986). The need for the study of adaptation in the children of parents with affective disorders. In M. Rutter, C. E. Izard, & P. B. Read (Eds.), *Depression in young people: Developmental and clinical perspectives* (pp. 189–220). New York: Guilford Press.

Berley, R. A., & Jacobson, N. S. (1984). Causal attributions in intimate relationships: Toward a model of cognitive-behavioral marital therapy. In P. C. Kendall (Ed.), *Advances in cognitive-behavioral research and therapy* (Vol. 3, pp. 1–60), Orlando, FL: Academic Press.

Bowlby, J. (1973). *Attachment and loss, Vol. 2: Separation: Anxiety and anger.* New York: Basic Books.

Briscoe, C. W., Smith, J. B., Robins, E., Marten, S., & Gaskin, F. (1973). Divorce and psychiatric disease. *Archives of General Psychiatry, 29,* 119–25.

Brodie, H. K., & Leff, M. J. (1971). Bipolar depression – a comparative study of patient characteristics. *American Journal of Psychiatry, 12,* 1086–90.

Cloninger, C. R., Bohman, M., & Sigvardsson, S. (1981). Inheritance of alcohol abuse: Cross-fostering of analysis of adopted men. *Archives of General Psychiatry, 38,* 861–8.

Cohen-Sadler, R., Berman, A., & King, R. (1982). Life stress and symptomatology: Determinants of suicidal behavior in children. *Journal of the American Academy of Child Psychiatry, 21,* 171–86.

Cornblatt, B., & Erlenmeyer-Kimling, L. (1984). Early attentional predictors of adolescent behavioral disturbances in children at risk for schizophrenia. In N. F. Watt, E. J. Anthony, L. C. Wynne, & J. E. Rolf (Eds.), *Children at risk for schizophrenia: A longitudinal perspective* (pp. 198–211). Cambridge University Press.

Crow, T. J. (1980). Molecular pathology of schizophrenia: More than one disease process? *British Medical Journal, 280,* 1–9.

Crowe, R. R. (1983). Antisocial personality disorders. In R. E. Tarter (Ed.), *The child at psychiatric risk.* Oxford University Press.

Despert, J. L. (1942). *Preliminary report on children's reactions to war.* New York Hospital and Department of Psychiatry, Cornell University Medical College, New York.

Doherty, W. J. (1981). Cognitive processes in intimate conflict: Extending attribution theory. *American Journal of Family Therapy, 9,* 35–44.

Emery, R. E. (1982). Interparental conflict and the children of discord and divorce. *Psychological Bulletin, 92,* 310–30.

Erlenmeyer-Kimling, L., & Cornblatt, B. (1978). Attentional measures in a study of children at risk for schizophrenia. In L. Wynne, R. L. Cromwell, and S. Matthysse (Eds.), *The nature of schizophrenia: New approaches to research and treatment* (pp. 359–65). New York: Wiley.

Erlenmeyer-Kimling, L., Marcuse, Y., Cornblatt, B., Friedman, D., Rainer, J. D., & Rutschmann, J. (1984). The New York High-Risk Project. In N. F. Watt, E. J. Anthony, L. C. Wynne, & J. E. Rolf (Eds.), *Children at risk for schizophrenia: A longitudinal perspective* (pp. 198–211). Cambridge University Press.

Erlenmeyer-Kimling, L., Wunsch-Hitzig, R. A., & Deutsch, S. (1980). Family formation by schizophrenics. In L. N. Robins, P. J. Clayton, & J. K. Wing (Eds.), *The social consequences of psychiatric illness* (pp. 114–34). New York: Brunner/Mazel.

Farber, S. (1981). *Identical twins reared apart: A reanalysis.* New York: Basic Books.

Fincham, F., & O'Leary, K. D. (1983). Causal inferences for spouse behavior in maritally distressed and non-distressed couples. *Journal of Social and Clinical Psychology, 1,* 45–52.

Friedman, R. C., Corn, R., Hurt, S. W., Fibel, B., Schulick, S., & Swirsky, S. (1984). Family history of illness in the seriously suicidal adolescent: A life-cycle approach. *American Journal of Orthopsychiatry, 54,* 390–7.

Friedman, R. C., Erlenmeyer-Kimling, L., & Vaughn, H. G. (1984). Event related evoked potential (ERP) methodology in high-risk research. In N. F. Watt, E. J. Anthony, L. C. Wynne, & J. E. Rolf (Eds.), *Children at risk for schizophrenia: A longitudinal perspective* (pp. 198–211). Cambridge University Press.

Garmezy, N. (1971). Vulnerability research and the issue of primary prevention. *American Journal of Orthopsychiatry, 41,* 101–16.

Garmezy, N. (1976). The experimental study of children vulnerable to psychopathology. In A. Davids (Ed.), *Child personality and psychopathology: Current topics* (Vol. 2, pp. 171–216). New York: Wiley.

Garmezy, N. (1981). Children under stress: Perspectives on antecedents and correlates of vulnerability and resistance to psychopathology. In A. Rubin, J. Aronoff, A. M. Barclay, & R. A. Zucker (Eds.), *Further explorations in personality* (pp. 196–269). New York: Wiley.

Garmezy, N. (1982). *Stress-resistant children: The search for protective factors.* Unpublished manuscript, University of Minnesota.

Garmezy, N. (1983). Stressors of childhood. In N. Garmezy & M. Rutter (Eds.), *Stress, coping, and development in children* (pp. 43–84). New York: McGraw-Hill.

Garmezy, N. (1986). Developmental aspects of children's responses to the stress of separation and loss. In M. Rutter, C. E. Izard, & P. B. Read (Eds.), *Depression in young children: Developmental perspectives* (pp. 297–323). New York: Guilford Press.

Garmezy, N., & Phipps-Yonas, S. (1984). An early crossroad in research on risk for schizophrenia: The Dorado Beach Conference. In N. F. Watt, E. J. Anthony, L. C. Wynne, & J. E. Rolf (Eds.), *Children at risk for schizophrenia: A longitudinal perspective* (pp. 6–18). Cambridge University Press.

Garmezy, N., & Rutter, M. (1985). Acute reactions to stress in children. In M. Rutter & L. Hersov (Eds.), *Child and adolescent psychiatry: Modern approaches* (2nd ed., pp. 152–76). Oxford: Blackwell Scientific.

Gershon, E. S. (1984). *The origins of depression: Current concepts and approaches.* New York: Springer.

Goldstein, M. J., & Rodnick, E. H. (1975). The family's contribution to the etiology of schizophrenia: Current status. *Schizophrenia Bulletin, 14,* 14–63.

Gotlib, I. H., & Hooley, J. M. (1988). Depression and marital distress: Current status and future directions. In S. Duck (Ed.), *Handbook of personal relationships* (pp. 543–71). New York: Wiley.

Gottesman, I. I., & Shields, J. (1972). *Schizophrenia and genetics: A twin study vantage point.* New York: Academic Press.

Hetherington, E. M. (1989). Coping with family transitions: Winners, losers, and survivors. *Child Development, 60,* 1–14.

Hoffman, M. L. (1970). Moral development. In P. H. Mussen (Ed.), *Carmichael's manual of child psychology* (pp. 261–359). New York: Wiley.

Holtzworth-Munroe, A., & Jacobson, N. S. (1985). Causal attributions of married couples: When do they search for causes? What do they conclude when they do? *Journal of Personality and Social Psychology, 48,* 1398–412.

Hooley, J. M. (1986). Expressed emotion and depression: Interactions between patients and high-versus low-EE spouses. *Journal of Abnormal Psychology, 95,* 237–46.

Hooley, J. M., Richters, J. E., Weintraub, S., & Neale, J. M. (1987). Psychopathology and marital distress: The positive side of positive symptoms. *Journal of Abnormal Psychology, 96,* 27–33.

Jacobson, N. S., McDonald, D. W., Follette, W. C., & Berley, R. A. (1985). Attributional processes in distressed and non-distressed couples. *Cognitive Therapy and Research, 9,* 35–50.

Kagan, J., & Freeman, M. (1963). Relation of childhood intelligence, maternal behaviors and social class to behavior during adolescence. *Child Development, 34,* 899–911.

Kokes, R. F., Fisher, L., Cole, R. E., Perkins, P. M., Harder, D. W., & Wynne, L. C. (1985). *Competent children at risk: Their parents and families: Markers of competent children.* Unpublished manuscript, University of Rochester.

Lambert, L., Essen, J., & Head, J. (1977). Variations in behavior ratings of children who have been in care. *Journal of Child Psychology and Psychiatry and Allied Disciplines, 18,* 335–46.

Lewine, R. R. J. (1984). Stalking the vulnerability marker: Evidence for a general vulnerability model of psychopathology. In N. F. Watt, E. J. Anthony, L. C. Wynne, & J. E. Rolf (Eds.), *Children at risk for schizophrenia: A longitudinal perspective* (pp. 545–607). Cambridge University Press.

Lewine, R. R. J., Watt, N. F., & Grubb, T. W. (1984). High-risk-for-schizophrenia research: Sampling bias and its implications. In N. F. Watt, E. J. Anthony, L. C. Wynne, & J. E. Rolf (Eds.), *Children at risk for schizophrenia: A longitudinal perspective* (pp. 557–64). Cambridge University Press.

Maccoby, E. E., & Martin, J. A. (1983). Socialization in the context of the family: Parent–child interaction. In M. Hetherington (Ed.), *Handbook of child psychology. Vol. IV: Socialization, personality, and social development* (pp. 1–101). New York: Wiley.

Mednick, S. A. (1965). Primary prevention and schizophrenia: Theory and research. In *Public health practice and the prevention of mental illness*. Copenhagen: World Health Organization.

Mednick, S. A. (1966). A longitudinal study of children at risk for schizophrenia. *Mental Hygiene, 50,* 522–35.

Mednick, S. A. (1967). Psychophysiology, thought processes, personality and social development of children at risk for schizophrenia. *Sociological Micro-Journal, 1,* 1–100.

Mednick, S. A., & McNeil, T. (1968). Current methodology in research on the etiology of schizophrenia. *Psychological Bulletin, 70,* 681–93.

Mednick, S. A., & Schulsinger, F. (1968). Some premorbid characteristics related to breakdown in children with schizophrenic mothers. *Journal of Psychiatric Research 6* (Suppl. 1), 354–62.

Meehl, P. E. (1954). *Clinical versus statistical prediction*. Minneapolis: University of Minnesota Press.

Meehl, P. E. (1962). Schizotaxia, schizotypy, schizophrenia. *American Psychologist, 17,* 824–38.

Moffitt, T. E., Mednick, S. A., & Cudeck, R. (1983). Methodology of high-risk research: Longitudinal approaches. In R. E. Tarter (Ed.), *The child at psychiatric risk* (pp. 54–79). Oxford University Press.

Moskovitz, S. (1983). *Love despite hate: Child survivors of the Holocaust and their adult lives.* New York: Schocken Books.

Murphy, L. B., & Moriarty, A. E. (1976). *Vulnerability, coping, and growth: From infancy to adolescence*. New Haven: Yale University Press.

Neale, J. M. (1984). Information processing and vulnerability: High-risk research. In M. Goldstein (Ed.), *Preventive intervention in schizophrenia: Are we ready?* Washington, DC: U. S. Department of Health and Human Services, Alcohol, Drug Abuse, and Mental Health Administration.

Neale, J. M., & Oltmanns, T. F. (1980). *Schizophrenia*. New York: Wiley.

Neale, J. M., Winters, K. C., & Weintraub, S. (1984). Information processing deficits in children at high risk for schizophrenia. In N. F. Watt, E. J. Anthony, L. C. Wynne, & J. E. Rolf (Eds.), *Children at risk for schizophrenia: A longitudinal perspective* (pp. 198–211). Cambridge University Press.

Oltmanns, T. F., Weintraub, S., Stone, A. A., & Neale, J. M. (1978). Cognitive slippage in children vulnerable to schizophrenia. *Journal of Abnormal Child Psychology, 6,* 237–45.

Plomin, R., & Daniels, D. (1987). Why are children in the same family so different from one another? *Behavioral and Brain Sciences, 10,* 1–60.

Reichenbach, H. (1938). *Experience and prediction*. University of Chicago Press.

Richters, J. E. (1987). Chronic versus episodic stress and the adjustment of high-risk offspring. In K. Hahlweg & M. J. Goldstein (Eds.), *The impact of family research on our understanding of psychopathology* (pp. 74–90). Heidelberg: Springer.

Richters, J. E., & Weintraub, S. (1986, August). *Children at risk: A critical look at critical periods*. Paper presented at the annual meeting of the American Psychological Association, Washington, DC.

Rolf, J. E. (1972). The social and academic competence of children vulnerable to schizophrenia and other behavior pathologies. *Journal of Psychology, 80,* 225–43.

Rolf, J. E., & Garmezy, N. (1974). The school performance of children vulnerable to behavior pathology. In D. F. Ricks, A. Thomas, & M. Roff (Eds.), *Life history research in psychopathology* (Vol. 3, pp. 87–107). Minneapolis: University of Minnesota Press.

Rosenthal, D. (1970). *Genetic theory and abnormal behavior.* New York: McGraw-Hill.

Rutter, M. (1966). Children of sick parents: An environmental and psychiatric study. *Institute of Psychiatry Maudsley Monographs, 16.* Oxford University Press.

Rutter, M., & Quinton, D. (1984). Parental psychiatric disorder: Effects on children. *Psychological Medicine, 14,* 853–80.

Sameroff, A. J., Bakow, H. A., McComb, N., & Collins, A. (1978). Racial and social class differences in newborn heart rate. *Infant Behavior and Development, 1,* 199–204.

Sameroff, A. J., Barocas, R., & Seifer, R. (1984). The early development of children born to mentally ill women. In N. F. Watt, E. J. Anthony, L. C. Wynne, & J. E. Rolf (Eds.), *Children at risk for schizophrenia: A longitudinal perspective* (pp. 482–514). Cambridge Univeristy Press.

Sameroff, A. J., & Zax, M. (1978). In search of schizophrenia: Young offspring of schizophrenic women. In L. C. Wynne, R. L. Cromwell, & S. Matthysse (Eds.), *The nature of schizophrenia: New approaches to research and treatment* (pp. 430–41). New York: Wiley.

Schwartz, J. C. (1979). Childhood origins of psychopathology. *American Psychologist, 34,* 879–85.

Spring, B., & Coons, H. (1982). Stress as a precursor of schizophrenia. In R. W. J. Neufeld (Ed.), *Psychological stress and psychopathology* (pp. 13–54). New York: McGraw-Hill.

Stanley, E., & Barter, J. (1970). Adolescent suicidal behavior. *American Journal of Orthopsychiatry, 40,* 87–96.

Stoffelmayr, B. E., Dillavou, D., & Hunter, J. E. (1983). Premorbid functioning and outcome in schizophrenia: A cumulative analysis. *Journal of Consulting and Clinical Psychology, 51,* 338–52.

Stone, A. A., Weintraub, S., & Neale, J. M. (1977). *Using information processing tasks to form groups of vulnerable and invulnerable children of schizophrenic parents.* Paper presented at the 85th annual convention of the American Psychological Association, San Francisco.

Strauss, J. S., Carpenter, W. T., & Bartko, J. J. (1974). The diagnosis and understanding of schizophrenia. Part II: Speculations on the processes that underlie schizophrenic symptoms and signs. *Schizophrenia Bulletin, 11,* 61–9.

Vaughn, B., Gove, F., & Egeland, B. (1980). The relationship between out of home care and the quality of infant–mother attachment in an economically disadvantaged population. *Child Development, 51,* 1203–14.

Wachs, T. D., & Gruen, G. E. (1982). *Early experience and human development.* New York: Plenum Press.

Walker, E., Hoppes, E., Mednick, S. A., Emory, E., & Schulsinger, F. (1981). Environmental factors related to schizophrenia in physiologically labile high-risk males. *Journal of Abnormal Psychology, 90,* 313–20.

Wallerstein, J. S. (1983). Children of divorce: Stress and developmental tasks. In N. Garmezy & M. Rutter (Eds.), *Stress, coping, and development in children* (pp. 265–302). New York: McGraw-Hill.

Walton, H. (1958). Suicidal behavior in depressive illness: A study of etiological factors in suicide. *Journal of Mental Science, 104,* 884–91.

Watt, N. (1984). In a nutshell. In N. F. Watt, E. J. Anthony, L. C. Wynne, & J. E. Rolf (Eds.), *Children at risk for schizophrenia: A longitudinal perspective* (pp. 572–95). Cambridge University Press.

Watt, N. F., Anthony, E. J., Wynne, L. C., & Rolf, J. E. (Eds.). (1984). *Children at risk for schizophrenia: A longitudinal perspective.* Cambridge University Press.

Weintraub, S. (1987). Risk factors in schizophrenia: The Stony Brook High-Risk Project. *Schizophrenia Bulletin, 13,* 439–50.

Weintraub, S., & Neale, J. M. (1984). The Stony Brook High-Risk Project. In N. F. Watt, E. J. Anthony, L. C. Wynne, & J. E. Rolf (Eds.), *Children at risk for schizophrenia: A longitudinal perspective* (pp. 243–63). Cambridge University Press.

Weintraub, S., Prinz, R., & Neale, J. M. (1978). Peer evaluations of the competence of children vulnerable to psychopathology. *Journal of Abnormal Child Psychology, 4,* 461–73.

Weiss, R. L. (1980). Strategic behavioral marital therapy: Toward a model for assessment and intervention. In J. P. Vincent (Ed.), *Advances in family intervention, assessment, and theory* (Vol. 1, pp. 229–71.). Greenwich, CT: J.A.I. Press.

Werner, E. E., & Smith, R. S. (1982). *Vulnerable but invincible: A longitudinal study of resilient children and youth.* New York: McGraw-Hill.

Wynne, L. C., Singer, M. T., Bartko, J. J., & Toohey, M. L. (1977). Schizophrenics and their families: Research on parental communication. In J. M. Tanner (Ed.), *Developments in psychiatric research.* London: Hodder & Stoughton.

Yarrow, M. R., Campbell, J. D., & Burton, R. V. (1970). Recollections of childhood: A study of the retrospective method. *Monographs of the Society for Research in Child Development, 35*(5, Serial No. 138).

Zubin, J., & Spring, B. (1977). Vulnerability – a new view of schizophrenia. *Journal of Abnormal Psychology, 86,* 103–26.

5   Hard growing: children who survive

*Marian Radke-Yarrow and Tracy Sherman, with the
collaboration of Anne Mayfield and Judy Stilwell*

Children are inherently vulnerable, but also they are strong in a determination to survive and grow. Over the generations of scientific study, these complementary themes have directed much research concerned with children's
physical and psychological development under conditions that threaten their
well-being or survival. The field of study known as "risk research" provides an
example of this dual orientation, with its focus on the individual's vulnerabilities and resistances to risk and stress (Garmczy, 1981)

One historical stimulus for the present era of risk studies is no doubt to be
found in the observations by Spitz and Wolf (1946) of infants' responses to
institutionalization and lack of mothering. Severe disturbances, described as
anaclitic depression, developed in some infants, and some of these infants
died. A little more than a decade later, Harry Harlow gave his American
Psychological Association presidential address on "The Nature of Love"
(1958). His findings, based on an animal model and an experimental paradigm, showed similar stark results with infant monkeys: Severe environmental
deprivation has profound effects on infants' social, emotional, cognitive, and
physical development and well-being. The multitude of studies that followed
almost all documented or elaborated the findings of deteriorative processes
set in motion when infant monkeys were deprived of mothering. Across a
wide range of studies on human infants who had suffered deprivations and
neglect, as reviewed by Yarrow (1961), there were similar conclusions concerning both immediate and enduring damage to children. In the voice of that
period, the primary message was that biological sufficiency was not sufficient,
that monkey and human infants alike depended on love and psychological
nurturance for their survival.

The authors would like to thank Barbara Belmont for her help in data management and analysis,
Frances Bridges-Cline for reading and commenting on an earlier draft of the manuscript, and Rita
Dettmers for managing the preparation of the manuscript and tables. This work was supported by
the National Institute of Mental Health and by the John D. and Catherine T. MacArthur Foundation (Research Network Award on the Transition from Infancy to Early Childhood).

97

Other messages latent in those research findings and other challenges for research were yet to be recognized. Specifically, little attention was paid to individual differences in responses. Questions concerning why, how, and to what extent infants managed to survive severe deprivation were not asked. For example, Spitz and Wolf's data provided clear evidence of tremendous individual variability. Of 123 institutionalized infants suffering mothering deprivation, 19 developed anaclitic depression in a severe form, and 23 in a moderate form. Interestingly, that meant that 79 infants did not succumb to such a dramatic extent. More generally, the conclusion of that era of research was that infants need love, but the processes that translate love from parent into successful development in the child were not studied. Recently, the field of risk studies has begun to integrate these varied messages and has required of itself investigation of the full range of questions. Researchers have begun to investigate competence and coping, as well as vulnerability, in children (Garmezy, 1974; Rutter, 1983).

Investigators in developmental psychopathology are attempting to deal with these several issues in a developmental framework. However, multiple tensions are apparent in these research efforts. One theoretical concern is whether vulnerability is best regarded as a threshold phenomenon in which a certain level of stress results in a massive breakdown in the child's adaptive behavior, or as a continuous dimension of behavior, moving from more successful to less successful adaptations to stress. For certain purposes, behavior can be defined as acceptable or unacceptable, healthy or unhealthy. For example, statements concerning the numbers of individuals who have received diagnoses and those who have not received diagnoses can be very useful, as can other threshold cutoffs, such as school dropout rates. In contrast, when investigation involves a search for mechanisms or processes, threshold models lose a tremendous richness of information and may conceal as much as or more than they reveal. As Norman and Bobrow (1975) wrote when describing human information processing, humans rarely, if ever, undergo catastrophic failure in processing – as when a computer "goes down." Rather, they suggested that the concept of *graceful degradation* in function more accurately describes human information processing. Even as input data become less accurate and less informative, and even as the system becomes increasingly overwhelmed by competing demands, the human mind continues to function, albeit in an increasingly less efficient manner. Similar continuing and eroding processes apply to the individual's adaptive behavior.

A second theoretical tension concerns the concepts of risk and protective factors. Should these be regarded as universally defined, or are they better defined in terms linked to the individual's developmental level? The meaning to the individual of particular life events or stressors is clearly dependent on the cognitive and emotional capacities of the individual. Perhaps an understanding of the factors or processes that protect the individual or increase the individual's vulnerability requires consideration of developmental issues as well.

Closely tied to these theoretical issues is a methodological question; namely, whether our understanding of risk and coping is best advanced by in-depth study of individuals or by large-sample research designs. Use of large-sample epidemiological studies clearly has been valuable for identifying factors that, in general, are predictive. Interest in mechanisms, however, forces another level of investigation, one that is sensitive to the individual.

The task of developmental psychopathologists is, then, to try in an interdisciplinary manner to integrate these different theoretical and methodological views in order to further our understanding of behavior in contexts of serious constitutional and environmental challenges to individual integrity. To achieve this objective, the range of inquiry must include as core issues the investigation of evolving maladaptive and adaptive behaviors in response to stress, in concert with normal developmental processes. Thus, the familiar concepts of vulnerability, invulnerability, resilience, and coping need definitions and assessments in terms of the changing capabilities and needs of the child. In addressing these more difficult questions, high demands must be placed on research methods.

When Anthony (1974) presented a paper on "The Syndrome of the Psychologically Invulnerable Child," he offered an assortment of questions about invulnerability. Is invulnerability a property developed gradually out of successive masteries of difficulties? Is it a natural "immunity," that is, an inborn higher threshold of sensitivity to stress? Is it useful to imagine coping behavior as drawing on a reservoir of resources that can eventually be "used up," with the costs appearing later in development? Is invulnerability a general trait, or are there very specific invulnerabilities, just as there are specific (Achilles' heel) vulnerabilities? These questions remain.

"Resilience" is a more thoroughly defined notion, having emerged from Lewinian, Wernerian, Murphian, and psychoanalytic concepts. A resilient individual is one who shows a composite of characteristics:

. . . to be generally resourceful, to show more "umveg" solutions when faced with a barrier, to be able to maintain integrated performance under stress, to be able to process simultaneously two or more competing stimuli, to be able to resist sets or illusions, to be able to both "regress in the service of the ego" when task requirements favor such a form of adaptation and, conversely, to be able to become adaptively obsessive and even compulsive under certain other environmental presses. (Block & Block, 1973, p. 5)

Assessment of resilience presents formidable difficulties and is rarely fully realized in research.

Both Anthony and the Blocks have chosen to highlight the positive side of children's coping with very difficult circumstances, thereby bringing attention to children who, like some of Spitz's infants or Harlow's baby monkeys, have not succumbed to their adverse situations. Just as the early work failed to acknowledge and follow the group of children who survived, so, too, there is a risk in the the study of resilient or invulnerable children of failing to attend to the costs that these children are paying for their "successful" survival. Clearly a balance is needed in investigating the total functioning of children, noting their strengths and their weaknesses.

How one evaluates whether or not and in what manner children are, in fact, "coping" with their life circumstances is not entirely clear. Is coping a reactive process, a measure of how children deal with stressors as they are presented? Or is it a process by which children come to have control over, or at least have some influence on, the levels and kinds of stresses encountered in life? What criteria should be used to evaluate more and less effective coping behaviors so that social and personal values will not impose themselves on what should be scientific criteria?

In this discussion we are viewing coping at three levels. At a biological level, children are said to be coping successfully if their behavior contributes to their chances of physical survival and health, and the continuation of the species. Risk factors are those influences that reduce children's chances of survival and of reaching the age of procreation. At a societal level, successful coping behaviors are those that contribute to the survival and well-being of others. At a psychological level, we regard positive coping as the exercise of behaviors that contribute to the well-being of the self. A child who becomes a survivor is one who is happy about one's self, who is physically healthy, whose behavior is masterful, and who is learning to be a positive contributor to one's immediate society. Our goal is to discern how children accomplish these levels of survival, to describe children's functioning in relation to the stressors in their lives, and to speculate on the implications of patterns of coping for the children's continuing development.

The problem

In this exploration, we are looking at children who seem to be surviving multirisk conditions of genetic and environmental origins. These are children who are being reared in chaotic and threatening conditions by affectively ill parents. These children could be labeled "invulnerable" or "resilient." We refer to them as survivors. We have defined survivorship in the following manner: These children have no psychiatric diagnoses, are performing at grade level in school, relate well to peers and to adult authorities in school and at home, and have a positive self-concept.

Our method of inquiry is to begin by examining a group of children whose familial circumstances would suggest unfavorable outcomes and then determine if there are children in the group who seem to be managing relatively well. Finding such children, we then move to an individual level of analysis to examine interactions among factors in the immediate environment and in the child's perceptions and behavior; finally, we consider likely trajectories in the child's development. We shall attempt to elucidate how the children we have

chosen for individual study seem to have succeeded in minimizing psychological and physiological costs and how their coping styles stem from strengths
with which they seem to have been born, as well as from protective factors or
processes operating in their particular environments – in spite of overarching
family impairment and chaos.

The data from developmental psychopathology (Garmezy, 1983; Rutter,
1983) indicate that factors such as intelligence, sex of child, age of child, and
family socioeconomic status have value as predictors of how well children *on
the average* will weather stresses. The challenge is to understand how and
when these and other factors can deflect risks and reflect processes that mediate the experiences of the individual child.

To anticipate what we shall be able to conclude: There exists a group of
children who have not been devastated by adversity, but even within that
group, the story of each child, in its way, shows that children cannot "walk
between the raindrops," that environmental and genetic risks are costly.

The data source

In order to search for processes, it is necessary to have a data base
that is informative on many levels. One needs to see or learn about a child's
behavior in a range of contexts, under various demands and risks, with a
variety of persons, and across time. One needs, also, to be able to provide an
atmosphere of trust so that one is allowed access to the thoughts and inner
world of the child. The NIMH child-rearing study (Radke-Yarrow, 1989)
provided the necessary data for this kind of exploration. It provided a
multiassessment data base of 123 families in which the mother or both parents
were depressed or in which both parents were without histories of psychiatric
disorder. In each of the families, there were at least two children at the time of
initial assessment: a 2- to 3-year-old who was reexamined at 5 to 6 years of
age, and a 5- to 8-year-old who was reexamined at 8 to 11 years of age. The
families were primarily of middle-class background. A subsample ($n = 9$) was
very disadvantaged economically. In the total study, 105 of the families were
Caucasian, 16 were black, and 2 were Oriental.

Information on the children and their families was integrated from many
data sources: repeated psychiatric assessments of each parent and child, family histories, family demographics, child developmental histories, reports of
marital relationships and life events of the family, reports of each child's
behavior from the mother on the Child Behavior Checklist (Achenbach,
1979) and from the teacher on the Child Behavior Checklist–Teacher's Report (Achenbach & Edelbrock, 1980), an IQ test for the younger children,
and extended observations of parent–child and sibling interactions in a laboratory apartment, in a range of situations representative of family life.

From the NIMH study we selected as our target sample families for which
there was an exceedingly high aggregation of unfavorable conditions of ge-

Table 5.1. *Sample characteristics*

Measure	Both parents affectively ill $(n = 25)$[a]		Both parents without history of psychiatric disorder $(n = 18)$[a]	
	$\bar{X}$	SD	$\bar{X}$	SD
Socioeconomic level[b]	46.16	18.37	56.11	12.42
Education of mother[c]	5.04	1.37	6.11	.83
Education of father[c]	6.10	1.10	6.00	1.64
Age of mother	32.16	5.12	32.33	3.73
Age of father	35.75	5.14	34.61	3.66
Mother's GAS score[d]	51.96	13.27		
Number of children in family	2.96	1.00	3.00	1.46

Note: None of the differences between groups is significant.
[a]Twenty of the ill group were white, and 5 were black. In the group without psychiatric disorder, 16 were white, and 2 were black.
[b]On the Hollingshead scale, a score of 40 is in the lower-middle-class range, 50 is middle-class, and 60 is upper-middle-class.
[c]On the Hollingshead scale, 5 is "some college" and 6 is "college graduate."
[d]This GAS score is a rating of the impairment in the mother's functioning during the most severe episode of illness in the lifetime of the younger child. A score of 50 describes a level of serious symptoms or impairment in functioning that most clinicians would think would require treatment or attention.

netic and environmental origins. Genetic risk was high by virtue of unipolar or bipolar depression in the mothers and minor, major, or bipolar depression in the fathers in all but 5 families. In those 5 families, the mothers had major affective illness, and the fathers were absent from the home. Environmental risk was high in terms of chronically chaotic, harsh, and unusual kinds of family life, as well as impaired and disturbed parental behavior associated with the parents' affective disorders. Twenty-five families met these criteria. A contrast sample of 18 families was chosen in which neither parent had a history of psychiatric disorder. These 18 families were intact, two-parent families in which life experiences varied from relatively calm and orderly to relatively chaotic. The sample characteristics are presented in Table 5.1.

Our analyses of the high-risk families and contrast families were of three sorts. We began with a between-groups analysis in which we compared how well the children in the two groups were coping at the time of follow-up assessment, when the younger child was between 5 and 6 years old and the older sibling was between 8 and 11 years. From the high-risk group we then singled out for intensive study 4 children (a younger and an older boy, and a younger and an older girl) who satisfied our criteria of "surviving." Third, we examined whether or not the protective factors identified by the case analysis

Table 5.2. *Percentages of children with psychiatric problems in the high-risk and normal families by age and sex*

Group membership	High-risk families[a]		Normal families[b]	
	%	(n/N)	%	(n/N)
5- to 6-year-olds[c]	32	(8/25)	6	(1/18)
8- to 11-year-olds[c]	48	(12/25)	17	(3/18)
All boys[c]	42	(8/19)	12	(2/17)
All girls[c]	39	(12/31)	11	(2/19)
Total group[c]	40	(20/50)	11	(6/36)

[a]$n = 25$ families, 50 children.
[b]$n = 18$ families, 36 children.
[c]One-tailed χ^2, $p < .05$.

discriminated between survivor and nonsurvivor children in the full sample of at-risk children.

Between-groups analyses

We compared the two groups of children on psychiatric assessments. Each child was given a standard psychiatric interview, the Child Assessment Schedule (CAS) (Hodges, McKnew, Cytryn, Stern, & Kline, 1982), at the time of the second assessment. Persons who conducted the interviews were blind to parental diagnoses. The mother's report on the Child Behavior Checklist (Achenbach, 1979) was a second source of information.

Within the high-risk sample (50 children), 40% of the children had serious problems; within the normal group (36 children), 11% of the children had serious problems. Detailed data on the psychiatric status of the children from the high-risk sample and the normal sample are presented in Table 5.2. The DSM-III categories are used to describe the areas of problems. Not only did more children in the risk group receive "diagnoses," but in many cases two diagnoses were given to a child. In most of these dual morbidity cases the two problem categories were depressive feelings and anxiety (Table 5.3).

In addition to these psychiatric assessments, teachers' reports on the Child Behavior Checklist (Achenbach & Edelbrock, 1980) were obtained for the older siblings only, who were in grades 3 to 6. Assessments were based primarily on teachers' written comments, with special attention to statements about the child's peer relationships, apparent loneliness, and conduct problems. (Data were missing on 3 children, 1 from the risk sample and 2 from the normal group.) In the high-risk sample, 9 children were described by their teachers as having problems interacting with peers, problems of apparent loneliness, and/or conduct problems. In the normal sample, teachers' reports indicated that 4 children were having problems evident in the school environment.

Table 5.3. *Problems of children by group, age, and sex*

Subjects	Major depression	Dysthymic disorder	Over-anxious disorder	Separation anxiety disorder	Conduct disorder (socialized, nonaggressive)	Oppositional disorder	Attention deficit disorder	Other
Risk group								
Younger boys (n = 9)				X				
					X			
							X, w/hyperactivity	
Younger girls (n = 16)				X			X, w/hyperactivity	
		X					X, w/hyperactivity	
		X		X				
						X		
								Adjustment reaction, w/depressed mood
Older boys (n = 10)			X					
				X				
					X			
		X		X			X	
		X	X					
Older girls (n = 15)					X			
		X	X					
	X		X					
			X					Sleepwalking disorder
				X				
		X						
				X				
Normal control group								
Younger boys (n = 7)		X	X					
Younger girls (n = 11)								
Older boys (n = 10)		X						
Older girls (n = 8)		X						Simple phobia
			X					

By integrating the data on psychiatric diagnosis, the data from the school on academic achievement, and the data on social and emotional functioning, we were able to identify a group of the older children who were functioning adequately in all domains. As expected, many more of the children from healthy homes than from high-risk homes were doing well in all three domains. From the healthy families, 69% of the children (5 of 8 boys, 6 of 8 girls) met the entire set of criteria for successful social, emotional, and cogni-

Table 5.4. *Percentages of older children from high-risk and normal families by criteria of survivorship*

Measure	High-risk families ($n = 24$)[a]		Normal families ($n = 16$)[a]	
	%	(n)	%	(n)
Psychiatric diagnosis and school problems	21	(5)	12	(2)
Psychiatric diagnosis only	25	(16)	7	(1)
School problems only	21	(5)	12	(2)
No diagnosis, no school problems	33	(8)[b]	69	(11)[b]

[a]Three children (2 from normal families and 1 from a high-risk family) were excluded from the determination of survival because school data were missing. They had no psychiatric diagnoses.
[b]One-tailed χ^2, $p < .05$.

tive functioning. From the risk families, only 33% of the children (2 of 9 boys, 6 of 15 girls) satisfied our criteria for being included in the survivor group. The breakdown of problems is presented in Table 5.4.

For the younger children we did not have school data. For these children the only criterion for survivorship was absence of problems on the psychiatric evaluation. Seventeen of 18 children from the normal group and 17 of 25 children from the risk group were without serious problems.

Thus, from the high-risk families, there were 6 younger boys and 11 younger girls and 2 older boys and 6 older girls who appeared to be managing reasonably well and were candidates for our case studies. We chose 4 children, one representative of each age and gender group, for further study.

Four case studies of survivors

We shall present brief vignettes of 4 children. All of these children come from very chaotic homes; in all cases the mother and father suffer from major affective disorders, either unipolar or bipolar depressive disorder. The parents have poor marital relationships: In two of the households, the children live with only one parent in residence; in the other two households the father is often absent. In each case, the mother is both physically and psychologically inconsistently available to her children; this is because of episodes of affective illness. In each of these families, the child's siblings are not faring as well as the child we have chosen to describe. We shall mention the siblings only to the extent that they help us understand what the processes might be that are allowing the target child to survive. We shall also comment on what appear to be the costs already incurred by the target child, which may eventually compromise the child's chances of survival: ability to procreate, psychological well-being, and likelihood of behaving lawfully. All names have been changed, and specific details have been altered to protect confidentiality.

Case 1

Dominique is the second daughter in a family of four daughters. Her mother, who has major depression, supports herself via prostitution and by participating at the minimal level required by various social agencies to get maximum benefits for her children and herself. Mrs. Adams has three siblings and three paternal half-siblings. Only she and one older half-sister have escaped serious problems with alcoholism and/or drug abuse. Mrs. Adams left home in adolescence to live with an older man, who unfortunately was unable to provide her an easier existence than she had experienced at home. Dominique's father is intermittently in her life. He also suffers from major depression and a serious marijuana abuse problem, typically using four to six reefers a day.

Dominique was separated from her mother from age 3 months to 15 months. During that time, Dominique was in her grandmother's home, a very small house in which lived both grandparents, three of Mrs. Adams's siblings, and a niece. Mrs. Adams visited at least once a month, except for the last 5 months, when she had a major depressive episode and was living on the street, was raped, and wanted to die. Mrs. Adams, when not ill, exhibits strong survival behaviors; she demands of and teaches her daughters explicit coping behaviors. Her manner with her children is "tough"; she yells at them much of the time. She gets what she wants even if she has to resort to physical violence.

Dominique is a healthy and sturdy little girl and has been since birth. Her mother's only complaint about Dominique is her silliness. Mrs. Adams is proud of Dominique's health. She also emphasizes Dominique's feminine qualities, spending the hours necessary to keep Dominique's hair stylishly braided.

When assessed at 2 years of age, Dominique was securely attached to her mother. By objective rating, Mrs. Adams was one of the angriest mothers in our sample, and Dominique herself showed little positive emotion. Nonetheless, their interaction was ongoing. Neither was isolated from the other. It was easy to observe that Dominique knew how to get contingent responses from her mother. Simply by walking on or kicking her mother's purse, Dominique could reliably elicit a yell or a swat from her mother. She would play for a while and then return to anger her mother. This may not be the idyllic, contingent mother described in the attachment literature, but it seemed to be working for Dominique and her mother. An especially informative episode was provided when Mrs. Adams was asked to have Dominique open a tightly sealed, relatively large (larger than the child's hands) plexiglass container with a toy inside. Dominique, like most of the children, declared she could not manage it. Mrs. Adams absolutely denied this conclusion, and by barking instructions, some physical assistance, and many loud and angry statements, she informed Dominique both that she could do it and how to do it. Dominique did succeed in opening the container by herself before Mrs. Adams would allow her to do anything else.

Life in this family was very disorganized, with frequent moves, changes in the mother's major male relationship, many changes in caretaker in any given day, being left alone, having little opportunity to attend school consistently or to attend one school for any period of time. Yet Dominique was securely attached at 2 years. Moreover, when evaluated by two psychiatrists, one observing the child in interaction with the mother, the other interacting with Dominique after she was separated from her mother, Dominique was observed to be a creative, curious, outgoing, and charming 2-year-old. Three years later, at the time of our second evaluation, Dominique was doing well in school in the first grade, was consistently healthy, showed an average amount of positive affect, and reported herself to be happy and unafraid. However, Dominique appeared to be surviving mainly by attending only to herself and, when necessary, to her mother's demands. For example, unlike her older sister, who set the table for the two of them and served food for both, Dominique served herself and then ate immediately. Despite these concerns, and despite the fact that Dominique came from one of our most chaotic home environments, she was clearly surviving.

Case 2

The second little girl survivor comes from an intact middle-class family. The mother is a very depressed individual who often remains in bed. The father is also depressed and often stays away at his father's home.

In the early years of Andrea's life, the family was living in an unfinished home, built by the father near to his extended family. The mother became depressed in that environment: She felt that she was not welcomed by his family, and she believed that molds in the house were contributing to her depression. She became so adamant that the house was a major source of her problems that she convinced her husband to move. The move brought her physically close to her extended family, but did not improve her mood. The mother then began to miss the old house and to bemoan the fact that they had sold it. The father was extremely unhappy to have sold the house he had built. Marital strife worsened.

When the family entered the study, Andrea, then age 6, had just been diagnosed as diabetic. She reported herself to be very anxious and sad. As an infant, Andrea had been a colicky baby. With the end of colic, her mother reported that Andrea became a happy, well-behaved toddler who was dearly loved and cared for by herself and by her own mother, who was also depressed. At our second assessment, Andrea was age 9, caring well for her diabetes, on her own. Her mother showed no signs of being able to help Andrea responsibly. Andrea described herself as happy, and she was reported by her teacher to be happy, well liked by adults and peers, and doing very well at school.

Between the first and second assessments, Andrea's father developed a serious problem with alcoholism, and Andrea's mother continued to have recurrent bouts of deep depression. Mr. Holmes had begun a night-shift job. Additionally, he had begun to see other women. He was rarely home and rarely saw his wife or the children. He reported that he had no close friends and that his moods were very bad, especially so when he was home. Andrea's younger brother had been identified as suffering from severe learning disabilities. Just as she had reacted to Andrea's diabetes, Mrs. Holmes had reacted to her son's problems by going to bed.

In our research apartment at the time of the second assessment, Andrea organized the family into a pretend game in which she was a one-woman restaurant. She seated and served her parents at one table, keeping her younger brother as peripheral as possible. Like Dominique, Andrea seemed to be surviving by cutting out social others who did not support her needs – her sibling. Unlike Dominique, she appeared to be more invested in people, and she sought out parents, adults in the neighborhood, and other children to fill her social and emotional needs. She visited neighbors frequently and bestowed affection and care on their children. Andrea's diabetes and her intense social seeking suggest to us a child who suffers more than Dominique.

Nevertheless, Andrea was doing well, socially and emotionally, at that time. She kept her reactions to her stress hidden; it did not break into her overt behavior. But her physical survival may already have been compromised. Research on elevated cortisol levels suggests that a contributing factor in Andrea's diabetes may have been heightened cortisol due to the stresses in her life (Levine, 1983). Her coping strategy seemed to be one that required large expenditures of emotional energy as she won love and affection from others. The social-emotional payoff appeared sufficient to the expenditure; one questions that this will continue.

Case 3

Steven is the youngest child and the only son in a blended family. His mother has two teenage daughters from a prior marriage. He also has a full sister 3 years older than he. Steven's parents run a summer resort as their main source of income. In the off-season, Steven's father works on maintaining the grounds and equipment, and also as a carpenter, which often involves his being away from home for long periods of time. Also, Mr. Marshall is a world-class athlete. Both his preparation for competitions and the actual competitions often take him away from home for extended periods of time.

Mr. Marshall had been depressed throughout his life, especially during the winter months. When he felt depressed, he would sit and think, or he would feel the need to go out and exercise, or he would wish to go away, and sometimes he did simply leave the family. He reported that he had no close friends, that there was no one he could trust; but he did like to help others.

Mrs. Marshall also suffers from major depressive disorder. Her first marriage caused her to be very unhappy. Her husband left her and their two girls. To supplement her child-support checks, she worked at the resort where she met Mr. Marshall. They married, but almost immediately began having marital difficulties. Both times that she was pregnant, Mr. Marshall left the home. He returned after Mary was born, and there was a period of relatively good relations. He became attached to Mary, and she was a happy child. But Mary's position changed dramatically when Steven was born. Both Mr. and Mrs. Marshall highly prize the fact that Steven is a boy. This family value is shared by all members and is known to all the children. Steven is well loved, and he reported this fact during the psychiatric interview. Mary reported wishing she were a boy, and wishing she could die. Apparently, this high valuing of maleness was true in Mr. Marshall's family of origin. His sister reported that he had never had to grow up and had never had true demands placed on him simply because he was born male. When Mr. Marshall abandoned his family during his wife's pregnancies, he returned to his parents' home, where he was welcomed. Following Steven's birth, Mr. Marshall threw Mrs. Marshall and the children out of their home because he did not approve of the names she had suggested for the baby. They were names from her family. During that period, it was Mr. Marshall's sister who provided Mrs. Marshall money to pay the rent.

The parents are very critical of one another and fight constantly. Their fighting is always in front of the children because of the nature of the house. Mr. Marshall is concerned with nature and ecology; so their home is a one-room construction that is energy-efficient. Open sleeping lofts are near to the roof; the kitchen and living area are below. Steven's biggest complaints were his difficulty in falling asleep and his wish that his parents would fight less.

Since the reconciliation following Steven's birth, Mr. Marshall has not abandoned the family. The only prolonged separation to which Steven was exposed was his father's stay in Europe to compete in international sports competition. Mr. Marshall's participation is a major point of family pride.

Despite Steven's prized status as a boy and his certainty of his loved position, he, too, is criticized and teased. The gist of much of this teasing is that he needs to be a tougher boy. There have been few concessions to Steven's young age. He is required to come home to an empty house after kindergarten because his father thinks there is nothing wrong with this. And he is required to wait for his father at outdoor construction sites even in bitter weather. Steven dislikes coming home to an empty house and dislikes standing out in the cold, but there is no question of the father ceding to the child's wishes on these matters. This is what father expects of his son.

At age 2, in our research apartment, Steven stayed close to his mother, demanding attention much of the time. At 2 years and again at 5 years, Steven was happy, active, and engaging. He seemed to like people, sought out his sister Mary as a playmate, and related warmly to both mother and father. He is well liked in school by both teachers and peers.

In his psychiatric interview, Steven appeared to have an accurate view of himself and his family. He also admitted to many fears. He did not deny the family situation, had clear complaints, and knew with certainty that he was loved by his parents, his sisters, and his grandparents. Interestingly, when introduced to a new female peer in our apartment, he immediately assumed the "Daddy" role, which involved the peer's fixing a pretend meal for him, and his finding many, many flaws in the quality of her cooking and the efficiency of her service. Although he did not like to listen to his parents fighting, he had learned the male role as defined by his family.

During the period between the first and second assessments, Steven's paternal grandmother committed suicide. That resulted in his father having an extended and deep period of depression. Currently, Mary (at age 8) is talking about suicide. Mrs. Marshall's depression has become continuous, and she has begun to suffer from panic attacks. Continuing family crises and continuing exposure to severe depression may become increasingly costly to Steven as he matures enough to understand more about the lives of the other members of his immediate family.

At this time, Steven appears to be coping quite well. Being the recipient of this family's small store of warmth and affection seems to be enabling him to withstand his parents' tensions and depressions and the age-inappropriate demands being placed on him. The question raised by his life situation is whether or not he will continue to be successful in meeting what will undoubtedly be increasing tests of his maleness. How will he fare if he cannot become an Olympic-quality athlete?

Case 4

Drew is an attractive child, and very personable. His mother and school and research personnel describe him as having charisma. He is the older of two children. He is the oldest of our 4 case study children (11 years), and he is showing more problem behaviors and less adequate coping than the other children we have studied. Still, at this time he is surviving, and he is doing better than any of the other older sons from our set of multiproblem families.

Drew was the result of an unplanned pregnancy early in his parents' marriage. Both parents were in college at the time. Unlike the other case study families, Drew's parents are not close to their families of origin. Mr. Connors is not in touch with his family at all. Mrs. Connors's parents did not approve of her marriage, and as problems have arisen in the marriage, Mrs. Connors felt that her parents would be more inclined to say "I told you so" than to be supportive. Her parents, too, have had a difficult marriage, but they have stayed together.

Mrs. Connors suffers from bipolar affective disorder (Bipolar II – periods of hypomania). Her first major depressive episode was at age 15. It was triggered by the loss of a boyfriend. Mr. Connors's first depressive episode took place when he was only 12 years of age. At that time he was hospitalized because of hysterical paralysis.

Mrs. Connors was happy to learn that she was pregnant with Drew because it suited her to have her children early so that she could then go on to pursue her career interest in business management. Mr. Connors was not happy about the pregnancy. Mrs. Connors reported that Drew was an extremely good and lovable baby and that she immediately incorporated him into her school routine, taking him to classes with her. That was a good period in her life. However, it was also during that period that she had her first hypomanic episode. When she became pregnant again, Mr. Connors left her. She was alone and very depressed. Two-year-old Drew was her only company and confidant. She said that she had always been close to Drew and had always been able to talk to him about her problems. Drew, however, communicated more easily with his father.

Following the birth of Drew's sister, Mr. Connors invited Mrs. Connors to live with him again. She agreed. Shortly thereafter, Mrs. Connors began graduate business school, made some new friends, and grew increasingly dissatisfied with her marriage. She began to have affairs. Mr. Connors also began to have affairs. The parents fought a great deal in front of the children. Both parents had repeated bouts of depression.

In the period between our two assessments of the family, Mr. Connors began to have hypomanic episodes. At the time of the second assessment, Mrs. Connors had moved to another city. There were plans for her daughter to join her and for Drew to stay with his father.

Through his childhood, Drew has been well liked by his father and his sister and by other children, but it is only in the past 2 to 3 years that Drew has seemed to have a best friend. The school reports that Drew is a born leader. Drew also excels in athletics. However, he has now begun to show problem behaviors in school and disobedient behavior at home. His behavior was most disturbed in the months preceding his mother's moving out. During that period, both parents repeatedly explained the situation from their points of view to the children. Since his mother has moved out, Drew's behavior has become less problematic in the school. He has, however, begun nocturnal enuresis, as has his sister.

In his interview at the time of the second assessment, Drew did not report any problems or any family conflicts. His denial with the interviewer is consistent with his mother's reports of Drew. However, in the apartment observations, he did reveal his feelings to his father during a task in which the parent is asked to show the children various pictures and discuss the moods and the situations of the people in the photographs.

Drew commented that the people in one picture were happy because they were a family that was all together. He described a boy in a second picture as being angry at his mother and as going to get a gun to shoot her. Drew's father made connections for him between his descriptions of the feelings of the people in the pictures and Drew's own feelings about himself and his family.

Drew is connected to people, he is able to lead other children, he is able to talk to his father, and, though he denies problems with his words, his behavior gets him attention and help when he needs it.

Our concerns for Drew are numerous. Now that the family is dissolved, he is denied contact with his mother and his sister, persons to whom he was very close. His father is planning to move the two of them to Greece. Drew's incredible charm may be culture-specific. How will he fare in a different culture? Also, part of Drew's leadership appeal with peers stems from his athletic superiority. An accident in early childhood left Drew with only minimal vision in one eye. As athletic participation becomes more demanding in adolescence, Drew's visual handicap may become more problematic and hurt his standing among his peers.

Case analysis findings

We have presented case descriptions of children from multiproblem families in the hope of discerning processes whereby a child succeeds in coping with adverse circumstances. Has the case study approach, against a background of information from the group data, provided us with information that will allow some generalizable conclusions concerning how these children are managing to survive? We believe so.

Each of these children is surviving biologically, although one child has a serious disease, juvenile diabetes, which puts into jeoparady her longevity and her ability to give birth to healthy infants. Each child has a core of positive self-esteem. All of the children have warm relationships with either the mother or father, despite parent illness and family disorder. Each child is mastering the tasks of school – performing at least at grade level and succeeding in developing and maintaining positive relationships with teachers and peers.

We interpret the successes seen in these 4 children as stemming from two complementary factors. One key factor is a *match* between a psychological or physical *quality* in the child and a core *need* in one or both of the parents that the child fulfills. The child quality in each case appears to be one with which the child was born. The second factor, an extension of the first, is the child's clear conception that there is something good and special about himself or herself. The child quality is then a source of positive self-regard for the child, as well as need-satisfying to the parent. These children receive the maximum social-emotional resources that their families are capable of providing (a fact brought into relief by the contrast between these 4 children and their siblings).

For the 4 children, we see the match beginning early and remaining stable over the time period studied. For Dominique, health and sturdiness are among the special qualities with which she was born, qualities that are valued by her mother. In contrast, Dominique's sisters have been anemic since birth, and this has been a source of tension for their mother. The mother prides herself on being good at taking care of her girls; she is angered and blames the girls when they are ill. Dominique avoids that negative interaction with her mother because she is healthy. Dominique's sturdiness is highly valued because it is one of the necessary components for the fight in which Mrs. Adams feels one must engage for survival. At age 5, Dominique shared these values: When asked what she was most proud of in herself, Dominique answered, "That I can do things for myself."

Steven's family values his gender. Both father and mother highly value male qualities, and the simple fact that Steven is a boy has given him a special place in his family. As reported earlier, Steven is at least a second-generation recipient of this prized status. In the structured interview, Steven repeatedly mentioned that he was loved. In contrast, his sister talked of wishing that she were a boy and of suicide.

Both Andrea and Drew had quiet, happy temperaments as infants and became the special love objects of their harried, depressed mothers. Their mothers reported that, beginning with toddlerhood, Andrea and Drew had been their confidants. The children know that they have functioned as important and successful social companions for their mothers, and it appears to us that this relates to these children's social confidence. Andrea, for example, reports that her best quality is her niceness.

An important consequence of the match is that the children's positive self-esteem and patterns of behavior that have developed within the family around these parent-valued traits are incorporated in the children's behaviors outside the family. Their styles of interacting are generalized to relationships with other adults and with peers. For the children observed, their manner of interacting has continued to engender positive social interaction with a broadening social world. This positive social regard from school and peers has then fed back to the family. Dominique, for example, is admired by other children as well as by her teachers as a very independent, competent child. The positive school reports cycle back into the family. They are a source of great joy to her mother, and Dominique receives high praise for bringing them home. Andrea's socially mature behavior, too, goes beyond the family. It makes her popular in the neighborhood. She creates many situations in which neighboring women value her and treat her very well as she showers their young children with competent care and affection. Drew manifests a maturity and leadership quality beyond his years, acknowledged in school as well as in the family. Steven's boyishness is appreciated by children and adults alike and especially by his male peers.

It is important that the "match" quality in the child functions to organize or draw together the family in such a way that the child becomes the recipient of the family's love and positive evaluation. If the match between the child's quality and the parental need functions to create antagonism within the family, the protective quality is lost. An example is provided by the case of a family in which the firstborn son is regarded by the mother as her special helper and friend. The boy's special position antagonizes the father, who is scornful of the child. The key element of matching is that it serves to elicit positive experiences for, and positive evaluations of, the child.

Beyond the special attributes that have been nourished by their families, these children share a cluster of positive features that are universally valued and protective. These attributes, too, contribute to the children's self-esteem and to having positive social experiences. The children are all alert and curious, and they impress observers as having a zest for living. All have winning smiles and are attractive, charming, and socially engaging. All have above-average intelligence. These attributes contribute, also, to the children's self-esteem. It seems that the children need both the universally valued traits as well as the special family-valued traits to do as well as they are doing.

Why then, have we discussed these children as experiencing "hard" growing? It is because we see extra challenges and developmentally inappropriate demands embedded in their special valued traits. Furthermore, in aspects of their styles of coping, we suggest that there are hidden costs that continuing life stresses or the tasks of normal developmental transitions may make manifest.

Even being a favored child does not put these children outside the influence of parental pathology. In fact, their favored status derives largely from the fact that they satisfy needs in their parents that entail behaviors and responsibilities that often are inappropriate to their years and definitely are inappropriate to their roles as children. On the one hand, they are pushed to competent maturity beyond their years; on the other hand, they do not have the opportunity within their families to make demands on the parents and have their own needs met. Steven has needed to be a man since infancy – for Dad. But Steven cannot get a parent to be waiting at home when he arrives from kindergarten. Andrea has been good and has been her mother's confidante. But Andrea cannot get either parent to help her to care for her diabetes.

We believe that we can see a structure to each child's manner of adaptation that might usefully be referred to as personality. The patterns by which children are managing with the stresses of parental impairment and family chaos appear to be the ways in which these children are organizing their lives in general. In each child's reaction patterns and manner of initiating interaction and dealing with others there is the basis for predicting to which stresses that child will be most vulnerable, to which kinds of stresses the child may be least sensitive, and to which type of psychopathology the child may be most susceptible. Evident in all of these children are characteristic patterns of expressing their felt distress. These patterns (defenses, coping styles) have had strong continuity over the 3-year period studied; they seem to have been there in the earlier years as well. In part, this continuity stems from the continuity in their environments. In all cases, the children's parents have remained depressed or have had episodes of depression with increasing frequency.

Dominique's coping pattern appears to be the one that is least involved and invested in other people. As a toddler in our laboratory apartment, Dominique explored the new environment and picked the toys she wanted to play with, seeking support from no one. Now that Dominique is age 5, her mother has already started to complain that Dominique is moving away from the family and beginning to associate with children who are too old for her. It appears to us that Dominique is searching out children like herself who are independent and want to have control over their own lives. Unfortunately, in her environment, the children who have the most control over their lives are the streetwise children. If her home life continues to be so stressful, we would expect that she will continue to distance herself from the family and not remain enmeshed in their chaotic existence. Like her mother, Dominique may leave her family at a young age for the support of another person. What we cannot know is whether that person from outside the family will offer Dominique any real alternative or will simply be one of the other street children. The research literature on survivors from lower-class environments (Garmezy, 1983; Rutter, 1983) has identified the importance of significant nonfamily adults for providing children with opportunities.

We would speculate that Dominique's personality may make her less vulnerable to loss, if she leaves her family, than would be the case for our other children. Therefore, she may be less susceptible than they to depression. On the other hand, mother and daughter alike strive for a better life. Mrs. Adams's depression came after some years outside her mother's home, when she felt that she had nothing to show for all the efforts to better her lot. If Dominique has no avenue to achieve the successes she and her mother dream of, she, too, may succumb to depression.

Steven, Andrea, and Drew are all much more people-oriented than Dominique. Both Andrea and Steven have devoted themselves to being lovable; Drew is acting out. In all three cases, however, we believe that the children are vulnerable to depression. Drew's situation has already become so stressful that he is manifesting behavior problems that appear to be his way of calling for help and of attempting to keep functioning. As mentioned earlier, Drew's style of coping since toddlerhood has been denial. It is difficult for him to admit openly, in words, that family life is hard or that he needs help. His acting-out behavior, however, has not been ignored at school. Drew's charisma and charm have thus far enabled him to avoid the label of "bad" boy. Rather, teachers report being fond of him and wishing he could get the appropriate help so that his behavior would again be as positive as they know it can be. Drew is now at a turning point in his life as he approaches adolescence. The dissolving of his family, his separation from his mother and sister, and his moving to another culture with his father, we predict, will all be stresses for him. We are concerned that the combination of stresses may be too much.

Andrea expends large amounts of energy in cultivating the friendships and attachments that she needs to feel connected and to feel loved. Moreover, she keeps her negative feelings of stress out of her behavior. We believe that this is a costly way of coping that will leave her vulnerable to loss or rejection. Perhaps her diabetes is a first sign of this costliness. At the present time in her development, Andrea has established a need-satisfying style of living. However, in adolescence, her need for acceptance and her hypothesized heightened vulnerability to rejection will be further stressed by the normal course of early heterosexual encounters. It is during this period that it is predicted that she may succumb.

Steven is loved because he is male. Even at this age, meeting a father's demands is difficult. His lovableness is contingent on his continuing to satisfy his father's definition of manliness. One would expect that the normal stresses of adolescence will be exacerbated for Steven by the family value system. Steven may do well if puberty is good to him – if it comes on time and leaves him big and strong and athletically skilled. If his physical development does not allow him to live up to the family expectations, we predict that he, too, will be at heightened risk for an exacerbation of the normal moodiness of adolescence. However, Steven's coping style has not involved denial as in Drew's case, or masking of feelings as in Andrea's case. His coping style is more open and flexible, and this may help Steven to continue to survive.

High-risk group analyses and findings

Protective factors that are emphasized in the literature include having above-average intelligence and qualities that elicit positive responses from others. These are present in the 4 children. We have suggested the importance also of the presence in the child of an attribute that functions to bring to the child whatever love and positive regard the family has to offer. For all of the children from our 25 high-risk families we have evaluated these three features to determine if they are characteristic of the group of children who are "surviving."

To be certain that children's social winningness or charm and the match between child and parents' needs were not the same factor, the two members of our research staff (Anne Mayfield and Judy Stilwell) who were most familiar with the families were asked to make consensual judgments on each child concerning these two qualities. There appeared to be no halo effect. Among the younger children, 14 received identical ratings for charm and match, and 11 received divergent ratings; among the older children, 12 received identical ratings, and 13 received divergent ratings.

IQ assessments were based on the McCarthy Scales of Children's Abilities for the younger children, and school records for the older children. IQs above 115 were considered above average. For the lower-SES families, IQs above 105 were considered above average. Examination of the 25 younger children (including Dominique and Steven) at ages 5–6 yielded a group of 6 children who had above-average intelligence, who were socially engaging, and who seemed to have a special positive place in their families. None of these 6 children has a diagnosed problem at this time. There are, in addition, 11 young children who do not have problems and yet do not have all of the protective factors operating in their favor.

The data on the older siblings offer a more complete test of our hypothesis than do the data on the younger children. This group of survivors has met all of our criteria – no psychiatric diagnosis, grade-level performance in school, and positive relationships with peers and adults. Also, because there is a trend for problems to become increasingly manifest as the children develop, these children are truly a select group. Among these 25 children (including Drew and Andrea) there are 5 children who satisfy the criteria of intelligence, social engagingness, and parental "match." Among these children, only 1 girl has a psychiatric diagnosis, separation anxiety disorder. Of the remaining 20 children who do not have the protective factors, only 4 meet all of our criteria for being labeled a survivor. Thus, there is some suggestion that, with development, the children who have the protective qualities continue to be without serious problems and to be functioning well academically and socially in school; in contrast, only a small percentage of the children who lack the triplet of protective qualities are still among our survivors.

Conclusions

This chapter has been concerned with conceptual and methodological considerations for research in developmental psychopathology. Especially it has been an attempt to understand the better-than-expected cognitive, social, and emotional adaptive functioning of children who are developing under conditions of genetic and environmental risk. Using a developmental framework, we have created a multifaceted research paradigm that has provided us with in-depth information about a large group of young children and their families. We have focused on families that by objective criteria present enormous risks for the children, and we have examined a few families in detail – those in which at least one child is surviving. Each of these families is expectedly idiosyncratic in its problems, its values, and the role the child plays in the family. Each child has developed an individual style of coping. Despite the uniqueness of the details of family life and child style, some commonalities in processes have emerged. First, we have not found invulnerable children. These children who are managing to grow up and develop under conditions of extreme stress might be called survivors, because we have also identified costs that the surviving child is already paying for having to grow under such adverse conditions. In order to understand the processes whereby some of the children are managing to survive, we have also identified protective factors. In addition to the generally established protective factors of intelligence, curiosity, pleasing physical appearance, and socially winning ways, each survivor-child has been found to fulfill a need of one or both ill parents that also serves the child positively, at least for the present. By meeting parents' needs, the child receives as much of the family's scant social and emotional resources as the family can muster – more than do other children from similar backgrounds of risk who are not faring as well. It is in the context of the match between child characteristics and parent need that we have observed the development of the child's positive self-regard and effective style of responding to stress and relating to others.

The processes underlying these children's relatively successful adaptations, however, also harbor the seeds of possible future serious problems. The child–family interaction patterns have enabled the children to cope and develop up to this point. We have speculated that with further development, especially with adolescence, these children will be able to satisfy their parents' needs and their own needs only at increasing costs to the children themselves. These children have undergone "hard growing," and we have hypothesized that the straight-jackets they have been forced to adopt will become increasingly difficult to wear as they continue to develop.

References

Achenbach, T. M. (1979). *Child Behavior Checklist for ages 4–16.* Bethesda, MD: National Institute of Mental Health.

Achenbach, T. M., & Edelbrock, C. (1980). *Child Behavior Checklist – Teacher's Report Form.* Burlington: University of Vermont.

Anthony, E. J. (1974). The syndrome of the psychologically invulnerable child. In E. J. Anthony & C. Koupernik (Eds.), *The child in his family. Vol. III: Children at psychiatric risk* (pp. 529–44). New York: Wiley.

Block, J., & Block, J. H. (1973). *Ego development and the provenance of thought: A longitudinal study of ego and cognitive development in young children.* Progress report for NIMH grant MH-16080.

Garmezy, N. (1974). The study of competence in children at risk for severe psychopathology. In E. J. Anthony & C. Koupernik (Eds.), *The child in his family. Vol. III: Children at psychiatric risk* (pp. 77–97). New York: Wiley.

Garmezy, N. (1981). Children under stress: Perspective on antecedents and correlates of vulnerability and resistance to psychopathology. In A. I. Rabin, J. Aronoff, A. M. Barclay, & R. A. Zucker (Eds.), *Further explorations in personality* (pp. 196–269). New York: Wiley.

Garmezy, N. (1983). Stressors of childhood. In N. Garmezy & M. Rutter (Eds.), *Stress, coping, and development in children* (pp. 43–84). New York: McGraw-Hill.

Harlow, H. (1958). The nature of love. *American Psychologist, 13,* 673–85.

Hodges, K., McKnew, D., Cytryn, L., Stern, L., & Kline, J. (1982). The Child Assessment Schedule (CAS) diagnostic interview: A report on reliability and validity. *American Academy of Child Psychiatry, 21*(5), 468–73.

Levine, S. (1983). A psychobiological approach to the ontogeny of coping. In N. Garmezy & M. Rutter (Eds.), *Stress, coping, and development in children* (pp. 107–32). New York: McGraw-Hill.

Norman, D., & Bobrow, D. (1975). On data-limited and resource-limited processes. *Cognitive Psychology, 7,* 44–64.

Radke-Yarrow, M. (1989). Family environments of depressed and well parents and their children: Issues of research method. In G. R. Patterson (Ed.), *Aggression and depression in family interactions* (pp. 169–84). Hillsdale, NJ: Erlbaum.

Rutter, M. (1983). Stress, coping, and development: Some issues and some questions. In N. Garmezy & M. Rutter (Eds.), *Stress, coping, and development in children* (pp. 1–41). New York: McGraw-Hill.

Spitz, R., & Wolf, K. (1946). Anaclitic depression. *Psychoanalytic Study of the Child, 2,* 313–42.

Yarrow, L. (1961). Maternal deprivation: Toward an empirical and conceptual reevaluation. *Psychological Bulletin, 58,* 459–90.

6 Children born at medical risk: factors affecting vulnerability and resilience

Margaret O'Dougherty and Francis S. Wright

What happens to medically vulnerable infants when they return home? How likely are these infants to develop normally without neurological handicap, cognitive impairment, or problems in psychosocial development? The existing literature contains widely divergent estimates of later disability for these infants, ranging from 10% to 40% of a sample displaying adverse sequelae (Field, Sostek, Goldberg, & Shuman, 1979; Holmes, Nagy, & Pasternak, 1984; Kopp, 1983; Stewart, 1983). In part, differences in incidences of disabilities reflect the fact that the category of infants "medically at risk" is broad, encompassing many subgroups of infants with markedly differing biological and environmental problems. These infants may have experienced a variety of genetic, prenatal, perinatal, and/or postnatal risk events that are associated with an increased probability of problems in cognitive, social, affective, physical, and neurological arenas. The purpose of this chapter is to explore the multiple dimensions of medical risk conditions, focusing on the processes within or external to the child that exacerbate or attenuate risk status. The usefulness of a risk model as a conceptual and empirical framework for predicting later competence and adaptation is specifically examined for infants medically vulnerable because of the experience of chronic hypoxia and open heart surgery following birth with a congenital cyanotic heart defect.

During the last two decades, various innovative approaches to the study of high-risk, medically vulnerable infants have emerged. The work of investigators in these areas extends to children considered to be at risk as a result of either biomedical or environmental problems. Within the biomedical area, two types of risk status have been identified: (a) infants diagnosed as having a medical disorder in which there exists an established risk for aberrant development; (b) infants presenting with a history of prenatal, perinatal, neonatal, and early developmental events suggestive of biological insult to the developing central nervous system (CNS) that, either singly or collectively, increase the risk for future disorder (Kopp & Krakow, 1983; Tjossem, 1976). Infants considered to be at risk for later difficulties as a result of depriving or damag-

120

ing environmental experiences demonstrate a third type of risk status. The interactions of these environmental and biological factors are of critical importance in either enhancing or diminishing the development of infants at risk (Gottfried, 1973; Parmelee, Sigman, Kopp, & Haber, 1975; Sameroff & Chandler, 1975; Sameroff & Seifer, 1983; Werner & Smith, 1977, 1982). Each of these categories is associated with marked diversity in outcome and provides an opportunity to explore the factors that differentiate between those vulnerable children who remain ill or impaired and those resilient children who do not.

Predictive validity of early risk factors

The concept of a "continuum of reproductive wastage" was first formulated by Lilienfeld and Parkhurst (1951) to describe the wide range of lethal (abortion, neonatal death, stillbirth), sublethal (cerebral palsy, epilepsy, hemiplegia), and subtle manifestations of disability (learning disability, hyperactivity, minimal brain dysfunction) that can result from early CNS trauma. During the next 10 years, Pasamanick, Knobloch, and Lilienfeld (1956; Pasamanick & Knobloch, 1966) elaborated this concept through a series of retrospective studies that expanded the range of deviant developmental outcomes that were thought to result from early damage. They subsequently employed the term "continuum of reproductive casualty" to encompass the range of minor motor, perceptual, learning, and behavioral disabilities associated with possible early cerebral insult. From this early retrospective research, a number of early risk factors such as anoxia, prematurity, obstetrical complications, malnutrition, and low socioeconomic status (SES) of the family were identified as negatively influencing the child's adaptation and heightening the risk for later disorder.

However, this strong association between early possible cerebral insult and subsequent disorder has not been confirmed by most follow-up studies and prospective longitudinal studies. Such studies have found only low, if any, correlations between many of the *single* perinatal or postnatal biomedical risk variables and later disabling sequelae. These findings are perhaps best illustrated by a comprehensive longitudinal study of perinatal anoxia conducted by Graham and her associates in St. Louis. These investigators examined several hundred infants in the newborn period (Graham, Matarazzo, & Caldwell, 1956), tested them again at 3 years of age (Graham, Ernhart, Thurston, & Craft, 1962), and followed them for final assessment again at 7 years of age (Corah, Anthony, Painter, Stern, & Thurston, 1965). They found that (a) anoxia was strongly associated with impaired neurological and developmental status in the newborn period, (b) anoxia was only weakly associated with impairment at age 3, and (c) by 7 years of age, previously anoxic infants were inferior to controls on only 2 of 21 cognitive and perceptual tests.

This finding of higher incidences of intellectual consequences of perinatal anoxia among infants and preschoolers than among older children has been well documented by other comprehensive longitudinal studies (Broman, Nichols, & Kennedy, 1975; Werner, Bierman, & French, 1971). In the Collaborative Perinatal Project of the National Institute of Neurological Diseases and Stroke, 53,000 infants (the products of 56,000 pregnancies) were studied during a 6-year period (1959–65) and received detailed pregnancy, birth, neonatal, 4-month, 8-month, early childhood, and elementary school assessments (Broman et al., 1975). The most consistent predictors of later cognitive competence were maternal education and socioeconomic factors, although documented early brain abnormality, rare neurological conditions, and developmental delay were significant as well. This comprehensive study provided a means of identifying factors influential in high-risk pregnancies and documented the importance of poverty and adverse environmental rearing conditions in childhood mortality and morbidity (Broman et al., 1975; Niswander & Gordon, 1972).

Another seminal longitudinal project originated in Hawaii on the island of Kauai in 1954 (Werner et al., 1971; Werner & Smith, 1977, 1982). A large multiethnic sample ($N = 857$ births) was followed from birth through adolescence, with assessments during the mother's pregnancy, at birth, and at 2, 10, and 18 years. In the first 2 years of life, information on perinatal and neonatal events and developmental, psychological, and nutritional status was recorded. Later, individual psychological assessments also incorporated information from the child's school record, as well as from social welfare and other agencies. By age 18, more than one-half of this predominantly lower-SES sample had learning or emotional problems. Severe perinatal stress was associated with later impairments of cognitive, physical, or emotional functioning only when accompanied by adverse environmental circumstances. This relationship was weaker, although still present, for those infants who had experienced moderate perinatal stress. The Kauai studies documented the importance of family socioeconomic conditions and child-rearing factors as crucial moderator variables.

In their most recent analysis of the later competence of these children, *Vulnerable but Invincible: A Longitudinal Study of Resilient Children and Youth,* Werner and Smith (1982) attempted to identify protective factors in the lives of the children who did not succumb to later adaptational difficulties. All 2-year-old children who had been identified at high clinical risk were classified into one of three groups at age 18: (a) those identified with significant problems by age 10, (b) those developing problems by age 18, and (c) those "resilient" children who remained without significant educational or psychosocial problems. The key protective factors identified included easy temperament, small family size, low numbers of stressful experiences within the family, positive parenting attitudes, low levels of family conflict, and counseling and remedial assistance. In their analysis of interactional effects, Werner and Smith found that many of the protective factors were contributory only in the presence of high-risk factors and adverse environmental conditions, with little or no explanatory power in the lives of less stressed, economically more advantaged children (Werner & Smith, 1982).

Taken together, these three major longitudinal studies underscore the importance of multidimensional assessments, allowing adequate time for recovery processes to occur following adverse perinatal events, and incorporating powerful contributory social, familial, and environmental factors. Based on these and other reviews of research in this area (Gottfried, 1973), Sameroff and Chandler (1975) proposed a "continuum of caretaking casualty" to replace the "continuum of reproductive casualty." In a recent review, Sameroff and Seifer (1983) discussed risk potential in the following way:

In defining the developmental risk associated with any specific child, the characteristics of the child must be related to the ability of the environment to regulate the development of that child toward social norms. In extreme cases of massive biological abnormality such regulations may be ineffectual. At the other extreme, disordered social environments might convert biologically normal infants into caretaking casualties. (p. 1255)

Because developmental outcome is undoubtedly multidetermined, a multivariate approach that can take into account the complex interactions of all these factors is essential. The eventual diagnostic classification that a particular child receives not only reveals unique characteristics of the child but also implicates transactions between the child and the child's social environment.

However, the recurring finding that outcome measures are strongly influenced by environmental factors resulted in a tendency on the part of some reviewers to discount the importance of biological variables and to minimize the impact of early CNS insult (Sameroff & Chandler, 1975). That resulted in a revival of the view that a young child's CNS possesses more plasticity and is capable of more recovery than that of the mature adult. In a critical review, St. James-Roberts (1979) argued that there was little evidence to support the view that the young brain has greater recovery potential. He stressed that there are many potentially interfering and confounding factors in studying brain behavior relationships and included foremost among these the failure to separate research studies in which brain damage has been *verified* (e.g., intraventricular hemorrhage, hemiplegia) and studies in which brain damage has been *presumed* (e.g., obstetrical complications, prematurity, anoxia) to have occurred on the basis of behavioral measures, though there was no validating evidence. Rutter (1983) concurred in the need to make this distinction. The presence of overt (e.g., verified, actual) brain injury *is* associated with markedly increased risks of both intellectual impairment and psychiatric disorder, and the evidence suggests that this association represents the causal influence of brain injury (Chelune & Edwards, 1981; Isaacson, 1975; Rutter, Chadwick, & Shaffer, 1983; Stewart, 1983). Questions about this association arise in dealing with "covert" rather than "overt" brain injuries. Returning to the earlier research pertaining to perinatal risk factors, Rutter (1983) pointed out that "the very weak associations between perinatal complications and brain damage syndromes can be expected simply because the few children with true brain injuries resulting from perinatal events will be diluted by the much larger number who experienced perinatal hazards but escaped cerebral damage" (p. 4).

Confounding possible risk indicators with known risk mechanisms has contributed to conceptual confusion in the high-risk area (Rutter, chapter 9, this volume). Unlike research with experimental animals, in which controlled cerebral changes can be produced and the precise nature of neural and behavioral changes can be studied, research with human subjects is done when the nature, extent, and focus of damage often remain both unknown and uncontrolled variables. The development of noninvasive brain imaging techniques [computed tomography (CT), positron emission tomography (PET), magnetic resonance imaging (MRI), brain electrical activity mapping (BEAM), evoked potentials, and real-time ultrasound] that allow in vivo visualization of the brain has been a major breakthrough in our ability to document the occurrence and severity of cerebral damage. Problems with the brain's functional integrity can now be visualized anatomically with CT imaging and MRI, metabolically with PET, and electrically with BEAM and evoked potentials. Repeat ultrasound evaluation of infants of very low birth weights has provided a means of identifying those infants who have sustained damage through cerebral hemorrhage, infarction, or asphyxia and has documented the relationship between the severity of these events and long-term neurodevelopmental handicaps (Palmer, Dubowitz, Levene, & Dubowitz, 1982; Pape et al., 1979; Stewart, 1983; Thorburn et al., 1981). In the study by Thorburn and associates (1981), only 4% of the low-birth-weight infants with normal ultrasound findings or grade I hemorrhage displayed major neurodevelopmental handicaps at follow-up, whereas 38% of those with more extensive hemorrhage or cerebral atrophy were adversely affected. Although both CT images and ultrasound can reliably detect cerebral hemorrhage, neither technique reliably identifies ischemic lesions until there has been actual tissue loss. Recent investigations with animals have utilized phosphorus MRI to explore the effects of transient ischemia. This technique may be particularly useful in monitoring infants who have suffered severe intrapartum asphyxia and whose ultrasound images show reduced pulsation of cerebral arteries. Phosphorus MRI scanning may provide a means of assessing prognosis as well as evaluating therapeutic interventions to reverse the ischemia (Delpy et al., 1982; Thulborn, du Boulay, Duchen, & Radda, 1982).

Thus, although the development of brain imaging and mapping techniques has provided valuable means of documenting cerebral damage, even among infants with known cerebral damage there is heterogeneity in outcome. Studies of these high-risk infants should provide a better understanding of the factors mediating resilience in those who are medically vulnerable. In addition to examinations of familial factors to account for such variation in outcome, a variety of other confounding variables that potentially could mediate recovery effects should be examined. These include factors such as (a) individual genetic variation, (b) sex, (c) experiential differences, (d) changes in medical technology affecting prognosis, (e) location and extent of the lesion or insult, (f) age at the time of the cerebral insult, (g) topography and redundancy of the neural system affected, (h) length of the recovery period prior to the evaluation period, (i) general developmental rate, and (j) the comprehensiveness of the particular tasks used in assessment (Reitan & Davison, 1974; Rourke, Bakker, Fisk, & Strang, 1983; St. James-Roberts, 1979). One of the greatest challenges facing researchers in this area is to develop measurement instruments that will be valid and sensitive enough to measure the effects of CNS insult. St. James-Roberts (1979) commented directly on this issue:

In this area, the insensitivity of testing used has pre-empted understanding of whether putatively insulting variables have no effect, a transient effect, a small effect which is remediable by good caretaking, or an enduring effect sometimes camouflaged by psychosocial variables. A significant source of obfuscation has been the tacit assumption that psychometric, and primarily IQ, tests provide direct measures of normal CNS function and are unaffected by experiential variables. This is an exaggeration of the properties of these tests. (p. 300)

Predictive validity of multivariate risk models

In part, some of the failures to identify pertinent biomedical risk factors that can accurately predict the degree of risk for an individual infant have resulted from a focus on *isolated* factors occurring solely within the neonatal period. Such an approach does not take into account the ongoing changes that affect outcome measures. An important new development in this regard has been an effort by some investigators (Cohen & Parmelee, 1983; Field et al., 1979; O'Dougherty, Wright, Garmezy, Loewenson, & Torres, 1983; Parmelee et al., 1975; Smith, Flick, Ferriss, & Sellman, 1972; Stewart, 1983) to develop a method of identifying infants at risk by using multiple assessments at different ages, measuring a wide range of variables. This use of sequential prediction stages has the advantage of employing multivariate analyses so that the contributions made by various measures independently, and in combination, can be identified. Subsequently it should be possible to design a more effective system for identification by eliminating those measures that do not contribute to the prediction of later performance. To make the data meaningful, investigators have begun to take into account many interrelated factors, such as (a) the special characteristics of the infant's medical problems, how severe the disturbance is, and the occurrence of multiple problems, (b) the time period under study and the medical treatments available, (c) whether the data were collected retrospectively or prospectively, (d) the comprehensiveness of developmental outcome measures in physical, cognitive, social, and emotional domains, and (e) the characteristics of the parents and the environment to which the infant was exposed on leaving the hospital. We need our research methodologies and statistical analyses to take these complex and interrelated factors into account, rather than employing study designs that correlate a single medical event with outcome. The number of risk events, the severity of each problem, and the presistence of these difficulties appear to heighten the infant's risk status and increase the probability of later dysfunction. The complex developmental interactions that exist among personal vulnerabilities and strengths in the child, the supportiveness of the environment, and the goodness or poorness of fit between the two that can result in either negative or positive transactions must be examined (Sameroff & Seifer, 1983).

Early risk status and later competence in children who survive severe heart defects

This section examines data collected on a sample of children each born with a cyanotic congenital heart defect (CHD) in which multiple biomedical and environmental risk factors were employed as a means of establishing more accurate identification of children at risk for future disability (O'Dougherty et al., 1983). This cohort was part of the "Project Competence" studies of stress resistance in children under the direction of Norman Garmezy.

Giving birth to a child with a congenital defect creates a crisis situation for most parents. Many feel a sense of guilt that they may have been responsible for the child's abnormality. Prolonged grief, loss of self-esteem, shock, disbelief, and intial attempts to deny the severity of the defect or the child's possible mortality frequently are observed (Garson, Benson, Ivler, & Patton, 1978; Travis, 1976). A review of the major findings on the impact of congenital heart disease indicates that there is the potential for widespread impact of such a disability on the parents and children (O'Dougherty, 1983). When an infant is diagnosed as having a CHD, the family must cope with the stresses associated with a chronic physical problem, poor health of the child prior to reparative closed or open heart surgery, repeated hospitalizations, repeated surgical intervention, and uncertainty of outcome. The seriousness of the condition will vary depending on the specific heart defect, the presence of associated anomalies, and the surgical risk.

The outlook for survival, however, has changed dramatically over the last 20 years. Improved surgical techniques and new methods of anesthesia have allowed earlier operative intervention and dramatic improvements in longevity (Vanden Belt, Ronan, & Bedynek, 1979). For many infants, corrective or reparative open heart surgery is possible using the technique of cardiopulmonary bypass with or without hypothermia. All of these factors have increased our awareness of the specific impact of a cardiac defect and the potentially detrimental effects such a defect may have on the child's subsequent psychological development. Ways in which parents can be helped to cope effectively with the diagnosis of a heart defect and the variety of biomedical, surgical, and psychosocial stresses related to it have just begun to be addressed (Garson et al., 1978; O'Dougherty, 1983; O'Dougherty et al., 1983).

Construction of a risk model for infants with transposition of the great arteries

Although there is no question that these infants have benefited from the medical advances that have taken place over the last two decades, little is known of the long-term effects of heart defects and open heart surgery on the developing CNS. A newborn infant with a cardiac defect experiences a variety of biomedical and surgical stresses during the neonatal and early infancy periods that are related to remediation of the heart defect and its physiological consequences. We believed that these biomedical and surgical factors could be viewed as possible risk factors that might heighten the possibility of later dysfunction. We developed a hypothetical risk model for one specific heart defect (transposition of the great arteries, TGA) that allowed for assessment of the effects of single and cumulative risk factors on development. All surviving school-age children (K–8) with TGA who had undergone reparative open heart surgery at the University of Minnesota Hospital were identified. This surgery was performed between 1967 and 1977 and utilized cardiopulmonary bypass at normothermia. Of the 34 children identified, all but 3 participated. This constituted 91% of all children with this CHD treated at this hospital during this time period.

Our studies with these children have attempted to delineate the risks and benefits of surgical treatment beyond the immediate operative period, in order ultimately to provide data for a prospective study to further define risk and protective factors for developmental outcomes in infants with cardiac defects.

Specific biomedical risk factors. Based on prior research with children who have cardiac defects, various biomedical and environmental risk variables were identified as possible predictive variables. The medical variables selected focused on the natural medical history of an infant with CHD and included such factors as the success or failure of palliative surgical procedures, the presence of neurological or medical complications, evidence of growth failure, congestive heart failure, or pulmonary vascular obstructive disease, the duration and severity of hypoxia prior to corrective open heart surgery, the duration of cardiac repair, and the length of hospitalizations. A medical inventory was then developed to evaluate each child's hospital chart with respect to these hypothetical risk variables. Table 6.1 includes a list of the potential variables considered. Those variables that could be reliably deter-

Table 6.1. *A hypothetical risk model for study of children with congenital heart defects*

Biomedical and surgical risk factors	Psychosocial risk factors
Congestive heart failure[a]	Psychological impact of diagnosis
Unsuccessful initial palliation[a]	Age at times of hospitalization and surgery, frequency and extent of separations from parents necessitated by hospitalizations[a]
Growth failure (height and weight)[a]	
Severity of hypoxia	
Duration of hypoxia[a]	Quality of substitute care the child received while away from home
Pulmonary obstructive disease[a]	Painful and frightening medical and surgical treatment
Complex heart anomalies[a]	
State of the art of medical-surgical technology[a]	Stress of restriction
Precipitously early surgery	Parents' attitude and behavior toward the ill child
Duration and degree of hypothermia	Family's mode of coping with these stressful events
Duration of cardiac repair[a]	
Duration of hospitalization[a]	Socioeconomic status of the family[a]
Major neurological complication prior to or following surgery (stroke, seizures, CNS infection)[a]	Other stressful events occurring within the family[a]
	Lack of social support

[a]These factors were included in the risk model.

mined for each child and that were subsequently included in the risk model are indicated in Table 6.1.

Psychosocial moderator variables. When the children's medical records were examined to identify early psychosocial risk factors, serious problems were encountered. Chart notes were examined to document possible effects of each child's heart defect on the family, the parents' attitude and behavior toward their ill child, the stress of the medical procedures on the child, the frequency and duration of separation from the parents, and the presence of social support for the family, but the case records were highly variable and impressionistic and did not consistently address these issues. Consequently, only the socioeconomic status of the family (based on occupation and education of the breadwinner) (Watt, 1976), current family stress (Garmezy, Tellegen, & Devine, 1981), and frequency and length of hospitalization were included as moderator variables that potentially could affect current adaptation.

Establishing risk potential. The relationship between each risk variable and later outcome was first examined individually. Subsequently, medical risk variables demonstrating significant relationships to later neurological and psychological outcomes were summed to obtain a cumulative medical risk score for each child (O'Dougherty et al., 1983). Children receiving similar cumula-

Table 6.2. *Neurological and psychological outcome measures*

Neurological function
Test data
   Neurological examination
   Electroencephalogram
   Visual evoked potential

Cognitive sphere
Test data
   Wechsler Intelligence Scale for Children–Revised (WISC-R)
   Peabody Individual Achievement Test

Biographical data
   Special services received in school
   Child's cumulative school record

Attentional sphere
Test data
   Continuous Performance Test
   Freedom from Distractibility Factor from the WISC-R

Psycholinguistic sphere
Test data
   Verbal Comprehension Factor from the WISC-R

Perceptual motor sphere
Test data
   Perceptual Organization Factor from the WISC-R
   Bender Visual Motor Gestalt Test
   Porteus Maze Test

Social and affective sphere
Observation data
   Examiner Behavior Profile
   Devereux Elementary School Behavior Rating Scale
   Parent Behavior Checklist

---

tive risk scores did not necessarily resemble each other in the similarity of their medical experiences, but did resemble each other in regard to the intensity, duration, and accumulation of stressful experiences. A combined biomedical and environmental cumulative risk score was also calculated that correlated .91 with the biomedical risk score. High-, mild-, and low-risk groups were determined on the basis of the cumulative risk scores.

Outcome measures. Multivariate outcome assessment measures focused on the child's current adaptation as assessed by neurological status, electrophysiological function, cognitive, linguistic, and perceptual motor function, sustained attention, inhibitory control, academic achievement, behavioral adjustment, and need for special services at school. A list of the specific tests included in the outcome assessment is presented in Table 6.2.

Developmental consequences of TGA. On follow-up evaluation, the developmental consequences of TGA were examined to determine if these children should be considered a group at risk for later adaptational difficulties. An attempt was made to determine if TGA children who had survived open heart reparative surgery were characterized by a greater magnitude of later adaptational difficulties than expected in the normal population. Next, our efforts were directed toward determining if such disabilities were characteristic of the sample as a whole or if the children evidenced diversity in their subsequent outcomes. The results indicated significantly greater variability in developmental outcomes. For this sample of TGA children there was both a higher proportion of mental retardation (6.5%) than in the normative sample (2.2%) and a higher incidence of superior intellectual functioning (15% vs. 9%). In addition, 42% of the TGA children required special class placement and/or individualized instruction for learning or behavioral disabilities (SLBP assistance) (O'Dougherty et al., 1983). Abnormal neurological findings were also prevalent. Only 23% of the children were rated as normal on neurological examination. Forty-eight percent of the children received a rating of mild neurological impairment, and 29% were rated as moderately to markedly abnormal (O'Dougherty, Wright, Loewenson, & Torres, 1985). This is in striking contrast to the 5% of normal children receiving such a rating (Bortner, Hertzig, & Birch, 1972). Finally, the incidence of abnormal EEG recordings in the TGA sample (32%) was also higher than that expected in a normal population (5–16%) (Lairy, 1975). These findings confirmed that these children were at risk.

In the attentional area, poor attentional functioning was evident for the majority of children irrespective of their cumulative biomedical risk score when compared with normal age-mates. In a further study (O'Dougherty, Nuechterlein, & Drew, 1984), the attentional performance of these children was compared with that of hyperactive and normal controls. Both the hyperactive and the TGA children demonstrated a lowered overall level of vigilance on the Continuous Performance Test (CPT), with hyperactive children displaying additional difficulty in inhibitory control, whereas the TGA children displayed additional difficulty sustaining their attention over time. In addition, a significant developmental component to the children's attentional problems was identified. When the effects of age were considered in our TGA sample, only the youngest children (kindergarten to third grade) displayed significant impairment in their overall vigilance level. Children in the fourth through sixth grades were not significantly different from normal controls in their attentional abilities. This finding suggested that the adverse consequences of the chronic hypoxia associated with this CHD may ameliorate with time following the resumption of normal oxygenation. Our results are consistent with the findings in the prospective studies of Graham and colleagues involving infants who had experienced a time-limited episode of perinatal anoxia (Corah et al., 1965; Graham et al., 1962). However, the period of time required for recovery in our sample was considerably extended. In the Graham studies, significant recovery of function had been obtained by age 3, with no further deficits evident by age 7. In our studies, the children's attentional functioning did not fall within the normal range until 10–12 years of age, with significant impairment evident for those in the early elementary school years. Although the TGA children resembled the hyperactive children in the severity of their attentional impairment, they did not display behavioral overactivity, suggesting that they may have represented a group with attention deficit disorder without hyperactivity.

In the behavioral area, both the TGA and the hyperactive children were rated as having less self-confidence and shorter attention spans. The hyperactive children showed greater dependence, less goal orientation, higher emotional reactivity, greater overt motor activity, impulsivity, and lower frustration tolerance than the normal or TGA children. In contrast, the TGA children, as compared with the hyperactive children, were rated as abnormally passive and less friendly, and they engaged in less communication (O'Dougherty et al., 1984). Later behavioral adjustment problems were only weakly related to early biomedical risk factors ($r = .29$). In general, the TGA sample as a whole experienced more behavioral adjustment problems than did the normative group, but we were not able to relate the presence of behavioral problems to any of the biomedical risk factors. The potentially significant early psychosocial variables that may have influenced the subsequent adjustment of these children could not be reliably documented in this follow-up study, with two exceptions: Both family stress and socioeconomic status showed small but significant correlations with behavioral adjustment, as discussed in the next section.

Relationship of early risk factors to later competence. In light of previous research (Broman et al., 1975; Corah et al., 1965; Werner & Smith, 1977, 1982) that found only low correlations between early cerebral insult and later adverse sequelae, individual risk factors were hypothesized to have a low but significant correlation with later competence. Significant correlations were anticipated even for the individual risk factors, because several of the factors represented more than a single isolated event. For example, the duration of hypoxia represented a risk factor that persisted until the time of reparative surgery, which occurred at different ages and developmental stages for these children (range 10–69 months). Similarly, growth failure suggests prolonged failure to acquire adequate nourishment. Other risk factors, such as CNS infection or stroke, represent serious CNS insults that occurred at various times prior to or following the open heart surgery. Overall, our data provided modest support for this hypothesis. Seven of the 11 early medical risk variables (duration of hypoxia, height growth failure, congestive heart failure, no shunting heart defects, unsuccessful palliation, CNS infection, and cerebrovascular accident) were significantly related to later intellectual competence and neurological measures. Biomedical risk variables not associated with subsequent performance included weight growth failure, duration of cardiac repair, number and length of hospitalizations, year of cardiac surgery, and seizures prior to or following surgery. There were no significant intercorrelations among the biomedical risk variables.

The two psychosocial risk variables that we were able to document reliably for each child were also significantly associated with current competence and adaptation. The socioeconomic status (SES) of the family related primarily to the child's verbal abilities and current behavioral adjustment, although the degree of relationship was modest ($r = -.30$; $r = .33$, respectively). The degree of current family stress (indexed by the Life Events Questionnaire) was significantly associated with verbal IQ ($r = -.43$), performance IQ ($r = -.44$), full-scale IQ ($r = -.43$), academic achievement ($r = -.35$), perceptual motor functioning ($r = -.40$), and behavioral adjustment ($r = .31$). Neither of these environmental variables was significantly related to neurological outcome as assessed by neurological examination, EEG, and visual evoked response. In this sample of predominantly working-class families, SES and current life stress were not significantly correlated ($r = .23$). This emphasized the importance of assessing current family stress in addition to SES when examining variations in current competence in different samples. Children from low-SES families did spend a significantly longer time in the hospital following open heart surgery ($r = -.40$), and children from families evidencing a high degree of current life stress experienced a longer duration of hypoxia ($r = .31$) and more significant weight growth failure ($r = .31$). Overall, the biomedical risk variables that were significantly related to outcome could be grouped into (a) factors affecting adequate oxygenation (duration of hypoxia, congestive heart failure, unsuccessful palliation) or (b) those potentially compromising CNS function or development (CNS infection, cerebrovascular accident, malnutrition).

Prior animal research has indicated that the CNS is highly vulnerable to the effects of oxygen deprivation (Cavazzuti & Duffy, 1982; Myers, 1975; Volpe, 1976). Human neuropathological studies have suggested time-dependent effects of chronic hypoxia on the developing brain (Gilles, Levinton, & Jammes, 1973). In children with CHD who died after 1 year of age, a large number had abnormalities in the parietal- and temporal-lobe white matter in comparison with CHD children who died under 2–4 months of age. Behavioral performance data have also indicated an adverse effect of chronic hypoxia on subsequent cognitive function. Early studies reported lower IQ scores, poorer motor coordination, impaired perceptual motor skills, and slower visual reaction times for cyanotic children than for acyanotic children (Aisenberg, Rosenthal, Wolff, & Nadas, 1977; Silbert, Wolff, Mayer, Rosenthal, & Nadas, 1969).

We examined the relationship between duration of hypoxia (indexed by age at reparative surgery) and later cognitive performance (O'Dougherty et al., 1983, 1985). The duration of hypoxia demonstrated a negative relationship to later attentional and perceptual motor performance ($r = -.45$ and $-.40$, respectively). Chronic hypoxia also correlated significantly with subsequent intellectual functioning (WISC-R Cognitive Index, $r = -.33$) and academic achievement ($r = -.44$). The results supported the hypothesis that prolonged chronic hypoxia can adversely affect a child's cognitive, perceptual motor, and attentional functioning. A subsequent study by Newberger and colleagues confirmed our finding that age at the time of surgical repair was inversely associated to subsequent intellectual functioning for cyanotic children (e.g., chronically hypoxic) but not for acyanotic children (Newberger, Silbert, Buckley, & Fyler, 1984).

Most investigators have described growth retardation in both height and weight among children with CHD (Bayer & Robinson, 1969; Ehlers, 1978; Linde, Dunn, Schireson, & Rasof, 1967). An earlier autopsy study of infants with CHD (Naeye, 1965) had revealed that the brain weights of these infants were approximately two standard deviations below the mean. Although the mechanisms by which growth is delayed are not yet clearly understood, Rosenthal and Castenada (1975) speculated that the infant with a cardiac defect may not receive sufficient nutrient and caloric intake because of a variety of factors, such as fatigue due to excessive respiratory effort, recurrent infection, cardiac decompensation, or possibly other psychological factors that may emerge as a result of chronic illness. Such malnutrition during the period of rapid brain growth (50% in the first year and 20% in the second year) may result not only in retarded physical growth but also in permanent anatomic or functional brain impairment.

Two indices of growth were used in this study: height and weight percentile for age. However, only height growth failure related significantly to outcome. In this study, height growth failure was associated with poorer intellectual functioning (WISC-R General Cognitive Index, $r = .31$), verbal abilities ($r = .33$), attentional functioning (WISC-R Freedom from Distractibility Factor, $r = .34$) and academic achievement ($r = .31$). These results suggested another approach to the study of the effects of early malnutrition on brain development and behavior. Typically, most investigations of the effects of malnutrition on subsequent cognitive function have confounded the effects of prenatal and postnatal malnutrition with psychosocial deprivation (St. James-Roberts, 1979; Stein & Susser, 1976). This does not permit the specification of CNS damage resulting from malnutrition to be differentiated from the effects of other psychosocial factors. In experiments in which social status variables have been controlled, often there have been no adult consequences of early malnutrition (St. James-Roberts, 1979). However, in our study, SES did not relate to growth failure ($r = .06$ and $.08$ for height and weight, respectively). The diminished cognitive and attentional functioning most likely resulted from consequences of abnormal heart functioning rather than from psychosocial factors. Our results provide some evidence for the deleterious effects of malnutrition on later competence skills.

Among the more severe neurological disturbances that may result from the complications of congenital heart disease are seizure disorder, cerebrovascular stroke syndrome, and CNS infection (meningitis, brain abscess). These neurological complications in children with TGA are significant and sometimes life-threatening events. In our study, children who had experienced a major neurological complication prior to or during open heart surgery were grouped and compared to the remaining TGA children to determine if these experiences limited the development of competence. When all neurological complications (e.g., stroke, seizures, CNS infection, brain abscess) were considered together, no significant differences emerged. However, this appeared to be primarily related to the fact that the 6 children who had experienced seizures with no other neurological complications performed comparatively well on follow-up. When the performances of children experiencing stroke and CNS infection were examined, deficits in intellectual and attentional functioning, academic achievement, and perceptual motor skills were apparent. The 3 children who had experienced more than one neurological complication evidenced marked disabilities on most of the competence measures, but the small numbers of children in these categories did not permit statistical analyses (O'Dougherty et al., 1983).

Cumulative risk score. Whereas the analyses pertaining to individual risk variables displayed a modest relationship to later outcome measures, the combination of multiple risk factors resulted in a considerable strengthening of the relationship with both neurological and psychological outcome variables. Significantly higher cumulative risk scores were characteristic of children who sustained abnormal neurological outcomes as indexed by an abnormal pattern of visual evoked responses, abnormal EEGs, and abnormal neurological examinations ($r = -.66$). Significant correlations between composite biomedical risk and intellectual functioning ($r = -.48$), academic achievement ($r = -.60$), and perceptual motor functioning ($r = -.48$) were also obtained. Differentiation of the TGA children into groups considered to be at low, mild, and high risk on the basis of their cumulative risk scores also provided strong validation of the risk model.

Wide diversity in outcomes was characteristic of this sample. Our findings indicated that TGA infants at low risk for subsequent dysfunction were characterized by initial successful palliation allowing more adequate oxygenation, a normal growth pattern, no major neurological complications, absence of congestive heart failure, shorter duration of hypoxia, and early reparative open heart surgery. On follow-up evaluation, children with these characteristics demonstrated high intellectual functioning (mean IQ = 112) and above-average academic achievement (PIAT Composite = 65%). Three of the 8 children in the low-risk group received IQ scores in the superior range of functioning. Such findings affirm the adaptive potential of some infants who experienced the biological stress of cyanotic heart disease and open heart surgery. Their high level of competence indicates that cyanosis is not incompatible with subsequent superior intellectual function. The repeated finding of a greater-than-average incidence of gifted intellectual abilities in children with CHD (Honzik, Buse, Fitzgerald, & Collart, 1976; Linde, Rasof, & Dunn, 1970) suggests the need to examine possible parenting factors that may foster the development of competence in children exposed to the stress of these experiences.

However, our follow-up data also illustrated that although the human infant can respond adaptively to a circumscribed period of biomedical stress, the infant becomes increasingly vulnerable as these stressful events extend, intensify, or accumulate over time. In our study, chronicity, multiplicity, or severity of the risk event was related adversely to outcome. The TGA children at high risk were those for whom initial palliative surgical intervention failed to ensure adequate arterial oxygen saturation, requiring further palliative procedures. These children may also have been subjected to growth failure, congestive heart failure, neurological complications, and the prolonged effects of chronic hypoxia. Reparative surgery typically had occurred after 2 years of age. On follow-up evaluation, these children exhibited considerable intellectual impairment (mean IQ = 79) and difficulty in academic achievement (PIAT Composite = 18%) (O'Dougherty et al., 1983).

The results of our initial studies emphasized the importance of using multiple medical and environmental risk factors in assessing the risk potential of children with CHD. This approach does not rely excessively on an isolated event that occurs only for a limited period but considers ongoing changes in the infant's medical status that may adversely affect outcome. The medical experiences and complications associated with the diagnosis and surgical correction of a CHD vary for each infant. Such variation emphasizes the need to study these infants in terms of a distribution from relatively low risk to a degree of risk or biological insult that might grossly interfere with these infants' development. Technological advances in monitoring cerebral blood flow and perfusion and in identifying CHD infants at risk for cerebral hemorrhage or infarction will undoubtedly aid in early identification and possible intervention for those at risk for adverse outcome.

Physiological techniques for identifying the CHD child at risk

In our current work we have extended our studies to include children from preschool through elementary school age with cyanotic and acyanotic heart defects. We have utilized an integrated, multidisciplinary approach to identify neurophysiological markers that are associated with the attentional and information processing deficits identified in these children through our previous research. We have examined a psychophysiological measure of the cardiac orienting response to nonsignal auditory and somatosensory stimuli that has been a useful autonomic indicator in the study of habituation, learning, discrimination, and attentional processes. Heart rate responses are also recorded continuously during vigilance performance on the CPT and on the Sternberg memory and reaction time task to evaluate phasic heart rate responses to the task stimuli. In addition, we have examined the cortical event-related potentials (ERPs) recorded from the scalp during these attentional and information processing tasks. The ERPs are sensitive indicators of the psychological state of the individual and of the information content of the stimulus (Hillyard, Picton, & Regan, 1978; Ritter, Simson, Vaughan, & Macht, 1982; Squires, Hillyard, & Lindsay, 1973). Taken together, these psychophysiological and electrophysiological measures can serve as markers for critical dimensions of cognitive and attentional performance. We believed that they might prove highly useful in the identification and assessment of children with CHD who are at risk for subsequent learning disorders (O'Dougherty, Berntson, Boysen, Wright, & Teske, 1988).

To briefly summarize the results of our ongoing research, all subject groups [controls, CHD, and attention deficit disordered (ADD)] displayed a predominantly deceleratory cardiac response to auditory and somatosensory stimuli, with a larger response to the somatosensory (vibrotactile) modality. This typical pattern indicates initial attention directed toward the stimulus. Significant group differences emerged in the magnitude and pattern of habituation of the cardiac response to the somatosensory stimulus. Normal children displayed an expected initial cardiac deceleration, with rapid habituation of the response. In contrast, CHD children failed to evidence habituation, and ADD children showed a lower initial cardiac response and an opposite sensitization response over repeated trials. Thus, both the CHD and ADD groups displayed overreactivity to nonsignal somatosensory stimuli. On the CPT, overall task performance was poorer for children with CHD and ADD. Cardiac measures revealed predominantly deceleratory responses to hits and correct rejections, with the normal subjects displaying the largest cardiac deceleratory response.

Because considerable functional heterogeneity was evident within each clinical group, the data were subjected to multiple regression analysis in order to identify psychophysiological variables that might predict poor attentional performance. Total error scores from the vigilance task (CPT) served as the criterion measure, with the following as predictor variables: age, base-line heart rate, cardiac response magnitudes for the auditory and somatosensory stimuli, habituation measures for each stimulus modality, and heart rate change to the stimuli of the vigilance task. The regression analysis revealed that approximately one-half of the variance in error scores on the vigilance task could be accounted for by the predictor variables ($R^2 = .47$), with cardiac reactivity to the somatosensory stimulus emerging as the only significant independent predictive factor ($r = -.54$; partial correlation $= -.46$). A larger magnitude of the cardiac response to the somatosensory stimulus was associated with higher error rates and lower overall perceptual sensitivity (d') on the CPT (O'Dougherty et al., 1988).

Preliminary analysis of the ERP studies of task performance has suggested a typical response pattern. We have found two late components of the ERP to emerge selectively to target stimuli, but not to nontarget stimuli, of the CPT. These include a positive (P_{300}) component with a latency of about 400–450 ms most apparent over the central vertex (Cz) region and a following positive slow component (Bernston, Wright, O'Dougherty, & Boysen, 1986). Appreciable correlations have emerged between the mangitude of the P_{300} and d', cardiac reactivity, and false alarm rate in the CPT. In contrast, no correlations existed between P_{300}, hit rate, or beta on the task. These data suggest that the P_{300} might be associated with the efficient discrimination of target stimuli from nontarget stimuli and may serve as a useful marker of attentional performance.

Congenital heart defect subjects who demonstrated performance deficits on the CPT task showed a diminished P_{300} to target stimuli and demonstrated a diminished positive slow potential. In this respect, their performance was similar to that of the ADD subjects who had no history of heart defect. These preliminary findings suggested that late ERP components may offer a sensitive index of cognitive dysfunction, applicable at early ages, that may provide an important method for identifying CHD children at risk for later learning problems.

We hope that these studies will reveal specific problem areas in attentional performance for a subgroup of children with congenital defects. Although the overall IQ for children who have suffered from CHD may be within normal limits, many of these children do experience difficulties in school similar to those of children with attentional problems and learning disabilities. The deficient skills identified in our studies may seriously interfere with the children's acquisition of early academic competence. Because these dysfunctions may have serious consequences for a child's eventual success in school, early diagnostic markers of such deficits could be extremely valuable to the parent and the school system in tailoring educational programs specific to a child's needs. Identification of such functional markers as cardiac reactivity, habituation of autonomic orienting responses, and anomalies in the endogenous components of event-related evoked potentials may lead to more accurate diagnosis and may facilitate the development of appropriate remediation strategies. Future research efforts need to be directed toward early detection of attentional and information processing deficits and to the refinement of electrophysiological and psychophysiological measures that might provide sensitive functional markers of such delays.

References

Aisenberg, R. B., Rosenthal, A., Wolff, P. H., & Nadas, A. S. (1977). Hypoxemia and auditory reaction time in congenital heart disease. *Perceptual and Motor Skills, 45,* 595–600.

Bayer, L. M., & Robinson, S. J. (1969). Growth history of children with congenital heart defects. *American Journal of Diseases of Children, 117,* 564–72.

Berntson, G. G., Wright, F. S., O'Dougherty, M., & Boysen, S. (1986). *Electrophysiological indices of attentional dysfunction in children with congenital heart defects.* Unpublished manuscript.

Bortner, M., Hertzig, M. E., & Birch, H. G. (1972). Neurological signs and intelligence in brain-damaged children. *Journal of Special Education, 6,* 325–33.

Broman, S. H., Nichols, P. L., & Kennedy, W. A. (1975). *Preschool IQ: Prenatal and early developmental correlates.* Hillsdale, NJ: Erlbaum.

Cavazzuti, M., & Duffy, T. E., (1982). Regulation of local cerebral blood flow in normal and hypoxic newborn dogs. *Annals of Neurology, 11,* 247–57.

Chelune, G. J., & Edwards, P. (1981). Early brain lesions: Ontogenetic-environmental considerations. *Journal of Consulting and Clinical Psychology, 49,* 777–90.

Cohen, S. E., & Parmelee, A. H. (1983). Prediction of five-year Stanford-Binet scores in preterm infants. *Child Development, 54,* 1242–53.

Corah, N. L., Anthony, E. J., Painter, P., Stern, J. A., & Thurston, D. L. (1965). Effects of perinatal anoxia after seven years. *Psychological Monographs, 79,*(3, Whole No. 596).

Delpy, D. T., Gordon, R. E., Hope, P. L., Parker, D., Reynolds, E. O. R., Shaw, D., & Whitehead, M. D. (1982). Noninvasive investigation of cerebral ischemia by phosphorus nuclear magnetic resonance. *Pediatrics, 70,* 310–13.

Ehlers, K. H. (1978). Growth failure in association with congenital heart disease. *Pediatric Annals, 7,* 750–9.

Field, T. M., Sostek, A. M., Goldberg, S., & Shuman, H. H. (Eds.) (1979). *Infants born at risk: Behavior and development.* New York: Spectrum Medical and Scientific Books.

Garmezy, N., Tellegen, A., & Devine, V. T. (1981). *Project competence: Studies of stress-resistant children.* Technical report, University of Minnesota.

Garson, A., Benson, R. S., Ivler, L., & Patton, C. (1978). Parental reactions to children with congenital heart disease. *Child Psychiatry and Human Development, 9,* 86–94.

Gilles, F. H., Levinton, A., & Jammes, J. (1973). Age-dependent changes in white matter in congenital heart disease. *Journal of Neuropathology and Experimental Neurology, 32,* 179.

Gottfried, A. W. (1973). Intellectual consequences of perinatal anoxia. *Psychological Bulletin, 80,* 231–42.

Graham, F. K., Ernhart, C. B., Thurston, D. L., & Craft, M. (1962). Development three years after perinatal anoxia and other potentially damaging newborn experiences. *Psychological Monographs, 76*(Whole No. 522).

Graham, F. K., Matarazzo, R. G., & Caldwell, B. M. (1956). Behavioral differences between normal and traumatized newborns: II. Standardization, reliability, and validity. *Psychological Monographs. 70*(Whole No. 428).

Hillyard, S. A., Picton, T. W., & Regan, D. (1978). Sensation, perception, and attention: Analysis using ERPs. In E. Callaway, P. Tueting, & S. H. Koslow (Eds.), *Event-related potentials in man* (pp. 223–321). New York: Academic Press.

Holmes, D. L., Nagy, J. N., & Pasternak, J. F. (1984). *The development of infants born at risk.* Hillsdale, NJ: Erlbaum.

Honzik, M. P., Buse, S. T., Fitzgerald, L. H., & Collart, D. S. (1976). Psychologic development. In L. J. Bayer & M. P. Honzik (Eds.), *Children with congenital intracardiac defects* (pp. 25–9). Springfield, IL: Charles C Thomas.

Isaacson, R. L. (1975). The myth of recovery from early brain damage. In N. R. Ellis (Ed.), *Aberrant development in infancy: Human and animal studies.* Hillsdale, NJ: Erlbaum.

Kopp, C. B. (1983). Risk factors in development. In M. Haith & J. Campos (Eds.), *Handbook of child psychology: Infancy and developmental psychobiology* (4th ed., pp. 1081–188). New York: Wiley.

Kopp, C. B., & Krakow, J. B. (1983). The developmentalist and the study of biological risk: A view of the past with an eye toward the future. *Child Development, 54,* 1086–108.

Lairy, G. C. (1975). The evolution of the EEG in normal children and adolescents from 1 to 21 years. In A. Remond (Ed.), *Handbook of electroencephalography and clinical neuro-physiology* (Vol. 6, Part B, III, The evolution of the EEG from birth to adulthood, pp. 6B-31-68). Amsterdam: Elsevier.

Lilienfeld, A. M., & Parkhurst, E. (1951). A study of the association of factors of pregnancy and parturition with the development of cerebral palsy: A preliminary report. *American Journal of Hygiene, 53,* 262–82.

Linde, L. M., Dunn, O. J., Schireson, R., & Rasof, B. (1967). Growth in children with congenital heart disease. *Journal of Pediatrics, 70,* 413–19.

Linde, L. M., Rasof, B., & Dunn, O. J. (1970). Longitudinal studies of intellectual and behavioral development in children with congenital heart disease. *Acta Paediatrica Scandinavica, 59,* 169–76.

Myers, R. E. (1975). Four patterns of perinatal brain damage and their conditions of occurrence in primates. *Advances in Neurology, 10,* 223–34.

Naeye, R. L. (1965). Organ and cellular development in congenital heart disease and in alimentary malnutrition. *Pediatrics, 67,* 447–58.

Newburger, J. W., Silbert, A. R., Buckley, L. P., & Fyler, D. C. (1984). Cognitive function and age at repair of transposition of the great arteries in children. *New England Journal of Medicine, 310,* 1495–9.

Niswander, K. R., & Gordon, M. (1972). *The women and their pregnancies: The collaborative perinatal study of the National Institute of Neurological Diseases and Stroke.* Philadelphia: Saunders.

O'Dougherty, M. (1983). *Counseling the chronically ill child: Psychological impact and intervention.* Lexington, MA: Lewis Publishing Co.

O'Dougherty, M., Berntson, G. G., Boysen, S. T., Wright, F. S., & Teske, D. (1988). Psychophysiological predictors of attentional dysfunction in children with congenital heart defects. *Psychophysiology, 25,* 305–15.

O'Dougherty, M., Nuechterlein, K. H., & Drew, B. (1984). Hyperactive and hypoxic children: Signal detection, sustained attention, and behavior. *Journal of Abnormal Psychology, 93,* 178–91.

O'Dougherty, M., Wright, F. S., Garmezy, N., Loewenson, R. B., & Torres, F. (1983). Later competence and adaptation in infants who survive severe heart defects. *Child Development, 54,* 1129–42.

O'Dougherty, M., Wright, F. S., Loewenson, R. B., & Torres, F. (1985). Cerebral dysfunction after chronic hypoxia in children. *Neurology, 35,* 42–6.

Palmer, P., Dubowitz, L. M. S., Levene, M. I., & Dubowitz, V. (1982). Developmental and neurological progress of preterm infants with intraventricular haemorrhage and ventricular dilatation. *Archives of Disease in Childhood, 57,* 748–53.

Pape, K. E., Blackwell, R. J., Cusick, G., Sherwood, A., Houang, M. T. W., Thorburn, R. J., & Reynolds, E. O. R. (1979). Ultrasound detection of brain damage in preterm infants. *Lancet, 1,* 1261–4.

Parmelee, A. H., Sigman, M., Kopp, C. B., & Haber, A. (1975). The concept of a cumulative risk score for infants. In N. R. Ellis (Ed.), *Aberrant development in infancy: Human and animal studies* (pp. 113–21). Hillsdale, NJ: Erlbaum.

Pasamanick, B., & Knobloch, H. (1966). Retrospective studies on the epidemiology of reproductive causality: Old and new. *Merrill-Palmer Quarterly of Behavior and Development, 12,* 7–26.

Pasamanick, B., Knobloch, H., & Lilienfeld, A. M. (1956). Socioeconomic status and some precursors of neuropsychiatric disorders. *American Journal of Orthopsychiatry, 26,* 594–601.

Reitan, R. M., & Davison, L. A. (Eds.). (1974). *Clinical neuropsychology: Current status and applications.* Washington, DC: Hemisphere Publishing.

Ritter, W., Simson, R., Vaughan, H. G., & Macht, M. (1982). Manipulation of event-related potential manifestations of information processing stages. *Science, 218,* 909–11.

Rosenthal, A. H., & Castenada, A. R. (1975). Growth and development after cardiovascular surgery in infants and children. *Progress in Cardiovascular Diseases, 18*, 27–37.

Rourke, B. P., Bakker, D. J., Fisk, J. L., & Strang, J. D. (1983). *Child neuropsychology: An introduction to theory, research, and clinical practice.* New York: Guilford Press.

Rutter, M. (1983). Introduction: Concepts of brain dysfunction syndromes. In M. Rutter (Ed.), *Developmental neuropsychiatry* (pp. 1–11). New York: Guilford Press.

Rutter, M., Chadwick, O., & Shaffer, D. (1983). Head injury. In M. Rutter (Ed.), *Developmental neuropsychiatry* (pp. 83–111). New York: Guilford Press.

St. James-Roberts, I. (1979). Neurological plasticity, recovery from brain insult, and child development. *Advances in Child Development and Behavior, 14*, 253–319.

Sameroff, A. J., & Chandler, M. J. (1975). Reproductive risk and the continuum of caretaking casualty. In F. D. Horowitz, M. Hetherington, S. Scarr-Salapatek, & G. Siegel (Eds.), *Review of child development research* (Vol. 4, pp. 187–244). University of Chicago Press.

Sameroff, A. J., & Seifer, R. (1983). Familial risk and child competence. *Child Development, 54*, 1254–68.

Silbert, A., Wolff, P. H., Mayer, B., Rosenthal, A., & Nadas, A. S. (1969). Cyanotic heart disease and psychological development. *Pediatrics, 43*, 192–200.

Smith, A. C., Flick, G. L., Ferriss, G. S., & Sellman, A. H. (1972). Prediction of developmental outcome at seven years from prenatal, perinatal, and postnatal events. *Child Development, 43*, 495–507.

Squires, K. C., Hillyard, S. A., & Lindsay, P. H. (1973). Vertex potentials evoked during auditory signal detection: Relation to decision criteria. *Perception and Psychophysics, 14*, 265–72.

Stein, Z. A., & Susser, M. W. (1976). Prenatal nutrition and mental competence. In J. E. Lloyd-Still (Ed.), *Malnutrition and intellectual development* (pp. 39–79). Littleton, MA: Publishing Sciences Group.

Stewart, A. (1983). Severe perinatal hazards. In M. Rutter (Ed.), *Developmental neuropsychiatry* (pp. 15–31). New York: Guilford Press.

Thorburn, R. J., Lipscomb, A. P., Stewart, A. L., Reynolds, E. O. R., Hope, P. L., & Pape, K. E. (1981). Prediction of death and major handicap in very preterm infants by brain ultrasound. *Lancet, 1*, 1119–21.

Thulborn, K., du Boulay, G. H., Duchen, L. W., & Radda, G. (1982). A $_{31}$P nuclear magnetic resonance in vivo study of cerebral ischaemia in the gerbil. *Journal of Cerebral Blood Flow and Metabolism, 2*, 299–306.

Tjossem, T. D., (Ed.). (1976). *Intervention strategies for high risk infants and young children.* Baltimore: University Park Press.

Travis, G. (1976). *Chronic illness in children: Its impact on child and family.* Stanford University Press.

Vanden Belt, R. J., Ronan, J. A., Jr., & Bedynek, J. L., Jr. (1979). *Cardiology: A clinical approach.* Chicago: Year Book Medical Publishers.

Volpe, J. J. (1976). Perinatal hypoxic-ischemic brain injury. *Pediatric Clinics of North America, 23*, 383–97.

Watt, N. F. (1976). *Two-factor index of social position: Amherst modification.* Unpublished manuscript available from N. F. Watt, University of Denver, 2460 S. Vine St., Denver, Colorado.

Werner, E. E., Bierman, J. M., & French, F. E. (1971). *The children of Kauai: A longitudinal study from the prenatal period to age ten.* Honolulu: University of Hawaii Press.

Werner, E. E., & Smither, R. S. (1977). *Kauai's children come of age.* Honolulu: University of Hawaii Press.

Werner, E. E., & Smith, R. S. (1982). *Vulnerable but invincible: A longitudinal study of resilient children and youth.* New York: McGraw-Hill.

7   A mediational model for boys' depressed mood

Gerald R. Patterson and Deborah M. Capaldi

Some variables embedded in the process of family interaction relate in a
number of ways to the development of children's depressed mood. This chapter provides a brief review of the relevant literature and a model that identifies several mechanisms we believe to be mediators between certain family
variables and children's depressed mood.

Depressed mood may be the outcome of a complex process that places the
child at risk for two kinds of experiences. Loss of support from the social
environment is signified by rejection by the normal peer group and by parents. For our preadolescent samples (fourth-grade boys), aversive events associated with repeated failures in school may also play a significant, albeit
secondary, role.

Reactions from the social environment are "natural," or at least predictable, reactions to the behaviors of antisocial children. The extreme noncompliance and coerciveness associated with antisocial (and perhaps hyperactive)
behaviors have their own natural consequences. As shown in Figure 7.1, the
child's deviant behavior pattern may well be the outcome of poor parenting
skills that, in turn, may relate to children's difficult temperament and contextual variables such as social disadvantage, divorce, and stress. The interaction
of these variables serves to fuel ongoing aversive processes; this defines our
social interactional approach to the study of delinquency.

We gratefully acknowledge the ongoing support provided by grant MH-37940 (Center for Studies
of Antisocial and Violent Behavior, NIMH, USPHS), grant DA-05304 (National Institute of
Drug Abuse, USPHS), grant MH-38318 (Mood, Anxiety and Personality Disorders Research
Branch, Division of Clinical Research, NIMH, USPHS), grant MH-38730 (Child and Adolescent
Disorders Research Branch, NIMH, USPHS), and grant HD-22679 (Center for Research for
Mothers and Children, NICHD, USPHS).

The model presented here is the direct outcome of extended discussions with our colleagues
L. Bank, T. J. Dishion, and M. Skinner. In a very real sense, this is their chapter as well as our
own.

141

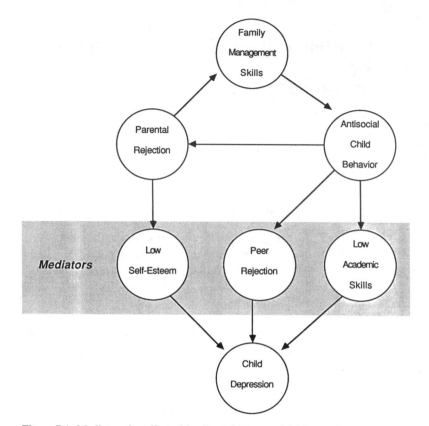

Figure 7.1. Mediators for effect of family variables on child depression.

Measuring depressed mood

Definition and incidence

In their scholarly comparison of four different diagnostic approaches to child depression, Cytryn, McKnew, and Bunney (1980) note that the following symptoms were listed by at least three diagnostic approaches: dysphoria, sadness, hopelessness, loss of appetite, sleep disturbance, loss of pleasure, psychomotor retardation, low concentration, aggressiveness, suicidal tendencies, guilt, loss of interest, somatic complaints, and loneliness. They also note the striking concordance in depressed symptoms for children and adults.

Gittelman-Klein (1977) and Wells, Deykin, and Klerman (1985) suggest that the defining characteristics for diagnosis of childhood depression may be pervasive loss of interest and decreased ability to experience pleasure. In this context, the accompanying symptoms, such as appetite loss or disruption in sleep, would be secondary symptoms. In a survey study of parental reports of child symptoms, Achenbach and Edelbrock (1981) noted a consistent increase in the reports of "child feels worthless" up to age 10. Child sadness peaked at age 13, according to parental reports.

McKnew, Cytryn, and Yahraes (1983) estimate that somewhere between 5% and 10% of children have clear symptoms of depression. Wells et al. (1985), summarizing the data from a number of researchers' estimates, suggest that as many as 20% of children might show a prevalence of dysphoric mood. The Danish studies (Kastrup, cited in Graham, 1979) also suggest 10% as a reasonable estimate for the incidence of childhood depression.

In keeping with the formulation about depressed adults by Lewinsohn and Hoberman (1982) and Forgatch (1986), the core symptom is dysphoric mood. Only a limited subset of those with depressed mood move on to be diagnosed as experiencing major depression. In the analyses of mothers of children referred for treatment of antisocial behavior, Forgatch found that given a significant cutting score (16 or more) on the CES-D, the likelihood that the mother would be given the diagnosis of major depression (SADS interview), for either a past or current episode, was 88%. The false positive rate for the cutting score was 60%.

We assume that there is a comparable transition matrix for children characterized by dysphoric moods recurring with increasing frequency and duration. A very small group of children move from this stage to diagnosable major depression. By adolescence, the number moving in and out of depressed moods will increase, as will the likelihood of moving from the depressed-mood state to major depression. The implicit hypothesis posits a continuity in dysphoric mood from childhood to adolescence and adulthood. At any point in this sequence, a small but significant proportion of individuals with recurring depressed moods will become clinically diagnosable as having major depression. Individuals with recurring dysphoric mood swings are most likely at greatest risk, although this hypothesis has not yet been tested in a longitudinal design.

The clinical studies reviewed by Rappaport (1977) indicate that most depressed adults were not depressed as children, but in the retrospective study of adult depressives by Amenson and Lewinsohn (1981), a sizable proportion reported that their first episode of depression occurred during childhood or adolescence. Making a systematic test of the continuity hypothesis as it applies to children involves several difficulties, however. First, major depression in children is such a low-base-rate event that if one uses it as the dependent variable, the hypothesis becomes untestable. For example, Rutter (1983) estimates that the incidence of diagnosable depression (DSM-III) for community samples of adolescents is from 2% to 4%. Lefkowitz and Desiny (1985) estimate the incidence of severe depression in third through fourth grade at 5.6% for girls and 4.8% for boys (using peer nomination data). With these low rates, it becomes almost impossible to demonstrate a relation between major depression in children and major depression in adults. In keeping with the hypothesis, however, a Venn diagram would show that the larger set of depressed adults would totally include the tiny subset of the adult population who had previously been diagnosed in childhood as having major depression.

A more testable form of the hypothesis would include an investigation of the continuity from depressed mood in childhood to adolescence. Children with recurring dysphoric moods presumably are at risk for persisting depressed mood as adolescents. Implicit in this hypothesis is the notion that depressed mood must occur at higher rates than major depressed episodes. The large-scale survey study by Kandel (1982) of adolescents showed that 15% reported themselves as having a severely depressed mood. The Kandel and Davies (1982) 9-year follow-up study showed that adolescent depression was, in fact, related to later adult depression.

Transient states and stability

In his review of longitudinal studies of children's antisocial behavior, Olweus (1980) demonstrated an average stability correlation of .63 for studies averaging 5-year test–retest intervals. It seems unlikely, however, that clinical depression is such a stable trait. For example, there are data suggesting that about 15% of all adults experience clinically significant depression in a given year (Lewinsohn & Hoberman, 1982). Of those who are depressed, about one-quarter remain in this state for a duration of 4 weeks, about one-half for 3 months, and the remainder for more than 1 year (P. M. Lewinsohn, personal communication, December 1986). The median length of time for clinical depression is roughly 22 weeks.

On the other hand, measures of depressed mood may be more traitlike in that the scores are stable across time. For a given sample of adults, the individuals most likely to be in a depressed mood at some future time are those who have been in such a state in the past. For example, in a follow-up study of single mothers, 71% of those who reported a depressed mood had so reported themselves a year earlier (Patterson & Forgatch, in press).

The fact that some individuals are more at risk than others over time for a depressed state points toward low but significant stability correlations. The magnitude of these correlations for samples of children is not expected to be of the order obtained for antisocial behavior, but should be sufficient for some predictive significance. In keeping with this, the Child Depression construct used in the present report (see following section) was assessed twice over roughly a 12-month time interval. At Time 2, only teacher and mother reports were collected. The stability correlation was .48 ($p < .001$). This is roughly equivalent to stability values for adult self-reported depression obtained in studies by Forgatch (1986) and Radloff (1977).

Reliability of assessment (multiple agents)

How does one set about obtaining a reliable estimate of children's dysphoric mood? There seem to be three principal methods of measurement: trained interviewers, parent or teacher reports, and child self-reports. As in our earlier studies, our general strategy is to require converging measures based on data from multiple agents (Patterson, 1986; Patterson & Bank, 1985, 1987).

If one relied only on trained interviewers working with children, one would immediately encounter a major problem. Gittelman-Klein (1977) found an exceedingly low test–retest reliability of .25 for two trained interviewers reinterviewing children over an interval as brief as 12 days. She also noted that Rutter and Graham (1966) found that items dealing with affect in children were the least reliable components of the psychiatric interview used in their survey study; the correlation between ratings on depression by two interviewers was only .30.

The test–retest reliabilities for *parents* reinterviewed after roughly a 9-day interval seemed to provide more encouraging results (Edelbrock, Costello, Dulcan, Kalas, & Conover, 1985). For parents of 6- to 9-year-old children in a highly structured interview, the correlation was .83.

Parent report seems promising as a data set. In keeping with these findings, the data from Cohort I in the present study showed a correlation of. 53 ($p <$ .001) between mothers and fathers. The findings also demonstrated that the parental picture of child depression was quite stable over time; the combined mother-father descriptions of child depression at Time 1 covaried .69 ($p <$ .001) with mother reports roughly 12 months later. Child self-reported depression in fifth grade tended to correlate less than .20 with parent ratings. The data for children in third to sixth grade reported by Reynolds, Anderson, and Bartell (1985) provided a comparably low stability correlation, and the disappointingly low test–retest correlation of .30 over a 9-day interval reported by Edelbrock et al. (1985) leads one to conclude that children of this age may not be reliable reporters of their own inner states.

The third major source of data about the incidence of sadness or depressed mood could be teachers and peers. The study by Lefkowitz and Desiny (1985) made a number of important contributions; chief among them was the development of a peer nomination measure for child depression. Their study of several thousand children in third to fifth grade showed that teacher ratings and peer nomination data correlated .36 for boys and .43 for girls. Peer nomination data and mothers' ratings of child self-report data tended to correlate .2 or less. In the present report, the data from Cohort I showed a stability correlation of .30 ($p < .001$) for teachers' ratings. Note that the bulk of the ratings would have been made by two different sets of teachers. As we shall see in a later section, there was moderately good convergence between teacher and parent ratings both at the initial testing (.29; $p < .01$) and at 1-year follow-up (.47; $p < .001$). It may be that the observed depressed mood was more noticeable to adult observers as the child grew older.

Hoberman (1984) also employed a multiple-agent approach in his study of child depression. In his review he noted that in comparison with parent reports and interviews, the child self-report data seemed to contain a very high false positive rate (i.e., the children described themselves as more sad, anxious, and so forth, than did the adults describing them). Hoberman used teacher and self-report data on depression to screen an at-risk sample, who were then assessed by the K-SADS interview (Chambers, Puig-Antich, & Tabrizi, 1978).

Family variables and child depressed mood

In his review of twin and adoption studies, Garmezy (1984) concludes that genetic factors are strongly implicated in bipolar depression and, to a lesser extent, unipolar depression. As he points out, however, the incidence rates require some combination of environmental and hereditary factors. In his study, 27% of patients with major affective illness had adult children who were also depressed. In our study, parent self-reported depression correlated .35 ($p < .01$) with the Depressed Mood construct (combined standardized scores) for children in Cohort I, but only .08 for Cohort II.

Studies of children of depressed parents have shown these children to be more likely to have a wider range of problems than children of normal parents (Billings & Moos, 1983; Bone, 1977; Radke-Yarrow, Cummings, Kuczynski, & Chapman, 1985). Notice that the link is between parental depression and a wide spectrum of childhood problems. In the Billings and Moos study, the likelihood of childhood problems given one depressed parent was .26; given a depressed parent plus high family stress, .38; and given all the above plus low family support, .41.

Rather than one simple path, many lead from parental pathology (including depression, antisocial behavior, substance abuse, etc.) to childhood problems (including depressed mood, antisocial behavior, and perhaps hyperactivity and withdrawal). Psychiatric illness may be only one of many variables associated with diminished parenting skills resulting in deviant child behaviors, which then place the child at risk for loss of environmental support, with depressed mood as one outcome. This is consistent with survey findings from studies by Hoberman (1984), Reynolds and Coats (1982), and Teri (1982), who report more negative interactions between parents and depressed children.

A number of investigators have attempted to study the relation between general aspects of the parent–child relationship and children's depression (Block, 1985; Hoberman, 1984; Kandel & Davies, 1982; Reynolds et al., 1985). This type of approach, however, has produced only inconsistent findings. Even when significant, the variables account for only a small proportion of the variance in measures of children's depressed mood.

We believe that part of the problem with the earlier studies lay in the lack of effective measures of family variables. Most of the studies relied on a single method of assessment, namely, self-report by the parent or by the child.

Coercion model and child depressed mood

Positive and negative life experiences

It may well be that some determinants for depressed mood are similar for adults and children. For most of us, happiness and depression covary as a function of some ratio of positive to negative events that characterize current life experiences. This is in keeping with the general formulations by Lewinsohn and Hoberman (1982) for depressed adults, by Patterson (1980, 1982) for mothers in general, and by Patterson and Forgatch (in press) for single mothers. A prolonged increase in negative or stressful life events may well be associated with increased risk for depressed mood. In the multivariate study by Patterson and Forgatch (in press), estimates of positive and negative life experiences contributed unique variance to measures of depression.

There is an interesting congruence between the models of social psychologists studying happiness and life satisfaction (Bradburn & Caplovitz, 1965; Campbell, Converse, & Rodgers, 1976) and research clinicians investigating adult depression (Lewinsohn & Hoberman, 1982). Both groups define the ratio of aversive to positive experiences as a prime mechanism determining happiness and its opposite, depression. Self-report measures of the two variables tend to be uncorrelated (i.e., an individual can have a great many negative and positive events occurring at the same point in life) (Campbell et al., 1976).

Lack of social skills

We assume that socially unskilled adults are particularly at risk for recurring depressed mood. Parents lacking in social skills are more likely to be ineffective in problem-solving skills, leading to increased stress and accompanying risk for dysphoric mood swings (Patterson, 1980, 1982). In keeping with this idea, Lewinsohn, Mischel, Chaplin, and Barton (1980) found that observers and depressed persons agreed in rating depressed individuals less competent than nondepressed persons.

Figure 7.1 illustrates that the child's lack of skill in interacting with the normal peer group leads to loss of support from that quarter. The findings from observation studies of normal peer groups show that antisocial behavior consistently covaries with rejection (Gottman, 1983; Hartup, 1983; Snyder & Brown, 1983). Experimental manipulations demonstrate that antisocial behavior produces low status within the peer group (Coie & Kupersmidt, 1983; Dodge, 1983). The correlational study by Patterson (1986) shows that abrasive interactions with the parents and daily rounds of conflicts with siblings covary with rejection by parents and by peers.

The antisocial child often lacks work skills ranging from failure to complete chores at home to failure in finishing homework. In the classroom setting, noncompliance is expressed by spending more time out of one's seat and disrupting other children. Classroom observation studies consistently support this assumption (Cobb, 1972; Cobb & Hops, 1973; Hops & Cobb, 1974). The same studies also demonstrated significant positive correlations between time on task and achievement test scores. For example, Walker, O'Neill, Shinn, and Ramsey (1986) found that normal boys (in the longitudinal sample reported here) spent 85% of their class time on task, as compared with only 68% for the antisocial boys in the same sample. By fifth grade, 38% of the latter group had already repeated at least one grade; an equivalent number were receiving special services. The review of the empirical literature by Knorr (1981) showed a consistent relation between completion of homework assignments and achievement scores.

The child's acceptance and status within the peer group are key measures of positive/negative life experiences: Children rejected or isolated from the peer group are at greater risk for recurring depressed mood. For fourth-grade children, academic competence is a second significant contributor. The emphasis on low academic skills and peer rejection as determinants for children's depression is in keeping with the findings in the study by Reynolds and Coats (1982). They asked several hundred adolescents what they thought produced their mood swings; 41% of those with depressed mood reported family problems as the prime cause, 19% cited academic causes, and 19% cited problems with friends. In Kandel's large-scale survey of early-teenage adolescents, those individuals who were either overly involved or isolated from the peer group tended to be in a depressed mood (Kandel, 1982). The multivariate analyses showed that both the peer and parent variables accounted for significant variance in children's self-reported depression. For girls, the amount of variance accounted for by peers was 8%, and by parents 12%; the comparable figures for boys were 5% and 5%.

Low self-esteem and depressed mood

In keeping with the developmental formulation by Harter (1983), we assume that for the younger child the parents' supportive reactions (involvement, positive reinforcement, and acceptance) serve as the prime determinants for child self-esteem. The structural equation modeling studies summarized in Patterson, Reid, and Dishion (in press) showed that these parental variables accounted for most of the variance in the child self-report measures of self-esteem. Alternative models that included peer relations and academic competence did not provide a fit to the data.

The implicit hypothesis is that one of the outcomes for some types of problem child behavior is the accompanying risk for children being rejected by their parents (Patterson, 1986). Therefore, the rather large set of children who have low self-esteem probably includes most children who are hyperactive, withdrawn, academic failures, immature, and, of course, antisocial. In keeping with this idea, our structural modeling analyses showed that our Antisocial Child Behavior construct accounted for 71% of the variance in the Low Self-Esteem construct.

The clinical literature suggests that low self-esteem may be one of the important precursors for depressed moods. Kandel and Davies (1986) note that measures of self-esteem consistently correlate with measures of depressed mood for both boys and girls. In our sample of fourth-grade children, the correlation between the two composite scores for the low Self-Esteem and Depressed Mood constructs was .33 ($p < .001$). The comparable figure for the Kandel and Davies (1982) large-scale survey study of 14- to 18-year-olds was $-.28$. In our fourth-grade sample, if a score was below the mean on self-esteem, the conditional for being perceived by adults as in a depressed mood was .25. Given that the child was perceived as depressed, however, the likelihood was .83 that the child would also report having low self-esteem. The hypothesis illustrated (but not tested) by these findings is that low self-esteem for young children might be thought of as an early stage for the development of depressed mood in later childhood. Children with adjustment problems are at significant risk for both low self-esteem and recurring depressed mood. We assume that children with adjustment problems probably are at greater risk for parent rejection, peer rejection, and academic failure.

Antisocial behavior and depressed mood

Clinical observers have long commented on the relation between conduct disorders and children's depressed mood. For example, Puig-Antich (1982) cited a clinical study of adolescent suicides that found antisocial behavior to be a strong component for three-quarters of the sample. In his own study of 43 children with major depression, 37% were described as also having a conduct disorder.

In their intensive clinical study of 37 children aged 6 to 12, Cytryn and McKnew (1972) identified three distinct types of childhood depression: acute, chronic, and masked. Masked depression often was accompanied by other problem behaviors such as scholastic failure, antisocial behavior, hyperactivity, and marginal relations with peers and adults. These children also seemed to come from chaotic and disorganized homes; again, the long-term prognosis was guarded. In the later reanalyses of these cases by Cytryn et al. (1980) it was decided that the primary diagnosis should be depression if all of the symptom requirements were met for that category. Conduct problems were the ancillary diagnosis.

The model we have examined stipulates that children's depressed mood is a product of the same process that produces antisocial behavior. Angst and Clayton (1986) studied several thousand young male military recruits reporting themselves as being aggressive, and they found higher incidences of both suicide and depression. Pulkkinen and Korpela (1986) noted a covariation between higher aggressiveness and dysphoric mood for boys in a reformatory, as compared with normal adolescents. In keeping with this idea, Kandel (1982) found that the more delinquent and peer-oriented adolescents were characterized by more frequent depressed moods. Interestingly enough, girls were most likely to be delinquent and depressed. This sex difference in covariates for depression also occurred in the large-scale study by Robins (1984).

We hypothesize that children's antisocial behavior is a prime determinant for, and precedes, both low self-esteem and depressed mood. It should be noted that one retrospective study of children with clinical episodes of depression suggested that depression preceded rather than followed the conduct disorder (Puig-Antich, 1982). A longitudinal study of toddlers by our colleague Beverly Fagot should provide the necessary data for determining what the sequence might be.

Models

The model to be tested assumes that constructs measuring peer rejection, low academic skills, and low self-esteem will each make significant contributions to a construct measuring children's depressed mood. The adequacy of this simple, direct-effects model will be compared to the adequacy of a model assuming that the effect of low academic skills on depressed mood is mediated by the effect it has on peer rejection.

Procedures

Sample characteristics

A cohort-sequential longitudinal design (Baltes, 1968; Schaie, 1965) was used in this study. The sample consisted of two cohorts of boys in fourth grade: the first cohort ($n = 102$) entered the study in the 1983–4 school year, and the second cohort ($n = 104$) entered the study 1 year later.

Schools were selected on the basis of high incidences of juvenile crime in their districts compared with the rest of the local area. The study took place in a medium-size metropolitan area (adjacent cities with a combined population of 150,000). All the fourth-grade boys in the selected schools were invited to participate in the study. The few exceptions were those who were declared ineligible for such reasons as not being fluent in English. The recruitment rates were 77% for Cohort I and 72% for Cohort II. Comparisons of teacher CBC scales for participants and nonparticipants showed the participants to have slightly higher means than nonparticipants on scales indicating psychopathological behaviors (Capaldi & Patterson, 1987).

These were mainly white, lower-class and working-class families, with a median household income of $10,000 to $15,000; one-third of the families received food stamps or welfare, and one-fifth of the families had no employed parent. Less than half (42%) the boys in the study lived with two biological parents; 35% lived in single-parent families, and 23% lived in step-parent families. Of the fathers present in the homes, 27% had adult criminal records in the state. The two cohorts looked very similar on demographic variables and were combined for the modeling analyses presented later in this chapter.

Each family participated in a comprehensive assessment procedure including a 2.5-hr interview, a videotaped problem-solving task, and a series of six brief telephone interviews. Three separate 1-hr observations were made at the families' homes. In addition, questionnaires were filled out by all members of each family, as well as by teachers and members of the peer group. The data collected at the school also included scholastic test scores and attendance. The details of the assessment battery are presented in Patterson et al. (in press).

Our general approach to building a construct is described in Patterson and Bank (1985, 1987) and in Patterson et al. (in press). We assume that each agent reporting and each method of assessment introduces some distortion in defining the meaning of a construct. Those measures accepted as part of the nomological network defining the construct are labeled as indicators. Although each indicator must be a reliable measure, it is also biased. Our working assumption is that some indicators, such as global judgments about self, child, and family, may be more biased than other indicators. The studies reviewed in Patterson (1980) showed a strong correlation between maternal depression and mothers' ratings of child deviance. In these studies, however, there were zero-order correlations between maternal depression and deviant behaviors observed in the home. The correlation of single mothers' depression with their ratings of child deviance was .43 ($p < .001$) (Forgatch, 1986). The teacher and mother ratings of child deviance correlated .24 ($p < .05$), but the correlation between teacher ratings and mother depression was .01.

The following decision rules were followed in building each construct:

1. Each of the assessment procedures was tailored a priori to measure a specific construct.
2. Each construct was measured by at least two different methods and, wherever possible, by data from two different reporting agents.
3. Whenever possible, an indicator was based on an aggregate of variates and shown to be internally consistent.

4.   Indicators that were reliable were then subjected to a principal-components factor analysis and forced to one factor to determine whether or not the latent construct loaded significantly (.30 or greater) on each indicator.

Each of the latent constructs used in the modeling analyses is briefly described in the following section. More detailed information is available in the technical reports that summarize the item analyses and factor-analytic results from both cohorts (Capaldi & Patterson, 1989). In order to prevent missing data due to listwise deletion for single parents, mother and father scale scores were standardized and combined to form a score for parent report. Final indicator scores were reversed where necessary so that scores were in the theorized direction: for example, low rather than high academic skills.

Low self-esteem

The boys' self-esteem was assessed by two self-report questionnaires: Child Self-Perception, which contains 7 items measuring global self-esteem (Kaplan, 1975), and the Child Skill Checklist, with 12 items assessing the social and academic domains. Alphas for the two measures and two cohorts ranged from .69 to .79, and correlations between the two indicators were .3 for Cohort I and .34 for Cohort II.

Low academic skills

This construct was defined by four indicators. Two of the indicators were based on items selected from the Child Behavior Checklist (CBC) (Achenbach & Edelbrock, 1981). Two scales were developed for parents (seven items for mother, six items for father), and one was developed for the teacher (eight items). The other two indicators included the Wide Range Achievement Test (Jastak & Jastak, 1976) and the mean of the reading, math, spelling, and language arts standardized tests administered once a year by the school districts.

Correlations among these indicators varied between .44 and .75, and alphas for the scales ranged from .70 to .93 for Cohorts I and II.

Good peer relations

This construct was defined by three indicators. Two of the indicators were based on CBC reports, one by the parents (four items each) and one by the teacher (three items).

Alphas for the three indicators varied form .69 to .88 for the two cohorts and correlations between these indicators varied between a low of .34 and a high of .57.

Table 7.1. *CBC items for a priori scale: Child Depressed Mood*

Item	Mother scale: item–total correlations	Father scale: item–total correlations
Items from parent CBC		
8 Can't concentrate	.25 (.49)[a]	.40 (.44)[a]
14 Cries a lot	.45 (.38)	.40 (.49)
33 Feels unloved	.44 (.51)	.60 (.68)
52 Feels guilty	.43 (.34)	.29 (.45)
88 Sulks a lot	.57 (.36)	.47 (.40)
91 Talks of committing suicide	.33 (.38)	—
102 Slow-moving, underactive	.37 (.21)	—
103 Unhappy, sad, depressed	.66 (.56)	.50 (.60)
Alphas	.73 (.70)	.70 (.76)
Items from teacher CBC		
8 Can't concentrate	.55 (.48)	
14 Cries a lot	.41 (.40)	
33 Feels no one loves him	.38 (.43)	
52 Feels too guilty	.33 (.20)	
88 Sulks a lot	.50 (.65)	
102 Underactive, slow-moving	.47 (.51)	
103 Unhappy, sad, depressed	.57 (.62)	
Alphas	.74 (.74)	

[a]Figures in the first column are for Cohort I; figures in parentheses are for Cohort II.

Depressed mood

Four indicators provided potential measures for Child Depressed Mood. These indicators represented four agents: mother, father, teacher, and trained observer. The indicators sampled two methods: the CBC and observer impressions. Child self-reported depressed mood was not collected until the second year of the study.

Items pertaining to depressed mood were selected a priori from the CBC. Somatic symptoms such as stomachaches and anxiety were not included. For the depressed mood scales, the items selected matched as closely as possible the DSM-III-R definition for child depression.

The items for the mother, father, and teacher scales from the CBC are listed in Table 7.1. The correlation of each item with the corrected total score is listed separately for each of the two cohorts. All three scales met the minimum requirements for internal consistency (alpha .60 or better).

The fourth potential measure of Child Depressed Mood was based on impressions from the observers following their visits to the home. The single variable was an Observer Impressions item filled out after each of three separate home

Table 7.2. *Principal-components factor analysis for indicators of the Child Depressed Mood construct*

Potential indicators	Factor loading (forced one-factor solution)	
	Cohort I	Cohort II
1. Mother CBC scale	.83	.81
2. Father CBC scale	.74	.74
3. Teacher CBC scale	.51	.64
4. Observer impression	.60	.34

observations by three different observers. The mean of the three ratings defined the variable. The item was "Child seemed sad or depressed."

The results from the principal-components factor analyses are summarized separately for the two cohorts in Table 7.2. As shown, the latent construct loaded higher than .3 on all four indicators involving adult reporters of children's depressed mood. Mothers, fathers, teachers, and home observers showed a moderate level of consensus about the boys' mood state. This is in agreement with the findings from the Reynolds et al. (1985) study. Parent ratings correlated significantly with teachers' ratings of child depression, with a correlation of .32 for the combined cohorts.

For the purposes of structural equation modeling (SEM), the final arbiter determining the usefulness of a set of indicators defining a construct is their performance in the model. The meaning of a construct is defined in part by its network of indicators or measures and in part by its function within the model as a whole. A significant replicated factor loading just means that an indicator is worth testing in a model.

Structural models for children's depressed mood: a methodological problem

A series of studies has led us to believe that merely having multiple indicators to define a latent construct is not a sufficient basis for adequately testing some models. An investigator, for example, might employ three self-report scales as multiple indicators to define a latent construct such as depression and three other self-report scales to define stress from the same agent. We believe such heavy use of a single agent across several constructs in a model would result in limited generalizability (Bank, Dishion, Skinner, & Patterson, in press).

As an alternative, we propose the use of SEM (Jöreskog & Sörbom, 1977) and a sampling of indicators across agent and method domains. As they demonstrate, using only self-report by the same agent for several constructs

Table 7.3. *Convergent and discriminant matrix for full set of indicators (Cohort I) for Good Peer Relations and Child Depressed Mood constructs*

Variable and source	Good Peer Relations			Child Depressed Mood		
	Parent	Teacher	Peer	Parent	Teacher	Observer
Peer Rejection						
Parent		.45*	.37*	.55*	.26*	.10
Teacher			.48*	.24*	.64*	.20*
Peer				.23*	.40*	.21*
Depressed Mood						
Parent					.32*	.21*
Teacher						.26*

*p < .01.

creates a situation in which even using LISREL VI will not protect the investigator from overestimating the structural relation between one construct and another. In addition, overlap in agent–method domains across adjacent constructs in a model often means the model will not work (a poor fit between data and the a priori model). Self-report data often may have discriminant validities as high as or higher than the convergent validities. We find that global self-report scales are particularly vulnerable to these problems, as demonstrated in the studies by Bank et al. (in press) and Forgatch, Patterson, and Skinner (in press).

By way of illustration, we examine our first test of the depression model, in which three indicators were developed for each of four constructs. In a theory-driven model there are three outcomes of being antisocial that directly or indirectly relate to boys' depressed moods. For boys this age, repeated failures to find acceptance by the peer group are the primary determinant, and poor self-esteem and academic failure are secondary sources.

In our initial model, two of the constructs (Depressed Mood and Peer Rejection) had indicators that overlapped by agent (mother and teacher) and method of assessment (CBC ratings). Peer nomination served as a nonoverlapping additional indicator for the Peer Rejection construct, and Observer Impressions ratings served a similar function for the Depressed Mood construct. The nature of the problem becomes evident if one examines the correlation for the convergent and discriminant validities for Peer Rejection and Depressed Mood for the combined cohorts in Table 7.3.

From the Campbell and Fiske (1959) perspective it can be seen that the convergent correlations were of about the same magnitude as the discriminant validities. The mean convergent validity was .35, whereas the mean discriminant validity was .31. The median convergent correlation among the three measures defining Peer Rejection was .43; the comparable value for Depressed Mood was .26.

The pattern of findings for the discriminant validities also gives the modeler pause. For example, although great care was exercised in the selection of items defining depression to see that there were no items in that scale refer-ring to Peer Rejection, also there were no items in the Peer Rejection scales referring to sadness or downcast mood. The correlation across traits, how-ever, was .64 for teachers and .55 for parents. The between-construct correla-tions were generally higher than any of the within-construct correlations. This means that the structural equations specifying relations between constructs are likely to be spuriously high and the model only poorly identified. In the present instance, the full model (four constructs) "exploded" when tested. The explosion was characterized by negative psi values and a path coefficient between Peer Rejection and Depressed Mood that was greater than 1.0. To push the matter even further, a confirmatory factor analysis examined the hypothesis that depression and peer rejection are really the same thing, rather than a two-factor solution. The chi-square analysis showed that the two alter-natives were equally acceptable. The outcome of this analysis was similar to that obtained when attempting to define the relation between stress and de-pression using mother self-report data for the full set of indicators (Forgatch et al., in press). Effective modeling requires that one meet the Campbell and Fiske criteria for convergent and discriminant validities. In our brief experi-ence, often it has not been possible to meet these standards if the indicators for adjacent constructs (in the model) consist of judgments (ratings) by the same agent(s). Adult raters more often operate from a general schema and tend to view a given child in a consistently positive or consistently negative light. From the perspective of the reporting adult, a child who gets on well with peers is viewed as nondepressed and as doing well in school. It may well be that this connection actually exists, but how does one partial out the distorting effect of theory-based schemas described by Dawes (1985)?

Two different means have been examined for surmounting the problem of overlapping indicators. The procedures are examined in detail in the report by Bank et al. (in press). One procedure is part of the structural modeling tradition and involves extracting one or more method constructs (e.g., in the preceding example, a separate method factor for teachers and parents). The model is then tested against the residual matrix. The second approach is to select nonoverlapping indicators for constructs specified by the theory-driven model to have significant path coefficients. In the present report, it is the second of the two procedures that will be followed.

Indicators were selected so that there was no overlap among the constructs. Two indicators for Low Self-Esteem were based on child self-report. Peer nomination and teacher ratings defined Peer Rejection, and observer and parent ratings defined Depressed Mood. Low Academic Skills was defined by two sets of achievement test scores. The two cohorts were combined to pro-vide a sufficiently stable sample size for the analyses.

Table 7.4 summarizes the correlations among the indicators. It can be seen

Table 7.4. *Correlation matrix for mediated model (combined cohorts)*

Item	Peer Rejection		Low Academic Skill		Low Self-Esteem		Depressed Mood	
	Teacher CBC	Peer nomination	Scholastic tests	WRAT	Child perception	Child skills checklist	Observer impressions	Parent CBC
Peer Rejection								
Teacher CBC	1.0							
Peer nominations	.465	1.0						
Low Academic Skill								
Scholastic tests	.192	.428	1.0					
WRAT	.111	.267	.626	1.0				
Low Self-Esteem								
Child perception	.082	.120	.162	.076	1.0			
Child skills checklist	.251	.227	.129	.105	.316	1.0		
Depressed Mood								
Observer impressions	.193	.194	.194	.153	.069	.240	1.0	
Parent CBC	.247	.244	.282	.161	.295	.165	.204	1.0

there that the convergence correlations are rather modest, particularly for the cognitive-emotional constructs in the model (Low Self-Esteem and Depressed Mood).

A confirmatory factor analysis was conducted using LISREL VI (Jöreskog & Sörbom, 1977) in order to assess the adequacy of the hypothesized measurement model (Anderson & Gerbing, 1988). Factor variances were standardized, nonhypothesized factor loadings were constrained to equal zero, and factors were allowed to intercorrelate. As often happens, the initial measurement model did not fit the data. The model was respecified to allow one pair of error terms to covary (from the parent CBC and the child perception questionnaire). The resulting measurement model showing factor loadings, correlations among the latent variables, and fit statistics is shown in Figure 7.2. The chi-square value of 14.19 ($p = .36$) showed that the respecified measurement model adequately accounts for the covariances.

It can be seen that all three constructs hypothesized to contribute to depressed mood are highly correlated with depressed mood. In addition, Peer Rejection is related to Low Self-Esteem and Low Academic Skills.

In the first path model, Peer Rejection, Low Academic Skills, and Low Self-

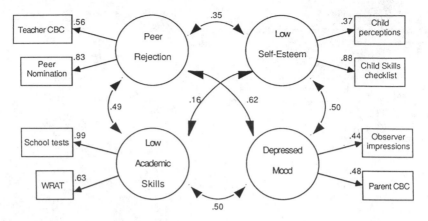

Figure 7.2. Child depressed mood measurement model (combined cohorts). $\chi^2_{(13)} =$ 14.19, $p = .36$; $N = 193$. Goodness-of-fit index $= .98$; adjusted goodness-of-fit index $= .95$; root mean-square residual $= .036$. Error terms allowed to covary: parent CBC and child perceptions.

Esteem were all assumed to contribute uniquely and significantly to Depressed Mood. However, such a model failed to fit the data. The modification indices suggested that information about the relation between academic achievement and peer relations was being omitted. A post hoc mediational model was hypothesized, with the effect of Low Academic Skills on Depressed Mood mediated through Peer Rejection. It was also hypothesized that Peer Rejection would have both a direct effect on Depressed Mood and an indirect effect mediated by Low Self-Esteem. Although the resulting model fit the data, two of the paths – from Peer Rejection to Low Self-Esteem and from Low Self-Esteem to Depressed Mood – fell just below significance.

In a second post hoc model, the path from Low Self-Esteem to Depressed Mood was dropped. This mediated model showed an acceptable fit to the data, and all paths were significant (Figure 7.3). The model accounted for 58% of the variance. A comparison of the mediated model with the measurement model was made by deducting the chi-squares, and the results showed that the difference between the measurement and mediated models was nonsignificant ($X^2 = 6.29$, $df = 3$, $p = .10$). This suggests that the mediated model adequately reproduced the measurement model. The fact that the major components of the model have been replicated for a sample of boys from single-mother families suggests that the mediational model is robust.

According to the mediational model, the relation of Low Academic Skills to Depressed Mood is best explained as mediated by Peer Rejection. However, an alternative model in which the path goes from Peer Rejection to Low Academic Skills fits the data just as well. This alternative model, therefore, places peer rejection in the role of the sole independent variable, explaining

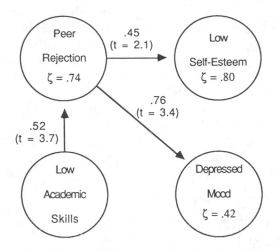

Figure 7.3. Child depressed mood mediated model (combined cohorts). $\chi^2_{(16)} = 20.48$, $p = .199$; $N = 193$. Goodness-of-fit index $= .975$; adjusted goodness-of-fit index $= .943$; root mean-square residual $= .043$. Error terms allowed to covary: parent CBC and child perceptions.

variance in low self-esteem, low academic skills, and depression. It is impossible to distinguish between the mediational and alternative models solely on the basis of concurrent data. However, for theoretical reasons, the mediational model is preferred, as it has been shown previously that academic improvement in low achievers leads to greater peer acceptance (Coie & Krehbier, 1984). In the mediational model, Low Self-Esteem does not account for significant additional variance in Depressed Mood over and above the variance explained by Peer Rejection. In fact, this model suggests that Low Self-Esteem and Depressed Mood may have similar etiologies with respect to Peer Rejection. Longitudinal and experimental data will be required to verify these findings.

Discussion

The data present here are consistent with a mediational model of boys' depressed mood, where the prime determinant seems to be rejection by the peer group. The finding of the relation of academic failure to depressed mood was consistent with that from the long-term follow-up study by Kellam, Brown, Rubin, and Ensminger (1983). They found that academic failure in elementary grades covaried significantly with later adolescent depression. At this age, child self-reported self-esteem did not explain additional variance in depressed mood. The present model differs from that of Kellam et al. in hypothesizing that the effect of poor achievement is mediated through its disrupting effect on peer relations.

The models presented here do not include many stressful life events that may be related to depressed mood. Such events as frequent moves (home and school), parental transitions (divorce, stepparents), failure in sports and extracurricular activities, or a simple lack of enjoyable life experiences would also be expected to contribute to depressed mood. Some of these stressful life events, such as school moves and failures in sports, may exacerbate peer rejection as academic failure appears to do. The effects of such events on depressed mood will be examined in later studies.

The data presented in this chapter are all from the first year of the study. Future longitudinal analyses with this sample will address further questions: What are the variables that contribute to the stabilities of depressed mood for adolescent boys? What are the relative contributions of peers, family, and stressor variables to depressed mood at age 10, age 12, and age 14? To answer these and other questions evolving in the course of data analyses, we need not only a developmental theory tracing the changes in the topography of depressed moods but also one tracing the network of controlling variables.

References

Achenbach, T. M., & Edelbrock, C. S. (1981). Behavior problems and competencies reported by parents of normal and disturbed children, ages 4 through 16 years. *Monographs of the Society for Research in Child Development, 46*(Serial No. 188).

Amenson, C. S., & Lewinsohn, P. M. (1981). An investigation into the observed sex difference in prevalence of unipolar depression. *Journal of Abnormal Psychology, 90*(1), 1–13.

Anderson, J. C., & Gerbing, D. W. (1988). Structural equation modeling in practice: A review and recommended two-step approach. *Psychological Bulletin, 103*(3), 411–23.

Angst, J., & Clayton, P. J. (1986, July). *Premorbid personality of depressed unipolar disorders, suicides, and sociopaths.* Paper presented at the annual meeting of the International Society for Research on Aggression, Evanston, IL.

Baltes, P. B. (1968). Longitudinal and cross-sectional sequences in the study of age and generation effects. *Human Development, 11,* 145–71.

Bank, L., Dishion, T. J., Skinner, M., & Patterson, G. R. (in press). Method variance in structural equation modeling: Living with "Glop." In G. R. Patterson (Ed.), *Aggression and depression in family interactions.* Hillsdale, NJ: Erlbaum.

Billings, A. G., & Moos, R. H. (1983). Comparisons of children of depressed and nondepressed parents: A social environmental perspective. *Journal of Abnormal Child Psychology, 11,* 463–86.

Block, J. (1985, October). *Some relationships regarding the self emanating from the Block and Block longitudinal study.* Paper presented at the SSRC Conference on Selfhood, Center for Advanced Study in the Behavioral Sciences, Stanford Research Institute, Stanford, CA.

Bone, M. (1977). *Preschool children and need for day care: A survey carried out on behalf of the Department of Health and Social Security.* Office of Population Census and Surveys, Social Survey Division, Her Majesty's Stationery Office, London.

Bradburn, N. M., & Caplovitz, D. (1965). *Reports on happiness.* Chicago: Aldine.

Campbell, A., Converse, P., & Rodgers, W. (1976). *The quality of American life: Perceptions, evaluations, and satisfactions.* New York: Russell Sage Foundation.

Campbell, D. T., & Fiske, D. W. (1959). Convergent and discriminant validation by the multitrait-multimethod matrix. *Psychological Bulletin, 56,* 81–105.

Capaldi, D., & Patterson, G. R. (1987). An approach to the problem of recruitment and retention rates for longitudinal research. *Behavioral Assessment, 9,* 169–77.

Capaldi, D., & Patterson, G. R. (1989). *Psychometric properties of fourteen latent constructs from the Oregon Youth Study.* New York: Springer-Verlag.

Chambers, W. J., Puig-Antich, J., & Tabrizi, M. A. (1978). *The ongoing development of the Kiddie-SADS (schedule for affective disorders and schizophrenia for school-age children).* Paper presented at the American Academy of Child Psychiatry annual meeting, San Diego, CA.

Cobb, J. A. (1972). The relationship of discrete classroom behaviors to fourth-grade academic achievement. *Journal of Educational Psychology, 63,* 74–80.

Cobb, J. A., & Hops, H. (1973). Effects of academic survival skill training on low achieving first graders. *Journal of Educational Research, 63*(1), 74–80.

Coie, J. D., & Krehbier, G. (1984). Effects of academic tutoring on the social status of low achieving, socially rejected children. *Child Development, 55,* 1465–78.

Coie, J. D., Kupersmidt, J. B. (1983). A behavioral analysis of emerging social status in boys' groups. *Child Development, 54,* 1400–16.

Cytryn, L., & McKnew, D. H. (1972). Proposed classification of childhood depression. *American Journal of Psychiatry, 129,* 63–9.

Cytryn, L., McKnew, D. H., & Bunney, W. E. (1980). Diagnosis of depression in children: A reassessment. *American Journal of Psychiatry, 137,* 22–5.

Dawes, R. M. (1985). *The distorting effect of theory-based schemas on responses to questionnaire items eliciting summaries of global judgment based on retrospective memory.* SSRC working paper (available from the author, Department of Social Science, Carnegie-Mellon University, Pittsburgh, PA 15213).

Dodge, K. A. (1983). Behavioral antecedents of peer social status. *Child Development, 54,* 1386–99.

Edelbrock, C. S., Costello, A. J., Dulcan, N. K., Kalas, R., & Conover, N. C. (1985). Age differences in the reliability of psychiatric interview of the child. *Child Development, 56,* 265–75.

Forgatch, M. S. (1986). *Negative emotion: A disruptor for family problem solving.* Unpublished manuscript (available from the author, Oregon Social Learning Center, Suite 202, 207 E. 5th, Eugene, OR 97401).

Forgatch, M. S., Patterson, G. R., & Skinner, M. L. (in press). A mediational model for the effect of divorce on antisocial behavior in boys. In E. M. Hetherington & J. D. Aresteh (Eds.), *Impact of divorce, single parenting, and step-parenting on children.* Hillsdale, NJ: Erlbaum.

Garmezy, N. (1984). Children vulnerable to major mental disorders: Risk and protective factors. In L. Grinspoon (Ed.), *Psychiatry update: The American Psychiatric Association annual review* (Vol. 3, pp. 91–104). Washington, DC: American Psychiatric Press.

Gittelman-Klein, R. (1977). Definitional and methodological issues concerning depressive illness in children. In J. Schulterbrandt & A. Raskin (Eds.), *Depression in childhood: Diagnosis, treatment, and conceptual models* (pp. 69–80). New York: Raven Press.

Gottman, J. M. (1983). How do children become friends? *Monographs of the Society for Research in Child Development, 48*(3, Serial No. 201).

Graham, P. J. (1979). Epidemiological studies. In H. C. Quay & J. S. Werry (Eds.), *Psychopathological disorders of childhood* (2nd ed., pp. 185–209). New York: Wiley.

Harter, S. (1983). Developmental perspectives on the self-system. In E. M. Hetherington (Ed.), *Handbook of child psychology. Vol. 4: Socialization, personality, and social development* (pp. 275–386). New York: Wiley.

Hartup, W. W. (1983). Peer relations. In E. M. Hetherington (Ed.), *Handbook of child psychology. Vol. 4: Socialization, personality, and social development* (pp. 413–57). New York: Wiley.

Hoberman, H. N. (1984). *Distinguishing psychosocial characteristics of a community sample of depressed children.* Unpublished doctoral dissertation, University of Oregon, Eugene.

Hops, H., & Cobb, J. A. (1974). Initial investigations into academic survival skill training: Direct instruction and first-grade achievement. *Journal of Educational Psychology, 66,* 548–53.

Jastak, J. F., & Jastak, S. R. (1976). *Wide range achievement test.* Wilmington, DE: Jastak Associates.

Jöreskog, K. G., & Sörbom, D. (1977). Statistical models and methods for analysis of longitudinal data. In D. J. Aigner & A. S. Golberger (Eds.), *Latent variables in socioeconomic models* (pp. 285–325). Amsterdam: North Holland.

Kandel, D. B. (1982). Epidemiological and psychosocial perspectives on adolescent drug use. *Journal of the American Academy of Child Psychiatry, 21,* 328–47.

Kandel, D. B., & Davies, M. (1982). Epidemiology of depressive mood in adolescents. *Archives of General Psychiatry, 39,* 1205–12.

Kandel, D. B., & Davies, M. (1986). Adult sequelae of adolescent depressive symptoms. *Archives of General Psychiatry, 43,* 255–62.

Kaplan, H. B. (1975). Increase in self-rejection as an antecedent of deviant responses. *Journal of Youth and Adolescence, 4*(93), 281–92.

Kellam, S. G., Brown, C. H., Rubin, B. R., & Ensminger, M. E. (1983). Paths leading to teenage psychiatric symptoms and substance abuse: Developmental epidemiological studies in Woodlawn. In S. B. Guse, F. J. Earls, & J. E. Barrett (Eds.), *Child psychopathology development* (pp. 17–51). New York: Raven Press.

Knorr, G. L. (1981, January). *A synthesis of homework, research and related literature.* Paper presented to the Lehigh chapter of the Phi Delta Kappa society, Bethlehem, PA.

Lefkowitz, N. M., & Desiny, E. P. (1985). Depression in children: Prevalence and correlates. *Journal of Consulting and Clinical Psychology, 53*(5), 647–58.

Lewinsohn, P. M., & Hoberman, H. M. (1982). Behavioral and cognitive approaches to treatment. In E. S. Paykel (Ed.), *Handbook of affective disorders* (pp. 338–45). Edinburgh: Churchill Livingstone.

Lewinsohn, P. M., Mischel, W., Chaplin, W., & Barton, R. (1980). Social competence and depression: The role of illusory self-perceptions. *Journal of Abnormal Psychology, 89*(2), 203–12.

McKnew, D. H., Cytryn, L., & Yahraes, H. (1983). *Why isn't Johnny crying?* New York: Norton.

Olweus, D. (1980). The consistency issue in personality psychology revisited: With special reference to aggression. *British Journal of Social and Clinical Psychology, 19,* 377–90.

Patterson, G. R. (1980). Mothers: The unacknowledged victims. *Monographs of the Society for Research in Child Development, 45*(5, Serial No. 186), 1–64.

Patterson, G. R. (1982). *A social learning approach. Vol. 3: Coercive family process.* Eugene, OR: Castalia Publishing Co.

Patterson, G. R. (1986). Performance models for antisocial boys. *American Psychologist, 41,* 432–44.

Patterson, G. R., & Bank, L. (1985). Bootstrapping your way in the nomological thicket. *Behavioral Assessment, 8,* 49–73.

Patterson, G. R., & Bank, L. (1987). When is a nomological network a construct? In D. R. Peterson & D. B. Fishman (Eds.), *Assessment for decision* (pp. 249–79). New Brunswick, NJ: Rutgers University Press.

Patterson, G. R., & Capaldi, D. M. (in press). Antisocial parents: Unskilled and vulnerable. In P. Cowan & E. M. Hetherington (Eds.), *The effect of transitions on families.* Hillsdale, NJ: Erlbaum.

Patterson, G. R., & Forgatch, M. S. (in press). Initiation and maintenance of processes disrupting single-mother families. In G. R. Patterson (Ed.), *Depression and aggression in family interaction.* Hillsdale, NJ: Erlbaum.

Patterson, G. R., Reid, J. B., & Dishion, T. J. (in press). *A social learning approach. IV: Antisocial boys.* Eugene, OR: Castalia Publishing Co.

Puig-Antich, J. (1982). Major depression and conduct disorder in prepuberty. *Journal of the American Academy of Child Psychiatry, 21,* 118–28.

Pulkkinen, L., & Korpela, K. (1986, July). *Adolescent boys' self-reports of their feelings and attitudes.* Paper presented at a meeting of the International Society for Research on Aggression, Evanston, IL.

Radke-Yarrow, M., Cummings, E. M., Kuczynski, L., & Chapman, M. (1985). Patterns of attachment in two- and three-year-olds in normal families and families with parental depression. *Child Development, 56,* 884–93.

Radloff, L. S. (1977). The CES-D scale: A self-report depression scale for research in the general population. *Applied Psychological Measurement, 1*(3), 385–401.

Rappaport, J. L. (1977). Pediatric psychopharmacology and childhood depression. In J. G. Schulterbrandt & A. Raskin (Eds.), *Depression in childhood: Diagnosis, treatment, and conceptual models.* New York: Raven Press.

Reynolds, W. M., Anderson, G., & Bartell, N. (1985). Measuring depression in children: A multimethod assessment investigation. *Journal of Abnormal Child Psychology, 13,* 513–26.

Reynolds, W. M., & Coats, K. (1982). *Depression in adolescents: Incidence, depth and correlates.* Paper presented at the Tenth International Congress of the International Association for Child and Adolescent Psychiatry, Dublin, Ireland.

Robins, L. N. (1984). *Conduct disorder and adult psychiatric diagnoses.* Unpublished manuscript (available from the author, Department of Psychiatry, Washington University School of Medicine, St. Louis, MO).

Rutter, M. (1983). Stress, coping and development: Some issues and questions. In N. Garmezy & M. Rutter (Eds.), *Stress, coping and development in children* (pp. 1–42). New York: McGraw-Hill.

Rutter, M., & Graham, P. (1966). Psychiatric disorder in 10- and 11-year-old children. *Proceedings of the Royal Society of Medicine, 59,* 382–7.

Schaie, K. W. (1965). A general model for the study of developmental problems. *Psychological Bulletin, 64,* 92–107.

Snyder, J. J., & Brown, K. (1983). Oppositional behavior and noncompetence in preschool children: Environmental correlates and skills deficits. *Behavioral Assessment, 5,* 333–48.

Teri, L. (1982). Depression in adolescence: Its relationship to assertion and various aspects of self-image. *Journal of Clinical Child Psychology, 11,* 101–6.

Walker, H. M., O'Neill, R., Shinn, M., & Ramsey, B. (1986) *Longitudinal assessment and long-term follow-up of antisocial behavior in fourth grade boys: Rationale, methodology, measures and results.* Unpublished manuscript (available from the first author, Department of Special Education, University of Oregon, Eugene, OR 97403).

Wells, V. W., Deykin, E. Y., & Klerman, G. L. (1985). Risk factors for depression in adolescents. *Psychiatric Development, 3,* 83–108.

8   A temperamental disposition to the state of uncertainty

Jerome Kagan, Jane L. Gibbons, Maureen O. Johnson,
J. Steven Reznick, and Nancy Snidman

An approach to temperament

The behaviors of young children that are classified as temperamental can be named with constructs that remain close to the events (a Baconian strategy that minimizes error) or constructs that are considerably more abstract. The broader concepts are preferred by most scholars, but they require a large corpus of reliable information and a unifying idea. Because facts have been thin and theory weak, the names for temperamental characteristics have usually, and properly, referred to observed qualities, such as activity level, lability of mood, crying, and approach or withdrawal to novelty (Buss & Plomin, 1975). During the last two decades, however, biologists and ethologists have produced rich descriptions of behavioral ontogeny in mammalian species that hold the promise of providing an initial rationale for parsing the dimensions of temperament from above rather than from below.

One of the many theoretical perspectives that might be used for the classification of temperament rests on four assumptions. The first, which is noncontroversial, assumes that all animals possess structures and functions that permit them to cope with at least four universal adaptational problems: eating, sleeping, reproduction, and protection from harm. The second, only a little less obvious, states that evolutionary changes within the mammals have involved alterations in the degree of preparedness to react to particular incentives and to issue specific motor actions that serve the adaptation domains. During mating, for example, rodents are prepared to be especially sensitive to chemical signals; primates are more sensitive to visual cues. When harm is a possibility, kittens are prepared to freeze to a threat; primate infants become excited and emit distress calls.

This research was supported in part by grants from the John D. and Catherine T. MacArthur Foundation and the National Institute of Mental Health, U.S. Public Health Service (MH-40619).

164

The third and fourth assumptions are less consensual. The third states that the anatomical structures and physiological processes that mediate the internal states of hunger, sleepiness, sexual arousal, and defensive fear may have changed less with evolution than have the structures and processes that mediate the perceptual and response preparednesses. For example, rats with septal lesions react to an intruding object by biting it; rabbits vocalize and try to escape; quail become submissive (Albert & Chew, 1980). Yet most scientists assume that the physiological states accompanying the three response classes are more similar. The final assumption claims that members of a given species vary in the excitability of those neural structures that mediate the internal states involved in the adaptational domains and, further, that this variation is the basis for strain differences in animal behavior and temperamental qualities in humans. To illustrate, the bodily state that leads to food seeking depends, in part, on discharge patterns in the lateral hypothalamus (we acknowledge that other structures participate in food seeking). If members of a species differ in the threshold of excitability of the lateral hypothalamus, they will vary in the probability of food seeking under equivalent conditions of deprivation. This hypothesis implies that anorexia and bulimia in humans could, in some instances, reflect temperamental qualities. Similarly, differential sensitivity of neurons in the hypothalamus to serotonergic axons from the raphe nucleus should be accompanied by stable individual differences in the amount of sleep required or the ease of falling asleep – another potential temperamental quality ignored in current essays.

Consider the limbic structures serving the family of related states that are called uncertainty, fear, and anxiety and the prepared responses of inhibition of action and/or withdrawal that often occur to these states, especially in young children. It is likely that here, too, individuals differ in the threshold of excitability of relevant limbic structures and, as a result, in the likelihood of inhibition of action or withdrawal to unfamiliar events that cannot be assimilated or to a threat for which there is no immediate coping reaction. The idea that humans differ in the ease with which inhibition of action and/ or withdrawal are evoked by such incentives is implicit in Aristotle, Plato, and Galen, Sheldon's tripartite typology, and Jung's theory of psychological types. Schneirla's suggestion (1959) that approach or withdrawal from events is a fundamental differentiating feature in animal species has been affirmed in many groups, including mice, rats, cats, dogs, wolves, pigs, and monkeys. Blizard (1981) has found strain differences in fearfulness among rats; Scott and Fuller (1965/1974) have discovered that timidity in the face of novelty is one of the two most differentiating characteristics in five breeds of dogs; both Suomi (1984) and Stevenson-Hinde, Stillwell-Barnes, and Zunz (1980) have reported that variation in fearful behavior is among the most stable qualities observed in macaque monkeys reared in a laboratory from infancy to puberty.

Bases for withdrawal

Although all newborns will withdraw a foot from the prick of a pin or move the head toward a source of food, the responses with which we are concerned refer to withdrawal from or approach toward events that are psychologically unfamiliar and not immediately assimilable. Such reactions are not present in newborns because they have not had sufficient experience to recognize most events as discrepant. Further, the newborn's central nervous system may not be sufficiently mature to mediate recognition of the unfamiliar in contexts other than the few that are biologically fundamental. It is not until 6 to 8 weeks of age that human infants will behave reliably in ways that suggest they recognize that an event in the perceptual field differs from one previously experienced, and it is not until 7 or 8 months that they will display obvious retreat and/or crying to a variety of unfamiliar events (Kagan, Kearsley, & Zelazo, 1978). Free-living chimpanzees also fail to show behavioral avoidance of unfamiliar animals and people until they are about 6 or 7 months old (Plooij, 1984). One possible explanation for the relatively late appearance of avoidance to unfamiliar events is that maturation of particular central nervous system functions is necessary before the animal is able to retrieve schemata that share features with the unfamiliar event in the perceptual field and to maintain both the retrieved schemata and the processed products of the contemporary percept on the "stage of short-term memory" long enough to permit attempted assimilation of the latter to the former. Failure of assimilation, despite effort, creates the occasion for a special state of arousal and the possibility of subsequent inhibition or withdrawal. It is the inability to cope with the unfamiliar event, not the stimulus qua stimulus, that generates both the arousal and the withdrawal. This conclusion is in accord with evidence from both animals and humans indicating that production of cortisol and/or catecholamines is most likely when the animal cannot cope with a novel intrusion.

Human data

Although individual differences in the probability of approach to or withdrawal from unfamiliar and challenging events are subtle before 7 months of age, they are unambiguous by the middle of the second year. It is relatively easy to distinguish between 18-month-olds who will become quiet and wary of an unfamiliar adult and those who will approach a stranger quickly, often with a smile and vocal greeting. The contexts that reveal these behavioral differences best during the second year are unfamiliar persons, rooms, and objects. Many investigators have reported that individual differences in behavioral withdrawal and inhibition of activity and vocalization to the unfamiliar are preserved from late infancy to the preschool and early school years, and from early to late childhood (Moskowitz, Schwartzman, & Ledingham, 1985; Elder, Liker, & Cross, 1984; Bronson, 1970; Bronson & Pankey, 1977). On occasion, the differences can persist into adolescence and adulthood, where they often assume the form of cautious reluctance to take risks, or social introversion (Kagan & Moss, 1962).

Follow-up investigations of clinical cases have revealed modest preservation of extreme forms of withdrawal behavior from childhood into adult life. A group of 66 children diagnosed as school-phobic when they were between 4 and 11 years of age were assessed by a psychiatrist when they were 12 to 21 years old. About one-quarter of the group had no symptoms and were regarded as well adjusted. Although another 40% were no longer phobic, they still displayed one or more other symptoms, especially poor school achievement and a sense of dependence on others. An additional one-third were still very anxious (Coolidge, Brodie, & Feeney, 1964). As might be expected, extremely shy, phobic children are likely as adults to select bureaucratic jobs with minimal risk (Morris, Soroker, & Burruss, 1954).

Although preservation of these two complementary classes of behavior does not require the assumption of biological factors, research implicates genetic influences. Studies of monozygotic and dizygotic twins – infants, adolescents, and adults – have revealed that the psychological characteristics yielding the best evidence for heritability are related to approach to or withdrawal from the unfamiliar; see Plomin (1986) for an extensive review of this literature. For example, examiners rated the test behaviors of a large number of twins six times between 3 and 24 months of age. Factor analysis revealed a factor of timidity and inhibition that showed evidence of heritability at 6, 12, and 24 months of age (Matheny, 1980). In a similar investigation, behavioral ratings were made on 350 twin pairs at 8 months and 4 and 7 years (Goldsmith & Gottesman, 1981). Differences in fearfulness, indexed by reluctance to separate from the mother at 7 years of age, were among the most heritable of the behavioral variables, especially for boys. Finally, the heritability of the social introversion score on the MMPI in adolescent twin pairs, which often is a developmental derivative of extreme withdrawal in childhood, was higher than any of the other MMPI scales, and again the coefficients were higher for male twins than for female twins (Gottesman, 1963); see also Eaves and Eysenck (1975) and Loehlin (1982).

Infant antecedents of inhibition

Preliminary evidence suggests a predictive link, albeit modest, between extreme irritability during the first months of life and behavioral timidity and inhibition in later childhood. Further, variation in infant irritability among twin samples shows evidence of heritability (Wilson, Brown, & Matheny, 1971; Goldsmith & Campos, 1985). For example, over one-third of inhibited 2- and 3-year-old children from two separate longitudinal cohorts, in contrast to less than 10% of the uninhibited children, were reported by their mothers to have been extremely irritable during the first year (Kagan, Reznick, Clarke, Snidman, & Garcia-Coll, 1984). Japanese newborns who became extremely upset by the repeated frustration of nipple withdrawal were highly irritable when they were observed in their homes at 3 months of age, were fearful of strangers at 7 months, and, at age 2, showed behavioral inhibition and withdrawal when faced with the unfamiliar (Chen & Miyake, 1983). This relation had been found earlier in American newborns. Infants who were extremely irritable to the frustration of nipple withdrawal became 2-year-olds who were shy with other children in a peer group situation. Although a replication of this investigation failed to find a significant association between newborn irritability and later shyness, the relation was in the same direction (Yang & Halverson, 1976); see also Matheny, Riese, and Wilson (1985).

Contribution of the limbic system

The data from both humans and animals imply that intraspecific variations in inhibition and withdrawal in the face of uncertainty are relatively stable qualities of an individual that appear to be influenced by inherent physiological processes. Recent research with cats has come close to specifying some of these physiological processes. Adamec and Stark-Adamec (1986) have found that domestic cats (*Felis catus*) display considerable variation in their tendencies to be defensive to novelty and to be nonaggressive with rats. This variation in defensiveness emerges during the second postnatal month, and once the individual bias to be either defensive or aggressive has appeared, it remains stable for many years. The defensive cats who do not attack rats are also inhibited when placed in an unfamiliar room, when placed with a familiar human in an unfamiliar environment, or when they hear a tape recording of conspecific threat vocalizations. Further, the defensive cats show greater piloerection, greater pupillary dilation, and more trembling – all signs of sympathetic arousal – when exposed to unfamiliar incentives. Although specific experiences early in life (e.g., rearing with conspecifics who serve as models for killing rats, periodic food deprivation, and exposure to killed prey) facilitate adult aggressive behavior, even within a group of cats who have experienced these same facilitating conditions there will be some who will not attack rats (Adamec, Stark-Adamec, & Livingston, 1983).

Careful developmental observations have revealed that the average kitten first approaches prey at about 22 days, a few days before it will display withdrawal behavior to the same incentive (about 27 days). However, the kittens who will become nonaggressive adults show larger-than-normal increases in withdrawal behavior at 1 month, whereas the kittens who will become aggressive adults fail to show this exaggerated increase in withdrawal.

The appearance of withdrawal behavior in kittens at the end of the first month has parallels in the appearance of similar behavior in wolf pups at the same age, fearfulness in monkeys at 2 months, and the anxiety of human infants when faced with a stranger at about 7 months of age. These remarkable concordances in the ages at which withdrawal and/or emotional distress to novelty emerge imply that particular forms of postnatal maturation of the brain are necessary before a state of uncertainty to novelty can mediate defensive behavior. It may not be a coincidence that the period from 1 to 2 months in the kitten corresponds to the time when the amygdala begins to modulate the hypothalamic substrate that may help to mediate defensive behavior (Kling & Coustan, 1964).

This corpus of facts led Adamec and his colleagues to perform a series of experiments suggesting that the responsiveness of the amygdala and related limbic structures is associated with defensive behavior. Defensive cats, compared with aggressive animals, have a lower threshold of seizure susceptibility in the amygdala and greater propagation of seizure activity from the amygdala to the thalamus and hypothalamus. The more defensive the cat, the stronger the evoked neural response in areas to which the amygdala projects, especially the ventromedial nucleus of the hypothalamus. In addition, while orienting to a rat, defensive cats show more prolonged increases in neural activity in both amygdala and hypothalamus. Finally, repeatedly induced electrical evocations of after-discharges in the perforant path of the ventrohippocampal system produced defensive behavior in *ordinarily nondefensive cats* for periods as long as 30 to 60 days. This induced defensiveness appeared to be mediated by an increase in excitability of synaptic transmission between the amygdala and the hypothalamus (Adamec & Stark-Adamec, 1983a,b,c,; Adamec et al., 1983).

We now present data on young children suggesting that consistently timid, shy, inhibited children show higher levels of arousal in one or more of the three systems that originate in the amygdala or hypothalamus and are responsive to novelty and threat, namely, the hypothalamic-pituitary-adrenal axis, the projections from the amygdala to the basal ganglia and motor system, and the sympathetic nervous system. It is possible that, as with cats, this stable behavioral variation is due in part to differential thresholds of responsiveness in amygdala and hypothalamus to unfamiliarity and challenge.

Longitudinal studies

We have been following two independent groups of Caucasian children from middle- and working-class families who were selected at either 21 or 31 months to be extremely shy and timid (inhibited) or socially outgoing and bold (uninhibited) when exposed to unfamiliar rooms, people, and objects. Classification into one of the two groups required that the child show either consistent withdrawal from or approach to a variety of incentives. We screened over 400 children to find initial groups of 60 behaviorally inhibited and 60 behaviorally uninhibited children, with equal numbers of boys and girls in each group. It may not be a coincidence that when kindergarten teachers in Munich, Germany, were asked to select only those children who were extremely shy, only 15% of the total school population of 1,100 was chosen – about the same proportion we found in our screening (Cranach et al., 1978).

The index of inhibited or uninhibited behavior in Cohort I, seen initially at 21 months, was based on the children's behaviors when faced with an unfamiliar female examiner, unfamiliar toys, a woman displaying a trio of acts that were difficult to recall, a metal robot, and temporary separation from their mothers. The signs of behavioral inhibition were long latencies before interacting with or retreating from the unfamiliar people or objects, clinging to the mother, and cessation of play or vocalization. The uninhibited children showed the opposite profile. They approached the unfamiliar quickly, rarely played close to their mothers, and talked early and frequently.

The original index of inhibited behavior in Cohort 2, seen at 31 months, was based primarily on behavior with an unfamiliar peer of the same sex and age and, secondarily, on behavior with an unfamiliar woman. The indices of inhibition were similar to those used with Cohort 1: long latencies before interacting with the child, adult, or toys, retreat from the unfamiliar events, and long periods of time proximal to the mother. Each of our two longitudinal samples has been seen on several occasions since the original selection, the most recent being at age 7.5 years for Cohort 1 and 5.5 years for Cohort 2, with about 10% attrition from the samples (Garcia-Coll, Kagan, & Reznick, 1984; Snidman, 1984; Kagan et al., 1984; Reznick et al., 1986). At 4 years of age for Cohort 1, and at 3.5 years for Cohort 2, the indices of inhibition were based primarily on behavior with an unfamiliar child of the same sex and age. At 5.5 years of age the index was based more broadly on behavior with an unfamiliar peer in a laboratory setting, behavior in a school setting, behavior with an examiner in a testing situation, and behavior in a room that contained unfamiliar objects mildly suggestive of risk (a balance beam, a black box with a hole). An aggregate index of inhibition for Cohort 1 was a mean standard score across the separate situations presumed to index an inhibited disposition. The assessment at 7.5 years of age is not yet complete, and only preliminary results are available.

The behaviors that characterized inhibited and uninhibited children were preserved from the original assessment to the later assessments at 4 and 5.5 years of age. The correlation for Cohort 1 between the index of inhibition at 21 months and the aggregate index at 5.5 years was $+.52$ ($p < .001$). The correlation between the indices at ages 4 and 5.5 was $+.67$ ($p < .001$). One of the scores in the aggregate index at 5.5 years was derived from observation of each child in kindergarten during the first week of school. An observer who did not know the child's prior classification noted every 15 s the occurrences of a small number of variables reflecting the child's physical proximity to other children and social interaction with them. The children classified as inhibited at 21 months were more often isolated from their peers and not engaged in any form of social interaction. The correlation between the index of inhibition at 21 months and low sociability during the first week of kindergarten was .39 ($p < .05$) (Gersten, 1986).

One of the assessments of Cohort 1 seen when they were 7.5 years old was made during a 90-min play group session, including supervised competitive games, with 9 or 10 children of the same age and sex, both inhibited and uninhibited, who were initially unfamiliar with each other when they entered a large laboratory play room. The videotape records of the five sessions, supplemented by taped narrations of each child's behavior by observers who did not know the child's prior history, were coded for six variables. The two most discriminating were (a) the total time each child was distant from and not interacting with another child (defined as greater than an arm's length from any other child) and (b) the number of spontaneous utterances. The 21 formerly inhibited children were more often distant from a peer and less often talking than were the 18 formerly uninhibited children. Further, significantly more of the inhibited children scored both high on total time distant from a peer and low on talkativeness, whereas the uninhibited children showed the opposite profile ($\chi^2 = 5.4$, $p < .05$, with Yates correction based on median division for each variable).

The numbers do not capture the consistency with which a majority of the inhibited children habitually and unselfconsciously moved away from unfamiliar peers. When the group was lined up for a game, usually it was one of the inhibited children who was at the far end of the line or was standing a few feet in back of the group. When an uninhibited child approached an inhibited child, the latter often would walk away within a few seconds. Throughout the session, an inhibited child would tend to move away from wherever the center of the group was located, whereas an uninhibited child usually would move toward that center. It was as if a small cluster of unfamiliar children constituted an aversive object to be avoided. These observations reminded us of Jung's definitions (1924) of the two psychological types: "Extraversion means an outward-turning of the libido . . . a positive movement of subjective interest towards the object [p. 542] . . . introversion means a turning inwards of the libido whereby a negative relation of subject to object is expressed. Interest does not move towards the object but recedes toward the subject" (p. 567).

There was more obvious preservation of uninhibited behavior than of inhibited behavior in both cohorts. This asymmetry in stability is reasonable because American parents, reflecting the values of their society, regard bold, spontaneous, sociable behavior as more adaptive than shyness and timidity. About 40% of the original groups of inhibited children became much less inhibited at 5.5 years, although only 2 children became as spontaneous as the typical uninhibited child. By contrast, less than 10% of the uninhibited children became more timid. There was, however, a gender asymmetry in the direction of change. More boys than girls changed from inhibited to uninhibited, whereas the small number of uninhibited children who became more inhibited usually were girls from working-class families. This pattern is in accord with the supposition that a proportion of working-class American parents value an obedient, quiet daughter – a standard that is less common among middle-class families.

There are also more inhibited children who are later-born than firstborn – about two-thirds of the groups – and more uninhibited children who are firstborn – a result affirmed by Snow, Jacklin, and Maccoby (1981). We interpret this finding to mean that later-born status may represent a chronic stress for those infants who are born with a biological disposition to be inhibited, but not for the average infant who does not begin life with this temperamental quality. A second interpretation of this vulnerability in later-borns, especially in males, assumes that fetal stress is less likely during the first pregnancy than during subsequent pregnancies. This explanation is in accord with a recent speculation that the H-Y antigen in the male fetus may evoke an immune response in some mothers that is more harmful to the later-born than to the firstborn son (Gualtieri & Hicks, 1985). Finally, it may be that the arrival of a new baby leads some parents to demand less fearful and more independent behavior from their firstborn child.

Physiological reactivity

The inhibited children were more likely than the uninhibited youngsters to show some of the consequences expected from the hypothesis of lower thresholds of reactivity in amygdala and hypothalamus. These physiological consequences include reactivities in the pituitary-adrenal axis, the skeletal motor system, and the sympathetic arm of the autonomic nervous system. In order to assess the responsivity of these stress circuits, eight physiological variables were quantified for Cohort 1 at 5.5 years of age: salivary cortisol levels obtained in the early morning at home and during a laboratory testing session as indices of activity in the pituitary-adrenal axis; mean heart period, heart period variability, pupillary dilation, and total urinary norepinephrine level during a laboratory session as indices of sympathetic activity; and variability of the pitch periods and standard deviation of the fundamental frequency of vocal utterances obtained under both base-line and stress conditions as indices of muscle tension (Coster, 1986). We transformed all scores so that a higher standard score indicated higher physiological arousal. The correlations between the mean standard score across the eight biological variables and an index of behavioral inhibition at each age for 22 inhibited and 21 uninhibited children revealed the highest coefficient with the original index of behavioral inhibition at 21 months ($r = .70$). However, the correlations were also significant with the behavioral index at age 4 ($r = .66$) and with the index at 5.5 years ($r = .58$). (All three coefficients were significant at $p < .001$.) It is important to note that the inhibited children who showed the highest values on the physiological profile were most likely to retain their behavioral inhibition across the 4 years of observation.

The heightened physiological responsivity among inhibited children could be due to special structural characteristics in parts of the limbic system or the three circuits, greater responsivity of the target organs, or differences in brain biochemistry that could influence the limbic system and in turn affect the probability of discharge of the stress circuits. Although each of these mechanisms is possible, current research favors the last hypothesis. One reasonable, albeit hypothetical, argument holds that the locus ceruleus, a brain-stem structure that is the main source of central norepinephrine, produces more of this neurotransmitter in inhibited children. If that is true, the limbic system may be at a higher level of excitability and prone to discharge to slight increases in uncertainty or challenge (Charney & Redmond, 1983). Kopin (1984) has suggested that genetic differences in the amounts of norepinephrine secreted to anticipated stress among different animal strains may be analogous to differences in proneness to anxiety among humans, and Charney, Heninger, and Breier (1984) believe that increases in central norepinephrine are causally related to attacks of panic anxiety in human patients.

There may be a modest relation between temperamentally based inhibition in childhood and risk for agoraphobia, or for the more extreme diagnosis of panic disorder in adulthood. Panic patients, who typically are women, report that they had been extremely anxious children who showed fear of leaving home and going to school because it required a separation from the mother (Gittelman & Klein, 1984; Raskin, Peeke, Dickman, & Pinsker, 1982; Berg, 1976). Additionally, panic patients have higher heart rates, lower finger temperatures (Freedman, Ianni, Ettedqui, Pohl, & Rainey, 1979), and higher levels of epinephrine, norepinephrine, and cortisol (Nesse, Cameron, Curtis, McCann, & Huber-Smith, 1985) than do patients from other diagnostic categories. Some investigators have hypothesized that panic attacks might be due to increased central noradrenergic activity attributable to the action of the locus ceruleus. The increase in plasma MHPG levels when panic patients are in fear-arousing situations is viewed as supportive of this idea (Ko et al., 1983). There is also support for the proposition that agoraphobia and panic are heritable, for about 25% of the relatives of panic patients (versus 2% for controls) have a form of anxiety disorder (Harris, Noyes, Crowe, & Chaudhry, 1983), and twin studies imply a genetic contribution to panic attacks, but not to generalized anxiety (Torgersen, 1983). These facts, together with the finding that imipramine has a therapeutic effect on panic but little or no beneficial effect on general anxiety disorder, imply a specific biological contribution to panic symptoms that might be similar to the mechanisms that mediate temperamentally based inhibited behavior in children.

It is of interest that among the 5.5-year-olds in Cohort 2, the inhibited children with high and stable heart rates had the largest numbers of fears, including fears of large animals, being left alone in the house, bodies of water, machines, unfamiliar children, going to school, and monsters on television or in movies. Ninety-one percent of the inhibited children who also had high and stable heart rates had two or more of these fears; over half were afraid of monsters, and one-third had unusual fears or night terrors. One child was afraid of Santa Claus, another was afraid of a kidnapper coming to the home, and several were afraid of going alone to their bedrooms at night. Not one of the uninhibited children had any of these atypical fears; their fears usually were of large animals or the dark.

Summary

Although the data summarized here suggest that extreme degrees of shyness with strangers and timidity in unfamiliar contexts (versus sociability and boldness) probably are influenced by biological qualities present at birth, the evidence also implies that both characteristics are malleable during childhood. Neither psychological bias is fixed indefinitely at birth. Further, in an industrialized society there are adaptive advantages to both inhibited and uninhibited behavior. Because extremely inhibited children are prone to avoid social relationships with peers, if they come from homes that value academic mastery they are a little more likely to invest effort in schoolwork and, if successful, may choose careers that involve intellectual work. Such careers typically lead to challenge, high status, and economic reward in industrialized societies. Finally, one's life course is under the influence of many factors, including the will to change one's characteristics; hence, we suspect that a biologically based temperamental disposition to be inhibited or uninhibited in early childhood probably contributes no more than 10% to the variation in the adult characteristics our society values.

It is likely that an uninhibited temperamental style will be associated with less vulnerability, and an inhibited style with greater vulnerability, to adult anxiety, panic disorder, or agoraphobia, especially in females. This suggestion is based on the fact that adult panic patients report being extremely shy as children; some even displayed a period of phobic avoidance of school. Moreover, we recently saw a group of children 4 to 7 years of age who had one parent with panic disorder, along with a matched group of control children who had a parent with depression or a sibling with attention deficit disorder. Significantly more of the former group were extremely inhibited in our laboratory. The two most sensitive indices of inhibition were a long latency before issuing the first spontaneous comment to an examiner and very few spontaneous comments over the 1-h testing session. About one-third of these children with anxious parents were qualitatively more inhibited than the typical inhibited child in our two longitudinal cohorts.

Additionally, a small proportion of inhibited boys may become impulsive adolescents because on tests with response uncertainty (the child had to decide which of a series of similar alternatives matched a standard), a small group of the inhibited children responded very quickly and made many errors. We interpret this fact to mean that under moderate psychological stress, some inhibited children become impulsive. However, the majority of behaviorally inhibited boys and girls are cautious and reflective on these tasks, suggesting that most inhibited children will be less likely than the average child to implement asocial behavior when they become adolescents. Additional data are needed to affirm both of these speculations.

Epilogue

The research on temperamental inhibition may have heuristic implications for contemporary behavioral science. During psychology's first half-century – roughly until World War II – most investigators unselfconsciously followed the models provided by the first cohorts of physicists, chemists, and biologists. These natural scientists believed that the most profitable way to set the foundations of a discipline was, first, to choose stable objects/events in nature and then study their characteristics in order to discover robust, functional relations between dimensions that gave intensional meanings to different sets of objects/events. Kepler, for example, selected planets and generated principles that related the shape of the earth's orbit around the sun to the distance between the two entities. Lavoisier chose the material changes in objects that follow combustion; Harvey selected the circulation of blood from and to the heart. The intellectual heirs of these scholars recognized that although a mature science is characterized by explanation of a set of functional relations among selected dimensions ascribed to entities in nature, the explanatory propositions summarizing the functional relations were inventions and therefore were fallible and subject to revision. The natural events, however – whether objects in the sky, piles of ash, or hearts – were not. This is why Newton urged scholars to argue from phenomena, and why Darwin suggested that observing baboons might provide a more profound insight into human mental life than reading John Locke.

The first cohort of psychologists also began their inquiries with natural entities, many of which were distinctive reactions in specific contexts. Salivation to food powder, verbal reports of sensations, temporary anesthesias, avoidance of crowds, and developmental changes in speech and motor coordination were among the events subjected to empirical analysis. The first generations of psychologists tried to invent coherent networks of principles that would unite dimensions induced from these events. Unfortunately, their praiseworthy ambitions exceeded the quality of their evidence, and dissatisfaction with their conclusions led to an ideological rebellion against their inductive strategy. But rather than begin anew with different events and deeper analyses, a proportion of the current cohort of social scientists abandoned their friendly attitude toward induction and began their research by positing a priori processes for which there were no consensual referents. Put plainly, and therefore with slight distortion, these investigators behaved as if the a priori processes they invented were the natural entities. They turned upside down the traditional sequence that has characterized the first profitable stage in most empirical sciences by assuming that ideas such as anxiety, concept, attachment, memory, love, individuation, and intelligence – to name only a few – were robust natural unities. As a result, a nontrivial segment of contemporary behavioral science consists of investigations that seek referents for a priori ideas rather than attempts to discover functional relations between dimensions of actual phenomena.

The work on individual variation in initial withdrawal from the unfamiliar, whether in animals or children, has heuristic value because it demonstrates the usefulness of analyzing the dimensions of natural events. Although many of the scientists who study this domain arrived at their current understanding through initially inductive investigations, they might have chosen this family of phenomena following reflection on the theoretical issue of adaptation discussed at the beginning of this chapter. But whether inquiry into the sources of temperamental variation is arrived at inductively or deductively, the observations and experimental procedures originate in and revolve around robust phenomena. That is the sense intended when we suggest that investigations of temperamental qualities in children may provide a balance to the current bias in the social sciences that favors beginning with Platonic processes rather than a family of reliable events. It has not escaped our notice that these conclusions are in accord with Norman Garmezy's continued effort to understand the bases for differences among children and adults in the ability to cope with stressful events and his intuition that attainment of this understanding is more likely if investigators keep the behavioral phenomena at the center of their inquiry.

References

Adamec, R. E., & Stark-Adamec, C. (1983a). Partial kindling and emotional bias in the cat: Lasting aftereffects of partial kindling of the ventral hippocampus. *Behavioral and Neural Biology, 38,* 205–22.

Adamec, R. E., & Stark-Adamec, C. (1983b). Partial kindling and emotional bias in the cat: Lasting effects of partial kindling of the ventral hippocampus. *Behavioral and Neural Biology, 38,* 223–39.

Adamec, R. E., & Stark-Adamec, C. (1983c). Limbic kindling in animal behavior – implications for human psychopathology associated with complex partial seizures. *Biological Psychiatry, 18,* 269–93.

Adamec, R. E., & Stark-Adamec, C. (1986). Limbic hyperfunction, limbic epilepsy and interictal behavior. In B. K. Doane & K. E. Livingston (Eds.), *The limbic system* (pp. 103–45). New York: Raven Press.

Adamec, R. E., Stark-Adamec, C., & Livingston, K. E. (1983). The expression of an early developmentally emergent defensive bias in the adult domestic cat in non-predatory situations. *Applied Animal Ethology, 10,* 89–108.

Albert, D. J., & Chew, G. L. (1980). The septal forebrain and the inhibitory modulation of attack and defense in the rat: A review. *Behavioral and Neural Biology, 30,* 357–88.

Berg, I. (1976). School phobia and the children of agoraphobic women. *British Journal of Psychiatry, 128,* 86–9.

Blizard, D. A. (1981). The Maudsley reactive and nonreactive strains. *Behavioral Genetics, 11,* 469–89.

Bronson, G. W. (1970). Fear of visual novelty. *Developmental Psychology, 2,* 33–40.

Bronson, G. W., & Pankey, W. B. (1977). On the distinction between fear and wariness. *Child Development, 48,* 1167–83.

Buss, A. H., & Plomin, R. A. (1975). *A temperamental theory of personality development.* New York: Wiley.

Charney, D. S., Heninger, G. R., & Breier, A. (1984). Noradrenergic function in panic anxiety. *Archives of General Psychiatry, 41,* 751–63.

Charney, D. S., & Redmond, D. E. (1983). Neurobiological mechanisms in human anxiety. *Neuropharmacology, 22,* 1531–6.

Chen, S., & Miyake, K. (1983). Japanese versus United States comparison of mother–infant interactions and infant development. In K. Miyake (Ed.), *Annual Report of the Research and Clinical Center for Child Development* (pp.13–26). Hokkaido University.

Coolidge, J. C., Brodie, R. B., & Feeney, B. (1964). A ten year follow-up study of 66 school phobic children. *American Journal of Orthopsychiatry, 34,* 675–84.

Coster, W. J. (1986). *Aspects of voice and conversation in behaviorally inhibited and uninhibited children.* Unpublished doctoral dissertation, Harvard University.

Cranach, B. V., Grote-Dham, R., Huffner, U., Marte, F., Reisbeck, G., & Mitterstadt, M. (1978). Das social Gehemmte Kind im Kindergarten. *Praxis der Kinderpsychologie und Kinderpsychiatrie, 27,* 167–79.

Eaves, L., & Eysenck, H. (1975). The nature of extroversion: A genetical analysis. *Journal of Personality and Social Psychology, 32,* 102–12.

Elder, G. H., Liker, J. K., & Cross, C. E. (1984). Parent–child behavior in the Great Depression. In *Lifespan, development and behavior* (Vol. 6, pp. 109–58). New York: Academic Press.

Freedman, R. R., Ianni, P., Ettedqui, E., Pohl, R., & Rainey, J. M. (1979). Psychophysiological factors in panic disorder. *Psychopathology, 16,* 392–7.

Garcia-Coll, C., Kagan, J., & Reznick, J. S. (1984). Behavioral inhibition in young children. *Child Development, 55,* 1005–19.

Garmezy, N. (1983). Stressors of childhood. In N. Garmezy & M. Rutter (Eds.), *Stress, coping and development in children* (pp. 43–84). New York: McGraw-Hill.

Gersten, M. (1986). *The contribution of temperament to behavior in natural contexts.* Unpublished doctoral dissertation, Harvard Graduate School of Education.

Gittelman, R., & Klein, D. F. (1984). Relationship between separation anxiety and panic and agoraphobic disorders. *Psychopathology, 17,* (Suppl. 1), 56–65.

Goldsmith, H. H., & Campos, J. J. (1985). Fundamental issues in the study of early temperament. In M. Lamb & A. Brown (Eds.), *Advances in developmental psychology.* (pp. 231–83). Hillsdale, NJ: Erlbaum.

Goldsmith, H. H., & Gottesman, I. I. (1981). Origins of variation in behavioral style: A longitudinal study of temperament in young twins. *Child Development, 52,* 91–103.

Gottesman, I. I. (1963). Heritability of personality. *Psychological Monographs,* (Whole No. 372), 1–26.

Gualtieri, T., & Hicks, R. E. (1985). An immunoreactive theory of selective male affliction. *Behavioral and Brain Sciences, 8,* 427–41.

Harris, E. C., Noyes, R., Crowe, R. R., & Chaudhry, D. R. (1983). Family study of agoraphobia. *Archives of General Psychiatry, 40,* 1061–6.

Jung, C. G. (1924). *Psychological types.* New York: Harcourt Brace & Co.

Kagan, J., Kearsley, R. B., & Zelazo, P. R. (1978). *Infancy: Its place in human development.* Cambridge, MA: Harvary University Press.

Kagan, J., & Moss, H. A. (1962). *Birth to maturity.* New York: Wiley.

Kagan, J., Reznick, J. S., Clarke, C., Snidman, N., & Garcia-Coll, C. (1984). Behavioral inhibition to the unfamiliar. *Child Development, 55,* 2212–25.

Kling, A., & Coustan, D. (1964). Electrical stimulation of the amygdala and hypothalamus in the kitten. *Experimental Neurology, 10,* 81–9.

Ko, G. N., Elsworth, J. D., Roth, R. H., Rifkin, B. G., Leigh, H., & Redmond, D. E. (1983). Panic induced elevation of plasma MHPG levels in phobic-anxious patients. *Archives of General Psychiatry, 40,* 425–30.

Kopin, I. J. (1984). Avenues of investigation for the role of catecholamines in anxiety. *Psychopathology, 17,* 83–97.

Loehlin, J. C. (1982). Are personality traits differentially heritable? *Behavior Genetics, 12,* 417–28.

Matheny, A. P. (1980). Bayley's infant behavior record: Behavioral components in twin analyses. *Developmental Psychology, 51,* 1157–67.

Matheny, A. P. Riese, M. L., & Wilson, R. S. (1985). Rudiments of temperament: Newborn to nine months. *Developmental Psychology, 21,* 486–94.

Morris, D. P., Soroker, E., & Burruss, G. (1954). Follow-up studies of shy, withdrawn children. I: Evaluation of later adjustment. *American Journal of Orthopsychiatry, 24,* 743–54.

Moskowitz, D., Schwartzman, A. E., & Ledingham, J. E. (1985). Stability and change in aggression and withdrawal in middle childhood and early adolescence. *Journal of Abnormal Psychology, 94,* 30–41.

Nesse, R. M., Cameron, O. G., Curtis, G. C., McCaan, D. S., & Huber-Smith, M. J. (1985). Adrenergic function in patients with panic anxiety. *Archives of General Psychiatry, 41,* 771–6.

Plomin, R. (1986). *Development, genetics and psychology.* Hillsdale, NJ: Erlbaum.

Plooij, F. X. (1984). *The behavioral development of free living chimpanzee babies and infants.* Norwood, NJ: Ablex.

Raskin, M., Peeke, H. V. S., Dickman, W., & Pinsker, H. (1982). Panic and generalized anxiety disorders. *Archives of General Psychiatry, 39,* 687–9.

Reznick, J. S., Kagan, J., Snidman, N., Gersten, M., Baak, K., & Rosenberg, A. (1986). Inhibited and uninhibited behavior: A follow-up study. *Child Development, 57,* 660–80.

Schneirla, T. C. (1959). An evolutionary developmental theory of biphasic processes underlying approach and withdrawal. In M. R. Jones (Ed.), *Nebraska symposium on motivation.* Lincoln: University of Nebraska Press.

Scott, J. P., & Fuller, J. L. (1974). *Dog behavior: The genetic basis.* University of Chicago Press. (Original work published 1965)

Snidman, N. (1984). *Behavioral restraint and the central nervous system.* Unpublished doctoral dissertation, University of California, Los Angeles.

Snow, M. E., Jacklin, C. N., & Maccoby, E. E. (1981). Birth order differences in peer sociability at 33 months. *Child Development, 52,* 589–95.

Stevenson-Hinde, J., Stillwell-Barnes, R., & Zunz, M. (1980). Subjective assessment of rhesus monkeys over four successive years. *Primates, 21,* 66–82.

Suomi, S. J. (1984). The development of affect in rhesus monkeys. In N. A. Fox & R. J. Davidson (Eds.), *The psychology of affective development* (pp. 119–59). Hillsdale, NJ: Erlbaum.

Torgersen, S. (1983). Genetic factors in anxiety disorders. *Archives of General Psychiatry, 40,* 1085–9.

Wilson, R. S., Brown, A. M., & Matheny, A. P. (1971). Emergence and persistence of behavioral differences in twins. *Child Development, 42,* 1381–98.

Yang, R. K., & Halverson, C. F. (1976). A study of the inversion of intensity between newborn and preschool age behaviors. *Child Development, 47,* 350–9.

Part III

Competence under adversity: individual and family differences in resilience

The chapters in this part are concerned with the roles of individual and family differences in how children adapt to stressful life experiences. They highlight *resilience*, the positive side of the study of adaptation in children at risk due to cumulative environmental stressors.

Michael Rutter sets the stage by defining and tracing the history of interest in the concepts of vulnerability and resilience. Rutter suggests that the focus of this area must shift from identifying protective variables to identifying the processes by which protection occurs, and he brings together a diverse set of empirical findings to illustrate possible mechanisms of resilience.

The next three chapters represent three large studies of adaptation in children at risk due to adverse life circumstances. Robert C. Pianta, Byron Egeland, and L. Alan Sroufe draw on longitudinal data from the Mother–Child Interaction Research Project at the University of Minnesota to examine the role of contextual stress and earlier developmental history in understanding the adaptational competence of their sample of first-grade children. Child and family qualities associated with resilience in this sample are also identified. Ann S. Masten, Patricia Morison, David Pellegrini, and Auke Tellegen describe the evolution and results of the "Project Competence" research program founded by Norman Garmezy to study competence under conditions of stress and disadvantage. Both these chapters suggest that individual and family differences play critical roles in the achievement and maintenance of competence despite stressful life challenges. Moreover, both studies suggest that sex differences are crucial to understanding protective processes within the family.

The role of the family as mediator of environmental risk is emphasized by Alfred L. Baldwin, Clara Baldwin, and Robert E. Cole in their chapter based on data from the Rochester Longitudinal Study initiated by Arnold Sameroff (see chapter 3). They distinguish between proximal and distal environmental risk factors, contrasting, for example, the proximal effect on a child of the irritability of an exhausted working single mother with the distal influence of social class. They draw on their data to show that a family may create a positive

179

proximal environment despite very risky distal circumstances. Their data also illustrate how the behavior of stress-resistant families may vary as a function of the environment, reminding us that interventions to promote competence in high-risk children must take into account the environmental context, because competent parents undoubtedly tailor their protective behaviors to the nature of the environmental risks as well as to their child's individual qualities.

The roles of individual and family differences as moderators of stress in school-age children are also examined in the chapter by Norman F. Watt, Olivia Moorehead-Slaughter, Debra M. Japzon, and Gloria G. Keller on adjustment to parental divorce. The quality of parent–child relationships emerges again as a key factor in predicting adjustment to a major stressor. Their observation that children may be "subdued" following divorce is consistent with results from Project Competence suggesting that certain children may become disengaged at high stress levels. The results from Watt and his collaborators also suggest that academic achievement may gradually erode following a major loss, such as divorce, unless a supportive relationship with an adult is present to buffer the loss.

In sum, the chapters in this part clearly indicate the necessity of studying the child in context if we are to make progress in understanding pathways toward and away from competence in development. These chapters illustrate the importance of knowing the nature of the challenge, the qualities of the child, the child's previous developmental history, the family milieu, and the neighborhood context if we are to identify protective processes that mitigate the effects of severe challenges to development.

9   Psychosocial resilience and protective mechanisms

Michael Rutter

During the past decade, the concept of "protective factors" has become firmly established in the field of psychiatric risk research (Garmezy, 1985; Masten & Garmezy, 1985; Rutter, 1979a, 1985a). It stems from the related notion of "resilience," the term used to describe the positive pole of the ubiquitous phenomenon of individual difference in people's responses to stress and adversity. For many years the phenomenon had been put aside as largely inexplicable and therefore of little interest (Ainsworth, 1962). However, the issue of individual differences would not go away, and there came a growing appreciation that it was a key topic in risk research and that an understanding of the mechanisms involved should throw crucial light on the processes involved in risk itself, as well as having implications for prevention and intervention (Rutter, 1979a). Thus, in 1972, the study of individual differences was singled out as the most important development in "maternal deprivation" research (Rutter, 1972).

Although it is difficult to identify the roots of the upsurge of interest in resilience, three fields of research clearly played crucial roles. First, the consistency of the findings of marked variations in outcomes in the quantitative research with high-risk populations, such as that into the offspring of mentally ill parents (Rutter, 1966, 1987a), forced investigators to appreciate how many children seemed to escape relatively unscathed. Second, research into temperament following the pioneering lead of Thomas, Birch, Chess, Hertzig, and Korn (1963) provided empirical evidence that children's qualities did indeed influence their responses to a variety of stress situations (Rutter, 1977). Third, Adolf Meyer (1957) had long argued for the developmental importance of the ways in which people met key life changes and transitions. His psychobiological approach placed emphasis on the importance of person–environment interac-

This work was supported in part by the John D. and Catherine T. MacArthur Foundation (Mental Health Research Network on Risk and Protective Factors in the Major Mental Disorders). A shorter version of this chapter appeared in the *American Journal of Orthopsychiatry*, 57(1987): 316–31.

181

tions at these key turning points in people's lives (Rutter, 1986). Similarly, Murphy's studies of coping and mastery (Murphy, 1962; Murphy & Moriarty, 1976) drew attention to the importance of variations in the ways people deal with threat and challenge. This last theme was vital in its emphasis on the *active* role of the individual. Resilience was not just a matter of constitutional strength or weakness; it was also a reflection of what one did about one's plight. Hinde's experimental studies of separation in rhesus monkeys drew attention to another crucial facet, namely, that individual responses were influenced by, and were part of, family interactions (Hinde & McGinnis, 1977; Hinde & Spencer-Booth, 1970). Factors outside as well as within the individual needed to be considered within the context of person–environment interactions. This third aspect of resilience research has now taken on a life of its own under the general concept of coping with stress (Lazarus & Folkman, 1984; Moos & Schaefer, 1986). Research has concentrated on the set of "tasks" or challenges or adaptations involved in managing a personal crisis.

It is apparent that the shift was not just from vulnerability to resilience but also from risk *variables* to the process of *negotiating* risk situations. It is in that context of risk negotiation that attention was turned to protective mechanisms. Before proceeding further, it is necessary to ask if that was more than a semantic change, reflecting a desire to inject some hope and optimism into the dispiriting story of stress and adversity. After all, family discord had been identified as a vulnerability factor at the same time as a good parent–child relationship was picked out as a protective one (Rutter, 1971a). Were these not opposite sides of the same coin? Would it not be more parsimonious simply to regard intimate relationships as comprising a continuum, with one end positive and the other negative with respect to risk? The criticism is pertinent, and if the concept of protective mechanisms is to have any separate meaning, it must be more than that.

The need to pose the question is underlined by Garmezy's review of research into stress-resistant children (Garmezy, 1985; Masten & Garmezy, 1985). He concluded that three broad sets of variables operated as protective factors: (a) personality features such as autonomy, self-esteem, and a positive social orientation, (b) family cohesion, warmth, and an absence of discord, and (c) the availability of external support systems that encourage and reinforce a child's coping efforts. This list is very familiar to risk researchers as the antonyms of risk variables. High self-esteem protects; low self-esteem puts one at risk. What have we gained by introducing the notion of protective factors? Not very much, if that is where we stop. The warning needs to be heeded. If research into resilience seeks to distill everything down to a few key global composites, we shall only end up where we started. Of course, the demonstration that these composites are highly robust predictors of resilience is important in showing that they are likely to play key roles in the processes involved in people's responses to risk circumstances. But they are of limited value as a means of finding new approaches to prevention. Instead of searching for broadly based protective factors, we need to focus on protective mechanisms and processes. That is, we need to ask why and how some individuals manage to maintain high self-esteem and self-efficacy in spite of facing the same adversities that lead other people to give up and lose hope. How is it that some people have confidants to whom they can turn? What has happened to enable them to have social supports that they can use effectively at moments of crisis? Is it chance, the spin of the roulette wheel of life, or did prior circumstances, happenings, or actions serve to bring about this desirable state of affairs? It is these questions that constitute the main focus of this chapter. The search is not for broadly defined protective factors but rather for the developmental and situational mechanisms involved in protective processes.

Resilience

Before turning to concepts of protective mechanisms, some general points need to be made about resilience as a whole. Resilience is concerned with individual variations in response to risk factors. For the concept to have any meaning it must apply to differences in responses to a given dose of the risk factor; that is, it is not just a dose effect by which the children who have the better outcome have been exposed to a lesser degree of risk. It will be appreciated that the criterion requires accurate knowledge of the risk *mechanism,* not just the risk indicator. There are numerous examples in the literature in which much of the observed variation in response has been an artifact resulting from a mistaken confusion of one for the other. For example, the literature in the 1960s made much of the finding that most children exposed to perinatal hazards developed normally and that those who did not do so tended to come from socially disadvantaged groups (Birch & Gussow, 1970). The finding is solid, but it is doubtful whether social factors play the crucial mediating role that they were supposed to in children's responses to perinatal damage. The development of noninvasive brain imaging techniques showed that the serious adverse sequelae were evident mainly in survivors who had suffered periventricular or intraventricular hemorrhage (Catto-Smith, Yu, Bajuk, Orgill, & Astbury, 1985; Stewart, 1983). The good outcome in the remainder was mainly a function of their not having suffered perinatal damage. The earlier research had to rely on unsatisfactory risk indicators; now that the most important biological mediating mechanism can be identified, the picture looks rather different. It remains to be seen if the supposed moderating role of social factors remains (of course, it does with respect to development in normal infants; the question is whether or not it interacts to modify the effects of biological damage).

A similar situation is evident with respect to the disputed association between early parental death and adult depression. Recent work by Brown, Harris, and Bifulco (1986) has shown that parental death has a long-term vulnerability effect only if it is followed by a serious lack of affectionate parental care. The good outcomes following bereavement were largely consequences of not having experienced the key risk variable. The lesson is that adequate study of resilience requires a prior understanding of risk mechanisms. Without that understanding, there is a danger that resilience will mean no more than that the person has not in fact experienced the crucial risk factor.

Although a clear identification of the operative risk mechanisms is necessary, it is important to note another feature of risk research findings – namely, that many risk factors do not seem to have a straightforward direct effect. Thus, for example, in our epidemiological studies of children living in London or on the Isle of Wight, we found that risk variables did not lead to an increased rate of psychiatric disorder if they occurred truly in isolation (Rutter, 1979a). On the other hand, the rate was much increased if there were two or more concurrent risk variables. This observation had not been made before, largely because the usual statistical approaches do not test for it; a significant main effect in an analysis of variance does not mean that the variable has an effect in the absence of other variables, even though it sounds as if that is what it means (Rutter, 1983). The finding is relevant in forcing us to rethink the matter of mechanisms. If, for example, family discord has its major adverse effect only when it is accompanied by other adversities (Emery & O'Leary, 1984), what does this mean in terms of the risk process? Similarly, one hospital admission is not followed by any appreciable psychiatric risk, but two admissions do indicate a risk, at least if the first admission is during the preschool years (Quinton & Rutter, 1976). This cannot be an additive effect because there is no long-term risk from one admission to be put into the sum. Or, again, recurrent admissions constitute a greater psychiatric hazard if they are associated with chronic psychosocial adversity. The implication is that the mediating mechanism is not quite what it seems at first sight. It may be that the study of protective processes could throw light on what is involved.

The last general point is that resilience cannot be seen as a fixed attribute of the individual. If circumstances change, the risk alters. For example, in our longitudinal studies of children whose parents were mentally ill, we found that the risk to the children that was associated with early separations as a result of family discord went down if family cohesion and harmony were subsequently restored (Rutter, 1971a), although this ameliorating effect was not seen with lesser, more short-lived improvements in family functioning (Rutter & Quinton, 1984). Conversely, there is evidence that serious stress and adversity in middle childhood may lead to psychiatric disorder even though all was well in infancy and early childhood (Rutter, 1985b).

Vulnerability and protective mechanisms

The concepts of vulnerability and protective mechanisms are more specific and more narrowly defined than that of resilience. The essential defining feature is that there is a modification of the person's response to the risk situation. Thus, it requires some form of intensification (vulnerability) or amelioration (protection) of the reaction to a factor that in ordinary circumstances leads to a maladaptive outcome. The effect is indirect and dependent on some type of interaction. It must be in some sense catalytic, in that it changes the effect of another variable, instead of (or in addition to) having a direct effect of its own. It will be appreciated that in this respect vulnerability and protection are the negative and positive poles of the same concept, not different concepts.

There is a temptation among psychological researchers to assume that the requirements of an interactive process can be confirmed or refuted by testing for a multiplicative statistical interaction effect. However, that assumption is mistaken, for a variety of different reasons (Rutter, 1983, 1987b). Four main problems should be emphasized. First, the key issue is whether or not the hypothesized vulnerability or protective factor has a direct effect on outcome in the absence of the risk factor (or provoking agent); as already noted, that is not tested for by examination of whether or not there is a main effect in an analysis of variance. Second, the statistical significance of an interaction effect is crucially dependent on the number of individuals for whom the modifying factor and risk variable co-occur. It is quite possible to have a strong interactive effect, but for it to be nonsignificant because it applies to only a small proportion of the sample (in other words, the proportion of variance explained is an inadequate measure of the strength of an effect). Third, the indirect vulnerability/protection effect may lie in an increase or decrease in the likelihood that a risk factor will be present (i.e., an effect on the rate of occurrence of the independent variable, rather than on its effect). Fourth, the interactive processes may rely on chains of connections over time rather than on a multiplicative effect at any single time. Interactions cannot be restricted to the statistical or psychological chemistry involved in a particular mix of variables at any one time. Nevertheless, the essence of the concept is that the vulnerability or protective effect is evident only in combination with the risk variable. Either the vulnerability/protective factor has no effect in low-risk populations or its effect is magnified in the presence of the risk variable. It is crucial that this interactive component be put to rigorous empirical test. Without its presence there is no point in differentiating risk mechanisms from vulnerability processes.

Throughout this discussion I have been careful to use the terms "process" and "mechanism" in preference to "variable" or "factor." That is because any one variable may act as a risk factor in one situation but a vulnerability factor in another. There has been much unhelpful dispute in the literature on the supposed buffering effect of social support, because most investigators have assumed that the vulnerability (or protection) lies in the variable rather than the process. It does not and cannot. Thus, for example, loss of a job through forced redundancy serves as a direct risk factor for depression in adults (Jackson & Warr, 1984; Melville, Hope, Bennison, & Barraclough, 1985; Warr &

Jackson, 1985); but not having a job (i.e., a long-standing lack of employment) may act as a vulnerability factor in relation to other threatening life events (Brown & Harris, 1978). Similarly, loss of a love relationship because of death or divorce serves as a direct precipitant of depression, but chronic lack of such a relationship constitutes a vulnerability factor in conjunction with other life stressors (Brown & Harris, 1978). In the field of depression, the direct risk effect tends to be seen with acute life changes of an adverse type, whereas the vulnerability or protective effects usually are found with long-standing life circumstances or happenings in the distant past. However, the acuteness of an environmental variable is not a good guide to the mechanisms. Thus, for example, chronic family discord has a direct risk effect for conduct disorder (Rutter, 1985b). It makes no sense to label variables as inherently of the direct risk or indirect vulnerability type. It is the process or mechanism, not the variable, that is one or the other.

As an extension of the same point, it is necessary to note that whether the *process* serves to increase or decrease the risk has no necessary connection with whether the variable (i.e., attribute or experience) itself will ordinarily be thought of as positive or negative. Protection is not a matter of pleasant happenings or socially desirable qualities of the individual (Rutter, 1981, 1985a). The search is not for factors that make us feel good but for processes that protect us against risk mechanisms. Like medicines that work, these are often of the type that tastes bad! Thus, immunization does not involve direct promotion of positive physical health. To the contrary, it comprises being exposed to, and successfully coping with, a small (or modified) dose of the noxious infectious agent. Protection in this case resides not in evasion of the risk but in successful engagement with it. The same applies for acute physical stressors (such as electric shock) when these bring about lasting structural and functional changes in the neuroendocrine system that are protective against later stressors (Hennessy & Levine, 1979). Studies of the anticipatory hormone changes that come with experience in parachute jumping (Ursin, Baade, & Levine, 1978) tell the same story. The protection stems from the adaptive changes that follow successful coping. The same may apply for psychosocial stresses and adversity.

It should be added that the protective process may even stem from a variable that itself provides a risk to health or to social functioning. For example, the sickle cell phenomenon causes disease, but protects against malaria. Also, adoption probably carries with it an increased psychiatric risk for children from advantageous backgrounds, but it may be protective for those born to deviant parents living in discord or deprivation.

Differences between vulnerability and protection

This defining feature of an interactive process applies to both vulnerability and protection. Is there, then, any point in retaining two concepts, if in reality they are no more than opposite poles of the same concept? There are several rather different reasons why the two terms need to be retained. To begin with, even if we use only one concept, we need words to describe the two poles. Thus, we have the two words "up" and "down" rather than just "up" and "not-up." But that example introduces another point, namely, that it is useful to have terms that emphasize the focus. "Not-up" is not quite the same as "down." Similarly, we talk about immunization as a protection, just as we do preparation of children for hospital admission. Logically, we could say that lack of immunization and lack of preparation are vulnerability factors, but we prefer to use the positive concept of protection, because the action taken concerns the positive pole. The choice of term in this case does no more than highlight where the action lies; the mechanism is the same as the vulnerability end of the continuum. Most of the differences between vulnerability and protection are of this kind. There are, however, some variations on this theme that are important because they add new dimensions, or at least facets, to the concept.

Perhaps the most important stems from the finding that many vulnerability or protective processes concern key *turning points* in people's lives, rather than long-standing attributes or experiences as such. For example, Brown et al. (1986) have shown this in connection with the ways in which girls deal with premarital pregnancies, and our own research has shown the same for decisions regarding whether or not to stay on at school to attain higher educational qualifications (Maughan & Rutter, 1986; Rutter, Maughan, Mortimore, Ouston, with Smith, 1979) and for the choice of marriage partner (Quinton, Rutter, & Liddle, 1984). In each case, the turning point arises because what happens then determines the direction of trajectory for the years that follow. It seems helpful to use the term "protective mechanism" when a trajectory that was previously a risk one is changed in a positive direction to one with a greater likelihood of an adaptive outcome. This would be so in the example of our school-based studies, in which the decision to stay on at school enabled black teenagers with previously poor educational attainments to gain improved scholastic qualifications that might serve to widen occupational opportunities (Maughan & Rutter, 1986). The same applies in the second example from our follow-up study of institution-reared girls, for whom the exercise of planning and foresight increased the likelihood of a harmonious marriage to a nondeviant man and by so doing much improved the chances of successful social functioning for the women themselves (Quinton et al., 1984; Rutter & Quinton, 1984). Conversely, the process will be labeled a vulnerability process when a previously adaptive trajectory is turned into a negative one, as, for example, by the sequelae that may follow the birth of an unwanted illegitimate child to a well-functioning teenager who is then rejected by the parents with whom she had previously had a good relationship. The point of emphasizing the turning points that change a developmental trajectory is to focus attention on the process involved. It is not enough, for example, to say that academic success and self-efficacy are protective (although they are); we must go on to ask how those qualities developed and how they changed the life course.

A second situation in which it may be preferable to speak of protective processes rather than an absence of vulnerability ones is when the mechanisms involved in protection seem different from those involved in the risk process. For example, there is tentative evidence that previous experience of happy separations renders young children less vulnerable to the stress of hospital admission (Stacey, Dearden, Phil, & Robinson, 1970). Even a previous hospital admission may have this effect in an older child (although it has the opposite effect in a preschooler). The implication is that knowledge and experience of other separations that have been negotiated successfully may be protective because they alter a child's cognitive appraisal of the event (the various ways of preparing children for admission to hospital probably do the same) (Ferguson, 1979; Wolfer & Visintainer, 1979).

In psychology and medicine more generally, there are well-documented examples of continuous variables or dimensions that have effects at both ends of the distribution, but in which such effects reflect different mechanisms at opposite poles. For example, IQ clearly functions as a dimensional variable. However, whereas the presence of organic brain damage is the main factor accounting for IQs below 50, it is not responsible for variations within the normal range (Rutter & Gould, 1985). Similarly, a lower IQ constitutes a relative risk variable throughout the IQ range, both normal and abnormal, but again the mediating mechanisms at the bottom end include the effects of organic brain dysfunction, whereas these are likely to be of negligible importance with respect to the variation in risk between, say, IQ 100 and 125 (Rutter, 1971b). The implication, once more, is the need to be concerned with processes, not just variables.

A third situation that suggests the use of the term "protective mechanism" arises when the main effect seems to derive from the positive end of the variable. For example, in our study of institution-reared women, we found that the presence of a supportive harmonious marital relationship had a marked protective effect with respect to the quality of parenting (Quinton et al., 1984). This was not just a matter of a poor marital relationship creating a vulnerability, because poor parenting was just as likely among women who lacked spouses (either because they had not married or, more often, because the marriage had broken down earlier). Of course, one could just as well talk about a lack of support as a vulnerability factor, but the focus on the positive forces one to ask what the support is doing that creates the protective effect.

In summary, the crucial difference between vulnerability/protection processes and risk mechanisms is that the latter lead directly to disorder (either strongly or weakly), whereas the former operate indirectly, with their effects apparent only by virtue of their interactions with the risk variable. The implication is that the psychological processes involved in risk and in protection are likely to differ in important respects. The key feature lies in the process, not in the variable, and the utility of the differentiation from risk lies in the focus on the mechanisms involved. The distinction between protective processes and a lack of vulnerability ones is less crucial, but again its value resides in the implications for mechanisms. The term "protection" is to be preferred over "lack of vulnerability" when the process involves a change in life trajectory from risk to adaptation (rather than the reverse) or when the mechanisms of protection seem to differ from those of vulnerability.

Meaning of interaction effects

Because interaction effects compose a crucial criterion for protective processes, it is necessary to ask what they might mean. Why should there be no effect in the absence of the risk variable? What kinds of psychological mechanisms might be implicated in the interaction? These have been little studied up to now, but a few leads are available.

Sex

Many investigators have shown that boys are more likely than girls to develop emotional/behavioral disturbances when exposed to marked family discord (Rutter, 1982). This is not just a matter of boys having a higher rate of disorder; the interactive component is shown by the finding that the *increase* in risk with family discord is greater for boys. Figure 9.1 shows the relevant data from our 4-year longitudinal study of children with mentally ill parents (Rutter & Quinton, 1984). The top left histogram shows the greater vulnerability of boys at the time of the initial assessment. However, as the top right histogram indicates, the sex difference in susceptibility waned with time. Girls took longer to develop emotional problems when exposed to discord, but the sex difference for persistent disturbances throughout the 4-year follow-up period (bottom histogram) was much less than that found initially. In short, the sex difference seems to be a matter of degree rather than kind. Various explanations for this sex difference in susceptibility have been considered (Rutter, 1970, 1982), but most theoretical speculations have concentrated on the overall sex difference in rates of disorder (Gualtieri & Hicks, 1985), rather than on the difference in responses to discord (or any other psychosocial stressor). However, the mechanisms probably are somewhat different. Males are more vulnerable to a wide range of physical hazards, and it is conceivable that there is a parallel, biologically determined greater susceptibility to psychosocial hazards (Earls, 1987; Eme, 1979), perhaps mediated in part by the greater incidence of neurodevelopmental impairment in boys (Brothwood, Wolke, Gamsu, Benson, & Cooper, 1986; Richman, Stevenson, & Graham, 1982). Nevertheless, it seems that other mechanisms are also operative. First, it may be that there is a difference between boys and girls in the extent to

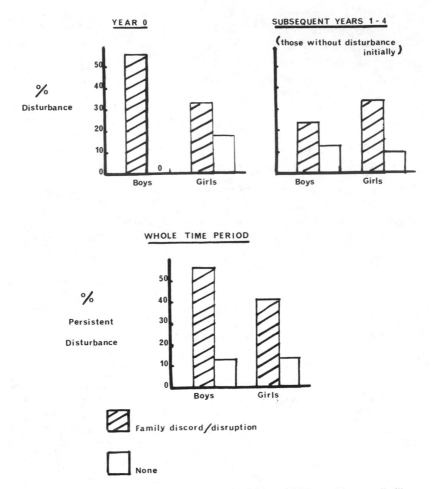

Figure 9.1. Marital discord and disturbance in children (children with mentally ill parents). (From Rutter & Quinton, 1984)

which discord impinges directly. Thus, Hetherington, Cox, and Cox (1982) noted that parents were more likely to quarrel in front of boys than in front of girls. Second, it appears that when a family breaks up, sons are more likely than daughters to be placed in some form of institutional care (Packman, 1986), a placement that serves to increase their psychiatric risk (Walker, Cudeck, Mednick, & Schulsinger, 1981). Third, boys are more likely than girls to react with disruptive oppositional behavior (Maccoby & Jacklin, 1974, 1980; Rutter, 1982) rather than with emotional distress – a type of reaction that is more likely to elicit a negative response from parents. Fourth, people tend to place different meanings on aggression in boys than on that in girls (Condry & Ross, 1985), so that aggression in boys is more likely to be met

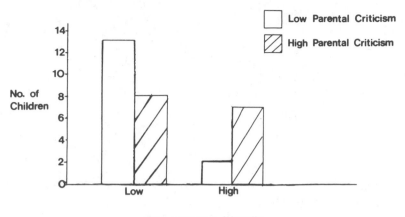

Figure 9.2. Temperamental adversity and parental criticism. (From Rutter, 1978)

with either punitive or backing-away responses from adults (Maccoby & Jacklin, 1983; Snow, Jacklin, & Maccoby, 1983) and negative responses from peers (Fagot, Hagan, Leinbach, & Kronsberg, 1985). Similarly, Hinde and Stevenson-Hinde (1986) and Simpson and Stevenson-Hinde (1985) found that whereas shyness in boys was associated with negative interactions with others, in girls it was associated with positive personal interchanges. The data of Dunn and Kendrick (1982) suggested that mothers were more punitive with sons than with daughters and were more consistently so over time, a response likely to lead to escalating negative behavior (Patterson, 1982). It may be inferred that the protection afforded by being female is in part a result of lesser exposure to the risk factor, a reduced exposure that is a consequence of the immediate family context, the chain of interactions that follows, and the sequelae of family breakdown.

Temperament

The data on temperament tell a similar story. Figure 9.2 shows the pattern evident in the longitudinal family illness study that has been mentioned earlier (Rutter & Quinton, 1984). Children with adverse temperamental features (a composite of low regularity, low malleability, negative mood, and low fastidiousness) were more likely than other children to be targets of parental hostility, criticism, and irritability. When parents are depressed, they do not "take it out" on all children to the same degree; often children with difficult temperaments tend to be scapegoated. Similarly, Lee and Bates (1985) found that toddlers with difficult temperaments were more resistant to maternal control, and their negative behavior was more likely to be met with coercive responses by mothers (Figure 9.3). As with sex, the interactive pro-

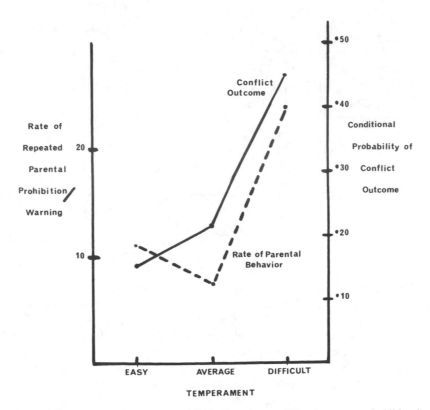

Figure 9.3. Repeated parental prohibition/warning, conflict outcome, and children's temperament. (Adapted from Lee & Bates, 1985)

cess reflects a pattern in which the children's attributes make them a focus for the discord (thus increasing exposure to the risk variable) and increase the probability that that exposure will set in motion a train of adverse interactions that will prolong the risk. It should be added that the overlap in the mechanisms applicable to sex and to temperament is partially a consequence of the children being the same. In both the studies mentioned, the composites of difficult temperament were more often evident in males (even though there were few sex differences on the individual traits that made up the composites).

Good parent–child relationships

In the same family illness study (Rutter, 1978) it was found that the presence of one good parent–child relationship served to reduce the psychiatric risk associated with family discord (Figure 9.4). The mechanisms involved in this effect are not known. It could simply mean that the overall level of discord was less when there was one harmonious relationship in the family.

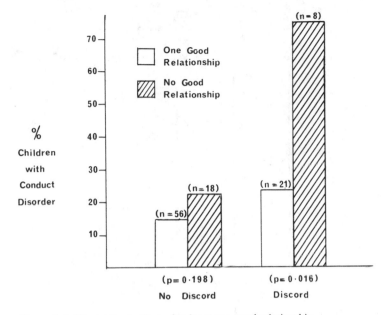

Figure 9.4. "Protective" effect of at least one good relationship.

Alternatively, it could reflect a process by which the parent with whom the child had a good relationship sought to ensure that the child was out of the way when the major rows occurred. Another possibility is that the security of that one good relationship increased the child's self-esteem and that it was this that exerted the protective effect. The process requires further study.

Marital support

Good marital relationships have been found to exercise a similar protective function, as shown in our follow-up of girls reared in institutions (Quinton et al., 1984; Rutter & Quinton, 1984). The institution-reared (ex-care) girls had a generally worse outcome than that for the comparison group, but it was found that their adult functioning was closely associated with their marital situations at the time. The level of good parenting by the ex-care women who had supportive spouses (as reflected in a harmonious marriage with warmth and confiding) was as high as that in the comparison group, but there was an absence of good parenting when such support was lacking (Figure 9.5). It is notable that the presence of marital support was less critical for good parenting in the comparison group. The implication is that protective mechanisms are more necessary in high-risk groups.

Similar protective processes associated with marital support or the presence of close confiding relationships have been found by other investigators

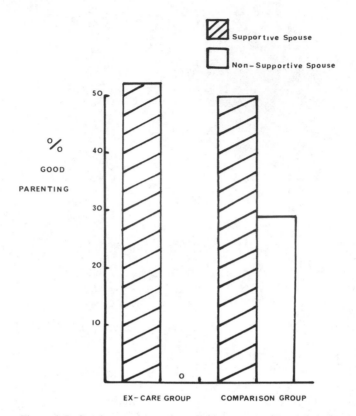

Figure 9.5. Good parenting and supportive spouse. (From Quinton & Rutter, 1988)

(Brown & Harris, 1978; Parker & Hadzi-Pavlovic, 1984). Figure 9.6 shows the data from a study by Campbell, Cope, and Teasdale (1983), replicating the Brown and Harris (1978) work. A lack of an intimate confiding relationship with a husband or boyfriend was associated with a nonsignificant increase in the risk for depression (i.e., some direct effect, albeit below statistical signifi-cance), but a significant 3.5-fold enhancement of the effect of the provoking agent (an enhancement that exceeds the sum of the two considered separately, i.e., 46% exceeds 13% and 11%).

Again there is uncertainty over how this protective effect operates (al-though detailed analyses indicated that it was most unlikely to be an artifact). Like a good parent–child relationship, it may operate through an effect on maternal self-esteem, as suggested by the data of Ingham, Kreitman, Miller, Sashidharan, and Surtees (1986). But also it might reflect a diffusion of task responsibilities by virtue of husbands sharing the parental role. Alternatively, the availability of someone with whom to discuss family problems may have served to increase social-problem-solving skills. Once more, research is

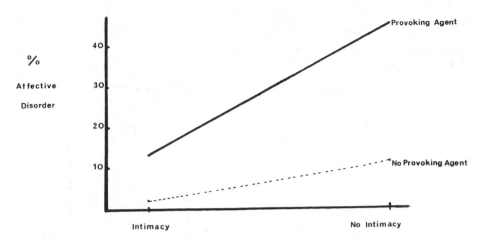

Figure 9.6. Intimacy, provoking agents, and affective disorder. (From Campbell et al., 1983)

needed to test these various possibilities. However, further questions need to be posed on the mechanisms by which some women made harmonious marriages to nondeviant men, whereas others did not. This issue was tackled in the same follow-up study of institution-reared girls.

Planning

The data (Rutter & Quinton, 1984) showed that the most important explanatory variable was whether or not the women exercised "planning" in their choices of a spouse (simply meaning that they did *not* marry for a negative reason, such as to escape from an intolerable family situation or in response to an unwanted illegitimate pregnancy, and that they had known their future spouses for 6 months or more). Within the ex-care group, but not the comparison sample, women who "planned" were much less likely to marry deviant men (Figure 9.7). A similar measure of "planning" was obtained for work (Quinton & Rutter, 1988). This overlapped greatly with planning for marriage, suggesting that the tendency to exercise foresight and to take active steps to deal with environmental challenges was a general one. Again, planning for work showed a significant association with outcome in the institution-reared sample, but a weaker association among the controls. It seems fairly straightforward to see why planning might be protective in the risk sample. It was associated with a significantly lower rate of teenage pregnancy (19% vs. 48%), so that the pressures to make a hasty marriage were less. Also, presumably, the "planning" style meant that the women took steps to avoid commitment to deviant men and to seek relationships with more suitable partners. However, why did this effect not apply within the compari-

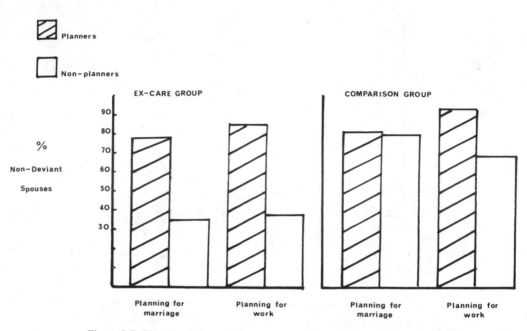

Figure 9.7. Planning and nondeviant spouses. (From Quinton & Rutter, 1988)

son group? Two reasons may be suggested. First, their peer group was much less likely to include seriously deviant males. Hence, even if they married by random allocation, they were quite likely to end up with well-functioning husbands. Second, most continued to live in supportive families throughout their teens, so that it may well be that parents would have sought to keep the girls from making seriously bad marriages, even if the girls seemed likely to drift into them. It may be inferred that planning operated as a way of avoiding risky situations, but if risky situations were less prevalent in the immediate social context, this was less necessary. As with marital support, the next question was how planning arose in some girls but not others.

Positive school experiences

The findings showed that within the ex-care group, but again not in the comparison group, the girls who showed planning were much more likely to have had positive school experiences (Figure 9.8). Such experiences could be academic or nonacademic (such as sports, drama, arts and crafts), but in the ex-care group most did not involve exam success, although they did in the comparison group. Because the effect was not found in the controls and because the positive experiences rarely included high scholastic attainments, it is unlikely that the variable was a proxy for high IQ. It should be added that the power of positive school experiences in this sample probably derived from

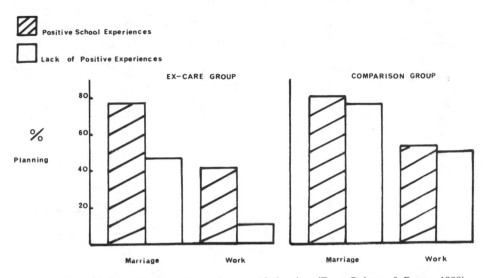

Figure 9.8. Positive school experiences and planning. (From Quinton & Rutter, 1988)

the policy at that time of sending these children to ordinary schools not linked with the Children's Homes and of ensuring that there were not too many children from the institution at any one school. The result was a marked disjunction between the Children's Homes and the school, thus allowing the experiences to be different in the two settings. Although the precise mediating mechanism is not known, it may be supposed that the experiences of pleasure, success, and accomplishment at school had helped the girls to acquire a sense of their own worth and their ability to control what happened to them. There is evidence from other research suggesting the importance of feelings of self-esteem and self-efficacy (Bandura, 1977; Harter, 1983). It is likely that the reason why the school effect was not seen in the comparison group was that most of the girls had ample sources of reward in the family, so that the additional experiences of success at school merely reinforced self-esteem, rather than creating it.

Neutralizing events

The findings on school experiences suggest that there may be many sources of self-esteem and self-efficacy and that a lack in one domain of life may be compensated for by the presence of relevant experiences in another domain. The concept of "neutralizing" life events (Tennant, Bebbington, & Hurry, 1981) takes the suggestion one stage further in postulating an effect that relies on a quality that substantially negates or counteracts the impact of an earlier threatening event or difficulty. Tennant and associates found that neurotic disorders in an adult community sample were more likely to remit if

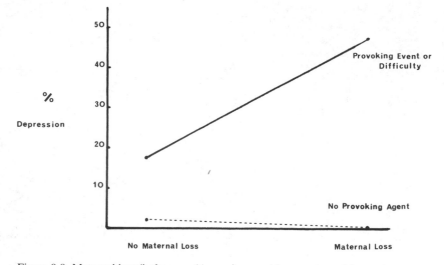

Figure 9.9. Maternal loss (before age 11 years), provoking agents, and depression. (From Brown & Harris, 1978)

there was a neutralizing event, but not if there was a positive life event that lacked that neutralizing quality.

The same notion might be applied to the finding of Stacey et al. (1970) that children who did not show distress following admission to hospital were more likely than distressed children to have had more "normal" separation experiences, such as staying overnight with friends or relatives, having baby-sitters, attending nursery school, and being left all day with a family person. In this case, of course, the neutralizing experiences antedated the risk experience, rather than following it. The same is true for the successful interventions designed to prepare children for admission to hospital (Ferguson, 1979; Wolfer & Visintainer, 1979). It appears that this is a consequence of a more positive mental set toward the experience and more effective coping as a result of a better understanding of what is involved in going into a hospital. It is notable in that connection that the main benefits are evident when the children return home, there being less effect on initial anxiety in hospital.

Early parental loss and poor parent–child relationships

Early parental loss has figured prominently in considerations of experiences in childhood that create a vulnerability to psychiatric disorders that do not become manifest until much later, and then only in association with direct risk variables. Figure 9.9 shows the data from the Brown and Harris (1978) study indicating that loss of the mother before the child was age 11 years had no association with adult depression in the absence of a provoking agent, but

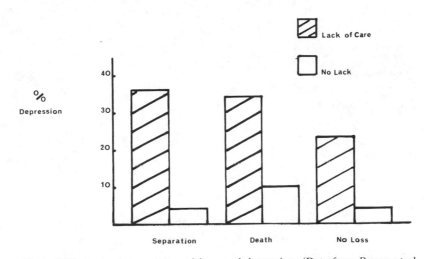

Figure 9.10. Lack of care, maternal loss, and depression. (Data from Brown et al., 1986)

a significant threefold enhancing effect when combined with a threatening life event or long-term difficulty.

Two major questions arise with this vulnerability interaction. First, what is it about maternal loss that creates the vulnerability? More recent data from Brown et al. (1986) clearly showed that in their sample, a serious lack of affectionate care in childhood was the key variable (Figure 9.10). It predicted depression both with and without maternal loss, whereas loss showed no association with depression in the absence of lack of care.

Second, there is the question of what change in the individual is brought about by the vulnerability factor. That is, what is the mediating variable that interacts with the later risk factor? Brown et al. (1986) have argued that it is a cognitive set of helplessness, and their data support this hypothesis. They also invoke the related concept of low self-esteem. The problem with both postulated variables is that they will be strongly influenced by the presence of depression. Accordingly, there is a need to assess the link in nondepressed individuals. Ingham et al. (1986) have done this, with the results shown in Figure 9.11 ("depressed" here includes anxiety as well as depressed states). Maternal loss was indeed associated with marked lack of self-esteem in both depressed and nondepressed individuals. Accordingly, it seems reasonable to assume that this may be involved in the mediation. It should be added, however, that although lack of parental care serves as a vulnerability factor for depression, other evidence suggests that it acts as a direct risk variable for conduct disorders and personality disturbance (Quinton & Rutter, 1988; Rutter, 1985b). Accordingly, it may well be that the mediating mechanisms extend much wider than low esteem. There is growing evidence to suggest

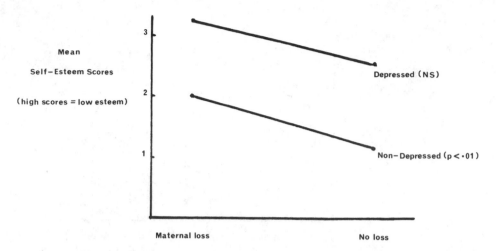

Figure 9.11. Early maternal loss and self-esteem in depressed and nondepressed women. (Data from Ingham et al., 1986)

that adverse life experiences make it more likely that people will act in ways that create threatening situations for themselves (Kandel & Davies, 1986; Miller et al., 1986; Robins, 1986).

The possible mediating role of a tendency to respond helplessly when faced with difficulties is also shown by the Lutkenhaus, Grossmann, and Grossmann (1985) comparison of 3-year-old infants who had been securely or insecurely attached at 12 months of age. They were given the task of building a tower of rings, the objective being to complete the tower faster than the experimenter. The children's responses to potential failure were assessed by whether they speeded up or slowed down their building after looking at the experimenter's tower. Children who had been securely attached tended to speed up, whereas those who had shown insecure attachments tended to slow down (Figure 9.12). The implication is that secure attachments led to a sense of confidence in their ability to meet challenges, whereas insecurity was followed by a tendency to give up under pressure.

Life turning points

The last interactive processes to consider are those concerned with turning points in people's lives. Their importance has been implicit in the role of planning for marriage and for work careers. Less directly, too, they are implicated in the effects of positive school experiences. In the first place, this is because the choice of school is likely to influence the likelihood that the child will have such experiences (Rutter, 1983; Rutter et al., 1979). However, it is also because personal decisions about staying on at school beyond the

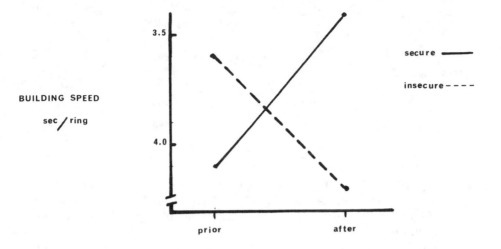

Figure 9.12. Building speed, failure feedback, and security of attachment. (From Lütkenhaus et al., 1985)

LEAVING INSTITUTION		Teenage Pregnancy	Marriage for Negative Reason	Deviant Spouse
	Return to Harmonious Family	30%	20%	40%
	Independent Living	41%	46%	39%
	Return to Discordant Family	64%	53%	61%

Figure 9.13. Leaving the institution, pregnancy, and marriage. (Data from Quinton & Rutter, 1988)

period of compulsory education will determine children's opportunities to take examinations, success in which could open up occupational opportunities (Gray, Smith, & Rutter, 1980).

Figure 9.13 shows the findings from the follow-up study of institution-reared girls for another life transition – namely, that at the time when they could leave the institution (Quinton & Rutter, 1988). Of those who left to return to discordant families, most (64%) experienced teenage pregnancy, compared with less than a third (30%) of those who went back to harmonious homes; the figure (41%) for those who stayed on longer in the Children's Home was intermediate. A similar contrast was evident in the proportions marrying for negative reasons (53%, 46%, and 20%, respectively). This re-

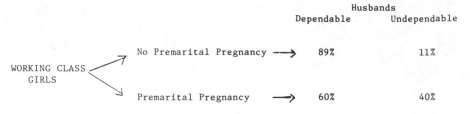

Figure 9.14. Premarital pregnancy and dependability of husband. (From Brown et al., 1986)

sulted in a comparable trend for the proportions marrying deviant men, meaning those with criminality or some form of mental disorder. This, in turn, was followed by differences in rates of lack of marital support, marital breakdown, and poor parenting.

Premarital pregnancy played a key role in this process. Figure 9.14 shows the data from the Brown et al. (1986) study on this turning point. Of the working-class girls who did not experience teenage pregnancy, only 11% married husbands who turned out to be undependable. In contrast, two-fifths (40%) of those who became pregnant in their teens married undependable men (undependability being assessed by features such as criminality, gambling, violence, poor work record, and infidelities). The qualities of the husband, in turn, were associated with a lack of a confiding relationship and a greater likelihood of depression.

Mediating mechanisms in protective processes

It will be appreciated that the data on the possible meanings of interaction effects were chosen to illustrate different possibilities, rather than to draw general conclusions. The findings vary in their strength and in the extent to which they have been replicated. Nevertheless, they provide some pointers to possible mechanisms that might act as predictors in protective processes. Four stand out as contenders: (a) reduction of risk impact, (b) reduction of negative chain reactions, (c) establishment and maintenance of self-esteem and self-efficacy, and (d) an opening up of opportunities.

Reduction of risk impact

It is clear that one crucial mechanism is a reduction of the impact of the risk factor on the individual. This seems likely to take place via two rather different routes; (a) alteration of the meaning or riskiness of the risk variable for that child and (b) alteration of the child's exposure to or intimate involvement with the risk situation.

Alteration of the riskiness itself. The first route reflects the fact that most risk factors do not constitute absolutes that are independent of the person's appraisal of them and cognitive processing of the experiences. For example, hospital admission constitutes a stress experience in early childhood, probably in part because it involves children's separation from their parents, in part because of the roster of discontinuous caregiving provided, and in part because of the frightening nature of some of the nursing, medical, and surgical procedures (Rutter, 1979b). Very young infants (under the age of 6 months or so) are less at risk, probably because they lack established selective attachments that could be threatened by separation. School-age children, on the other hand, are less at risk, probably because they have the cognitive capacity to maintain relationships over a period of separation and to appreciate why admission is necessary and what is involved. The riskiness of admission can be reduced by seeking to avoid admitting children to hospital during the period of greatest risk, by giving them appropriately graded experiences of happy separations in circumstances in which they will feel secure, and by preparing them for the admission experience.

As discussed earlier in the chapter, physiological studies suggest that "inoculation" against stress may be best provided by controlled exposure to the stress in circumstances in which successful coping or adaptation can take place (Meichenbaum, 1985). Life involves unavoidable encounters with all manners of stressors and adversities. It is not realistic to suppose that children can be so sheltered that they can avoid such encounters. Rather, protection may lie in the "steeling" qualities that derive from success in coping with the hazards when the exposure is of a type and degree that is manageable in the context of the child's capacities and social situation. This aspect of protection has been little explored up to now in relation to psychosocial hazards, and it warrants further investigation.

In the example of hospital admission, the cognitive processing of the experience that reduced its negative impact took place at the time, but it has been suggested that this may also take place long after the events. For example, this has been put forward to explain how some individuals who have experienced an adverse upbringing themselves may nevertheless integrate their painful experiences into a coherent and adaptive "internal working model" of relationships (Main, Kaplan, & Cassidy, 1985; Ricks, 1985). This may take place as a result of later positive experiences that enable these people to reevaluate their own negative relationships with their parents not as being due to their own failings but rather as consequences of, say, a mother's depressive disorder or disadvantageous social circumstances or problems with a husband's excessive drinking. In this way, it is postulated that the meaning of the prior risk experience is altered in a direction that reduces the riskiness for that individual.

The possible role of "neutralizing" life events introduces another possibility for reduction of risk. The hypothesis is that threatening life events create a psychiatric risk because they lead to a damaging alteration in a person's self-concept (Brown & Harris, 1978). Thus, the loss of a love relationship (through rebuff, bereavement, or separation) is important not so much because a loss is painful in itself but because it causes people to question their own ability to maintain relationships. The concept of "neutralization" suggests that if the threatening life event is accompanied or followed by some other event that counteracts this damage to self-esteem or self-efficacy, the risk should be reduced. However, the concept implies specificity. Thus, a new love relationship should reduce the impact of the loss of a previous love relationship, but success at work (however positive in itself) would not. Similarly, a task failure (such as by dismissal from a job or failure to get an expected promotion) would need to be accompanied by task success in order to be neutralized. There is a lack of adequate evidence on whether or not this postulated mechanism in fact operates in the way proposed, but the possibility warrants further study.

A further alternative is that there may be a reduction in the task demands that bring out the risk effect. For example, good marital support lessens the likelihood of poor parenting in women who are at risk because of seriously adverse childhood experiences (Quinton & Rutter, 1988). There is continuing uncertainty on precisely how support exercises its protective function, and that issue constitutes a major research need for the future. However, one possibility with respect to parenting is that the task of parenting is itself made easier because the supportive spouse shares the burden, because alternative approaches can be discussed, and because the supportive spouse backs up the other parent at times of difficulty or confrontation. In short, the support is, in a sense, practical rather than emotional, although the distinction between the two is necessarily blurred.

Alteration in exposure to or involvement in the risk. The second way in which risk impact may be reduced is through mechanisms that alter the child's exposure to the risk situation or that reduce involvement in its risky aspects. Thus, Wilson (1974, 1980) found that strict parental supervision and regulation of children's peer group activities outside the home reduced the risk of delinquency for children reared in a high-risk environment; the findings of Patterson and Stouthamer-Loeber (1984) suggest that perhaps most urban neighborhoods are risky in this respect. Efficient parental monitoring of children's play and friendships (through knowing whom they were with, where they were, and what they were doing) presumably means that there is the chance of directing young people away from risk and toward prosocial peer group activities and, in addition, allows the parents to provide firm feedback to the children on which behaviors are and which are not acceptable.

The findings on gender differences and on temperamental variations emphasize that within any one family that provides a risk environment by virtue of, say, parental depression or family discord, all children are not equally at risk.

Children with easy temperaments are less likely than those with difficult ones to be scapegoated or to become the target for parental irritation; similarly, family discord is less likely to impinge on girls than on boys. The protection in this case resides in the qualities of the child that make for more harmonious interactions. Equable mood, malleability, predictability of behavior, mild to moderate intensity of emotional reactions, and an approaching style to new situations have all been implicated in the composites that make up an easy temperament, but a sense of humor (Masten, 1986) probably should be added to the list.

Children's own actions in physically removing themselves, or physically distancing themselves, from an unalterably bad situation may also be important in reducing effective exposure to risk (Rutter, 1985a). For example, children reared by seriously mentally ill parents may cope effectively by developing their social ties with other family members or with people outside the family and by developing the ability to accept that the poor relationships in the home are functions of illness rather than any lack in themselves or malevolent feelings on the part of the parents.

Reduction of negative chain reactions

The second group of protective mechanisms comprises those that reduce the negative chain reactions that follow risk exposure and that serve to perpetuate the risk effects. These chain reactions probably play a crucial role in the long-term adverse sequelae that may stem from risk experiences (Rutter, 1985a, 1987b). For example, animal studies of separation (Hinde & McGinnis, 1977) and human studies on the birth of a sibling (Dunn & Kendrick, 1982) both bring out the importance of the vicious cycles of coercive or anxiety-producing interchanges that may be set in motion. Being female and having an easy temperament not only reduce the initial impact of some risk situations but also reduce the likelihood that maladaptive patterns of interaction will become established. It is noteworthy that the protective function does not simply reside within the individual. In addition to any intrinsic qualities that may be relevant in relation to constitutional vulnerability, such qualities have an effect through their influence on other people's reactions. Because, to a substantial extent, the protective mechanism lies in the interaction rather than in the individual attribute as such, there is scope for it to be made use of in interventions.

At a molar level, the negative chain reactions include changes in patterns of child care. Thus, the ill effects of parental loss in early childhood seem to stem from the lack of affectionate care or from the institutional admission that follows the loss in some cases, not from the loss itself (Brown et al., 1986). The implication is that protection should be found in the support necessary to enable the remaining parent to function adequately or in the provision of high-quality alternative care that will ensure continuity in relationships.

Promotion of self-esteem and self-efficacy

There is a growing body of literature that attests to the importance of people's concepts and feelings about themselves, their social environment, and their ability to deal with life's challenges and to control what happens to them. These concepts and feelings are both cognitive and affective. The terms used to refer to them have included self-esteem (Harter, 1983), self-efficacy (Bandura, 1977), internal working models of relationships (Bowlby, 1969/1982, 1973, 1980; Bretherton, 1985), the self-concept (Epstein, 1980), and (expressed in terms of the negative pole) learned helplessness (Brewin, 1985; Seligman, 1975). The available evidence suggests that it is protective to have a well-established feeling of one's own worth as a person together with confidence and conviction that one can successfully cope with life's challenges. Some theorists would add that it is adaptive for the self-concepts to have a coherence that accepts the reality of the bad experiences and less desired attributes as well as the presence of the good qualities and happenings. Although it would be premature to claim that it is well established that high self-esteem and self-efficacy are truly protective, the empirical findings point in that direction. For an understanding of the protective processes, however, it is necessary to ask further questions about how these self-concepts develop and which experiences can strengthen them for individuals in high-risk situations.

The limited available evidence suggests that two main types of experiences are most influential: (a) secure and harmonious love relationships and (b) success in accomplishing tasks that are identified by individuals as central to their interests.

Secure and supportive personal relationships. In early childhood the most important relationships in this connection are children's selective attachments with their parents. The long-term results of secure early attachments are not known, but the available data from short-term prospective studies (Bretherton, 1985), from retrospective recall of adults (Main et al., 1985; Ricks, 1985), and from intergenerational studies of high-risk populations (Rutter, 1987b, 1989) suggest that the experience of secure early attachments does make it more likely that children will grow up with feelings of high self-esteem and self-efficacy. To that extent, secure, harmonious parent–child relationships provide a degree of protection against later risk environments.

Self-concepts, however, are not set in early (or even late) childhood. There is much evidence that they continue to be modified according to the nature of the life experiences encountered. It appears that good intimate relationships, even in adult life, can do much to bolster people's positive concepts about themselves and their worth in other people's eyes. The evidence is mainly correlational at present; we lack good evidence from prospective studies that good relationships *cause* beneficial changes in self-esteem and self-efficacy.

Nevertheless, it is plausible that they might do so, and the possibility should be investigated further.

It remains uncertain that the apparent benefits that stem from "social support" work in this way. There is considerable evidence that effective social supports do contribute to mental health and some evidence that they may provide a buffering protective function against psychosocial risk (Cohen & Wills, 1985; Parry & Shapiro, 1986). However, numerous questions remain. In the first place, it is uncertain what aspects of social support are crucial. Is it the practical help or the opportunity to discuss strategies and tactics with others? Or is it the well-being that comes from being part of a larger social group, or the satisfactions that come from shared activities? Or is it the presence of just one intimate relationship that gives the feeling of being loved and needed enough? Second, it is unclear how far the support can be conceptualized as external to the individual, as distinct from a consequence of effective social functioning determined in part by personality attributes. What evidence there is suggests that the number of available social contacts is not the crucial dimension and that the quality of social relationships and the use made of them are important. Third, insofar as social supports are protective, by what means do they serve that function? Is it, as supposed, through their effects on enhancing self-esteem and self-efficacy, or are the mechanisms quite different? These questions remain unanswered.

Task accomplishment. The second type of experience that seems to lead to high self-esteem and self-efficacy is task accomplishment of one kind or another. Our findings (Quinton et al., 1984) on the benefits stemming from positive school experiences suggest that "tasks" should be interpreted very broadly in this connection. There seemed to be benefits from a wide range of "accomplishments" that included social success, the taking of positions of responsibility, and success in nonacademic pursuits such as sports or music or craftwork, as well as traditional successes in examination performance. Other research suggests the same. Thus, our studies of inner London secondary schools showed that those that gave the children many opportunities to take responsibility tended to have better pupil outcomes (Rutter et al., 1979). Similarly, Elder's study (1974, 1979) of children growing up in the Great Depression showed that the taking on of domestic responsibilities and part-time work proved strengthening for many of the older children. This was not so for younger children, suggesting that it is important that the tasks or challenges be within children's coping capacities. Also, Werner and Smith's study (1982) of children in Kauai noted that resilience was associated with the taking of responsibility for younger siblings.

As with most of the other variables considered, there is uncertainty as to exactly which aspect is protective. Is it the learning of effective coping or social problem-solving skills (Moos & Schaefer, 1986; Pellegrini, 1985) that matters most? In other words, are the specific skills acquired crucial? Or do the benefits derive from the self-knowledge that one has succeeded in coping with challenges in the past, with the implication that it is likely that one will be able to do so again in the future – with the concept of self-efficacy the mediating mechanism? Alternatively, perhaps what is protective is the feeling of one's own worth as an individual that derives from the positive appraisal by others – so that the mechanism depends on self-esteem.

Turning points. It would be misleading to view either self-esteem or self-efficacy as a fixed attribute of the individual. Undoubtedly, there are important continuities over time and situation, but also changes take place as a result of new experiences. Such experiences may be viewed as potential turning points in people's lives. Thus, when children start school, they enter a new arena, with challenges in peer group relationships as well as scholastic work. Success in coping with these challenges may be protective in children from seriously disadvantaged homes, just as failure may create psychiatric vulnerability or risks. Later on, it could be that success in an absorbing free-time interest (e.g., sports, photography, music, modeling) might also create a similar turning point. Such interests have been subjected to remarkably little investigation so far, although they seem to play an important part in the lives of some young (and older) people. Adolescence (with its challenges in love relationships and in personal autonomy), work careers, marriage, and parenting all provide further possible turning points whereby "success" in the form of personal relationships or task accomplishment may change the life course onto a more adaptive trajectory. Elder (1986) has shown that military service may do the same for some young men from disadvantaged backgrounds.

Opening up opportunities

The last mechanism, the opening up of opportunities, also concerns turning points in people's lives. Its operation is most strikingly evident in the educational process when success in taking examinations provides the passport to higher education or the credentials for entry to skilled jobs. Those who drop out of schooling or who do not apply for training courses thereby lose the opportunity to obtain experiences that may be protective. However, important though these education-to-work transitions may be, there are many other equally important turning points in people's lives when opportunities are opened up or closed down. For example, teenage motherhood for a girl from a seriously deprived background (as with the institution-reared girls we studied) tends to mean a continuing tie to the adversities of childhood, either because of marriage to a man with a similarly disadvantaged upbringing or because of the social and financial restrictions of unsupported parenting. Postponement of pregnancy and marriage until later may increase the opportunity for obtaining a widening range of experiences and increase the social network and hence the range of possible marriage partners. A geographical move may have a similar beneficial effect by changing the peer group. Thus, West (1982) found that the delinquency rate dropped in boys from inner London who moved with their families away from the metropolis. Elder (1986) noted that for some disadvantaged young men, army service performed a similar function, allowing opportunities for personality growth in a structured setting, providing sources of self-esteem, and delaying marriage (with an associated increase in marital stability).

Conclusions

All studies of risk factors for psychiatric disorder in childhood and adult life have noted the marked individual variations in people's responses to stress and adversity; some succumb, and some escape damage. The phenomenon of maintaining adaptive functioning in spite of serious risk hazards has been termed "resilience." The factors promoting resilience remain poorly understood, but it is clear that part of the explanation lies in the overall level of risk. Frequently the individuals who develop disorders have suffered accumulations of greater risks experienced over longer periods of time. However, that does not seem to be the whole story. In addition, there are vulnerability/protection processes by which there is a catalytic *modification* of a person's response to the risk situation. This interactive mechanism applies to both vulnerability and protective processes, the latter term being used when the focus is on factors that counter risk, when the process involves a change of life trajectory from risk to adaptation, and when the mechanisms of protection seem to differ from those of vulnerability.

Much of the research on protective influences has concentrated on a search for protective *variables,* often with the aim of distilling the findings down to provide identification of the few key global attributes or experiences that are crucial in this connection. An almost inevitable consequence of this approach, however, is confusion among risk, vulnerability, and protection. It is argued that the focus needs to be on protective *processes* or mechanisms, rather than on variables. By definition, these involve interactions of one sort or another. Moreover, because of the importance of developmental linkages involving discontinuities and turning points, as well as continuities, the required research needs to be longitudinal as well as epidemiological. In particular, a focus is needed on the mechanisms involved in changes in life trajectory. Because these often are best considered in terms of altered states or circumstances, there is a need to use categorical as well as dimensional variables. Mechanisms should be examined in terms of situational effects and interactive processes over time, with high-risk versus low-risk comparisons to test the hypothesis of interaction effects with little effect in the absence of the risk situation.

The limited evidence available so far suggests that protective processes include (a) those that reduce the risk impact by virtue of effects on the riskiness itself or through alteration of exposure to or involvement in the risk, (b) those that reduce the likelihood of negative chain reactions stemming from the risk encounter, (c) those that promote self-esteem and self-efficacy through the availability of secure and supportive personal relationships or success in task accomplishment, and (d) those that open up opportunities. Protection does not reside in the psychological chemistry of the moment but in the ways in which people deal with life changes and in what they do about their stressful or disadvantaging circumstances. Particular attention needs to be paid to the mechanisms operating at key turning points in people's lives, when a risk trajectory may be redirected onto a more adaptive path.

References

Ainsworth, M. D. (1962). The effects of maternal deprivation: A review of findings and contro-versy in the context of research strategy. In *Deprivation of maternal care: A reassess-ment of its effects*. Geneva: World Health Organization.

Bandura, A. (1977). *Social learning theory*. Englewood Cliffs, NJ: Prentice-Hall.

Birch, H. G., & Gussow, J. D. (1970). *Disadvantaged children: Health, nutrition and school failure*. New York: Grune & Stratton.

Bowlby, J. (1973). *Attachment and loss. II: Separation anxiety and anger*. London: Hogarth Press.

Bowlby, J. (1980). *Attachment and loss. III: Loss, sadness and depression*. London: Hogarth Press.

Bowlby, J. (1982). *Attachment and loss. I: Attachment*. London: Hogarth Press. (Original work published 1969)

Bretherton, I. (1985). Attachment theory: Retrospect and prospect. In I. Bretherton & E. Waters (Eds.), *Growing points of attachment theory and research. Monographs of the Society for Research in Child Development, 50*(Series No. 209, No. 1–2).

Brewin, C. (1985). Depression and causal attributes: What is their relation? *Psychological Bulle-tin, 98*(2), 297–309.

Brothwood, M., Wolke, D., Gamsu, H., Benson, J., & Cooper, D. (1986). Prognosis of the very low birthweight baby in relation to gender. *Archives of Disease in Chlidhood, 61*, 559–64.

Brown, G. W., & Harris, T. O. (1978). *Social origins of depression: A study of psychiatric disorders in women*. London: Tavistock Publications.

Brown, G. W., Harris, T. O., & Bifulco, A. (1986). The long term effects of early loss of parent. In M. Rutter, C. E. Izard, & P. B. Read (Eds.), *Depression in young people* (pp. 251–96). New York: Guilford Press.

Campbell, E. A., Cope, S. J., & Teasdale, J. D. (1983). Social factors and affective disorder: An investigation of Brown and Harris's model. *British Journal of Psychiatry, 143*, 548–53.

Catto-Smith, A. G., Yu, V. Y., Bajuk, B., Orgill, A. A., & Astbury, J. (1985). Effect of neonatal periventricular haemorrhage on neurodevelopmental outcome. *Archives of Disease in Childhood, 60*, 8–11.

Cohen, S., & Wills, T. A. (1985). Stress, social support, and the buffering hypothesis. *Psychologi-cal Bulletin, 98*(2), 310–57.

Condry, J. C., & Ross, D. F. (1985). Sex and aggression: The influence of gender label on the perception of aggression in children. *Child Development, 56*, 225–33.

Dunn, J., & Kendrick, C. (1982). *Siblings: Love, envy and understanding*. London: Grant McIntyre.

Earls, F. (1987). Sex differences in psychiatric disorders: Origins and developmental influences. *Psychiatric Developments, 1*, 1–23.

Elder, G. H. (1974). *Children of the Great Depression.* University of Chicago Press.

Elder, G. H. (1979). Historical change in life patterns and personality. In P. B. Bates & O.G. Brim (Eds.), *Life span development and behaviour* (Vol. 2, pp. 118–59). New York: Academic Press.

Elder, G. H. (1986). Military times and turning points in men's lives. *Developmental Psychology, 22*(2), 233–45.

Eme, R. F. (1979). Sex differences in childhood psychopathology: A review. *Psychological Bulletin, 86,* 574–95.

Emery, R. E., & O'Leary, K. D. (1984). Marital discord and child behaviour problems in a non-clinic sample. *Journal of Abnormal Child Psychology, 12,* 411–20.

Epstein, S. (1980). The self concept: A review and the proposal of an integrated theory of personality. In E. Straub (Ed.), *Personality: Basic aspects and current research.* Englewood Cliffs, NJ: Prentice-Hall.

Fagot, B. I., Hagan, R., Leinbach, M. D., & Kronsberg, S. (1985). Differential reactions to assertive and communicative acts of toddler boys and girls. *Child Development, 56,* 1499–505.

Ferguson, B. F. (1979). Preparing young children for hospitalization: A comparison of two methods. *Pediatrics, 64*(5), 656–64.

Garmezy, N. (1985). Stress resistant children: The search for protective factors. In J. Stevenson (Ed.), *Recent research in developmental psychopathology.* Oxford: Pergamon Press (a book supplement to the *Journal of Child Psychology and Psychiatry, Number 4*).

Gray, G., Smith, A., & Rutter, M. (1980). School attendance and the first year of employment. In I. Hersov & I. Berg (Eds.), *Out of school: Modern perspectives in truancy and school refusal* (pp. 343–70). New York: Wiley.

Gualtieri, T., & Hicks, R. (1985). An immunoreactive theory of selective male affliction. *Behavior and Brain Sciences, 8,* 427–41.

Harter, S. (1983). Developmental perspectives on self-system. In E. M. Hetherington (Ed.), *Socialization, personality, and social development. Vol. 4: Mussen's handbook of child psychology* (4th ed., pp. 275–385). New York: Wiley.

Hennessy, J. W., & Levine, S. (1979). Stress, arousal, and the pituitary-adrenal system: A psychoendocrine hypothesis. In J. M. Sprague & A. N. Epstein (Eds.), *Progress in psychobiology and physiological psychology* (pp. 133–78). Academic Press: New York.

Hetherington, E. M., Cox, M., & Cox, R. (1982). Effects of divorce on parents and children. In M. Lamb (Ed.), *Nontraditional families* (pp. 223–88). Hillsdale, NJ: Erlbaum.

Hinde, R. A., & McGinnis, L. (1977). Some factors influencing the effect of temporary mother–infant separation: Some experiments with rhesus monkeys. *Psychological Medicine, 7,* 197–212.

Hinde, R. A., & Spencer-Booth, Y. (1970). Individual differences in the responses of rhesus monkeys to a period of separation from their mothers. *Journal of Child Psychology and Psychiatry, 11,* 159–76.

Hinde, R. A., & Stevenson-Hinde, J. (1986). Relating childhood relationships to individual characteristics. In W. W. Hartup & Z. Rubin (Eds.), *Relationships and development* (pp. 37–50). Hillsdale, NJ: Erlbaum.

Ingham, J. G., Kreitman, N. B., Miller, P. M., Sashidharan, S. P., & Surtees, P. G. (1986). Self-esteem, vulnerability and psychiatric disorder in the community. *British Journal of Psychiatry, 148,* 375–85.

Jackson, P. R., & Warr, P. B. (1984). Unemployment and psychological ill-health: The moderating role of duration and age. *Psychological Medicine, 14,* 605–14.

Kandel, D. B., & Davies, M. (1986). Adult sequelae of adolescent depression symptoms. *Archives of General Psychiatry, 43,* 255–62.

Lazarus, R. S., & Folkman, S. (1984). *Stress, appraisal and coping.* New York: Springer.

Lee, C. L., & Bates, J. E. (1985). Mother–child interaction at age two years and perceived difficult temperament. *Child Development, 56,* 1314–25.

Lütkenhaus, P., Grossmann, K. E., & Grossmann, K. (1985). Infant–mother attachment at twelve months and style of interaction with a stranger at the age of three years. *Child Development, 56,* 1538–42.

Maccoby, E. E., & Jacklin, C. N. (1974). *The psychology of sex differences.* Stanford University Press.

Maccoby, E. E., & Jacklin, C. N. (1980). Psychological sex differencess. In M. Rutter (Ed.), *Scientific foundations of developmental psychiatry* (pp. 92–100). London: Heinemann Medical.

Maccoby, E. E., & Jacklin, C. N. (1983). The "person" characteristics of children and the family as environment. In D. Magnusson & V. Allen (Eds.), *Human development: An interactional perspective* (pp. 75–91). New York: Academic Press.

Main, M., Kaplan, N., & Cassidy, J. (1985). Security in infancy, childhood and adulthood. In I. Bretherton & E. Waters (Eds.), *Growing points of attachment theory and research. Monographs of the Society for Research in Child Development, 50*(Serial No. 209, No. 1–2), 66–106.

Masten, A. S. (1986). Humor and competence in school-aged children. *Child Development, 57,* 461–73.

Masten, A. S., & Garmezy, N. (1985). Risk, vulnerability, and protective factors in developmental psychopathology. In B. B. Lahey & A. E. Kazdin (Eds.), *Advances in clinical child psychology* (Vol. 8, pp. 1–52). New York: Plenum Press.

Maughan, B., & Rutter, M. (1986). Black pupils' progress in secondary schools. II: Examination attainments. *British Journal of Developmental Psychology, 4,* 19–29.

Meichenbaum, D. (1985). *Stress inoculation training.* Oxford: Pergamon Press.

Melville, D. I., Hope, D., Bennison, D., & Barraclough, B. (1985). Depression among men made involuntarily redundant. *Psychological Medicine, 15*(4), 789–93.

Meyer, A. (1957). *Psychobiology: A science of man.* Springfield, IL: Charles C Thomas.

Miller, P. M., Dean, C., Ingham, J. G., Kreitman, N. B., Sashidharan, S. P., & Surtees, P. G. (1986). The epidemiology of life events and long-term difficulties, with some reflections on the concept of independence. *British Journal of Psychiatry, 148,* 686–96.

Moos, R. H., & Schaefer, J. A. (1986). Life transitions and crises: A conceptual overview. In R. H. Moos (Ed.), *Coping with life crises: An integrated approach* (pp. 3–28). New York: Plenum.

Murphy, L. B. (1962). *The widening world of childhood: Paths towards mastery.* New York: Basic Books.

Murphy, L. B., & Moriarty, A. E. (1976). *Vulnerability, coping and growth from infancy to adolescence.* New Haven, CT: Yale University Press.

Packman, J. (1986). *Who needs care.* Oxford: Blackwell Scientific.

Parker, G., & Hadzi-Pavlovic, D. (1984). Modification of levels of depression in mother-bereaved women by parental and marriage relationships. *Psychological Medicine, 14,* 125–35.

Parry, G., & Shapiro, D. A. (1986). Social support and life events in working class women: Stress buffering or independent effects. *Archives of General Psychiatry, 43,* 315–23.

Patterson, G. R. (1982). *Coercive family process.* Eugene, OR: Castalia.

Patterson, G. R., & Stouthamer-Loeber, M. (1984). The correlation of family management practices and delinquency. *Child Development, 55,* 1299–307.

Pellegrini, D. (1985). Training in social-problem solving. In M. Rutter & L. Hersov (Eds.), *Child and adolescent psychiatry: Modern approaches* (2nd ed., pp. 839–50). Oxford: Blackwell Scientific.

Quinton, D., & Rutter, M. (1976). Early hospital admissions and later disturbances of behaviour: An attempted replication of Douglas' findings. *Developmental Medicine and Child Neurology, 18,* 447–59.

Quinton, D., & Rutter, M. (1988). *Parenting breakdown: The making and breaking of intergenerational links.* Aldershot, Hants: Avebury.

Quinton, D., Rutter, M., & Liddle, C. (1984). Institutional rearing, parenting difficulties and marital support. *Psychological Medicine, 14,* 107–24.

Richman, N., Stevenson, J., & Graham, P. J. (1982). *Pre-school to school: A behavioural study.* London: Academic Press.

Ricks, M. H. (1985). The social transmission of parental behaviour: Attachment across generations. In I. Bretherton & E. Waters (Eds.), *Growing points of attachment theory and research. Monographs of the Society for Research in Child Development, 50*(Serial No. 209, No. 1–2).

Robins, L. N. (1986). The consequences of conduct disorder in girls. In D. Olweus, J. Block, & M. Radke-Yarrow (Eds.), *Development of antisocial and prosocial behavior* (pp. 385–408). New York: Academic Press.

Rutter, M. (1966). *Chlidren of sick parents: An environmental and psychiatric study* (Maudsley Monograph No. 16). London: Oxford University Press.

Rutter, M. (1970). Sex differences in children's responses to family stress. In E. J. Anthony & C. Koupernick (Eds.), *The child in his family* (Vol. 1, pp. 165–96). New York: Wiley.

Rutter, M. (1971a). Parent–child separation: Psychological effects on the children. *Journal of Child Psychology and Psychiatry, 12,* 233–60.

Rutter, M. (1971b). Psychiatry. In J. Wortis (Ed.), *Mental retardation: An annual review. III* (pp. 186–221). New York: Grune & Stratton.

Rutter, M. (1972). *Maternal deprivation reassessed.* Harmondsworth: Penguin.

Rutter, M. (1977). Individual differences. In M. Rutter & L. Hersov (Eds.), *Child psychiatry: Modern approaches* (pp. 3–21). Oxford: Blackwell Scientific.

Rutter, M. (1978). Early sources of security and competence. In J. S. Bruner & A. Garten (Eds.), *Human growth and development* (pp. 33–61). London: Oxford University Press.

Rutter, M. (1979a). Protective factors in children's responses to stress and disadvantage. In M. W. Kent & J. E. Rolf (Eds.), *Primary prevention in psychopathology. Vol 3: Social competence in children* (pp. 49–74). Hanover, NH: University Press of New England.

Rutter, M. (1979b). Separation experiences: A new look at an old topic. *Journal of Pediatrics, 95,* 147–54.

Rutter, M. (1981). Stress, coping and development: Some issues and some questions. *Journal of Child Psychology and Psychiatry, 22,* 323–56.

Rutter, M. (1982). Epidemiological-longitudinal approaches to the study of development. In W. A. Collins (Ed.), *Minnesota Symposia on Child Psychology. Vol. 15: The concept of development* (pp. 105–44). Hillsdale, NJ: Erlbaum.

Rutter, M. (1983). Statistical and personal interactions: Facets and perspectives. In D. Magnusson & V. Allen (Eds.), *Human development: An interactive perspective* (pp. 295–319). New York: Academic Press.

Rutter, M. (1985a). Resilience in the face of adversity: Protective factors and resistance to psychiatric disorder. *British Journal of Psychiatry, 147,* 598–611.

Rutter, M. (1985b). Family and school influences on behavioural development. *Journal of Child Psychology and Psychiatry, 26,* 349–68.

Rutter, M. (1986). Meyerian psychobiology: Personality development and the role of life experiences. *American Journal of Psychiatry, 143,* 1077–87.

Rutter, M. (1987a). Parental mental disorder as a psychiatric risk factor. In R. E. Hales & A. J. Frances (Eds.), *American Psychiatric Association Annual Review* (Vol. 6, pp. 647–63). Washington, DC: APA.

Rutter, M. (1987b). Continuities and discontinuities from infancy. In J. Osofsky (Ed.), *Handbook of infant development* (2nd ed., pp. 1256–96). New York: Wiley.

Rutter, M. (1989). Intergenerational continuities and discontinuities in serious parenting difficulties. In D. Cicchetti & V. Carlson (Eds.), *Child maltreatment* (pp. 317–48). Cambridge University Press.

Rutter, M., & Gould, M. (1985). Classification. In M. Rutter & L. Hersov (Eds.), *Child and adolescent psychiatry: Modern approaches* (2nd ed., pp. 304–21). Oxford: Blackwell Scientific.

Rutter, M., Maughan, B., Mortimore, P., Ouston, J., with Smith, A. (1979). *Fifteen thousand hours: Secondary schools and their effects on children.* Cambridge, MA: Harvard University Press.

Rutter, M., & Quinton, D. (1984). Long-term follow-up of women institutionalized in childhood: Factors promoting good functioning in adult life. *British Journal of Developmental Psychology, 18,* 225–34.

Seligman, M. E. P. (1975). *Helplessness: On depression, development and death.* San Francisco: Freeman.

Simpson, A. E., & Stevenson-Hinde, J. (1985). Temperamental characteristics of three- to four-year-old boys and girls and child–family interactions. *Journal of Child Psychology and Psychiatry, 26,* 43–53.

Snow, M. E., Jacklin, C. N., & Maccoby, E. E. (1983). Sex-of-child differences in father–child interactions at one year of age. *Child Development, 54,* 227–32.

Stacey, M., Dearden, R., Pill, R., & Robinson, D. (1970). *Hospitals, children and their families: The report of a pilot study.* London: Routledge & Kegan Paul.

Stewart, A. (1983). Severe perinatal hazards. In M. Rutter (Ed.), *Developmental neuropsychiatry* (pp. 15–31). New York: Guilford Press.

Tennant, C., Bebbington, P., & Hurry, J. (1981). The short-term outcome of neurotic disorders in the community: The relation of remission to clinical factors to "neutralizing" life events. *British Journal of Psychiatry, 139,* 213–20.

Thomas, A., Birch, H. G., Chess, S., Hertzig, M. E., & Korn, S. (1963). *Behavioral individuality in early childhood.* New York University Press.

Ursin, H., Baade, E., & Levine, S. (1978). *Psychobiology of stress: A study of coping men.* New York: Academic Press.

Walker, E. F., Cudeck, R., Mednick, S. A., & Schulsinger, F. (1981). Effects of parental absence and institutionalization on development of clinical symptoms in high-risk children. *Acta Pyschiatrica Scandinavica, 63,* 95–109.

Warr, P., & Jackson, P. (1985). Factors influencing the psychological impact of prolonged unemployment and of re-employment. *Psychological Medicine, 15,* 795–807.

Werner, E. E., & Smith, R. S. (1982). *Vulnerable, but invincible: A longitudinal study of resilient children and youth.* New York: McGraw-Hill.

West, D. J. (1982). *Delinquency: Its roots, careers and prospects.* London: Heinemann Educational.

Wilson, H. (1974). Parenting in poverty. *British Journal of Social Work, 4,* 1–254.

Wilson, H. (1980). Parental supervision: A neglected aspect of delinquency. *British Journal of Criminology, 20,* 203–35.

Wolfer, J. A., & Visintainer, M. A. (1979). Prehospital psychological preparation for tonsillectomy patients: Effects on children's and parents' adjustment. *Pediatrics, 64*(5), 646–55.

10   Maternal stress and children's development: prediction of school outcomes and identification of protective factors

Robert C. Pianta, Byron Egeland, and L. Alan Sroufe

The extent to which contextual stress in families affects children's development is a research topic that has been given considerable emphasis within the emergent field of developmental psychopathology (Garmezy, 1983, 1984; Garmezy, Masten, & Tellegen, 1984). This chapter presents research findings relating maternal stress and children's school outcomes, conducted as part of the Mother–Child Interaction Research Project at the University of Minnesota. The Mother–Child Project has accumulated data on the role of maternal stress in predicting child maltreatment (Egeland, Breitenbucher, & Rosenberg, 1980; Pianta, Egeland, & Erickson, 1989) and as a factor related to the quality of attachment relationships (Erickson, Sroufe, & Egeland, 1985; Egeland & Farber, 1984). These studies have suggested that maternal stress played a major role in determining certain parenting and child outcomes in this sample. Specifically, in this chapter we present data on the effects of maternal and family psychosocial stress on children's development in the early school years and the factors related to competence in a high-stress subsample. These introductory sections address issues germane to the study of contextual stress and its effects on children.

Risk research and the study of stressful life events

By and large, studies that have examined the role of contextual stress in child development have chosen one of two possible strategies for measuring contextual stress, both of which have certain advantages and disadvantages. The first uses life events scales as measures of general environmental stress, and the second involves identification of subjects on the basis of exposure to a particular stressor, such as divorce (Wallerstein, 1983) or parental mental

This research was supported by a grant from the Maternal and Child Health Service of the U.S. Department of Health, Education, and Welfare (MC-R-270416-01-0). This research is currently supported by a grant from the Office of Special Education, Department of Education (G00830029), and by the William T. Grant Foundation.

illness (see chapters 11 and 12 in this volume). These measurement strategies have been applied within prospective risk research designs and concurrent or retrospective designs. From a methodological standpoint, the prospective designs have provided a more powerful data base from which to make inferences regarding the causal nature of stress and other risk factors (Garmezy, 1977). However, issues related to the advantages and disadvantages of the measurement strategy chosen to study contextual stress (life events scale or single stressor) may have implications for theory building that are as important as the nature of the research design.

Life events scales as measures of contextual stress

Life events scales and their use as predictors have come under a great deal of justified criticism. Investigators have cited the need for these scales to contain items representative of subjects' experiences, to control for retrospective collection of data, and to collect and score responses so as to gain some assessment of the relative stressfulness of a particular event for a subject (Brown & Harris, 1978; Cochrane & Robertson, 1973; Derogatis, 1982; Dohrenwend & Dohrenwend, 1974). Other weaknesses of this approach have to do with the assumption that subjects' endorsements or reports of wide-ranging experiences lie along a common dimension of nonspecific stress and can therefore be composited to form a single score that can then be used as a predictor variable. This assumption has proved tenuous in light of research on the multidimensionality of these scales (Skinner & Lei, 1980). The life events literature has also lacked studies of a prospective, multivariate nature and thereby has confused cause and consequence (Rabkin & Streuning, 1976).

Despite these shortcomings, the life events methodology has proved amenable to a number of adaptations that have been quite useful in improving it as a strategy for measuring contextual stress. The advantages of using life events scales as measures of contextual stress lie predominantly in the fact that they survey a wide range of stressors and are adaptable to use within a semi-structured interview format whereby subjects' subjective interpretations of events can be analyzed. If gathered frequently across time, the information from these scales can be applied prospectively (Brown & Harris, 1978; Derogatis, 1982; Dohrenwend, Krasnoff, Askensky, & Dohrenwend, 1982; Perkins, 1982). Egeland et al. (1980) applied a scoring technique in which ratings were assigned to the disruptiveness of life events items on mothers' functioning (Egeland & Deinard, 1975), and they found the scores from this rating technique to be predictive of maltreatment, whereas simple event occurrence was not. Skinner and Lei (1980) have investigated the multidimensional nature of these scales, as have Pianta (1986) and Herzog (1985), and it is clear that there is potential for development of subscales that will measure specific stressors. Issues that remain to be addressed include continued work on the multidimensionality of life events scales and the nature of relations among subscales measuring specific stressors, as well as the relations of these measures to outcomes.

Research on single stressors

There have been several research programs that have focused attention on the developmental sequelae of exposure to a single major stressor. Research on the effects of parental divorce is one example of this approach (Hetherington, Cox, & Cox, 1979; Wallerstein, 1983), as is research on the effects of family violence (Straus, 1983) or parental mental disorder (Watt, Anthony, Wynne, & Rolf, 1984). This approach to research on stress is attractive in that some believe that it may encompass a somewhat more circumscribed field of influences than does research that relies on life events scales, and it has led to the development of data bases for generating theoretical statements regarding particular stressors (Rutter, 1983). Unfortunately, there is the strong possibility that many of the subjects chosen for inclusion in this type of investigation, by virtue of their exposure to the stressor of interest, will have been exposed to a number of other stressors as well, so that there will be considerable overlap among subjects within and between investigations in the extent to which they represent multiple stressful experiences. This can result in difficulty in making statements about the effects of a particular kind of stress, such as divorce, when in fact there may be a number of families in a sample chosen for divorce that have also been exposed to other stressors, such as violent behavior or changes in income or employment status.

The possibility of exposure to multiple stressors in families chosen as "at risk" because of a single stressor suggests a need to assess contextual stress, even in research on single stressors, in such a way as to be able to capture and analyze the relations among and effects of a variety of stressors. From this perspective, the life events literature and the research on single stressors converge on the need to develop measurements of contextual stress that are wide-ranging enough to have adequate face and content validity and that also acknowledge the multidimensional nature of contextual stress. The use of life events scales as a basis for forming subscales representative of specific stressors may be useful in this regard, because this approach allows the researcher to sample many different types of contextual stress and also examine the many ways in which events may be classified and related to one another and to criterion variables (Herzog, 1985).

Recent investigations have shown promise in beginning to establish a more solid empirical base for the roles that contextual stresses may play in child development by using a risk research design and measuring stress using life events scale total scores. Maternal and/or child stresses have been related to changes in attachment classification (Egeland & Farber, 1984), child maltreatment (Pianta et al., 1989), and children's academic and behavioral outcomes in school (Garmezy et al., 1984; Lewis, Feiring, McGuffog, & Jaskir, 1984). These studies have not attempted to measure or analyze the effects of specific stressors. Data presented in a later section of this chapter address this issue by using measures of specific stressors derived from life events scales to predict developmental outcomes within a risk research design.

Risk research, life events, and protective factors

Accounting for deflections in development both away from and toward competence has been a major focus of risk research, although historically interest has been focused toward those factors accounting for deflections away from competence. Protective factors have, until recently, received less attention, despite their potential to facilitate efforts directed at primary prevention of nonoptimal outcomes (Garmezy, 1984; Rutter, 1979, 1983; Sroufe & Rutter, 1984). In a recent summary of the literature, Garmezy (1984) identified three factors that appear to differentiate between competent and incompetent children within highly stressful environments across a wide range of investigations: personal characteristics of the child, a relationship with a warm, empathic adult, and a social environment that reinforces and supports the child's coping efforts. This suggests that attempts to identify protective factors must take into account individual child characteristics, including previous developmental history, the characteristics of parents and parent–child relationships, and larger, system variables such as the support available for parents in the social network.

The Mother–Child Interaction Research Project has been specifically designed to address many of the issues involved in studying the effects of contextual risk, stress, and protective factors. By means of a risk research design, data have been collected periodically on approximately 200 families in the areas of child competence and development since birth, parental characteristics (including personality and intelligence), maternal and family life events, and characteristics of parent–child interaction and the social network. As such, the Mother–Child Project provides an oppportunity to examine a number of aspects of the relations among contextual stress, protective factors, and development. Our purpose in the following sections of this chapter is to present project data to address three questions related to issues identified in these introductory sections:

1. Within a sample selected for economic disadvantage, are there significant relations among specific types of stressful maternal experiences?
2. To what extent do specific types of stressful maternal experiences predict children's school outcomes?
3. Among children of mothers experiencing high levels of stress, are there factors that differentiate developmental paths toward and away from competence?

Method

Subjects

Our subjects were 133 mothers and their firstborn children selected from primiparous women seen for prenatal care at the Minneapolis Public Health Clinic and considered to be at risk for caretaking problems by virtue of their disadvantaged economic status. In addition to low socioeconomic status, the risk factors included low educational level (41% had not completed high school), age ($X = 20.5$ range $= 12$–34), lack of support (62% single at the time of the baby's birth), generally unstable living conditions, and what appeared to be exposure to a variety of environmental stressors. Eighty-six percent of the pregnancies were unplanned. The racial and ethnic composition of the sample was 80% white, 13% black, and 7% Hispanic or Native American. Fifteen percent of the children were of mixed racial background. By the time the children had reached the second grade, approximately 40% had been identified for some form of special education or mental health services.

Measures and procedures

Measurement of and relations among specific stressors. Maternal stress was assessed using a scale adapted from Cochrane and Robertson (1973) for use with this specific population (Egeland & Deinard, 1975). The adaptation process involved addition of items and rewriting of items to capture stressors specific to a low income population. This scale was used to assess life stress at 54 and 64 months and in the summer following the first grade. The data in this chapter are based on maternal stress assessed at 54 and 64 months and in the summer following the first grade. These data were composited by summing item scores across these three time periods to form a measure of maternal stress in the 2 years prior to the child's year in the first grade.

The procedure for collecting the maternal stress data involved a semistructured interview with each mother covering the 39 items on the scale. The interviewer asked if a particular event or condition had occurred since the previous assessment or was ongoing at the time. The interviewer then elicited the mother's feelings about the experience and the extent to which it had had an effect on family functioning. This allowed the mother to elaborate on each item and enabled us to make certain judgments about her subjective experiences.

Each Life Events Scale (LES) item was scored on a 3-point scale reflecting the extent to which the experience was disruptive to family functioning (Egeland et al., 1980). The rating of disruptiveness was based on both the frequency of occurrence of the item since the previous assessment and the extent to which it involved a person with whom the mother shared a close relationship. A close relationship was defined as one that the mother shared with an immediate family member (e.g., a child, husband, boyfriend) or someone on whom the mother was financially or emotionally dependent (e.g., a close friend, parents, siblings). Interviewers were instructed to use probing and follow-up questions to gather the information necessary to make the rating of disruptiveness. The reliability of this scoring technique was established by determining interrater agreement across several raters for the ratings done at each assessment period. Raters must have achieved a minimum interrater agreement of .85 during training, and the average interrater agreement obtained after the scales were scored was .86.

Two types of procedures (empirical and rational) were used to derive subscales from the 39-item scale. Using a factor analysis of the composited 39-item scale (Pianta, 1986), 27 items were chosen with loadings of greater than .30 on the large first factor. These items represented a less diverse range of experiences than the entire 39-item scale, but were still somewhat heterogeneous in content. Because these items appeared to assess stressful experiences in the mothers' interpersonal relationships, the subscale formed from summing the scores of these items was named the Personal Stress subscale. The items forming the Personal Stress subscale were further subdivided on a rational/theoretical basis to assess more specific or content-homogeneous stressors. These subscales included Family Relationship Transitions, Family Violence, and Chemical Dependency. These rationally derived subscales were nonoverlapping with each other.

The Family Relationship Transitions subscale was a 12-item subscale representative of a range of family entrance and exit events: gain of a new family member, period of homelessness, miscarriage, abortion, pregnancy, marriage, boyfriend/husband moving in or out, other people moving in or out, marital separation, divorce, reconciliation, and separation of mother and child. This subscale provided a measure of family stability and structure. Family violence experienced by the mother was measured by the 2-item Family Violence subscale indicating the mothers' involvement in physical fights and receiving threats. Chemical Dependence was a 2-item subscale that measured alcohol and drug abuse in the mother's extended family and immediate family. Scores for these subscales were obtained by summing a subject's scores on the items composing a particular subscale.

Correlations were computed among these subscales in an effort to address the first research question regarding the need to assess the relations among diverse stressors within a high-risk population.

Prediction of school outcomes from specific maternal stressors. Children's first-grade outcomes were assessed in the academic/cognitive and socioemotional/behavioral domains. Socioemotional and behavioral functioning was assessed by the Internalizing, Externalizing, and Total scores from the Child Behavior Checklist – Teacher report form (CBC-T) (Achenbach & Edelbrock, 1980). Teachers were also asked to fill out Teachers' Ratings of Cognitive Competence

(TRCC), which is the teacher report analogue to the Perceived Competence Scale for Children (Harter, 1982). The Total score from the Peabody Individual Achievement Test (PIAT) (Dunn & Markwardt, 1971) was used as an independent, standardized measure of the child's academic and cognitive competence.

The second research question noted earlier involves the extent to which first-grade outcomes were predicted by the more heterogeneous Personal Stress subscale and the set of three rationally derived content-homogeneous subscales. Multiple regression procedures were used to investigate this question. There were two sets of multiple regression analyses for each sex. In each set of analyses, mother IQ and child IQ, as assessed by the Wechsler Adult Intelligence Scale (WAIS) and Wechsler Preschool and Primary Scale of Intelligence (WPPSI), were entered into the equation first in order to control for individual differences in outcomes that might be due to intelligence. The next regression step corresponded to the content homogeneity of the subscale. In the first set of analyses, the Personal Stress subscale was entered in the second step in order to determine the predictive validity of an empirically derived, more heterogeneous measure of stress. In the second set of analyses, the three content subscales were entered stepwise, after mother IQ and child IQ, in order to examine the possibility that rationally derived measures of specific content-homogeneous stressors would account for unique variance in outcomes.

Comparisons of competent and incompetent children of highly stressed mothers. The third research question noted earlier involves the identification of factors that lead to competent development under conditions of significant risk. The analyses designed to address this question were somewhat dependent on the results of the first two phases of this investigation and therefore will be described in detail following presentation of the relevant preliminary results.

Results

Relations among separate stressors in a high-risk sample

Correlations were calculated separately for boys and girls for the relations among the maternal stress subscales. For mothers of boys, there was a strong correlation between Family Violence and Chemical Dependence ($r = .57$, $p < .05$) and a moderate relations between Family Violence and Family Relationship Transitions ($r = .27$, $p < .05$). There was not a significant relations between Chemical Dependence and Family Relationship Transitions for mothers of boys ($r = .15$). All three specific subscales shared items with the Personal Stress subscale; so, not surprisingly, all three were significantly correlated with it for mothers of both boys and girls. For mothers of girls, among the rationally derived subscales, Family Relationship Transitions was significantly correlated with both Family Violence ($r = .41$, $p < .05$) and

Table 10.1. *Summary of regressions of Grade 1 outcomes on maternal stress subscales and mother and child IQs for boys (N = 57)*

Scale	Internalizing[a] β	ΔR²	Externalizing β	ΔR²	Total β	ΔR²	PIAT β	ΔR²	TRCC β	ΔR²
Set 1										
WAIS	.30		.26		.31		.07		−.25	
WPPSI	−.40	.18**	−.44	.19**	−.45	.20**	.67	.47**	.58	.31**
Set 2										
Personal Stress	.13	ns	.33	.11*	.30	.09*	−.07	ns	−.17	ns
Family Violence	—[b]	—[b]	.28	.08*	.24	.06*	—[b]	—[b]	−.27	.07*
Chemical Dependence	—	—	−.01	ns	−.03	ns	—	—	.02	ns
Family Relationship Transitions	—	—	.11	ns	.07	ns	—	—	−.08	ns

*p < .05; **p < .01.
[a]Figures reported are β and change in R^2.
[b]No variables entered.

Chemical Dependence ($r = .31, p < .05$), and Family Violence and Chemical Dependence were also correlated ($r = .43, p < .05$). These results suggest that in this low-income sample there were relations of only moderate degrees among different stressors. This finding supports a point made earlier regarding the possibility of multiple stress experiences in families chosen as "at risk," and it suggests a need for further research to identify linkages and possible potentiating relations (Rutter, 1979) among stressful experiences in these families.

Predicting school outcomes from maternal life events scales

As noted earlier, the second question addressed by this research involves the extent to which measures of different stressors derived from life events scales can be used to predict children's school outcomes. Table 10.1 summarizes the results of the regression of outcomes on the different subscales derived from the maternal life events scale. The data presented above as Set 1 in Table 10.1 are the results of regressing the outcomes on maternal IQ and child IQ. Set 2 (Personal Stress) is a summary of the results of adding the Personal Stress subscale to the equation after accounting for maternal IQ and child IQ. The remainder of Set 2 is a summary of stepwise entry of the three rationally derived, content-specific subscales after maternal IQ and child IQ were accounted for. The results are presented in the same format for girls in Table 10.2.

Table 10.2. *Summary of regressions of Grade 1 outcomes on maternal stress subscales and mother and child IQs for girls (N = 70)*

Scale	Internalizing[a] β	ΔR^2	Externalizing β	ΔR^2	Total β	ΔR^2	PIAT β	ΔR^2	TRCC β	ΔR^2
Set 1										
WAIS	−.01		−.06		.00		.02		.12	
WPPSI	−.16	.03	−.11	.02	−.14	.02	.65	.43**	.45	.27**
Set 2										
Personal Stress	.24	.05*	.28	.08*	.20	ns	−.10	ns	−.30	.08**
Family Violence	−.04	ns	—[b]	—[b]	—[b]	—[b]	—[b]	—[b]	−.05	ns
Chemical Dependence	.07	ns	—	—	—	—	—	—	−.01	ns
Family Relationship Transitions	.30	.09**	—	—	—	—	—	—	−.30	.08**

*p < .05; **p < .01.
[a]Figures reported are β and change in R^2.
[b]No variables entered.

As indicated in Table 10.1, Personal Stress was predictive of outcomes in the socioemotional/behavioral domain for boys, even after accounting for maternal IQ and child IQ. Mothers' Personal Stress accounted for 11% of the variance in boys' Externalizing scores and 9% of their CBC Total scores. Within the set of rationally derived, content-specific subscales, Family Violence was the only significant predictor of boys' first-grade outcomes. Using stepwise entry, Family Violence was the first subscale entered into the equation after maternal IQ and child IQ were entered on a previous step and accounted for 8% of the variance in the boy's Externalizing scores, 6% in their CBC Total scores, and 7% in the TRCC.

The results for girls are presented in Table 10.2. The empirically derived measure of mothers' Personal Stress accounted for 5% of the variance in the girls' Internalizing scores, 8% in their Externalizing scores, and 8% in the TRCC. For the set of rationally derived, content-specific subscales entered stepwise, Family Relationship Transitions accounted for 9% of the variance in the girls' Internalizing scores and 8% in the cognitive competence rating. As for the boys, no additional rationally derived subscales were entered into the equation.

These results suggest that for boys and girls in this low-income sample, an empirically derived, somewhat heterogeneous measure of maternal stress in interpersonal relationships was a potentially important predictor of socioemotional/behavioral outcomes and was also predictive of ratings of girls' cognitive competence by their classroom teachers. The rationally derived measures of specific stressors did not appear to be independent enough of one another to result in each accounting for unique variance in outcomes; so the subscale with the highest correlation with the outcomes was the first and only rationally derived scale to be entered for both boys and girls. Interestingly, the single rationally derived scale that was a significant predictor was different for boys and girls. These results may suggest a very tentative hypothesis that when measures of specific stressors are used, boys and girls may be differentially vulnerable to different types of maternal stresses. Otherwise, the broader, more heterogeneous measure of maternal stress appeared to be as useful for predicting boys' outcomes as it was for girls, with the interresting corollary finding that maternal stress did appear to affect teachers' perceptions of girls' classroom performances, but was not predictive of their scores on a standardized achievement test.

We then attempted to address the third research question noted earlier, namely, whether or not factors could be identified that would differentiate between competent and incompetent children from within a group of families in which the mothers were highly stressed.

Competence for children exposed to high stress: protective factors

Clearly, not all of the children exposed to high levels of maternal stress in the preschool period were functioning in an incompetent fashion in school; the range of outcomes appeared large. In the following section we present analyses used to determine why some children exposed to high levels of maternal stress were functioning competently. Specifically, we addressed the question of what child or parent characteristics, parent–child interaction patterns, or life circumstances "protected" children from the negative effects of stress. To answer this question, the children were divided at the median on their mothers' Personal Stress scores, because that measure appeared to be a useful predictor for both boys and girls but was also sufficiently general to encompass a wide range of experiences and outcomes. Children in the top half of the Personal Stress distribution were then divided into competent and incompetent groups based on CBC-T ratings obtained in kindergarten and the first and second grades.

Identification of competence groups. Competence groups were derived using hierarchical cluster analyses on the CBC-T factor profile scores for each sex at each grade level. These analyses resulted in patterns of scores that were common for different groups of boys and girls at each grade level, identifying groups of children labeled as clearly competent, average, or clearly incompetent on the basis of their patterns of factor scores determined by the clustering procedure. For each grade and sex, a three-, four-, or five-group cluster solution best fit the data. Each solution resulted in identification of one group that was clearly competent and another that was clearly incompetent. The remaining groups in each cluster solution were classified as average. For each grade level, children were assigned competence scores depending on the cluster group in which they were classified. They received a score of 1 if they fell into the incompetent group, 2 if in the average group, and 3 if in the competent group. The scores were summed across the three grade levels for each child. Scores ranged from a high of 9 to a low of 3. Children who received a 7 or higher were placed in the competent group, those with scores below 7 were classified as less competent. There were 17 competent boys and 17 less competent boys and 18 competent girls and 13 less competent girls who had been exposed to high levels of maternal life stresses during the preschool years.

Measures used to compare competent and less competent groups. The competent and less competent groups were compared on the following variables:

1. Maternal characteristics: mother's age, education, and personality characteristics. The mother's IQ was assessed using the Comprehension, Block Design, and Similarities subtests of the WAIS, which was administered at the 48-month assessment. The mother's personality was assessed using the Form E of the 16PF (Cattell, Eber, & Tatsuoka, 1976). The items are forced-choice and arc intended to assess pathological rather than normal aspects of a subject's personality.

2. Child characteristics: language skills, IQ, and ability to cope with frustration. At 42 months, the child was given the Zimmerman Preschool Language Scale (Zimmerman, Steiner, & Pond, 1979), which is an age scale yielding an auditory comprehension and verbal ability score. To assess intelligence, four subtests of the WPPSI were administered (Vocabulary, Comprehension, Block Design, and Animal House) to the child at 64 months. The measure of frustration tolerance and self-control consisted of observing the child in a barrier-box situation (Harrington, Block, & Block, 1978). This situation involved allowing a child to play with attractive toys, then removing the toys and telling the child that she or he could play with similar toys that were in a locked plexiglass box. The child was rated on 11 scales, including self-esteem, ego control, withdrawal, flexibility, dependence, and positive and negative affect.

3. Mother–child interaction: At 42 months the mother and child were observed in a series of teaching tasks. The four tasks included building copies of a block tower from a set of smaller blocks, the mother asking the child to name as many objects as possible that have wheels, a matrix sorting task requiring the child to sort chips according to size, color, and form, and the mother asking the child to trace a pattern drawn on the screen of an Etch-A-Sketch. The mothers were rated on six 7-point scales: supportive presence, respect for autonomy, structure and limit setting, hostility, quality of instruction, and confidence. The children were rated on persistence, enthusiasm, negativity expressed to mother, compliance, experience in the session, reliance on the mother, affection for the mother, and avoidance of the mother.

4. Mother's relationship status: At each assessment (12, 18, 24, 30, 42, 48, 54, and 64 months and first grade), the status of the mother's relationship with

husband or boyfriend was determined. For those mothers involved with a male, the relationship was judged as stable (consistent and ongoing) or unstable (separations and transient relationships) on the basis of interview questions. The mother also reported the degree of her satisfaction with the relationship and whether or not she was being abused by her husband/boyfriend.

5. Quality of organization and stimulation in the home environment: During the first-grade visit, observers completed the Home Observation for Measurement of the Environment (HOME) (Caldwell & Bradley, 1984). This inventory is designed to sample aspects of the quality and quantity of social, emotional, and cognitive support available to the child in the home. The nine scales include organization of a stable and predictable environment, developmental stimulation, quality of language support, responsiveness and avoidance of restrictions, fostering maturity and independence, emotional climate, breadth of experience, aspects of the physical environment, and provision of play material.

Comparisons between the competent and less competent children who were exposed to high levels of maternal stress resulted in significant differences on a number of variables. These results are presented in Table 10.3 for boys and Table 10.4 for girls.

Results of comparing competent and less competent groups. Competent boys of mothers who experienced high levels of stress had better auditory comprehension and overall language ability and were more intelligent than the less competent sons of highly stressed mothers. Differences were found on the Animal House and Block Design subtests and total score on the WPPSI. These high-stress boys classified as competent in school also had a history of competence as judged by their functioning on the barrier-box and teaching tasks at 42 months. These boys displayed more positive affect and were more creative in dealing with the frustration of the barrier-box task than their less competent peers. In the teaching situation, the less competent group lacked persistence, enthusiasm, and affection for their mothers, displayed more negative affect, and were avoidant of their mothers. The experience in the teaching tasks was basically a negative one for the less competent boys. The highly stressed mothers of the competent boys were more emotionally responsive and supportive than were mothers of less competent boys. Highly stressed mothers of less competent boys had a history of poor functioning with their sons, as evidenced by their lack of respect for autonomy, poorer quality of instruction, and lack of structure and limit setting.

There were no differences between the two groups of boys in terms of the percentage from intact families. However, the overall quality of the relationships reported by the highly stressed mothers was more satisfying for mothers of competent boys (59% satisfied) than for those from the less competent group (35% satisfied). The high-stress mothers of competent boys were also less likely to be in abusive relationships (18% abused) than were mothers of less competent boys (35% abused).

Table 10.3. *Protective factors: differences between competent and less competent boys of mothers experiencing high stress in preschool period*

Factor	Less compe-tent (n = 17)	Competent (n = 17)	t	p
Child characteristics				
Zimmerman language, 42 months				
Auditory comprehension	96.19 (16.36)	115.40 (16.42)	−3.26	.003
Language ability	98.20 (19.70)	114.33 (17.72)	−2.36	.026
Barrier box, 42 months				
Creativity	1.94 (1.12)	2.81 (1.17)	−2.16	.039
Positive affect	2.50 (0.89)	3.25 (0.93)	−2.32	.027
Quality of the home environment				
HOME: Grade 1				
Total	58.71 (13.54)	69.29 (8.62)	−2.64	.011
Organization	2.76 (1.72)	4.24 (1.44)	−2.71	.011
Stimulation	6.12 (2.62)	7.88 (0.83)	−2.28	.030
Emotional climate	6.58 (1.81)	8.12 (1.50)	−2.69	.011
Physical environment	11.07 (3.38)	13.88 (1.50)	−2.64	.017
Content characteristics				
Emotional support of mother, 42 months	3.53 (1.13)	4.47 (1.42)	−2.14	.040
Characteristics of mother–child interaction				
Teaching task, 42 months, mother ratings				
Supportive presence	8.35 (3.32)	10.35 (1.94)	−2.15	.041
Structure & limits	8.18 (2.72)	10.00 (2.42)	−2.06	.047
Respect for autonomy	8.59 (2.85)	10.53 (1.42)	−2.51	.019
Quality of instruction	8.53 (3.11)	10.76 (1.20)	−2.77	.012
Teaching task: child ratings				
Persistence	7.24 (2.86)	9.12 (1.58)	−2.38	.026
Enthusiasm	6.59 (2.83)	8.76 (1.92)	−2.62	.013
Negativity	5.24 (3.70)	2.88 (1.22)	2.49	.022
Experience in session	7.18 (3.30)	9.29 (1.57)	−2.39	.026
Affection for mother	6.29 (3.10)	8.47 (2.65)	−2.20	.035
Avoidance of mother	5.18 (3.80)	3.00 (1.37)	2.22	.038
Maternal characteristics				
No significant differences				

Note: Groups compared on all variables described in the section on methods; only significant results reported.

Mothers of competent boys were also able to provide a structured, organized environment for their children. The homes of the competent boys were judged to be more stimulating, better organized, and emotionally "warmer" than the homes of the less competent boys. These groups also differed on the appropriateness of the physical environment and the total HOME score.

It appeared that despite experiencing high levels of interpersonal stress, there was a subset of mothers who were able to support their children both emotionally and through providing structure; it was these boys who were later

Table 10.4. *Protective factors: differences between competent and less competent girls of mothers experiencing high stress in the preschool period*

Factor	Less competent ($n = 13$)		Competent ($n = 18$)		t	p
Child characteristics						
Zimmerman language, 42 months						
Verbal ability	99.08	(19.09)	115.00	(20.54)	−2.11	.044
Barrier box, 42 months						
Ego control	2.31	(1.11)	3.83	(1.62)	−2.93	.007
Creativity	1.54	(0.87)	2.44	(1.38)	−2.08	.047
Help seeking	4.62	(1.33)	3.28	(1.45)	2.63	.014
Negative affect	3.15	(1.63)	1.72	(1.41)	2.62	.014
WPPSI, 64 months						
Vocabulary	8.85	(3.31)	11.11	(2.98)	−1.99	.056
Animal House	10.00	(2.55)	11.72	(2.22)	−2.00	.054
Quality of the home environment						
HOME: Grade 1						
Foster independence	11.08	(2.75)	12.87	(1.89)	−2.03	.053
Emotional climate	6.38	(2.18)	7.75	(1.13)	−2.18	.038
Content characteristics						
Emotional support of mother, 42 months	3.08	(1.19)	3.94	(1.16)	−2.03	.051
Characteristics of mother–child interaction						
No significant differences						
Maternal characteristics						
Education at child's birth	10.31	(.95)	12.11	(1.84)	−3.55	.001
WAIS 3-subtest total	26.62	(5.59)	32.94	(6.44)	−2.82	.009
16 PF						
Ego strength	4.54	(1.56)	5.94	(1.48)	−2.46	.021
Enthusiastic	5.38	(1.56)	6.63	(1.75)	−2.00	.056
Venturesome	4.62	(2.26)	6.63	(1.89)	−2.61	.015
Apprehensive	6.38	(1.50)	4.38	(2.36)	2.66	.013
Tense	7.92	(2.50)	6.00	(1.97)	2.32	.028
Group-dependent	6.08	(2.14)	4.00	(1.71)	2.91	.007

classified as competent in school. These mothers also tended to be involved in satisfying relationships with men. In turn, their sons developed competently; they had a history of competent functioning as early as 3.5 years that appeared to continue on into the first grade. These competent boys of highly stressed mothers were also relatively intelligent and had good communicative skills prior to school entry. Generally these boys appeared better suited for adaptive functioning prior to school entry, an impression borne out by their competence in school.

The comparisons between the competent and less competent girls of mothers who experienced high levels of personal stress are presented in Table 10.4. The factors that were associated with school competence for girls were quite different from those associated with boys' competence.

The characteristics of mothers were important protective factors for girls. Compared with the mothers of the less competent group, highly stressed mothers of girls classified as competent in school were better educated, more intelligent, and differed on a number of personality variables. Comparisons on the 16PF scales indicated that highly stressed mothers of competent girls were emotionally more mature and stable, enthusiastic and cheerful, adventurous, self-confident, relaxed, and self-sufficient. In general, these mothers appeared to be characterized by positive affect, good social skills, and a sense of positive self-esteem, despite their stressful experiences, whereas the mothers of the less competent girls were characterized as anxious, restricted, depressed, and socially restrained.

Language and intelligence were also protective factors for girls of high-stress mothers. Competent girls obtained higher scores on the Verbal Ability scale of the Zimmerman and tended to score higher on the Vocabulary and Animal House subtests of the WPPSI. In response to the frustration of the barrier-box tasks, girls who were competent in the first grade displayed better self-control, more creativity, and less negative affect and help seeking than did the girls later identified as less competent. Surprisingly, there were no differences between the competent and less competent groups on any of the mother or child ratings during the teaching tasks.

Highly stressed mothers of competent girls also provided a higher quality of environment within their homes. Homes of competent daughters of highly stressed mothers were rated as fostering more independence and providing a better emotional climate than were the homes of girls classified as less competent in school.

There were no differences between the two competence groups of girls regarding factors related to the mothers' relationships with their husbands/boyfriends.

In contrast to the protective factors identified for the boys, those identified for the girls appeared to have more to do with the characteristics of their highly stressed mothers than with factors associated with parent–child interaction or the quality of the home environment, which were the important protective factors for boys. These points will be addressed in more detail in the following section.

Discussion

In this section we discuss the findings that address the three issues outlined earlier: the overlap among stressful experiences within an economically disadvantaged sample, the extent to which different measures of maternal stress predict children's school outcomes, and the identification of factors distinguishing between competent and less competent children within a high-stress subsample.

Measuring contextual stress

As noted at the beginning of this chapter, measurement and methodological issues pervade research on contextual stress, especially the life events literature (Goldberger & Breznitz, 1982). Our research has addressed these issues by using a life events scale with items representative of the life experiences of the subjects, deriving content subscales as a means of examining relationships among, and prediction by, measures of specific stressors, and using a multivariate prospective research design.

The use of life events scales as a basis for measuring specific stressors breaks with the life events research paradigm, which considers stress to be a nonspecific entity subsuming any and all experiences requiring coping or adaptation, however broadly defined these may be (Dohrenwend & Dohrenwend, 1974). An important conceptual and methodological issue addressed by our research involves overlapping and shared variance among stressors in populations identified on the basis of some broad risk factor such as socioeconomic status (or even personal stress). We have presented data indicating that there are significant relations between specific stressors (e.g., family violence and chemical dependence) within our low-income sample. With regard to prediction, such overlap could lead to considerable empirical and theoretical confusion if not examined. Our research has addressed the collinearity issue through the use of stepwise regression. The findings from those analyses indicated that, at least empirically, measures of separate stressors did little to increase the amount of outcome variance accounted for, because it was perhaps the variance shared by the stress measures that was also the predicted outcome variance. These results could be used in support of an argument for the use of general, heterogeneous measures of stress (total scores); however, there is an alternative approach to conceptualizing and analyzing these relationships among specific stressors.

This alternative approach to conceptualizing and analyzing the issue of stressor overlap might involve assessing the extent to which some stressors (e.g., violence) "cause" or lead to other stressors (e.g., divorce or separation). For example, the results presented earlier suggest relationships among family violence, chemical dependence, and changes in family relations. Analysis of the causal hierarchy among stressors and the factors that serve to break causal chains among stressors (i.e., protective factors) may be highly useful in understanding and treating families with multiple stresses. This approach would emphasize specification of stressors, and relations among specific stressors would be viewed as a relevant and researchable domain, as opposed to a nuisance that must be controlled.

Measuring contextual stress by identifying specific stressors has led to results that suggest linkages between coherent subsets of maternal experiences and child outcomes. This is helpful from the perspective of generating testable hypotheses about cause and consequence; otherwise, the use of a total score makes it difficult to comprehend the meaning of significant relationships because the total score is so heterogeneous (Perkins, 1982; Rutter, 1983). For example, the finding that interpersonal stresses on mothers were predictive of children's school outcomes was a consequence of measuring a specific type of stress. Interestingly, when we measured stress at a level of even greater specificity using the rationally derived subscales, relations between types of stressors and outcomes were obtained that were gender-related.

The predictive validity of interpersonal stresses could be explained by the possibility that this class of events taxed mothers' emotional and psychological resources to the extent that they were less able to provide appropriate care for their children. Similar hypotheses have been suggested for divorce as a stressor (Bloom, Asher, & White, 1978; Hetherington, 1979). An alternative hypothesis for the interpersonal stress–outcome relation may be that some stressors that were part of the Personal Stress subscale (e.g., violence, separation) affected children's competences directly, whether through internal psychological processes such as anxiety or through a process of observational learning (Straus, 1983). In the case of either possible explanation, prior specification of stressors can assist in a clearer conceptualization of the processes underlying the predictive relation by identifying a class of events that could meaningfully fit into existing theories of development in a way that general, nonspecific notions of stress cannot.

Competence in children of highly stressed mothers

Our findings comparing competent and less competent children of highly stressed mothers support Garmezy's identification (1984) of three types of protective factors. We identified protective factors having to do with child characteristics, such as intelligence, environmental support (as indicated by the HOME), positive relationships with adults (as measured by mother–child interaction), and personal characteristics of mothers. Boys' competence seemed to be especially related to characteristics of the home environment and mother–child interaction, whereas girls' competence was distinguished by characteristics of mothers. The roles of child characteristics, environmental support, and mother–child relationships as protective factors will be the focus of the following discussion.

Child characteristics and environmental support. One set of factors distinguishing the competent and less competent children included the characteristics of the children themselves. Both boys and girls classified as competent in school had a history of prior competence as early as 42 months. This suggests that the child has a role as an active agent in the coping process. Also, the results of the comparisons between the competent and less competent children supported the view that environmental support was an important part of producing competence under stress. The relative contributions of endogenous and environmental influences on children's coping skills have implications for the goals and methods of early intervention and prevention efforts based on risk research in light of the fact that developmental history is itself a product of a dynamic relation between the child and the environment. Interestingly, our data suggested that the nature of protective environmental support was different for boys and girls.

For example, the quality of direct environmental support for learning coping skills appeared most salient for boys' competence, as evidenced in the findings that HOME measures and the ratings of mother–son interaction distinguished the competence groups. For girls, it appeared to be the case that maternal characteristics were the predominant features distinguishing competent development under stress. For boys, these environmental protective factors were related to actively facilitating competence and coping skills. "Protective" environments for boys were structured, organized, emotionally supportive, and distinguished by good teaching by mothers.

For girls, it appeared that it was not as important for them to be provided with such active environmental support in order to develop competently within a stressful household. This could have been due to resilience related to endogenous child characteristics, as noted earlier, or to cultural expectations that might have influenced whether or not coping skills were taught to girls. In any case, it appeared important for the mothers of girls to have a set of positive social and problem-solving characteristics that might be effective in buffering or shielding the girls from stress, in a manner that was not the same for boys, or that could be transmitted to the girls through some process of identification or observational learning and thereby become a part of the girls' repertoire of coping skills. Aspects of the relationship between the child and the caregiver that might mediate or produce protective influences will be discussed in the following section.

Child–caregiver relationships and protective factors. Our data indicate that among a group of mothers who experienced large amounts of personal stress, there were differences in competence among their children that were related to both the sex of the child and factors that had to do with the quality of the mother–child relationship and maternal characteristics. The consistent variable across these sets of measures was the mother. Therefore, it may be useful to look for explanations of these findings by examining the nature of the relationships between these mothers and their daughters and sons.

We identified the group of high-stress mothers for the competence group comparisons on the basis of their scores on the Personal Stress subscale.

Because that subscale contained a majority of items having to do with experiences with men (e.g., violence, separations, conflict), it is reasonable to assume that high scores on that index were reflective of dysfunctional relationships with males. For mothers of boys, relationships with males provided both a source of stress and a pattern for caregiving. From the perspective of an internal working model (Bowlby, 1980; Sroufe & Fleeson, 1986), it is plausible that mothers' beliefs and feelings about their relationships with men might be manifest in their interactions, as caregivers, with their sons (Pianta, Egeland, & Hyatt, 1986). This link between internal working models and caretaking behaviors may also be influenced by the complexity of the mother's understanding of the caretaking process (Newberger & Cook, 1983; Sameroff & Feil, 1985). Providing the types of environments that led to boys' competence, when the mothers were stressed by relationships with males, may have been influenced by the extent to which the mothers could differentiate their attitudes and feelings about their sons from their experiences in relationships with men.

From the perspective of an internal working model, it was not surprising to find that a girl's competent development was related to the personal characteristics of the mother and a home environment that was emotionally warm and fostered independence. Because there was no gender similarity between the source of stress and the object of caregiving, there may have been less of a tendency for mothers to interact with their daughters in a manner that validates internal models influenced by relationships with men. In this way, the gender difference between the source of stress and the object of caretaking facilitates a mother's efforts to keep attitudes and feelings about these relationships separate. Conversely, the girls' internal models would be strongly influenced by what they observed and experienced with their mothers. Therefore, in addition to being exposed to home environments that were emotionally warm and encouraged independence, the competent girls may also have internalized their mothers' positive personal characteristics.

Conclusion

Despite the progress made by risk research in the areas of schizophrenia and other biologically related conditions in identifying the relationships between risk factors and outcomes (Watt et al., 1984; chapters 19 and 20 in this volume), research in the domain of contextual stress continues to struggle with issues of conceptualization and measurement of contextual stress and generation of empirically based explanatory models. The questions we posed at the beginning of this chapter reflect our effort to deal with these issues in a systematic fashion. We believe the results presented here indicate support for greater specificity in conceptualization and measurement of stress, provide evidence for the importance of prior developmental history in a risk/protective factors model, and suggest the extent to which factors related to competent development under stress are woven into the nature of child–environment and child–caregiver relationships.

References

Achenbach, T. M., & Edelbrock, C. S. (1980). *The Child Behavior Checklist: Teacher Report Form.* Burlington: University of Vermont Department of Psychiatry.

Bloom, B., Asher, S., & White, S. (1978). Marital disruption as a stressor. *Psychological Bulletin, 85,* 867–94.

Bowlby, J. (1980). *Loss.* New York: Basic Books.

Brown, G. W., & Harris, T. (1978). *Social origins of depression.* New York: Free Press.

Caldwell, E., & Bradley, R. (1984). *Home observation for measurement of the environment.* Little Rock: Center for Early Development and Education.

Cattell, R. B., Eber, H. W., & Tatsuoka, M. M. (1976). *Sixteen PF.* Champaign, IL: Institute for Personality and Ability Testing.

Cochrane, R., & Robertson, A. (1973). The life events inventory: A measure of the relative severity of psycho-social stressors. *Journal of Psychosomatic Research, 17,* 135–9.

Derogatis, L. (1982). Self report measure of stress. In L. Goldberger & S. Breznitz (Eds.), *Handbook of stress* (pp. 270–94). New York: Free Press.

Dorhenwend, B. S., & Dohrenwend, B. P. (1974). *Stressful life events: Their nature and effects.* New York: Wiley..

Dohrenwend, B. S., Krasnoff, L., Askensky, A., & Dohrenwend, B. P. (1982). The psychiatric epidemiology research interview life events scale. In L. Golberger & S. Breznitz (Eds.), *Handbook of stress* (pp. 320–31). New York: Free Press.

Dunn, L., & Markwardt, F. (1971). *The Peabody Individual Achievement Test.* Circle Pines, MN: American Guidance.

Egeland, B., Breitenbucher, M., & Rosenberg, D. (1980). Prospective study of the etiology of child abuse. *Journal of Consulting and Clinical Psychology, 48,* 195–205.

Egeland, B., & Deinard, A. (1975). *Life stress scale and manual.* Minneapolis: University of Minnesota.

Egeland, B., & Farber, E. (1984). Infant–mother attachment: Factors related to its development and changes over time. *Child Development, 55,* 753–71.

Erickson, M. F., Sroufe, L. A., & Egeland, B. (1985). The relationship between quality of attachment and behavior problems in preschool in a high risk sample. In I. Bretherton & E. Waters (Eds.), *Growing points of attachment theory and research. Monographs of the Society for Research in Child Development, 50,* 147–66.

Garmezy, N. (1977). On some risks in risk research. *Psychological Medicine, 7,* 1–6.

Garmezy, N. (1983). Stressors of childhood. In N. Garmezy & M. Rutter (Eds.), *Stress, coping and development* (pp. 43–84). New York: McGraw-Hill.

Garmezy, N. (1984). Stress-resistant children: The search for protective factors. In J. E. Stevenson (Ed.), *Aspects of current child psychiatry research* (*Journal of Child Psychology and Psychiatry* book supplement No. 4). Oxford: Pergamon Press.

Garmezy, N., Masten, A., & Tellegen, A. (1984). The study of stress and competence in children: A building block for developmental psychopathology. *Child Development, 55,* 97–111.

Goldberger, L., & Breznitz, S. (1982). *Handbook of stress.* New York: Free Press.

Harrington, D., Block, J. H., & Block, J. (1978). Intolerance of ambiguity in preschool children: Psychometric considerations, behavioral manifestations and parental correlates. *Developmental Psychology, 14,* 242–56.

Harter, S. (1982). The perceived competence scale for children. *Child Development, 53,* 87–97.

Herzog, J. (1985). *Life events as indices of family stress: Relationships with children's current levels of competence.* Unpublished doctoral dissertation, University of Minnesota.

Hetherington, E. M. (1979). Divorce: A child's perspective. *American Psychologist, 34,* 851–8.

Hetherington, E. M., Cox, M., & Cox, R. (1979). Family interaction and the social, emotional and cognitive development of children following divorce. In V. Vaughn & T. B. Brazelton (Eds.), *The family: Setting priorities.* New York: Science and Medicine.

Lewis, M., Feiring, C., McGuffog, C., & Jaskir, J. (1984). Predicting pathology in six-year-olds from early social relations. *Child Development, 55,* 123–36.

Newberger, C. M., & Cook, E. H. (1983). Parental awareness and child abuse: A cognitive developmental analysis of urban and rural samples. *American Journal of Ortho-psychiatry, 53,* 512–24.

Perkins, D. V. (1982). The assessment of stress using life events scales. In L. Goldberger & S. Breznitz (Eds.), *The handbook of stress* (pp. 320–31). New York: Free Press.

Pianta, R. (1986). *The longitudinal effects of maternal life stress on the developmental outcomes of first grade children in a high risk sample.* Unpublished doctoral dissertation, University of Minnesota.

Pianta, R., Egeland, B., & Erickson, M. (1989). The antecedents of child maltreatment: The results of the Mother–Child Interaction Research Project. In D. Cicchetti & V. Carlson (Eds.), *Child maltreatment: Research consequences and theoretical perspectives* (pp. 203–53). Cambridge University Press.

Pianta, R., Egeland, B., & Hyatt, A. (1986). Maternal relationship history as an indicator of developmental risk. *American Journal of Orthopsychiatry, 56,* 385–98.

Rabkin, J., & Streuning, E. (1976). Life events, stress and illness. *Science, 194,* 1013–20.

Rutter, M. (1979). Protective factors in children's responses to stress and disadvantage. In M. Kent & J. Rolf (Eds.), *Primary prevention of psychopathology: Social competence in children* (pp. 49–74). Hanover, NH: University Press of New England.

Rutter, M. (1983). Stress, coping and development: Some issues and some questions. In N. Garmezy & M. Rutter (Eds.), *Stress, coping and development* (pp. 1–42). New York: McGraw-Hill.

Sameroff, A., & Feil, L. (1985). Parental concepts of development. In I. Sigel (Ed.), *Parental belief systems: The consequences for children* (pp. 83–105). Hillsdale, NJ: Erlbaum.

Skinner, H., & Lei, H. (1980). Differential weights in life change research: Useful or irrelevant? *Psychosomatic Medicine, 12,* 367–70.

Sroufe, L. A., & Fleeson, J. (1986). Attachment and the construction of relationships. In W. W. Hartup & Z. Rubin (Eds.), *Relationships and development* (pp. 51–72). Cambridge University Press.

Sroufe, L. A., & Rutter, M. (1984). The domain of developmental psychopathology. *Child Development, 55,* 17–29.

Straus, M. (1983). Ordinary violence, child abuse and wife beating: What do they have in common? In D. Finkelhor, R. Gelles, G. Hotaling, & M. Straus (Eds.), *The dark side of families: Current family violence research.* Beverly Hills, CA: Sage.

Wallerstein, J. (1983). Children of divorce. In N. Garmezy & M. Rutter (Eds.), *Stress, coping and development* (pp. 265–302). New York: McGraw-Hill.

Watt, N. F., Anthony, E. J., Wynne, L. C., & Rolf, J. (1984). *Children at risk: A longitudinal perspective.* Cambridge University Press.

Zimmerman, I., Steiner, G., & Pond, R. (1979). *Preschool Language Scale.* Columbus, OH: Charles E. Merrill.

11 Competence under stress: risk and protective factors

Ann S. Masten, Patricia Morison, David Pellegrini, and Auke Tellegen

Developmental psychopathology is finally gaining recognition as a viable interdisciplinary perspective, providing an impetus for sustained studies of risk and protective factors in childhood (Cicchetti, 1984; Masten & Braswell, in press; Sroufe & Rutter, 1984). It has taken the field over a decade to catch up with Norman Garmezy and a few other pioneering psychopathologists who recognized the need for a developmental perspective and the theoretical and clinical significance of studying adaptation in children vulnerable to psychopathology (Garmezy, 1970, 1973, 1974a,b).

Over the past two decades at the University of Minnesota, Garmezy has translated his interest in positive responses to high-risk conditions into a research program that has encompassed a variety of studies under the rubric of "Project Competence." These studies of adaptation have focused on normative samples as well as high-risk samples, including children at risk for maladaptation because of such factors as mental illness in a parent (see chapter 20, this volume), physical disability (Raison, 1982; Silverstein, 1982), and life-threatening birth defects (see chapter 6, this volume). Common to these diverse studies has been the focus on competence, correcting psychologists' traditional neglect of successful adaptation under adverse conditions (Garmezy, 1981; Garmezy & Devine, 1984; Garmezy & Tellegen, 1984).

The Project Competence studies of children were a natural outgrowth of Garmezy's earlier studies of schizophrenic adults that led him to an interest in premorbid competence (Garmezy & Rodnick, 1959; see chapter 22, this volume) and then to the study of adaptation in children at risk for schizophrenia (Garmezy, 1970, 1971). Garmezy participated in the consortium of risk researchers who undertook the first generation of high-risk studies in psychopathology, following the early lead of Fish, Mednick, and Schulsinger to study offspring of schizophrenic parents (Garmezy, 1974c,d).

The "Project Competence" work described here has been supported by grants from the National Institute for Mental Health (RO1-MH-33222), the William T. Grant Foundation, and the University of Minnesota Computer Center.

The goals, methodologies, successes, and even the predictive "failures" of high-risk studies (Watt, Anthony, Wynne, & Rolf, 1984) bore unanticipated fruit for developmental psychopathology in its infancy and for systematic studies of stress resistance in children. These high-risk studies inevitably led to longitudinal designs and to a concern with developmental changes in adaptation. Looking for early signs of psychopathology, most of these investigators found a wide range of individual differences in adaptation (although not necessarily related to risk for schizophrenia) that had a great deal to do with variations in socioeconomic status, adversity of rearing conditions, family stability, birth complications, intelligence, and so forth. Similarly, studies of infants with perinatal complications and the precursors of delinquency pointed to the importance of similar risk and protective factors (Garmezy, 1984; Masten & Garmezy, 1985).

During the past decade, Garmezy's Project Competence program turned to studies of a normative community sample in addition to specific risk populations. The purpose of these normative studies was to explore the apparent ability of some children to adapt very well in spite of highly disadvantageous life events. Gradually these studies became focused on the search for risk and protective factors for competence in middle childhood and adolescence, posing such questions as these:

· What are the characteristics of competent children, particularly those who have been exposed to stressful life circumstances?
· What are potential risk and protective factors that increase or reduce the negative effects of stress exposure?
· What are the long-term predictors of adaptation in adolescence from middle childhood?
· What are the implications for intervention?

These studies began by defining adaptation under adversity ("stress resistance") as the manifestation of competence in children despite exposure to stressful life circumstances. Consequently, two constructs had to be operationalized: stress exposure and competence. When the pilot studies and planning for these studies began more than a decade ago, there had been virtually no systematic studies predicting competence in middle childhood, and studies of stress in children were also few and far between. Given the paucity of empirical studies, careful attention was directed to measuring the two constructs. In many cases, measures had to be developed or revised for the study at hand, and then tested for reliability, stability, and validity.

The design of the community cohort studies has been described in more detail elsewhere (Garmezy, Masten, & Tellegen, 1984; Garmezy & Tellegen, 1984; Masten et al., 1988). The participants were recruited from two elementary schools in an urban Minneapolis community. Their socioeconomic backgrounds varied, but they were predominantly from lower- and middle-class

Table 11.1. *Project Competence community cohort: overview of procedures*

Year 1
Life events survey by mail: Life Events Questionnaire
Child competence assessment at school:
   Teacher ratings: Devereux Elementary School Behavior Rating Scale
   Peer ratings: Revised Class Play (Masten, Morison, & Pellegrini, 1985)
   Achievement: school record data
Parent interviews initiated: three 2-hr sessions (Linder, 1985)
   I. Family structure, history, activities, relationships
   II. Child's behavior, activities, relationships
   III. Contextual life events
   Developmental Questionnaire
   Home Rating Scales by interviewer
   Family Rating Scales by interviewer

Year 2
Stressful life events reassessed
Child competence at school reassessed:
   Teachers, peers, school records
   Peabody Individual Achievement Test (PIAT) (Dunn & Markwardt, 1970)
Child attributes measured:
   Intellectual ability
   Social cognition (Pellegrini, 1985)
   Humor (Masten, 1986)
   Divergent thinking (Masten, 1982)
   Reflectivity–impulsivity (Ferrarese, 1981)
Child interviews: 2 1-hr sessions (Finkelman, 1983; Morison, 1987)
   Topics: School, activities, friends, family, aspirations, plans, self-concept, life events

Follow-up study (7–8 years later)
In progress: adaptation in late adolescence

families. Twenty-eight percent of the final sample of children represented ethnic minorities, and 45% were from intact families.

An overview of the procedures is provided in Table 11.1. The study was initiated by sending a life event survey to all parents of third- to sixth-graders in two schools ($N = 610$). The Life Events Questionnaire (LEQ) was based on Coddington's revision (1972a,b) of the Holmes and Rahe (1967) method, and it provided a rapid and relatively objective count of recent life events. A negative life events score was compiled by a simple tally of 30 of the 50 events on the LEQ that were both negative and unlikely to be the result of the child's own behavior or competence (e.g., death of a parent, friend moved away). Fifty-nine percent of the parents returned the LEQ. These respondents were subsequently invited to participate in more extensive research activities.

Parents of the 205 children who eventually participated in the complete set of procedures were interviewed about the family (history, relationships, activities, social support, etc.) the target child (behavior, activities, relationships, response to discipline, etc.), and their life events. These interviews took place over three home visits. The final interview session was designed to make detailed inquiry about all the life events of the past 2 years, in an attempt to place the events in a more individually meaningful context (Linder, 1985).

Another perspective on stress exposure was provided by the interviewer, who at the conclusion of the home interviews rated the family on a 30-item set of scales designed to tap global clinical impressions of the family. Three of the items on the Family Rating Scales specifically concerned the interviewer's assessment of the level of family stress exposure.

The measurement of competence, defined in terms of effective functioning in important environments, required a developmental perspective (Waters & Sroufe, 1983). Measures had to be selected that would assess the qualities of functioning appropriate to the developmental level of the sample, in this case middle childhood. Garmezy (1973), following Whitehorn, described these tasks as the ability to work well, play well, and love well. In middle childhood these tasks included school adjustment, peer acceptance, and positive familiy relationships.

Measurement of competence in the school context was emphasized because of the importance of school in the lives of elementary school children. Multiple perspectives on child competence at school were obtained, including teacher ratings, peer ratings, classroom grades, and performance on standardized achievement tests.

One of the first goals of the community project was to identify the structure of competence. Competence was assumed to be multidimensional, and the different dimensions were expected to vary in salience with the sources of the information. Results from a factor analysis of schoolwide assessments of competence indicated that two dimensions based on ratings by teachers and peers at school were particularly salient, and these were named Engaged–Disengaged and Classroom Disruptiveness (Garmezy et al., 1984). The former dimension reflected the quality of involvement with peers and classroom activities, and the latter reflected reputation among peers and teachers as disruptive, aggressive, or oppositional. The correlation of these two competence dimensions was modest ($r = -.25$ in Year 1).

Academic achievement was deliberately maintained as a separate variable representing a distinct aspect of school competence, readily defined by grade point average and achievement on standardized tests, which were highly correlated. For the same school year, grade point average was moderately related to the Engaged dimension ($r = .56$ in Year 1) and modestly related to Disruptive ($r = -.30$).

Other measures, as well as information obtained from the interviews, were designed to assess potential modifiers of the relation of stress exposure to competence, in other words, to search for risk and protective factors. These included individual attributes such as intellectual ability, social cognition and humor, and environmental attributes such as socioeconomic status (SES) and family qualities.

Information from interviews with mothers provided two perspectives on family qualities. One consisted of the mothers' own responses to the questions posed. Answers to these questions were coded, and 28 family composite scores were formed through rational classification and factor analysis. The 28 composites included topics such as the extent of maternal social support, family mobility, and mother–child closeness. Two second-order composites were also derived, combining many items from these 28 composites, and these were named Family Stability/Organization and Family Cohesion. The former included items concerned with the mobility of the family, changes in marital status, and number of parental jobs, as well as the general adequacy of the home, including its appearance and maintenance. The latter included items concerned with the social involvements of the family, such as the quality of the mother–child relationship, amount of socializing with family and relatives, and discipline.

The second perspective on family qualities based on the interview came from the interviewers themselves, who completed a set of 30 Family Rating Scales at the conclusion of their three home visits. These 30 scales entailed global 5-point ratings, most of which concerned perceived family qualities, such as "consistency of family rules" and "quality of parent–child relationship," as well as family stress (described earlier). Factor analysis suggested that three dimensions were measured by this instrument (Masten et al., 1988). The most salient dimension and largest set of items appeared to measure maternal competence in relation to parenting and was labeled Parenting Quality. Other dimensions were Family Sociability and Family Stress.

Correlates of competence and stress exposure

The correlates of the school competence criteria (Engaged, Disruptiveness, and achievement) suggested that certain individual and family characteristics were associated wth currently successful adaptation in these children. Selected correlations are presented in Table 11.2.

Children with high quality involvement in the school environment, who were engaged and achieving, generally had more personal and environmental assets, such as greater intellectual ability, higher SES, and more positive family qualities. As noted elsewhere, competent children were found to have a variety of other cognitive qualities as well, including better interpersonal awareness and social comprehension, a more reflective cognitive style, more divergent thinking, and more ability to appreciate and generate humor (Masten, 1986; Pellegrini, 1985; Pellegrini, Masten, Garmezy, & Ferrarese, 1987).

Sex differences in social competence emerged in the teacher ratings. These elementary school teachers rated girls as more positively engaged in classroom activities (more cooperative, motivated, attentive and compliant), as well as less disruptive (less oppositional and aggressive). Separate regression analyses (Masten et al., 1988) suggested that intellectual ability was a better

Table 11.2. *Correlates of school competence and stressful life events*

	Dimensions of school competence			Negative life events
Attribute	Engaged	Disruptive	Grade point average	
Individual attributes				
Sex	.22***	−.19**	.04	−.01
IQ	.36***	−.21**	.55***	−.17**
Demographic data				
SES	.20**	−.17**	.29***	−.21**
Income	.13*	−.17**	.12*	−.31***
Mother's education	.08	−.12*	.23***	−.05
Family size	.02	.09	−.08	.16**
Intact family	.05	−.20**	.04	−.29***
Family qualities				
Global Parenting Quality[a]	.36***	−.25***	.38***	−.27***
Family Sociability[a]	.32***	−.05	.16*	−.02
Family Stability/ Organization[b]	.16**	−.32***	.22***	−.42***
Family Cohesion[b]	.25***	−.11	.10	−.16*

*$p < .05$; **$p < .01$; ***$p < .001$.

Note: Year-1 data; $N = 194–207$.

[a]Composite scores from the Family Rating Scales completed by parent interviewers after three visits to the home.

[b]Composite scores based on responses by the parent to the interview questions.

predictor of disruptive behavior for boys, whereas Parenting Quality was a better predictor of disruptiveness for girls.

The variable Family Stability/Organization was an equally good negative predictor of disruptiveness for both boys and girls. Children with a history of instability in the environment (e.g., frequent moves, changes in parental marital status) and current disorganization in the home (e.g., poor maintenance and housekeeping) were more likely to be rated as disruptive by peers and teachers.

The correlates of recent life events in Table 11.2 suggest that recent adversity is associated with a history of adverse events or chronic disadvantages, such as marital disruptions, moving, or poverty. The number of life events reported in 1 year also was correlated with the level of events reported the following year ($r = .50$).

It is also evident in Table 11.2 that children with more resources tended to be exposed to fewer life events. Unfortunately, it is children with the fewest assets who are most likely to be challenged by adverse life events. However, as noted elsewhere (Masten et al., 1988), exposure to life stress was associated only modestly with impaired competence. A modest association was observed regardless of whether stress was indexed by a simple count of negative life events, by a weighted event score, or by interviewers' clinical judgments based on rich contextual information. The effort to link stress exposure to adaptation must go beyond simple correlations.

Protective factors: assets tested by adversity

Implicit in the concept of protective factors is the idea that adaptation has been challenged (Rutter, 1979). The assets described earlier as simple correlates of competence may or may not function as protective factors under adversity. To test specifically the idea that these characteristics associated with competence play a "protective" role, we have examined whether or not they *moderate* the relation of stress exposure (recent life events) to competence (Masten et al., 1988). For example, four of the resources listed in Table 11.2 were empirically identified through regression analyses as moderators of stress exposure: IQ, SES, and two scores from the Family Rating Scales (Parenting Quality and Family Sociability).

A consistent but complex pattern has emerged in the way these resources operate, revealing the importance of individual differences as well as the importance of the chosen criterion of competence. For example, when the criterion was Classroom Disruptiveness, IQ and SES showed protective (moderator or interaction) effects for both boys and girls. Family qualities, such as global Parenting Quality and Family Sociability, however, apppeared to be protective with respect to disruptiveness only for girls.

When the criterion was the quality of engagement, these assets did not appear to be protective. Instead, such advantaged children appeared to be somewhat more vulnerable to high levels of stress exposure. Advantaged children who had experienced high levels of stress exposure showed significantly lower competence in the Engaged dimension than did similar children with few recent life events.

The general pattern of the findings can be illustrated by comparing the competence of children with many resources and the competence of children with few resources at different levels of stress exposure. The four variables previously identified as moderators were viewed as resources or risk factors for competence and composited, by summing z scores, to form a risk-versus-resources index. Competence was then plotted as a function of life events to compare the patterns of high-risk and low-risk children. For purposes of illustration, high- and low-risk groups were defined as the bottom third and top third of scores on the composite of the four resources (IQ, SES, Parenting Quality, and Family Sociability). Results for boys and girls were plotted separately so that their patterns could be compared. Two levels of stress exposure were plotted: low (0–2 events) and high (4 or more events). For each level of life events, the actual average mean level of competence (Engaged, Disruptive, Grade Point Average) was plotted. Results are presented in Figure 11.1.

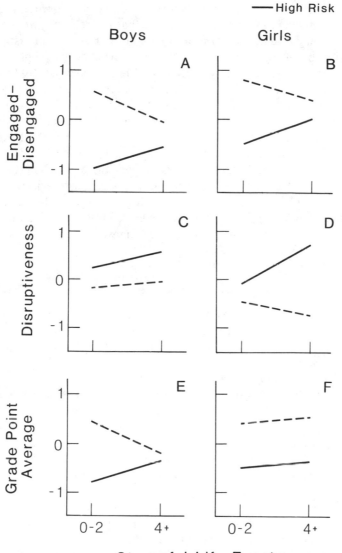

Figure 11.1. The relation between number of stressful life events and competence shown as a function of risk. Boys and girls are shown separately. The four variables summed into the index of risk-versus-resources were SES, IQ, Parenting Quality, and Family Sociability. Low risk was defined as the upper third of the distribution of the combined resources (i.e., possessing many advantages), with high risk as the lower third.

These figures suggest that risk status as defined in this study was highly related to school competence, particularly for positive classroom engagement and academic achievement. The data suggest that the relations of life events to competence may differ not only as a function of risk status but also according to the criterion of competence and the sex of the children. High-risk boys appear to be more disengaged in school than high-risk girls. At low stress levels, high-risk children of both sexes were relatively more disengaged, less achieving, and more disruptive than their low-risk peers. With high stress exposure, high-risk children appeared to become *more* disruptive, although the level of their engagement in school did not vary much with stress exposure. For low-risk/advantaged children, engagement appeared to decrease as a function of stress exposure, but only boys showed higher levels of disruptiveness in the context of high stress exposure; low-risk girls showed low levels of disruptiveness even when stress exposure was high. School grades did not vary significantly as a function of negative life events, although there appears to have been a trend for achievement to decline somewhat in advantaged boys at very high stress levels.

The single-case approach: learning from exemplars and exceptions

These potential patterns of adaptation, based on analyses of group trends, take one far away from individual children. Although it is crucial for the advancement of our science to generalize beyond the single case, intensive study of single cases can enrich our understanding of statistical results and aid our search for clues about why outcomes may have been "mispredicted." Single-case exemplars and exceptions to predicted patterns of data can both be informative. The "case for the single case" has been well stated by Garmezy (1982).

Therefore, we undertook to identify individuals in our sample who would exemplify the patterns of adaptation described earlier. The particular focus on identifying stress-resistant children implies two key criteria for the selection of such children: high stress exposure and high competence. Thus, all children who had experienced five or more life events and who were above the sample mean on at least two of the three school-based competence measures were nominated. The risk factors for each of these 23 children were then examined to identify those at highest and lowest risk. The case of Sarah exemplifies well the child whose many advantages (i.e., low-risk status) may have protected her against very stressful life circumstances, although not granting her "invulnerability."

When her family first joined our study, Sarah was in the fourth grade. She had one younger sister and lived with her biological parents. That year, Sarah's mother, who was pregnant, had been hospitalized for a serious progressive illness. She chose to postpone further treatment, although this placed her at greater risk, until after the baby was born. The baby, who was born after a difficult delivery requiring an emergency cesarean, had serious medical problems that required several hospitalizations during the first year.

The preceding year had also been a very stressful one for the family. Events that year included multiple deaths in the extended family, a brief hospitalization for Sarah, and the father's hospitalization for an orthopedic problem.

Despite two consecutive years of sustained life stressors, a subsequent assessment of competence revealed that Sarah was functioning quite well at school. Her grade point average was approximately one standard deviation above the mean. Her score on Classroom Disruptiveness, which reflects the extent to which her teacher and her peers viewed her as disruptive, aggressive, and oppositional in the classroom, was one standard deviation below the mean. Her teacher and peers also viewed her as relatively disengaged (well below average on Engaged). Her peer reputation suggests that at that time she was viewed positively, but as rather isolated, and something of a loner. Similarly, her teacher described her as well below average on a scale measuring active involvement in class activities. Sarah appeared particularly unlikely to initiate classroom discussion, tell stories, or bring things in to class. On the other hand, her teacher described her as persistent, showing high comprehension in class and likely to know academic material. Overall, Sarah appeared to be disengaged in her classroom, somewhat isolated from others, and perhaps self-contained, although her academic competence and comprehension remained high. This pattern of adjustment is highly consistent with the overall findings for "low-risk" children with multiple advantages, but experiencing high stress exposure, pictured in Figure 11.1.

Sarah's family was above the mean for this sample on indices of SES and income. Her father was personnel manager for a small company, and her mother, a college graduate, had a part-time position as a librarian. Her parents owned a modest home where the family had lived since before Sarah was born. The home was described by the project interviewer as sufficient in every way for meeting the child's needs; it was neat and well maintained. This family was rated quite highly by the interviewer on indices of social involvement and receipt of support from both extended family and friends. Quite striking in Sarah's case history was the competence of Sarah's mother, who impressed the interviewer as a remarkably resilient person.

Sarah's parents received the highest score in the sample on the composite Parenting Quality scale. This family showed clear communication among members and a high degree of respect for one another's opinions, and it was very child-centered. The mother (as primary caregiver) appeared to be exceptionally perceptive about Sarah's needs and personality and to express positive feelings toward Sarah. School achievement, independent thinking, and the ability to get along with other people were all highly encouraged by these parents. When asked to describe their views about child rearing, they talked about "self-reliability . . . being able to take care of herself" (father); "I believe in talking to kids and that you don't ever talk down. And you explain what's happening to them from the best of your point of view [and] from day one opening her up to as many different experiences as she possibly can have" (mother).

When Sarah's mother was interviewed, life was still stressful for this family because of continuing concerns about their infant's medical condition and the mother's poor medical prognosis. She described the family's biggest stress as being the fact that they were "still waiting." The mother was open and verbal in the interview and described in an articulate manner her style of coping with these ongoing stressors. She referred to herself as a fighter who had been made tougher because of what had happened, and she was proud of her ability to bounce back quickly after setbacks; she saw herself as strong and determined. She had made a determined effort to go on with life, keeping as much to a routine as possible.

Despite their setbacks, family members were busy and involved in many interests and activities. Sarah, too, was encouraged to stay involved and active. The mother expressed her view that it was important to expose her child to the world so that she would "know what's out there [and] not be afraid of it or grow up naive and unaware." She stressed independence and skill building in her children: "the more you know, the more you have to build with."

Sarah's mother's approach to dealing with her own illness had been practical and cautious and yet positive. She had been open and candid about her illness with Sarah because she believed in preparing members of the family to the fullest. She described her ability to know when she could handle something herself and when she needed to seek help from family and friends. Physical exercise as an antidote to stress was also emphasized. Sarah and her mother regularly attended exercise classes together. After surgery, this mother began a regimen of physical exercise to gain strength and mobility.

Sarah's mother described her marriage as strong and "closer than ever." She felt that the many events that had happened to their family had helped them to retain a perspective about what was important and "made living all that more valuable."

Sarah herself appeared to possess a number of personal resources. As our findings predicted, she was quite intelligent (more than 1 SD above the mean). For several summers she had been placed in a Talented Youth Summer Program. In an interview done when she was 10 years old, Sarah reported that when she grew up she wanted to be "a person that does research on dinosaurs and digs up their bones." In the interview, she appeared to be highly motivated, articulate, reflective, curious, academically confident, conscientious, compliant, and polite. In addition, Sarah was rated as empathic, as self-aware about emotions, and as showing good judgment. She also appeared to be somewhat lonely, although she seemed to possess the qualities necessary to have friends. A close friend of Sarah's had moved away the first year of the study. Sarah expressed the desire for more friends and seemed to possess insight about possible reasons for some of her peer difficulties. A conscientious student, prepared when the other children were not, she commented: "I feel like they don't like me because I have all the answers." Despite her social disengagement, Sarah came across as a resourceful child coping successfully with highly stressful circumstances.

As part of a follow-up study, we have recently located Sarah, now an adolescent, and learned that her mother had died and her father had been recurrently hospitalized for his physical disability. Nevertheless, preliminary indications are that Sarah continues to function well. She lives with her grandmother. She is excelling at school, plans to study science in college, has several close friends, and is active in sports and music. She views herself as a competent, attractive person who is pleased with herself and the way her life is going.

Sarah provides an example that fits the picture emerging from our data analysis. She appears to be a resilient child who has had many resources and has used them well. But we were also interested in looking for subjects who did not fit the picture so well, those whose adaptational patterns were unexpected. To identify such a subject, we examined the same list of children who manifested both high stress exposure (5 or more life events) and high competence (above the mean on two of three criteria). This time, however, we searched for children who had maintained competence without the advantage of the protective assets identified in our data analysis.

The case of John illustrates a boy who was doing well despite his high-risk, high-stress status. When this family joined our study, John was in the fifth grade and was living with his father. The 2 years preceding our initial contact with John had been extremely stressful for him. His parents had been separated for a number of years, and his father had remarried. John had been living with his mother, but she died suddenly in an auto accident. Subsequently, John moved back and forth for a time to live with various relatives, but primarily lived with either his father or his aunt. John's father was hospitalized that year because of an injury at work. Because of his injury, the father lost his job and had to go on welfare. During that same year, just before the study began, the father and stepmother separated for a brief period. Food stamps were cut off, and the family's financial situation, previously difficult, worsened. In addition, the stepmother returned home, became pregnant, and had the baby shortly after the study began.

Despite the preceding two extremely difficult years, John appeared to be doing quite well at school when competence data were collected. His achievement and the quality of his engagement at school were considerably above average. Examination of the components of the Engaged score suggested that his peers viewed him positively, not as likely to be withdrawn or isolated. His teacher rated him high on a subscale measuring cooperative and initiating behavior and indicated that he was particularly likely to initiate classroom discussion, offer to do things for the teacher, and seek out the teacher after class to talk. He also was rated as exhibiting high comprehension in the classroom, as likely to know material when called on, and as extremely capable at applying what he had learned to new situations.

John's overall score on Classroom Disruptiveness was about average. Although his peers did not rate him as disruptive or aggressive, his teacher described him as somewhat more disruptive than average. She described John as particularly likely to interfere with the work of his classmates, to be quickly drawn into the talking or noisemaking of others, and to need reprimanding by her during class. His behaviors suggested behavioral immaturity and unsatisfied needs for attention, rather than a more ominous aggressive pattern of behavior.

John's family fell well below the mean on SES indices. His father, poorly educated, read with difficulty. The family received an extremely low score (2 SDs below the mean) on Parenting Quality as well. John's father and stepmother were difficult to interview, and conflict was evident between them. The father had many complaints about the stepmother and her inability to properly care for children. Whereas the stepmother fought constantly with John, his father appeared to be more patient and understanding of the abilities and needs of the children.

John seemed to act as a kind of interpreter for the parents – they relied on him to explain things they could not understand. John appeared to cope with the difficult home situation by avoiding home as much as possible. Sent on an errand, often he would not return. John reportedly spent a great deal of time with a paternal aunt who lived nearby.

When interviewed at age 12, John appeared to be a child with many internal resources. His intellectual ability was above average. Although he was somewhat subdued and reserved during the interview, particularly when discussing his mother's death, the interviewer found him to be a colorful, likable boy with a positive outlook on his life. He seldom spoke negatively or critically about things and appeared to be quite happy with himself, proud of his accomplishments, and extremely self-confident. When faced with problems, he said has was unlikely to confide in his parents, stating that "I mostly handle [problems] by myself." When asked what he liked most about himself, he replied "my sportsmanship and my humor." He repeatedly invoked his good sense of humor – stating, for example, that he gets along well with other kids because "I can pull out a punch line any time." When asked what makes him feel mad or angry, John replied "I don't get mad very easily. Most of the time if I have a bad situation, I just laugh at it."

John was rated as involved and enthusiastic about his activities. He chose reading as his favorite activity, with sports a close second. He appeared to feel competent athletically and to participate enthusiastically in sports. The interviewer rated him as quite "gutsy" and self-assured. He described himself as a risk taker, saying "Dangerous – that's probably my middle name right there." Although somewhat rambunctious, John appeared to be capable of reasoning about and controlling his own behavior.

In addition, John was rated as possessing considerable psychological insight, and as compassionate and empathic. When he won money once in a contest, he gave some of it away to a children's cancer fund because he had known a child with the disease. He spoke often and with much affection about his young cousins; he apparently had responsibility for watching them every day after school and on weekends. He appeared to assume responsibility well; when talking about his chores, he explained that his father wanted him to do chores because "he thinks the more I do, the more responsible I'm gonna get." John stated that it was important to do well in school "because my dad wants me to become a doctor." Apparently, he and his father had discussed this, and John planned to be either a doctor or a lawyer.

The case of John illustrates a child with few obvious environmental assets handed down who had to rely on himself and had figured out ways to do so. One might say that John's "received" environment was poor, but that the environment actively "acquired" by him personally provided substantial compensation; although the received–acquired terminology is ours, the distinction is essentially that proposed by Scarr and McCartney (1983) between "passive" and "active" environments. Perhaps another adult, such as his aunt, provided him with some of the parenting he had lacked. His father also may have provided an enduring source of nurturance, despite his other limitations. His father impressed a recent interviewer as being extremely proud of John and his accomplishments. Whatever his environmental resources, however, John clearly had multiple internal resources that promoted his resilience. Furthermore, recent contacts with John, who is now in high school, have confirmed his continued competence. Although his grades are just average, he still outlines plans to go to graduate school in either medicine or law. He has many friends, is involved in sports and weightlifting, and is active at a local boys' club, where he recently took a part-time job supervising activities for younger children. He appears to feel attractive, competent in many arenas, and happy with the way his life is going. One might characterize John's adaptation as "positive-emotional," that is, characteristic of someone not only temperamentally disposed to react positively to his environment but also disposed to generate encounters and experiences that engender a sense of mastery and well-being.

Conclusions and implications for the future agenda of developmental psychopathology

What can be concluded about stress and adaptation from this project? First, we have recognized that the search for protective processes is complex. We surmise that there is no general "immunity" to stress. Instead, there may be different patterns of stress responding that are more or less adaptive, depending on the context, the circumstances, and the developmental stage of the child. For example, there may be an *internalizing* pattern of stress response (disengaged but not disruptive) that is more common in girls, as exemplified by Sarah, and more acceptable than other patterns in the elementary school context with teachers and peers. If short-lived, this pattern may be adaptive, or at least without adverse consequences. If persistent or extreme, this pattern may be associated with vulnerability to affective or anxiety disorders, particularly later during adolescence.

There may also be an *externalizing* pattern of stress response (disengaged plus disruptive) that is more common in boys and more aversive to both teachers and peers in elementary school. This pattern appears to be maladaptive in the school context. In extreme or persistent cases, we would surmise that it would be very damaging to development and social integration. It is conceivable, however, that in other subcultures or circumstances, this pattern in less extreme form may be acceptable and even adaptive.

Competent children appear to have many resources on which to draw. Some are predictable and can be observed and documented empirically (in part because quantity counts). Examples would be IQ or high parenting quality, as in the case of Sarah. Resources such as these tend to co-occur. Other important resources, however, may be more idiosyncratic or more difficult to detect for other reasons. The roles played by John's apparent ability to use adults effectively outside the home and by his humor may be difficult to discern in the analysis of aggregated data.

Given the multiplicity and renewability of resources of competent children, we expect that competence itself may be the best predictor of future competence unless there are dramatic changes in circumstances. Moreover, we expect competent children to be the most resilient in the face of acute stressors and to recover well from whatever emotional or behavioral difficulties they do experience. Competence may reflect, in part, the capacity for resilience, because in order to have achieved competence in middle childhood, children must have mastered, perhaps excelled at, the normative challenges of early childhood, such as school entry.

Many of the questions raised by this study point to items for a future research agenda in developmental psychopathology:

1. Can replicable patterns of adaptation to stressors be discerned that vary with sex, cognitive abilities, family variables, and age? Our findings require cross-validation and extension. It will be important to undertake intensive short-term longitudinal studies of competence before, during, and after the occurrence of acute stressors in order to determine if these patterns actually reflect responses to stress exposure.

2. Are such patterns consistent across different types of stressors? For example, a diverse literature on stressors of childhood suggests that boys tend to be disruptive following stressful experiences (Emery, 1982; Garmezy & Rutter, 1985). However, the heterogeneity of subjects is confounded in many studies with a heterogeneity of stressors, as in Project Competence. Even in "single-stressor" studies (studies of children of divorce, children with life-

threatening illness, etc.), inevitable variations occur in the profiles of life stressors within a given sample that might constitute critical contextual modifiers of the primary stressor of interest. Further study is necessary to determine if a given child's responses to stressors as diverse as family dissolution, economic hardship, and life-threatening illness are more similar than different.

- What shape do patterns of adaptation assume over time? There may be different recovery functions for children with different combinations of asset and risk factors, as well as for different types of stressors.
- Assuming that adaptational patterns reflect ongoing developmental processes, do major changes occur in the forms of stress responses during periods of developmental transition, such as puberty?
- Is there continuity in adaptational patterns across development?
- How may patterns of stress response be related to symptoms, clinic referral, diagnostic categories, or other taxonometric systems? One might expect a low-asset child with acute stressors to become disruptive on top of an already manifest disinterest in school and low achievement. This combination is likely to precipitate referral. One might also ask if somatic symptoms are more likely to occur in children who respond to high stress exposure with disengagement but not disruptiveness, in what appears to be an internalizing pattern.

Ultimately, these inquiries can be posed in broad terms: What are the relations among psychopathology, competence, risk, and protective factors, patterns of adaptation, and individual differences in children across age? Answers to this question in all its manifestations – the search for greater understanding of the process of adaptation – can only serve to enhance our efforts to help children in trouble.

Understanding competence, particularly competence under adversity, can guide efforts to promote adaptation. For example, diverse investigations over the past two decades have identified many of the underlying skills and behavioral correlates of socially competent children. These findings have been translated into a variety of social skills training (SST) programs that have generated considerable interest and enthusiasm in recent years. Whereas some of these SST programs focus on the specific behavioral components of effective social behavior (Oden & Asher, 1977), others emphasize the development of social cognitive skills that are presumed to be more "generic" to social adaptation (Shure & Spivack, 1979). Systematic evaluations of the effectiveness of both program approaches have been largely limited to secondary prevention efforts with children showing signs of emerging social maladjustment, such as aggressive and disruptive social behavior, social isolation, and peer rejection, without regard to the origins of such difficulties [e.g., the Hahnemann program (Spivack, Platt, & Shure, 1976) and the Cincinnati Social Skills Development Program (Kirschenbaum, 1979)]. The viability of SST for primary prevention purposes has yet to be demonstrated convincingly (Durlak, 1985; Pellegrini & Urbain, 1985).

Nevertheless, SST programs hold considerable promise for preventing the development of maladaptive social behavior and status that might arise as a consequence of unavoidable life stressors. Children could be identified for inclusion in preventive SST programs based on their experience of targeted life events (e.g., parental divorce), as opposed to being selected after maladaptive social behaviors have emerged (along with other children whose behavior may be more resistant to change as a result of more distant, more complex, or more deep-seated origins). The content of such training could also be tailored to enhance the development of social skills pertinent to the stressor of interest (e.g., for children of divorce, how to negotiate with parents for preferred times of visitation, how to resolve conflicts with stepsiblings, etc.).

Similarly, the concept of "stress inoculation training" has gained popularity. The idea behind these programs is to provide graduated manageable doses of stress that the individual can master, gaining experience and confidence in coping with stress that will facilitate future adaptation. One method developed by Meichenbaum and colleagues (Meichenbaum, 1977, 1985) includes education about the nature of stress, analysis of the clients' stress responses, training in coping skills drawn largely from the cognitive behavioral armamentarium, practice, and "booster" training. Ayalon (1983) has developed a similar intervention called COPE (Community Oriented Preparation for Emergency) to better prepare Israeli children for the possibility of terrorism. Through this program, schoolchildren are taught general cognitive coping skills, learn to ventilate emotions, and are encouraged to respond to stress with action. Both of these stress inoculation programs emphasize the development of generic coping skills.

These interventions assume that effective resources can be improved, either by expanding the repertoire of resources or by learning to use more effectively those resources that are readily available. As an adaptive species, we have developed a myriad of coping strategies. Adaptation is undoubtedly the result of many attributes operating together, although different areas of functioning may require different combinations of resources. It follows that interventions focusing on one resource, one attribute, one cognitive style, or one social skill would not be expected to show large changes in functioning across situations.

In connection with contrasting concepts such as SST and stress inoculation, it may become important to distinguish among personal qualities, experiences, or treatments geared to optimize *positive* experiences of well-being and self-efficacy and those relating to minimizing *negative* experiences of stress and disorganization. The management of joy and distress may involve not so much opposite extremes of a single adaptational dimension but rather different, if interacting, dimensions requiring their own distinctive constructs of temperament, environmental input, development, and intervention (Tellegen, 1985).

Our work also emphasizes that consideration of individual differences will be important in planning interventions. Those designing prevention programs aimed at improving the general capacity to adapt to stressors must be mindful that differences in sex and in personal and environmental resources may well play a role in the needs of individual children.

Studies of adaptation to specific stressors have the potential to identify particular strategies most effective for coping with a given stressor. Here again, however, children who face ostensibly the same stressor may have different patterns of responses dependent on their individual characteristics and resources. A bright, achieving but withdrawn girl who is adjusting to parental divorce will not have the same needs as a peer-rejected, aggressive boy with learning problems who is in a similar situation.

Good clinicians undoubtedly already adjust their interventions in a single case according to the child's personal and environmental resources, as well as according to their understanding of normal development, maladaptation, and stress. One goal of our study and studies like it is to provide more knowledge for that process so that treatments of maladaptation can be more systematically matched to the child and also evaluated more effectively. Reciprocally, the informed clinician, expert at analyzing the single case, can offer researchers insights into the processes of stress and adaptation that can set them onto overlooked trails of empirical exploration (Garmezy & Masten, 1986).

This study began as an expedition into largely unknown territory, guided by Norman Garmezy. Our methodology has evolved as we have learned a little about competence and its relation to stress exposure. Perhaps most important, we have learned how to ask better questions in this complex area. We remain convinced that study of the positive aspects of adaptation, including competence, protective factors, and resilience, is a necessary part of the knowledge base to which we all must contribute if we are to enhance the prevention and treatment of disorders, as well as the education of children.

References

Ayalon, O. (1983). Coping with terrorism: The Israeli case. In D. Meichenbaum & M. E. Jaremko (Eds.), *Stress reduction and prevention* (pp. 293–339). New York: Plenum Press.

Cicchetti, D. (1984). The emergence of developmental psychopathology. *Child Development, 55*, 1–7.

Coddington, R. D. (1972a). The significance of life events as etiologic factors in the diseases of children. I: A survey of professional workers. *Journal of Psychosomatic Research, 16*, 7–18.

Coddington, R. D. (1972b). The significance of life events as etiologic factors in the diseases of children. II: A study of a normal population. *Journal of Psychosomatic Research, 16*, 205–13.

Dunn, L. M., & Markwardt, F. C. (1970). *Peabody Individual Achievement Test.* Circle Pines, MN: American Guidance Service.

Durlak, J. A. (1985). Primary prevention of school maladjustment. *Journal of Consulting and Clinical Psychology, 53*(5), 623–30.

Emery, R. E. (1982). Interparental conflict and the children of discord and divorce. *Psychological Bulletin, 92*, 310–30.

Ferrarese, M. J. (1981). Reflectiveness-impulsivity and competence in children under stress (Doctoral dissertation, University of Minnesota). *Dissertation Abstracts International, 42,* 4928B.

Finkelman, D. G. (1983). The relationships of children's attributes to levels of competence and familial stress (Doctoral dissertation, University of Minnesota). *Dissertation Abstracts International, 44,* 2891B.

Garmezy, N. (1970). Vulnerable children: Implications derived from studies on an internalizing–externalizing symptom dimension. In J. Zubin & A. M. Freedman (Eds.), *The psychopathology of adolescence* (pp. 212–39). New York: Grune & Stratton.

Garmezy, N. (1971). Vulnerability research and the issue of primary prevention. *American Journal of Orthopsychiatry, 41,* 101–16.

Garmezy, N. (1973). Competence and adaptation in adult schizophrenic patients and children at risk. In S. R. Dean (Ed.), *Schizophrenia: The first ten Dean Award Lectures* (pp. 163–204). New York: MSS Information Corp.

Garmezy, N. (1974a). *The study of children at risk: New perspectives for developmental psychopathology.* Distinguished Scientist Award address presented to Division 12, Section III, at the 82nd annual convention of the American Psychological Association, New Orleans.

Garmezy, N. (1974b). The study of competence in children at risk for severe psychopathology. In E. J. Anthony & C. Koupernick (Eds.), *The child in his family: Children at psychiatric risk* (Vol 3., pp. 77–97). New York: Wiley.

Garmezy, N. (1974c). Children at risk: The search for the antecedents of schizophrenia. Part I: Conceptual models and research methods. *Schizophrenia Bulletin, 8,* 14–90.

Garmezy, N. (1974d). Children at risk: The search for the antecedents of schizophrenia. Part II: Ongoing research programs, issues and intervention. *Schizophrenia Bulletin, 9,* 55–125.

Garmezy, N. (1981). Children under stress; Perspectives on antecedents and correlates of vulnerability and resistance to psychopathology. In A. I. Rabin, J. Aronoff, A. M. Barclay, & R. A. Zucker (Eds.), *Further explorations in personality* (pp. 196–269). New York: Wiley.

Garmezy, N. (1982). The case for the single case in research. In A. E. Kazdin and A. H. Tuma (Eds.), *Single-case research designs* (pp. 5–17). San Francisco: Jossey-Bass.

Garmezy, N. (1984). Children vulnerable to major mental disorders: Risk and protective factors. In L. Grinspoon (Ed.), *Psychiatry update* (Vol. 3, pp. 91–104). Washington, DC: American Psychiatric Press.

Garmezy, N., & Devine, V. T. (1984). Project Competence: The Minnesota studies of children vulnerable to psychopathology. In N. Watt, E. J. Anthony, L. C. Wynne, & J. E. Rolf (Eds.), *Children at risk for schizophrenia* (pp. 289–303). Cambridge University Press.

Garmezy, N., & Masten, A. M. (1986). Stress, competence, and resilience: Common frontiers for therapist and psychopathologist. *Behavior Therapy, 17,* 500–21.

Garmezy, N., Masten, A. S., & Tellegen, A. (1984). The study of stress and competence in children: A building block for developmental psychopathology. *Child Development, 55,* 97–111.

Garmezy, N., & Rodnick, E. H. (1959). Premorbid adjustment and performance in schizophrenia: Implications of interpreting heterogeneity in schizophrenia. *Journal of Nervous and Mental Disease, 129,* 450–66.

Garmezy, N., & Rutter, M. (1985). Acute reactions to stress. In M. Rutter & L. Hersov (Eds.), *Child and adolescent psychiatry: Modern approaches* (2nd ed., pp. 152–76). Oxford: Blackwell Scientific.

Garmezy, N., & Tellegen, A. (1984). Studies of stress-resistant children: Methods, variables, and preliminary findings. In F. Morrison, C. Lord, & D. Keating (Eds.), *Advances in applied developmental psychology* (Vol. 1, pp. 231–87). New York: Academic Press.

Holmes, T. H., & Rahe, R. H. (1967). The social readjustment rating scale. *Journal of Psychosomatic Research, 11,* 213–18.

Kirschenbaum, D. S. (1979). Social competence intervention and evaluation in the inner city: Cincinnati's Social Skills Development Program. *Journal of Consulting and Clinical Psychology, 47,* 778–80.

Linder, H. D. (1985). *A contextual life events interview as a measure of stress: A comparison of questionnaire-based versus interview-based stress indices.* Unpublished doctoral thesis, University of Minnesota.

Masten, A. S. (1982). Humor and creative thinking in stress-resistant children (Doctoral dissertation, University of Minnesota). *Dissertation Abstracts International, 43,* 3737B.

Masten, A. S. (1986). Humor and competence in school-aged children. *Child Development, 57,* 461–73.

Masten, A. S., & Braswell, L. (in press). Developmental psychopathology: An integrative framework for understanding behavior problems in children and adolescents. In P. R. Martin (Ed.), *Handbook of behavior therapy and psychological science: An integrative approach.* New York: Pergamon.

Masten, A. S., & Garmezy, N. (1985). Risk, vulnerability, and protective factors in developmental psychopathology. In B. B. Lahey & A. E. Kazdin (Eds.), *Advances in clinical child psychology* (Vol. 8, pp. 1–52). New York: Plenum Press.

Masten, A. S., Garmezy, N., Tellegen, A., Pellegrini, D. S., Larkin, K., & Larsen, A. (1988). Competence and stress in school children: The moderating effects of individual and family qualities. *Journal of Child Psychology and Psychiatry, 29,* 745–64.

Masten, A. S., Morison, P., & Pellegrini, D. S. (1985). A revised class play method of peer assessment. *Developmental Psychology, 21,* 523–33.

Meichenbaum, D. (1977). *Cognitive-behavior modification: An integrative approach.* New York: Plenum.

Meichenbaum, D. (1985). *Stress inoculation training.* New York: Pergamon Press.

Morison, P. (1987). *Interview-derived attributes of children as related to competence and familial stress.* Unpublished doctoral dissertation, University of Minnesota.

Oden, S., & Asher, S. R. (1977). Coaching children in social skills for friendship making. *Child Development, 48,* 495–506.

Pellegrini, D. S. (1985). Social cognition and competence in middle childhood. *Child Development, 56,* 253–64.

Pellegrini, D. S., Masten, A. S., Garmezy, N., & Ferrarese, M. J. (1987). Correlates of social and academic competence in middle childhood. *Journal of Child Psychology and Psychiatry, 28,* 699–714.

Pellegrini, D. S., & Urbain, F. S. (1985). An evaluation of interpersonal cognitive problem solving training with children. *Journal of Child Psychology and Psychiatry, 26,* 17–41.

Raison, S. B. (1982). *Coping behavior of mainstreamed physically handicapped students.* Unpublished doctoral dissertation, University of Minnesota.

Rutter, M. (1979). Protective factors in children's responses to stress and disadvantage. In M. W. Kent & J. E. Rolf (Eds.), *Primary prevention of psychopathology. Vol. 3: Social competence in children* (pp. 49–74). Hanover, NH: University Press of New England.

Scarr, S., & McCartney, K. (1983). How people make their own environments: A theory of genotype–environmental effects. *Child Development, 54,* 424–35.

Shure, M. B., & Spivack, G. (1979). Interpersonal cognitive problem solving and primary prevention: Programming for preschool and kindergarten children. *Journal of Clinical Child Psychology, 2,* 89–94.

Silverstein, P. R. (1982). *Coping and adaptation in families of physically handicapped children.* Unpublished doctoral dissertation, University of Minnesota.

Spivack, G., Platt, J. J., & Shure, M. (1976). *The problem-solving approach to adjustment.* San Francisco: Jossey-Bass.

Sroufe, L. A., & Rutter, M. (1984). The domain of developmental psychopathology. *Child Development, 55,* 17–29.

Tellegen, A. (1985). Structures of mood and personality and their relevance for assessing anxiety, with an emphasis on self-report. In A. H. Tuma & D. Maser (Eds.), *Anxiety and the anxiety disorders* (pp. 681–716). Hillsdale, NJ: Erlbaum.

Waters, E., & Sroufe, L. A. (1983). Social competence as a developmental construct. *Developmental Review, 3,* 79–97.

Watt, N. F., Anthony, E. J., Wynne, L. C., & Rolf, J. E. (Eds.). (1984). *Children at risk for schizophrenia: A longitudinal perspective.* Cambridge University Press.

12 Stress-resistant families and stress-resistant children

Alfred L. Baldwin, Clara Baldwin, and Robert E. Cole

The purpose of this chapter is to help explain why some children in high-risk circumstances develop more cognitive competence than would be expected considering their backgrounds. One of the factors, we believe, is a certain stress resistance in their families.

The sample of families that we are investigating includes some whose children may become school dropouts, delinquent, drug users, or pregnant within the next 5 years. We have, however, seen some high-risk families whose children appear to have escaped these outcomes. We shall report on the characteristics of these families that seem likely to prevent the poor outcomes that so often befall children in these neighborhoods.

Garmezy (1982) has stimulated great interest in the study of stress-resistant children. In our study we have been impressed by the fact that some high-risk families protect their children from the dangers that surround them. In these cases it seems to us that it is the families, rather than the children, that are stress-resistant. This is not to deny that there are factors in the children that help them resist the influence of a high-risk environment. Even if exposed to such dangers as drugs or alcohol, they are able to cope with them.

Proximal versus distal variables

One purpose of this chapter is to distinguish between stress-resistant children and stress-resistant families. In order to conceptualize this difference we need to recognize that risk variables differ from one another in the degree to which they directly impinge on the child. Social class, for example, is an impor-

Dr. Ellen Nakhnikian, a clinical psychologist, has been primarily responsible for the child assessments in this research. She has been an invaluable colleague and research associate throughout the project. We thank her for her thoughtful comments during the writing of this chapter. Jennifer Fray has served as our research assistant, and we are grateful for her many hours of work at the computing center, running analysis after analysis. The Rochester Longitudinal Study (Adolescent) (RLS-A) is partially supported by a grant from the National Institute of Mental Health.

tant risk variable – we shall see later how powerfully social class predicts cognitive outcome. But social class does not impinge directly on the child. Its effects are mediated through a number of more proximal variables – we do not even know what all the mediators are. The mother must work full time, but cannot afford help in the household. Thus, she may face a day's load of housework after she returns home tired after a full day of work. Her irritability may be one proximal variable resulting from poverty that impinges directly on her children, or, as another result of poverty, the overburdened working mother may leave her children alone in the house or neighborhood without supervision and thus expose them to a multitude of directly impinging influences.

We distinguish between distal risk variables that do not directly impinge on the child, but act through mediators, and the proximal risk variables that do impinge directly on the child. The terms "distal" and "proximal" should be thought of as the ends of a continuum. Some distal variables are more distal than others. Poverty, for example, is a distal variable. Maternal anxiety is closer to the proximal end of the scale, but its effect on the child is still mediated through maternal behaviors such as irritability, restriction of the child's freedom, or excessive nurturance. We picture a causal chain beginning with the distal variable, proceeding through its consequences (the mediating variables), and finally impinging on the child through one or more proximal variables.

Another feature of this causal network is that frequently the link between a distal variable and its consequence is not inevitable. For example, families of lower socioeconomic status (SES) are less likely to provide their children books than are more prosperous families, but this consequence of SES is not inevitable. Poor, tired working mothers are not necessarily irritable. We have interviewed some economically disadvantaged mothers who buy their children the books they want even if it means sacrificing something else. The important distal variables are linked to outcome only by a probability statement, not by a firm causal link.

It is this fact, among others, that makes it possible for children from a high-risk group to have positive outcomes. A child may belong to a group in which the probability for a negative outcome is quite high, but because the mediating variables are more favorable than one would expect from the probabilities associated with the distal variables, the child may actually be in a more favorable proximal environment than the distal variables would indicate.

Because the family is in control of so many of the direct proximal variables in a child's life, the child's distal environment may be a high-risk environment, but the family environment may be much more favorable. We would like to call such families stress-resistant families to distinguish their children from children who are truly stress-resistant. A stress-resistant child, for various internal reasons, succeeds in resisting the dangers of a high-risk proximal environment. A child from a stress-resistant family may or may not have some of the same characteristics, but the important fact is that such a child is shielded from many of the risks of the environment by a protective family that creates a low-risk proximal environment despite living in a high-risk distal environment.

It is also important to recognize that the proximal variables related to a successful outcome in a high-risk environment may not be the same as the variables related to a successful outcome in a low-risk environment. Families living in a high-risk environment operate in a context different from that of families living in a low-risk environment.

Family policies that will shield a child from noxious elements in a high-risk environment may unnecessarily limit a child's opportunities in a low-risk environment. Similarly, encouraging what would be reasonable self-reliance for a child in a low-risk environment might overwhelm the coping abilities of a child living in a high-risk environment. To truly understand family processes it is essential to recognize the nature of the environment. If we are to recommend parenting strategies for families in high-risk environments, we must select those strategies that will operate successfully in a high-risk environment.

Statistical analysis of proximal and distal variables

In terms of statistical analysis, the variable B is a mediator between A and C if the correlation between A and C is significantly reduced if B is partialed out. If we could control the complete set of variables that describe the proximal environment, then the distal variables would make no contribution. The practical flaw in actually carrying out this strategy is that important distal variables, such as social class, operate through so many different proximal variables that it is almost impossible to control all of the proximal mediators of the distal variable. Furthermore, there are other relationships between variables that lead to a reduction in the correlation of one variable with the dependent variable when another is partialed out.

In this analysis, therefore, we are adopting a different strategy, namely, to look at the differences in the correlations between various proximal variables and the outcome in two different groups: a high-risk group and a low-risk group. Risk is defined in terms of a set of distal variables.

Significant correlations of variable X with outcome in both the high-risk and the low-risk samples indicate that the addition of variable X to the predictors that define risk in the multiple regression equation would add significantly to the multiple correlation. Significantly different correlations with outcome in the high- and low-risk samples, particularly if they are opposite in sign, indicate that there is a nonlinear component in the regression line relating variable X to outcome. In either case we can improve the multiple correlation by adding variable X to the prediction equation.

If restrictiveness of regulations in the home is positively correlated with an outcome variable in a high-risk group and negatively correlated with the outcome variable in a low-risk group, then it is clear that knowledge of the

Table 12.1. *Demographic characteristics of the sample*

Boys	Girls	Total N
75	77	152
Minority	Nonminority	
57	95	152
Intact	Nonintact	
102	50	152

proximal variable adds to the predictability of the outcome over and above what the distal variable alone would provide.

In addition to comparing the correlations with outcome in the high-risk and low-risk samples, we have divided each risk group into a successful subsample and an unsuccessful subsample by dividing the group at the mean cognitive outcome score for the entire sample. In this way we can actually examine the differences between the mean values of variables in the successful and unsuccessful high-risk subsamples. Because the number of cognitively successful children in the high-risk sample may well be small – if the risk variables have been well chosen – the difference in means may be a less stable statistic than the correlation coefficient, but it does provide concrete information about the precise sample in which we are interested (i.e., the successful families in the high-risk group).

The empirical data

Sample

The sample on which this study was based was a longitudinal sample of families originally studied by Sameroff, Seifer, and Zax (1982) from 1971 to 1974. The mothers were first interviewed late in their pregnancies. Earlier findings on this sample have been published (Sameroff et al., 1982; Sameroff & Seifer, 1983).

These children were 12 to 14 years old when the data for this study were collected. The details of the instruments and the data collection will be published soon. The sample was composed of 152 families. The sample included a wide range of socioeconomic levels, both minority and nonminority families, and sizable subsamples of both intact and single-parent families. The distribution of this sample on these demographic characteristics is shown in Table 12.1.

Procedure

The mothers of these children (and their husbands if they were available) were interviewed in the Psychology Department of the University of

Rochester. Each child was interviewed at the same time in a separate interview room. The parent interview began with an open-ended interview along the lines of the Camberwell Family Interview (Leff & Vaughn, 1985) designed to elicit expressions of feelings and emotions from the parent or parents about the child. The interview raised questions pertaining to a standard set of topics. It began with a request for the parent to describe the child in the parent's own words, and to describe how they got along together. If more information was needed, we asked about the kinds of activities that the parent and the child enjoyed doing together and about the child's helpfulness and consideration. We asked about the activities in which the parent was proud of the child. We also asked about sources of friction, specifically doing homework, cleanliness of the child's room, and dating rules, if they were not mentioned spontaneously. From pretest interviews we had learned that these were frequent sources of stress between parents and 12–14-year-olds. For the last 58 families the interview also contained a set of questions about child-rearing practices that could be rated on a set of seven Fels Parent Behavior Scales.

After the open-ended interview, the parent or parents reported on the occurrence of 28 life events for the child (Herzog, Linder, & Samaha, 1982) and were given the Community Mental Health Interview (CMHI) (Ikle, Lipp, Butters, & Ciarlo, 1983) in an interview format. This interview asks the parents for a variety of information about the child's behavior at home and in school. The interview provides scores on 15 subscales. The analysis of these data will be reported elsewhere. The child and the parents responded independently to the CMHI and also to a life events questionnaire, so that we have both the parents' judgments of the child and the child's self-judgments.

After the CMHI, the parents independently filled out several questionnaires, including a ranking of the parental values studied by Kohn (1977), the Concepts of Development Questionnaire (CODQ) developed by Sameroff and Feil (1985), the Beck Depression Scale (Beck, 1967), and the Rutter Malaise Scale (Rutter, Tizard, Yule, Graham, & Whitmore, 1976). Finally, the parents responded to the Shipley Intelligence Scale (Shipley, 1939), and the Quick Test (Ammons & Ammons, 1962).

Each child was tested on four subtests of the WISC-R (Wechsler, 1974) and on the spelling and arithmetic tests from the WRAT (Jastak & Wilkinson, 1984). In addition, each child's school achievement was scored -1, 0, or $+1$, depending on grade placement in relation to age and whether the child was in a section receiving special remedial help or was placed in an advanced group in any subject. For the purposes of this study, cognitive achievement outcome is the average of the IQ, arithmetic achievement score, and school achievement score. These measures all correlate above .60 with each other. The spelling achievement score could be included without affecting the results, but the arithmetic achievement score has a slightly higher correlation with IQ.

These children also filled out a number of instruments assessing their self-perceptions (Harter, 1978), their perceptions of their social environment

(Furman & Buhrmeister, 1985), and their locus of control (Connell, 1985). Children also rated their physical maturity on the Tanner (1962) scale. Two 35-mm pictures were taken of each child, and these are being rated for the child's physical attractiveness. Height and weight were also measured.

The hypothesis

In the course of interviewing these families, we met many middle-class families in which the children were functioning well. These families were verbal; they did not need to control their children closely and gave them quite a bit of free choice in their activities. They discussed policies with their children when they felt that they needed to set limits.

What came as a surprise was the number of successful families of relatively low SES. The jobs held by the parent or parents were neither high-paying nor high-prestige; their education had been restricted, and many of these families lived in the inner city in high-crime areas. In many cases the mother was a single parent. Some of these families seemed to the interviewer to be raising well-functioning children. Their pattern of child rearing, however, clearly was much more restrictive than that in the middle-class families. These mothers frequently were legitimately worried about the dangers of the neighborhood and temptations from peer groups. They were warm and loving, but strict and authoritarian.

We developed the hypothesis that the successful parents in high-risk families show a pattern of parental variables different from that shown by successful parents in low-risk families.

Definition of the risk groups

In order to test this hypothesis, we first divided the sample into a high-risk group and a low-risk group. We chose to concentrate on cognitive outcome (IQ, achievement test scores, and academic achievement in school). We chose four important risk variables that fit our criterion of being distal variables. These were family occupation level, family education level, minority status, and absence of the father. Family occupation level was defined in terms of the nine occupational levels developed by Hollingshead. However, we combined the mother's and father's occupations in a manner different from that of Hollingshead (Hollingshead & Redlich, 1958). If both parents were at home and both employed, we defined the family occupation as the maximum of the levels of the two parents. Averaging the two as Hollingshead recommends frequently distorts the picture when the mother is employed. For a variety of reasons, mothers frequently take jobs well below their educational levels. The family social status seems much better geared to the father's level in these families. We also had a few families in which the mother's occupation was of higher socioeconomic level than the father's. In these families, averaging also seemed inappropriate. Similarly, the family education level was the maximum value for the two parents if the family was intact. Minority status was defined as either black or Hispanic. We did not have any other minority groups represented in this sample. Absence of the father was the fourth risk variable. It indicated whether or not the family was intact, but we did not in this analysis did not try to distinguish between absent fathers who never saw their children and those who saw their children regularly.

These risk variables were translated into z scores to make them comparable and then averaged to give a "distal risk" score. The high-risk sample was defined as those families in the highest third of the total sample in terms of risk, and the low-risk group comprised the remainder.

The outcome variable used in these analyses was a cognitive outcome, namely, the mean of IQ, arithmetic achievement, and school achievement. These risk variables made a major contribution to the prediction of cognitive outcome. The four variables had a multiple R^2 of .47, equivalent to a correlation of .685. On our composite cognitive z score, the means of the low- and high-risk groups were $.92\sigma$ and -1.88σ. The range of cognitive scores for the low-risk group was -4.3σ to $+6.4\sigma$, and for the high-risk group the range was -5.4σ to $+4.9\sigma$. The standard deviations of the two groups were both about 2σ. The difference between the two groups was, of course, highly significant ($t = 7.1$; $p < .0001$), but still each group had a broad enough range of cognitive scores to permit significant improvement in predictions.

The high-risk and low-risk groups were each divided into a cognitively successful subgroup and a cognitively unsuccessful subgroup at the mean score for the entire sample (i.e., the same standard for success was established for the two risk samples). As would be expected, that procedure selected a much larger successful subgroup from the low-risk group than from the high-risk group – 68 of the 102 children in the low-risk group were in the high-cognitive group, whereas only 8 of the 50 children in the high-risk group were above the mean in the cognitive score. Those were precisely the families about which we wanted to know more. What information would help us understand how these eight families produced cognitively successful children?

Comparisons of the risk groups on the parenting variables

The seven parenting scales based on the tapes of the parent interviews were labeled (1) restrictiveness of regulations, (2) explanation of policy, (3) democracy of policy, (4) readiness of enforcement, (5) severity of penalties, (6) clarity of policy, and (7) effectiveness of policy. Six of these were used in the analyses, because of the low reliability of one (readiness of enforcement).

Champney (1941) distinguished between parental rules or policy and parental suggestions or orders made on the spur of the moment. We asked the parents about the rules they expected their children to obey without being

Table 12.2. *Reliability of parenting variables*

Variable	Intraclass correlation
Restrictiveness	.78***
Explanation	.59***
Democracy	.61***
Readiness	.002
Severity	.42**
Clarity	.44**
Effectiveness	.85***

$*p < .05; **p < .01; ***p < .001.$

reminded. The restrictiveness score rated how much freedom the child had if the parental policy was completely obeyed. For example, some families required their children to stay in the house if the parent was not there; others required merely that the parent know where the child was. The score on clarity of policy measured how clearly the child understood the policy. We asked ourselves – and the parents if necessary – how well the children could tell us what the rules were. The explanation score measured how fully the parent explained the reasons for the rules (e.g., "You could be mugged or raped if you wander around this neighborhood after dark by yourself"). The score on democracy of policy measured how much the child was consulted about the policy and how much influence the child had over the policy. Toward the low end of the scale, but not at the very bottom, it included the parent taking the child's wishes into account even without actual consultation.

The severity score measured the severity of punishments reported by the parents. Finally, the overall success of the policy (i.e., how well the child conformed to it) was measured on the effectiveness scale.

The children were rated on these scales on the basis of the audiotapes of the interviews by the interviewers, along with the judgments of expressed emotion in the Camberwell Family Interview (Leff & Vaughn, 1985). The interviewers met regularly and discussed their ratings. In order to measure reliability, four interviewers and a research assistant rated tapes of all the other interviewers and discussed any disagreements. The reliability measures are based on the agreement before the discussion of a particular interview. The intraclass correlations were quite satisfactory (greater than .60) for restrictiveness, democracy, and effectiveness. The reliabilities were satisfactory (greater than .40) for all the rest, except readiness of enforcement (Table 12.2).

Table 12.3 shows the means for the high- and low-risk groups on each parenting variable and the directions and significances of those differences, as well as the correlations with outcome within each group. The important confirmation of the hypothesis lies in the strikingly different correlations of restrictiveness with cognitive outcome. The mean values in the high- and low-risk

Table 12.3. *Relationships between cognitive outcome and parenting variables*

Variable	Mean	Difference	Correlation with cognitive outcome
Restrictiveness			
Low risk	50.9		−.26
High risk	58.6	+7.5*	+.63
Severity of penalties			
Low risk	44.4		−.10
High risk	59.6	+15.2**	−.08
Justification of policy			
Low risk	59.4		+.24
High risk	50.8	−8.6 ns	+.20
Democracy of policy			
Low risk	53.2		+.42
High risk	35.0	−18.2**	+.29
Clarity of policy			
Low risk	67.7		+.35
High risk	63.7	−4.0 ns	+.68
Effectiveness of policy			
Low risk	71.8		+.36
High risk	58.7	−13.1**	+.20

*$p < .05$; **$p < .01$; ***$p < .001$; ns, not significant.

samples were not unexpected. The high-risk sample was more restrictive and less democratic; these parents justified the policy less. They were more severe in their punishments. Clarity scores were nearly the same in the two samples. The low-risk sample was judged to be more effective in its policy. In the high-risk sample, however, success went along with being restrictive, and because these families were not democratic, clarity of policy was an essential for success. The cognitively successful high-risk subgroup had a mean restrictiveness score of 68.3, more than 10 points higher than the mean for any of the other three subgroups (Table 12.4). The same small subgroup had a higher clarity score (75) than even the cognitively successful low-risk subgroup. The unsuccessful high-risk subgroup had a mean clarity score of 60, the lowest for any of the subgroups (Table 12.4).

The low-risk group contained more democratic families, as seen by the significant difference in the means. The successful high-risk families were not democratic. Their mean score of 41 was higher than that for the unsuccessful high-risk families, but it was not as high as that for the unsuccessful low-risk families (Table 12.4). Some of the parents in the low-risk group said that they did not have any specific rules; they talked things out, and the children did not need specific rules. Many parents described having had clear rules when their

Table 12.4. *Mean parenting scores for four subgroups*

	Low risk[a]	High risk[a]	Significance
Clarity			
Successful	70.5	75.0	Success $p < .05$
Unsuccessful	62.6	60.0	
Explanation			
Successful	60.8	55.0	ns
Unsuccessful	57.1	49.4	
Effectiveness			
Successful	74.1	58.3	Risk $p < .01$
Unsuccessful	67.9	58.8	Success $p < .05$
Restrictiveness			
Successful	47.9	68.3	ns
Unsuccessful	56.2	56.6	
Democracy			
Successful	57.6	41.7	Risk $p < .01$
Unsuccessful	45.6	32.8	Success $p < .01$
Severity			
Successful	44.8	66.7	Risk $p < .01$
Unsuccessful	43.8	57.2	

Note: The significance statements are from an ANOVA testing the two main effects and the interaction.
[a]Number of cases: low-risk successful, 30; low-risk unsuccessful, 17; high-risk successful, 3; high-risk unsuccessful, 9.

children were younger, but at age 12 to 14 "they simply know what is expected of them."

The successful high-risk families were also more severe in their punishments than were the unsuccessful families, despite the lack of an overall correlation. This fits the general picture, although we shall see soon that it must be modified.

The table of correlations of the parenting variables with each other confirms this general interpretation (Table 12.5). In the low-risk families, restrictiveness was negatively correlated with democracy, whereas in the high-risk families it was positively correlated with democracy. In the low-risk families, restrictiveness had a chance relation with effectiveness, whereas in the high-risk families it was positively correlated. In low-risk families, severity was negligibly related to the effectiveness scale, but in high-risk families it was strongly negatively correlated. Note, however, that it was not strongly correlated with cognitive outcome.

Democracy, clarity, and justification were "good" traits in both samples in that they were correlated with the children's cognitive outcomes and the interviewers' ratings of effectiveness. Restrictiveness in the high-risk sample

Table 12.5. *Intercorrelations of parenting variables*

	Restrictiveness	Justification	Democracy	Clarity	Severity	Effectiveness
Restrictiveness		−.20	−.46	+.25	+.54	−.00
		+.60	+.49	+.90	−.47	+.32
Justification			+.67	+.53	−.18	+.28
			+.63	+.59	−.44	+.44
Democracy				+.27	−.39	+.49
				+.59	−.43	+.61
Clarity					+.44	+.50
					−.61	+.58
Severity						−.01
						−.86
Effectiveness						

Note: The top figure in each cell represents the low-risk families ($N = 47$). The bottom figure represents the high-risk families ($N = 12$).

was also one of the "good" variables and was correlated with the others. In the low-risk families it was not. Severity was a "bad" trait in high-risk families, but unimportant in the low-risk sample.

Democracy was a "good" trait in both samples, but in the high-risk families its mean value was so low that it did not mean that the parent consulted the child about policy. It meant merely that the parent took the child's wishes into account. Thus, it was more a measure of warmth than of democratic child rearing.

Recently, we finished additional analyses that strengthen the preceding interpretation. These analyses were based on multiple regression models rather than on the correlations of cognitive outcome with parenting in the high- and low-distal-risk groups. The differences in the correlations for the two risk groups were evaluated by introducing an interaction term – parenting multiplied by distal risk – in the multiple regression.

Restrictiveness of policy and justification of policy were found to show significant interactions with distal risk. Table 12.6 shows the results. It was our interest to try to understand how the distal risk variables operated. The mothers in the high-risk group who seemed to be successful frequently spoke of the risks their children faced in the neighborhood. The risk of being the victim of a crime was one source of anxiety, and in many cases the restrictions on the children's actions were dictated by that risk. One mother, for example, walked with her child to school and met the child after school every day. When the child complained that her mother did not trust her, the mother said that it was not the child, but the weirdos in the neighborhood, she did not trust.

In order to see how much that threat influenced the effect of parenting on cognitive outcome, we obtained, with the cooperation of the Rochester police department, crime statistics for each "lemras" block in the city of Rochester.

Table 12.6. *Regression coefficients of cognitive outcome on predictors, with and without interaction terms*

Variable	Without interaction[a]	With interaction[a]
Restrictiveness	−.06	−.21
Justification	+.20	+.18
Risk group	−.36	−1.13
Restrictiveness × risk group		1.44
Justification × risk group		−.62
R^2	.2237**	.3091[b]

*$p < .05$; **$p < .01$.
[a]Number of cases = 60. Predictive equation for high-risk group:

Cognitive outcome = −7.99 + .15 · Restrictiveness − .06 · Justification

Predictive equation for low- and moderate-risk group:

Cognitive outcome = 1.31 − .05 · Restrictiveness + .04 · Justification

[b]Improvement due to interaction: $R^2 = .0854$*.

A lemras block is a spatial unit used in describing the geographical distribution of crime in the city. It is an area varying in size, but comprising a number of city blocks. The police department furnished us with the total number of police calls for each lemras block over the preceding 2 years, classified according to the 31 FBI categories of crime.

In order to allow for the varying sizes of lemras blocks, we divided the number of crimes by the area of each lemras block. This index, we thought, was a fair representation of how likely a child would be to encounter such a crime in wandering about the neighborhood. For our purpose, the area rather than the population of the lemras block seemed an appropriate divisor. Thus, we had, for each child in the study (provided the child lived in the city of Rochester), the density of crimes per thousand square feet in area in which the child lived.

Unfortunately, the police departments in the suburbs did not keep crime statistics in this same way; so we could not obtain comparable figures for children outside the city limits. About half of these children lived in the city.

Next we directed our attention to two classes of crimes: (1) those that a child might be enticed into committing and (2) those in which a child might become the victim. The first included criminal mischief, larceny, drug offenses, and disorderly conduct. The second included robbery, rape and sex offenses, murder, and assault. Other categories of crime, such as automobile violations, forgery, or embezzlement, seemed unlikely to be sources of risk to these 13-year-olds.

It was our hypothesis that the high distal risk these children faced might be concretely described for this purpose in terms of high-crime neighborhoods.

Table 12.7. *Regression of cognitive outcome on interactions with crime rate (victim)*

Variable	Without interaction	With interaction
Restrictiveness	−.03	−.57
Justification	+.25	+.38
Crime rate	−.42*	−1.40
Restrictiveness × crime rate		+2.77**
Justification × crime rate		−1.66*
R^2	.28888	.6258[a]

*p < .05; **p < .01; ***p < .001.
[a]Improvement due to interaction: R^2 = .33***.

Obviously, there were other risks these high-risk children faced, but this risk seemed important to these parents and may have been the instigation for some of their restrictive parental policies.

Thus, we again calculated multiple regression coefficients for predicting cognitive outomes on the basis of parental restrictiveness, parental justification, crime rate, and the interaction of each parenting variable with crime rate. These parenting variables were selected because they were the ones showing differences in the high- and low-distal-risk groups. The results are shown in Table 12.7. Crime rate included only crimes in which a child might be a victim. The multiple R^2 value for restrictiveness, justification, and crime rate was .29. When the two interaction terms (restrictiveness × crime rate, justification × crime rate) were added into the equation, the multiple R^2 value jumped to .63. The equations for predicting cognitive outcomes for the low- and high-crime-rate groups were as follows:

High-crime-rate group,

Cognitive outcome = −7.02 + .18 · Restrictiveness − .14 · Justification

Low crime rate group,

Cognitive outcome = .145 − .12 · Restrictiveness + .12 · Justification

Restrictiveness was counterproductive in the low-crime-rate families, and justification facilitated cognitive development, whereas in the high-crime-rate families the reverse was true. These differences were larger and more significant when the families were classified by crime rate than when they were classified by distal risk. It was not merely that crime rate was correlated with distal risk (which, of course, it was) but that the effect of distal risk was better described in terms of crime rate than in terms of the distal risk variables. In this case, crime rate was the proximal variable through which distal risk operated.

These results were for a small sample, N = 24, because only the children in the city of Rochester for whom we had parenting scores had both variables measured, but even with such a small sample the findings were highly signifi-

Table 12.8. *Correlations of ratings on values with cognitive outcome*

| | Mean values | | | Correlations | |
	Low risk (N = 102)	High risk (N = 49)	Difference	Low risk	High risk
1. Considerateness	4.1	6.8	+2.7***	+.18	+.30*
2. Interested[a]	8.4	9.1	+.7 ns	+.14	−.09
3. Responsible	4.1	6.3	+2.2***	+.28*	+.01
4. Self-control	7.0	6.9	−.1 ns	+.04	+.26*
5. Good manners	8.4	5.9	−2.5***	−.23*	−.22
6. Neat and clean	9.7	8.0	−1.7**	−.43	−.22
7. Good student	8.1	7.2	−.9 ns	+.17	+.13
8. Honest	2.3	4.7	+2.4***	+.14	+.15
9. Obedience	6.6	4.7	−1.9***	−.37	−.15
10. Good judgment	4.8	7.9	+3.1***	+.29	+.16
11. Sex-typed behavior[b]	11.7	7.5	−4.2***	−.29	−.34
12. Tries to succeed	7.6	7.8	+.2 ns	+.13	−.01
13. Peer sociability[c]	8.1	8.8	+.7 ns	+.16	+.11

*$p < .05$; **$p < .01$; ***$p < .001$; ns, not significant.
[a]Interested – "Interested in how things work" (Kohn list).
[b]Sex-typed behavior – "Behaves the way a boy (or girl) should" (Kohn list).
[c]Peer sociability – "Gets along well with other children" (Kohn list).

cant. They will be described more fully in a forthcoming publication describing the entire study of the 13-year-olds in the Rochester Longitudinal Study (RLS).

Comparison of the ranking of Kohn's values

There were other relevant variables on these families that were available for the entire sample. We now present a similar analysis of those variables – comparing the correlations with cognitive outcome for the high-risk and low-risk groups.

The first data to be presented are the rankings of parental values developed and studied by Kohn (1977). There were 13 values listed, and the parents were asked to rank them (the value they considered most important for their children being ranked 1, and the least important value being ranked 13). Table 12.8 shows the mean rankings and the correlations of each value with cognitive outcome for the low-risk and high-risk groups. In Table 12.8, the mean ranking is the actual rank; 1 is the highest rank, and 13 the lowest. Because a high rank is a low number, the correlations are apparently reversed; therefore, the correlations have all been changed in sign so that a positive correlation represents a correlation with the importance the parent gave to that value.

Table 12.9. *Mean rankings of selected parental variables for four subgroups of parents*

Variable	Low risk[a]	High risk[a]	Significance
Good judgment			
Successful	4.2	6.2	Risk $p < .0001$
Unsuccessful	6.0	8.0	Success $p < .05$
Obedience			
Successful	7.6	5.5	Risk $p < .0001$
Unsuccessful	4.7	3.2	Success $p < .0001$
Neat and clean			
Successful	10.4	9.0	Risk $p < .01$
Unsuccessful	8.2	7.8	Success $p < .05$
Responsibility			
Successful	3.7	4.8	ns
Unsuccessful	4.8	6.6	
Self-control			
Successful	7.3	4.5	Interaction $p < .01$
Unsuccessful	6.6	7.2	
Sex-typed behavior			
Successful	12.1	11.7	Risk $p < .0001$
Unsuccessful	11.0	6.7	Success $p < .0001$
Good student			
Successful	7.7	7.2	ns
Unsuccessful	8.9	7.2	

Note: Items were ranked by parents from 1 (most highly valued) to 13 (least valued).
[a]Number of cases: low-risk successful, 67, low-risk unsuccessful, 34; high-risk successful, 8; high-risk unsuccessful, 40.

In general, the correlations had much the same pattern, but slightly different levels. For the low-risk parents, responsibility and good judgment were both highly valued and also were the most highly correlated with cognitive success. For the high-risk parents self-control was significantly correlated with success; it was more highly valued by the successful high-risk parents than by any other subgroup. For the unsuccessful high-risk parents its value was low. Responsibility was not significantly correlated with success in the high-risk group, but the successful high-risk parents valued it as highly as did the low-risk parents. For high-risk parents, success depended on the children following the rules and resisting the temptation to deviate. For both kinds of families, success depended on the children using their own judgment and being responsible.

Among low-risk parents, obedience ranked only sixth or seventh and was negatively correlated with outcome. High-risk parents, in general, valued obedience more than did low-risk parents, but the successful valued it less than the unsuccessful (Table 12.9).

In both risk groups, sex-typed behavior was significantly negatively corre-lated with outcome. For low-risk parents, sex-typed behavior was the least important value – many of them practically discarded that item and did not have to think about how to rank it. In the high-risk sample the picture was quite different. There was a subgroup of parents who ranked sex-typed behav-ior at the very top of the list, and that was more common among the high-risk parents. But the successful high-risk parents gave it a much lower value (Table 12.9). The size of the negative correlation with success was partly because of the enlarged range of ranking in the high-risk group. The standard deviation of the ranking for this item was twice as large in the high-risk group as in the low-risk group.

The same relation holds for item No. 6, "being neat and clean." Next to sex-typed behavior, it was least valued among low-risk parents and was strongly negatively correlated with success. In the high-risk group it was more highly valued, on the average, and the standard deviation was large, reflecting high diversity of opinion. The successful high-risk parents valued it much less than did the unsuccessful ones, and along with good manners it was negatively correlated with success.

These rankings of the values gave us a better picture of the successful families in the two risk groups. Many of the same values accompanied success in the two groups. In the interviews with the high-risk group, we believed that the values of the successful parents were not widely held and that they were in fact almost deviant in their community. The mean values for the successful high-risk group confirmed that impression.

Warmth and criticism

Let us turn now to the interview variables concerned with parental expression of feeling toward the child. These variables were based on the taped interviews with the parents. Following the protocol developed for the Camberwell Family Interview (CFI) (Leff & Vaughn, 1985), we counted the number of remarks by the mother that met the criteria for critical com-ments, and on the basis of the entire interview we made a global rating of warmth.

In the literature reporting studies of the relationship between these ex-pressed emotions and rehospitalization of the patient-offspring, the critical comments variable has been the best predictor of rehospitalization. There was no reason to expect that the same variable would be most significant in the groups in our study. The children in our sample were not mentally ill, nor had they necessarily posed any stressful problems for their parents (although in some cases they certainly had). In the CFI studies, the parents recounted the offspring's breakdown and hospitalization. They welcomed a ready listener to whom they could pour out their troubles. In our RLS study the interviewer was ready to listen, but few of the parents had a tale of woe. Some did, but

Table 12.10. *Correlations between expressed emotions and cognitive outcome*

Variable	Mean value (N = 101)			Correlation (N = 48)	
	Low risk	High risk	Difference	Low risk	High risk
Critical comments	1.1	1.8	+.7*	−.20*	−.02
Warmth	3.3	2.8	−.5*	+.24*	+.13

*p < .05.

Table 12.11. *Correlations of parental variables with cognitive success*

Variable	Mean value			Correlation	
	Low risk	High risk	Difference	Low risk	High risk
CODQ	1.2	0.6	−.6***	+.29	+.53
Shipley IQ	110.8	90.9	19.9***	+.44***	+.50***

***p < .001.

generally these parents presented a balanced picture of life with a young teenager, and some of the parents were quite content with their children and explained in the interview how rewarding their children were.

The correlations between cognitive outcome and these scores on expressed emotion are shown in Table 12.10. Both of these correlations were significantly different from zero. There were no striking differences in the correlations for the two risk groups. In general, warmth was related to success, and critical comments were negatively related. That was true for both the high- and low-risk groups. In the interviews, we did not get any feeling that the successful low-risk families were anything but warm in their feelings toward their children. Some of the other parent variables that were relevant to outcome are shown in Table 12.11. The correlations between these variables and outcome were generally quite sensible. The differences between the correlations in the high- and low-risk groups were also significant for the CODQ (Sameroff & Feil, 1985). Here the correlation with outcome was higher in the high-risk group than in the low-risk group. The CODQ measures how perspectivistic rather than categorical are the parents' beliefs about child development and child rearing. A categorical parent is one who believes that there is only one way to raise children; a perspectivistic parent is one who believes that there are many different circumstances that should influence one's child-rearing policy. Our hypothesis seemed to suggest that the successful high-risk parents were somewhat rigid, and by comparison with low-risk parents they were, but by comparison with the unsuccessful high-risk parents, they were perspectivistic. One successful high-risk parent said "I don't whup him because it don't do no good." A less successful high-risk parent said "I whup him all the time but it don't do no good."

Parental IQ was highly correlated with success in both samples. That finding was not unexpected.

In summary, we have evidence that among these high-risk families, success was related to restrictiveness, clarity, vigilance, and warmth, whereas in low-risk families, success was related more to democracy of policy and warmth. A high cognitive outcome for the child was associated with parents who put a high value on responsibility and good judgment and, in the successful high-risk subgroup, on self-control. Furthermore, it was associated in both the high-risk and low-risk groups with a perspectivistic rather than categorical outlook in the CODQ.

Comparisons with an earlier study

Prior to the RLS research project reported here, we were collaborators in the University of Rochester Child and Family Study (URCAFS) (Baldwin, Cole, & Baldwin, 1982). The URCAFS sample was quite different from the RLS sample in that all of the URCAFS parents were white, and none of them were in the lowest socioeconomic class. There was, however, a range of SES levels from class I to class IV. In the URCAFS project we made direct observations of family interactions in a free play setting and in the consensus Rorschach (Watt, Anthony, Wynne, & Rolf, 1984). In that sense we had measures of the most proximal variables, actual counts of different kinds of interactions. Therefore, it seemed important to examine the differences between the high- and low-risk URCAFS families on the correlations with cognitive outcome. In URCAFS, this outcome was the full WISC-R IQ.

For this analysis, risk was defined in exactly the same way: family education, family occupation, father's presence, and minority status (except that none of the URCAFS families belonged to minority groups). Because one parent in each family had been hospitalized, we had a measure of the GAS (global assessment score) for each patient-parent at the time of the observations. The results did not change if the GAS score was included as a risk variable.

Because the URCAFS sample did not contain the lowest levels of SES, it seemed important to compare the high- and low-risk groups in the two samples. These data are shown in Table 12.12. The same table shows the correlations of these risk variables with cognitive outcome. The score for father's presence is the percentage of families in which the father was present, and that for minority status is the percentage of minority group members in the sample.

The variables measured during the observation of the free play period included a count of the number of behavior requests and the number of acts that conveyed warmth. Each of these counts was available for the mother, for

Table 12.12. *Risk variables in the RLS and URCAFS samples*

	RLS sample						URCAFS sample[a]					
	Low risk		High risk				Low Risk		High risk			
Variable	Mean	Correlation	Mean	Correlation			Mean	Correlation	Mean	Correlation		
Family education	5.4	.43	3.5	.35			5.3	.55	3.9	.15		
Family occupation	5.9	.46	2.3	.21			6.6	.33	4.2	.29		
Father present	75%	-.07	26%	-.17			89%	-.08	56%	-.55		
Minority status[a]	14%	-.40	86%	-.26								

[a]URCAFS had no minority representatives.

Table 12.13. *Correlations of free play variables with cognitive success*

Variable	Low risk		High risk	
	Mean	Correlation	Mean	Correlation
Mother behavior request	.07	−.06	.06	−.07
Father behavior request	.15	+.04	.14	−.53
Mother warmth	.26	−.13	.26	+.52
Father warmth	.24	+.11	.22	+.02
Family behavior request	20.2	.22	19.6	−.72
Family warmth	55.6	.20	51.8	+.58

the father, and for the two parents combined. In the data shown here, the counts were reduced to percentages of the total number of acts during the free play period in order to adjust for the differences in overall activity levels.

The number of behavior requests seemed, perhaps, to be the variable most similar to restrictiveness as measured in the RLS study, but they were not closely similar. Champney (1941) made the distinction between policy and suggestions. One of the Fels scales, *frequency of suggestions,* measures the frequency of behavior requests. Restrictiveness describes established rules and policy, whereas behavior requests during free play are almost always momentary requests, such as "Hook the engine onto the coal car" or "Close up the bars faster" on the shoot-the-moon game. Rarely in the free play did family policy emerge, although occasionally it would become involved (e.g., "You must put away the game you have been playing with before you get out another").

The mean level of each variable and its correlation with the full IQ are shown in Table 12.13. The results for behavior requests seemed exactly opposite to the findings on restrictiveness and contrary to the hypothesis. The difference, however, between a restrictive policy and bossiness in interpersonal interaction on nonpolicy issues is important. Restrictive rules, if they are reasonable and nonarbitrary, obviate the necessity for moment-to-moment dominance. The most dominant URCAFS families (which were also very high in activity levels) were the parents who supervised every aspect of their children's behaviors. Among the RLS successful high-risk families, it was important that the children not need constant supervision, because many single-parent mothers worked full-time and had to leave their children on their own for periods of the day.

In light of these considerations, it was surprising that behavior requests and activity levels were negatively related to cognitive outcome. Finding that warmth was positively correlated with outcome, however, was not surprising. In families with strict rules, warmth was an important factor in making such a restrictive policy function effectively.

Discussion

Our original hypothesis emphasized the differences between the child-rearing practices of high- and low-risk families who succeeded in raising children who were above average in cognitive functioning. The findings, taken together, confirm the hypothesis that the cognitive competence of children from high-risk families is related to the parenting variables in a different way than is the cognitive competence of children from low-risk families. Our successful high-risk families were more restrictive and authoritarian in their policies and were more vigilant in monitoring their children's compliance than were successful low-risk families. These findings are in essential agreement with those in Baumrind's study of black families (Baumrind, 1982).

We also found many variables related to the development of cognitive competence that were similar for low- and high-risk families. Parental intelligence was, of course, one of these, and we did not expect that parental IQ would be differently related to children's cognitive functioning in the two subsamples.

From the analysis of the parental rankings on 13 Kohn values, it appeared that responsibility and good judgment in children were consistently valued higher in the successful homes, regardless of risk status. On the other hand, obedience, good manners, being neat and clean, and behaving in a sex-typed way were consistently given lower rankings in the successful homes. Self-control, however, was highly valued in high-risk homes, but that was not true for any other subgroups.

The higher restrictiveness of the successful high-risk subgroup reflects some of the very real temptations and risks faced by those children, namely, drugs, delinquency, and early pregnancy. These are risks from which children can to some degree be sheltered by restrictions on their freedom – provided that the restrictions do not arouse the negativism of a teenage child. In other words, if children conform to parental restrictions, they are partially protected from these environmental influences.

Another major problem for this high-risk sample is school failure. Here, again, parental requirements that children do their homework and close parental supervision of children's school conduct and progress can be effective. To some degree, school failure may result from the same kinds of peer pressures that may entice children into drugs or antisocial conduct. Truancy leads to school failure and also exposes children to damaging environmental influences.

These risks are those associated with a lower-SES inner-city environment, and for protection against those influences, restrictiveness can be effective. Other kinds of risks, such as the risks associated with being raised by a psychotic mother, are quite different, and there is no reason to suppose that restrictiveness would be an effective protection against those risks.

Following our interviews, we came to believe that in this sample, another feature of the successful high-risk homes was church membership. Many of these high-risk families were black, and in the successful families particularly we were impressed by the importance of the church in their lives as they reported it to us. We had no variable that would measure this directly, although assessment of the social environment might reveal the influence of the church on these children. There is nothing magical about the church per se, but a social support group that reinforces the parental policy and also provides peer influences that are consonant with the parental values may be an important element in the success of such children.

The picture we have drawn of these successful high-risk families indicates that they are fighting against the influences of the neighborhood and in some respects are actually deviant in relation to it. Thus, an institution that supports the parental values probably is an important ally of the parents. This seems quite different from the situation in low-risk, middle-class suburbia, where many community influences support high achievement and good conduct.

This line of thought led us to ask if the influence of the family was perhaps more important for cognitive competence in the children of high-risk successful families than for low-risk successful families, for whom nonfamilial influences may provide alternative motivations for high standards.

In order to get some empirical data relating to this question, we hypothesized that familial influences would make a more important contribution to cognitive outcome for high-risk children than for low-risk children. The findings were quite consistent with that hypothesis. The multiple R^2 for the five significant parenting variables and the CODQ in predicting cognitive outcome was .34 for the low-risk families, but .57 for the high-risk group. Similarly, the multiple R^2 for significant Kohn values was .27 for low-risk children, but .35 for high-risk children.

These findings are quite relevant to intervention. At one time we thought, somewhat naively, that knowing the major risk factors would point the way to intervention, because removing the risk factors might prevent the development of problem behavior. It is clear, however, that without social revolution we are not going to remove the risk variables of lower SES, divorce, and minority prejudice. If there is going to be intervention, it must operate through the proximal rather than the distal variables. We must help these families and their children to cope with the risks in their environment, rather than attempt the futile task of removing the large-scale risk factors themselves. We could conceive of a psychoeducational program that would teach families how to protect their children from these malignant influences by restricting the children's freedom if necessary, by making family rules quite clear and explicit, and by monitoring the children's behavior closely.

It is interesting to speculate whether or not the successful middle-class pattern of child rearing could be effective in the risky environment in which high-risk families live. Probably part of the reason for the success of low-risk children derives from the many other community influences in middle-class neighborhoods that support the value system of the family. In that case, the middle-class strategies for success might not work in high-risk lower-class environments.

On the other side, would a more restrictive authoritarian family pattern be successful in middle-class homes? Part of the reason for the success of the restrictiveness in the high-risk environment is that the restrictions are realistic responses to the environment and can be defended on the basis of reason if the child objects. That is, they are not arbitrary. The same restrictions in a suburban environment might seem both arbitrary and unduly harsh to the child and to the neighbors – witness the effectiveness of the well-known argument that "all the other kids get to do it."

On the other hand, restrictiveness does work well in some middle-class environments. In the Fels studies, the pattern of behavior labeled "casual autocratic" (Baldwin, Kalhorn, & Breese, 1945) was found largely in rural homes, but was quite effective there. Again, however, a farm environment contains more realistic pressures and more threatening risks to safety than does the suburban home. So perhaps restrictiveness tends to emerge in those successful homes in which risks are clear and present and are understood by both the parents and the children.

All of these speculations simply reinforce what was said earlier: that to design a successful intervention program, it is important to determine which strategies will be successful in the environment in which it is to be applied, and not generalize too freely from successful child rearing in one environment to a quite different kind of environment.

References

Ammons, R. B., & Ammons, C. H. (1962). *The Quick Test (QT): Provisional manual.* Missoula, MT: Psychological Test Specialists.

Baldwin, A. L., Cole, R. E., & Baldwin, C. P. (1982). *Parental pathology, family interaction, and the competence of the child in school. Monographs of the Society for Research in Child Development, 47*(No. 197).

Baldwin, A. L., Kalhorn, J., & Breese, F. H. (1945). Patterns of parent behavior. *Psychological Monographs, 58,* 268.

Baumrind, D. (1982). An explanatory study of socialization effects on black children: Some black–white comparisons. *Child Development, 43,* 261–7.

Beck, A. T. (1967). *Depression: Causes and treatment.* Philadelphia: University of Pennsylvania Press.

Champney, H. (1941). The measurement of parent behavior. *Child Development, 43,* 131–66.

Connell, J. P. (1985). A new multidimensional measure of children's perception of control. *Child Development, 56,* 1018–41.

Furman, W., & Buhrmester, D. (1985). Children's perceptions of the personal relationships in their social networks. *Developmental Psychology, 21,* 1016–24.

Garmezy, N. (1982, July). *Stress resistant children: The search for protective factors.* Address to the 10th international congress of the International Association for Child and Adolescent Psychiatry and allied professions. Dublin, Ireland.

Harter, S. (1978). *Perceived Competence Scale for Children.* University of Denver.

Herzog, J., Linder, H., & Samaha, J. (1982). *The measurement of stress: Life events and interview-*

ers' ratings (from the research programs of Project Competence: Studies of stress resistant children). University of Minnesota.

Hollingshead, A. B., & Redlich, F. C. (1958). *Social class and mental illness.* New York: Wiley.

Ikle, D. N., Lipp, D. O., Butters, E. A., & Ciarlo, J. (1983). *Development and validation of the adolescent community mental health questionnaire.* Denver: Mental Systems Evaluation Project.

Jastak, S., & Wilkinson, G. (1984). *The Wide Range Achievement Test – Revised.* Jastak Assessment Systems.

Kohn, M. L. (1977). *Class and conformity* (2nd ed.). University of Chicago Press.

Leff, T., & Vaughn, C. (1985). *Expressed emotion in families: Its significance for mental illness.* New York: Guilford Press.

Rutter, M., Tizard, J., Yule, W., Graham, P., & Whitmore, K. (1976). Research report: Isle of Wight studies 1964–1974. *Psychological Medicine, 6,* 313–32.

Sameroff, A. J., & Feil, L. A. (1985). Parental concepts of development. In I. Sigel (Ed.), *Parental belief systems: The psychological consequence for children* (pp. 84–104). Hillsdale, NJ: Erlbaum.

Sameroff, A. J., & Seifer, R. (1983). Familial risk and child competence. *Child Development, 54,* 1254–68.

Sameroff, A. J., Seifer, R., & Zax, M. (1982). *Early development of children at risk for emotional disorder. Monographs of the Society for Research in Child Development, 47*(Serial No. 199).

Shipley, W. C. (1939) *Shipley Institute of Living Scale for measuring intellectual impairment: Manual of directions and scoring key.* Hartford: The Institute of Living.

Tanner, J. M. (1962). *Growth at adolescence.* Oxford: Blackwell.

Watt, F. N., Anthony, J. E., Wynne, L. C., & Rolf, J. E. (Eds.). (1984). *Children at risk for schizophrenia: A longitudinal perspective.* Cambridge University Press.

Wechsler, D. (1974). *Manual for the Wechsler Intelligence Scale for Children–Revised.* New York: Psychological Corporation.

13 Children's adjustment to parental divorce: self-image, social relations, and school performance

Norman F. Watt, Olivia Moorehead-Slaughter, Debra M. Japzon, and Gloria G. Keller

Background of the problem

There is legitimate public concern for children whose parents divorce. No longer uncommon, divorce permeates every corner of society. The U.S. Census Bureau (1980) reported a 79% increase in the number of single-parent families since 1970. Divorce rates have doubled since 1970 and tripled since 1960 (Select Committee on Children, Youth, and Families, 1983). About 9 million children, one of every seven, experience parental divorce, and by 1990 33% of our children may experience family dissolution before age 18 (Glick, 1979).

Despite a recent surge of interest in the effects of divorce on the lives of children (Wyman, Cowen, Hightower, & Pedro-Carroll, 1985), the number of controlled studies that have been carried out has been disappointing in view of the urgency of the problem (Levitin, 1979). Potentially damaging effects on children's adjustment include increased likelihood of aggressive, undercontrolled behaviors (Emery, 1982; Felner, Farber, & Primavera, 1983; Stolberg & Anker, 1984), anger at the parents for breaking up the family (Wallerstein & Kelly, 1974), fear, depression, and guilt (Hetherington, 1979), more sexual behavior, delinquency, and subjective psychological symptoms (Kalter, 1977), and more anxiety, lower cognitive competence, and fewer social supports (Marsden, 1969; Pearlin & Johnson, 1977; Wyman et al., 1985).

The negative impact of such factors may be more pervasive and enduring

We wish to express our sincere gratitude to Georgia Imhoff, who contributed generously to the funding of this project because of her genuine interest in and dedication to the field of mental health. Special thanks are also due to Lee Kirkpatrick for statistical advice, Michael McCormick for assisting with the home visits, and Rose Molendyk for typing and clerical assistance. Expert advice on research design, instrument selection, and conceptualization was provided by Wyndol Furman, Howard Markman, Mindy Rosenberg, Robbie Rossman, Phil Shaver, and Irving Weiner. We are also indebted to the principals and faculty at the Hill, Kepner, Kunsmiller, and Smiley Middle Schools in Denver and, of course, to the families who welcomed us so openly in their homes.

for boys than for girls (Guidubaldi, Cleminshaw, Perry, & McLoughlin, 1983; Kurdek, Blisk, & Siesky, 1983), despite some contrary evidence (Copeland, 1985; Kurdek & Berg, 1983). Boys from divorced families have shown more behavior disorders and problems at home and in school, and it appears that they receive less support and nurturance than girls (Hetherington, Cox, & Cox, 1978; Santrock, 1975; Santrock & Trace, 1978). A child's age at the time of the divorce may also be important, as one study found negative sequelae for self-concept only in girls under 6 years of age (Kalter, Riemer, Brickman, & Chen, 1985).

Marital conflict has been identified as a principal mediating variable that associates divorce with children's maladjustment (Emery, 1982; Stolberg & Bush, 1985; Stolberg, Camplair, Currier, & Wells, 1984; Block, Block, & Gjerde, 1986). Children show more evidence of maladjustment if parental discord persists after the separation than if the divorce is harmonious (Hetherington, Cox, & Cox, 1976; Jacobson, 1978), and children whose parents have divorced peaceably have fared better than children from intact but conflict-ridden homes (Hetherington et al., 1978; Rutter, 1980a,b; Werner & Smith, 1982).

Looking beyond the potential damage from parental divorce, we might consider compensating factors that may assist some children to cope with its emotional consequences. Under stress, compensatory mechanisms often reestablish the balance of emotional forces in human relationships (Beal, 1979). A harmonious relationship with one parent may buffer the child from some of the negative impact of divorce (Hetherington, Cox, & Cox, 1979). If neither parent is able to meet a child's emotional needs, compensating support can be sought from relatives, teachers, or friends (Wallerstein & Kelly, 1980), especially other children of divorce (Kurdek et al., 1983). The developmental literature also suggests that interpersonal relationships change as children mature into young adults (Berndt, 1979; Hunter & Youniss, 1982). Peer friendships gain prominence and influence as children approach adolescence, while parental influence wanes (Hartup, 1970). Others dispute Hartup's view, arguing that these two sources of support are relatively independent because they meet different needs of the children. Security, affection, enhancement of worth, practical advice, and guidance are obtained primarily from parents (Berndt, 1981; Furman & Robbins, 1985; Hunter & Youniss, 1982; Kon & Losenkov, 1978; Youniss, 1980), but if specific support is not available from one source, the young adolescent may seek it out elsewhere.

Rationale for this investigation

The purpose of this study was an empirical examination of areas of maladjustment in children from divorced or separated families. In addition, we tested five theoretical hypotheses about potential causal factors in psychological adjustment following parental divorce, based on correlational analyses of the data from the divorce sample itself. Finally, we tested four theoretical hypotheses about the influence of peer relationships as compensating sources of support for coping with parental divorce, based on comparisons of children from divorced or separated families and children from intact families. Although more parental conflict was expected in the divorced sample, we did not try to control for that difference, nor to compare the divorced and intact samples for differential effects of conflict. The basic premise of the investigation, consistent with the prevailing tenor of the research literature, was that in most cases parental divorce or separation would create psychological stresses that would place children at risk emotionally, socially, and scholastically, at least for a number of years. We therefore expected to see maladjustments in these areas by the time the children reached adolescent age (about 4 years after the divorce, on the average, in this sample), their severities depending partly on the intensities of various stresses (e.g., the level of marital conflict prior to the separation) and partly on the sources of support available subsequently (e.g., peer relationships and rapport with the custodial parent). The specific hypothetical postulates are listed next, with a brief word of explanation following each.

Correlational analyses within the divorce sample

1. *The level of marital conflict in a divorcing family is negatively related to an adolescent's scholastic competence, perceived self-worth, and quality of relationships with peers and with the custodial parent, and it is directly related to the adolescent's level of behavioral and psychological problems.* This is intended to test the theory of Emery (1982) that the intensity of marital conflict is a primary cause of stress for the offspring when parents divorce, but it offers no contrast with the effects of conflict in intact families.

2. *Effective participation in an extended social network is negatively related to an adolescent's level of behavioral and psychological problems and directly related to the level of rapport with the custodial parent.* An adolescent who is able to find emotional support from an extended social network will have a better relationship with the custodial parent and generally will be better adjusted because the strain on the parent to provide "nurturance supplies" will be shared more widely with other people. There is a kind of "hydraulic" mechanism implied here: Because "distancing" is an important maneuver used by some adolescents to cope with the stress of divorce, those who are able to find activities of interest outside the home and spend more time with peers are likely to experience less conflict in the relationship with the custodial parent. The respite from the stressful home situation is seen as a buffer for the parent–child relationship.

3. *The level of economic decline in a divorcing family is negatively related to*

an adolescent's scholastic competence, perceived self-worth, and relationships with the custodial parent and peers, and it is directly related to the level of behavioral and psychological problems. The general level of stress should be greater for adolescents who have experienced considerable changes in their life-styles because of financial difficulties. Stability of life-style is believed to be the important factor here, not the absolute level of family income.

4. *Following parental divorce, boys tend to manifest lower perceptions of self-worth, more behavioral and psychological problems, and more conflicted relations with the custodial parent than do girls.* This is intended to test a widely held theory cited earlier, but it does not specify differential effects as a function of a child's age or the gender of the custodial parent.

5. *The level of marital conflict in divorcing families is negatively related to adolescents' perceptions of their bodies and self-images and directly related to the level of openness in their sexual attitudes.* Youngsters who observe their identification models in highly conflictual relationships may question their own adequacy in heterosexual relations, leading to disturbances in self-perception. That may give rise to a compensating need to prove their own sexual prowess, perhaps taking the form of expressing more liberal sexual attitudes.

Specific contrasts with children from intact families

1. *Adolescents from divorced families obtain affection, reliable alliance, intimacy, companionship, and enhancement of worth from friends and supply nurturance to friends more than do adolescents from intact families.* This prediction presumes that children turn to their peers as a means of compensating for parental support lost through the divorce, regardless of the level of parental conflict.

2. *Peer social support is more closely associated with school performance, nonacademic school adjustment, and self-esteem in children of divorce than in control children.* Because of the psychological vulnerability of children following parental divorce and the increased importance of peers, it is expected that success in scholastic and personal adjustment will be more directly contingent on social support from peers than is typical of their classmates, regardless of parental conflict.

3. *In divorced families, children who have strong or harmonious rapport with the custodial parent turn less to peers for nurturance and enhancement of worth than do those who have weak or conflictual rapport with the custodial parent.* The expectation here is that children whose rapport with the custodial parent is good do not differ from normal controls in their dependence on peer support because their emotional needs are adequately met at home. By contrast, those with poor parental rapport are doubly deprived, having lost support from the noncustodial parent through the divorce and currently lacking support from the custodial parent because they do not get along. Hence, these

youngsters are expected to become especially dependent on peers as sources and objects of esteem.

4. *In divorced families, children who have weak or conflictual rapport with the custodial parent function less well at school in terms of classroom behavior and academic performance and have lower self-esteem than do children who have strong or harmonious rapport with the custodial parent.* By similar reasoning, youngsters who do not get along with the custodial parent adjust less well than do intact controls, whereas those who do get along at home do not differ significantly from the controls in their general adjustment. This reasoning does not specify differences as functions of the gender of either parents or children.

Method

Subjects

The subjects were solicited from four public middle schools in Denver: 50 children of separated ($n = 11$) or divorced ($n = 39$) parents, and 31 children living with both their natural parents. Eight children in the experimental sample were siblings of index subjects, included because of their availability. The children's ages ranged from 12 to 15 (10 to 14 for the siblings, seven of whom attended elementary schools). There were 32 girls and 18 boys in the experimental group, including 1 Asian-American, 4 blacks, 18 Hispanics, and 27 whites. The control group comprised 14 girls and 17 boys, with 3 blacks, 6 Hispanics, and 22 whites. Their families ranged from upper middle class to lower social class, with average scores close to the national mean, and the control group's mean slightly higher than the experimental group's mean. In the divorce group, the interval since the parents initially separated ranged from 1 to 139 months, with an average of 51 months. Six of the 42 custodial parents were fathers.

Measures

Social class was measured by the Two-Factor Index of Social Position (Hollingshead & Redlich, 1957), which is based on the occupational level and education of the breadwinner.

The Personal Relationships Questionnaire (PRQ) assessed seven relationship qualities (Furman & Buhrmester, 1985): reliable alliance (durability of the bond), affection, enhancement of worth (from another), companionship, nurturance (of another), satisfaction, and conflict. Parents rated their relationships with their children and children rated their relationships with parents, friends, grandparents, and teachers, on five-point Likert scales ranging from least to most characteristic of their relationships.

The Self-Perception Profile for Children (SPP) measured the children's own views of their scholastic competence, social acceptance, behavior/conduct, and self-worth on 21 four-point scales, ranging from least to most favorable self-evaluation (Harter, 1983).

The Self-Image Questionnaire (SIQ) contains 55 items that measure impulse control, emotional tone (mood), body image and self-image, sexual attitudes, and psychopathology (Offer, Ostrov, & Howard, 1981). The item scores (on six-point scales) were modified for clarity of presentation here so that a high score would be most descriptive of the respondent.

Teachers rated each child on 28 five-point behavioral scales of the Pupil Rating Form (PRF), yielding four factors: scholastic motivation, extraversion, interpersonal harmony, and emotional stability (Watt, Stolorow, Lubensky, & McClelland, 1970; Shay, 1978).

Parents and children completed the Conflict Tactics Scale (CTS) as an index of marital conflict (Straus, 1979). They rated how frequently 21 conflictual events had occurred in the preceding 4 to 5 years and how often the child had witnessed them. The sum of the verbal aggression and violence scores from Form N provided a general conflict score.

The Short Marital Adjustment scale was administered to the parents to assess marital satisfaction and adjustment (Locke & Wallace, 1959). We obtained the numbers of each child's friends and extracurricular activities in a structured interview.

Procedures

Letters were sent to families at the four target middle schools describing the research project and soliciting participation from children and custodial parents from divorced families. Presentations were made to the students at three of the schools to discuss the project and answer questions. A short memorandum was distributed, and qualified children volunteered by returning the memorandum to the school. A follow-up letter to interested families explained the purpose and experimental procedures. After obtaining informed consent by mail, arrangements were made to interview and administer the questionnaires to the child and the custodial parent in the home, for which each child received a $10 stipend. The children were offered six 1-hr counseling group sessions in a Divorce Support Group program held after school, for which each of the 25 participating children received $10 more.

Each child nominated two major-subject teachers to evaluate his or her classroom behavior. If the student's first-choice teacher was unwilling to cooperate, the second-choice teacher was asked to make the ratings. Each child also nominated three friends living with their natural parents who might serve as control subjects. These friends were assumed to be similar to the index subject in age, intelligence, ethnic status, and neighborhood location. One was randomly chosen for invitation to participate (also for a $10 stipend). If that one declined, another was randomly chosen from the remaining nomi-

Table 13.1. *Summary of multiple analyses of variance for major clusters of dependent variables*

Cluster of variables[a]	F values for tests of effects		
	Group (G)	Sex (S)	Interaction (G × S)
Marital conflict (5)	21.05****	0.69	1.96*
Scholastic performance (5)	3.95***	1.36	0.39
Emotional adjustment (3)	2.98**	0.50	0.55
Social relations (3)	2.14*	2.53*	0.22
Peer rapport (8)	1.07	2.34**	1.30
Parent–child rapport (16)	1.03	1.09	1.76*

*p < .10; **p < .05; ***p < .005; ****p < .001.
[a]The number of variables in each cluster analyzed is given in parentheses after each cluster name.

nees. With minor exceptions, the data collection procedures were identical for experimental and control subjects.

Results

We present first our analysis of the general premise that divorce has damaging effects on children's adjustment, followed by the findings regarding the specific hypotheses stated earlier. Because there were more than 40 variables to test for group differences, some significant results could be expected by chance alone. Therefore, to control for that possibility, we conducted preliminary multiple analyses of variance for six major clusters of variables, which are presented in Table 13.1. The summary shows that there were substantial differences between the "divorced" and "intact" groups on four of the clusters (marital conflict, scholastic performance, emotional adjustment, and social relations), but not on the peer rapport and parent–child rapport clusters. Appreciable sex differences were found for two clusters (social relations and peer rapport), and noteworthy group × sex interactions were obtained for marital conflict and parent–child rapport. Therefore, with reservations about the group differences for the peer rapport and parent–child rapport measures, we proceeded with the univariate analyses. Comparisons of children from divorced and intact families were made with *t* tests and were repeated using covariance control for social class. Significant group differences were reanalyzed with two-way unweighted-means ANOVAs to test for sex differences and sex × group interactions. Six custodial parents in the divorce group were fathers. Analyses that found significant differences from the control sample were repeated after omitting those six cases, without changing any finding. The term "custodial parent" is used here when the data for these six cases are included; otherwise, the term "mother" is used.

Table 13.2. *Summary of family relations variables that significantly differentiated the divorced sample from the controls*

Variable	Divorced	Controls	t	df	p
Marital satisfaction: mother's view	53.89[a] (26.19)[b]	114.16[a] (23.40)[b]	10.30	73	< .001
Marital conflict: mother's view	2.33 (1.55)	1.02 (0.54)	5.07	72	< .001
Marital conflict: child's view	2.20 (1.37)	1.20 (0.84)	3.98	76	< .001
Marital conflict seen by child: mother's view	1.88 (1.53)	0.72 (0.51)	4.59	72	< .001
Marital conflict seen by child: child's view	1.34 (1.66)	0.96 (0.78)	2.90	76	< .005
Marital conflict concealed from child: child's view	0.52 (0.74)	0.24 (0.50)	2.01	76	< .05
Positive qualities in maternal relationship: child's view	3.10 (0.67)	3.70 (0.85)	3.30	79	< .005
Conflict with mother: child's view	1.89 (0.61)	2.67 (0.98)	-3.92	79	< .001
Child's nurturance of mother: child's view	3.88 (0.95)	3.27 (1.19)	2.33	73	< .025

[a]Mean.   [b]Standard deviation.

Family relations

The analyses summarized in Table 13.2 exclude the data for the six custodial fathers. Predictably, experimental mothers reported less marital satisfaction and more marital conflict than did control mothers, and their evaluations of conflict were corroborated by their children. Mothers and children likewise agreed that experimental children were exposed to more marital conflict than were control children. The children of divorce believed that more of the conflict was concealed from them than from the controls, but that view was not corroborated by the mothers. In their current maternal relationships, the controls perceived both more positive qualities and more conflict than did the children of divorce. This might suggest that the controls currently were more "engaged" in the maternal bond. On the other hand, the children of divorce felt obliged to provide more nurturance for their mothers than did the controls, perhaps reflecting how much stress divorce creates for mothers and families alike. Interpretations concerning the children's relations with their mothers must be made cautiously, because the group effect from the MANOVA did not reach significance, but that lack of significance was at least partially accounted for by the conflict variable "competing" with the differences in nurturance and positive qualities perceived.

Table 13.3. *Summary of significant differences in self-image and social relations perceived by children from divorced and intact families*

Variable	Divorced	Controls	t	df	p
Nurturance given to peers	3.60[a]	4.01[a]	1.97	78	= .05
	(1.00)[b]	(0.85)[b]			
Enhancement of worth received from peers	3.75	4.15	2.15	78	< .05
	(1.00)	(0.68)			
Child's rapport with the extended social network	1.17	1.55	2.32	78	< .025
	(0.83)	(0.62)			
Self-perceived scholastic competence	2.71	3.07	2.31	79	< .025
	(0.65)	(0.72)			
Self-perceived emotional tone or mood	3.14	3.52	2.20	79	< .05
	(0.85)	(0.70)			

[a]Mean.   [b]Standard deviation.

Subjective perceptions of self and relationships with others

Table 13.3 summarizes the group differences in self-image and current social relations. Children of divorce claimed that they gave less nurturance to their peers and gained less esteem from them in return. In view of the nonsignificant MANOVA results for the peer rapport cluster, these two differences could be attributed to chance alone. However, they were consistent with the finding that experimental subjects also felt less rapport with members of their extended social networks, which included their peers. Finally, the children in the divorce group rated themselves less scholastically competent and more vulnerable emotionally than the controls.

To capture an impression of the salient features of the self-images of the children in the experimental group, Table 13.4 lists the items on the SIQ and the SPP that distinguished them from the controls. Children of divorce reported feeling more lonely, sad, and tense. They considered themselves less competent than controls in several areas. Academically, they acknowledged having trouble figuring out answers, not doing well at their classwork, and worrying about their ability to do the schoolwork assigned to them. In their social functioning, they claimed to have fewer friends than did controls. However, when asked to list their friends by name, the numbers for the two groups were similar.

Scholastic performance and school behavior

Objective measures of scholastic performance and behavior ratings by teachers confirmed the children's perceptions of their scholastic competence. Table 13.5 shows that children in the divorce group earned lower grade point averages (GPA) and lower scholastic aptitude scores in both reading and

Table 13.4. *Summary of SIQ and SPP items that differentiated children from divorced and intact families*

Item	Divorced ($n = 50$)	Controls ($n = 31$)	t	p
Emotional tone (SIQ)				
52. I feel so very lonely.	3.28[a]	2.00[a]	3.47	< .001
	(2.05)[b]	(1.27)[b]		
51. I frequently feel sad.	3.52	2.52	2.83	< .01
	(1.79)	(1.39)		
25. I feel relaxed under normal circum-	3.51	4.00	1.68	< .10
stances.	(1.47)	(1.13)		
Scholastic competence (SPP)				
21. [I] have trouble figuring out the an-	1.52	0.90	3.07	< .005
swers in school. . . .	(0.95)	(0.83)		
17. [I] don't do very well at [my]	1.12	0.65	2.52	< .025
classwork.	(0.98)	(0.71)		
1. [I] worry about whether [I] can	1.42	0.97	1.97	= .05
do the school work assigned. . . .	(0.99)	(1.02)		
Social competence (SPP)				
6. [I] don't have very many friends.	1.04	0.55	2.52	< .025
	(1.18)	(0.57)		

[a]Mean.   [b]Standard deviation.

mathematics. The GPA group difference remained significant even when scholastic aptitude and social class were statistically discounted through covariance analysis ($F_{1,63} = 4.50$, $p < .05$), suggesting that the impairment in scholastic performance could not be attributed entirely to sampling differences in ability or background. A significant main effect for sex in that analysis of covariance ($F_{1,62} = 4.80$, $p < .05$) reflected primarily that experimental girls achieved higher GPA scores than did experimental boys ($t_{35} = 2.38$, $p < .025$). According to the teachers, the two groups behaved differently in the classroom (Tables 13.5, 13.6, and 13.7). Experimental children were judged to be clearly less motivated scholastically, with lower ratings for achievement, motivation, maturity, attentiveness, independence, orderliness, and organization. Teachers also rated them marginally less dependable and less confident. Their ratings for interpersonal harmony were lower, with item differences showing them less cheerful, less popular, less well adjusted, and marginally less pleasant than the controls.

The experimental children characterized themselves as low in extracurricular participation (Table 13.5), which is consistent with their self-descriptions of social isolation and loneliness. However, teachers did not rate the groups differently on the extraversion or the emotional stability factor. Some interesting item differences emerged nevertheless (Table 13.7). Teachers considered

Table 13.5. *Summary of significant differences in scholastic performance and school behavior for children from divorced and intact families*

Variable	Divorced	Controls	t	df	p
Grade point average	2.39[a]	3.20[a]	4.11	72	< .001
(GPA)	(0.90)[b]	(0.80)[b]			
Reading aptitude: CTBS[c]	56.78	76.80	3.24	65	< .005
percentile	(27.20)	(23.30)			
Mathematical aptitude:	58.03	77.93	3.71	65	< .005
CTBS percentile	(29.20)	(22.20)			
Scholastic motivation:	3.08	3.83	3.17	67	< .005
teacher rating	(0.98)	(0.93)			
Interpersonal harmony:	3.58	4.06	2.18	67	< .05
teacher rating	(0.81)	(0.92)			
Extracurricular activities:	1.34	2.19	2.32	79	< .025
self-report	(1.78)	(1.49)			

[a]Mean. [b]Standard deviation. [c]California Test of Basic Skills.

the children of divorce more deliberate and somewhat less active than their classmates, but less controlled emotionally. We might infer from this configuration that parental divorce leads children to be somewhat depressed (less spontaneous and energetic), but also more volatile temperamentally. The competition between the ratings for deliberateness and emotional control explains why the groups did not differ significantly on the overall emotional stability factor

Correlational patterns within the divorce sample

Extensive correlational analyses were presented by Moorehead (1986); a succinct narrative summary of those analyses is presented here. Several of the hypotheses tested involved measures of marital conflict prior to and during the divorce that were assessed independently by the custodial parent and by the child; so we had two separate measures of the conflict. Preliminary analyses revealed a significant inverse relation between marital conflict and social class: $r_{47} = -.34$ and $p < .02$ when conflict was evaluated by the custodial parent, and $r_{45} = -.43$ and $p < .005$ when rated by the child. This meant that there was more intense marital conflict in lower-class families. We considered a correlational finding reliable only if it held after covariance for social class and was corroborated by both parent and child assessments of the conflict. The correlations with marital conflict reported here cite first the association with the parent's view of the conflict and then the association with the child's view of the conflict.

Regarding the first hypothesis, it was found that marital conflict was not correlated with the child's scholastic competence, subjective assessments of

Table 13.6. *Scholastic motivation of children from divorced and intact families: teacher rating means and statistical results for individual items*

Item	Divorced (n = 42)	Controls (n = 26)	t	p
13. Achieving	2.81[a] (1.38)[b]	4.12[a] (1.28)[b]	3.97	< .001
23. Motivated	3.17 (1.45)	4.12 (1.21)	2.91	< .005
20. Mature	3.05 (1.19)	3.92 (1.26)	2.84	< .01
7. Attentive	3.14 (1.34)	3.88 (1.14)	2.44	< .025
16. Independent	3.07 (1.18)	3.69 (0.93)	2.41	< .025
1. Orderly	3.07 (1.26)	3.77 (1.18)	2.31	< .025
19. Organized	2.95 (1.29)	3.69 (1.32)	2.27	< .05
25. Dependable	3.39 (1.24)	3.96 (1.22)	1.86	< .10
2. Confident	2.79 (1.18)	3.31 (1.26)	1.70	< .10

[a]Mean.   [b]Standard deviation.

peer rapport, nor behavioral and psychological problems. Marital conflict was inversely correlated, as predicted, with the child's perceived self-worth ($r_{47} = -.41, p < .005, r_{45} = -.34, p < .05$) and with the child's view (but not with the parent's view) of current rapport between the child and the custodial parent ($r_{47} = -.43, p < .005, r_{45} = -.42, p < .005$). Hence, there was only limited support for the hypothesis that marital conflict may adversely affect the self-esteem of the offspring and may be associated in some way with subsequent rapport with the custodial parent.

The second hypothesis postulated that effective social participation outside the home would correlate with good psychological adjustment and favorable rapport with the custodial parent. It was found that social participation, as measured by the child's number of extracurricular activities and number of friends, was not related to current rapport with the custodial parent. Rapport with the extended social network, as judged by the child, however, was correlated with favorable emotional tone ($r_{47} = +.28, p < .05$), good conduct ($r_{47} = +.42, p < .005$), and good rapport with the custodial parent ($r_{47} = +.28$ and $p < .05$ with parental rapport judged by the parent; $r_{47} = +.55$ and $p < .001$ with parental rapport judged by the child). All but one of these significant correlations were between self-report measures from the children themselves. Because of the obvious possibility of response bias inflating these correla-

Table 13.7. *Summary of teacher ratings of general classroom behavior that distinguished children of divorce from controls: item means and statistical comparisons*

Item	Divorced (n = 42)	Controls (n = 26)	t	p
Interpersonal harmony				
8. Cheerful	3.17[a]	3.92[a]	2.72	<.01
	(1.15)[b]	(1.09)[b]		
15. Popular	3.19	3.88	2.62	<.025
	(1.22)	(0.95)		
27. Well adjusted	3.41	4.00	2.03	<.05
	(1.07)	(1.20)		
17. Pleasant	3.83	4.36	1.92	<.10
	(1.10)	(1.08)		
Emotional stability				
28. Deliberate	3.13	2.35	−3.11	<.005
	(1.14)	(0.89)		
24. Controlled	3.15	3.84	2.26	<.05
	(1.33)	(1.11)		
Extraversion				
6. High activity level	3.00	3.58	1.84	<.10
	(1.29)	(1.24)		

[a]Mean.   [b]Standard deviation.

tions, we were inclined to discount confirmatory findings when the child was the sole source of evaluation. We can say with confidence that objective counts of social participation were not related to rapport with the custodial parent, whereas the children's subjective assessments of rapport with the extended social network were positively associated with parent–child rapport, providing limited support for the hypothesis.

The third hypothesis predicted that an economic decline following parental divorce would have adverse effects on children's scholastic competence, self-esteem, general psychological adjustment, and current rapport with peers and with the custodial parent. The psychological "penalties" expected to result from economic decline were not found. The only significant correlation showed more open (less prudish) sexual attitudes associated with extreme economic decline ($r_{47} = +.30$, $p < .05$). This one positive result (among 16 tested) could be attributed to chance alone. Analyses partialing out the length of time since marital separation had occurred did not alter these findings (nor did they alter most of the other findings in the study). Our conclusion is that either economic decline is not a major stressor for children following parental divorce or its negative impact dissipates within a few years.

Boys and girls in our study did not differ significantly on any of the dependent measures of self-worth, self-image, or current rapport with the custodial parent, regardless of the sex of the parent. Moreover, in most cases the correlations showing conflict with the custodial parent were somewhat larger for girls than for boys, which contradicts the popular theory that parental divorce has greater negative impact on boys, but is consistent with the findings of Kalter et al. (1985). We should add the caveat that marital conflict prior to the divorce was judged by the custodial parents to have been more extreme in the families of our girls than in the families of our boys ($t_{47} = 2.78$, $p < .01$). This may have added to the level of stress with which the girls and their families had to cope.

As predicted in the fifth hypothesis, we found that youngsters whose parents had intensely conflicted marriages reported more negative images of themselves and their bodies: $r_{47} = -.43$ and $p < .005$ when the parent judged the conflict, and $r_{45} = -.36$ and $p < .01$ when the child judged the conflict. The analyses of sexual attitudes yielded inconsistent results that clearly did not support the hypothesis that marital conflict may foster more liberal sexual attitudes in the offspring.

Tests of the compensatory model

The synopsis presented here is a highly condensed version of more extensive analyses by Japzon (1986). The essence of the compensatory model is that children who experience parental divorce may turn to peers for emotional support, especially if rapport with the custodial parent is poor; and if that coping strategy is successful, it will have positive ramifications for their general adjustment in adolescence. The first hypothesis derived from this model was that children from divorced families would have greater rapport with their peers than would children from intact families (i.e., more affection, reliable alliance, intimacy, nurturance, companionship, and enhancement of worth). That hypothesis was soundly disconfirmed. On all six variables the group differences favored the controls, most prominently for nurturance ($t_{78} = 1.97$, $p = .05$) and enhancement of worth ($t_{78} = 2.15$, $p < .05$). In both cases, experimental boys showed the least rapport in peer relations. Significant main effects for sex in all six analyses showed consistently stronger peer relations for girls than for boys.

The second hypothesis predicted that peer social support would correlate positively with scholastic performance, classroom adjustment, and self-esteem in children of divorce, with a corollary that those correlations would be higher for the experimental group than for the control group. Only one of the nine predicted correlations was significant, associating the child's view of the positive qualities in peer relations with GPA ($r_{40} = +.34$, $p < .05$). The comparable correlation for the control group was negative ($r_{28} = -.34$, $p < .10$), yielding a significant difference between the two correlations ($t_{70} = 2.82$, $p < .01$). The overall configuration of results does not support the hypothesis, but this one specific finding is consistent with the view that peer rapport may contribute, at least in a limited way, to the scholastic performance of children following parental divorce.

The third hypothesis predicted that a child who had poor rapport with the custodial parent would invest more in peer relations for emotional support, deriving thereby more enhancement of worth and supplying more nurturance to peers. Rapport with the custodial parent was measured from the perspective of the child and that of the parent. Every analysis emphatically disconfirmed the hypothesis. Considering first the parent's view, children with low parental rapport acknowledged less nurturance given to peers than did the controls ($t_{55} = 2.26$, $p < .05$) and less enhancement of worth derived from peers ($t_{55} = 2.56$, $p < .025$). Experimental children with good parental rapport did not differ from the controls nor from the experimental children with poor parental rapport. From the child's perspective, experimental children with low parental rapport acknowledged less nurturance for peers than did controls ($t_{58} = 3.65$, $p < .001$) or experimental children with high parental rapport ($t_{47} = 4.59$, $p < .001$), as well as less enhancement of worth received from peers than did controls ($t_{58} = 4.08$, $p < .001$) or experimental children with high parental rapport ($t_{47} = 5.53$, $p < .001$). The controls and experimental children with high parental rapport did not differ on either variable. The conclusion from these analyses is unequivocal: Following parental divorce, children who do not get along with the custodial parent have the poorest relationships with peers, whereas those who do get along with the custodial parent enjoy peer relationships that are indistinguishable from those of classmates from intact families (Rutter, 1980a,b).

The last hypothesis also derives from the compensatory model. On the assumption that a supportive relationship with the custodial parent can serve to buffer the adjustment process of adolescents after parental divorce, it was predicted that children who had poor rapport with the custodial parent would function less well at school in academic performance and classroom behavior and would have lower self-esteem than would children who had harmonious relations with the custodial parent. Those who had good rapport with the custodial parent were predicted to be indistinguishable from the controls.

The results resoundingly confirmed most of the principal elements of the theory. The experimental subjects with poor parental rapport differed significantly from the control subjects on 12 of the 16 variables analyzed, showing lower scores for self-esteem, for all three of the objective measures of scholastic performance (GPA, reading achievement, mathematics achievement), and for two of the classroom behavior measures (scholastic motivation, interpersonal harmony). Within the experimental sample, the low-rapport subgroup differed from the high-rapport subgroup, as predicted, on interpersonal harmony, self-esteem, and (in one of two analyses) GPA, but the two subgroups did not differ on scholastic motivation, reading achievement, or mathematics achievement. The high-rapport subgroup differed significantly from the controls on all three of the scholastic performance variables, but not on any of the behavioral and psychological variables.

Several conclusions can be drawn from these analyses. Interpersonal harmony observed by teachers at school and self-esteem acknowledged by the youngsters themselves were associated more clearly with parent–child rapport than with the experience of parental divorce per se (Block et al., 1986). In other words, it is only when the divorce experience is coupled with a poor relationship to the custodial parent that the child's self-esteem and classroom interaction style are adversely affected. Only the low-rapport subgroup differed significantly from the controls on teacher-rated scholastic motivation. We infer from this that poor rapport with the custodial parent may mediate the association between parental divorce and a decline in academic effort. Parental support for academic discipline is, after all, a key ingredient in the collaboration between home and school to achieve an education for the child. This observation is potentially important when considering possibilities for preventive intervention. Conceivably, the powerful motivational deficits reported in Tables 13.5 and 13.6 do not materialize when the rapport with the custodial parent develops favorably. A plausible implication here is that therapeutic intervention to nurture that rapport may pay dividends over the long term in the adolescent's efforts toward scholastic achievement. Finally, scholastic achievements are impaired by parental divorce, but are not consistently associated with subsequent rapport with the custodial parent. Contrary to our expectations, the deficits in most of the objective measures of scholastic performance were almost as great for the high-rapport subgroup as for the low-rapport subgroup.

Accessibility of the parents

Systematic study of parental rapport assumes that parents are available and willing to engage in a companionate relationship with their children. In order to test this assumption, we asked the adolescents in our study several questions about the accessibility of their parents and the quality of parental support. There were no significant differences between the experimental and control groups on any evaluation of the mothers. Children of divorce did not consider their mothers to be less available to them for help and advice than did the control subjects. For the fathers, however, differences emerged on every evaluation, most emphatically for father's availability, expecting a favorable response when father's help is requested, and obtaining helpful suggestions when advice is sought from the father. The lack of accessibility and lack of helpfulness of fathers in the divorce group probably relates to the very small proportion who had primary custody of their children; apparently, noncustodial fathers are less involved than usual in child rearing. This pattern of results suggests that relationships with noncustodial fathers are seriously strained as a result of parental divorce, with potentially grave consequences for subsequent development of the offspring.

Discussion

It is no surprise to find that marital relationships that end in divorce are characterized by parents and children alike as unsatisfying and troubled by conflict. It is instructive to learn that little of that conflict is concealed from the children in such families, although the children themselves may exaggerate the concealment. It is also apparent from this study that divorce is not an isolated event but a dynamic part of developmental processes in the lives of children and families. It is important to understand what happens after the divorce takes place, as children and parents strive to cope with the financial strains, emotional stresses, and practical dislocations that typically follow when a marriage dissolves. Our sample was limited to preadolescent children at the time of the divorce, and our perspective on the children's adjustment was limited to a cross-sectional observation of the early years of adolescence. That is a period of special vulnerability in childhood development, when children experience dramatic changes in cognitive perspectives, physical maturation, social and emotional awakening, and personal identity. As anticipated, the data have shown that parental divorce during this critical phase is associated with serious difficulties in children's scholastic functioning, emotional adjustment, social relations, and rapport with parents.

Partly owing to those changes in the children, it is also a time of testing and challenge for parents in their marital and parental roles. Divorced adults are reported to have more health and emotional problems, even after the initial crisis period, than do married adults (Bloom, Asher, & White, 1978). This study adds some insights concerning the roles that children play as their parents (primarily mothers) try to reconstruct their families and their lives after divorce. The children in this sample saw relatively few positive qualities in their current relationships with their custodial parents, but the children also reported less conflict with them and claimed to provide more nurturance for them than did their classmates from intact families. This configuration of findings suggests that children regard their divorced parents as needy, less capable than average to cope physically and psychologically with their own lives and their family responsibilities. The nurturance scale items that express this view of their parents include helping them with things they cannot do by themselves, protecting and looking out for them, and taking care of them, all of which imply helplessness and vulnerability. We infer that the children disengage themselves to some extent from their parents, finding fewer virtues to praise and fewer parental restrictions to oppose. These changes in attitude may be attributable in part to the fact that the children are driven prematurely out of their filial roles in the family and are forced to take on more reciprocal obligations toward their parents (Youniss, 1980).

From the group differences presented in Table 13.3 we infer that the experience of parental divorce takes some toll in the social development of children, as reflected in reduced support for peers, less esteem gained from them, and generally lower rapport with social contacts that extend beyond the family. This means that children of divorce feel deprived of important sources of emotional support at a critical time in their lives when such support probably is in short supply at home. Our evidence associating these peer problems with the intensity of marital conflict previously observed was inconsistent, but there was a strong negative correlation between the children's ratings of esteem gained from peers and the parental evaluations of previous marital conflict witnessed by the children: $r_{46} = -.42, p < .005$. Though not corroborated by the children's views of marital conflict, this correlation might be interpreted to imply that previous exposure to intense marital conflict may contribute causally to the lack of peer esteem felt by adolescents in divorced families.

Our subjects emphasized the limitations in their peer relations, especially if rapport with the custodial parent was strained, claiming to provide less support for their friends and to receive less esteem from them in return. This finding supports the views of Hetherington et al. (1979) that a positive relationship with one parent may buffer the child to some extent against the negative impact of the divorce experience, especially in peer relations. We should note, however, that the two samples in this study did not differ significantly in most aspects of their peer relations: intimacy, satisfaction, reliable alliance, conflict, affection, and companionship. Hence, the limitations in peer relations appear to be restricted to exchanges of support and esteem. General sex differences on all the peer relationship variables favored the girls in every case, indicating that peer friendships are important sources of emotional support for them. This may account in part for the observation that preadolescent boys are more vulnerable under stress (Rutter, 1983), as well as our finding that boys felt more peer isolation than did girls after parental divorce.

We can construct a mosaic impression of the emotional state of these children following divorce on the basis of self-image results and teacher ratings of their behaviors at school. Subjectively, that image was captured most poignantly by their emphatic endorsement of two items on the SIQ: "I feel so very lonely" and "I frequently feel sad." Secondarily, they revealed some emotional strain by denying that they felt relaxed under normal circumstances. Their teachers provided objective validation, rating them as very deliberate (vs. impulsive or spontaneous), somber (vs. cheerful), and rather low in activity level, but emotional (vs. controlled or even-tempered). Assembling the pieces of the mosaic in this way, we see a group of young adolescents who feel somewhat depressed, tense, and isolated, with an undertone of temperamental volatility that might plausibly be traced to unresolved anger over painful past events. They may not be clinically depressed or severely disturbed psychologically, but their mood is observably subdued.

The feeling of social isolation in the children of divorce is clearly indicated by their perceived lack of friends and extracurricular activity. The latter finding is interesting, because they listed as many friends (by first name) as the control subjects did, and their teachers did not rate them significantly more introverted than the controls on any of eight extraversion scales! Children's sense of well-being and personal adjustment depends more on the *perception* of social support than on the objective features of their social network (Barrera, 1981; Wyman et al., 1985). Apparently, the quality rather than the quantity of the peer relations of our subjects (and perhaps some biased expectancies traceable to the divorce experience) led them to feel exceptionally isolated.

The clinical observations of academic decline by Wallerstein and Kelly (1976) and the controlled study of self-perceived cognitive competence by Wyman et al. (1985) support the theory that parental divorce often leads to dysfunction at school. Our findings offer compelling empirical evidence that by the time they reach adolescent age, children of divorced parents have lower scholastic aptitude in both reading and mathematics, lower academic performance in the classroom, and less confidence in their cognitive ability than do comparable classmates from intact families. The teacher ratings justify attributing the deficiencies in aptitude and performance in part to poor scholastic motivation, as shown on seven of the nine PRF scales that measure it. It may be quite realistic for such youngsters to deprecate their scholastic ability now, after many years of disappointments, but the deficits observed here probably evolved gradually in interactive cycles of performance tests and progressive discouragement, ultimately leading to profound scholastic demoralization. We need prospective research to establish the causal patterns in these developments, but it is certainly plausible to infer that parental divorce plays a part in setting the process of demoralization in motion. In this connection, we should emphasize that our data yielded exceedingly large differences in scholastic performance between divorced and control groups, but *not* a significant correlation between scholastic performance and interparental conflict within the divorced group.

The social frictions observed by teachers in the areas of mood, popularity, adjustment, and disposition suggest social as well as academic troubles at school. This may be traced partly to the ambience of defeat that the academic setting has acquired for them and partly to the depressive emotions that drain psychological energy for social engagement with schoolmates. We consider it plausible that parental divorce takes a direct toll on the scholastic achievements of the offspring, but rapport with the custodial parent is apparently a key variable in determining their attitudinal orientation to academic endeavors, social participation, and self-perception. The rationale offered to explain this is that a good relationship with the custodial parent creates a supportive, loving environment that buffers the negative impact of divorce on scholastic motivation, social interactions, and self-esteem. We need to consider here the possibility of reciprocal causation, because it is also plausible that abrasive, unmotivated, and insecure adolescents cause damage to parent–child rapport.

Conclusion

When a marriage dissolves, every family member is potentially a victim. Some injuries are obvious. Violent emotions erupt; cruel and sometimes bitter financial hardships must be endured; and transformations in work loads, personal relationships, and life-styles may take their toll. Other wounds are more subtle, wreaking mischief insidiously, like a slow virus. Undoubtedly, children suffer acutely from immediate disruptions and parental hostility, even violence, but they may pay even greater progressive costs for latent psychological insults: loss or tarnishment of primary identification figures, erosion of life structure, feelings of stigma and isolation among peers, and prematurely imposed self-reliance.

Children's struggles to cope with the most tangible hazards are compounded by the burden of supporting precipitously needy parents, typically traumatized mothers. This turn of events preempts carefree exploration of stimulating natural interests and hampers inclinations to develop sources of emotional support outside the home. Many children lack the emotional resilience required for more mature, reciprocal relationships with their mothers. Scholastic development is also adversely affected if more fundamental preoccupations disqualify their mothers as major sources of support and discipline for meeting school demands. If these conditions persist, children naturally become demoralized, like the subjects in this study.

In this study, marital conflict was associated with low self-esteem in the offspring, negative images of themselves and their bodies, and troubled rapport with the custodial parent. Otherwise there was no support for Emery's theory (1982) that marital hostility is a principal medium associating divorce with children's maladjustment. Children's rapport with their custodial parents was not correlated with objective indices of their social activities outside the home, but was correlated with subjective judgments of their rapport with the extended social network. Hence, we found little constructive value in the children leading an active social life away from home. The evidence discounted the importance of economic decline as a factor influencing psychological adjustment after parental divorce. Interviews with the custodial mothers suggested that initial financial deprivation gave way in many cases to favorable developments in their own vocational situations, remarriages, and psychological attitudes, that are not fully reflected in monetary terms. Except for some indications that the peer relations of boys suffered more than those of girls, our findings did not support the popular theory that boys are more adversely affected by parental divorce than girls. This may be specific to the particular age range of the children we studied, namely, early adolescence.

There was little evidence to support the compensatory model of children's adjustment to parental divorce. Children from broken homes did not report better-than-average rapport with peers. With one exception (GPA), peer social support was generally not associated with good adjustment. Contrary to the prediction from the model, adolescents who did not get along with their custodial parents also had the poorest peer relationships. In striking contrast to the other tests of theory, there was strong confirmation of the prediction that good rapport with the custodial parent would be associated with self-esteem and harmonious social relations at school. On the other hand, parental rapport did not seem to relate consistently with objective scholastic performance.

Relieving pressures on the parents should free the children to pursue more age-appropriate tasks, such as school performance, social camaraderie, and skill development. Children such as we studied may benefit from knowing that their peer relations are not as barren as they believe. Addressing deterioration in school functioning is a more formidable task. Granted, children may benefit from tutoring and counseling services at school, but even well-organized educational efforts may not replace parental support. If we were to single out a primary target for intervention, based on this study, it would be to strengthen the relationship bond between children and parents, both custodial and noncustodial, after the divorce takes place.

References

Barrera, M. (1981). Social support in the adjustment of pregnant adolescents. In B. Gottlieb (Ed.), *Social networks and social support* (pp. 69–96). Beverly Hills, CA: Sage.

Beal, E. W. (1979). Children of divorce: A family systems perspective. *Journal of Social Issues, 35*, 141–54.

Berndt, T. J. (1979). Developmental changes in conformity to peers and parents. *Developmental Psychology, 15*, 608–16.

Berndt, T. J. (1981). Relations between social cognition, non-social cognition, and social behavior: The case of friendship. In J. H. Flavell & L. Ross (Eds.), *Social cognitive development: Frontiers and possible futures* (pp. 176–99). Cambridge University Press.

Block, J. H., Block, J., & Gjerde, P. F. (1986). The personality of children prior to divorce: A prospective study. *Child Development, 57*, 827–40.

Bloom, E. A., Asher, S. J., & White, S. W. (1978). Marital disruption as a stressor. A review and analysis. *Psychological Bulletin, 85*, 867–94.

Copeland, A. P. (1985). Individual differences in children's reactions to divorce. *Journal of Clinical Child Psychology, 14*, 11–19.

Emery, R. E. (1982). Interparental conflict and the children of discord and divorce. *Psychological Bulletin, 92*, 310–30.

Felner, R. D., Farber, S. S., & Primavera, J. (1983). Transitions and stressful life events: A model for primary prevention. In R. Felner, L. Jason, J. Moritsugu, & S. Farber (Eds.), *Preventive psychology: Theory, research and practice* (pp. 199–215). New York: Pergamon.

Furman, W., & Buhrmester, D. (1985). Children's perceptions of their personal relationships. *Developmental Psychology, 21*, 1016–22.

Furman, W., & Robbins, P. T. (1985). What's the point? Issues in the selection of treatment objectives. In B. H. Schneider, K. H. Rubin, & J. E. Ledingham (Eds.), *Children's peer relations: Issues in assessment and intervention* (pp. 41–54). New York: Springer.

Glick, P. C. (1979). Children of divorced parents in demographic perspective. *Journal of Social Issues, 35,* 170–82.

Guidubaldi, J., Cleminshaw, H. K., Perry, J. D., & McLoughlin, C. S. (1983). The impact of parental divorce on children: Report of the nationwide NASP study. *School Psychology Review, 12,* 300–23.

Harter, S. (1983). *Supplementary description of the Perceived Competence Scale for Children: Revision.* Unpublished manuscript, University of Denver.

Hartup, W. W. (1970). Peer interaction and social organization. In P. H. Mussen (Ed.), *Carmichael's manual of child psychology* (Vol. 2, 3rd ed., pp. 361–456). New York: Wiley.

Hetherington, E. M. (1979). Divorce: A child's perspective. *American Psychologist, 34,* 851–8.

Hetherington, E. M., Cox, M., & Cox, R. (1976). Divorced fathers. *Family Coordinator, 25,* 417–28.

Hetherington, E. M., Cox, M., & Cox, R. (1978). The aftermath of divorce. In J. H. Stevens & M. Matthews (Eds.), *Mother–child, father–child relations* (pp. 149–76). Washington, DC: National Association for the Education of Young Children.

Hetherington, E. M., Cox, M., & Cox, R. (1979). Play and social interaction in children following divorce. *Journal of Social Issues, 35,* 26–49.

Hollingshead, A. B., & Redich, F. C. (1957). *Social class and mental illness.* New York: Wiley.

Hunter, F. T., & Youniss, J. (1982). Changes in functions of three relations during adolescence. *Developmental Psychology, 18,* 806–11.

Jacobson, D. S. (1978). The impact of marital separation/divorce on children. II: Interpersonal hostility and child adjustment. *Journal of Divorce, 2,* 3–20.

Japzon, D. M. (1986). *Children's adjustment to parental divorce.* Unpublished master's thesis, University of Denver.

Kalter, N. (1977). Children of divorce in an outpatient psychiatric population. *American Journal of Orthopsychiatry, 47,* 40–51.

Kalter, N., Riemer, B., Brickman, A., & Chen, J. W. (1985). Implications of parental divorce for female development. *Journal of the American Academy of Child Psychiatry, 24,* 538–44.

Kon, I. S., & Losenkov, V. A. (1978). Friendship in adolescence: Values and behavior. *Journal of Marriage and the Family, 40,* 143–55.

Kurdek, L. A., & Berg, B. (1983). Correlates of children's adjustment to their parents' divorces. In L. A. Kurdek (Ed.), *New directions in child development: Children and divorce* (pp. 47–60). San Francisco: Jossey-Bass.

Kurdek, L. A., Blisk, D., & Siesky, A. E. (1983). Correlates of children's long-term adjustment to their parents' divorce. *Developmental Psychology, 17,* 565–79.

Levitin, T. E. (1979). Children of divorce: An introduction. *Journal of Social Issues, 35,* 1–25.

Locke, H. J., & Wallace, K. M. (1959). Short marital adjustment and prediction tests: Their reliability and validity. *Marriage and Family Living, 21,* 251–5.

Marsden, D. (1969). *Mothers alone: Poverty and the fatherless family.* London: Penguin Press.

Moorehead, O. D. (1986). *The emotional impact of divorce on adolescents.* Unpublished doctoral dissertation, University of Denver.

Offer, D., Ostrov, E., & Howard, K. I. (1981). *The adolescent: A psychological self-portrait* (pp. 30–79). New York: Basic Books.

Pearlin, L. I., & Johnson, J. S. (1977). Marital status, life strains, and depression. *American Sociological Review, 42,* 704–15.

Rutter, M. (1980a). *Changing youth in a changing society: Patterns of adolescent development and disorder.* Cambridge, MA: Harvard University Press.

Rutter, M. (1980b). Protective factors in children's responses to stress and disadvantage. In M. Kent & J. Rolf (Eds.), *Primary prevention of psychopathology. Vol. 3: Promoting social competence and coping in children* (pp. 49–74). Hanover, NH: University Press of New England.

Rutter, M. (1983). Stress, coping, and development: Some issues and some questions. In N. Garmezy & M. Rutter (Eds.), *Stress, coping, and development in children* (pp. 1–41). New York: McGraw-Hill.

Santrock, J. W. (1975). Father absence, perceived maternal behavior and moral development in boys. *Child Development, 46,* 753–7.

Santrock, J. W., & Trace, R. L. (1978). Effect of children's family structure status on the development of stereotypes by children. *Journal of Educational Psychology, 70,* 754–7.

Select Committee on Children, Youth, and Families, 98th Congress (1983). *U.S. Children and their families: Current conditions and recent trends.* Washington, DC: Foundation for Child Development.

Shay, J. J. (1978). *A methodological investigation of reliability, validity, and factor structure of the Amherst Pupil Rating Form.* Unpublished doctoral dissertation, University of Massachusetts at Amherst.

Stolberg, A. L., & Anker, J. M. (1984). Cognitive and behavioral changes in children resulting from parental divorce and consequent environmental changes. *Journal of Divorce, 7,* 23–41.

Stolberg, A. L., & Bush, J. P. (1985). A path analysis of factors predicting children's divorce adjustment. *Journal of Clinical Child Psychology, 14,* 49–54.

Stolberg, A. L., Camplair, C., Currier, K., & Wells, M. (1984). *Individual, familial, and environmental determinants of children's post-divorce adjustment and maladjustment.* Unpublished manuscript.

Straus, M. A. (1979). Measuring intrafamily conflict and violence: The Conflict Tactics (CT) scales. *Journal of Marriage and the Family, 41,* 75–88.

U.S. Census Bureau. (1980). *Statistical abstract of the United States.* Washington, DC: USCB.

Wallerstein, J. S., & Kelly, J. B. (1974). The effects of parental divorce: The adolescent experience. In E. J. Anthony & C. Koupernik (Eds.), *The child in his family: Children at psychiatric risk* (pp. 479–505). New York: Wiley.

Wallerstein, J. S., & Kelly, J. B. (1976). The effects of parental divorce: Experiences of the child in later latency. *American Journal of Orthopsychiatry, 46,* 256–69.

Wallerstein, J. S., & Kelly, J. B. (1980). *Surviving the break-up: How children and parents cope with divorce.* New York: Basic Books.

Watt, N. F., Stolorow, R. D., Lubensky, A. W., & McClelland, D. C. (1970). School adjustment and behavior of children hospitalized for schizophrenia as adults. *American Journal of Orthopsychiatry, 40,* 637–57.

Werner, E. E., & Smith, R. S. (1982), *Vulnerable but invincible: A study of resilient children.* New York: McGraw-Hill.

Wyman, P. A., Cowen, E. L., Hightower, A. D., & Pedro-Carroll, J. L. (1985). Perceived competence, self-esteem, and anxiety in latency-aged children of divorce. *Journal of Clinical Child Psychology, 14,* 20–6.

Youniss, J. (1980). *Parents and peers in social development: A Sullivan-Piaget perspective.* University of Chicago Press.

The challenge of adolescence
for developmental psychopathology

Part IV focuses on psychopathological processes during adolescence and on factors that may influence such processes. Adolescence has long been considered to be a period of particular developmental change and challenge. The chapters in this part offer the reader both a useful macroscopic theoretical perspective on the developmental psychopathology of adolescence and more specific consideration of possible factors in the development of individual disorders.

The initial chapter by Aaron T. Ebata, Anne C. Petersen, and John J. Conger uses knowledge of normative adolescent development to provide an excellent overview of prominent theoretical issues concerning psychopathological processes during adolescence. The authors highlight prevalent myths about adolescent psychopathology, such as the belief that psychopathological disturbances are normative and necessary during adolescence. Further, they urge that consideration of adolescent development include not only individual maturational processes but also specific social-context factors and dynamic transactions between the individual and the social environment. Ebata, Petersen, and Conger emphasize that adolescent psychopathological development can be usefully viewed as representing extreme poles on continuous dimensions of emotional development. This view leads to consideration of specific forms of psychopathology as differing patterns of adaptation that are negative deviations from the individual's developmental trajectory, products of interactions between the individual's adaptive coping skills and the changing social context.

Jack Block and Per F. Gjerde present data from a large-scale study that used one of the most direct methods of assessing developmental trajectory and precursors of psychopathology: the longitudinal follow-through design. This method is one that Norman Garmezy often has emphasized as critical to developmental psychopathology (Garmezy, 1971; Garmezy & Streitman, 1974). In this chapter, Block and Gjerde examine the personality precursors of late-adolescent depressive symptoms, using California Q-set data collected at ages 3–4, 7, 11, and 14 to predict self-reported depression at age 18.

305

Extensive personality antecedents of 18-year-old depressive symptoms are found at age 14, although relatively few are present at earlier ages. These precursors show striking gender differences, suggesting that the developmental pathways to late-adolescent depression may differ for males and females. Block and Gjerde relate their findings to the construct of ego resilience as well as to psychoanalytic views of depression.

In the next chapter, Judith Rodin, Ruth H. Striegel-Moore, and Lisa R. Silberstein identify known and hypothesized risk and protective factors for bulimia nervosa, a disorder that usually develops in adolescence or early adulthood. Their perspective encompasses individual as well as social-context factors within an interactive orientation that is highly compatible with that emphasized by Ebata, Petersen, and Conger. Rodin, Striegel-Moore, and Silberstein integrate their own data as well as the data of others to support the roles of the sociocultural milieu (e.g., an unrealistically thin beauty ideal), family context (e.g., low support of independence and insufficient training in self-regulation), and genetic factors (e.g., family history of affective disorder) in bulimia nervosa. The authors note that the time is right for application of prospective research designs to bulimia nervosa, as advocated by Garmezy for other disorders, to allow a clearer test of possible risk factors and to begin to identify protective factors.

In the last chapter of this section, Jon Rolf and Jeannette Johnson highlight the relevance of a developmental psychopathology perspective for the acquired immunodeficiency syndrome (AIDS), a disorder that is typically viewed primarily from a physical-disease viewpoint. As Rolf and Johnson note, a developmental perspective on AIDS is particularly likely to be fruitful for adolescence, the period during which experience with the risk factors of sexual contact and intravenous drug use often begins. Developmental studies would focus on the processes by which high-risk individuals either protect themselves from or make themselves more vulnerable to HIV exposure. The roles that personality characteristics, such as poor planning skills and external locus of control, and maladaptive coping strategies, such as excessive denial of personal risk, play in moderating exposure to the HIV virus need to be examined. Rolf and Johnson also suggest several protective factors that might be enhanced for adolescents, including social support for a positive perception of self-efficacy in AIDS prevention and peer models in the media who demonstrate responsible regulation of sexual activity. Appropriate prospective studies of the interaction of risk and protective factors in AIDS are critically needed.

Taken as a whole, this part of the volume demonstrates the wide range of potential risk and protective factors that need to be incorporated in sophisticated approaches to developmental psychopathology during the adolescent period. The integration of the developmental psychology of adolescence with psychopathology research is still in its infancy, but the prospects for such approaches appear exciting.

References

Garmezy, N. (1971). Vulnerability research and the issue of primary prevention. *American Journal of Orthopsychiatry, 41,* 101–16.

Garmezy, N., & Streitman, S. (1974). Children at risk: The search for the antecedents of schizophrenia. Part I: Conceptual models and research methods. *Schizophrenia Bulletin, 1*(8), 14–90.

14 The development of psychopathology in adolescence

Aaron T. Ebata, Anne C. Petersen, and John J. Conger

Our society holds contradictory beliefs about adolescent psychopathology. Some of these beliefs are myths that have impeded adequate conceptualization of psychopathology in adolescence and have encouraged stereotypes about "normal" adolescent development as well. In this chapter we briefly discuss these myths relative to the empirical evidence. We then provide an overview for a developmental perspective on psychopathology in adolescence, along with the related implications and issues.

Myths about adolescent psychopathology

Myth 1: Psychopathology is a normal state in adolescence

The belief that psychopathology in adolescence is normative stems primarily from psychoanalytic theory (Blos, 1962; Freud, 1958). Psychoanalytic theory proposed that disturbances in adolescence, leading to neurotic or psychotic states, were created as a result of the effects of pubertal changes on impulses (Kestenberg, 1968). According to Blos (1962), these impulses, particularly sexual impulses, threatened the parent–child relationship and required greater separation and differentiation between child and parent. From that perspective, adolescent upheavals and disturbances, though often difficult to distinguish from "true" pathology, were considered normal and healthy expressions of adolescent development (Freud, 1958). Rebellion and conflict with parents were similarly viewed as normative. Resolution of this developmental crisis was thought to be necessary for normal development to proceed. Failure to resolve this crisis, manifested in adolescent turmoil, would lead to

The preparation of this chapter was supported in part by grant MH-30252/38142 from the National Institute of Mental Health to Anne C. Petersen. Portions of this chapter are based on an invited address to Division 12, Section 3, at the annual meeting of the American Psychological Association, Toronto, August 1984. We would like to acknowledge previous collaborations with W. Edward Craighead and the helpful comments of our colleague, Jay Belsky.

repression of the conflict, resulting in a reemergence of the conflict later in life, typically in a "middle-life crisis" (Vaillant, 1977).

In contrast, epidemiological research, both in the United States and in other countries, suggests that no more than 20% of youngsters in the adolescent age span manifest diagnosable disorders during these years (Graham, 1979). Variations in incidence have depended on the specific populations studied, the ages of the adolescents studied, their gender, the sources of information, and the criteria used to assess particular disorders; see the reviews by Gould, Wunsch-Hitzig, and Dohrenwend (1981) and Links (1983).

Several empirical studies involving nonclinical subjects (Douvan & Adelson, 1966; Grinker, Grinker, & Timberlake, 1962; Offer, 1969; Offer & Offer, 1975) have demonstrated that adolescence is not tumultuous for all young people. For example, the Offers (1975) found three routes that would describe most adolescent boys. The development of about one-fourth of their adolescents was characterized as "continuous," involving no periods of difficulty or turmoil. The development of approximately one-third of their boys could be characterized as "surgent," with progressions and regressions in development. The remainder of the boys in their sample did experience significant tumult, in what was characterized as the "tumultuous" route. If we were to extrapolate the results of that research on a selected sample to a population not selected for normality, we might expect to see about half of our adolescents manifesting tumult, about one-fifth showing continuous development, and about one-fourth characterized by surgent growth. It has been assumed that girls show similar patterns, though perhaps in different proportions; relevant data on girls are lacking at this time. None of these longitudinal studies of adolescence has yet followed subjects into middle adulthood, but as yet there is no evidence that adolescents manifesting continuous growth inevitably experience a mid-life crisis.

Myth 2: Adolescent psychopathology is something one outgrows

This myth is a corollary of Myth 1. The view that psychopathology in adolescence was normative led to this second myth and to overuse of the diagnosis of "adolescent adjustment disorder." The study by Weiner and DelGaudio (1976) and data from England (Rutter, Graham, Chadwick, & Yule, 1976) show that adolescents with the diagnosis of adjustment disorder are just as likely to seek psychotherapy and be diagnosed as schizophrenic in young adulthood as are those with more serious diagnoses during adolescence. The implication of this research is that difficulties among adolescents ought to be viewed as seriously as problems seen in older age groups. At any age, however, temporary disorder may occur because of specific stresses. The disorders seem to pass as either the stresses abate or the individual adapts favorably to the presence of the stress. These "good" outcomes appear, however, to require good characteristics both in the individual and in the environment.

At the heart of this myth is the issue of continuity of behavioral disorders from adolescence into adulthood. Findings pertinent to such continuity vary depending on the nature of the disorders and the criteria used to assess them. For example, Zeitlen, as reported by Rutter (1986), found that most children in a hospital sample who were initially diagnosed as depressed were *not* diagnosed as depressed when they became adults. When operational criteria based on symptomatology were used to classify these adults, however, 31 of 37 cases met the criteria for depression.

There is consistent evidence that antisocial behavior and aggression (typically diagnosed as conduct disorder) often persist into adulthood (Robins, 1966; Robins & Ratcliff, 1979) and that predictability from childhood through adolescence is increased with knowledge of the age of onset of the problems, the frequency and severity of problems, and whether or not problem behavior is exhibited in multiple settings (Loeber, 1982). Early acting-out behavior, however, is also associated with a wide range of adjustment problems later in life, including schizophrenia (Kohlberg, LaCrosse, & Ricks, 1972; Robins & Ratcliff, 1979). Although there may not be isomorphism in behaviors reflecting particular disorder syndromes, early adaptational difficulties may predict later ones (Sroufe & Rutter, 1984).

Myth 3: With regard to psychopathology, adolescents are (a) like adults or (b) like children

Textbooks on abnormal psychology must assume either (a) or (b), because most include no discussion of adolescent psychopathology. To be fair, we ought to clarify our definition of adolescence. The definition usually used in developmental research is that adolescence includes the phase of life beginning with puberty and extending until the individual takes on adult work and family roles. Because that span may be different for different individuals, this definition of adolescence is of limited use to those who wish to refer to a uniform period across individuals. For practical purposes, then, it is more sensible to designate as adolescence the second decade of life. Using that definition, early adolescence is more like childhood, and later adolescence is more like adulthood. But there is a transitional phase between childhood and adulthood, varying in duration for different individuals, to be considered adolescence. As we shall describe, it involves developmental aspects distinct from either childhood or adulthood. There is a special nature of adolescence that warrants consideration with regard to many issues, particularly psychopathology.

"Normal" adolescence in a developmental perspective

What makes adolescence distinctive? The traditional view of adolescent development, typically based on psychoanalytic theory, is too narrow and often focuses only on individual maturation. Developmental outcomes during adolescence can more readily be understood by taking a developmental perspective that considers two essential components: (a) the social contexts for individual development and (b) the dynamic processes involved with development (Baltes, 1968; Belsky, Lerner, & Spanier, 1984; Lerner, 1978).

First, development is influenced by the contexts in which development takes place (Bronfenbrenner, 1979). The family environment of an individual is critically important to the developmental outcomes of the individual, but there are other important socializing contexts as well, with the school and peer group highly salient during childhood and adolescence. Development from birth to adulthood takes place in an increasingly complex and widening array of social contexts, and the relative impacts of particular contexts may vary across the life span. With increasing age, each context becomes more complex in terms of the nature of the relationships between individuals within the context and the specific demands and challenges posed by the particular context.

Second, development is most appropriately seen as a transactional process involving continuous interactions between the individual and the various relative social contexts (Sameroff, 1975). Social contexts, like the developing individual, may change over time, and continuities and discontinuities in individual development are influenced by stability or change in the contexts of development. It is important to note that the relationships between an individual and various contexts involve reciprocal influences (Bell & Harper, 1977; Lerner & Spanier, 1980). Although we tend to speak of the socializing influences of various contexts on the child, the child is just as likely to influence the context (Lerner, 1982). For example, adolescents with serious problems may have dramatic impacts on their parents and siblings.

This view of development as *process* also acknowledges (a) that there may be multiple pathways to a particular outcome, as well as a range of possible outcomes given similar prior conditions (Ogbu, 1981), (b) that individuals are capable of change, and (c) that constructs of developmental interest may require different indicators at different ages because of qualitative transformations as well as quantitative change (Sroufe & Rutter, 1984). These and other developmental propositions have recently been applied to the study of pathol ogy, creating an emerging field of "developmental psychopathology" (Sroufe & Rutter, 1984). Several important issues raised by the application of these principles and propositions are discussed next.

Developmental changes in adolescence

This section briefly describes some of the changes that occur in several developmental domains and social contexts during adolescence. These changes reflect what seem to be general developmental trends that have been identified by cross-sectional and longitudinal studies. There are, of course, variations in these trends reflecting specific individual characteristics and conditions. As will be shown, individual differences in developmental trajectories, relationships between developmental domains, and continuity or discontinuity within and between social contexts are major aspects of the developmental perspective on psychopathology. This perspective requires the study of (a) normative developmental capacities that can serve as either intrapersonal resources or liabilities, (b) the contexts in which they develop, and (c) the transactional processes that influence later functioning.

Biological change. During adolescence, changes are seen in each of the areas of lifelong biological change: the brain, somatic development, and physiological change (Petersen & Taylor, 1980). For normal individuals, puberty also marks the completion of growth in size, the attainment of mature body shape, and the attainment of reproductive potential (Petersen & Taylor, 1980; Tanner, 1962).

Cognitive change. During adolescence, a major change in cognitive development often takes place as well (Inhelder & Piaget, 1958; Keating, 1980). During this phase of life, young people are first able to think abstractly or "think about thinking." It is important to note that although abstract thinking typically first appears during adolescence, many adolescents (as well as adults) never manifest the capacity to think abstractly, at least as assessed by the standard measures of abstract thinking or formal operational thought (Elkind, 1975).

Change in self-perception. Adolescence is marked by an increase in self-esteem from the beginning to the end of adolescence (Damon & Hart, 1982), with some evidence that there may be a specific dip in self-esteem during early adolescence (Simmons, Rosenberg, & Rosenberg, 1973). Over adolescence, individuals decrease their attributions to themselves of the responsibility for failure, whereas attributions of success remain stable over these years (Harter, 1983).

Family changes. The changes that occur during adolescence may include changes in relationships (i.e., interactions between family members) as well as structural changes within the family – both of which influence further development. As for the parent–adolescent relationship, Montemayor (1983) concluded that although most families report positive relations, conflict "increases during early adolescence, is reasonably stable in middle adolescence, and declines when the adolescent moves away from home" (p. 89). Adolescents' increased needs for autonomy (Conger & Petersen, 1984) often require transformations in adolescent–parent relationships (Papini & Datan, 1983; Steinberg, 1981; Steinberg & Hill, 1978).

Besides having to deal with developing children, however, families are also developing and may be going through additional structural changes (e.g., death, divorce, change in work status). Parents themselves often are faced with their own developmental issues in terms of career, relationships, and personal well-being (Aldous, 1978; Chilman, 1968; Hill & Mattesich, 1979; Vaillant, 1977).

Peers and social development. During adolescence, the peer group increases in size and complexity (Crockett, Losoff, & Petersen, 1984). By the beginning of adolescence, more time is spent (and enjoyed) with chosen friends than with classmates (Csikszentmihalyi & Larson, 1984). Relative to children, adolescents experience greater involvement with peers, often accompanied by more emphasis on intimacy, particularly shared thoughts and feelings (Hartup, 1983). Peer status, however, seems to be stable over time, especially for children who are "rejected" (Coie & Dodge, 1983). Studies of preadolescents show that this stability is maintained despite changes in the peer group (Coie & Kupersmidt, 1983) and is more a result of individual behavior than of "reputation" (Dodge, 1983).

Schools. A major change in the school context appears during early adolescence, when young people move from elementary school to junior high or middle schools (Schulenberg, Asp, & Petersen, 1984). Whereas elementary schools typically involve a single classroom, one teacher, and a single set of classmates, junior high or middle schools typically involve multiple classrooms with multiple teachers and multiple sets of classmates. The transition to these more complex school settings challenges the coping resources of young adolescents, leading to lower grades in schoolwork and decreased perceptions of control on the part of young adolescents (Blyth, Simmons, & Carlton-Ford, 1983). The number and timing of school transitions during early adolescence influence mental health outcomes (Crockett, Petersen, Graber, Schulenberg, & Ebata, 1989). If older cohorts of adolescents are present in a school, there will be increases in the amounts of violence, drug and alcohol use, and sexual behavior, as well as decreased self-esteem among younger adolescents (Blyth, Hill, & Smith, 1981).

Broader society. Although too little research has focused on the impact of the broader society on adolescents, we can observe the dramatic impact that the communications media have through the various messages that are sent to adolescent consumers concerning what clothes to wear and which kinds of soda to drink, among other behaviors. Research has documented the effects of advertising on cognition (Linn, deBenedictis, & Delucchi, 1982) and the effects of body image depictions on boys' and girls' self-images (Faust, 1983).

Implications of developmental change for adolescent behavior

In general, an adolescent experiences increasing expectations and demands, in large part because of changes in the adolescent's size, appearance, and behavior. These changes may be considered as presenting either crisis or challenge: invoking stresses that can undermine development, or revealing resources and opportunities for growth (Garbarino, 1985). In any case, these changes often involve an expectation of greater individual "responsibility" for behavior (Petersen & Spiga, 1982).

At the same time, the various developing capacities of adolescents allow for greater potential for impact on the environment and on their own development. There is a greater ability to draw on one's own resources (which in most cases are expanding) and to draw on resources from the environment in order to maintain some level of psychological well-being, choose or create their own niches, and "fit in" with the existing environment. Thus, the study of adolescent development involves examining how an individual deals with changing environmental expectations and demands and how individual characteristics and capacities, previous experiences, and particular contextual conditions influence this adaptation.

Psychopathology in adolescence

Although we would like to present psychopathology as part of a normative, continuous construct such as emotional development, such constructs have been neglected in research (Yarrow, 1979), except in infancy (Emde, 1980). This status of knowledge seems especially ironic given the frequent attributions concerning adolescent mood swings and emotional changes. Although one study, for example, found that there were more mood fluctuations among adolescents than among adults (Larson, Csikszentmihalyi, & Graef, 1980), much more research on emotional development in adolescence is needed.

Nevertheless, our conceptual frame assumes that there are continuous dimensions of emotional well-being represented with specific aspects of psychopathology at one extreme. We find, for example, that relevant aspects of self-image, a normative construct, are lower in adolescents who also report specific kinds of psychopathology (Petersen, Schulenberg, Abramowitz, Offer, & Jarcho, 1984). We also find that adolescents reporting significant episodes of depression and anxiety are lower in those self-image scales involving psychopathology and emotional tone than are adolescents who report no such experiences of depression or anxiety (Petersen et al., 1984).

Rather than present an exhaustive review of psychopathology during adolescence, three categories of psychopathology will be presented as the most common examples: anxiety, depression, and conduct disorders. This review is based on a previous review by Craighead (Petersen & Craighead, 1986).

Anxiety

Anxiety is considered here to involve both apprehension and fear, and it has emotional, behavioral, physiological, and cognitive components.

There do appear to be developmental changes in anxiety, with possibly greater frequency in adolescents, as well as a changed form in adolescence relative to childhood (Chapman, 1974; Senn & Solnit, 1968). By middle adolescence, anxiety is more closely related to social situations and includes more abstract phobias, such as agoraphobia (Marks & Gelder, 1966). Anxiety appears to be two to three times more common in girls than in boys. Although few data are available on the long-term stability of anxiety, the existing evidence does suggest that a subset of anxious children become anxious adults, and a somewhat larger subset of anxious adolescents become anxious adults (Gersten, Langer, Eisenberg, Simcha-Fagen, & McCarthy, 1976). Most anxious adults were anxious adolescents (Pritchard & Graham, 1966).

Depression

In recent years, research on depression in childhood and adolescence has experienced explosive growth. Current data suggest that by late adolescence, 3–5% of individuals are diagnosable with severe depression, and 12–15% of individuals are diagnosable with moderate depression (Craighead, Kennedy, & Raczynski, 1984). Several studies have found rates of mild to moderate feelings of depression in the 20–35% range, including our own study (Albert & Beck, 1975; Kandel & Davies, 1982; Kaplan, Hong, & Weinhold, 1984; Mullins, Siegel, & Hodges, 1985; Teri, 1982).

There are developmental changes in the occurrence and experience of depression as well. The cross-sectional Isle of Wight study (Rutter et al., 1976) found a 100-fold increase in clinical depression from about age 10 to about age 15 (although the incidence at age 10 was very low). They also observed an approximately fourfold increase in depressive feelings and moodiness over the same age span. Depression appears to occur about two to three times more often in girls than in boys by middle adolescence. Although more children experience feelings of depression as they get older, recent evidence suggests that those who experience clinical depression earlier in childhood are at greater risk for more prolonged problems than are those who first experience depression at a later age (Kovacs, Feinberg, Crouse-Novak, Paulaustkas, & Finkelstein, 1984).

Depression, like anxiety, has affective, cognitive, physiological, and behavioral characteristics. Recent studies have shown that attributional styles typical of depressed adults are also found in depressed children (Seligman & Peterson, 1986). A depressive attributional style is more typical of females than of males, a finding replicated in studies involving adolescent subjects (Craighead, Smucker, & Duchnowski, 1981). Of note is the recent finding by Craighead et al. (1984) that when diagnostic categories of anxiety are differentiated from depression, this specific attributional style is typical only of subjects in whom anxiety is found. Depressed subjects manifest this attributional style only if they are also anxious.

Conduct disorders

Children and adolescents with conduct disorders provide an interesting contrast to those with anxiety and depression. For one thing, this diagnosis is three times more likely for boys than for girls (Graham, 1979). In addition, the longitudinal course in conduct disorders is quite distinct from that seen with anxiety or depression. Conduct disorders typically are manifested early, especially once youngsters begin school. Children manifesting conduct disorders in middle childhood may become adolescent delinquents and antisocial adults.

Several longitudinal studies have pointed to aggressive and antisocial behaviors as risk factors for a variety of adjustment problems. Aggressive tendencies have been conceptualized and assessed in a variety of ways, including parent and teacher reports of "externalizing" problems, teacher and peer ratings of aggressive behavior, and sociometric ratings of peer rejection. Several findings from studies of peer assessments should be noted. First, peer ratings show that some children are scored high on both aggressive behavior and withdrawal behavior, and those children are at greater risk for later maladjustment than are children who score high on only one of the two, aggression or withdrawal (Ledingham, Schwartzman, & Serbin, 1984). Second, although peer rejection is most often related to aggressive behavior, not all aggressive/antisocial children are rejected. Those who are aggressive/ antisocial and who also do not get along with peers seem to be at highest risk for poor adjustment later in life.

A more integrated view

Although scholarly articles on psychopathology in adolescents typically consider each diagnostic category separately, recent evidence suggests that individuals often manifest more than one disorder or at least experience overlapping symptoms. The extent to which individuals are likely to manifest more than one diagnosable disorder or a combination of maladaptive behaviors is something that deserves further examination.

In addition to research looking within psychopathologies, we need more research linking psychopathology with developmental changes. The meager body of research thus far suggests that there are some synergistic effects of less optimal development that lead to pathological outcomes. For example, in our own data, we found that high-anxious girls reported worsening body image from grade six through grade eight. We have several other findings showing similar links between psychopathological status and developmental change.

A recent study by Kovacs and Paulaustkas (1984) was unusual in its simultaneous examination of developmental status and psychopathological status. They found that among depressed patients, those who were prepubertal when admitted manifested more chronic depression and more prolonged recovery from depression than did those who were already pubertal at first admission. These results ran counter to Kovacs's hypotheses that disorder was precipitated by pubertal and cognitive change, as proposed by psychoanalytic theory and her interpretation of Piagetian cognitive development theory. The results are more consistent, however, with a model for psychopathology based on the life-span developmental perspective. Kovacs and Paulaustkas (1984) acknowledge that early onset may reflect greater genetic or psychosocial vulnerability to depression and that younger, less mature children may lack a "sophisticated repertoire of internal and external coping responses" (p. 76) that might help resolve distress, thereby prolonging depression. Early onset may also reflect certain environmental conditions or changes that persist in the child's life, and it may be indicative of the chronic presence of stresses and/or lack of resources in the caretaking environment.

Any consideration of the development of psychopathology during adolescence needs to address several interrelated issues. It is important, for example, to distinguish between adolescent problems that may first develop (or become apparent) during adolescence and those problems that have continued (or could have been predicted) from childhood. The etiological factors that lead to the occurrence of a problem in adolescence may be quite different from those that initially contributed to and maintained problems from childhood. The prognoses for these problems may differ as well. For example, Rutter et al. (1976) found several differences between psychiatric problems that arose during adolescence and those persisting from childhood. In particular, an adolescent onset was more commonly observed in girls; cases persisting since childhood often were associated with early educational difficulties, whereas adolescent-onset cases were not; and adverse family factors were less often found in adolescent-onset cases than in cases that had an early onset and persisted into adolescence.

In a prospective study of prepubertal clinically referred children, Kovacs et al. (1984) found that three types of depression commonly diagnosed in adults could be distinguished in their sample on the basis of differences in age of onset, duration of episodes, presence of other psychiatric problems, and time to recovery. Children were diagnosed (using DSM-III criteria) as suffering from major depressive disorder (MDD), dysthymic disorder (DD), or adjustment disorder with depressed mood (ADDM), or they were nondepressed clinical controls. Although MDD was distinguished by a later age of onset and shorter recovery time than DD, subjects in these two diagnostic categories shared some characteristics that might reflect different expressions of a single underlying process. They were similar in terms of the presence and incidences of other psychiatric symptoms, they showed inverse relationships between age at onset and time to recovery, and MDD was often diagnosed in DD patients. These studies show (a) that chronic, "subsyndromal" depression (dysthymia) is found in children and adolescents, (b) that these symptoms may persist for several years and perhaps into adulthood, (c) that acute episodes of depression can be distinguished from more chronic forms, and (d) that chronic depression is accompanied by other types of problems that may impair adaptive functioning, with the most common problems including poor school performance, interpersonal difficulties, feelings of aggression and hostility, and conduct problems (Puig-Antich et al., 1985a,b).

Developing a model of adolescent psychopathology

Thus far, we have presented research results describing the phenomena of adolescence and of psychopathology during adolescence. But how does psychopathology develop? The existence of some consistent findings across studies and across related variables leads to the question whether or not there is a common developmental pathway for several adolescent problems, including mental illness, as well as behavioral problems as diverse as drug abuse and eating disorders. The general part of the developmental pathway involves the set of individual and context factors that are likely to weaken the individual's capacity to cope with life's challenges. A second general part of this model concerns those life phases that involve inherent challenges to the individual; we hypothesize that the transitions into and out of adolescence constitute challenging developmental phases. What is specific in the model are those factors, in the individual or context, that result in one particular problem, and not others.

Coping and adaptation

The individual's capacity to cope with the new challenges involved at successive phases of development plays a key role in whether the outcomes are healthy or pathological. By "coping capacity" we mean the individual characteristics that the person brings into a situation. Adaptation or the resulting coping performance is the interaction among coping capacity, availability of social resources, and extent of challenge in the situation (French, Rodgers, & Cobb, 1974; Lazarus & Launier, 1978). Adaptive coping (and optimal development) results from a good fit or balance between the power of the person and the power of the situation. This is similar to the goodness-of-fit concept proposed by Thomas and Chess (1977) with regard to temperament, but extended by the Lerners to a variety of aspects of development (Lerner, 1983).

The importance of fit between developmentally relevant contexts and individual coping capacity may be seen in Werner's longitudinal study of development. She and her colleagues (Werner & Smith, 1982) found that constitutional factors (e.g., temperament) played major roles in outcomes early in development, that school and cognitive factors were keys to adjustment during middle childhood, and that interpersonal as well as "self" factors were involved with adjustment during adolescence. Relationships with parents were important throughout these age periods, but the specific ways in which they were important changed over time. What is important about this example is that at each phase of life, the factors in the individual that are important seem to be those that are brought out by the salient social contexts at that phase. Constitutional factors, such as temperament, are important for family interactions, the primary context for early development. During middle childhood, as children begin to attend school, the ability to achieve becomes critical. In adolescence, when the peer group and other aspects of that social context become crucial, the ability to develop interpersonal relationships as well as to feel good about oneself become dominant factors.

Behavioral health, in this model, involves the extent to which adaptive coping takes place. Certain behaviors will occur in any case, and though adaptive in the short term, in the long run they may be damaging or may be likely to facilitate the development of behaviors and capacities that are maladaptive. For example, a young adolescent overwhelmed by the challenges of a new school structure with the transition to a junior high school may become depressed. Although components of this depression, such as withdrawal, may enable the young person to maintain some sort of equilibrium, the inability to cope adaptively with the school change is likely to lead to simultaneous difficulties in other areas, such as with peer relations or with parents, and is likely to make development in subsequent stages more difficult.

Another example may be seen in the middle adolescent, about 15 to 16 years of age, who finds the demands of cliques and pressures to date increasingly stressful and begins to drink alcohol as a way of coping with these social situations. Again, the drinking coping mechanism can enable this young person to continue to go to parties and interact socially, but it is unlikely to facilitate social development or other aspects of development during middle adolescence and, in addition, is likely to make subsequent development more difficult.

Although general pathways, or common underlying constructs such as "social disability" (Vance, 1973), have been proposed in the past, it has been only quite recently in the emerging field of developmental psychopathology that the need to examine *patterns of adaptation* has been proposed, integrating both "outcomes" and "processes" from a variety of theoretical and empirical bases (Cicchetti & Schneider-Rosen, 1984, 1986; Greenspan, 1981; Greenspan & Porges, 1984; Sroufe & Rutter, 1984; Waters & Sroufe, 1983). Although others have stressed the need to consider competent, healthy functioning, particularly as it relates to specific environmental demands and resources (Sundberg, Snowden, & Reynolds, 1976), these approaches typically have addressed *developmental* issues only superficially.

Greenspan (Greenspan, 1981; Greenspan & Porges, 1984), Sroufe (Sroufe, 1979; Waters & Sroufe, 1983), and Cicchetti (Cicchetti & Schneider-Rosen, 1984, 1986) have outlined adaptational or organizational models of development (focused primarily on infants and young children) that focus on one's ability to organize one's behavioral capacities to engage the environment and on the ability of the environment to foster these abilities. There are different "developmental issues" that need to be addressed at different points in the life span that both influence the development of these capacities and can serve as indicators of current capacities. Both Greenspan and Sroufe stress that the manner in which individuals address developmental issues at a given time influences how later issues will be addressed. Sroufe, in particular, argues that there is coherence in individual development in terms of adaptational capacity that may not be reflected in behavioral isomorphism across time (Sroufe, 1979). Rather, it is the underlying coping process that is more enduring in the individual. This is not to say that change is impossible, but rather that continuity in individual capacities is more probable given continuities in the environment. Here, "continuity of context," as in individual continuity, does not necessarily mean no change. Rather, it means that though specific aspects of the context may vary, the changes may be appropriate for meeting the changing needs of the developing individual. For example, parental "support" may manifest itself in different ways across the childhood years. During adolescence, being supportive may mean relinquishing controls and limits that previously were in place and expressing care and support in ways other than (or in addition to) hugs and kisses.

Regressive coping

Some ways of coping with contextual or maturational demands can be considered regressive and can have serious consequences for subsequent development. Baumrind and Moselle (1985) develop this idea well in a paper focused on drug abuse during adolescence. They describe three consequences of maladaptive methods of coping, such as that represented by drug abuse. Regressive coping involves developmental lags, frequently involves specific developmental change, and typically includes psychosocial maladjustment. Baumrind and Moselle (1985) specifically identify six ways in which these regressive methods of coping produce developmental lag: (a) by obscuring the differentiation between the context of work and the context of play, (b) by promoting a false consciousness of reality, (c) by reinforcing egocentrism, (d) by enabling the adolescent to avoid realistic confrontation of environmental demands, (e) by consolidating cultural relativism and idealism of adolescents, and (f) by masquerading as an emancipatory effort.

Although not all regressive ways of coping involve specific developmental damage, examples can be identified for drug abuse, particularly the amotivational syndrome that is associated with marijuana use and the actual physiological damage or brain damage that can result from other forms of substance abuse. Because developmental change is quite serious, it is extremely important to identify the ways that this might occur with various problems. With serious depressive episodes, for example, there is likely to be developmental damage resulting from long hospitalizations, because these adolescents will miss important social and academic learning experiences.

Psychosocial dysfunction is perhaps less serious than developmental damage and involves behaviors that diminish optimal functioning. Escapism, egocentrism, an external locus of control, and alienation and estrangement are all examples of psychosocial dysfunction. Specific forms of psychopathology are also appropriate for this list, particularly both depression and anxiety.

Developmental trajectory

Although we think of adaptation or coping capacity as consisting of many component parts, we may consider this as the result of an individual's developmental history. There is some evidence to suggest that certain factors can predict a course of greater versus poorer adaptation and that certain earlier characteristics and experiences put individuals on particular trajectories. Deviations from expected trajectories are also of interest to us as "casualties" or "resilient" individuals.

By "developmental trajectory" we refer to a pattern of growth or development, a path that an individual has traveled and is likely to travel in the future. It includes a person's developmental history and connotes some sense of direction or value (i.e., positive versus negative, growth or maturation versus retardation or regression, health versus illness). The "results" of growth, in our use of the term, include several aspects of adjustment. It involves adaptive capacity, as assessed by both psychological well-being and adaptational success (Kellam & Brown, 1986; Kohlberg et al., 1972). It also includes the situations, events, and experiences in an individual's life, be it by chance or choice.

Adaptive efforts during adolescence also influence and perhaps constrain the likelihoods of particular future trajectories, not just in terms of adaptive capacity but also in terms of life "choices" and patterns of adaptation in the roles and responsibilities expected of young adults: for work and self-sufficiency, involvement in an intimate relationship (which may result in marriage), and parenting.

Taking a developmental perspective on adolescent psychopathology, then, requires not only asking where it comes from and how it develops but also asking where it goes: What are the consequences of adolescent problems?

Three sets of questions should be asked in this regard. First, is there continuity in a problem over time? Do symptoms persist or abate? Are there transformations in the nature of a problem or set of problems? Second, what factors are related to the continuity or change in problems? Finally, what are the consequences of problems for other domains of functioning later in life? Are problems predictive of life outcomes beyond measures of the problem itself?

Cicchetti and Schneider-Rosen (1984, 1986) have outlined a model for the relationship between competence and depression during childhood that addresses some of these issues, and a study of the adult sequelae of depressive symptoms during adolescence by Kandel and Davies (1986) directly examined these questions. High scores on depressive mood during adolescence were related to a history of psychiatric hospitalization and consultation with a mental health professional over the next 9 years for women, but not for men. Those reporting high levels of depression as adolescents also scored high on a variety of other symptom measures and reported feeling less happy with life. Men and women who had been depressed as adolescents were more likely to have dropped out of school and to have been involved in deviant and delinquent activities. Women who had been depressed as adolescents were more likely to be working, to be mothers, and to be divorced. Previously depressed males experienced greater numbers of unemployment spells than did their previously nondepressed peers. Those who had been depressed as adolescents reported feeling less close and less satisfied in their relationships with their partners and attending fewer social activities with their partners. Women who previously had been depressed also reported feeling less close and less satisfied in their relationships with both parents, as they had earlier in adolescence. Thus, the presence of problems during adolescence had consequences not only for later psychological functioning but also for social functioning, particularly in the acquisition of social roles and adjustment within those roles.

A framework for understanding adaptation in adolescence

A developmental outcome in adolescence (adaptive coping or disturbance) can be seen as a result of the interaction between what an individual brings into this period (one's developmental trajectory) and the nature of the challenges and resources available during this period. This conception requires identifying (a) individual characteristics and capacities that could be considered strengths or weaknesses, (b) social resources available before and during the transition, (c) specific challenges (demands) that occur during adolescent transitions and the capacities and coping responses needed for adaptation, and (d) how developmental trajectories, challenges, and resources interact in determining outcome (Figure 14.1).

Individual eliciting factors

Biological substrate. This model assumes that at least some disorders involve a biological, particularly genetic, component. Such a component is likely to provide for specificity of disorder, particularly regarding the type and severity of the disorder. For example, an adolescent probably will not develop schizophrenia without the genes establishing such a potential (Erlenmeyer-Kimling et al., 1984). We might argue that individuals with such genetic potential

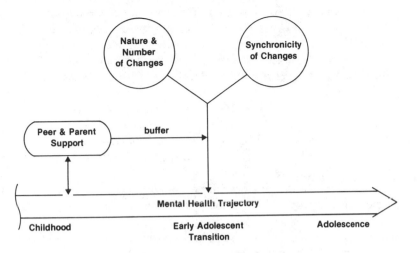

Figure 14.1. A model for the effect of early adolescent transition on the development of mental health.

manifest schizophrenia if certain conditions exist in the environment. Because concordance rates are only about 50% for monozygotic twins, we can hypothesize that the differential appearance of disorder is due to environmental factors. Fluctuations or other genetic factors could be involved as well. Late adolescence and early adulthood are peak times for the onset of schizophrenia, a development we could attribute to the challenges of the late adolescent transition to the work and family roles of adulthood.

Similarly, there is general agreement that diabetes has a biological component to its causation. It is less common, however, to talk about the environmental aspects that permit, elicit, or facilitate diabetes. Epidemiological research (Drash, 1979) indicated a high incidence of onset of diabetes during early adolescence. That observation led to hypotheses about the role of puberty in the initiation of diabetes, particularly because onset in this age group averages 6–12 months earlier in girls (Drash & Berlin, 1985). Another increase in the incidence of diabetes at about age 6 (Drash, 1979) suggests that beginning school, or changing the school environment, may prove sufficiently stressful to individuals with the biological potential to stimulate the onset of juvenile diabetes (more correctly termed insulin-dependent diabetes mellitus in juveniles).

Gender. In our earlier review of psychopathology, we noted that depression and anxiety are two to three times more common in girls than in boys. In contrast, conduct disorders are more common in boys than in girls. Although the factors leading to these gender ratios are not known at present, gender is clearly an important factor, and the various existing hypotheses need thorough investigation. A major gender difference not noted earlier is that almost any kind of problem or psychopathology during childhood has a higher incidence among boys than among girls, whereas by middle adolescence almost all these ratios seem to be reversed except for personality disorders and schizophrenia (Eme, 1979; Gove & Herb, 1974; Werner & Smith, 1982).

Psychological factors. In considerations of risk and protective factors in developmental psychopathology, Garmezy's conceptualizations and research (Garmezy, 1985) have been critically important. The risk factors are attributed primarily to the social environment and will be discussed in the next section. Several of the protective factors that operate to produce better outcomes even when poor social conditions prevail are individual factors. These include psychological factors such as self-esteem, feelings of control, a view of the environment as predictable, and a view of life as a basically positive experience, as well as the ability to elicit positive responses from the environment (e.g., good temperament, sociability, and social competence) and the possession of sufficient intelligence (Garmezy, 1985).

Children who have suffered a great deal of personal distress, whether from social conditions (e.g., extreme poverty, disrupted families) or from individual characteristics (e.g., debilitating illness, severe learning disorder), are less likely than other children to attain psychologically healthy states. Nevertheless, Garmezy (1985) has effectively argued that some children cope effectively and even seem to derive greater strength from their adverse circumstances.

Eliciting effects of the social contexts

Social contexts also appear to have differential potentials to elicit specific outcomes in an individual, depending on the fit between individual characteristics and the features of the social context. Ideally, the challenges of the social contexts should be difficult for the individual and should require some coping. For example, school transitions are not difficult for everyone. On the other hand, the transition to junior high school typically is difficult for most children, although more so for girls than for boys. The divorce of parents is another social context change that is generally difficult for young people, although in some cases it provides a maturity-enhancing opportunity. Again, there may be gender differences in vulnerability. Werner and Smith (1982) found that whereas permanent absence of the father and maternal employment were related to resilience among high-risk girls, the same conditions were destructive for boys.

There are, however, some generally debilitative social circumstances. These have been identified by Garmezy (1985) as risk factors and include severe marital discord within the family, low social status and poverty, large family size, a pattern of criminality in the parents or child, psychiatric disorder of some family member (particularly the mother), and care of the child by local authorities at some point. Some social factors, however, play protective roles. A child can experience positive outcomes despite an otherwise poor environment if there is a close personal bond with at least one member of the family, preferably an adult member. Similarly, a positive school environment can play a protective role.

Challenge of the adolescent transition

Whereas research consistently shows the negative effects of chronic environmental adversity (such as poverty, or living with a mentally ill parent) on adjustment in children and adolescents, the literature is less clear on the effects of other life changes. Research in this area either follows the stressful life events paradigm (with emphasis on the amount of change) or involves studies on the effects of specific types of changes (e.g., effects of divorce, death of parent, school transitions).

Studies using the stressful life events paradigm (Dohrenwend & Dohrenwend, 1974) rarely distinguish between changes that can be considered normative (either biologically or socially) and those that are nonnormative (McCubbin & Patterson, 1986; Swearingen & Cohen, 1985). For adolescents, normative changes would include changes that all or most adolescents would experience within a fairly predictable time period, such as puberty and, for American youth, making the transition from an elementary school to a junior high or middle school. Nonnormative changes – events that are unpredictable and are not time- or age-dependent – include family changes such as death, illness, divorce, and job changes.

Studies show that the timing of normative changes, as well as the occurrence of multiple simultaneous changes, can affect outcomes (Coleman, 1978; Simmons & Blyth, 1987). For example, we find that "too early" school transitions to a secondary school format are worse than later transitions (Petersen & Ebata, 1986). The most extensively studied timing effects have included the effect of deviant pubertal timing on psychological adaptation, generally showing especially poor outcomes for girls who mature early (Petersen & Taylor, 1980). Simmons and Blyth (1987) found that greater numbers of changes experienced in early adolescence were related to poorer outcomes.

Beyond the factors that could be applied to any age period, there are special features of adolescence that make it more likely to be difficult. First, it is a period between childhood and adulthood, two periods of recognized, "legitimate" status. Adolescents are neither, and they are attempting to move from one to the other. Two transitional periods are involved in adolescence: into and out of the period. As described earlier, the transition into adolescence is characterized by changes in every aspect of individual development and every important social context (Petersen, 1987). The child is thrust from a relatively secure world into one in which the demands increase at the same time that the skills to meet the new demands are only beginning to be developed.

Whereas the transition into adolescence may be viewed as offering increased opportunity, as well as increased risk, the transition out of adolescence typically involves constriction of opportunity, as young people move into adult work and family roles. The fact of this transition is likely to affect and condition development during much of adolescence, at least from the middle through the later phases. Young people must begin to make decisions that will have major implications for their paths through life. The importance of the decisions may overwhelm young people who fear them or who cannot face expected decisions (e.g., following in "father's footsteps," recognizing a lack of the resources needed to pursue a particular career), resulting in breakdown.

Up until now, we have considered changes, transitions, and events as potential risk factors, factors that may contribute to maladjustment or prevent the development of adaptive capacities. Others (Garbarino, 1985) have argued, however, that these changes may also bring challenges and opportunities for growth. Having a new peer group from which to select friends, experiencing more extensive challenges and opportunities in school, and being freed of a conflicted parental marital relationship may be beneficial to the development of most adolescents. Garmezy and others (Rutter, 1981) have argued that a certain amount of challenge may be necessary for healthy development. The study of developmental challenges, then, must acknowledge the holism of any change or event, that risk and opportunity may be two faces of the same coin, and that what may be crucial is to identify for whom a particular type of change may be problematic and for whom it may be enhancing.

Cumulative processes

The outcomes of one developmental phase become integrated into the maturation of the individual or the change in the social context, or both, at the next developmental phase. Adverse outcomes at an earlier phase may weaken the individual but not yet produce illness. Some challenge during a subsequent phase may be the crucial one, the proverbial "straw that broke the camel's back" in terms of breakdown.

It is important to note, however, that specific stress can produce temporary distress, the distress being temporary given a good constitution, a stable family, and so forth. The persistence of problems is related to the continuation of poorer maturational outcomes and social contexts over time. For example, problems such as chronic poverty or psychopathology in a parent are conditions that are likely to continue through the child's lifetime and to have cumulative effects.

In general, specific environmental conditions and specific life changes can be interpreted as sources of stress, risk, or weakness or as sources of opportunity, depending on particular individual characteristics and previous environmental conditions. Contextual factors are crucial during infancy and childhood in influencing how individuals organize their cognitive, affective, motivational, and behavioral capacities to adapt to the social context. As a child approaches adolescence, however, individual capacities and proclivities become more important in the "selection" of other contexts and experiences that may influence further development. Particularly during adolescence, individual characteristics and capacities play more important roles in producing their own (further) development (Lerner, 1982; Lerner & Busch-Rossnagel, 1981).

For example, social support has been found to be an important mediator between stress and well-being, and it may be the case that certain people are better at procuring (as well as perceiving and accepting) this support from others during times of stress. Thus, good relationships and social support are related to healthy psychological adjustment, and it may be that the processes or capacities necessary to establish and maintain good interpersonal relationships are at the core of adaptive functioning and psychological well-being.

Summary

Developmental factors are important for an understanding of psychopathology. Adolescence, in particular, involves several changes that challenge the individual, both in the social contexts of this age and in individual maturation. Whether an adolescent is able to cope adaptively and enhance subsequent developmental outcomes or copes maladaptively and jeopardizes future developmental outcomes depends on previous maturation in the individual, as well as the nature of previous challenges presented and resources provided by the social contexts, together with the nature of the fit between the current challenges and the individual's resources for coping.

Attempts to predict relative success or failure in developing adaptive capacities during adolescence thus require several considerations. First, both individual capacities and contextual factors must be taken into account. The individual factors considered should include (a) capacities and characteristics that may be essential for successful adaptation during adolescence (e.g., good social skills) and (b) characteristics that either promote or prevent acquisition of further adaptive skills that might be important later in life, either through their effects on individual ability (e.g., extremely low IQ, congenital handicaps) or through their effects on relevant social contexts that in turn influence the individual (e.g., aggressive behavior alienating peers and teachers). The contextual factors considered should include conditions and events in relevant settings that may be stressful or be supportive, in order to assess the availability of resources and opportunities for challenge and growth, as well as failure and maladjustment.

Second, those factors unique to the adolescent period should be distinguished from more general factors that are important during childhood as well as over the entire life span. For example, good parenting may be generally important, but are the same qualities required to parent an infant as an adolescent? If not, what are the necessary changes for successfully parenting an adolescent?

Finally, capacities, conditions, and their interactions must be followed across time to examine individual differences in developmental trends and the conditions under which these differences arise and continue, abate, or become transformed.

This model for the interaction between changing social contexts and changing individual maturation proposes a developmental framework for investigating and understanding a diverse set of physical and mental illnesses, as well as less serious problems that occur during adolescence. The model has been derived from our research, but it requires further tests on additional samples, with examination of its limits and the extent to which it can be generalized.

References

Albert, N., & Beck, A. T. (1975). Incidence of depression in early adolescence: A preliminary study. *Journal of Youth and Adolescence, 4,* 301–7.

Aldous, J. (1978). *Family careers: Developmental changes in families.* New York: Wiley.

Baltes, P. B. (1968). Longitudinal and cross-sectional sequences in the study of age and generation effects. *Human Development, 11,* 145–71.

Baumrind, D., & Moselle, K. A. (1985). A developmental perspective on adolescent drug abuse. *Advances in Alcohol and Substance Abuse, 4,* 41–67.

Bell, R. Q., & Harper, L. V. (1977). *Child effects on adults.* Hillsdale, NJ: Erlbaum.

Belsky, J., Lerner, R. M., & Spanier, G. B. (1984). *The child in the family.* Reading, MA: Addison-Wesley.

Blos, P. (1962). *On adolescence: A psychoanalytic interpretation.* New York: Free Press.

Blyth, D., Hill, J. P., & Smith, C. K. (1981). The influence of older adolescents on younger adolescents: Do grade level arrangements make a difference in behaviors, attitudes, and experiences? *Journal of Early Adolescence, 1,* 85–110.

Blyth, D., Simmons, R., & Carlton-Ford, S. (1983). The adjustment of adolescents to school transitions. *Journal of Early Adolescence, 3,* 105–20.

Bronfenbrenner, U. (1979). *The ecology of human development.* Cambridge, MA: Harvard University Press.

Chapman, A. H. (1974). *Management of emotional problems of children and adolescents.* Philadelphia: Lippincott.

Chilman, C. S. (1968). Families in development at mid-stage of the family life cycle. *Family Coordinator, 17,* 297–331.

Cicchetti, D., & Schneider-Rosen, K. (1984). Toward a transactional model of childhood depression. In D. Cicchetti & K. Schneider-Rosen (Eds.), *Childhood depression* (pp. 5–27). San Francisco: Jossey-Bass.

Cicchetti, D., & Schneider-Rosen, K. (1986). An organizational approach to childhood depression. In M. Rutter, C. E. Izard, & P. B. Read (Eds.), *Depression in young people: Developmental and clinical perspectives* (pp. 71–134). New York: Guilford Press.

Coie, J. D., & Dodge, K. A. (1983). Continuities and changes in children's social status: A five-year longitudinal study. *Merrill-Palmer Quarterly, 29,* 261–82.

Coie, J. D., & Kupersmidt, J. B. (1983). A behavioral analysis of emerging social status in boys' groups. *Child Development, 54,* 1400–16.

Coleman, J. C. (1978). Current contradictions in adolescent theory. *Journal of Youth and Adolescence, 7,* 1–11.

Conger, J. J., & Petersen, A. C. (1984). *Adolescence and youth* (3rd ed.). New York: Harper & Row.

Craighead, W. E., Kennedy, R. E., & Raczynski, J. M. (1984). Affective disorders: Unipolar. In S. M. Turner & M. Hersen (Eds.), *Adult psychopathology: A behavioral perspective.* New York: Wiley.

Craighead, W. E., Smucker, M. R., & Duchnowski, A. (1981, August). *Childhood depression and attributional style.* Paper presented at the meeting of the American Psychological Association, Los Angeles.

Crockett, L., Losoff, M., & Petersen, A. C. (1984). Perceptions of the peer group and friendship in early adolescence. *Journal of Early Adolescence, 4,* 155–81.

Crockett, L. J., Petersen, A. C., Graber, J. A., Schulenberg, J. E., & Ebata, A. T. (1989). School transitions and adjustment. *Journal of Early Adolescence, 9,* 181–220.

Csikszentmihalyi, M., & Larson, R. (1984). *Being adolescent: Conflict and growth in the teenage years.* New York: Basic Books.

Damon, W., & Hart, D. (1982). The development of self-understanding from infancy through adolescence. *Child Development, 53,* 841–64.

Dodge, K. A. (1983). Behavioral antecedents of peer social status. *Child Development, 54,* 1386–99.

Dohrenwend, B. S., & Dohrenwend, B. P. (Eds.). (1974). *Stressful life events: Their nature and effects.* New York: Wiley.

Douvan, E., & Adelson, J. (1966). *The adolescent experience.* New York: Wiley.

Drash, A. L. (1979). The child with diabetes mellitus. In B. A. Hamburg, L. F. Lipsitt, G. E. Inoff, & A. L. Drash (Eds.), *Behavioral and psychosocial aspects of diabetes: Proceedings of a national conference* (NIH Publication No. 80-1993, pp. 33–42). Washington, DC: U.S. Government Printing Office.

Drash, A. L., & Berlin, N. (1985). Juvenile diabetes. In N. Hobbs & J. M. Perrin (Eds.), *Issues in the care of children with chronic illness* (pp. 155–82). San Francisco: Jossey-Bass.

Elkind, D. (1975). Recent research on cognitive development in adolescence. In S. E. Dragastin & G. H. Elder (Eds.), *Adolescence in the life cycle: Psychological change and social context* (pp. 49–61). Washington, DC: Hemisphere.

Emde, R. M. (1980). Levels of meaning for infant emotions: A biosocial view. In A. Collins (Ed.), *Minnesota symposia on child psychology* (Vol. 13, pp. 1–37). Minneapolis: University of Minnesota Press.

Eme, R. (1979). Sex differences in childhood psychopathology: A review. *Psychological Bulletin, 86,* 514–95.

Erlenmeyer-Kimling, L., Marcuse, Y., Cornblatt, B., Friedman, D., Rainer, J. D., & Rutschmann, J. (1984). The New York High-Risk Project. In N. F. Watt, E. J. Anthony, L. C. Wynne, & J. E. Rolf (Eds.), *Children at risk for schizophrenia: A longitudinal perspective* (pp. 169–89). Cambridge University Press.

Faust, M. S. (1983). Alternative constructions of adolescent growth. In J. Brooks-Gunn & A. C. Petersen (Eds.), *Girls at puberty: Biological and psychological perspectives* (pp. 105–26). New York: Plenum.

French, J. R., Rodgers, W., & Cobb, S. (1974). Adjustment as person–environment fit. In G. V. Coelho, D. A. Hamburg, & J. E. Adams (Eds.), *Coping and adaptation* (pp. 316–33). New York: Basic Books.

Freud, A. (1958). *Adolescence: Psychoanalytic study of the child* (Vol. 13). New York: International Universities Press.

Garbarino, J. (1985). *Adolescent development: An ecological perspective.* Columbus, OH: Charles Merrill.

Garmezy, M. (1985). Stress-resistant children: The search for protective factors. In J. E. Stevenson (Ed.), *Recent research in developmental psychopathology* (pp. 213–33). Oxford: Pergamon Press.

Gersten, J. C., Langer, T. S., Eisenberg, J. B., Simcha-Fagen, O., & McCarthy, E. D. (1976). Stability and change in types of behavioral disturbance of children and adolescents. *Journal of Abnormal Child Psychology, 4,* 111–27.

Gould, M. S., Wunsch-Hitzig, R., & Dohrenwend, B. (1981). Estimating the prevalence of childhood psychopathology. *Journal of the American Academy of Child Psychiatry, 20,* 462–76.

Gove, W. R., & Herb, T. R. (1974). Stress and mental illness among the young: A comparison of the sexes. *Social Forces, 53,* 256–65.

Graham, P. (1979). Epidemiological studies. In H. C. Quay & J. S. Werry (Eds.), *Psychopathological disorders of childhood* (2nd ed., pp. 185–209). New York: Wiley.

Greenspan, S. I. (1981). *Psychopathology and adaptation in infancy and early childhood: Principles of clinical diagnosis and preventive intervention.* New York: International Universities Press.

Greenspan, S. I., & Porges, S. W. (1984). Psychopathology in infancy and early childhood: Clinical perspectives on the organization of sensory and affective-thematic experience. *Child Development, 55,* 49–70.

Grinker, R. R., Sr., Grinker, R. R., Jr., & Timberlake, I. (1962). Mentally healthy young males (homoclites). *Archives of General Psychiatry, 6,* 311–18.

Harter, S. (1983). Developmental perspectives on the self-system. In E. M. Heatherington (Ed.), P. H. Mussen (Series Ed.), *Handbook of child psychology. Vol. 4: Socialization, personality and social development* (pp. 275–386). New York: Wiley.

Hartup, W. W. (1983). Peer relations. In P. H. Mussen (Ed.), *Handbook of child psychology* (Vol. 4, pp. 103–96). New York: Wiley.

Hill, R., & Mattesich, P. (1979). Family development theory and life-span development. In P. B. Baltes & O. G. Brim, Jr. (Eds.), *Life-span development and behavior* (Vol. 2, pp. 162–204). New York: Academic Press.

Inhelder, B., & Piaget, J. (1958). *The growth of logical thinking from childhood to adolescence.* New York: Basic Books.

Kandel, D. B., & Davies, M. (1982). Epidemiology of depressive mood in adolescents. *Archives of General Psychiatry, 39,* 1205–12.

Kandel, D. B., & Davies, M. (1986). Adult sequelae of adolescent depressive symptoms. *Archives of General Psychiatry, 43,* 255–62.

Kaplan, S. L., Hong, G. K., & Weinhold, C. (1984). Epidemiology of depressive symptomatology in adolescents. *Journal of the American Academy of Child Psychiatry, 23,* 91–8.

Keating, D. P. (1980). Thinking processes in adolescence. In J. Adelson (Ed.), *Handbook of adolescent psychology* (pp. 211–46). New York: Wiley.

Kellam, S. G., & Brown, C. H. (1986). Social adaptational and psychological antecedents in the first grade of adolescent psychopathology ten years later. In G. L. Klerman (Ed.), *Suicide and depression among adolescents and younger adults* (pp. 149–83). Washington, DC: American Psychiatric Press.

Kestenberg, J. (1968). Phase of adolescence with suggestions for correlation of psychic and hormonal organizations. Part III: Puberty growth, differentiation, and consolidation. *Journal of the American Academy of Child Psychiatry, 6,* 577–614.

Kohlberg, L., LaCrosse, J., & Ricks, D. (1972). The predictability of adult mental health from childhood behavior. In B. Wolman (Ed.), *Manual of child psychopathology* (pp. 1217–84). New York: McGraw-Hill.

Kovacs, M., Feinberg, T. L., Crouse-Novak, M. A., Paulaustkas, S., & Finkelstein, R. (1984). Depressive disorders of childhood. I: A longitudinal prospective study of characteristics and recovery. *Archives of General Psychiatry, 41,* 229–37.

Kovacs, M., & Paulaustkas, S. L. (1984). Developmental stage and the expression of depressive disorders in children. In D. Cicchetti & K. Schneider-Rosen (Eds.), *Childhood depression* (pp. 59–80). San Francisco: Jossey-Bass.

Larson, R., Csikszentmihalyi, M., & Graef, R. (1980). Mood variability and the psychosocial adjustment of adolescents. *Journal of Youth and Adolescence, 9,* 469–90.

Lazarus, R. S., & Launier, R. (1978). Stress-related transactions between person and environment. In L. A. Pervin & M. Lewis (Eds.), *Perspectives in interactional psychology* (pp. 282–327). New York: Plenum Press.

Ledingham, J. E., Schwartzman, A. E., & Serbin, L. A. (1984). Current adjustment and family functioning of children behaviorally at risk for adult schizophrenia. *New Directions for Child Development, 24,* 99–112.

Lerner, J. V. (1983). The import of temperament for psychosocial functioning: Tests of a goodness of fit model. *Merrill-Palmer Quarterly, 30,* 177–88.

Lerner, R. M. (1978). Nature, nurture, and dynamic interactionism. *Human Development, 21,* 1–20.

Lerner, R. M. (1982). Children and adolescents as producers of their own development. *Developmental Review, 2,* 342–70.

Lerner, R. M., & Busch-Rossnagel, N. A. (1981). Individuals as producers of their own development: Conceptual and empirical bases. In R. M. Lerner & N. A. Busch-Rossnagel (Eds.), *Individuals as producers of their development: A life span perspective* (pp. 1–36). New York: Academic Press.

Lerner, R. M., & Spanier, G. B. (1980). *Adolescent development: A life span perspective.* New York: McGraw-Hill.

Links, P. S. (1983). Community surveys of the prevalence of childhood psychiatric disorders: A review. *Child Development, 54,* 531–48.

Linn, M. C., deBenedictis, T., & Delucchi, K. (1982). Adolescent reasoning about advertisements. *Child Development, 53,* 1599–613.

Loeber, R. (1982). The stability of antisocial and delinquent child behavior: A review. *Child Development, 53,* 1431–46.

McCubbin, H. I., & Patterson, J. M. (1986). Adolescent stress, coping, and adaptation: A normative family perspective. In G. K. Leigh & G. W. Petersen (Eds.), *Adolescence in a family context.* Cincinnati: South-Western Publisher.

Marks, I., & Gelder, M. (1966). Different ages of onset in varieties of phobia. *American Journal of Psychiatry, 123,* 218–21.

Montemayor, R. (1983). Parents and adolescents in conflict: All families some of the time and some families most of the time. *Journal of Early Adolescence, 3,* 83–103.

Mullins, L. L., Siegel, L. J., & Hodges, K. (1985). Cognitive problem-solving and life event correlates of depressive symptoms in children. *Journal of Abnormal Child Psychology, 13,* 305–14.

Offer, D. (1969). *The psychological world of the teenager: A study of normal adolescent boys.* New York: Basic Books.

Offer, D., & Offer, J. (1975). *From teenage to young manhood: A psychological study.* New York: Basic Books.

Ogbu, J. U. (1981). The origins of human competence: A cultural ecological perspective. *Child Development, 52,* 413–29.

Papini, D., & Datan, N. (1983, April). *Transition into adolescence: An interactionist perspective.* Paper presented at the biennial meeting of the Society for Research in Child Development, Detroit.

Petersen, A. C. (1987). The nature of biological–psychosocial interactions: The sample case of early adolescence. In R. M. Lerner & T. T. Foch (Eds.), *Biological–psychological interactions in early adolescence: A life-span perspective* (pp. 35–61). Hillsdale, NJ: Erlbaum.

Petersen, A. C., & Craighead, W. E. (1986). Emotional and personality development in normal adolescents and young adults. In G. Klerman (Ed.), *Preventive aspects of suicide and affective disorders among adolescents and young adults* (pp. 19–52). New York: Guilford Press.

Petersen, A. C., & Ebata, A. T. (1986, March). *Effects of normative and non-normative changes on early adolescent development.* Paper presented at the first biennial meeting of the Society for Research on Adolescence, Madison, WI.

Petersen, A. C., Schulenberg, J. E., Abramowitz, R. H., Offer, D., & Jarcho, H. D. (1984). A Self-Image Questionnaire for Young Adolescents: Reliability and validity studies. *Journal of Youth and Adolescence, 13,* 93–111.

Petersen, A. C., & Spiga, R. (1982). Adolescence and stress. In L. Goldberger & S. Breznitz (Eds.), *Handbook of stress: Theoretical and clinical aspects* (pp. 515–28). New York: Macmillan.

Petersen, A. C., & Taylor, B. (1980). The biological approach to adolescence. In J. Adelson (Ed.), *Handbook of adolescent psychology* (pp. 117–55). New York: Wiley.

Pritchard, M., & Graham, P. (1966). An investigation of a group of patients who have attended both the child and adult departments of the same psychiatric hospital. *British Journal of Psychiatry, 112,* 603–12.

Puig-Antich, J., Lukens, E., Davies, M., Goetz, D., Brennan-Quattrock, J., & Todak, G. (1985a). Psychosocial functioning in prepubertal major depressive disorders. I: Interpersonal relationships during the depressive episodes. *Archives of General Psychiatry, 42,* 500–7.

Puig-Antich, J., Lukens, E., Davies, M., Goetz, D., Brennan-Quattrock, J., & Todak, G. (1985b). Psychosocial functioning in prepubertal major depressive disorders. II: Interpersonal relationships after sustained recovery from affective episode. *Archives of General Psychiatry, 42,* 511–17.

Robins, L. (1966). *Deviant children grown up: A sociological and psychiatric study of sociopathic personality.* Baltimore: Williams & Wilkins.

Robins, L., & Ratcliff, K. S. (1979). Risk factors in the continuation of childhood antisocial behavior into adulthood. *International Journal of Mental Health, 7,* 96–116.

Rutter, M. (1981). Stress, coping, and development: Some issues and some questions. *Journal of Child Psychology and Psychiatry, 22,* 323–56.

Rutter, M. (1986). The developmental psychopathology of depression: Issues and perspectives. In M. Rutter, C. Izard, & P. Read (Eds.), *Depression in young people: Developmental and clinical perspectives* (pp. 3–30). New York: Guilford Press.

Rutter, M., Graham, P., Chadwick, O., & Yule, W. (1976). Adolescent turmoil: Fact or fiction? *Journal of Child Psychology and Psychiatry, 17,* 35–56.

Sameroff, A. J. (1975). Transactional models in early social relations. *Human Development, 18,* 65–79.

Schulenberg, J. E., Asp, C. E., & Petersen, A. C. (1984). School from the young adolescent's perspective: A descriptive report. *Journal of Early Adolescence, 4,* 107–30.

Seligman, M. E. P., & Peterson, C. (1986). A learned helplessness perspective on childhood depression: Theory and research. In M. Rutter, C. E. Izard, & P. B. Read (Eds.), *Depression in young people: Developmental and clinical perspectives* (pp. 223–48). New York: Guilford Press.

Senn, M. J. E., & Solnit, A. J. (1968). *Problems in child behavior and development.* Philadelphia: Lea & Febiger.

Simmons, R. G., & Blyth, D. A. (1987). *Moving into adolescence: The impact of pubertal change and school context.* New York: Aldine.

Simmons, R. G., Rosenberg, F., & Rosenberg, M. (1973). Disturbance in the self-image at adolescence. *American Sociological Review, 38,* 553–68.

Sroufe, L. A. (1979). The coherence of individual development. *American Psychologist, 34,* 834–41.

Sroufe, L. A., & Rutter, M. (1984). The domain of developmental psychopathology. *Child Development, 55,* 17–29.

Steinberg, L. D. (1981). Transformants in family relations at puberty. *Developmental Psychology, 7,* 833–40.

Steinberg, L. D., & Hill, J. P. (1978). Patterns of family interaction as a function of age, the onset of puberty, and formal thinking. *Developmental Psychology, 14,* 683–4.

Sundberg, M. D., Snowden, L. R., & Reynolds, W. M. (1976). Toward assessment of personal competence and incompetence in life situations. *Annual Review of Psychology, 29,* 179–221.

Swearingen, E. M., & Cohen, L. H. (1985). Life events and psychological distress: A prospective study of young adolescents. *Developmental Psychology, 21,* 1045–54.

Tanner, J. M. (1962). *Growth at adolescence* (2nd ed.). Philadelphia: Davis.

Teri, L. (1982). The use of the Beck Depression Inventory with adolescents. *Journal of Abnormal Child Psychology, 10,* 277–84.

Thomas, A., & Chess, S. (1977). *Temperament and development.* New York: Brunner/Mazel.

Vaillant, G. E. (1977). *Adaptation to life.* Boston: Little, Brown.

Vance, E. T. (1973). Social disability. *American Psychologist, 28,* 498–511.

Waters, E., & Sroufe, L. A. (1983). Social competence as a developmental construct. *Developmental Review, 3,* 79–97.

Weiner, I., & DelGaudio, A. (1976). Psychopathology in adolescence. *Archives of General Psychiatry, 33,* 187–93.

Werner, E. E., & Smith, R. S. (1982). *Vulnerable but invincible: A longitudinal study of resilient children and youth.* New York: McGraw-Hill.

Yarrow, L. J. (1979). Emotional development. *American Psychologist, 10,* 951–7.

15   Depressive symptoms in late adolescence: a longitudinal perspective on personality antecedents

Jack Block and Per F. Gjerde

We have witnessed, over the last decade or so, growing interest in integrating the developmental and clinical aspects of depression. Researchers have attempted to delineate age-related manifestations of depressive symptoms from early childhood through adolescence and to trace the socioemotional and environmental antecedents of this disorder (Bemporad & Wilson, 1978; Rutter & Garmezy, 1983; Rutter, Izard, & Read, 1986; Sroufe & Rutter, 1984).

This research effort has identified adolescence as a period during which depressive symptoms and moods are especially evident. Of course, recognition of the mood fluctuations of the adolescent is not new; psychoanalysts have traditionally offered this perception (Freud, 1958; Lorand, 1967). Recent empiricism, however, has provided additional insights into the nature of adolescent depression. Following puberty there is a sharp increase in the frequency of depression, most notably among girls, a rise in the occurrence of manic moods, intensification of grief reactions, and greater frequency of suicide attempts (Rutter, 1986; Rutter & Garmezy, 1983). Although depression during early adolescence (age 13–16) may still be manifested via age-constrained expressions – possibly due to adolescent egocentrism, insufficiently developed time perspective, and limited life experiences (Bemporad & Wilson, 1978; Malmquist, 1971) – depression during late adolescence (age 16–18) is likely to be more truly comparable to the kind of depressive disorders characterizing adults (Weiner, 1975). This development is likely to derive both from an age-related maturation of cognitive structures (i.e., expressions of depression are no longer constrained by cognitive level) and from what has become, over time and living, a sufficient internalization of feelings and experiences. The deep similarities between adult depression and adolescent depres-

This study was supported by National Institute of Mental Health grant MH-16080 to Jack and Jeanne H. Block. Per F. Gjerde gratefully acknowledges additional support from the Japanese Society for the Promotion of Sciences.

sion notwithstanding, Weiner (1975) has noted that adolescents may continue to express an underlying depressive disorder through behaviors differing from the traditional manifestations of adult depression, including some behaviors that are not always recognized as depression-related (e.g., drug usage).

In research on the psychological causes of depression, a distinction is commonly drawn between vulnerability (or susceptibility) factors on the one hand and precipitating factors (or provoking agents) on the other (Brown & Harris, 1978; Cicchetti & Schneider-Rosen, 1986; Radloff & Rae, 1979). In this view, the chance of precipitating factors bringing about depression is greatly increased if an individual already is vulnerable to this disorder; distinct precipitating factors are therefore in many cases necessary but not sufficient causes of depression. Although the distinction between vulnerability factors and precipitating factors is not always entirely clear (Warren & McEachern, 1983), precipitating factors are most often defined as important life events that include elements of significant loss, disappointment, or major ongoing life stresses (Brown, Harris, & Bifulco, 1986). In contrast, susceptibility factors encompass relatively enduring, biologically and/or psychologically based characteristics – factors that have been established relatively early in life and certainly long prior to any given precipitating event. Of these two sets of causes, susceptibility factors are less understood, if only because they are more likely to have been established in the dim past, long before the depressive episode itself – the event that brings the depressed individual to the attention of the clinician/researcher. The poignant intensity of a depressive reaction has drawn clinical and research inquiry into the life experiences and stresses that immediately precede, elicit, or accompany this psychological disorder, as well as inquiry into how depressed individuals cope with and appraise the events of daily living (Folkman & Lazarus, 1986; Paykel, 1979). But historical knowledge of what depressed individuals were like long before recognition of their depression has been difficult to come by.

The purpose of the study reported here was to examine whether or not depressive symptoms in late adolescence (age 18) could be foretold by longitudinal observations of personality obtained much earlier – during the preschool period, preadolescence, and early adolescence. The importance of scanning for personality characteristics that may give rise to subsequent depressive disorders has been repeatedly emphasized (Chodoff, 1970, 1972; Salzman, 1975). Indeed, many depression-predisposing characteristics have been proposed. These susceptibility factors are commonly considered to develop early in life, often as a consequence of early experiences in the family context, and by definition they are said to precede depression. They include self-attributed inability to create and maintain affectional relationships (Bowlby, 1980), insufficient confidence in one's autonomous abilities (Bemporad & Wilson, 1978), excessive dependence on other individuals or excessive preoccupation with life goals (Arieti & Bemporad, 1980), a proclivity toward strong self-criticism (Blatt, 1974), maladaptive attributional styles (or self-schemata) characterized by helplessness and self-devaluation (Abramson, Seligman, & Teasdale, 1978; Kovacs & Beck, 1978), low self-esteem, especially in the interpersonal domain (Hirschfeld, Klerman, Chodoff, Korchin, & Barrett, 1976), introversion (Akiskal, Hirschfeld, & Yerevanian, 1983), and early incompetence (Cicchetti & Schneider-Rosen, 1986).

Although researchers generally converge in attributing the hypothesized vulnerability to depression, however conceived, to the early personal history of the individual, convincing empirical evidence for this position has been sparse. Currently, support for this position derives either from retrospective analyses of the depressed person's past or from comparisons of currently (or formerly) depressed individuals with normal controls. Neither approach is methodologically satisfactory. Although we are appreciative of the knowledge that can be gained from intensive and prolonged therapeutic contact (Arieti & Bemporad, 1980), retrospective analyses cannot replace prospective methods in the study of depression. First, retrospective data in general are subject to a number of biases, such as faulty memory and differential willingness to discuss painful memories. As Freud noted a long time ago, looking backward it is almost always possible to uncover a past event that can be said to explain a subsequent outcome. Second, it may well be the case that the use of retrospective methods is likely to be particularly inadequate in research on depression. More than other individuals, depressives appear to construe personal experience in an idiosyncratic fashion – as "representing defeat, deprivation, and disparagement" (Beck, 1967, p. 225); they tend to selectively monitor negative events and to activate negative cognitive schemata more easily than positive schemata (Ingram, 1984). This evaluative bias may produce seriously distorted interpretations of a wide range of phenomena, including events belonging to the depressed individual's past.

The second approach, comparison of depressed (or formerly depressed) individuals and normal controls, is also unlikely to produce strong evidence about the antecedents of depression. Although depressed and nondepressed individuals have been found to differ in terms of character structure (Altman & Wittenborn, 1980; Cofer & Wittenborn, 1980), we remain unsure whether these reported differences precede the depressive disorder or reflect personality changes induced by the experience of depression itself. If the latter is the case (and that possibility cannot be excluded), these observed personality differences between depressed and nondepressed individuals do not directly address the issue of susceptibility to this disorder (Akiskal et al., 1983). Additionally, developmental considerations suggest the need to distinguish between the concomitants of depression and its early precursors. Although low self-esteem often distinguishes currently depressed individuals from nondepressed individuals (Hirschfeld et al., 1976), during early childhood the construct of self-esteem cannot be invoked because children have not yet reached the age at which they have stable self-schemata and can engage in meaningful introspective and self–other comparisons. For these several reasons, a longitudinal method is required to search for early personality characteristics predisposing individuals to depression disorders.

The subjects included in this prospective study of personality and depressive symptoms have now been followed for 15 years, starting when the children were 3 years old and in nursery school; for further description of the study, the reader should consult Block and Block (1980b). The subjects, now young adults, were most recently assessed when they were graduating from high school at age 18. During the course of this study, each participant had been earlier assessed on multiple occasions (ages 3, 4, 5, 7, 11, and 14) by independent sets of personality assessors. Each assessment included a wide variety of experimental situations and objective tests tapping various psychological functions.

During the most recent assessment, conducted when they were in late adolescence (age 18), the subjects completed the widely used Center for Epidemiological Studies depression scale (CES-D scale) (Radloff, 1977). By relating depression, as reflected by this scale, to personality evaluations independently obtained as much as 15 years earlier, when the subjects were still in nursery school, we sought to evaluate the extent to which depressive symptoms and moods in late adolescence can be foretold by personality characterizations obtained between the ages of 3–4 and 14 years. In other words, we sought to examine whether or not depressive symptoms in nonclinical samples of 18-year-olds have characterological roots stretching back as far as nursery school – early characteristics that, by implication, may predispose these individuals to subsequent depression.

The CES-D scale is a 20-item self-report instrument originally developed to assess depressive symptoms in the general population. The 20 items tap four content subdomains: (a) depressed affect (e.g., "I felt sad"), (b) positive affect (e.g., "I was happy"), (c) somatic/vegetative signs (e.g., "I did not feel like eating"), and (d) interpersonal distress (e.g., "I felt that people disliked me") (Radloff, 1977). The CES-D scale is becoming widely used for assessing depressive mood and symptoms in nonclinical samples consisting of both adolescents and adults (Radloff & Locke, 1985; Schoenbach, Kaplan, Grimson, & Wagner, 1982; Schoenbach, Kaplan, Wagner, Grimson, & Miller, 1983). Previous research has indicated that the CES-D scale has good internal consistency and test–retest reliability. The scale has also been found to be acceptable to subjects of different ages, educational levels, and ethnic backgrounds; for further information concerning the CES-D scale and its psychometric properties, see Lin, Dean, and Ensel (1986), Radloff (1977), Radloff and Locke (1985), Roberts (1980), and Roberts and Vernon (1983). Furthermore, the CES-D scale has been found to discriminate well and in predictable ways between clinical patients and community samples and among subgroups of psychiatric patients. Compared with a community-population average score of approximately 9, a mixed-diagnosis sample of psychiatric patients will receive an average score of about 24, an acutely depressed group of outpatients will receive a score of about 38, and a sample of mixed-diagnosis outpatients in a mental health clinic will receive an average score of 27 (Craig & Van Natta, 1976; Husaini, Neff, Harrington, Hughes, & Stone, 1980; Weissman, Sholomskas, Pottenger, Prusoff, & Locke, 1977). In community samples, a cutoff score of 16 (or 17) is commonly used to designate "probable" cases of depression.

A final and prolonged caveat: Although the CES-D scale appears to possess satisfactory reliability and validity as a measure or reflection of depressive symptoms, the degree to which high scores on this scale are indicative of major, clinically observed depression remains unresolved. As indications of this problem, consider the following: Lewinsohn and Teri (1982) reported that of those classified as depressed on the basis of their CES-D scores (i.e., those scoring 17 or higher), less than half were judged to be clinically depressed on the basis of a 2-hr semistructured clinical interview. The CES-D items are simply added to produce a single total score for depression. However, as Lewinsohn and Teri observed, a diagnosis of depression requires that depressive symptoms be organized into a specific syndrome. The CES-D scale is believed to be relatively more accurate for identifying nondepressed subjects: Lewinsohn and Teri reported that a CES-D score lower than 17 resulted in an 82% accuracy rate. Finally, in using the CES-D scale, overreporting as well as underreporting of symptoms may occur. Using a CES-D score of 16 as a cutoff score and clinical diagnosis of major depression as criterion, less than 20% of CES-D scale respondents were categorized as false positives, whereas 40% were identified as false negatives, a finding suggesting that underreporting of depressive symptoms may constitute a more severe problem than overreporting.

A recent study by Boyd, Weissman, Thompson, and Myers (1982) is particularly important in evaluating the validity of the CES-D scale. In addition to comparing CES-D scores with diagnosed depression (Research Diagnostic Criteria, RDC) (Spitzer, Endicott, & Robins, 1978), Boyd and associates also tried to identify and explain discrepancies between self-report and interview outcomes. As many as 81% of those scoring over the CES-D threshold (cutoff threshold was 16) had depressive symptoms. However, only a third of these had major current depression, as evaluated via RDC criteria. Nineteen percent of those subjects scoring over the CES-D threshold were excluded because of an insufficient number of clinical symptoms and received a depressive RDC diagnosis other than major depression (e.g., minor depression, depressive personality, cyclothymic personality, or grief). Ten percent had symptoms of depression secondary to medical illness, a condition excluded by the RDC. Seven percent had symptoms of depression but showed an absence of another crucial RDC criterion – role impairment. Seventeen percent received another nondepressive RDC diagnosis (e.g., anxiety, phobia, somatization disorder). Finally, 12% of those scoring above the CES-D threshold denied all symptoms of depression during the interview. These subjects were classified as having no disorder, although the interviewer, ignorant of the subjects' CES-D scores, had the impression that these subjects were depressed. According to Boyd et al. (1982), the CES-D scale was more sensitive than the interview in these cases. This latter finding is important because it demonstrates that a diagnosis based on a clinical interview should not be taken as the ultimate and final criterion for deciding who shall receive the diagnosis of major depression. The concordance rates between self-report scales and clinical interviews should be evaluated in light of this realization.

Self-report measures assessing depressive symptoms in clinically unselected samples have been subjected to several types of criticism. As Depue and Monroe (1978) have noted, the relatively mild depressive states reported by nonclinical subjects may only represent the mood component of depression, not the psychosomatic and vegetative manifestations, the somaticized anxiety, and the other extreme and overt behaviors commonly found in more severe, clinically judged depression. Self-report depression scales may also measure a construct considerably broader than depression (e.g., general distress) (Gotlib, 1984), with scores being temporarily elevated because of transient physical or emotional disturbances (Amenson & Lewinsohn, 1981). Nor does a single scale score do justice to the likely heterogeneity of depressive disorders: Subtypes of depression may be characterized by different causes. Although these several criticisms have been leveled primarily against the Beck Depression Inventory (Beck, Ward, Mendelson, Mock, & Erbaugh, 1961), they apply as well to other depression scales, such as the CES-D scale. As Lin et al. (1986) have remarked, in most uses of self-report scales measuring depressed mood or symptoms, the incidences or intensities of various depressive symptoms in a group have been measured, rather than the presence in an individual of an organized psychiatric syndrome. However, increased knowledge of the antecedents of subclinical varieties of depression may, in itself, be important and help elucidate the processes leading to major depressive disorders. For example, Kovacs and colleagues (Kovacs, Feinberg, Crouse-Novak, Paulauskas, & Finkelstein, 1984a; Kovacs et al., 1984b) showed that among children, dysthymia developed into a major depressive disorder within the next 5 years for as many as two-thirds of their initial sample.

In sum, the inferential leap from depressive symptoms, as expressed via self-report, to depression, as a psychiatric disorder, remains uncertain and therefore arguable. To respect this uncertainty, throughout this chapter, we use the phrase "depressive symptoms" or "depressive tendencies" to indicate that our results, based on a self-report scale, may not be applicable or fully generalizable to clinical depression as defined in psychiatry.

Method

Subjects

Our subjects were 106 adolescents, 54 girls and 52 boys, participating in a longitudinal study of ego and cognitive development conducted by Jack and Jeanne Block at the University of California, Berkeley; see Block and

Block (1980b) for a comprehensive description of this study. The analyses reported in this chapter are based on 88 adolescents for whom CES-D scores were available. The exact number of subjects in any analysis will vary somewhat. These subjects live primarily in urban settings and are heterogeneous with respect to social class and parents' educational levels. About 66% of the subjects are white, 25% are black, and 5% are Asian.

Subjects were initially recruited into the study at the age of 3, while attending either a university-run nursery school or a parent-run cooperative nursery school. The children, now adolescents, were assessed via wide-ranging batteries of personality and cognitive measures at ages 3, 4, 5, 7, 11, 14, and 18.

Procedures

Measuring depression: the CES-D scale. During the age-18 assessment, each subject completed an extensive personality inventory. This inventory, consisting of 678 questions, included many separate scales measuring various aspects of personality and family relationships, and among these was the CES-D scale (Radloff, 1977).

The CES-D scale is a 20-item self-report instrument. Four of the 20 items are worded in a positive direction, whereas the remaining 16 items are worded in a negative direction. The scores on the 4 positively worded items are reflected, and a total sum score is created for each subject. Possible scores range from 0 to 60. High scores indicate more depressive symptoms. In this study, the internal consistency (alpha) reliability of the CES-D was .90.

To prevent the subjects from quickly realizing the common intention behind the 20 CES-D items, the 20 items were never presented consecutively, but, as is often the case, were interspersed among items belonging to other personality scales. In this study, subjects were asked how well each symptom applied to them. Responses were rated on a four-point scale: 0, does not apply at all; 1, does not apply particularly well; 2, applies somewhat; 3, applies quite well. Readers familiar with the CES-D scale will immediately realize that this response format deviates somewhat from the standard CES-D version. Usually, the CES-D asks how often each of the 20 symptoms included in the scale has occurred *during the preceding week*. The change in response format, a consequence of our decision to intersperse the presentation of items deriving from many scales, was deemed necessary to prevent too frequent changes in the response format. Whereas these changes in the way the CES-D items were presented to the subjects seem likely to have increased depressive symptoms scores, primarily because the subjects were not limited to considering the preceding week only, that should not have important consequences for the rank ordering of subjects on the depression symptoms dimension. In this study, the ranking of subjects provides the crucial information on which our correlational analyses depend.

In responding to the inventory questions, the subject was seated in front of a personal computer. The questions appeared, one by one, on the screen. The subject was required to provide an answer by pressing the appropriate key on the keyboard. The age-18 assessment program included six separate sessions, each of which lasted, on average, 2.5 to 3 hr. In most cases, there was a full week between sessions. Either prior to or following each main session, each subject was asked to complete part of the computer-assisted inventory. During each session, each subject was asked to work on the inventory for approximately 20 min. Therefore, it was unlikely that many subjects would have completed all 20 CES-D items in the course of a single session.

Measuring personality. The children's personality characteristics were described by their nursery-school teachers at age 3 and at age 4, by their public-school teachers and psychologist-examiners at age 11, and by psychologist-examiners at age 14. When the children were brought in for assessment at ages 3, 4, 7, and 11, the assessors used the standard vocabulary of the California Child Q-set (CCQ) to describe the subjects (Block & Block, 1980a,b). The CCQ is an age-appropriate modification of the California Adult Q-set (CAQ) (Block, 1961/1978) and consists of 100 widely ranging statements about the personalities and cognitive and social characteristics of children. When the subjects were seen at age 14, the 100 items of the adult form (CAQ) of the California Q-set was employed (Block, 1961/1978).

At age 3, each child was described by three nursery-school teachers who had worked with the children a minimum of 6 months before completing the descriptions. Previously, these teachers had received training and calibration experience in the use of the Q-set method in this context. At age 4, each child was again described via the CCQ procedure, but by an entirely different set of three nursery-school teachers who also had been trained. At age 7, each child was described by one elementary-school teacher and by two psychologist-examiners. When the subjects were 11 years old, four different psychologist-examiners, who had observed the subjects while administering a variety of experimental procedures tapping different aspects of personality and cognitive functioning, provided their descriptions. Finally, at age 14, a different set of four psychologist-examiners described each subject. These assessors had also observed the children during experimental sessions eliciting a wide variety of behaviors.

Judges described each child by arranging the Q-set items in a forced nine-step distribution according to the evaluated salience of each item with respect to a particular child. The judges worked independently of each other. At age 3, and again separately at age 4, the three independent Q-set formulations for a child were averaged to form a composite Q-set description. These two composite Q-descriptions were in turn composited to form an overall composite of each child during the preschool years. This last overall composite was used in the analyses reported here. At ages 7, 11, and 14, the several Q-descriptions available for each subject were also composited, but separately for each age level. The CCQ descriptions were completed by a total of 11 different nursery-school teachers when the children were at age 3, by an entirely different set of 9 nursery-school teachers when the children were at age 4, and by 67 elementary-school teachers when the children were at age 7. Because no judge contributed Q-descriptions more than once, the personality assessments at the different ages were strictly independent of each other.

The estimated internal consistency reliabilities of the Q-items, based on correlations among observers, averaged .65 at ages 3 and 4, .47 at age 7, .70 at age 11, and .72 at age 14. The relatively low average item reliability at age 7 was partly the result of having used only three raters at that age. These reliability data not only provide important information about the relative quality of the personality data employed but also give perspective on the possible magnitude of correlations that can be expected when these measures are related to our criterion variable, the CES-D scale (Block, 1963, 1964; Epstein, 1979, 1980).

Establishing criterion definitions of ego resilience and ego undercontrol. In addition to using the Q-set descriptions directly, item by item, we developed criterion scores based on the CCQ to index two dimensions of particular relevance for this study. Three experienced clinical psychologists were asked to consider the personality implications of the construct of ego resilience (Block 1965, 1982; Block & Block, 1980b), a construct that involves the assimilative and accommodative capacities of individuals under conditions of environmental stress, uncertainty, conflict, or disequilibrium. They were also asked to consider the behavioral implications of ego undercontrol (Block, 1950, 1951, 1965; Block & Block, 1980b; Block & Gjerde, 1986), the pole of the dimension of ego control that involves inability to delay gratification, impulsivity, behavioral spontaneity, short-term commitments, and other manifestations of an insufficient modulation or direction of motivations. In sum, for each construct, the psychologists were asked to use the CCQ set to portray the personality characteristics of a hypothetical ego-resilient child and a hypothetical ego-undercontrolled child. In each instance there was high agreement among the psychologists, or criterion definers, the reliability of the ego-resilience portrayal being .91, and the reliability of the ego-undercontrol portrayal being .90. These two composite formulations can be viewed as prototype or criterion definitions of each underlying construct (Block, 1957, 1961/1978).

Subsequently, the *actual* Q-descriptions of each subject were correlated, separately for each age, with each of the two criterion definitions. The resulting correlations can be said to index the similarity between the personality characteristics of each subject, as judged by the independent sets of teachers and examiners, and the prototype definition for each of the two constructs. If these correlations are relatively high, that subject is relatively

Table 15.1. *CCQ items characterizing the ego-resilient and ego-undercontrol prototypes*

Ego-resilient prototype	Ego-undercontrol prototype
Most characteristic items	
Is vital, energetic, and lively	Has rapid shifts in mood
Is resourceful in initiating activities	Is unable to delay gratification
Is curious and exploring	Has transient interpersonal relationships
Is self-reliant, confident	Has rapid personal tempo
Is creative in perception, thought, work, and play	Overreacts to minor frustrations
Least characteristic items	
Tends to become rigidly repetitive under stress	Tends to keep thoughts and feelings to self
Is inappropriate in emotive behavior	Is reflective
Tends to go to pieces under stress	Likes to be alone
Is inhibited and constricted	Is inhibited and constricted
Appears to feel unworthy	Is physically cautious

ego-resilient or relatively ego-undercontrolled; if these correlations are moderately low or negative, that subject is relatively ego-brittle or relatively ego-overcontrolled. These subsequent correlations are scores that we find useful for summarizing the position of each subject on the dimensions of ego resilience and ego undercontrol. Independent Q-formulations existed for these subjects from the assessments made at ages 3–4, 7, 11, and 14. It was therefore possible to compute, for each sex, entirely independent ego-resilience and ego-undercontrol behavior scores for each of the four ages. The correlation between the prototypical definitions of ego resilience and ego undercontrol was .10. In order to present briefly the meanings of these two constructs as they are conveyed by these Q-portrayals, Table 15.1 lists, separately for each construct, the five CCQ items most characteristic of each construct and the five CCQ items most uncharacteristic of each construct.

Measuring self-esteem. During the assessment conducted at age 14, the subjects were asked to describe themselves, using a 43-item Adjective Q-set (Block & Block, 1980b). In a separate session, they again used the 43-item Adjective Q-set to describe the person each would ideally like to be, an "ideal self." To the extent that one's self-characterization is relatively congruent with one's characterization of an ideal self, one may be said to have self-esteem. An estimate of the subject's self-esteem is thus obtainable by correlating the two descriptions – the self-concept and the ideal self. If this correlation is relatively high, the subject is said to rate relatively high on self-esteem; if this correlation is relatively low or negative, the subject is said to rate relatively low on self-esteem. This approach has long been employed to index self-esteem (Block & Thomas, 1955; Rogers & Dymond, 1954).

Measuring drug usage. When our subjects were age 14, extensive individual interviews lasting 55 to 75 min were conducted by a skilled clinician. All interviews were videotaped. In addition to questions about topics such as schoolwork, family dynamics, peer relations, current activities, and future aspirations, our subjects were asked about their use of the following drugs: wine and/or beer, liquor, tobacco, marijuana, and other "harder" drugs. In addition to their verbal responses, subjects indicated which drugs they had used by checking off the appropriate items on a drug-use checklist.

Data from the drug-use portion of the interview were independently coded or scored by two raters. Agreement on coding was high, and in the few cases of discrepancy, items were discussed to reach consensus. For each of the drugs, information was coded on (a) frequency of use, (b) context of use, and (c) school grade in which use was initiated. For this report, we focus on the information regarding use of marijuana and the "harder" drugs (i.e., hashish through heroin). A more complete report on the pattern of use of all drugs by our adolescent subjects can be found in Keyes and Block (1984).

For marijuana, information on use and frequency of use was scored on a scale from 0 to 5 as follows: 0, never used marijuana; 1, used once or twice; 2, used sometimes, occasionally; 3, used once a month; 4, used once a week; 5, used more than once a week. Only one subject reported use without providing an indication of frequency of use. This individual was classified in group 2 (used sometimes, occasionally). Examination of other items from this subject's protocol indicated that this choice (group 2) was somewhat likely to underrepresent, not overrepresent, her use of marijuana. Scores on the marijuana-use variable thus ranged from 0 to 5. For the sample of girls, the mean score on the marijuana-use variables was 1.38, with a standard deviation of 1.80; for the sample of boys, the mean marijuana-use score was 1.31, with a standard deviation of 1.56. These were highly skewed distributions: 49% of the total sample had never used marijuana, 13% has used it only once or twice, and only 10% used it more than once a week.

For the harder drugs, information on frequency of use was less complete. As a result, a score was derived that was simply the total number of these harder drugs that had been tried at least once on a recreational, nonprescription basis. Scores ranged from 0 to 9. For the sample of girls, the mean hard-drug-use score was .87, with a standard deviation of 1.74; for the sample of boys, the mean hard-drug-use score was .54, with a standard deviation of 1.18. Again, the distribution of use of harder drugs was highly skewed. To provide some perspective on frequency of use, 12% of the full sample had tried a hallucinogen, 18% had tried cocaine, 7% had tried amphetamines, and 5% had tried barbiturates; see Keyes and Block (1984) for further details on usage frequencies. It will be observed that the female sample was somewhat higher than the male sample with respect to both the marijuana-use and harder-drug-use variables, although neither of these differences approached statistical significance.

The marijuana-use and harder-drug-use variables correlated highly with each other (Pearson correlations of .58 and .73 in the female and male samples, respectively; corresponding Spearman correlations of .70 and .69). On the basis of ordering psychometric standards, these correlations would be considered sufficient to automatically warrant a summing or compositing of the two variables for purposes of data reduction and to achieve a more generalized index. However, close analysis of the correlations differentially generated by the marijuana and hard-drug variables indicated that maintaining a separation of these two drug variables would provide important recognitions that otherwise would be lost.

Results

This section is organized as follows: First, we present descriptive statistics pertaining to our use of the CES-D scale. We then report the correlations between CES-D scores and the control variables of intelligence and social class. Third, we present the correlates of the CES-D scores with the CCQ and CAQ personality evaluations obtained at ages 3–4, 7, 11, and 14. These latter analyses consider individual CCQ items, overall patterns in the Q-correlates of the CES-D score, and personality prototypes. Finally, the relations between the CES-D depression score and the two self-report variables (self-esteem and drug use) are reported.

Descriptive statistics for the CES-D scale

In this sample, with the version of the CES-D we used, the mean CES-D score was 22.50 ($SD = 11.10$, $n = 46$) for girls and 19.77 ($SD = 10.75$, $n = 42$) for boys. Whereas these mean values were not significantly different for girls and boys ($t = 1.17$, ns), they were considerably higher than the mean values obtained using the conventional CES-D scale with community populations, where the mean values generally have fallen between 8 and 14, depending on the subpopulation being studied (Amenson & Lewinsohn, 1981; Lin et al., 1986; Radloff, 1977).

We believe that the higher CES-D scale mean values reported in our study were primarily due to the different response orientation used in this study. Some additional possibilities should also be considered: First, the context in which the CES-D scale was completed in this study differed considerably from the relatively impersonal assessment situation characterizing most other studies in which this instrument has been employed. In our study, the subjects completed the CES-D scale within the familiar context of a longitudinal project in which they had participated since preschool age – a context in which they would be likely to and indeed had become accustomed to reflecting on the quality of their lives. Second, the individual CES-D items were interspersed among items belonging to other scales tapping constructs such as anxiety, well-being, loneliness, family relationships, and so forth. This assessment context, we propose, was more likely to have sensitized our subjects to their emotional states and inner lives than would be the case for the more impersonal assessment situation in which the CES-D scale typically has been completed. Finally, as Radloff (1977) observed, high CES-D scores tend to be associated with youth. We believe that the combination of these factors may explain the relatively high mean CES-D scores reported in this study.

CES-D score, intelligence, and demographic variables

When our subjects were 4 years old, they completed the Wechsler Preschool and Primary Scale of Intelligence (WPPSI); when they were 11 years old, they completed the Wechsler Intelligence Scale for Children (WISC). For girls, the correlations between the CES-D scores and WPPSI-measured intelligence were all positive: .09 (ns) for verbal intelligence, .33 (p < .05) for performance intelligence, and .24 (ns) for full-scale intelligence (n = 37). For boys, the corresponding values were all negative: $-.25$ (ns), $-.33$ (ns), and $-.34$ (p < .05) (n = 35). Comparing these independent correlations for girls and boys, using McNemar's formula (McNemar, 1969), nursery-school girls who subsequently were relatively high on the CES-D scale at age 18 were, compared with nursery-school boys, relatively high on the performance IQ subscale (z = 2.76, p < .01) and on the full IQ scale (z = 2.41, p < .05). WISC-measured intelligence at age 11 showed the same pattern of relations with the CES-D scores for both sexes, although falling short of statistical significance. For girls, the correlations between the CES-D scores and WISC-measured intelligence were again all positive: .16 for verbal intelligence, .10 for performance intelligence, and .16 for full-scale intelligence. For boys, the corresponding values were again all negative: $-.23$, $-.20$, and $-.25$. In the sample of girls, there was a tendency (p < .10) for the depression symptoms score to be positively associated with the social status (Duncan, 1961) of fathers (p < .10) and negatively associated with the social status of mothers (p < .10). In the sample of boys, there was no indication of an association between CES-D scores and parental social status.

Personality antecedents of depressive symptoms in late adolescence

From age 3–4 to age 11. In the sample of girls, few of the CCQ items evaluated at ages 3–4, 7, and 11 were found to correlate with subsequent depressive symptoms in late adolescence. Nonetheless, because the set of items that reached statistical significance in childhood appears to present a psychologically coherent picture of the young girl who later reports depressive symptoms at age 18, because longitudinal data of the kind presented here appear to be unprecedented in the study of depressive symptoms, and because (as we shall see) the childhood portraits of subsequently depressed adolescents seem to be

Table 15.2. *Childhood CCQ correlates of subsequent depressive symptoms (CES-D scores) at age 18: girls*

CCQ item	r
Age 3–4 (n = 46)	
Is attentive and able to concentrate	.33*
Is verbally fluent	.32*
Seeks others to affirm self-worth	−.32*
Is inappropriate in emotive behavior	−.30*
Age 7 (n = 41)	
Develops close and genuine relationships	.41*
Likes to be alone	.39*
Is shy and reserved	.35*
Is jealous and envious of others	−.42**
Has transient interpersonal relationships	−.36*
Has unusual thought processes	−.34*
Age 11 (n = 44)	
Is restless and fidgety	−.31*

$*p < .05; **p < .01.$

appreciably different for girls and boys, we report, in Table 15.2, these findings, albeit acknowledging their tentativeness. According to these results, 18-year-old girls who had depressive tendencies when they were age 3–4 were described by their nursery-school teachers as more attentive, more verbally fluent, less likely to seek out others to affirm self-worth, and less inappropriate in their emotive behavior than the girls who did not later admit to depressive symptoms. At age 7, female depressiveness in late adolescence is foretold by attempts to develop close relationships, by preference for solitude, by shyness, by an absence of jealousy, by conventionality of thought processes, and by enduring interpersonal relationships. At age 11, only an absence of restlessness significantly relates to subsequent depressive tendencies in these girls at age 18.

Few CCQ evaluations obtained between the ages of 3–4 and 11 presage age-18 depressive tendencies in the male sample. Nevertheless, we choose to report, in Table 15.3, these relationships. Relatively depressed 18-year-old boys had been described 14 years earlier by their nursery-school teachers as having transient interpersonal relationships and as being unable to admit to their own negative feelings. At age 7, relatively depressed 18-year-old boys had been evaluated as being more likely to stretch limits and to try to be the center of attention, and as less likely to imitate others, less responsive to reason, and less proud of their own accomplishments. At age 11, relatively depressed 18-year-old boys had been described as more likely to stretch limits and more stubborn, and also as less likely to look to adults for help, less likely to have high performance standards, less eager to please, and less helpful.

Table 15.3. *Childhood CCQ correlates of subsequent depressive symptoms (CES-D scores) at age 18: boys*

CCQ item	r
Age 3–4 (n = 41)	
Has transient interpersonal relationships	.44**
Can admit to own negative feelings	−.31*
Age 7 (n = 29–35)	
Generally stretches limits	.36*
Tries to be the center of attention	.35*
Tends to imitate those admired	−.47**
Proud of his accomplishments	−.38*
Uses and responds to reason	−.36*
Age 11 (n = 42)	
Is stubborn	.37*
Generally stretches limits	.34*
Eager to please	−.38*
Performance standards for self are high	−.36*
Helpful and cooperative	−.34*
Looks to adults for help	−.31*

*$p < .05$; **$p < .01$.

Compared with 11-year-old girls who subsequently described themselves as depressed at age 18, these young boys appear to have been more under-controlled and less concerned with establishing satisfying interpersonal relationships.

Early adolescence. It was not until our subjects reached early adolescence (age 14) that personality characterizations began to display extensive prospective relationships to depressive symptoms evaluated via the CES-D at age 18. The CAQ items from the age-14 assessment that correlated significantly with CES-D scores 4 years later are presented in Table 15.4 for the sample of girls and in Table 15.5 for the sample of boys.

Female adolescents who tended to report depressive symptoms at age 18 had been described 4 years earlier as follows: likely to lack a sense of meaning in life, concerned with self-adequacy, anxious, unconventional in thought processes, ruminating, unpredictable, likely to have bodily symptoms of anxiety, brittle, and vulnerable to threat. At age 14, these girls had been described as introspective about themselves, not likely to manifest social poise, not likely to be turned to for advice, not calm, not objective or rational, and not sex-typed in their behavior.

Among males, a quite different set of CAQ relationships at age 14 related to CES-D scores 4 years later. At age 14, these boys had been described as relatively self-indulgent, likely to perceive different contexts in sexual terms, interested in the opposite sex, able to enjoy sensuous experiences, self-

Table 15.4. *Early adolescence (age 14) CAQ correlates of subsequent depressive symptoms (CES-D scores) at age 18: girls (n = 46)*

CAQ item	r
Feels a lack of personal meaning in life	.46**
Concerned with own adequacy as a person	.41**
Is basically anxious	.38**
Unconventional thought processes	.36*
Tends to ruminate	.35*
Anxiety finds outlet in body symptoms	.32*
Is unpredictable	.32*
Has a brittle ego defense system	.30*
Vulnerable to threat	.29*
Is subjectively unaware of self concern	−.40**
Has social poise and presence	−.37*
Is turned to for advice	−.35*
Is calm, relaxed in manner	−.34*
Prides self on being objective, rational	−.32*
Behaves in sex-typed manner	−.30*

*$p < .05$; **$p < .01$.

Table 15.5. *Early adolescence (age 14) CAQ correlates of subsequent depressive symptoms (CES-D scores) at age 18: boys (N = 41)*

CAQ item	r
Is self-indulgent	.42**
Perceives different contexts in sexual terms	.40**
Interested in members of the opposite sex	.38*
Enjoys sensuous experiences	.34*
Tends to be self-defensive	.33*
Is subtly negativistic	.33*
Is guileful, deceitful, and manipulative	.33*
Is sensitive to criticism	.32*
Has hostility toward others	.32*
Is unpredictable	.32*
Basically distrustful of people	.31*
Productive, gets things done	−.40**
Behaves in ethically consistent manner	−.37*
Favors conservative values	−.36*
Sympathetic and considerate	−.35*
Able to see to heart of important problems	−.35*
Appears straightforward, candid	−.35*
Prides self on being objective, rational	−.34*
Genuinely values intellectual matters	−.32*

*$p < .05$; **$p < .01$.

Table 15.6. *Comparing overall patterns of personality correlates of the CES-D scale*

	Age of personality assessment			
	Age 3–4	Age 7	Age 11	Age 14
Age 3–4	—	.38	.46	−.31
Age 7	−.30	—	.61	.01
Age 11	−.12	.59	—	−.15
Age 14	−.04	.43	.81	—

Note: The CCQ was employed at ages 3–4, 7, and 11; the CAQ was employed at age 14. Above the dashes are the congruence indices for the sample of girls; below the dashes are the congruence indices for the sample of boys.

defensive, negativistic, guileful, deceitful, manipulative, sensitive to criticism, hostile, unpredictable, and distrustful of others. In addition, these boys who subsequently expressed depressive tendencies had been described as not productive, not ethically consistent, not conservative, not sympathetic and considerate, not straightforward and candid, not able to see to the heart of important problems, not objective and rational, and not likely to value intellectual matters.

Comparing overall patterns of Q-correlates foretelling depression

To evaluate the degree to which relationships between depressive symptoms and Q-set-based personality evaluations were similar across the four ages 3–4, 7, 11, and 14, we compared the vector of Q-item correlations with depressive symptoms obtained for one age level (e.g., age 3–4) with the vectors obtained for other age levels. In these analyses, only the 55 Q-items that had analogous versions in the CCQ and CAQ sets were included. Correlating the ordered set of 55 Q-item correlations of the CES-D score from one age level with the ordered set of 55 Q-item correlations from another age level provides, in a single coefficient, an index of the pattern similarity or congruence of the findings for the two age levels being related. A high congruence index means that relatively high (low) Q-item correlations with the CES-D score characterizing one age level tend to go along with relatively high (low) Q-item correlations with the CES-D score characterizing another age level. Thus, patterns of Q-correlations are being evaluated for their congruence across age levels. The congruence indices, themselves correlations, are presented in Table 15.6 for the two sexes; they, of course, are only descriptive and cannot be referred to sampling distributions for evaluation of their statistical significance.

In the sample of girls, the patterns of Q-item correlations associated over time with the CES-D scores are relatively similar from age 3–4 to age 11 (*r* values range from .38 to .61). The patterns of Q-item correlates of the CES-D scores at these three early age levels are unrelated to the patterns of Q-item correlates obtained later, at age 14 (*r* values range from −.31 to .01).

In the sample of boys, a different pattern of cross-time relationships can be discerned: The pattern of Q-correlates characterizing preschool boys (age 3–4) is essentially unrelated to the patterns of Q-correlates characterizing the remaining three age levels (*r* values range from −.30 to −.04). But beginning at age 7, and continuing at ages 11 and 14, appreciable pattern congruence exists in the Q-item correlates of the CES-D scores (*r* values range from .43 to .81). Thus, among girls, these congruence indices suggest that the patterns of personality characteristics during preschool (age 3–4), school age (age 7), and preadolescence (age 11) that foretell depressive symptoms in late adolescence are quite different from the pattern of early adolescent personality characteristics (age 14) foretelling depressive symptoms in 18-year-olds. In contrast, among boys, the patterns of personality characteristics that foretell depressive tendencies in late adolescence are quite similar for ages 7, 11, and 14. There is a suggestion in these results that the constellation of early personality characteristics associated with depressive tendencies in late adolescence stabilizes earlier for boys than for girls.

Additionally, we compared the patterns of Q-item personality correlates associated with the CES-D scores for girls and boys, separately for each age level. At ages 3–4, 7, and 11, the patterns of Q-correlates foretelling depressive tendencies in late adolescence are quite different for girls and boys, the congruence estimates being −.14, −.05, and −.46, respectively. Only at age 14 are the patterns of Q-correlations characterizing depressed 18-year-old girls and boys reasonably similar, the congruence index being .58.

CES-D depression related to personality prototypes

The CES-D depression score was then related to the scores derived from the two CCQ-based personality prototypes described earlier – ego resilience and ego undercontrol. At age 14, adolescents of both sexes who later described themselves as depressed were significantly more likely to be ego-brittle or nonresilient than were adolescents who later did not describe themselves as depressed, the correlation between the CES-D score and the ego-resilience prototype being −.29 (*p* < .10) for males and −.35 (*p* < .05) for females. For the preschool and early school ages (ages 3–4 and 7), none of the two prototype scores related to subsequent depressive tendencies in either sex.

CES-D depression related to self-esteem

Among girls, self-esteem evaluated at age 14 was negatively related to depressive symptoms 4 years later (*r* = −.34, *p* < .05). Among boys, there was no relationship between self-esteem at age 14 and later scores on the CES-D scale, the correlation being as low as $-.04$.

CES-D depression related to drug use

Compared with boys who received low scores on the CES-D scale, boys who described themselves as depressed at age 18 were significantly more likely to report having used marijuana at age 14 (Spearman $r = .30, p < .06$), but not harder drugs (Spearman $r = .18$, ns). Among girls, drug use did not foretell subsequent depressive tendencies, the Spearman correlations being $-.09$ and $.06$, respectively.

Discussion

Using a prospective design spanning a period of 15 years, this study sought to evaluate whether or not observations of personality obtained between nursery school and early adolescence would predict depressive symptoms in 18-year-old adolescents. Our results indicate that depressive symptoms in late adolescence are only moderately associated with the preschool and childhood personality characteristics assessed in our longitudinal study. It is worth noting, however, that the set of personality characteristics that reached statistical significance was psychologically coherent and that the childhood portraits of the subsequently depressed 18-year-olds were appreciably different for the sexes in a direction consistent with the findings obtained for later ages. Therefore, these preschool and childhood findings appear to be anticipatory of later and stronger findings.

When our male subjects approached preadolescence (age 11) and our female subjects approached early adolescence (age 14), observations of personality began to display multiple and substantial relationships to depressive symptoms seen at age 18. It is noteworthy, moreover, that when such prospective relations began to emerge, their natures continued to differ importantly for the samples of girls and boys. Fourteen-year-old girls who subsequently would express depressive tendencies at age 18 were seen as ego-brittle; they were vulnerable, anxious, somaticizing, concerned with their adequacy, ruminative, and likely to feel a lack of personal meaning in their lives. Their self-perceptions at age 14 expressed low self-esteem that, after another 4 years, eventuated in depressive symptoms. In sum, relatively depressed 18-year-old girls had possessed personality characteristics at age 14 that had been psychologically meaningful and, from several standpoints, theoretically expectable.

Consistent with the results obtained for the same-age girls, 14-year-old boys who later would receive high scores on the CES-D scale also were ego-brittle. In the main, however, they displayed a constellation of personality characteristics that was importantly different from that shown by girls. Unlike same-age girls, however, these boys displayed, as early as age 11, antisocial proclivities.

By age 14, the antisocial and hostile characteristics of these boys had become even more prominent (cf. the significant relations between drug use at age 14 and subsequent depressive tendencies observed in boys). It is noteworthy that, compared with the sample of girls, introspective concern with the adequacy of self appeared to be a less salient issue in the sample of boys. In sum, this set of prospective relationships suggests that, beginning in preadolescence, the personality structures that will later prove to be associated with depressive symptoms at age 18 differ substantially for the sexes.

The prospective relationships observed between early ego resilience and CES-D-measured depressive tendencies have certain implications: They connect observer-based indices of a well-established and central dimension of personality (ego resilience) observed at one time with a quite separate psychiatric dimension based on an entirely different source of data evaluated much later: self-reported depressive symptoms. Because of the demonstration of a relationship between earlier ego resilience and later depressive symptoms, further evidence is presented for the predictive utility of the construct of ego resilience. This construct (Block, 1965, 1982; Block & Block, 1980b; Gjerde, Block, & Block, 1986) has been extensively studied in different research contexts and has been found to relate to many cognitive and personality variables, both prospectively and concurrently, from early childhood through adolescence. The results presented here relate ego resilience to the psychodynamic organization underlying the emergence of depressive symptoms in adolescents of both sexes.

What is the relevance of these results for our understanding of depression? One major finding emerging from these analyses is the degree to which depressive symptoms in 18-year-old boys, but not in 18-year-old girls, can be foretold on the basis of hostility and antisocial tendencies manifested in a period stretching back all the way to preadolescence. This gender-differentiated outcome is particularly interesting in light of the long-standing theoretical interest in the relationships among hostility, anger, and depression – an issue that goes back to the earliest psychoanalytic speculations on this topic (Abraham, 1927; Freud, 1917/1968). A central feature of those early theories, however, was that they conceptualized depression as hostility and anger turned inward, rather than expressed openly in social relationships. It was this inhibition of hostility and anger that, according to the early psychoanalysts, underlay depression.

Whereas modest empirical evidence exists for an association between depression and hostility-anger directed inward (Gershon, Cromer, & Klerman, 1968; Gottschalk, Glesser, & Springer, 1963), other investigators have reported depression to be related to openly expressed hostility-anger in two patient populations (Friedman, 1970; Weissman, Klerman, & Paykel, 1971) and in clinically unselected samples (Wessman, Ricks, & Tyl, 1960). Yet other studies have reported equal numbers of depressives turning hostility-anger inward and outward (Schless, Mendels, Kipperman, & Cochrane, 1974). In general, however, more recent psychodynamic thinking has deemphasized the role of hostility and anger and has favored the importance of problems of self-esteem in understanding depressive disorders (Bibring, 1953; Hirschfeld et al., 1976).

The findings reported here, especially for the age of 14, take on special interest in the context of these deliberations regarding the psychodynamics of depression. Our results indicate that elements of hostility-anger and of self-esteem are involved in depressive symptoms, but that their relative importances are strongly moderated by gender: In depressed adolescent males, hostility and anger are centrally involved; in depressed adolescent females, inadequate self-esteem is the salient issue. We are not alone in suggesting that the key psychodynamic issues underlying depressive symptoms may differ importantly for the sexes (Kaplan, 1986; Radloff, 1980; Weissman & Klerman, 1979; Weissman & Paykel, 1974). We also note that for boys, our results suggest that hostile feelings tend to be expressed openly and directly, rather than, as psychoanalysts have postulated, being turned inward. Direct expression of hostility among depressed subjects has also been reported by other researchers working with older, concurrently depressed individuals (Kahn, Coyne, & Margolin, 1985), suggesting that our findings are not limited by age.

The sex-differentiated outcomes reported here illustrate the importance of performing separate analyses for males and females – an analytical approach often not implemented in depression research. Note that these sex differences in personality correlates emerged even though significant gender differences in mean levels of CES-D scores were not found. Gender differences in how personality characteristics are organized may be more important than gender differences in average scores (Block, 1976).

Although the essential results reported here are fully prospective (and unusual in research on depression), they do not permit clear-cut conclusions regarding the direction of causality between depressive symptoms per se and broader aspects of personality. We cannot say, for example, that low self-esteem in girls and high hostility-anger in boys are of primary and causal importance for the development of depressive symptoms. Although that possibility cannot be excluded, the converse possibility – that these characteristics emerge in response to the experience of depressive symptoms – is also psychologically tenable. Rather than preceding depressive symptoms in a causal manner, characteristics such as hostility and anger may serve to control or neutralize the emergent experience of depressive moods. That is, they may take on a defensive function (McCranie, 1971). As Schless et al. (1974) noted with respect to hostility, this latter position is congruent with recent conceptualizations of depression as a primary emotional state that acts as a signal emotion (Bibring, 1953). Further, the sex-differentiated prospective correlates of depressive symptoms at age 18 raise the possibility that girls and boys respond differentially to depressive experiences in ways that are compatible with their socialization history: girls by becoming passive, introverted, and concerned with self – an "internalizing" pattern of symptom expression – boys by being more likely to "act out" hostile and aggressive impulses – an "externalizing" pattern of symptom expression.

Some complicating considerations about the direction of causality inherent in the results reported here concern limitations in the design of our research. In particular, because we assessed depressive symptoms only once (at age 18), we do not know if the personality characteristics observed at age 14 to anticipate expressed depressive tendencies 4 years later truly preceded the experience of depression or, alternatively, if the age-14 adolescents with these personality characteristics also would have expressed depressive feelings on the CES-D concurrently at age 14, or even earlier. In any event, the results reported here indicate that depressive feelings in late adolescence manifest themselves differently for girls and boys – a finding that has important implications for the detection of depression-prone adolescents. To identify adolescents at risk for depressive disorders, we may have to look for different patterns of behaviors in girls and boys.

The relatively few early childhood predictors of depression in the personality domain in 18-year-olds deserve comment. In recent years, we have conducted a number of prospective analyses based on the same longitudinally followed sample from which the results reported here derive (Block, Block, & Keyes, 1988; Block, Gjerde, & Block, 1986; Gjerde et al., 1986). Especially for the sample of boys, it has generally been the rule rather than the exception that personality observations obtained during early childhood foretell a wide range of behavioral characteristics throughout the period of adolescence. Among girls, on the other hand, we have found such coherent relations over time to be less common. This gender difference has led us to suggest that girls are more likely than boys to experience a reorganization in psychodynamic structure as they approach or pass through puberty (Block et al., 1986; Gjerde et al., 1986). It is against this background that the relatively few preschool and childhood personality precursors of depressive tendencies in late adolescence take on special interest – especially for boys. It may be the case that the characterological roots of depression, especially when this disorder is, as was the case in our study, identified uniquely in terms of its subjective experience and is not tied to behavioral signs and manifestations, are difficult to foretell using observational ratings of personality. Depressed affect is intimately but variously linked to cognitive maturation, achieved internalization of experiences and feelings, and the ability and willingness to introspect. Therefore, it is easy to understand why relatively few simple relations were obtained between depressive symptoms in late adolescence and personality characteristics evaluated at periods prior to these developmental transformations.

This is not to say that early childhood personality characteristics may not influence the probability of depressive symptoms in late adolescence. More complex analyses, designed to take account of childhood personality characteristics in the context of both family experiences and more recent life events, are needed in order to better evaluate the extent to which early personality characteristics predispose individuals to depressive symptoms.

Because the early childhood personality antecedents of late adolescence depression are few in number, the prospective results pertaining to intelligence become all the more noteworthy. They suggest that a child's early intellectual competence influences the probability of depressive symptoms 14 years later. On the basis of the Waters and Sroufe (1983) definition of competence as an ability to use internal and external resources to achieve satisfactory developmental adaptation, Cicchetti and Schneider-Rosen (1986) proposed that lack of competence during the early stages of life plays an important etiological role, both directly and indirectly, in the development of depression in young persons. Although our analyses did not achieve the level of complexity required by the model advanced by Cicchetti and Schneider-Rosen, and although the constructs of intelligence and competence are not conceptually equivalent, our results for boys nonetheless provide support for the more general conjecture that early intellective incompetence increases the probability of later depressive symptoms. For girls, on the other hand, it is intellective competence, if anything, that early foretells depressive symptoms. This divergence calls attention yet again to the possibility that depression in adolescent boys and girls emerges via different developmental pathways.

References

Abraham, K. (1927). Notes on the psycho-analytical investigation and treatment of manic-depressive insanity and allied conditions. In K. Abraham (Ed.), *Selected papers of psychoanalysis* (pp. 137–56). London: Hogarth Press. (Original work published 1911)

Abramson, L. Y., Seligman, M. E. P., & Teasdale, J. D. (1978). Learned helplessness in humans: Critique and reformulation. *Journal of Abnormal Psychology, 87,* 49–74.

Akiskal, H. S., Hirschfeld, R. M. A., & Yerevanian, B. I. (1983). The relationship of personality to affective disorders. *Archives of General Psychiatry, 40,* 801–10.

Altman, J. H., & Wittenborn, J. P. (1980). Depression-prone personality in women. *Journal of Abnormal Psychology, 89,* 303–8.

Amenson, C. S., & Lewinsohn, P. M. (1981). An investigation into the observed sex difference in prevalence of unipolar depression. *Journal of Abnormal Psychology, 90,* 1–13.

Arieti, S., & Bemporad, J. (1980). The psychological organization of depression. *American Journal of Psychiatry, 137,* 1360–5.

Beck, A. T. (1967). *Depression: Clinical, experimental, and theoretical aspects.* New York: Hoeber.

Beck, A. T., Ward, C. H., Mendelson, M., Mock, J. E., & Erbaugh, J. K. (1961). An inventory for measuring depression. *Archives of General Psychiatry, 4,* 561–71.

Bemporad, J., & Wilson, A. (1978). A developmental approach to depression in childhood and adolescence. *Journal of the American Academy of Psychoanalysis, 6,* 325–52.

Bibring, E. (1953). The mechanism of depression. In P. Greenacre (Ed.), *Affective disorders* (pp. 13–48). New York: International Universities Press.

Blatt, S. J. (1974). Levels of object representation in anaclitic and introjective depression. In *Psychoanalytic study of the child* (Vol. 29, pp. 107–59). New York: International Universities Press.

Block, J. (1950). *An experimental investigation of the construct of ego control.* Unpublished doctoral dissertation, Stanford University.

Block, J. (1957). A comparison between ipsative and normative ratings of personality. *Journal of Abnormal and Social Psychology, 54,* 50–4.

Block, J. (1963). The equivalence of measures and the correction for attenuation. *Psychological Bulletin, 60,* 152–6.

Block, J. (1964). Recognizing attenuation effects in the strategy of research. *Psychological Bulletin, 62,* 214–16.

Block, J. (1965). *The challenge of response sets.* New York: Appleton-Century-Crofts.

Block, J. (1978). *The Q-sort method in personality assessment and psychiatric research.* Palo Alto, CA: Consulting Psychologists Press. (Original work published 1961)

Block, J. (1982). Assimilation, accommodation, and the dynamics of personality development. *Child Development, 53,* 281–95.

Block, J., & Block, J. H. (1980a). *The California Child Q-set.* Palo Alto, CA: Consulting Psychologists Press.

Block, J., Block, J. H., & Keyes, S. (1988). Longitudinally foretelling drug usage in adolescence: Early childhood personality and environmental precursors. *Child Development, 59,* 336–55.

Block, J., & Gjerde, P. F. (1986). Distinguishing between antisocial behavior and undercontrol. In D. Olweus, J. Block, and M. Radke-Yarrow (Eds.), *Development of antisocial and prosocial behavior: Research, theories, and issues* (pp. 117–206). New York: Academic Press.

Block, J., Gjerde, P. F., & Block, J. H. (1986). Continuity and transformation in the psychological meaning of categorization breadth. *Developmental Psychology, 22,* 832–40.

Block, J., & Thomas, H. (1955). Is satisfaction with self a measure of adjustment? *Journal of Abnormal and Social Psychology, 51,* 254–9.

Block, J. H. (1951). *An experimental study of a topological representation of ego structure.* Unpublished doctoral dissertation, Stanford University.

Block, J. H. (1976). Issues, problems, and pitfalls in assessing sex differences: A critical review of *The psychology of sex differences. Merrill-Palmer Quarterly, 22,* 283–522.

Block, J. H., & Block, J. (1980b). The role of ego-control and ego-resiliency in the organization of behavior. In W. A. Collins (Ed.), *The Minnesota Symposia on Child Psychology* (Vol. 13, pp. 39–101). Hillsdale, NJ: Erlbaum.

Bowlby, J. (1980). *Loss: Sadness and depression. Attachment and loss* (Vol. 3). New York: Basic Books.

Boyd, J. H., Weissman, M. M., Thompson, W. D., & Myers, J. K. (1982). Screening for depression in a community sample. *Archives of General Psychiatry, 39,* 1195–200.

Brown, G. W., & Harris, T. (1978). *Social origins of depression.* New York: Free Press.

Brown, G. W., Harris, T., & Bifulco, A. (1986). Long-term effects of early loss of parent. In M. Rutter, C. E. Izard, & P. M. Read (Eds.), *Depression in young people* (pp. 251–98). New York: Guilford Press.

Chodoff, P. (1970). The core problem in depression: Interpersonal aspects. In J. H. Masserman (Ed.), *Depression: Theories and therapies* (pp. 56–61). New York: Grune & Stratton.

Chodoff, P. (1972). The depressive personality. *Archives of General Psychiatry, 27,* 666–73.

Cicchetti, D., & Schneider-Rosen, K. (1986). An organizational approach to childhood depression. In M. Rutter, C. E. Izard, & P. B. Read (Eds.), *Depression in young people* (pp. 71–134). New York: Guilford Press.

Cofer, D. H., & Wittenborn, J. R. (1980). Personality characteristics of formerly depressed women. *Journal of Abnormal Psychology, 89,* 309–14.

Craig, T. J., & Van Natta, P. A. (1976). Recognition of depressed affect in hospitalized psychiatric patients: Staff and patient perceptions. *Journal of the Diseases of the Nervous System, 37,* 561–6.

Depue, R. A., & Monroe, S. M. (1978). Learned helplessness in the perspective of the depressive disorders: Conceptual and definitional issues. *Journal of Abnormal Psychology, 87,* 3–20.

Duncan, O. (1961). A socioeconomic index for all occupations. In A. J. Reiss, Jr. (Ed.), *Occupations and social status* (pp. 109–38). New York: Free Press.

Epstein, S. (1979). The stability of behavior. I: On predicting most of the people much of the time. *Journal of Personality and Social Psychology, 37,* 1097–126.

Epstein, S. (1980). The stability of behavior. II: Implications for psychological research. *American Psychologist, 35,* 790–806.

Folkman, S., & Lazarus, R. S. (1986). Stress processes and depressive symptomatology. *Journal of Abnormal Psychology, 95,* 107–13.

Freud, A. (1958). Adolescence. In *Psychoanalytic study of the child* (Vol. 13, pp. 255–78). New York: International Universities Press.

Freud, S. (1968). Mourning and melancholia. In J. Strachey (Ed.), *The standard edition of the complete works of Sigmund Freud* (Vol. 14). London: Hogarth Press. (Original work published 1917)

Friedman, A. S. (1970). Hostility factors and clinical improvement in depressed patients. *Archives of General Psychiatry, 23,* 524–37.

Gershon, E. S., Cromer, M., & Klerman, G. L. (1968). Hostility and depression. *Psychiatry, 31,* 224–35.

Gjerde, P. F., Block, J., & Block, J. H. (1986). Egocentrism and ego resiliency: Personality characteristics associated with perspective-taking from early childhood to adolescence. *Journal of Personality and Social Psychology, 51,* 423–34.

Gotlib, I. H. (1984). Depression and general psychopathology in university students. *Journal of Abnormal Psychology, 93,* 19–30.

Gottschalk, L. A., Glesser, G. C., & Springer, K. J. (1963). Three hostility scales applicable to verbal samples. *Archives of General Psychiatry, 9,* 254–79.

Hirschfeld, R. M. A., Klerman, G. L., Chodoff, P., Korchin, S., & Barrett, J. (1976), Dependency–self-esteem–clinical depression. *Journal of the American Academy of Psychoanalysis, 4,* 373–88.

Husaini, B. A., Neff, J. A., Harrington, J. B., Hughes, M. D., & Stone, R. H. (1980). Depression in rural communities: Validating the CES-D scale. *Journal of Community Psychology, 8,* 137–46.

Ingram, R. E. (1984). Toward an information-processing analysis of depression. *Cognitive Therapy and Research, 8,* 443–78.

Kahn, J., Coyne, J. C., & Margolin, G. (1985). Depression and marital disagreement: The social construction of despair. *Journal of Social and Personal Relationships, 2,* 447–61.

Kaplan, A. (1986). The "self-in relation": Implications for depression in women. *Psychotherapy, 23,* 234–42.

Keyes, S., & Block, J. (1984). Prevalence and patterns of substance use among early adolescents. *Journal of Youth and Adolescence, 13,* 1–14.

Kovacs, M., & Beck, A. T. (1978). Maladaptive cognitive structures in depression. *American Journal of Psychiatry, 135,* 525–33.

Kovacs, M., Feinberg, T. L., Crouse-Novak, M. A., Paulauskas, S. L., & Finkelstein, R. (1984a). Depressive disorders in childhood. I: A longitudinal prospective study of characteristics and recovery. *Archives of General Psychiatry, 41,* 229–37.

Kovacs, M., Feinberg, T. L., Crouse-Novak, M. A., Paulauskas, S. L., Pollack, M., & Finkelstein, R. (1984b). Depressive disorders in childhood. II: A longitudinal study of the risk for a subsequent major depression. *Archives of General Psychiatry, 41,* 636–44.

Lewinsohn, P. M., & Teri, L. (1982). Selection of depressed and nondepressed subjects on the basis of self-report data. *Journal of Consulting and Clinical Psychology, 50,* 590–1.

Lin, N., Dean, A., & Ensel, W. M. (1986). *Social support, life events, and depression.* New York: Academic Press.

Lorand, S. (1967). Adolescent depression. *International Journal of Psychoanalysis, 48,* 53–60.

McCranie, E. J. (1971). Depression, anxiety, and hostility. *Psychiatric Quarterly, 45,* 117–33.

McNemar, Q. (1969). *Psychological statistics.* New York: Wiley.

Malmquist, C. (1971). Depression in childhood and adolescence. I and II. *New England Journal of Medicine, 284,* 887–93, 955–61.

Paykel, E. S. (1979). Recent life events in the development of depression. In R. A. Depue (Ed.), *The psychobiology of depressive disorders: Implications for the effects of stress* (pp. 245–62). New York: Academic Press.

Radloff, L. S. (1977). The CES-D scale: A self-report depression scale for research in the general population. *Applied Psychological Measurement, 3,* 385–401.

Radloff, L. S. (1980). Risk factors for depression. What do we learn from them? In M. Guttentag, S. Salasin, & D. Belle (Eds.), *The mental health of women* (pp. 93–110). New York: Academic Press.

Radloff, L. S., & Locke, B. Z. (1985). The community mental health assessment survey and the CES-D scale. In M. M. Weissman, J. K. Myers, & C. E. Ross (Eds.), *Community surveys of psychiatric disorders* (pp. 177–89). New Brunswick, NJ: Rutgers University Press.

Radloff, L. S., & Rae, D. S. (1979). Susceptibility and precipitating factors in depression: Sex differences and similarities. *Journal of Abnormal Psychology, 88,* 174–81.

Roberts, R. E. (1980). Reliability of the CES-D scale in different ethnic contexts. *Psychiatry Research, 2,* 125–34.

Roberts, R. E., & Vernon, S. W. (1983). The Center for Epidemiological Studies depression scale: Its use in a community sample. *American Journal of Psychiatry, 140,* 4–46.

Rogers, C., & Dymond, R. (1954). *Psychotherapy and personality change.* University of Chicago Press.

Rutter, M. (1986). The developmental psychopathology of depression: Issues and perspectives. In M. Rutter, C. E. Izard, & P. B. Read (Eds.), *Depression in young people* (pp. 3–32). New York: Guilford Press.

Rutter, M., & Garmezy, N. (1983). Developmental psychopathology. In P. Mussen (Ed.), *Handbook of child psychology* (4th ed., Vol. 4, pp. 775–911). New York: Wiley.

Rutter, M., Izard, C. E., & Read, P. B. (Eds.). (1986). *Depression in young people.* New York: Guilford Press.

Salzman, L. (1975). Interpersonal factors in depression. In F. F. Flack & S. C. Droghi (Eds.), *The nature and treatment of depression* (pp. 43–56). New York: Wiley.

Schless, A. P., Mendels, J., Kipperman, A., & Cochrane, C. (1974). Depression and hostility. *Journal of Nervous and Mental Disease, 159,* 91–100.

Schoenbach, V. J., Kaplan, B. H., Grimson, R. C., & Wagner, E. H. (1982). Use of a symptom scale to study the prevalence of a depressive syndrome in young adolescents. *American Journal of Epidemiology, 116,* 791–9.

Schoenbach, V. J., Kaplan, B. H., Wagner, E. H., Grimson, R. C., & Miller, F. T. (1983). Prevalence of self-reported depressive symptoms in young adolescents. *American Journal of Public Health, 73,* 1281–7.

Spitzer, R. L., Endicott, J., & Robins, E. (1978). Research diagnostic criteria. *Archives of General Psychiatry, 35,* 773–83.

Sroufe, L. A., & Rutter, M. (1984). The domain of developmental psychopathology. *Child Development, 55,* 17–29.

Warren, L. W., & McEachern, L. (1983). Psychosocial correlates of depressive symptomatology in adult women. *Journal of Abnormal Psychology, 92,* 151–60.

Waters, E., & Sroufe, L. A. (1983). Competence as a developmental construct. *Developmental Review, 3,* 79–97.

Weiner, I. B. (1975). Depression in adolescence. In F. F. Flack & S. C. Droghi (Eds.), *The nature and treatment of depression* (pp. 99–117). New York: Wiley.

Weissman, M. M., & Klerman, G. L. (1979). Sex differences and the etiology of depression. In E. S. Gomberg & V. Franks (Eds.), *Gender and disordered behavior* (pp. 381–425). New York: Brunner/Mazel.

Weissman, M. M., Klerman, G. L., & Paykel, E. S. (1971). Clinical evaluation of hostility in depression. *American Journal of Psychiatry, 128,* 261–6.

Weissman, M. M., & Paykel, E. S. (1974). *The depressed women: A study of social relationships.* University of Chicago Press.

Weissman, M. M., Sholomskas, D., Pottenger, M., Prusoff, B. A., & Locke, B. Z. (1977). Assessing depressive symptoms in five psychiatric populations: A validation study. *American Journal of Epidemiology, 106,* 203–14.

Wessman, A. E., Ricks, D. F., & Tyl, M. M. (1960). Characteristics and concomitants of mood fluctuation in college women. *Journal of Abnormal and Social Psychology, 60,* 117–26.

16 Vulnerability and resilience in the age of eating disorders: risk and protective factors for bulimia nervosa

Judith Rodin, Ruth H. Striegel-Moore, and
Lisa R. Silberstein

Over the past two decades, bulimia nervosa has emerged as a significant mental health problem. The syndrome of bulimia nervosa is characterized by recurrent episodes of binge eating, during which the individual experiences a lack of control, followed by regular engagement in self-induced vomiting, laxative use, or severely restrictive dieting. Today, as a female passes through adolescence and enters adulthood, she is at considerable risk for developing bulimia nervosa (Striegel-Moore, Silberstein, & Rodin, 1986b). The pioneering work of Garmezy on risk and protective factors in the development of psychopathology (Garmezy, 1974, 1976, 1981; Garmezy & Streitman, 1974) has stimulated us to consider further in this chapter those factors that serve a risk or protective function in the development of bulimia nervosa. Following Garmezy's ground-breaking work on schizophrenia, we suggest that research on bulimia nervosa must encompass not only the study of bulimic individuals but also the study of women who appear resistant to the disorder.

In this chapter we consider what is known about the risk and protective factors for bulimia nervosa.[1] The information is incomplete and often tentative. Research on protective factors, in particular, has been virtually nonexistent in the study of eating disorders. We propose that they merit empirical study in the important tradition of theory and research begun by Garmezy and his students and colleagues (Garmezy, 1984, 1985a).

Two basic risk factors for bulimia nervosa set the stage for this discussion. First, the individuals at greatest risk for bulimia nervosa are women (90% of all bulimics are female[2]); see Pyle (1985) and Connors and Johnson (1987) for

---

[1] We shall discuss here risk and protective factors for bulimia nervosa, but not for other eating disorders such as anorexia nervosa. The question of common versus unique risk factors for anorexia and bulimia nervosa deserves further attention and research to resolve the current controversy over the relationship between the two disorders; see Fairburn and Garner (1986) for a discussion.

[2] At present, there are not sufficient data to discuss the causes of the disorder in the 10% of bulimics who are men. Some of the risk factors specified for women may relate to men as well.

361

reviews. Second, it has been found that before a woman becomes bulimic, she demonstrates significant body-image dissatisfaction and has engaged in multiple weight-reduction efforts. However, these are not uniquely predictive signs of bulimia nervosa; body-image dissatisfaction and concerns with weight have been found to be pervasive among women in general. The "typical" woman reports feeling fat, even though she is likely to be of normal weight (Huon & Brown, 1984; Pyle, Halvorson, Neuman, & Mitchell, 1986), and by age 13, 80% of girls (compared with 10% of boys) have already been on a weight-loss diet (Mellin, Scully, & Irving, 1986). We have dubbed this widespread weight concern and dieting behavior women's "normative discontent" (Rodin, Silberstein, & Striegel-Moore, 1985). We contend that normative discontent poses a second basic risk factor for bulimia nervosa.

We conceptualize that all women lie on a continuum of eating disorders and weight concerns; at one end are those who are not concerned with weight and who eat normally, in the middle are those experiencing normative discontent with their weight and showing moderately disregulated/restrained eating, and at the other end are those with bulimia nervosa (Rodin et al., 1985). The matter of risk and protective factors, therefore, can be seen as a question of what variables will move a woman along this continuum to bulimia nervosa, and what variables will protect her from such a course.

In this chapter we discuss three clusters of factors that may contribute to or protect against the development of bulimia nervosa: the sociocultural milieu, the family context, and individual characteristics.

The sociocultural milieu

Although isolated cases of bulimia nervosa have been described for centuries (Ziolko, 1985), bulimia nervosa has become a major health problem only in the past two decades. Its increase in recent years (Pyle et al., 1986) suggests that an understanding of the risk for bulimia nervosa will need to take into account sociohistorical factors.

The attractiveness stereotype

Consistent and persuasive data have been accumulated to suggest that the risk for bulimia has increased because of modern societal stereotypes regarding attractiveness (Garner, Rockert, Olmsted, Johnson, & Coscina, 1985; Hawkins & Fremouw, 1984; Johnson, Lewis, & Hagman, 1984; Rodin et al., 1985). Attractive individuals are believed to possess seemingly limitless numbers of desirable personality attributes, and they are judged to live happier and more successful lives than do less attractive persons. Furthermore, attractive individuals have been found to be at an advantage in a variety of interpersonal situations; see Hatfield and Sprecher (1986) for a review. The attractiveness stereotype is held by and applies to people of all ages. Furthermore, and most important, this stereotype is applied more strongly to women than to men (Rodin et al., 1985). Attractive women profit more, and unattractive women suffer more, in occupational, interpersonal, and educational settings than do attractive and unattractive men. In short, appearance matters in the life of a woman in our society.

Although all women are exposed to these sociocultural attitudes, women differ in the extent to which they internalize and emphasize the mores of attractiveness. We predict that women who accept the mores about attractiveness most fully will be at greater risk for bulimia, and, conversely, women who emphasize attractiveness less should be less vulnerable. To explore this hypothesis, we developed a series of attitude statements based on these sociocultural values (e.g., "attractiveness increases the likelihood of professional success"). Preliminary analyses suggest that women with disordered eating express substantially greater acceptance of these attitudes than do non-eating-disordered women (Striegel-Moore, Silberstein, & Rodin, 1989).

The contemporary beauty ideal

Although history suggests that attractiveness stereotypes date back for centuries, the *particular* beauty ideal changes with time (Banner, 1983; Rudofsky, 1971). Especially important to our understanding of the emergence of bulimia nervosa is the fact that the beauty ideal for women has become increasingly and unrealistically thin. Changes in measurements toward increasing thinness over time have been documented in Miss America contestants, *Playboy* centerfolds, and female models in magazine advertisements (Agras & Kirkley, 1986; Garner, Garfinkel, Schwartz, & Thompson, 1980; Silverstein, Peterson, & Perdue, 1986b). During the same time period, however, the average body weight for women under 30 years of age has actually increased (Metropolitan Life Foundation, 1983). The vast majority of female undergraduates desire to be thinner than their current sizes, in contrast to their male peers, who are as likely to want to be heavier as thinner (Silberstein, Striegel-Moore, Timko, & Rodin, 1988).

Therefore, there is an increasing discrepancy between the thin ideal and women's actual weight. We hypothesize that women who aspire to the thinnest ideal will be at greater risk for bulimia nervosa than will those who adopt a more moderate weight goal. Research has confirmed this prediction: The body ideal for bulimic women is significantly thinner than that for nonbulimic women (Williamson, Kelley, Davis, Ruggiero, & Blouin, 1985).

A major historical development has been that fashion has become more democratic, and so, too, have eating disorders. With the advent of mass media and the development of sophisticated photographic technology, the beauty ideal has become more universally similar and more widely distributed, and the beauty ideal is presented to the public as attainable by everyone. For example, photographs of models in magazines are seen as *realistic* representations of what people look like, as compared with painted figures that are more readily acknowledged to be artistic creations (Lakoff & Scherr, 1984).

The media glamorization of thinness thus contributes to a sociocultural risk factor for women's normative discontent with weight and for bulimia nervosa. Significant social change could provide an important protective factor, but that seems unlikely in the short run. Although the women's movement has made significant strides in reducing many (although certainly not all) sexist stereotypical portraits of women, little energy has been directed toward liberating women from the strict standards of thinness that define beauty in our culture. Perhaps this is because feminist leaders have not themselves escaped the oppression of the obsession with weight (Steinem, 1983).

What might such social change involve? A two-pronged approach can be conceptualized. First, it might begin with a deliberate effort to broaden our aesthetic sensibility. Beauty can certainly come in all sizes. (If we move beyond our cultural egocentrism, it is not difficult to imagine how our current thin ideals could be perceived as markedly unattractive.) The "Black is beautiful" component of the civil rights movement similarly strove to create a counteraesthetic. The second, more profound agenda for social change would be a reduction of the importance of physical beauty (of any sort) in our assessment and valuing of women.

Prescriptions for achieving the ideal

Society disseminates not only what the beauty ideal is but also the strategies for how to attain it. Over the ages, women have been advised about how to constrict their bodies in order to achieve the current beauty standards. In previous eras, the constraints were external, such as corsetting and footbinding; modern prescriptions to diet have moved the controls from external to internal (Brownmiller, 1984).

A look at the mass media today quickly reveals the plethora of advice about how to achieve the perfect body. The mass-market weight-control industry popularizes damaging rituals such as restrictive dieting and even purging (Wooley & Wooley, 1982). In addition to these media influences, females more directly teach each other how to diet, and how to binge and purge and starve. For example, Schwartz, Thompson, and Johnson (1981) found that a college woman who purges almost always knows another female student who purges, whereas a woman who does not purge rarely knows someone who does. Although eating pathology is not merely learned behavior, we believe that the public's heightened awareness of the bulimic syndrome and a young woman's likelihood of personal exposure to its symptoms may be significant factors in the increased emergence of this eating disorder in the last several years.

Whereas the seventies brought us the thinness craze, the eighties brought a redefinition of the ideal female body, which now is characterized not merely by thinness but also by firm, shapely muscles (though avoiding too much muscularity). Although the potential health benefits from increased exercise are real, the current emphasis on physical fitness may itself be contributing to the increased incidence of bulimia nervosa. The strong implication is that exercising helps achieve the thin, healthy-looking ideal and that such attainment is a direct consequence of personal effort. Inability to achieve the "aerobics instructor look" is attributed to insufficient effort and may leave women feeling defeated, ashamed, and desperate. The pursuit of fitness becomes another preoccupation, compulsion, even obsession for many.

If the pursuit of fitness represents a step beyond even the pursuit of thinness, so, too, does cosmetic surgery. Using procedures ranging from suction removal of fat to face-lifts, women in increasing numbers are seeking to match the template of beauty with ever more complicated, invasive, and expensive surgery (Adler et al., 1985). The message, again, seems to be that beauty is a matter of effort, that beauty is worth limitless expenditures of energy, and that failure to attain the beauty ideal makes one personally culpable.

The trend of escalating efforts directed toward reshaping one's body reflects the underlying cultural belief that the body is infinitely malleable. Efforts that today appear extreme and are considered appropriate only for models, actresses, and the wealthy may be adopted by the mainstream tomorrow. The consequences of such drastic measures are yet unknown. We propose that stemming the tide of the ever-proliferating methods for altering one's body will serve an essential protective function.

Subcultures intensifying the sociocultural pressures toward thinness

Although these powerful sociocultural forces are ever-present for all women in our society, thus placing all women at risk, it is only a minority of women who develop bulimia nervosa. To begin to answer the question of why some women, but not others, develop bulimia nervosa, we shall next consider factors that increase vulnerability.

Certain social contexts appear to increase the risk for bulimia nervosa for their participants. For example, boarding schools and colleges have been described as "breeding grounds" for eating disorders such as bulimia (Squire, 1983). Although precise epidemiological data are not yet available, it appears that the incidence of bulimia nervosa is considerably higher among college women than in the general female population (Pyle, 1985). As stressful and semiclosed environments, campuses may serve to intensify the sociocultural pressures to be thin. The competitive school environment may foster not only academic competition but also competition regarding the achievement of a beautiful (i.e., thin) body. Attractiveness is particularly important during this developmental period because of its role in relationships: For women, more than for men, appearance affects popularity and heterosexual appeal (Hatfield & Sprecher, 1986).

Other kinds of subcultures also appear to amplify sociocultural pressures and hence place their members at greater risk for bulimia nervosa. Illustrative examples are subcultures that demand, explicitly or implicitly, a certain weight. Members of professions that dictate a certain body weight, such as dancers, models, and actresses, are more likely to show pathological eating behavior than are individuals whose job performance is unrelated to their appearance and weight (Brooks-Gunn, Burrow, & Warren, 1988; Crago, Yates, Beutler, & Arizmendi, 1985; Garner & Garfinkel, 1978, 1980; Joseph, Wood, & Goldberg, 1982). The onset of eating pathology typically is observed after a woman enters one of these subcultures (Crago et al., 1985), and it has been shown to be correlated with the extent to which the subculture emphasizes appearance and weight (Garner & Garfinkel, 1980).

A question that remains open is whether or not any professional focus on the body increases risk for bulimia nervosa. It would be informative to study a population of athletes, because all sports require attention to the body, but only some focus on weight in particular. We would predict that sports that demand a thin body, such as gymnastics and figure skating, would increase the risk for bulimia nervosa. Participation in sports that focus on strength and endurance (e.g., tennis, volleyball) may have a positive effect on body image and self-esteem (Vanfraechem & Vanfraechem-Raway, 1978). Sports that foster an appreciation of the body as an agent rather than as an aesthetic object may increase a woman's resistance to becoming preoccupied with weight.

Virtually unexplored empirically is the question whether or not there are subcultures that serve a protective function regarding weight and eating-related concerns. For example, it has been reported that lesbian women place less emphasis on physical appearance than do heterosexual women and that the lesbian culture challenges our society's beauty ideals (Blumstein & Schwartz, 1983). Hence, one might argue that lesbians should be more accepting of their bodies than are heterosexual women. Initial research, however, failed to confirm that hypothesis (Striegel-Moore, Tucker, & Hsu, in press).

Another unresearched question concerns the types of peer groups that might serve to heighten or reduce the risk for bulimia nervosa. A female's attitudes toward weight may be influenced by the extent to which her friends emphasize thinness. For females, dieting often is a group activity, and by participating, a girl or woman affirms her group membership. Talking about weight and dieting may serve as a means of female "bonding" or, conversely, as a form of female competition. It has been found that women who reported having more friends who dieted also had more eating disorder symptoms themselves (Crandall, 1988; Gibbs, 1986). Our clinical experience suggests that male friends or partners represent another potential source of risk. Men vary in the degree to which they emphasize thinness as an important attribute. For an already weight-preoccupied woman, a boyfriend's negative comment about her weight may initiate a "tailspin" of dieting and subsequent binge eating. The ways in which significant others may potentiate risk for bulimia nervosa need to be researched.

Conversely, same-sex and cross-sex relationships may serve a protective function. At a concrete level, if friends or romantic partners have well-regulated eating habits and are relatively unconcerned with issues of weight, this may provide a buffer against some of the factors that increase risk. At a more psychological level, successful interpersonal relationships satisfy needs that might otherwise be displaced onto food. In our clinical work, we frequently observe that developing a satisfying intimate relationship co-occurs with a lessening of bulimic symptoms.

The central role of beauty in the female sex-role stereotype

Women's pursuit of the current thin ideal cannot be understood completely without a consideration of the role beauty plays in the female experience. Being concerned with one's appearance and making efforts to enhance and preserve one's beauty are central features of the female sex-role stereotype (Brownmiller, 1984). Several studies have documented that physically attractive women are perceived as more feminine (Cash, Gillen, & Burns, 1977; Gillen, 1981; Gillen & Sherman, 1980; Unger, 1985), and unattractive women as more masculine (Heilman & Saruwatari, 1979). It has also been shown that the mesomorphic male silhouette is associated with perceived masculinity, whereas the ectomorphic female silhouette is associated with perceived femininity (Guy, Rankin, & Norvell, 1980). Hence, thinness and femininity appear to be linked.

Interestingly, there also appears to be a relationship between certain types of eating behavior and femininity. Women who were described as eating small meals were rated significantly more feminine, less masculine, and more attractive than women who ate large meals, whereas meal size descriptions had no effect on ratings of male targets (Mori, Chaiken, & Pliner, 1987). The same study suggests that women may actually restrict their food intake in the service of making a favorable impression on men (Mori et al., 1987). Women ate significantly less in an experimental condition in which their feminine identity was threatened than when their feminine identity was confirmed (Mori et al., 1987).

It may seem paradoxical that bulimia nervosa has increased at a time when women appear to be less limited in their choices, personally and professionally, than were women of earlier eras. The literature on the impact of employment on women's health has documented that women with "multiple roles" (i.e., women who are gainfully employed *and* are wives and/or mothers) enjoy better physical and mental health than do women whose roles are limited to those of wife and mother (Baruch, Barnett, & Rivers, 1983; Crosby, 1982; Verbrugge, 1983). These findings may lead one to assume that having access to multiple roles serves as a protective factor regarding the development of disordered eating. Indeed, if a woman can base her sense of self on the multiple domains of her life (including career, family, personal interests), rather than on her appearance, she should be less vulnerable to bulimia nervosa.

However, it seems that being occupationally successful does not relieve women of the need to be beautiful (i.e., thin). Women who have achieved occupational success and have abandoned many traditional dictums for female behavior and roles still worry about their weight and pursue thinness (Lakoff & Scherr, 1984). One possible reason for such weight concerns among professional women is that thinness represents the antithesis of the ample female body associated with woman as wife and mother (Beck, Ward-Hull, & McLear, 1976), and a curvaceous build may be associated with being less competent and intelligent than a thinner build (Silverstein, Perdue, Peterson, Vogel, & Fantini, 1986a). A second reason may be found in these women's very orientation to success. They set high standards for themselves, and thinness represents a personal accomplishment. Research has documented relationships between perfectionism and symptoms of eating disorders (Garner, Olmsted, & Polivy, 1983; Garner, Olmsted, Polivy, & Garfinkel, 1984; Striegel-Moore, McAvay, & Rodin, 1986a) and between competitiveness and disordered eating (Striegel-Moore, Silberstein, Grunberg, & Rodin, 1989). At the same time, thinness may serve an instrumental and somewhat paradoxical function of furthering a woman's success in a man's world, for femininity gives a woman a "competitive edge" (Brownmiller, 1984). It also may be difficult for women to abandon femininity wholesale. Looking feminine, even while demonstrating "unfeminine" ambition and power, may serve an important function in affirming, to herself as well as to others, a woman's feminine identity.

Our bulimic clients often express confusion about their roles and about what it means to be feminine. Evidence suggests that when gender identity is challenged, individuals will engage in sex-role-appropriate behaviors to reaffirm their gender identity (Mori et al., 1987; Spence, 1985). Although many aspects of the contemporary female sex-role stereotype are unclear, being concerned and preoccupied with one's beauty has remained a hallmark of femininity. Thus, when a woman faces challenges to her feminine identity, she may be compelled to intensify her focus on her appearance as a way of affirming her gender identity.

For most women today, the expansion of roles has resulted not in an array of alternatives among which to choose but rather in a proliferation of roles that must be filled. For some roles, it is at least possible to relegate duties (i.e., household work and child care, for which surrogates can be hired), but there are no surrogates who can do women's beauty regimens. The current cultural myth of the "superwoman" embodies this view that a woman can expand her number of responsibilities infinitely without compromising quality. A study of adolescent girls found that they shared a common picture of the ideal superwoman who "has it all": career, family, and beauty. Interestingly, those girls who saw the superwoman as consonant with their own goals had elevated scores for eating pathology, whereas the non-eating-disordered girls had more modest goals for themselves (Steiner-Adair, 1986). Another study asked women to rate the importance of a wide array of roles to their sense of self. Women who viewed many roles as central to their sense of self scored higher on a measure of disordered eating than did women who considered fewer roles to be important (Timko, Striegel-Moore, Silberstein, & Rodin, 1987). Both of these studies support the view that adopting fully the current female ideal places a woman at increased risk for bulimia nervosa. Gilligan (1982) has argued that the process of female development in our androcentric society makes it difficult for girls and women to find and use their own "voice." We would contend that when women can critically evaluate the socio-culturally defined voice, they then become able to recognize the female ideal as unrealistically successful and unrealistically thin. A developmental process that enables women to find their own voice will allow them to formulate more moderate personal goals and thus serve a protective function.

The family context

The family represents a highly specific social context within which attitudes and behaviors related to weight, appearance, and eating are developed. Research on the contribution of family characteristics to the development of bulimia nervosa is in its initial stages. Three dimensions of family life will be considered here: parental attitudes toward weight, eating patterns in the family, and family dynamics.

Parents' attitudes toward weight

Certain family characteristics may amplify the sociocultural imperatives described earlier. For example, the risk for bulimia is relatively increased in girls whose families place heavy emphasis on appearance and thinness. A mother's efforts to control her own weight may convey to her daughter the importance of thinness as well as strategies to attain it. It probably is no accident that bulimia nervosa has become a major health problem among the daughters of the first generation of women in the Weight Watchers program (Boskind-White & White, 1983).

The family conveys attitudes about weight in a multitude of ways. Parents' comments about their own weight, or about other people's weight, have a subtle influence on children's developing attitudes about appearance. In addition, parents may comment directly on and criticize a child's weight, and such comments can have a profound and lasting effect on the child's body image. We hear striking numbers of inappropriate comments about children's bodies, as if they should be as flat-stomached and gaunt as adult fashion models. The current boom in designer clothes for children reflects this: Children's clothes are simply scaled-down versions of the adult models (Conant, 1986).

On the other hand, having parents who have resolved their own weight issues, or who are aware of the potentially harmful influence of our society's attractiveness bias, may serve as a protective factor. Most people currently do not view anti-fat attitudes as a form of prejudice. Therefore, consciousness raising will be required in order for parents to be able to rise above their own ingrained beliefs about weight and attractiveness. Parents who are aware that they have not completely outgrown their racial prejudice still may be committed to trying to liberate their children from similar biases. Similarly, parents who are aware of their own weight prejudices may be able, with deliberate effort, to limit the extent to which such concerns will influence their children.

In addition to the parental influence, siblings may increase or decrease the risk for disordered eating. In particular, we hypothesize that the presence of older sisters may prove significant. An older sister's concern with weight and dieting efforts may accelerate a girl's exposure to and personal involvement in this domain, much as an older sibling's drug or alcohol use often prompts precocious use by a younger sibling.

Eating patterns in the family

Several authors have speculated about the potential importance of early feeding interactions. In general, it has been proposed that a lack of contingencies between an infant's behavior and the immediate environment may lead to an increased risk of psychopathology (Thoman, 1980). Bruch (1973), for example, speculated that when a mother responds indiscriminantly to an infant's distress signals by providing food, the infant will not learn to regulate food intake adequately. Others have suggested that mothers who experience conflict regarding eating patterns and their own weight, regardless of how much they actually weigh, may engage in inconsistent and emotionally charged infant feeding practices that may interfere with an infant's learning of self-regulatory skills concerning food and eating (Wooley & Wooley, 1985).

In the context of family life, meals are important events. Research on family meals and the role of food in the family environment would be highly informative. Some of our bulimic patients have described a childhood of chaotic and irregular family meals, and, not surprisingly, these women have never learned consistent meal patterns. Other patients seem to have grown up in homes with stable meal patterns, but they developed disturbed eating behaviors on leaving home. Among the many challenges faced on leaving home, young women have to begin regulating their own food intake. That can prove difficult if prior eating patterns were completely controlled by the parents.

Given the sociocultural biases against overweight females, it is understandable that parents often become concerned about and involved in a daughter's eating behavior. Costanzo and Woody (1985) argue that when parents are highly invested in a domain of their child's life, they tend to utilize a restrictive parenting style to influence the child's behavior in that domain. Such high-concern/high-constraint parenting leads to a seemingly paradoxical outcome: The child experiences considerable anxiety and guilt over eating, and at the same time is deficient in the skills required for effective self-regulation of eating. Importantly, parents who are highly anxious about a daughter's weight may use this parenting style regardless of her actual weight. The result is that girls of any weight are at risk for developing high anxiety and low self-regulatory competence in regard to eating.

Family dynamics

The "psychosomatic family" model predicts that enmeshment, parental overprotectiveness, rigidity, and lack of conflict resolution will increase the risk for psychosomatic illness in a family (Minuchin, Rosman, & Baker, 1978). Consistent with that model, bulimic women tend to describe their families of origin as being characterized by insufficient encouragement of the daughter's independence, low tolerance for open expression of feelings, and high levels of conflict. However, contrary to the model, bulimic women usually perceive low cohesiveness in their families of origin (Humphrey, 1986; Humphrey, Apple, & Kirschenbaum, 1986; Johnson & Flach, 1985; Ordman & Kirschenbaum, 1985; Strober, 1981). A methodological concern is that all the families in those reports were studied after the onset of bulimic symptoms. Furthermore, none of those family studies described interactional patterns that were unique to bulimic families. The characteristics found in this line of research may represent general risk factors for the development of psychopathology in a family member. We would expect that when these family dynamics converge with the specific risk factors discussed in this chapter, bulimia nervosa is a likely outcome.

Mother/daughter and father/daughter relationships have received some initial attention. A challenge faced by women today is that in pursuing education and vocation, they often are surpassing their mothers' achievements in these domains (Chernin, 1985; Wooley & Kearney-Cooke, 1986). It has been argued that this dynamic produces considerable conflict for the daughter, who may feel torn between her own aspirations and her loyalty to the role model provided by her mother. An eating disorder represents an attempt to resolve this conflict: It allows the daughter who feels ambivalent about her competence to be incompetent in one domain, and permits displaced expression of her complex feelings. Given that feeding provided the initial basis for a relationship between mother and daughter, eating may be a likely arena for later expression of mother/daughter dynamics.

It would be interesting to look at variables that contribute to protection against or healthy resolution of these dynamics. Furthermore, it will be informative to observe the current daughters as they become mothers. For the next generation of daughters, surpassing one's mother may be a less prominent issue and therefore should be a less potent risk factor. On the other hand, new and yet uncharted risk factors seem likely for daughters whose mothers composed the first generation of bulimic women.

Considerably less attention has been directed to the father/daughter relationship as a source of risk or protection. In his clinical work with bulimic women, Hawkins (1983) observed a sudden shift at adolescence in the father/daughter relationship, with the father withdrawing abruptly from an earlier close attachment. The lack of conceptual and empirical efforts to understand the contribution of the father to the daughter's development of bulimia nervosa represents a significant omission. Bulimia nervosa research needs to follow the example of developmental psychology, which has begun to recognize the important role of the father in child development (Lamb, 1976).

Individual characteristics

We shall now discuss three general domains of individual characteristics that may contribute to differential risk for bulimia: biological variables, the development of body image, and personality and behavioral characteristics.

Influence of biological variables

Biological determinants of body weight. Because body weight has a normal distribution in the population, the current beauty ideal of extreme thinness represents a biologically unrealistic goal for the majority of women. In contradiction to popular belief, one's weight appears to be determined more by one's genetic endowment than by behavior (Stunkard et al., 1986). We conjecture that those women who are genetically predisposed to be heavier than the svelte ideal will be at higher risk for bulimia than those women who are naturally thin. Evidence suggests that a woman who is heavier than her peers may be more likely to develop bulimia nervosa (Fairburn & Cooper, 1983; Johnson, Stuckey, Lewis, & Schwartz, 1982).

One possible mediating factor is the way in which women try to cope with the discrepancy between the socially prescribed weight and their own genetically determined weight. For example, a 1978 Nielsen survey found that 56% of women between ages 24 and 54 were on a diet (Nielsen, 1979). Many researchers now believe that dieting is an ineffective way to achieve long-term weight loss, and it may in fact contribute to subsequent weight gain and binge eating (Polivy & Herman, 1985, 1987; Rodin et al., 1985). Dieting leads to numerous physiological changes that result in increased efficiency of food utilization and a higher proportion of fat in the body's composition (Polivy & Herman, 1987). When one resumes normal caloric intake, these physiological changes do not immediately rebound to the pre-diet state. In fact, a longer period of dieting will prolong the time it takes for the body to readjust to its original functioning (Even & Nicolaidis, 1981). Thus, even normal eating after a period of dieting may lead to weight gain. In addition, animal research suggests that regaining weight occurs significantly more rapidly after a second dieting cycle than after the first (Brownell, Greenwood, Stellar, & Shrager, 1986).

Concurrent with these biological ramifications, dieting also produces psychological results that are self-defeating. Typically, dieters feel deprived of their favorite foods; then, when "off" their diets, they are likely to overeat. The more restrictively one diets, the more likely one will be to develop food cravings (particularly for foods that one does not allow oneself as part of the diet) and eventually to yield to these cravings (Polivy & Herman, 1985).

Several studies have found a high correlation between dieting and binge eating, suggesting that food restriction may be an important causal antecedent to binging (Leon, Carroll, Chernyk, & Finn, 1981a; Polivy & Herman, 1985). Thus, a prolonged history of repeated attempts at dieting appears to be a risk factor for bulimia nervosa. We conjecture that those women who have engaged in repeated dieting attempts will be the least successful at achieving their target weights by dieting. These women may be most vulnerable to consider other, increasingly drastic weight-loss strategies, including severely restrictive diets, laxative abuse, and purging.

A protective strategy would be to educate the public about the ineffectiveness of dieting as a means of weight control and about its destructive side effects. However, it is anticipated that the multi-billion-dollar diet industry will pose an obstacle. As long as new "cures" for unwanted pounds are marketed, consumers will continue to be tempted and persuaded.

Genetic disposition to bulimia nervosa. In addition to an inherited predisposition to a specific body weight, it is possible that a predisposition to an eating disorder may be genetically transmitted. Research on this issue is at an early stage, but initial findings suggest familial clustering of eating disorders. Studies have documented significantly higher incidences of both anorexia nervosa and bulimia nervosa among the first-degree female relatives of anorexic patients than among the immediate families of control subjects (Strober, Morrell, Burroughs, Salkin, & Jacobs, 1985), and monozygotic twins have a considerably higher concordance rate for anorexia than do dizygotic twins; see Scott (1986) for a review. Research has not yet directly addressed the question of the heritability of bulimia nervosa. Studies of the relatives of bulimic women might provide important insights into risk and protective factors.

Affective instability has been proposed as another biogenetic risk factor for bulimia (Hawkins & Fremouw, 1984; Johnson et al., 1984; Strober, 1981). Several family studies have revealed a high incidence of affective disorders among first-degree relatives of bulimic patients; see Scott (1986) and Halmi (1985) for reviews. Studies using twin and adoption populations and family aggregation methods are needed to further our understanding of the relationship between affective disorder and bulimia.

Development of body image

Developmental studies have documented that girls readily internalize societal messages on the importance of pursuing attractiveness (Rodin et al., 1985). Among grade-school children, weight is already found to be critical in the relationship between body image and self-concept: The thinner the girl, the more likely she is to report feeling attractive, popular, and successful academically (Guyot, Fairchild, & Hill, 1981).

Female body-image dissatisfaction is intensified during adolescence (Davies & Furnham, 1986). Adolescence is a period that provokes challenging questions of identity, self-esteem, and interpersonal acceptance. For the adolescent, these questions are integrally interwoven with physical appearance. The extensive biological changes associated with pubertal development render perceptions of the body highly salient in the adolescent's overall self-perception. Pubertal development poses a particular challenge for girls. For boys, pubertal maturation results in body changes that bring them closer to the ideal masculine body (i.e., tall, muscular, and broad-shouldered). In contrast, puberty is associated with a considerable increase in fat tissue for girls. Puberty thus brings an increased discrepancy between the girl's actual build and the ideal female body. Not surprisingly, adolescent girls perceive weight as their leading concern about their appearance (Rosenbaum, 1979) and are harshly self-critical of their bodies (Crisp & Kalucy, 1974). In response to the distressing increase in fat that accompanies puberty, the majority of adolescent females embark on the first of many weight-loss efforts. We speculate that dieting in adolescence may be particularly damaging to the body's regulatory processes, interfering with the complex biological changes in progress and with the attainment of a new hormonal equilibrium.

Female adolescence thus becomes a time of heightened risk for bulimia nervosa. Indeed, it is during adolescence that bulimia nervosa begins to emerge as a major clinical problem. In addition, girls who enter puberty early may be at even greater risk. They tend to be heavier than their peers, and this weight difference persists after puberty. Girls who mature early perceive themselves as less attractive and seem to be particularly unhappy with their weight (Peskin, 1973; Simmons, Blyth, & McKinney, 1983; Tobin-Richards, Boxer, & Petersen, 1983). Bruch (1981) suggested that early development may place a girl at risk for anorexia nervosa. Empirical studies are needed to examine our hypothesis that precocious development may be a risk factor for bulimia nervosa as well.

The adolescent's increased preoccupation with weight and dieting behavior becomes intertwined with her search for identity. At a time when feeling accepted by peers is of prime importance, achieving the cultural beauty ideal holds the promise of popularity and acceptance. In addition, against the background of the turbulence of adolescence, weight represents a concrete domain that, allegedly, can be self-controlled (Hood, Moore, & Garner, 1982). Because our society views weight-loss efforts as a sign of maturity (Steele, 1980), dieting attempts may reflect a girl's desire to show others, as well as herself, that she is growing up. Hence, dieting may be a part of or a metaphor for independence.

On the other hand, attempts to lose weight may provide a refuge from the developmental challenges regarding independence that are posed to the adolescent. Losing weight may represent an effort to defy the bodily changes signaling maturity and adulthood. Dieting may be an attempt to reverse or arrest physical maturation, perhaps reflecting a desire to remain in childhood (Bruch, 1973; Crisp, 1980; Leon, Lucas, Colligan, Ferdinande, & Kamp, 1985b; Selvini-Palazzoli, 1978).

Although adolescence represents the initial period of increased risk for bulimia nervosa, the risk factors persist and may proliferate in early adulthood. Women's "normative discontent" with weight does not dissipate after adolescence, but rather continues throughout the life span (Blumstein & Schwartz, 1983). To some extent, then, weight and eating remain areas vulnerable to potential disregulation throughout the female life cycle. At the current time, bulimia nervosa emerges most frequently in adolescence and young adulthood. Perhaps there are protective factors in adulthood that prevent women in later life from moving from normative discontent to bulimia nervosa. Or perhaps we soon shall begin to observe the development of bulimia nervosa in middle and late adulthood. Most research to date has examined bulimia nervosa in the narrow age range of high school and college students. A recent study found that patients with late-onset bulimia nervosa were more likely to report concomitant problems such as drug abuse and depression than were patients with early-onset bulimia nervosa (Mitchell, Hatuskami, Pyle, Eckert, & Soll, 1987). Our understanding of risk and protective factors for bulimia nervosa will be expanded by studying a broader age spectrum.

Personality and behavioral characteristics

Various personality characteristics may increase the risk for bulimia nervosa. A limitation of the research to date is that it has focused on women who already exhibit the clinical syndrome; see Mizes (1985) for a review. As Garmezy and Streitman (1974) discuss, such a focus on the disordered adult is not sufficient for the identification of risk factors. We shall briefly review the personality and behavioral characteristics that have been found common among bulimic women. However, to determine which of these characteristics will increase the risk for bulimia nervosa, prospective studies will be required.

Several authors have argued that women define themselves primarily via their relations and connections to others (Chodorow, 1978; Gilligan, 1982; Miller, 1976). We conjecture that if a woman's own needs and opinions are eclipsed as she accommodates others' needs and opinions, she will be at greater risk for bulimia nervosa. In lieu of other forms of self-nurturance, she may rely on food. In addition, heightened concern about others' opinions may make her more vulnerable to subscribing to the societal emphasis on appearance and thinness. Support for this conceptualization comes from clinical descriptions of bulimic women as exhibiting a strong need for social approval, avoiding conflict, and experiencing difficulty in identifying and asserting needs (Boskind-White & White, 1983). Initial research has found that bulimic women have a greater need for approval than do control subjects (Dunn & Ondercin, 1981; Katzman & Wolchik, 1984) and show low levels of assertiveness (Hawkins & Fremouw, 1984). Conversely, it would be predicted that having little need for approval and being self-directed and assertive would serve a protective function.

On the Minnesota Multiphasic Personality Inventory (MMPI), bulimic women were found to have significantly high scores on the clinical scales Depression, Psychopathic Deviate, Psychasthenia, and Schizophrenia (Hatsukami, Owen, Pyle, & Mitchell, 1982; Leon et al., 1985b; Orleans & Barnett, 1984; Wallach & Lowenkopf, 1984). Among the subgroups that have emerged from this line of research are a group with obsessive-compulsive problems and a group with addictive behaviors (Hatsukami et al., 1982). Some have argued that bulimia nervosa is basically a substance abuse disorder (Brisman & Siegel, 1984; Wooley & Wooley, 1981). Having family members with substance abuse disorders may constitute a risk factor for bulimia nervosa: A high incidence of substance abuse has been reported among the members of bulimic women's families of origin (Leon et al., 1985a; Strober, Salkin, Burroughs, & Morrell, 1982). There is also a subgroup of bulimics who do not show psychopathology in areas other than their eating disorder.

On the basis of their clinical work, Johnson and Connors (1987) distinguish two types of bulimics: borderline and false-self. The borderline bulimic suffers from a deficient sense of self and an inability to modulate affect and impulses; her relationship to food mirrors her volatile interpersonal and intrapersonal relationships. The false-self bulimic presents a facade of competence and self-assurance, while internally experiencing herself as fraudulent, out of control, and needy; food is used as a regulator of tension and a self-contained means of gratifying needs.

The research on personality characteristics underscores the heterogeneity of women who develop bulimia nervosa. We greatly need further developments in conceptual models and empirical research to define risk and protective factors for subgroups of bulimics. It is possible that certain risk factors may contribute uniquely to the development of bulimia nervosa for a particular subgroup, but may be irrelevant for other groups.

Investigators who focus on behavior rather than personality have proposed that inadequate coping skills compose a risk factor for bulimia nervosa. For example, bulimic women appear deficient in their ability to cope with stressful situations (Hawkins & Fremouw, 1984; Katzman & Wolchik, 1984; Shatford & Evans, 1986). In addition, women who reported more stress were found to score higher on measures of binge eating; see Cattanach and Rodin (1988) for a review. It remains unclear whether or not bulimic women are exposed to greater stress, subjectively experience situations as more stressful, and/or are less skilled in coping with stress. In order to determine if competence in the face of stress serves a protective function, prospective studies will be necessary. As illustrated by the work of Garmezy and his colleagues (Garmezy, 1981; Garmezy, Masten, Nordstrom, & Ferrarese, 1979; Garmezy & Neuchterlein, 1972), it will be important to differentiate the specific domains of competence that relate to invulnerability to bulimia nervosa.

Conclusion

Our efforts to understand bulimia nervosa from a perspective of risk and protective factors have generated more questions than answers. It is now time for researchers in the eating disorders field to incorporate the framework that Garmezy has developed for studying the development of psychopathology, learning from his experience with challenging but fruitful prospective research designs (Garmezy, 1976, 1984, 1985b). We need to identify and verify those factors that appear to place a woman at increased risk for bulimia nervosa. As we have illustrated in this chapter, risk factors for bulimia nervosa stem from widely disparate sources. Thus, a multidimensional model of causation is needed (Garmezy, 1976). The fact that bulimia nervosa is influenced strongly by sociohistorical developments poses a challenge: Bulimia researchers are striving to hit a "moving target."

It is striking that no research has investigated women who appear to be resilient in the face of risk factors for bulimia nervosa. Garmezy's work on resistant children has illuminated our understanding of the development of schizophrenia and other forms of psychopathology. Similarly, a focus on women who prove resistant to bulimia nervosa will shed light on the causes of this eating disorder.

References

Adler, J., Raine, G., McCormick, J., Morris, H., Gosnell, M., Jackson, T., & Namuth, T. (1985). New bodies for sale. *Newsweek,* May 27, 64–9.

Agras, W. S., & Kirkley, B. G. (1986). Bulimia: Theories of etiology. In K. D. Brownell & J. P. Foreyt (Eds.), *Handbook of eating disorders* (pp. 367–78). New York: Basic Books.

Banner, L. W. (1983). *American beauty.* New York: Knopf.

Baruch, G., Barnett, R., & Rivers, C. (1983). *Life prints: New patterns of love and work for today's women.* New York: McGraw-Hill.

Beck, J. B., Ward-Hull, C. J., & McLear, P. M. (1976). Variables related to women's somatic preferences of the male and female body. *Journal of Personality and Social Psychology, 34,* 1200–10.

Blumstein, P. W., & Schwartz, P. (1983). *American couples.* New York: Morrow.

Boskind-White, M., & White, W. C. (1983). *Bulimarexia: The binge/purge cycle.* New York: Norton.

Brisman, J., & Siegel, M. (1984). Bulimia and alcoholism: Two sides of the same coin? *Journal of Substance Abuse Treatment, 1,* 113–18.

Brooks-Gunn, J., Burrow, C., & Warren, M. P. (1988). Attitudes toward eating and body weight in different groups of female adolescent athletes. *International Journal of Eating Disorders, 7,* 749–57.

Brownell, K. D., Greenwood, M. R. C., Stellar, E., & Shrager, E. E. (1986). The effects of repeated cycles of weight loss and regain in rats. *Physiology and Behavior, 38,* 459–64.

Brownmiller, S. (1984). *Femininity.* New York: Simon & Schuster.

Bruch, H. (1973). *Eating disorders: Obesity, anorexia nervosa and the person within.* New York: Basic Books.

Bruch, H. (1981). Developmental considerations of anorexia nervosa and obesity. *Canadian Journal of Psychiatry, 26,* 212–17.

Cash, T. F., Gillen, B., & Burns, D. S. (1977). Sexism and "beautyism" in personnel consultant decision making. *Journal of Applied Psychology, 62,* 301–10.

Cattanach, L., & Rodin, J. (1988). Psychosocial components of the stress process in bulimia. *International Journal of Eating Disorders, 7,* 75–88.

Chaiken, S., & Pliner, P. (in press). Women, but not men, are what they eat: The effect of meal size and gender on perceived femininity and masculinity. *Personality and Social Psychology Bulletin.*

Chernin, K. (1985). *The hungry self: Women, eating, and identity.* New York: Random House.

Chodorow, N. (1978). *The reproduction of mothering: Psychoanalysis and the sociology of gender.* Berkeley: University of California Press.

Conant, J. (1986). Bringing up baby in style. *Newsweek,* December 22, 58–9.

Connors, M., & Johnson, C. J. (1987). Epidemiology of bulimia and bulimia behaviors. *Addictive Behaviors, 12,* 165–79.

Costanzo, P. R., & Woody, E. Z. (1985). Domain-specific parenting styles and their impact on the child's development of particular deviance: The example of obesity proneness. *Journal of Social and Clinical Psychology, 3,* 425–45.

Crago, M., Yates, A., Beutler, L. E., & Arizmendi, T. G. (1985). Height-weight ratios among female athletes: Are collegiate athletics the precursors to an anorexic syndrome? *International Journal of Eating Disorders, 4,* 79–87.

Crandall, C. (1988). The social contagion of binge eating. *Journal of Personality and Social Psychology, 55,* 589–99.

Crisp, A. H. (1980). *Anorexia nervosa: Let me be.* London: Academic Press.

Crisp, A. H., & Kalucy, R. S. (1974). Aspects of the perceptual disorder in anorexia nervosa. *British Journal of Medical Psychology, 47,* 349–61.

Crosby, F. J. (1982). *Relative deprivation and working women.* Oxford University Press.

Davies, E., & Furnham, A. (1986). Body satisfaction in adolescent girls. *British Journal of Medical Psychology, 59,* 279–87.

Dunn, P., & Ondercin, P. (1981). Personality variables related to compulsive eating in college women. *Journal of Clinical Psychology, 37,* 43–9.

Even, P., & Nicolaidis, S. (1981). Changes in efficiency of ingestants are a major factor of regulation of energy balance. In L. A. Cioffi, W. P. T. James, & T. B. Van Itallie (Eds.), *The body weight regulatory system: Normal and disturbed mechanisms* (pp. 115–23). New York: Raven Press.

Fairburn, C. G., & Cooper, P. J. (1983). The epidemiology of bulimia nervosa. *International Journal of Eating Disorders, 2,* 61–7.

Fairburn, C. G., & Garner, D. M. (1986). The diagnosis of bulimia nervosa. *International Journal of Eating Disorders, 5,* 403–19.

Garmezy, N. (1974). Children at risk: The search for the antecedents of schizophrenia. Part II: Ongoing research programs, issues, and intervention. *Schizophrenia Bulletin, 9,* 55–125.

Garmezy, N. (1976). The experimental study of children vulnerable to psychopathology. In A. Davids (Ed.), *Child personality and psychopathology: Current topics* (Vol. 2, pp. 171–216). New York: Wiley.

Garmezy, N. (1981). Children under stress: Perspectives on antecedents and correlates of vulnerability and resistance to psychopathology. In A. L. Rabin, J. Aronoff, A. M. Barclay, & R. A. Zucker (Eds.), *Further explorations in personality* (pp. 196–269). New York: Wiley.

Garmezy, N. (1984). Children vulnerable to major mental disorders: Risk and protective factors. In L. Grinspoon (Ed.), *Psychiatric update* (Vol. 3, pp. 91–104). Washington, DC: American Psychiatric Press.

Garmezy, N. (1985a). Stress-resistant children: The search for protective factors. In J. E. Stevensen (Ed.), *Recent research in developmental psychopathology* (pp. 213–33). *Journal of Child Psychiatry and Psychology* (Book Supplement 4). Oxford: Pergamon Press.

Garmezy, N. (1985b). The NIMH–Israeli high risk study: Commendations, comments, and cautions. *Schizophrenia Bulletin, 11,* 349–53.

Garmezy, N., Masten, A., Nordstrom, L., & Ferrarese, M. (1979). The nature of competence in normal and deviant children. In M. W. Kent & J. E. Rolf (Eds.), *Promoting social competence and coping in children. Primary prevention of psychopathology* (Vol. 3, pp. 23–43). Hanover, NH: University Press of New England.

Garmezy, N., & Neuchterlein, K. H. (1972). Invulnerable children: The fact and fiction of competence and disadvantage. *American Journal of Orthopsychiatry, 77,* 328–9.

Garmezy, N., & Streitman, S. (1974). Children at risk: The search for the antecedents of schizophrenia. Part I: Conceptual models and research methods. *Schizophrenia Bulletin, 8,* 14–90.

Garner, D. M., & Garfinkel, P. E. (1978). Sociocultural factors in anorexia nervosa. *Lancet, 2,* 674.

Garner, D. M., & Garfinkel, P. E. (1980). Sociocultural factors in the development of anorexia nervosa. *Psychological Medicine, 10,* 647–56.

Garner, D. M., Garfinkel, P. E., Schwartz, D., & Thompson, M. (1980). Cultural expectations of thinness in women. *Psychological Reports, 47,* 483–91.

Garner, D. M., Olmsted, M. P., & Polivy, J. (1983). Development and validation of a multidimensional eating disorder inventory for anorexia nervosa and bulimia. *International Journal of Eating Disorders, 2,* 15–34.

Garner, D. M., Olmsted, M. P., Polivy, J., & Garfinkel, P. E. (1984). Comparison between weight-preoccupied women and anorexia nervosa. *Psychosomatic Medicine, 46,* 255–66.

Garner, D. M., Rockert, W., Olmsted, M. P., Johnson, C., & Coscina, D. V. (1985). Psychoeducational principles in the treatment of bulimia and anorexia nervosa. In D. M. Garner & P. E. Garfinkel (Eds.), *Handbook of psychotherapy for anorexia nervosa and bulimia* (pp. 513–72). New York: Guilford Press.

Gibbs, R. (1986). Social factors in exaggerated eating behavior among high school students. *International Journal of Eating Disorders, 5,* 1103–7.

Gillen, B. (1981). Physical attractiveness: A determinant of two types of goodness. *Personality and Social Psychology Bulletin, 7,* 277–81.

Gillen, B., & Sherman, R. C. (1980). Physical attractiveness and sex as determinants of trait attributions. *Multivariate Behavioral Research, 15,* 423–37.

Gilligan, C. (1982). *In a different voice: Psychological theory and women's development.* Cambridge, MA: Harvard University Press.

Guy, R. F., Rankin, B. A., & Norvell, M. J. (1980). The relation of sex-role stereotyping to body image. *Journal of Psychology, 105,* 167–73.

Guyot, G. W., Fairchild, L., & Hill, M. (1981). Physical fitness, sport participation, body build and self-concept of elementary school children. *International Journal of Sport Psychology, 12,* 105–16.

Halmi, K. A. (1985). Relationship of the eating disorders to depression: Biological similarities and differences. *International Journal of Eating Disorders, 4,* 667–80.

Hatfield, E., & Sprecher, S. (1986). *Mirror, mirror: The importance of looks in everyday life.* New York: SUNY Press.

Hatsukami, D., Owen, P., Pyle, R., & Mitchell, J. (1982). Similarities and differences on the MMPI between women with bulimia and women with alcohol or drug abuse problems. *Addictive Behaviors, 7,* 435–9.

Hawkins, R. C., II. (1983). *Cognitive processes in bulimia.* Paper presented at the annual meeting of the Association for the Advancement of Behavior Therapy. Washington, DC.

Hawkins, R. C., II, & Fremouw, W. J. (1984). *The binge–purge syndrome: Diagnosis, treatment and research.* New York: Springer.

Heilman, M. E., & Saruwatari, L. R. (1979). When beauty is beastly: The effects of appearance and sex on evaluations of job applicants for managerial and non-managerial jobs. *Organizational Behavior and Human Performance, 23,* 360–72.

Hood, J., Moore, T. E., & Garner, D. M. (1982). Locus of control as a measure of ineffectiveness in anorexia nervosa. *Journal of Consulting and Clinical Psychology, 50,* 3–13.

Humphrey, L. L. (1986). Family relations in bulimic-anorexic and nondistressed families. *International Journal of Eating Disorders, 5,* 223–32.

Humphrey, L. L., Apple, R. F., & Kirschenbaum, D. S. (1986). Differentiating bulimic–anorexic from normal families using interpersonal and behavioral observational systems. *Journal of Consulting and Clinical Psychology, 54,* 190–5.

Huon, G., & Brown, L. B. (1984). Psychological correlates of weight control among anorexia nervosa patients and normal girls. *British Journal of Medical Psychology, 57,* 61–6.

Johnson, C., & Flach, A. (1985). Family characteristics of 105 patients with bulimia. *American Journal of Psychiatry, 142,* 1321–4.

Johnson, C., Lewis, C., & Hagman, J. (1984). The syndrome of bulimia. *Psychiatric Clinics of North America, 7,* 247–74.

Johnson, C. L., & Connors, M. (1987). *The etiology and treatment of bulimia nervosa: A biopsychosocial perspective.* New York: Basic Books.

Johnson, C. L., Stuckey, M. R., Lewis, L. D., & Schwartz, D. M. (1982). Bulimia: A descriptive survey of 316 cases. *International Journal of Eating Disorders, 2,* 3–16.

Joseph, A., Wood, J. K., & Goldberg, S. C. (1982). Determining populations at risk for developing anorexia nervosa based on selection of college major. *Psychiatry Research, 7,* 53–8.

Katzman, M. A., & Wolchik, S. A. (1984). Bulimia and binge eating in college women: A comparison of personality and behavioral characteristics. *Journal of Consulting and Clinical Psychology, 52,* 423–8.

Lakoff, R. T., & Scherr, R. L. (1984). *Face value: The politics of beauty.* London: Routledge & Kegan Paul.

Lamb, M. E. (1976). *The role of father in child development.* New York: Wiley.

Leon, G. R., Carroll, K., Chernyk, B., & Finn, S. (1985a). Binge eating and associated habit patterns within college student and identified bulimic populations. *International Journal of Eating Disorders, 4,* 43–57.

Leon, G. R., Lucas, A. R., Colligan, R. C., Ferdinande, R. J., & Kamp, J. (1985b). Sexual, body-image, and personality attitudes in anorexia nervosa. *Journal of Abnormal Child Psychology, 13,* 245–58.

Mellin, L. M., Scully, S., & Irving, C. E. (1986). *Disordered eating characteristics in preadolescent girls.* Paper presented at the annual meeting of the American Dietetic Association, Las Vegas.

Metropolitan Life Foundation (1983). *Statistical Bulletin, 64,* 2–9.

Miller, J. B. (1976). *Toward a new psychology of women.* Boston: Beacon.

Minuchin, S., Rosman, B. L., & Baker, L. (1978). *Psychosomatic families: Anorexia nervosa in context.* Cambridge, MA: Harvard University Press.

Mitchell, J. E., Hatsukami, D., Pyle, R. L., Eckert, E. D., & Soll, E. (1987). Late onset bulimia. *Comprehensive Psychiatry, 28,* 323–8.

Mizes, S. (1985). Bulimia: A review of its symptomatology and treatment. *Advances in Behavior Research and Therapy, 7,* 91–142.

Mori, D., Chaiken, S., & Pliner, P. (1987). "Eating lightly" and the self-presentation of femininity. *Journal of Personality and Social Psychology, 53,* 693–702.

Nielsen, A. C. (1979). *Who is dieting and why?* Chicago: A. C. Nielsen Company.

Ordman, A. M., & Kirschenbaum, D. S. (1985). Cognitive-behavioral therapy for bulimia: An initial outcome study. *Journal of Consulting and Clinical Psychology, 53,* 305–13.

Orleans, C. T., & Barnett, L. R. (1984). Bulimarexia: Guidelines for behavioral assessment and treatment. In R. C. Hawkins II, W. J. Fremouw, & P. F. Clement (Eds.), *The binge–purge syndrome.* New York: Springer.

Peskin, H. (1973). Influence of the developmental schedule of puberty on learning and ego functioning. *Journal of Youth and Adolescence, 2,* 273–90.

Polivy, J., & Herman, C. P. (1985). Dieting and binging: A causal analysis. *American Psychologist, 40,* 193–201.

Polivy, J., & Herman, C. P. (1987). Diagnosis and treatment of normal eating. *Journal of Consulting and Clinical Psychology, 55,* 635–44.

Pyle, R. L. (1985). The epidemiology of eating disorders. *Pediatrician, 12,* 102–9.

Pyle, R., Halvorson, P., Neuman, P., & Mitchell, J. (1986). The increasing prevalence of bulimia in freshman college students. *International Journal of Eating Disorders, 5,* 631–47.

Rodin, J., Silberstein, L. R., & Striegel-Moore, R. H. (1985). Women and weight: A normative discontent. In T. B. Sonderegger (Eds.), *Nebraska symposium on motivation. Vol. 32: Psychology and gender* (pp. 267–307). Lincoln: University of Nebraska Press.

Rosenbaum, M. (1979). The changing body image of the adolescent girl. In M. Sugar (Ed.), *Female adolescent development* (pp. 234–52). New York: Brunner/Mazel.

Rudofsky, B. (1971). *The unfashionable human body.* New York: Doubleday.

Schwartz, D. M., Thompson, M. G., & Johnson, C. L. (1981). Anorexia nervosa and bulimia: The socio-cultural context. *International Journal of Eating Disorders, 1,* 20–36.

Scott, D. W. (1986) Anorexia nervosa: A review of possible genetic factors. *International Journal of Eating Disorders, 5,* 1–20.

Selvini-Palazzoli, M. (1978). *Self-starvation: From individuation to family therapy in the treatment of anorexia nervosa.* New York: Aronson.

Shatford, L. A., & Evans, D. R. (1986). Bulimia as a manifestation of the stress process: A LISREL causal modeling analysis. *International Journal of Eating Disorders, 5,* 451–73.

Silberstein, L. R., Striegel-Moore, R. H., Timko, C., & Rodin, J. (1988). Behavioral and psychological implications of body image dissatisfaction: Do men and women differ? *Sex Roles, 19,* 219–32.

Silverstein, B., Perdue, L., Peterson, B., Vogel, L., & Fantini, D. (1986a). Possible causes of the thin standard of bodily attractiveness for women. *International Journal of Eating Disorders, 5,* 907–16.

Silverstein, B., Peterson, B., & Perdue, L. (1986b). Some correlates of the thin standard of bodily attractiveness for women. *International Journal of Eating Disorders, 5,* 895–905.

Simmons, R. G., Blyth, D. A., & McKinney, K. L. (1983). The social and psychological effects of puberty on white females. In J. Brooks-Gunn & A. C. Petersen (Eds.), *Girls at puberty* (pp. 229–78). New York: Plenum Press.

Spence, J. T. (1985). Gender identity and its implications for the concept of masculinity and femininity. In T. B. Sonderegger (Ed.), *Nebraska symposium on motivation. Vol. 32: Psychology and gender* (pp. 59–95). Lincoln: University of Nebraska Press.

Squire, S. (1983). *The slender balance: Causes and cures for bulimia, anorexia, and the weight-loss/weight-gain seesaw.* New York: Putnam.

Steele, C. I. (1980). Weight loss among teenage girls: An adolescent crisis. *Adolescence, 15,* 823–9.

Steinem, G. (1983). *Outrageous acts and everyday rebellions.* New York: Holt, Rinehart, & Winston.

Steiner-Adair, K. (1986). The body politic: Normal female adolescent development and the development of eating disorders. *Journal of the American Academy of Psychoanalysis, 14,* 95–114.

Striegel-Moore, R. H., McAvay, G., & Rodin, J. (1986a). Psychological and behavioral correlates of feeling fat in women. *International Journal of Eating Disorders, 5,* 935–47.

Striegel-Moore, R. H., Silberstein, L. R., Grunberg, N., & Rodin, J. (1989). *The relationship between achievement orientation and disordered eating among female college students.* Manuscript submitted for publication.

Striegel-Moore, R. H., Silberstein, L. R., & Rodin, J. (1986b). Toward an understanding of risk factors for bulimia. *American Psychologist, 41,* 246–63.

Striegel-Moore, R. H., Silberstein, L. R., & Rodin, J. (1989). *Attitudes toward attractiveness in bulimic and control women.* Unpublished manuscript, Yale University.

Striegel-Moore, R. H., Tucker, N., & Hsu, J. (in press). Body image dissatisfaction and disordered eating in lesbian college students. *International Journal of Eating Disorders.*

Strober, M. (1981). The significance of bulimia in juvenile anorexia nervosa: An exploration of possible etiological factors. *International Journal of Eating Disorders, 1,* 28–43.

Strober, M., Morrell, W., Burroughs, J., Salkin, B., & Jacobs, C. (1985). A controlled family study of anorexia nervosa. *Journal of Psychiatric Research, 19,* 239–46.

Strober, M., Salkin, B., Burroughs, J., & Morrell, W. (1982). Validity of the bulimia-restrictor distinction in anorexia nervosa. *Journal of Nervous and Mental Disease, 170,* 345–51.

Stunkard, A. J., Sorensen, T. I. A., Hanis, C., Teasdale, T. W., Cakraborty, R., Schull, W. J., & Schulsinger, F. (1986). An adoption study of human obesity. *New England Journal of Medicine, 314,* 193–8.

Thoman, E. B. (1980). Disruption and asynchrony in early parent–infant interaction. In D. B. Sawin, R. C. Hawkins, L. O. Walker, & J. H. Penticuff (Eds.), *Exceptional infant: Psychosocial risk in infant–environment transactions* (Vol. 4, pp. 91–119). New York: Brunner/Mazel.

Timko, C., Striegel-Moore, R. H., Silberstein, L. R., & Rodin, J. (1987). Femininity/masculinity and disordered eating in women: How are they related? *International Journal of Eating Disorders, 6,* 701–12.

Tobin-Richards, M. H., Boxer, A. M., & Petersen, A. C. (1983). The psychological significance of pubertal change. Sex differences in perceptions of self during early adolescence. In J. Brooks-Gunn & A. C. Petersen (Eds.), *Girls at puberty* (pp. 127–54). New York: Plenum Press.

Unger, R. K. (1985). Personal appearance and social control. In M. Safir, M. Mednick, I. Dafna, & J. Bernard (Eds.), *Woman's worlds: From the new scholarship* (pp. 142–51). New York: Praeger.

Vanfraechem, J. H. P., & Vanfraechem-Raway, R. (1978). The influence of training upon physiological and psychological parameters in young athletes. *Journal of Sports Medicine, 18,* 175–82.

Verbrugge, L. (1983). Multiple roles and physical health of women and men. *Journal of Health and Social Behavior, 24,* 16–30.

Wallach, J. D., & Lowenkopf, E. L. (1984). Five bulimic women. MMPI, Rorschach, and TAT characteristics. *International Journal of Eating Disorders, 3,* 53–66.

Williamson, D. A., Kelley, M. L., Davis, C. J., Ruggiero, L., & Blouin, D. C. (1985). Psychopathology of eating disorders: A controlled comparison of bulimic, obese, and normal subjects. *Journal of Consulting and Clinical Psychology, 53,* 161–6.

Wooley, S. C., & Kearney-Cooke, A. (1986). Intensive treatment of bulimia and body-image disturbance. In K. D. Brownell & J. P. Foreyt (Eds.), *Handbook of eating disorders* (pp. 476–502). New York: Basic Books.

Wooley, S. C., & Wooley, O. W. (1981). Overeating as substance abuse. *Advances in Substance Abuse, 2,* 41–67.

Wooley, S. C., & Wooley, O. W. (1982). The Beverly Hills eating disorder: The mass marketing of anorexia nervosa. *International Journal of Eating Disorders, 1,* 57–69.

Wooley, S. C., & Wooley, O. W. (1985). Intensive outpatient and residential treatment for bulimia. In D. M. Garner & P. E. Garfinkel (Eds.), *Handbook of psychotherapy for anorexia nervosa and bulimia* (pp. 391–430). New York: Guilford Press.

Ziolko, H. U. (1985). Bulimie. *Fortschritte der Neurologischen Psychiatrie, 53,* 231–57.

17   Protected or vulnerable: the challenges of AIDS to developmental psychopathology

Jon Rolf and Jeannette Johnson

The acquired immunodeficiency syndrome (AIDS) plague is truly pandemic and spreading rapidly. It will challenge the coping and adaptive processes of typical and atypical persons at all stages of development, but especially those persons entering adolescence and young adulthood. The AIDS epidemic will cause adapting individuals to significantly alter their timing and experiencing of normative life choices, producing extremes not seen in developed countries since the world wars and the Great Depression. The epidemic's relevance to developmental psychopathology is clear, because studying developmental risk and protective processes during normative and nonnormative stressful life transitions is this discipline's core research strategy.

Developmental psychopathology as an emerging field has been defined and described in various ways in this volume. There is agreement that it should combine the methods and perspectives of clinical and normal developmental research in order for its practitioners to understand adaptation during development over the life span. The criteria for subject selection in order to demonstrate risk and protection differ, as would be expected for an interdisciplinary field. Typically, subjects have been selected for study on the basis of their possession of personal (e.g., biological or behavioral) attributes or exposure to contextual (e.g., family, peer group, and community) factors hypothesized to affect adaptation positively or negatively. For developmental psychopathologists, the AIDS epidemic will be a time for intensive efforts with new descriptive research, but it must also be a time for commitment to leading preventive intervention efforts. This chapter outlines how the developmental psychopathology research variables involving risk, vulnerability, and protection can be applied to the AIDS challenge and adapted for lifesaving preventive interventions.

The AIDS challenge

AIDS is a lethal disease. Since its discovery in 1981, it has become epidemic around the world. AIDS is caused by a retrovirus, human immunodeficiency virus (HIV-1), which is transmitted sexually and by other direct exchanges of body fluids containing infected cells. The U.S. Public Health Service estimates that virtually all persons infected with HIV will become mortally ill. Some 20–35% of those infected will develop full-blown AIDS within 5 to 7 years; most of these will become progressively demented. Others will develop AIDS-related complex (ARC) and experience significant health problems, eventually resulting in death. The World Health Organization (WHO) is attempting to coordinate the reporting of incidence and prevalence statistics. Not surprisingly, the reports thus far have been biased by political considerations and limited by the epidemiological research capacities of the various countries. For example, the United States and Canada are reporting the most cases, whereas the Eastern Bloc countries are just beginning to report some cases. No country is certain of the exact incidence, but the numbers of HIV-infected persons will be enormous worldwide.

The rate of spread of AIDS has been staggering in some areas. In the United States, the Centers for Disease Control estimate that approximately 270,000 Americans will have died or will be dying of AIDS by 1991; others estimate mortality at that time to be closer to 600,000 (Finkbeiner, Hancock, & Schneider, 1986). In April 1989 there were approximately 85,000 confirmed U.S. AIDS cases, with an additional 20 to 30 times as many asymptomatic carriers of the AIDS virus. Most of these early cases in the United States have occurred among members of high-risk groups (homosexual and bisexual men, intravenous drug users, and hemophiliacs), but it has begun to spread to the general population. In some regions of Africa the HIV contagion is more advanced, with millions of people in the general population infected, and up to half of the population of reproductive age in some localities estimated to be capable of transmitting the virus. Unfortunately, those infected with the virus usually show no symptoms, nor are they aware that they are agents by which the infection may be spread. Consequently, some regions in Africa are facing the loss of a generation of young people due to AIDS, and other regions of the world may face a similar catastrophe unless effective prevention programs are undertaken.

Research on AIDS is advancing on several fronts, with the majority of studies involving virology and epidemiology (Liskin, Blackburn, & Maier, 1986). In the forefront are studies that strive to detect and describe the characteristics of the virus itself (Chervin, Sloane, Gordon, & Gold, 1986; MacDonald, 1986), epidemiological studies of the syndrome (Hopkins, 1986; Kaplan et al., 1985; Peterman, Drotman, & Curran, 1985; Sander, 1986; WHO, 1984), studies on ARC and the diseases associated with advanced HIV infections (Institute of Medicine & National Academy of Sciences, 1986), and identification of antiviral treatments (Dowdle, 1986). To date there have been only initial reports of preventive interventions, and these have appropriately been directed at selected target groups who are at very high risk, such as homosexual men with many partners (Arno, 1986; Goulden, Todd, Hay, & Dykes, 1984; Ross, 1985; Van Druten et al., 1986).

By 1987 there had been little research on the mental health aspects of AIDS in the general population. What research has been done has been directed toward AIDS victims and their families and intimate friends. Much of the initial work, much of it supported by grants from the National Institute of Mental Health (NIMH), tended to focus on those victims within high-risk groups (such as male homosexuals) who have been the first to suffer the tragic consequences of the disease. The affective and cognitive consequences of AIDS, including shock, grief, and anger (often combined with expression of a revenge motive), have been reported (Goulden et al., 1984; NIMH, 1986). Studying the emotional consequences among those testing positive for HIV has also begun to be explored. Providers of mental health services and clinical researchers have also been interested in the affective responses and possible disruptions of normal functioning in family members and the loss of natural support groups for AIDS victims. Clearly, the stigma associated with being an AIDS victim, an AIDS virus carrier, or a member of such a person's family should be studied as a potent risk factor for mental disorders.

Developmental psychopathology research is needed to gather data on developmental and contextual variables that will influence the mental health consequences of the AIDS epidemic and to assess the effectiveness of preventive interventions for AIDS. By the end of 1987 there had been no published developmental psychopathological studies of the processes by which persons at risk for AIDS may have rendered themselves more vulnerable or more protected from HIV infection or the psychological disorders associated with anxiety about infection. In 1988 the U.S. Public Health Service research support institutes began to encourage grant proposals in this area. Our research group at Johns Hopkins responded to an NIMH/NICHD request for proposals on developmental aspects of behavioral vulnerability to HIV infection. Beginning in the fall of 1988, NIMH began funding our 4-year project called "HIV in Street Youth: Epidemiology and Prevention" (Halsey et al., 1988). It will be conducted in Belo Horizonte, Brazil, and in Baltimore, Maryland, and will attempt to identify and reinforce protective processes among homeless children who have been compelled by family and economic circumstances to resort to prostitution for survival.

AIDS and developmental psychopathology variables

Because adaptation to the AIDS threat involves complex processes resulting from the interplay of personal and environmental factors, prospective research will require that some of the risk and protective variables be both initially identifiable and subsequently observable over time. In designing AIDS developmental psychopathology research programs, one can begin with the specification of individual factors (including biological, psychological, and social factors), as well as environmental contextual factors, that are believed to contribute to risk dosage and to vulnerability and protective processes.

For the purposes of this chapter, we have defined two complementary sets of variables, *factors* and *processes,* that lead to risk for or protection from an AIDS-related illness or maladaptation. *Risk factors* are those variables that have proven or presumed effects that can directly increase the likelihood of a maladapted outcome. Conversely, *protective factors* are those that have proven or presumed effects that directly increase the probability of adaptive or "non-bad" outcomes. Our use of these terms differs somewhat from that of Rutter (chapter 9, this volume), who seems to reserve "protective variables" for association only with interactive processes and mechanisms, not with factors with direct protective effects. As we shall show, AIDS protective factors probably exist. We are in agreement, however, with Rutter's definitions of process variables. *Vulnerability processes* are defined as interactive operations that enhance the potency of a given risk dosage for an individual and thus increase the likelihood of the expression of a bad outcome. The *protective processes* are defined as interactive operations that diminish risk effects and thus reduce the probability of bad outcomes. Thus, protective processes enhance one's chances for positive adaptation and a good outcome.

Although Rutter (chapter 9, this volume) prefers not to use the concept of protective factors, it seems limiting for theoretical causal model building to accept the possibility of direct risk variables without also accepting the possibility of factors providing direct protection. Certainly, one usually can make a case for most relevant causal paths of risk and protection that involve moderator processes. For example, medication that prevents the progression from HIV virus contact to seropositivity (or from seropositivity to the expression of ARC or AIDS) should qualify as a protective factor. How the protective factor (medicine) interacts with the individual's biological and behavioral attributes will, of course, also become part of the protective and vulnerability processes. However, it seems extreme to view the agent that produces disease resistance as a "process" variable, while viewing the agent that causes the disease as a singular "factor" variable.

With respect to AIDS, it will be important for developmental psychopathologists to consider how both risk and protective factors can be studied as independent and dependent variables making up the biological, psychological, and social processes by which individuals develop adaptively and maladaptively for certain periods of time in certain contexts. In the paragraphs that follow, we will consider these variables and how they may be incorporated into descriptive and preventive intervention research.

Risk factors for AIDS

The primary direct risk for AIDS is exposure to the HIV-1 virus. Other factors can increase the risk for actual infection by placing the virus in hospitable environments (sexual secretions and blood) from which it may be transmitted to others. Another type of risk factor for AIDS involves the means by which the virus contacts a potential host. The risk for infection is increased when the donor's HIV-positive body fluid contacts a recipient whose internal immune processes cannot be sufficiently protective. Such is the case when HIV is introduced into the body through intravenous injection, prenatal exposure (as with a fetus carried by an HIV-positive mother), or sexual behavior involving multiple exposures and physical trauma (as is the case with anal intercourse among homosexual men) (Darrow et al., 1987).

Many of the risks for AIDS can be viewed as variables interacting with other health, behavior, and contextual variables. For example, the potential host's state of health may well be either a risk or protective variable. An illness may produce lesions that permit direct access by HIV (as would be the case with most sexually transmitted diseases), or an illness may require therapeutic injections or transfusions, with some potential for transmitting HIV. A healthy person, of course, would not require HIV-risking intrusive medical treatment nor have skin lesions that would seroconvert with a single HIV contact.

Individual variables implicated in vulnerability

Risk and protection from the biological and psychological dangers of AIDS involve a variety of behaviors. Therefore, individual-difference variables generally implicated in vulnerability processes for developmental disorders and psychopathology are important to examine in regard to AIDS. These variables include gender, age, developmental stage, personality, cognitive abilities, and affective attributes.

Gender

There are important sex differences in AIDS incidence rates. In early 1987 in the United States, eight times as many men as women had AIDS, but the gender ratio was more nearly equal in Africa. In large part, this fact probably reflects the differences in rates of certain social behaviors, disorders of psychosocial adaptation, and health problems that are commonly observed between girls and boys or men and women. For example, boys outnumber girls in referrals for behavioral and adjustment problems until puberty; after puberty, these overall sex differences are much reduced. Similarly, there are many differences in rates of illness and injuries between the sexes as a function of biological, behavioral, and cultural role differences. Males tend to engage in more rough-and-tumble play and injury-risking activities, including physical aggression with peers. Males also engage at earlier ages in more health-compromising behaviors outside the home, such as experimentation with drugs and alcohol.

Whereas gender-related differences in health-risking behaviors and social roles are implicated in the current gender difference related to the degree of risk for AIDS, we know of no gender difference in resistance to HIV once it gets into the bloodstream. Thus, the sexes may well be equally vulnerable to infection via transfusion of HIV-positive blood or an HIV-contaminated hypodermic needle. In economically developed countries, where blood is screened and the needles used in therapeutic injection of medicines are adequately sterilized, the observed HIV infection rates will show gender differences associated with social roles and health-risking behaviors. Unfortunately for epidemiologists, most gender-related risk factors co-occur and interact. For example, in the United States up to 1987, the group at highest risk for HIV infection was intravenous drug users, among whom there are more males than females. Nevertheless, females associated with the drug culture are at increased risk for AIDS because of their sexual contacts. Female intravenous drug users often are prostitutes, and many females who do not use drugs work as prostitutes to help support the intravenous drug habits of their mates. Thus, within the drug culture, men may be more at risk for HIV infection through shared needles (especially so with cocaine addicts), but the multiple sexual contacts of their mates diminish the gender difference in HIV infection over time.

Women have a unique role in the vertical transmission of the AIDS virus. About half of the offspring of women with HIV infection will become HIV-positive and will die of AIDS during the first year of life. Unfortunately, HIV-seropositive women can be as fertile as non-HIV-infected women for many years (Boulos et al., 1987). Those in the attending obstetrical staff are also placed at risk, as they are never entirely safe from infection by the maternal blood or amniotic fluid of an HIV-positive mother. In the United States, "vertical transmission" (i.e., perinatal) AIDS cases have occurred overwhelmingly among women associated with the intravenous drug culture. More depressing is that about 80% of these pediatric AIDS victims are born to black and Hispanic women, a statistic reflecting the overrepresentation of these minorities within the drug culture. Thus, sex differences in (a) drug use patterns, (b) affiliations with the drug culture, (c) reproductive function, and (d) occupational roles are all involved in the levels of risk for AIDS and will need to be taken into account in preventive intervention programs.

Gender differences in risks for sexual transmission of the HIV virus will be important to researchers interested in describing the development of psychopathology in association with the AIDS threat. As mentioned previously, HIV is transmittable through semen and other sexual secretions containing live cells secreted during intercourse. Recipients of semen are seemingly more at risk, and the risk is roughly proportional to the dose of HIV-infected cells received, the number of sexual interactions with HIV-positive donors, and the presence of lesions in or on sexual organs.

In many cultures there are important differences in the initiation, type, and circumstances of sexual behavior. On average, men (especially homosexual men in the United States) are more likely than women to strive to enhance their self-images through sexual encounters with multiple partners. Men more than women also tend to frequent prostitutes or engage in other promiscuous activity with persons who are not prostitutes (e.g., swingers, bisexuals, and gays). Behaviors during sex that increase the likelihood of placing HIV-infected cells in proximity to the recipient's circulatory system (e.g., anal intercourse combined with the use of inhalants that raise blood pressure and rupture capillaries) are associated with significantly increased risks. The sexual behavior risks associated with seroconversion among homosexual men have recently been described in a longitudinal study of 785 randomly selected homosexual men who had participated in a 1979–80 hepatitis B survey in San Francisco (Darrow et al., 1987). That study could not identify any sexual behavior that appeared to be a protective factor.

Age and developmental stage

There are clearly different degrees of risk for HIV infection associated with age and stage of development. At lower risk are persons who are either too old or too young for sexual activity or who are protected because of cultural norms that proscribe sexual activity. The great majority of pediatric AIDS patients in the United States were infected prenatally or perinatally. Prevention of these cases will depend in large part on prevention of HIV infection among those who could potentially be parents. Particularly in need of preventive intervention efforts are adolescents and young adults who are in the process of developing a sexual identity and intimacy skills and those children and youths who must use sex as a means to survive on the streets. For example, in Belo Horizonte, Brazil, where street youth as young as age 7 are commonplace, the HIV seropositive rate was estimated to be about 9% in early 1988 (Halsey et al., 1988).

Adolescents and young adults are two groups within the general population that are at increasing biological and psychological risk for AIDS. This is because, as a function of a normative developmental expression of maturation and social behavior, these young people will be motivated to engage in sexual activity, perhaps with a number of new partners, and in other behaviors (e.g., experimenting with illicit drugs) that will magnify their risk for HIV exposure (Black, 1986; Cowell, 1986; Dembo & Lundell, 1979; Keeling, 1986; Liskin et al., 1986; Tauer, 1983). Further, psychological casualties will increase as youths are made more aware of the AIDS threat by the communications media and are touched by the occurrence of an AIDS or ARC case within their families and/or social networks.

Psychological factors

The cognitive and affective traits of developing individuals will certainly be involved in the degree of successful adaptation to the AIDS threat. Important among the research questions are (a) how one's developmental stage is related to increased psychological vulnerability, (b) how cognitive development moderates anxiety resulting from knowledge gained about one's personal risk status and peer group risk status, and (c) the effects of delusional (but perhaps emotionally self-protective) denial of this risk by acting on one's belief of invulnerability to the AIDS virus.

From the opposite perspective, there are also questions about how AIDS information and the fear of AIDS may influence mental development. For example, what are the relationships between normative developmental challenges and basic adaptive mechanisms involving psychological variables such as self-esteem, locus of control, efficacy beliefs, and personality traits? Presented next are brief discussions of how these psychological variables may be studied as contributors to vulnerability and protective processes.

Vulnerability processes at the level of the individual

Cognitive processes

The basic tenet of prevention efforts from the perspective of health education is that the risk for exposure to HIV should be proportional to ignorance of the facts concerning infection and to deficiencies in causal reasoning. However, now that the facts about AIDS are becoming well disseminated through public health advertising campaigns, there remain individual differences in reasoning about personal risks and consequences that will influence an individual's vulnerability. Chief among these are poor planning skills and a system of causal beliefs that is characterized by an excessively external locus of control and a deficiency of self-efficacy beliefs.

Poor planners may understand consequences and contingencies, but often they fail to prepare for them or fail to avoid situations in which absence of preparation will increase the chances of negative outcomes. With respect to AIDS, poor planners who indulge in opportunistic sex with many partners will need to be overtrained in "last ditch" preparedness habits. They will need to carry condoms everywhere, regardless of the expected social situation. Their intimate friends could also be recruited to monitor these poor planners in high-risk situations, as, for example, when going to places where contact with sexual partners is likely (e.g., parties, singles bars).

An external locus of control and externality of causal reasoning in the areas of health and illness can increase vulnerability to AIDS. At its simplest, belief in fate or in God as the primary determinant of who gets AIDS may diminish the motivation to take protective measures. Different levels of attributional reasoning about the transmission of AIDS will be negatively affected by "response independence," which is associated with high external scores on locus-of-control tasks. Response independence is characterized by the belief that the outcome is independent of one's behavior. For some hostile environments in which rapid-onset diseases are prevalent and health services are relatively impotent, externality and response independence beliefs may even influence a nation's health policies. For example, in some regions of Africa, the policy has been not to inform infected persons or spouses of seropositivity, because "nothing can be done," and such news would be depressing. In our survey of Baltimore college freshmen (Rolf, Mamon, Baldwin, & Chandra, 1988b; Rolf et al., 1988c), we found somewhat weak correlations between our health locus-of-control measure and measures of AIDS-related worry and personal and peer risk perceptions. However, the data suggest that those with a more external locus of control may be more prone to inaccurate risk perceptions and lower levels of worry about AIDS. More work is needed to assess the utility of the locus-of-control scale in identifying more vulnerable subgroups within the general population.

Negative self-efficacy beliefs have also been shown to be important barriers to effective coping with health problems such as cancer, sexually transmitted diseases, and coronary disease. Self-efficacy beliefs are proving to be relevant to AIDS vulnerability, as they determine an individual's efforts to maintain health and prevent illness. Self-efficacy beliefs concerning health are modifiable, as has been shown by studies using Bandura's social learning theory techniques (Bandura, 1977). Self-efficacy concepts are being applied to AIDS preventive education programs (Rolf, Ewart, Mamon, Joffe, & Radius, 1987). In the aforementioned study of college freshmen, we developed a preliminary scale for perceived self-efficacy regarding condom use in various scenarios and other AIDS protective behaviors (e.g., avoiding partners who have had many partners). The initial scaling properties were fairly robust (standardized-item Cronbach alpha = 0.80; two factors identified); however, as with the health locus of control, we found only weak correlations with measures of AIDS worry and risk perceptions.

Depressive affect

Beliefs concerning personal helplessness, worthlessness, or self-blame for failures may also be involved in vulnerability to AIDS-related anxiety and depressive disorders. Seligman's reformulated theory of learned helplessness as a cause of depression seems particularly relevant (Seligman et al., 1984). Persons at high risk for depression, characterized by an internal stable, global causal attribution for bad events, should be especially prone to feelings of helplessness related to the avoidance of AIDS or the chances of finding a compatible HIV-free mate. Prospective studies of persons who initially differ in their tendencies for negative causal attributions and then confront the challenges of the AIDS plague may provide developmental psychopathology researchers with an important test of Seligman's model.

Invulnerability beliefs

In contrast to helplessness and hopelessness, excessive denial of personal risk is a cognitive process that should contribute to personal vulnerability to HIV risk, but not necessarily to mental distress. This denial, which was rather pervasive at the onset of the AIDS epidemic, involves identifying oneself with a no-risk group. Many heterosexuals have denied the possibility that AIDS will infect nonhomosexuals or that there are any risks associated with conventional sex practices. An all too common expression of personal invincibility is the belief that "none of my friends have it because they're clean and not gay. Therefore, I don't need to protect myself." One hears this repeatedly from adolescents who are being warned about AIDS (Haffner, 1987). For these typically very healthy, high-energy youths, death from illness is virtually unthinkable. In our survey of detained male juvenile delinquents in Baltimore (Rolf et al., 1988d), we found that these youths' self-perceptions of health status typically were quite positive, and their knowledge levels regarding the cause and transmission of AIDS were high. Nonetheless, these youths were at substantial behavioral and attitudinal risk for HIV infection. In spite of considerable self-reports of intravenous drug abuse, poor contraceptive behavior, and AIDS-risking sexual contacts, they reported low levels of AIDS-related worry and did not perceive themselves or their peers to be at risk for AIDS. In fact, there was a disturbing tendency for those delinquents at higher behavioral risk to see themselves at low risk for HIV infection.

As we shall point out later in our discussion of preventive interventions, youths must acquire a sufficient dose of reality-based fear to counter their denial and sense of excessive optimism. On the other hand, too much prevention-program-induced fear, without compensatory messages advocating developmentally appropriate risk-reduction skills, may actually prove counterproductive. This is a critical concern to address in order to avoid increasing the vulnerability of deniers by precipitating avoidance of anxiety-producing information or by increasing their denial tendencies.

Personality

Personality variables are involved in behavioral tendencies and should be considered in conjunction with developmental psychopathology studies of vulnerability to AIDS. Among these are self-concepts and clusters of tendencies for risk-enhancing behaviors, including impulsiveness, aggressiveness, emotional lability, dependence, negative self-concepts, and ineptness in social skills. Because AIDS will primarily be transmitted either sexually or by intravenous drug use for the general population in developed countries, one's choices of friends and the contexts in which risky social and sexual behavior can be monitored are important. Personality traits and self-concepts that lead to affiliation with high-risk social groups will be important to vulnerability processes. Also, youths prone to impulsive expression of sexual and affective urges will be especially vulnerable. For example, angry and aggressive delinquents who act out with intentional contempt for the conventional rules of health-promoting behavior will be extremely vulnerable to HIV infection. In our initial studies of incarcerated delinquent males (Rolf et al., 1988d), 53% admitted that they were "worried a lot" about getting AIDS, whereas only 24% stated that their friends were worried about getting AIDS. This level of peer worry assessment was much lower than was found in our sample of college freshmen (Rolf et al., 1988b,c), and it may reflect the generally more health-risking life-style of the delinquents' peer groups, as compared with the college students' peer groups. Many of these delinquent youths run away from home and adult supervision to engage in aggressive, sexual, and other risky behaviors in environments harboring society's lower classes and drug culture. For example, in our delinquent youth sample (Rolf et al., 1988d), large percentages were daily substance users; 5.4% reported sharing intravenous drug works, and 14.4% reported having sex with an intravenous drug user. Further, delinquents with more HIV-risking sexual contacts were significantly more likely to precede sex with alcohol or drug use.

Traits contributing to low self-esteem make one vulnerable to excessive dependence on others' approval. One's choice of peers or the availability of health-promoting mentors from whom to seek support may determine whether low self-esteem contributes to vulnerability or protection.

Protective processes at the level of the individual

Protection from nonsexual HIV infection should be achievable. Persons in need of transfusions must accept only donors who have been screened for HIV. When screening is not possible, only donors with verifiable (or very credible) low-risk histories should be used. Transfusion and intravenous drug injection equipment can be made safe from HIV infection (e.g., as has been shown by Dutch programs providing needle exchanges and U.S. programs teaching easy-to-do chlorine baths for cleaning needles). Evidence is mounting that addicts who use drugs with long latencies between injections (e.g., heroin) are more modifiable in their intravenous drug abuse behavior.

Protection from sexual transmission is more complicated, even though the same protective cognitive and affective processes (self-efficacy, etc.) may apply. Developmental issues may also be more important. Persons who are or are about to be sexually active must know how to adapt their sexual behaviors to the AIDS risks, while at the same time fulfilling their developmental tasks of intimate social relations with peers, mate selection, or reproduction in a new family context.

On the basis of our discussion of processes implicated in vulnerability to AIDS and AIDS-related mental disorders we can list some potential protective processes: good foresight and planning for avoidance of risk dosage, an internal locus of control and positive self-efficacy beliefs, and positive beliefs concerning the nonglobality of the causes of bad life events, coupled with modest use of denial of blame for personal failures in order to preserve self-esteem. These variables must be included when planning potent and practical behavioral AIDS-prevention programs.

A reduction in task demands is one of Rutter's protective processes discussed in conjunction with the benefits of social support for highly stressed individuals (chapter 9, this volume). Peer groups, families, and even a generational cohort may be mobilized to provide social support via reductions in performance standards in developmental tasks and challenges. For example, the sexual revolution in the United States and other Western countries in the 1960s encouraged experimentation, multiple partners, and a reduction in the disparity between dual standards of sexuality for men and women. The 1970s and 1980s have seen increased numbers of sexually active single women who are delaying marriage and childbearing until their third or fourth decade. Also, both men and women are dissolving marriages and forming new ones to the point that in the United States, children are now more likely to experience growing up in families with a stepparent and/or a single parent than to experience growing up with both biological parents. It seems reasonable to expect that new norms of premarital sexual experience will develop to cope with the AIDS threat: (a) there may be less emphasis on the social desirability of advertising or overtly expressing sexuality. (b) The criteria for "modern" successful adaptation may come to involve fewer short-term relationships, with one or two longer-term monogamous relationships prior to marriage and childrearing. (c) Middle-age adults may remain contented with their current spouses and may not seek further self-actualization through divorce, even though they are financially capable of independent living.

Among youths, the developmental challenge to achieve socially acceptable sexual competence may also be modified. Among unmarried sexually active women ages 15–19, 27% have never used any method of birth control, 39% have used one method inconsistently, and 34% have used one method consistently (Zelnick & Kantner, 1980). In the 1980s in the United States by age 17 about half of male and female adolescents have had sexual intercourse (Chilman, 1980). This norm may be temporally shifted to a later age. Moreover, the proportion of teenagers having sex with older partners must be diminished. It has been estimated that 70% of births to teenage mothers are fathered by men age 20 or older (Haffner, 1987). These older men are likely to have had more sexual partners; thus, their greater risk for HIV infection serves to magnify the risk for their teenage partners.

Another unnecessarily high risk for HIV infection for teens involves sexual identification and preference. About 10% of adolescents are estimated to be homosexual or bisexual. Among these males, it is common to have intercourse with older men (usually strangers). It is also fairly common for them to "turn tricks" downtown and then return to their suburban neighborhoods in order to date girlfriends with whom they will also have sex. Further, it is estimated that there are 125,000 convicted adolescent prostitutes and 1 million runaways who support themselves by prostitution (Haffner, 1987). In a recent study of 110 runaways using a free health clinic in Los Angeles (Yates, MacKenzie, Pennbridge, & Cohen, 1988), 57% reported having sex before age 15 (19% before age 10), 26% were engaging in "survival sex" (sex for money, food, or shelter), and 34.5% had used intravenous drugs. These norms of unprotected sex *must* be changed, because sex with an HIV carrier can give a death sentence, and pregnancy for an HIV-positive woman can kill her baby within months of birth. If sexual intercourse is to occur, youths must come to believe that (a) having no protection during sex is an unthinkable assault and (b) reliance on a non-HIV-protecting method (such as birth control pills) makes one a grossly incompetent sexual partner. Adolescents must come to expect mastery of condom use through practice prior to embarking on sexual relations with their peers. They have a long way to go, as only about 15% used condoms in 1986 (Haffner, 1987). In our sample of minority college freshmen (Rolf et al., 1988b,c), about half reported using a condom during their last intercourse, but a much lower number reported that they *always* used a condom. Obviously, adapting successfully to this norm will require individual planning skills, as previously discussed.

Gaining a perception of positive alternatives to AIDS-risking behaviors will be part of the protective process among adaptive individuals and social groups. Some persons will emerge as leaders in applying the effective coping skills necessary to monitor and maintain safe sexual behavior. For many others, identification with, imitation of, and vicarious learning from positive role models will be the psychological processes with the greatest potential for preventive interventions targeting adaptive development in a world threatened by AIDS. Communications media campaigns facilitating these processes will work if they include role models of the appropriate age, gender, and subcultural affiliation to stimulate rapid behavioral changes in all relevant segments of the population. Advertising campaigns can depict the types of persons at risk (nearly everyone) and attempt to instill both identification and fear. It is important that we mobilize self-protective behaviors and avoid fostering denial and avoidance of protective behaviors. An even more potent impetus for behavioral change will be knowing someone (especially someone just like oneself) who has already contracted AIDS or had an HIV-positive test. As the epidemic spreads, this will be the most powerful motivation for ceasing risky behaviors among current high-risk groups. Many homosexuals who have known and identified with the early AIDS victims are reducing their numbers of partners and substituting lower-risk practices (e.g., mutual masturbation) for high-risk practices (e.g., unprotected anal intercourse). Ironically, for those concerned with prevention of HIV infection among adolescents, the 5- to 10-year latency period between HIV infection and the onset of AIDS (Centers for Disease Control, 1988) means that there will never be many teenage AIDS cases to provide a graphic caution to other teenagers.

In the near future, safe-sex peer models should replace sexual athletes and overachievers in the social sexual hierarchy. Already, those who have changed to lower-risk behaviors are being advertised as positive role models by the AIDS action groups, such as Baltimore's HERO (Health Education and Research Organization). Both those serving as models and those who imitate models of positive coping should gain increased self-esteem and self-efficacy. Observation of these models should also provide opportunities for vicarious learning of the positive consequences of self-protective behaviors and provide the foundation of preventive educational campaigns. With time, vicarious learning from positive models could reduce the incidence of negative sequelae (Rutter's "chain of bad events") for persons who are failing to cope. For example, HIV-negative intravenous drug users and persons who have been engaging in high-risk sexual practices but who are still HIV-free must be helped to interrupt their chain of high-risk activities.

There is another type of deadly chain to be cut. Those unlucky persons who are already HIV-positive could pass the infection on to others. Some will intentionally do so in anger, to "pay back" the human race, or to bring down even blameless others who are perceived as too advantaged with their current good health and prospects for a future. In other cases, HIV carriers may not be aware of the danger to their lovers, spouses, or future offspring. Screening of high- and low-risk persons planning to marry or to have children should be encouraged by society's leaders as a voluntary act of good citizenship and altruism.

Finally, the low-risk volunteers who will be the first subjects in AIDS vaccine trials should be accorded the honor of heroes by society. They not only will be risking their health but also will be agreeing to bear forever the AIDS stigma of HIV antibody seropositivity. These brave people deserve intensive social support to boost their protective processes against future stress-related mental disorders.

Contextual variables

Environmental contexts are of great concern when evaluating epidemiological data on AIDS or the effects of preventive intervention efforts (DiClemente, Zorn, & Temoshok, 1986; Rolf et al., 1987). Some further consideration of contexts should preface our discussion of prevention research from a developmental psychopathology perspective.

We have discussed ways in which individual-level variables, including biological, cognitive, and affective processes, will be involved in shaping the general knowledge, motives, and health-risking or -protecting practices of those persons at risk for maladaptive development in the face of the AIDS challenge. Some indication has been given of the importance of environmental contexts in which the effects of vulnerability and protective processes will be expressed. However, we wish to borrow a phrase from a Paul Simon song to call attention to a problem concerning the relativity of an individual's vulnerability to biological and mental health risks associated with the AIDS epidemic: "One man's ceiling is another man's floor." It reminds us that for youths in some developing countries with already high mortality from other infectious diseases, as well as for many youths belonging to disadvantaged and forgotten groups in more developed countries, AIDS may seem like just another threat of death, even a relatively remote threat. If one is preoccupied with survival in the face of starvation or civil strife today, one may not be able to worry much about finding an HIV-free mate a few years down the road. Even among middle-class young people in more developed countries, their relative freedom from most forms of infectious diseases makes it difficult for them to perceive their risk for AIDS. For those at low risk for HIV infection, important mental health problems could be created by excessive worry about contracting HIV and its permanent stigma, while at the same time trying to master the normative developmental challenges of increasing independence from the family, sexual maturation, and practicing intimate relationships with peers.

In developmental psychopathology research, one is interested in predicting changes in persons who are undergoing developmental transitions, especially when such individuals are changing from one type of social environment to another. Therefore, the development-in-context perspective (Bronfenbrenner & Crouter, 1982) seems particularly relevant. Furthermore, as the physical and social environments change during these transitions, the individual's perception of and reaction to the differences will also be influenced by individual-difference variables (e.g., gender, experience, and knowledge). As described previously, these individual differences may well contribute to vulnerability and protection processes.

For youth, the prime environmental contexts are the family, peer groups, and work/educational settings. The latter is worth careful consideration. Certainly, educational institutions are pervasive in our culture and are natural choices for mass-outreach educational programs to promote health and prevent disease. Therefore, it seems reasonable and probably necessary to begin our experimental education programs dealing with preventive intervention there: with children, adolescents, and young adults who are students at schools, colleges, and universities. For children and adolescents in elementary and secondary schools in the United States, the political and religious aspects of the issue have mostly blocked the start of meaningful preventive education regarding AIDS. However, in our experience, colleges and universities (Keeling, 1986) and schools serving delinquents and minority groups in high-risk environments have proved to be more accessible. In the United States the American College Health Association established a task force on AIDS in 1985 because colleges and universities represent "a population that is on behavioral grounds at risk with individuals who need to be educated for their own protection" (Keeling, 1986, p. 123).

For educational environments, a program on AIDS prevention may in fact work best when integrated with good programs on sex education. In the

United States, only 12% to 15% of schools offer "comprehensive health education," mostly in high schools. The peer group is the primary source of sex education. It is recognized that new AIDS-relevant education programs need development and evaluation to prevent the spread of sexually transmitted diseases, including AIDS (Benson, Perlman, & Sciarra, 1986; Luckhurst, 1986; Parcel, Luttman, & Flaherty-Zonis, 1985; Romanowski & Harris, 1984). However, societal barriers similar to those that are slowing AIDS prevention are also limiting the number of informative studies in the research literature on sex education. Of those studies that have been conducted concerning sex education in schools, many have focused on assessing young people's knowledge, beliefs, and attitudes toward sexually transmitted diseases and, more recently, AIDS (Arafat & Allen, 1977; Chapman, 1977; DePietro & Clark, 1984; DiClemente et al., 1986; Finkel & Finkel, 1975; Giusti & Angela, 1981; Hillard, Kitchell, Turner, Keeling, & Shank, 1984; Yacenda, 1974; Zabin, Hirsch, Smith, & Hardy, 1984). In general, these studies have revealed that several behavioral factors and beliefs, such as perceived threat, response efficacy, personal efficacy, skills attainment, and peer support, appear to be associated with adopting risk-reducing behaviors (Becker, 1974; Bennett & Dickinson, 1980; Jordheim, 1975; Lawrance & McLeroy, 1986; Orr & Vickery, 1983; Thompson & Spanier, 1978). Consequently, our research team at Johns Hopkins University School of Hygiene and Public Health has initiated pilot research projects on preventive intervention at colleges (Rolf et al., 1988c) and at a school for delinquents (Rolf et al., 1988d) that combine elements of education regarding sexually transmitted diseases, discussion of normative social and sexual behaviors, preventive methods for "safe sex," and new skills for reducing anxiety when practicing new intimacy skills, all in the context of developmental and social challenges confronting the students. The data from these pilot studies are now being used to extend outward to other community environments, such as Bureau of Indian Affairs schools serving Navajo youth in the U.S. Southwest (Rolf, Alexander, Sorensen, & Armao, 1988a).

Of the educational programs on preventive intervention for AIDS that have been developed and published, many have been directed toward and run by groups in the high-risk gay population. Relevant to any proposed project are reports supporting the assumption that increased knowledge about AIDS will lead to modification of high-risk sexual behavior among some gay men, as seen by the marked drop in other sexually transmitted diseases among gay men in San Francisco and other U.S. cities (Arno, 1986; Liskin et al., 1986; Riesenberg, 1986; Romanowski & Brown, 1986; William, 1984). There have been several published reports of public health campaigns directed at alerting the general population to take self-protective measures (Cowell, 1986; DeYoung, 1986; Echenberg, 1985; Wykoff, 1986). AIDS education and preventive interventions for the general population as well as high-risk groups must soon be implemented (Check, 1985; Cowell, 1986; DeYoung, 1986; Echenberg, 1985; Henry, 1986; Mason, 1985). The key audiences, other than members of high-risk groups and their sexual partners, include young people, parents, teachers, employers, the national and local communications media, and health policy-makers. Certainly, controlled research programs are even now overdue, and evaluations of new campaigns and educational programs must be undertaken as soon as possible. Indeed, the Surgeon General of the United States (Koop, 1986) and the National Academy of Sciences Special Task Force on AIDS (Institute of Medicine & National Academy of Sciences, 1986) have urged massive mobilization of efforts to educate the public about the dangers of AIDS and the means of preventing HIV infection.

Researchers have emphasized that there are limits to the efficacy of AIDS educational programs, including advertising campaigns, because sexual behavior is so heavily mediated by psychological factors (Ross, 1985). In developing intervention strategies for reducing high-risk behavior among gay men, McKusick, Conant, and Thomas (1984) stated that a campaign via communications media will not work unless it is coordinated with support groups and systems tailored to meet the specific needs of a particular community or a particular subgroup. Such a multimethod, contextually relevant intervention plan is included in the design of our prevention projects.

Therefore, in order to develop research protocols regarding education to prevent AIDS, in the absence of a sufficient body of research information on prevention programs for AIDS, one must turn to research on other health problems that have been dealt with by public health programs and psychologically oriented interventions. Among the prime examples are smoking cessation (Flay, 1987), coronary heart disease (Ewart, Stewart, Gillilan, & Kelemen, 1986a; Ewart et al., 1986b), sexually transmitted diseases (Bennett & Dickinson, 1980; Gram, Cowen, & Deering, 1981; Jordheim, 1975), and cancer (Mamon & Zapka, 1985). Each of these areas of public health concern has a unique message for AIDS prevention researchers. Together they provide both positive clues and causes for concerns. With regard to the latter, it is surprising to see how difficult it is to change health-risking habits even when an individual is motivated by sound knowledge of the need for protective behavior and has been shown the means to accomplish it. We have also found in our AIDS surveys of delinquents and college freshmen that generally there are insignificant correlations among AIDS knowledge, past behavioral risks, current efforts to reduce risks, and intentions for future HIV risk reductions (Rolf et al., 1988b,d). Furthermore, sexually transmitted diseases such as AIDS pose difficult problems in that much of the necessary information has by custom been considered taboo and kept out of general circulation, and especially out of education programs for youth, as illustrated by the controversy over advertisements and public service announcements on the benefits of condoms for the prevention of AIDS and other sexually transmitted diseases. Therefore, educational programs in the communications media and community-based self-help organizations for prevention of AIDS must overcome some well-entrenched barriers in the culture and in local communities.

The near future

It is hoped that developmental psychopathologists will join in AIDS research and strive to find ways for youth to adapt safely and to become healthy adults. At Johns Hopkins, we have formed an interdisciplinary research team to design, implement, and evaluate the effectiveness of our proposed project's preventive interventions to educate, motivate, and reinforce self-protective attitudes and behaviors toward AIDS and other sexually transmitted diseases among adolescents and young adults in educational settings. Our Johns Hopkins research projects aim to identify factors facilitating or impeding preventive behaviors among normal and higher-risk adolescents and young adults who are beginning to be exposed to increased risk because of penetration of the HIV virus into the general population, where developmentally normative and high activity levels of nonprotected sexual behavior may lead to rapid spread of the disease. We have selected as informative study subjects (a) students in public and private colleges, (b) juvenile offenders in detention facilities in the greater Baltimore area, (c) homeless youth on the streets of Belo Horizonte, Brazil, and Baltimore, Maryland, and (d) Navajo youth living on or near reservations. The project includes (a) a survey study of the knowledge, motives, and health-risking and -protecting practices among these graduating high school seniors, college undergraduates, and juvenile offenders and (b) a controlled intervention study that includes communications media, classroom-based education programs, and intensive skill training. A third component, the dissemination study, involves securing community support for prevention, intended to increase the motivation for maintaining HIV/AIDS prevention efforts and to link our project's education strategies for preventive intervention against AIDS to existing health and educational services. We pray for resilience in coping with our difficulties in this often defeating research area.

References

Arafat, I., & Allen, D. E. (1977). Venereal disease: College students' knowledge and attitudes *Journal of Sex Research, 13,* 223–30.

Arno, P. S. (1986). The non-profit sector's response to the AIDS epidemic: Community-based services in San Francisco. *American Journal of Public Health, 76,* 1325–30.

Bandura, A. (1977). *Social learning theory.* Englewood Cliffs, NJ: Prentice-Hall.

Becker, M. H. (1974). The health belief model and personal health behavior. *Health Education Monographs, 2,* 326–508.

Bennett, S. M., & Dickinson, W. B. (1980). Student–parent rapport and parent involvement in sex, birth control, and venereal disease education. *Journal of Sex Research, 16,* 114–30.

Benson, M. D., Perlman, C., & Sciarra, J. J. (1986). Sex education in the inner city. *Journal of the American Medical Association, 255,* 43–7.

Black, J. L. (1986). AIDS: Preschool and school issues. *Journal of School Health, 56,* 93–5.

Boulos, R , Halsey, N., Holt, E., Brutus, J., Quinn, T., Boulos, L., & Boulos, C. (1987). *Two-and-one-half and five-year follow-up of HIV and HTLV-1 seropositive Haitian women.* Paper presented at the 27th ICAAA meeting, New York.

Bronfenbrenner, U., & Crouter, A. C. (1982). Work and family through time and space. In S. B. Kamerman & C. D. Hayes (Eds.), *Families that work: Children in a changing world*. Washington, DC: National Academy Press.

Centers for Disease Control (1988). Fewer AIDS symptoms in teenagers. *CDC AIDS Weekly*, May 2, p. 14.

Chapman, R. L. (1977). Undergraduate knowledge and attitude toward sexually transmitted disease. *Dissertation Abstracts International, 38*, 1947–8.

Check, W. (1985). Public education on AIDS: Not only the media's responsibility. *Hastings Center Report*, 27–31.

Chervin, D. D., Sloane, B. C., Gordon, K. A., & Gold, R. S. (1986). Achieving the health objectives for the nation in higher education. *Journal of American College Health, 35*(5), 15–20.

Chilman, C. S. (1980). *Adolescent sexuality in a changing American society: Social and psychological perspectives* (NIH Publication No. 80-1426). Washington, DC: U. S. Department of Health, Education, and Welfare.

Cowell, S. (1986). Emerging risk factors for AIDS and risk reduction education. *Journal of American College Health, 34*(5), 216–19.

Darrow, W., Echenberg, D., Jaffe, H., O'Malley, P., Byers, R., Getchell, J., & Curren, J. (1987). Risk factors for Human Immunodeficiency Virus (HIV) infections in homosexual men. *American Journal of Public Health, 77*, 479–90.

Dembo, M. H., & Lundell, B. (1979). Factors affecting adolescent contraception practices: Implications for sex education. *Adolescence, 14*, 657–64.

DePietro, R., & Clark, N. M. (1984). A sense-making approach to understanding adolescents' selection of health information sources. *Health Education Quarterly, 11*, 419–30.

DeYoung, K. (1986). Britain sets health unit: Ad campaign on AIDS. *The Washington Post*, November 22, p. A15.

DiClemente, R. J., Zorn, J., & Temoshok, L. (1986). Adolescents and AIDS: A survey of knowledge, attitudes and beliefs about AIDS in San Francisco. *Public Health Briefs, 76*(12), 1443–5.

Dowdle, W. (1986). The search for the AIDS vaccine. *Public Health Reports, 101*(3), 232–3.

Echenberg, D. F. (1985). A new strategy to prevent the spread of AIDS among heterosexuals. *Journal of the American Medical Association, 254*, 2129–30.

Ewart, C. K., Stewart, K. J., Gillilan, R. E., & Kelemen, M. H. (1986a). Self-efficacy mediates strength gains during circuit weight training in men with coronary artery disease. *Medicine and Science in Sports and Exercise, 18*(5), 531–40.

Ewart, C. K., Stewart, K. J., Gillilan, R. E., Kelemen, M. H., Valenti, S. A., Manley, J. D., & Kelemen, M. D. (1986b). Usefulness of self-efficacy in predicting over-exertion during programmed exercise in coronary heart disease. *American Journal of Cardiology, 57*, 557–61.

Finkbeiner, A., Hancock, E., & Schneider, S. (1986). Just the facts . . . from specialists at Johns Hopkins. *Johns Hopkins Magazine*, December, 15–27.

Finkel, M. L., & Finkel, D. J. (1975). Sexual and contraceptive knowledge, attitudes and behavior of male adolescents. *Family Planning Perspectives, 7*, 255–60.

Flay, B. R. (1987). Mass media and smoking cessation: A critical review. *American Journal of Public Health, 77*(11), 153–60.

Giusti, O., & Angela, L. (1981). Family life education: Knowledge, attitudes, and behavior among undergraduate college students at the University of Puerto Rico. *Dissertation Abstracts International, 66*(1), 42–9.

Goulden, T., Todd, P., Hay, R., & Dykes, J. (1984). AIDS and community supportive services. *Medical Journal of Australia, 141*, 582–6.

Gram, J. M., Cowen, J. R., & Deering, C. D. (1981). Preventive education and treatment for difficulties related to sexuality: A method for organizing campus resources. *Journal of American College Health, 29*(6), 306–7.

Haffner, D. (1987, April). *Teens and AIDS.* Paper presented at the conference "AIDS and Adolescents," sponsored by the Center for Population Options, held at the Brookings Institute, Washington, DC.

Halsey, N., Ruff, A., Rolf, J., Greco, D., Kendall, C., & Colman, P. (1988). HIV in street youth: Epidemiology and prevention (NIMH/NICHD Grant No. RO1 HD25030-01).

Henry, K. (1986). Condoms and the prevention of aids. *Journal of the American Medical Association, 256,* 1442–3.

Hillard, J. R., Kitchell, C. L., Turner, U. G., Keeling, R. P., & Shank, R. (1984). Knowledge and attitudes of university health service clients about genital herpes: Implications for patient education and counseling. *Journal of American College Health, 33*(3), 112–17.

Hopkins, D. R. (1986). Key epidemiologic questions about AIDS and infection with HTLV-III/LAV. *Public Health Reports, 101*(3), 234–7.

Institute of Medicine & National Academy of Sciences. (1986). *Confronting AIDS: Directions for public health, health care and research.* Washington, DC: National Academy Press.

Jordheim, A. E. (1975). A comparison of the effects of peer teaching and traditional instruction in venereal disease education with criterion measures of knowledge, attitudes, and behavioral intentions. *Dissertation Abstracts International, 35,* 5970–1.

Kaplan, J. E., Oleske, J. M., Getchell, J. P., Kalyanaraman, V. W., Minnefor, A. B., & Zabala-ablan, M. (1985). Evidence against transmission of human T-lymphotropic virus/lymphadenopathy-associated virus (HTLV-III/LAV) in families of children with acquired immunodeficiency syndrome. *Pediatric Infectious Disease, 4,* 468–71.

Keeling, R. P. (1986). AIDS on the college campus. *Journal of American College Health, 35*(3), 123 -33.

Koop, C. E. (1986). *Surgeon General's report on acquired immune deficiency syndrome.* Washington, DC: U. S. Department of Health and Human Services.

Lawrance, L., & McLeroy, K. R. (1986). Self-efficacy and health education. *Journal of School Health, 56*(8), 317–21.

Liskin, L., Blackburn, M., & Maier, J. (1986). AIDS: A public health crisis. *Population Reports, Series L,* No. 6 (Vol. 14, No. 3).

Luckhurst, D. G. (1986). Content, adequacy of sex education programs. *American Journal of Public Health, 76,* 589.

MacDonald, D. I. (1986). Coolfont report: A PHS plan for prevention and control of AIDS and the AIDS virus. *Public Health Reports, 101*(4), 341–8.

McKusick, L., Conant, M., & Thomas, J. C. (1984). The AIDS epidemic: A model for developing intervention strategies for reducing high-risk behavior in gay men [Summary]. *Proceedings of the Consensus Symposium,* held at the University of California, San Francisco, 229–34.

Mamon, J., & Zapka, J. (1985). Improving frequency and quality of breast self-examination: Effectiveness of an education program. *American Journal of Public Health, 75,* 618 -24.

Mason, J. O. (1985). Public health service plan for the prevention and control of acquired immune deficiency syndrome (AIDS). *Public Health Reports, 100*(5), 453–5.

NIMH (1986). *AIDS and AIDS related research.* Rockville, MD: Health and Behavior Branch, NIMH.

Orr, D. P., & Vickery, M. L. (1983). A values clarification workshop experience for residents. *Journal of Adolescent Health Care, 3,* 256–63.

Parcel, G. S., Luttman, D., & Flaherty-Zonis, C. (1985). Development and evaluation of a sexuality education curriculum for young adolescents. *Journal of Sex Education and Therapy, 2*(1), 38–45.

Peterman, T. A., Drotman, D. P., & Curran, J. W. (1985). Epidemiology of the acquired immunodeficiency syndrome (AIDS). *Epidemiologic Reviews, 1,* 1–21.

Riesenberg, D. E. (1986). AIDS-prompted behavior changes reported. *Journal of the American Medical Association, 255,* 171–6.

Rolf, J., Alexander, C., Sorensen, M., & Armao, F. (1988a). HIV/AIDS prevention project for Navajo youth. Grant proposal under review by the Robert Wood Johnson Foundation.

Rolf, J., Ewart, C., Mamon, J., Joffe, A., & Radius, S. (1987). AIDS prevention studies for youths at risk. Grant proposal submitted to NIMH, February 1987, Parklawn Building, Rockville, MD.

Rolf, J., Mamon, J., Baldwin, J., & Chandra, A. (1988b, March). *Perceptions of invulnerability to AIDS and ability to effect self-protective behaviors in the future*. Paper presented at the Symposium on Adolescents, Risk Taking and AIDS, Society for Research on Adolescence, Alexandria, VA.

Rolf, J., Mamon, J., Chandra, A., Baldwin, J., Joffe, A., Thompson, L., & Delahunt, M. (1988c, November). *Adolescents' perceptions of risks for AIDS: Implications for prevention of psychological vulnerability*. Paper presented at APHA Conference, Boston.

Rolf, J., Nanda, J., Thompson, L., Chandra, A., Baldwin, J., & DelaHunt, M. (1988d, June). *HIV/AIDS behavioral risks and prevention issues for delinquents*. Paper presented at a conference on prevention and treatment of aids among adolescents with serious emotional disturbances, sponsored by NIMH, NIDA, and the Georgetown Child Development Center, Washington, DC.

Romanowski, B., & Brown, J. (1986). AIDS and changing sexual behavior. *Canadian Medical Association, 134,* 872.

Romanowski, B., & Harris, J. R. W. (1984). Sexually transmitted diseases. *Clinical Symposia, 36,* 2–32.

Ross, M. W. (1985). Interventions to minimize AIDS. *Medical Journal of Australia, 142,* 279–80.

Sande, M. A. (1986). Transmission of aids: The case against casual contagion. *New England Journal of Medicine, 314,* 380–2.

Seligman, M. E. P., Peterson, C., Kaslow, N. J., Tannenbaum, R. L., Alloy, L. B., & Abramson, L. Y. (1984). Attributional style and depressive systems among children. *Journal of Abnormal Psychology, 93,* 235–8.

Tauer, K. M. (1983). Promoting effective decision-making in sexually active adolescents. *Nursing Clinics of North America, 18,* 275–92.

Thompson, L., & Spanier, G. B. (1978). Influence of parents, peers and partners on the contraceptive use of college men and women. *Journal of Marriage and the Family, 40*(3), 481–92.

Van Druten, J. A. M., de Boo, T., Jager, J. C., Heisterkamp, S. H., Coutinho, R. A., & Ruitenberg, E. J. (1986). Aids prevention and intervention. *Lancet, 8485,* 852–3.

William, D. C. (1984). The prevention of AIDS by modifying sexual behavior. *Annals of the New York Academy of Sciences, 437,* 283–5.

World Health Organization (1984). Acquired immunodeficiency syndrome – an assessment of the present situation in the world: Memorandum from a WHO meeting. *Bulletin of the World Health Organization, 62,* 419–32.

Wykoff, R. F. (1986). Preventing the spread of AIDS. *Journal of the American Medical Association, 255*(13), 1706–7.

Yacenda, J. A. (1974). Knowledge and attitudes of college students about venereal disease and its prevention. *Health Service Reports, 89,* 170–6.

Yates, G. L., MacKenzie, R., Pennbridge, J., & Cohen, E. (1988). A risk profile comparison of runaway and non-runaway youth. *American Journal of Public Health, 78*(37), 820–1.

Zabin, L. S., Hirsch, M. B., Smith, E. A., & Hardy, J. B. (1984). Adolescent sexual attitudes and behavior: Are they consistent? *Family Planning Perspectives, 16,* 181–5.

Zelnick, M., & Kantner, J. F. (1980). Sexual activity, contraceptive use and pregnancy among metropolitan-area teenagers: 1971–1979. *Family Planning Perspectives, 12,* 230–7.

Part V

Factors in the development of schizophrenia and other severe psychopathology in late adolescence and adulthood

Part V focuses on risk and protective factors in the initial development and evolving course of schizophrenia and other severe psychopathology, an area of study to which Norman Garmezy has made contributions for over three decades. Research on this topic has yielded direct benefits for our understanding of schizophrenia, as well as broader indirect benefits for the emerging field of developmental psychopathology. A direct result has been the identification of several personal characteristics and environmental factors that are associated with risk for schizophrenia and that may have an influence on the development and course of schizophrenia and related disorders. Work in this area also has led to conceptual advances that should aid future attempts to clarify the roles that potential risk and protective factors play in developmental pathways toward schizophrenia. Furthermore, as the chapters in this part show, research that began in this area has made a wide range of conceptual and empirical contributions to developmental psychopathology more generally, ranging from clarifying the predictive role of early competence for later psychopathology to focusing attention on specific ways in which genetic and environmental influences might interact during the epigenesis of psychopathology.

This part begins with a chapter in which Michael J. Goldstein presents the current evidence for family environmental factors as one set of stressors relevant to the onset and recurrence of schizophrenic episodes. Integrating evidence from his longitudinal study of disturbed adolescents and the ongoing Finnish Adoption Study by Tienari and colleagues, Goldstein concludes that interactions between a child's genetic vulnerability and disturbances in the family environment may be important in the epigenesis of schizophrenia. Furthermore, he summarizes work on the recurrence of schizophrenic episodes indicating that familial criticism and emotional overinvolvement play predictive roles, a possibility that is linked conceptually to the schizophrenic behavioral deterioration noted by Norman Garmezy and Eliot Rodnick in their studies of responses to social censure. Finally, Goldstein reviews recent intervention studies that suggest that changing a negative

405

affective family climate may be influential in reducing the likelihood of schizophrenic relapse.

In the next chapter, Daniel R. Hanson, Irving I. Gottesman, and Leonard L. Heston present a sobering analysis of the difficulties of predicting adult schizophrenia from childhood characteristics, given a multifactorial model of etiology and the low base rate for schizophrenia in the general population. They note parallels between schizophrenia and other genetically influenced disorders that suggest that such predictions must include consideration of changes over time in trait-relevant environmental factors and in the effective genotype. As an illustration of the diverse developmental paths characterizing children identified as at risk for schizophrenia, Hanson, Gottesman, and Heston report preliminary data from a follow-up in young adulthood of the offspring of schizophrenic patients whose childhood characteristics they had examined in 1976. In addition, Minnesota Multiphasic Personality Inventory (MMPI) data from a follow-up of individuals who eventually developed schizophrenia, drawn from the Hathaway-Monachesi sample of 15,000 adolescents who were administered the MMPI in the ninth grade, are used to show that some precursors track the progression of the development of psychiatric symptoms over time rather than identify the vulnerable genotype. Hanson, Gottesman, and Heston argue that other endophenotypic indicators are needed to isolate the vulnerable genotype.

The next two chapters report progress in two other attempts to identify endophenotypes relevant to vulnerability to schizophrenia. Keith H. Nuechterlein, Susan Phipps-Yonas, Regina Driscoll, and Norman Garmezy summarize and integrate their findings from the Minnesota High-Risk Studies. They found that an impairment in signal–noise discrimination during visual vigilance tasks with high processing loads characterized a subgroup of children of schizophrenic mothers, but not children of mothers with disorders outside the schizophrenia spectrum. The performance deficit was not a wholly generalized deficit, as it was not apparent in cross-modal reaction time or incidental learning tasks. Furthermore, new analyses suggest that this impairment in visual discrimination during vigilance is independent of and not secondary to social anomalies of children of schizophrenic mothers. Finally, Nuechterlein, Phipps-Yonas, Driscoll, and Garmezy report an intriguing bimodal distribution of scores comparing the visual vigilance levels of children of schizophrenic mothers and those of individually matched normal children.

Another promising endophenotype is described by Philip S. Holzman, who provides a broad-ranging analysis of the studies that he and others have recently conducted on abnormalities in smooth pursuit eye movements in schizophrenia. Disruptions in pursuit eye movements have been found to characterize 50% to 86% of schizophrenic patients, as well as about 40% of their first-degree relatives. Furthermore, twin studies suggest that impaired pursuit tracking is probably genetically transmitted. Although some bipolar patients have been found to have impaired pursuit tracking, Holzman notes that current evidence suggests that this impairment is related to lithium medication and also does not characterize the relatives of bipolar patients as it does the relatives of schizophrenic patients. Several studies point to a cortical localization for the disruptions in smooth pursuit eye movements in schizophrenia. Holzman outlines a latent-trait model developed by Matthysse, Holzman, and Lange that posits that pursuit eye tracking disruptions and schizophrenia are two indicators of a central nervous system disease process determined by a single major gene locus.

Moving away from specific vulnerability factors for schizophrenia to broader issues in adult developmental psychopathology, the final two chapters focus on relationships between major mental disorders and nonpathological aspects of development. Marion Glick and Edward Zigler describe a program of research concerned with the relationship between positive attributes of development, summarized as premorbid competence, and the development and course of mental disorder. This research began with a series of studies of schizophrenia, but has in recent years included a much broader range of psychopathology in an attempt to examine the generalizability of these relationships. The developmental framework described by Glick and Zigler assumes that premorbid competence is a benchmark for maturity level and that each maturity level has effective coping patterns and pathological deviations. They discuss the support for their view that higher premorbid competence, as evidenced in educational level, occupational level, employment history, marital status, and intelligence, is predictive of less likelihood of mental disorder, later onset age, and better outcome within disordered groups. Thus, Glick and Zigler extend the implications of the process-reactive subtypes that were originally investigated within schizophrenic groups to demonstrate that a more general relationship exists across diagnoses between premorbid competence level and adult psychopathology.

Finally, John Strauss and Courtenay Harding provide a stimulating conceptual discussion of the interrelationships between mental disorder and adult development, starting with the contrasting assumptions of natural history theories and psychoanalytic theories of mental disorder. Using many examples from research on schizophrenia and mood disorders, Strauss and Harding note that advances in our knowledge about mental disorders fail to support the view that these disorders have a natural history that unfolds independent of the influences of the individual and of environmental factors. Similarly, concepts of adult development have moved away from models positing fixed developmental stages. Strauss and Harding advocate a framework that views major mental disorders and adult development as highly interactive domains, rather than independent domains, and they provide examples of the application of this framework in longitudinal studies of individual patients. They call for further research emphasis on identification of repeated coping patterns that characterize individual patients over time, evaluated in relation to the developmental situation.

18　Family relations as risk factors for the onset and course of schizophrenia

Michael J. Goldstein

Most contemporary investigators accept the notion that the origins of schizo-phrenia are best understood within a vulnerability–stress model (Zubin & Spring, 1977). Persons are vulnerable to the disorder on the basis of genetic predisposition and prenatal and postnatal integrity. This vulnerability can be modified by stressful life events occurring throughout life. If life events have a negative effect on subsequent development, they are said to enhance the risk for this disorder. On the other hand, if the probability of subsequent disorder is reduced by certain life events, these events are said to be protective.

If the concept of a protective factor is to be meaningful, then it must be other than the inverse of a risk factor. In order to establish a protective role for life events, at any point in development, one must be able to document that the previously established expectancy of disorder has been reduced. This implies that we have robust vulnerability markers for schizophrenia that per-mit this type of analysis, a doubtful situation at the present time. In fact, the very existence of this volume indicates the interest in summarizing the current state of knowledge with regard to risk and protective factors so as to point the way to the next generation of studies in this area.

Because we lack clear-cut vulnerability markers for schizophrenia that can be applied to individuals early in their lives to estimate their risk for the disorder, does this mean that we are unable to investigate the other side of the equation regarding stressful life events? I do not think so, because it is still reasonable to explore whether or not there are relationships between certain definable life events and the subsequent probability of the development of a schizophrenic disorder or its recurrence. Should these investigations provide negative data, then there will be little point in searching for more complex interactions with vulnerability factors. If, on the other hand, strong relation-ships are found between the quality or quantity of life events and subsequent schizophrenia, then there will be good reason to explore the more complex model when robust vulnerability markers are available.

Presumptive evidence for adverse effects of life events on subsequent devel-

408

opment of schizophrenia can be obtained from longitudinal prospective studies. However, lacking robust vulnerability markers for the disorder, such studies can provide only weak evidence regarding any role for life events as protective factors.

Family relations as stressors for the onset of schizophrenia

The term "stressful life event" is vague and can apply to many things. It can refer to a particularly traumatic acute event in late adolescence (rejection, failure in school) that appears to trigger a schizophrenic episode, or it can refer to a chronic condition existing since childhood, as in a child-abusing family environment. It should help to distinguish between stressors as predisposing factors, as in the latter example, and stressors as potentiators, as in the former.

Most theories of schizophrenia have assumed that a triad of factors is necessary for the development of schizophrenia: (a) vulnerability, (b) predisposing stressors, and (c) potentiating stressors.

The bulk of research on predisposing stressors has focused on the intrafamilial environment and has speculated on how attributes of this environment might enhance the probability of the disorder. The earliest writers in this area (Bateson, Jackson, Haley, & Weakland, 1956; Bowen, 1960; Lidz, Cornelison, Fleck, & Terry, 1957; Wynne & Singer, 1964) operated from a strongly environmental bias, such that these stressful family relationships were necessary and sufficient conditions for the development and maintenance of the disorder. Later, as evidence from genetic studies became more convincing, stressful family relations were viewed within a vulnerability-stress model as modifiers of the genetic predisposition for the disorder.

The earliest studies in this area were done with families containing young adult schizophrenic offspring. Reviews of the many studies carried out in the 1950s and 1960s (Goldstein & Rodnick, 1975; Jacob, 1975; Liem, 1980) indicated that certain distinctive patterns of intrafamilial relationships were observed in these families, such as disordered communication styles and a negative affective climate, particularly involving criticism of the index offspring. The intricate series of experimental studies carried out by Garmezy and Rodnick represented an attempt to go beyond clinical observation to specify whether or not, and in what ways, parental criticism resulted in deterioration of behavior in schizophrenic patients; see Rodnick and Garmezy (1957) and Garmezy and Rodnick (1959) for summaries of those studies.

Despite the recurrence of these observations in studies of families containing schizophrenic offspring, the significance of these observations was ambiguous. Were these family patterns antecedents of, or reactions to, the presence of a schizophrenic relative in the family? Were these patterns in any way specific to schizophrenia, or did they represent nonspecific stressful environments likely to increase the risk for psychopathology in general? These questions required a different research strategy involving a longitudinal prospective design. At the present time, only two studies have provided data on the role of family relationships as antecedents of schizophrenia: the UCLA Family Project (Goldstein, 1985a; Goldstein, Judd, Rodnick, Alkire, & Gould, 1968; Rodnick, Goldstein, Doane, & Lewis, 1981) and the Finnish adoption study (Tienari et al., 1983). The latter study has only recently been converted to a longitudinal prospective design, although it has already provided important data on potential gene–environment interactions in the development of schizophrenia. We shall now review these studies.

The UCLA Family Project

Studies of family factors require clear specification of the family processes believed to be stressful for the vulnerable offspring. Two types of variables have been suggested as particularly stressful for the vulnerable person: disordered communication among family members, termed "communication deviance" (CD) by Wynne, Singer, Bartko, and Toohey (1977), and a negative affective climate in the family, termed "high expressed emotion" (high EE) (Vaughn & Leff, 1976) or, as indexed in direct interaction, "negative affective style" (AS) (Doane, West, Goldstein, Rodnick, & Jones, 1981).

These variables, primarily measured on parents, were utilized in a longitudinal prospective study carried out by Goldstein and associates (Doane et al., 1981; Goldstein, 1985a,b; Goldstein et al., 1968), in which a sample of 64 families of mild to moderately disturbed adolescents were studied for the 15 years following their assessment at an outpatient psychological clinic. A key part of this assessment was intensive study of parental communication style, affective attitudes, and interactive behavior, as well as data on the form of adolescent behavioral disturbance. The parental data were coded blindly for CD (high, intermediate, or low), EE (high or low), and AS (benign, intermediate, or negative), then related to subsequent psychiatric assessments carried out on the former teenagers (and their siblings, where relevant) at 5-year and 15-year follow-ups. Data on psychiatric status for 54 of the 64 cases were available for analysis.

Goldstein (1985a,b) reported that the incidences of schizophrenia and related disorders (schizotypal, paranoid, schizoid personality disorders) were highest in the families that had been classified as high in CD 15 years earlier. In fact, there were no cases of schizophrenia in the low-CD families, and only one case diagnosed in the extended schizophrenia spectrum (a schizoid personality) (Figure 18.1). Further, the addition of measures of affective climate (high EE or negative AS) yielded increased ability to identify those cases likely to manifest schizophrenia spectrum disorders in the follow-up period.

Although these family measures did identify family units at high risk for offspring schizophrenia or related disorders, there also were a notable number of offspring with diagnoses of borderline personality disorder in the high-CD

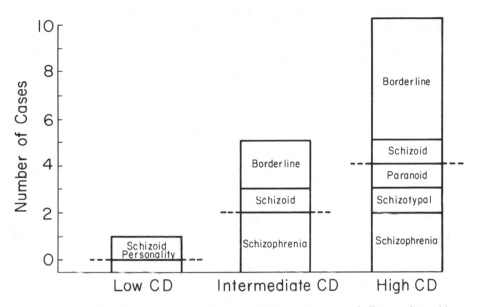

Figure 18.1. Number of cases (index or sibling as most severe) diagnosed as schizo-phrenia spectrum at follow-up, by parental CD group. Dashed lines distinguish be-tween "hard" and "soft" spectrum cases, as reported by Kendler and Gruenberg (1984).

cohort, raising the question whether or not the high-CD, high-EE, negative-AS aggregation of family attributes has any specific linkage to schizophrenia spectrum disorders or measures high-stress family units linked to severe off-spring psychopathology in general. A recent study by Miklowitz (1985) that contrasted parents of schizophrenics and parents of manic patients, in which equal levels of CD were found in the two groups, argued against the specific-ity of high CD to schizophrenia.

Unfortunately, the Goldstein study did not find interactions between attri-butes of the offspring (form of adolescent behavioral difficulties) and parent attributes. That limited the ability of that study to test interactions between an individual vulnerability factor and family stress. That study also lacked the kind of vulnerability markers, particularly those measuring attentional and information processing deficits, found promising in the other high-risk stud-ies, so that precise tests of the interactions of these processes with family stress factors were not feasible; see Asarnow and Goldstein (1986) for a review of these studies.

The findings of the Goldstein et al. (1968) study indicate that there are correlations between certain family stress factors and the subsequent probabil-ity of schizophrenia or related disorders in an offspring. That study does not, however, provide a test or a causal link between the two, as the study began relatively late in the lives of the offspring, and complex transactions between child and parent attributes may have shaped the observed patterns. That study merely indicates two things: first, that further investigations of these markers of family stress may be profitable in samples studied much earlier in life in order to evaluate their epigenesis; second, that these measures may be useful in prevention-oriented research in identifying family units with moderately disturbed teenagers who may be at higher-than-average risk for schizophrenia or schizophrenia spectrum disorders.

The Finnish adoption study

The second study that bears on this issue is that of Tienari et al. (1983) in Finland, which considers vulnerability to schizophrenia by contrasting the psychiatric status of adopted-away offspring of schizophrenic mothers and adopted-away offspring of mothers without psychiatric diagnoses. The subjects were drawn from a nationwide sample of schizophrenic women and matched controls, all of whom gave away offspring for adoption by nonrelatives. Two control cases were selected for each index case.

Though this study is still under way, as of April 1985 (Tienari et al. 1985), 247 adoptive families (112 index and 135 controls) have been studied. This study attempts to investigate both genetic and environmental factors in the development of schizophrenia as it assesses the incidence of schizophrenia in offspring as a function of the quality of the rearing environment. Ratings of the interactional patterns in the family are based on (a) a joint interview with the whole family, (b) a joint interview with the parents only, (c) a family interaction task based on the conjoint Rorschach procedure, and (d) ratings on the Interpersonal Perception Methods (Laing, Philipson, & Lee, 1966). In addition, each adoptive parent receives an individual interview, Rorschach test, and portions of the Wechsler Adult Intelligence Scale (Wechsler, 1981).

To date, these various measures of family relationships have been reduced to categorical ratings ranging from healthy to severely disturbed. Though ratings of the measures used in the Goldstein et al. (1968) study cited earlier (CD, EE, AS) are available from the data collected in the Tienari et al. (1985) study, they have not been completed as yet.

The data reported thus far (Tienari et al., 1985) strongly support a role for genetic factors in schizophrenia; of the 10 psychotic offspring in the sample, 8 were found among the adopted-away offspring of schizophrenic mothers (7.14%), whereas the population base rate was found in the control families (2/135 = 1.48%).

However, the data support a vulnerability–stress model, because all of the schizophrenic cases in the 92 families rated thus far occurred in families rated as disturbed (Table 18.1). In fact, the adopted-away offspring of schizophrenics with rearing environments rated as "healthy" had a rate of schizophrenia at or below the general population rate.

These data also weaken the argument against purely environmental causes of schizophrenia, because similar patterns of family disturbances did not re-

Table 18.1 *Incidence of psychosis observed in adopted-away offspring of schizophrenic mothers as a function of rearing family environment*

	Adoptive family rearing environment	
Offspring diagnosis	Healthy ($n = 49$)	Seriously disturbed ($n = 43$)
Psychotic[a]	0%	16.3%
Borderline psychotic	0%	20.9%

[a]Five diagnosed as schizophrenic, two as paranoid psychosis.
Source: Tienari et al. (1985).

late to a notable incidence of schizophrenia among the adopted-away off-spring of biological parents without psychiatric diagnoses.

Though the data from the Tienari project are intriguing, their limitations must be recognized. The study was not prospective, at least in its original conception, and it is entirely possible that disturbed family relationships evolved concurrent with or after the emergence of psychiatric disorder in an offspring. In order to addresss this criticism, the study is being continued as a high-risk project in which the unaffected offspring of index and control parents will be studied prospectively to determine if ratings of the rearing environment antedate the emergence of schizophrenia and related disorders.

Summary of stress factors as precursors of schizophrenia

As indicated earlier, only two studies have examined the question whether or not one type of stress (disturbed family relationships) interacts with individual vulnerability to increase the risk for onset of schizophrenia. Each of those studies has notable limitations; yet the congruence between them suggests that family stress may be a significant component in the epigenesis of schizophrenia. More research is needed on the roles of these family factors much earlier in life in order to understand the complex transactions among the emerging signs of individual vulnerability and caretaker–child interaction.

Family factors as stressors for recurrence of schizophrenia

One can interpret most of the research during the 1950s and 1960s on family relationships related to schizophrenia as documenting a particular sensitivity of the schizophrenic patient to attributes of the family environment *after* the disorder has emerged. In fact, one can, with the clarity of hindsight, recognize in the studies carried out at Duke University by Garmezy and

Rodnick (1959; Rodnick & Garmezy, 1957) that parental criticism induced a notable deterioration in functioning in the already schizophrenic patients.

In the early writings from this group, these findings were interpreted as documenting potential antecedents of the disorder, and their relevance to recurrence was not recognized. This is particularly ironic because this research utilized a powerful prognostic indicator, premorbid adjustment, to stratify the sample and found that the sensitivity to parental, particularly maternal, criticism was most pronounced in those patients with a poor premorbid (poor-prognosis) history. At that time, Garmezy and Rodnick did not recognize these patients' sensitivity to criticism as a possible mediating mechanism to account for the poor clinical course of these patients with a poor premorbid history.

Recent studies that originated in Great Britain at the Medical Research Council (MRC) Unit for Social Psychiatry in London focused more directly on the issue of predicting the clinical course of schizophrenia. Note that the process of predicting clinical course in the 1950s and 1960s involved somewhat different issues than are involved in studies that began in the 1960s and continue to this day. The earlier studies were designed to predict whether or not patients would recover at all and would be capable of leaving the hospital (these studies used months or years of hospitalization as dependent variables!), whereas the studies in Great Britain began after the early experiments in deinstitutionalization and were focused on how well patients (and this referred to almost all of them) could survive in the community after discharge.

Research on expressed emotion

A recent paper by Brown (1985) summarizes the history of this research, which began originally with a finding, not subsequently replicated, that patients who returned to family homes had poorer clinical courses than did those who left the hospital and went to an independent living environment. That finding stimulated a series of studies, summarized by Leff and Vaughn (1985), designed to identify attributes of the family environment associated with higher rates of relapse in the 9-month period following hospital discharge.

Those investigations led to the concept of expressed emotion (EE), in which a stressful family environment was defined by two parameters: high rates of criticism directed at the index patient and/or a marked degree of what is termed "emotional overinvolvement." So, in part, these British studies confirmed the original work of Garmezy and Rodnick in supporting the particular sensitivity of schizophrenic patients to criticism. They may also support Garmezy and Rodnick's findings of poor-prognosis patients' sensitivity to maternal cues, because high levels of EE based on emotional overinvolvement are almost exclusively present in the mothers of schizophrenics, and this attribute is rarely seen without high criticism as well.

Whereas the term "high expressed emotion" refers to behaviors expressed within the family, the studies that followed the earliest studies by Brown (1959) (which did involve home observation) measured EE status on the basis of a relative's verbal and paraverbal responses during administration of a semistructured interview, termed the Camberwell Family Interview (CFI). So the later EE studies observed behavior with a non–family member, the interviewer, and concluded that these high-EE attitudes were probably expressed at home toward the patient.

A number of investigations carried out by our research group at UCLA (Miklowitz, Goldstein, Falloon, & Doane, 1984; Valone, Norton, Goldstein, & Doane, 1983) have in fact confirmed this supposition, because relatives' behaviors during a direct observation task in which family members discussed conflictual problems did, in general, parallel these attitudes on the CFI. In fact, one study by members of our research group (Strachan, Leff, Goldstein, Doane, & Burtt, 1986) found similar attitude–interactional behavior overlap in a British sample testing using the identical interactional measurement techniques used in our UCLA studies.

Since the original studies by Brown, Monck, Carstairs, and Wing (1962) and Brown, Birley, and Wing (1972) and the replication by Vaughn and Leff (1976), a number of replication studies have appeared in both Great Britain and the United States (Jenkins et al., 1986; MacMillan, Gold, Crow, Johnson, & Johnstone, 1986; Nuechterlein et al., 1986; Vaughn, Snyder, Jones, Freeman, & Falloon, 1984) in which the prognostic value of high-EE attitudes has been confirmed.

Relationship of EE research to studies of premorbid adjustment

Though other replication studies are needed, in view of the fact that there are two reports of nonreplication in the literature (Dulz & Hand, 1986; Hogarty, 1985), the emphasis has shifted to questions of interpretation. For example, in the original Duke studies by Garmezy and Rodnick, a known prognostic variable, poor premorbid adjustment, was correlated with high sensitivity to parental criticism. It seems possible that patients with poor premorbid histories are more likely to be the recipients of more criticism and are also more likely to return to high-EE homes. If so, high EE possesses prognostic value merely because of its overlap with poor premorbid adjustment. This issue was investigated by our research group (Miklowitz, Goldstein, & Falloon, 1983), and no relationship was found between parental EE level and good or poor premorbid adjustment.

When we examined only those parents who were classified as high-EE based on the criticism criterion, we found that the premorbid adjustment levels of their patient-relatives did not differ from those for patient-relatives of low-EE parents. In fact, both groups had patient-relatives with reasonably good premorbid adjustment. We did, however, find that parents classified as high-EE solely on the emotional overinvolvement criterion had schizophrenic offspring who were uniformly poor in premorbid adjustment. Because mothers were most likely to be classified as high-EE on the basis of emotional overinvolvement, it appears that patients, largely male schizophrenics, with the poorest premorbid levels of social attainment came from families in which the mothers were rated as emotionally overinvolved, but *not* critical, on the CFI.

Of course, the latter findings suggest a number of different possibilities that we cannot resolve, namely, whether maternal overinvolvement is a precursor to poor social relations, a reaction to perceived social failure in childhood and adolescence, or a reaction to the actual emergence of schizophrenia.

These same trends have been replicated in a slightly different fashion in a more recent study of recent-onset schizophrenia currently being carried out with Keith Nuechterlein at UCLA. This study involves a longitudinal investigation of the course of schizophrenia in a sample of young, predominantly first-lifetime-episode schizophrenic patients. Our part of this study involves the collection of family assessment data shortly after the patient leaves the hospital, using a modification of the direct interaction task used in our longitudinal prospective study described earlier in this chapter. These data on parental interactions are coded by the AS coding system developed by Doane et al. (1981). Parental units are divided into groups: those above and those below the median of the sample of 41 family units on expressions of criticism toward their schizophrenic offspring. In fact, 63% of the parents of patients with good premorbid histories were rated high in criticism by this criterion, whereas 36% of parents of patients with poor premorbid histories were so rated, confirming the earlier finding of Miklowitz et al. (1983) that patients with good premorbid histories were more likely to be the recipients of critical attitudes or critical interactions with parents.

It is possible that it is not the rate of parental criticism that discriminates the family patterns for patients with good and poor premorbid histories, but rather differences in the patients' modes of coping with these expressions. In order to address this question, we developed, with the assistance of our colleagues Keith Valone and Dorothy Feingold, a coping style (CS) coding system applicable to patient responses to parental remarks in these same direct interaction tasks. The CS system evaluates five general categories of verbal behavior: (a) statements of self-worth, (b) negative self-statements, (c) behavior critical of, or oppositional to, parental suggestions, (d) statements of personal efficacy, and (e) statements supportive of the parents.

The rates for these five classes of statements were examined for patients with good and poor premorbid histories who were exposed to parents rated as high or low in criticism. To parallel the earlier experimental studies of Garmezy and Rodnick, we restricted these analyses to the 34 male schizophrenics in our sample, because their original studies involved predominantly male patients as well. We also considered which family attribute, parental

Table 18.2. *Male patient coping style in direct interaction with parents as a function of premorbid status in families (a) high or low on criticism or (b) high or low EE*

AS criticism level

CS code	Good premorbids		Poor premorbids	
	High criticism ($n = 11$)	Low criticism ($n = 5$)	High criticism ($n = 5$)	Low criticism ($n = 13$)
Self-worth statements	1.09	3.00	1.60	1.38
Oppositional-critical statements	3.82	5.80	10.40	2.53

EE attitude level

CS code	Good premorbids		Poor premorbids	
	High EE	Low EE	High EE	Low EE
Self-efficacy	0.69	4.00	0.60	1.13

attitude (high or low EE) or parental interactional behavior (high or low in observed criticism), showed the strongest association with patient coping style. Statements of self-worth ($p < .05$) and oppositional-critical behavior ($p < .05$) revealed significant interactions with premorbidity and AS criticism level, but no relationship to EE attitudes. On the other hand, statements of self-efficacy (e.g., the patient claims to have talents, plans, etc., worthy of pursuing) revealed interactions with EE and premorbidity, but not with the actual rate of expressed criticism in the interaction (AS level). No effects were found for supportive statements. These patterns are presented in Table 18.2. The data in this table indicate that for two of the measures (self-worth and self-efficacy) the significant interactions with premorbidity were carried largely by the good premorbids, who showed higher rates of positive self-image (self-worth and self-efficacy statements) when parent criticism levels were low (either in attitude [low EE] or actual interactional behavior [low AS criticism level]). The dramatic effect for the poor premorbids was found for oppositional-critical behavior, in which high levels of behaviorally expressed parental criticism were associated with extraordinarily high rates of refusal to follow parental suggestions, combined with marked countercriticism of the parents. The trend in the good premorbids was, in fact, in the opposite direction. So if there is a specific response of poor premorbids to parental criticism, it is to adopt a negativistic stance when parental suggestions or directions are offered.

These data do not directly parallel the original Garmezy-Rodnick findings of a deficit in perceptual discrimination in schizophrenics with poor premorbid historios under conditions of criticism, but they certainly support the notion that premorbid adjustment is a determinant of the patient's *mode* of response to criticism. Schizophrenics with poor premorbid histories, shortly after hospital discharge, show more negativistic responses to parental pressure when this pressure is associated with a critical attitude toward the patient. The good premorbids, on the other hand, are most likely to express a higher sense of self-esteem when parents avoid criticizing them, a pattern not seen in poor premorbids, who rarely express high self-esteem under either condition.

Issues in the interpretation of these findings

The greatest controversy in research on family affective climate and the course of schizophrenia has to do with the interpretation of these findings and their implications regarding the direction of effects. In both of the Brown et al. (1962, 1972) studies, relationships were found between patients' ratings on "behavioral disturbance" in the 3-month prehospitalization period and patients' subsequent relapses. However, when this patient attribute was entered into a prediction equation with EE status, it failed to add anything to prediction on the basis of EE status. The Vaughn and Leff (1976) study found that ratings of the severity of psychopathology at discharge were unrelated to EE status, a finding subsequently confirmed by Miklowitz et al. (1983) in the United States.

Along a similar line of investigating a possible link between EE status of relatives and the history of the patient's illness, MacMillan et al. (1986) reported an association between preadmission duration of illness (the time between the reported initial signs of the first episode of schizophrenia and first lifetime hospital admission for the disorder) and EE status, with longer history associated with greater probability of high-EE attitudes. These authors further concluded, from logistic regression analyses, that EE was not a significant predictor of relapse when the duration of illness was also entered as a predictor.

Unfortunately, these authors failed to consider that the same data sources frequently were used for rating duration of illness and EE attitudes, so that common attitudes toward a relative's illness (an early acknowledgment of deviance and a critical response after a full-blown episode in high-EE relatives, and a denial of deviance in both the premorbid and postmorbid phases by low-EE relatives) may reflect the same underlying stance toward a relative.

Statistical removal of the duration of untreated illness from the predictor equation does not eliminate the significance of EE attitude for the future course of the patient's disorder. It is one thing to clarify the origins of contemporary attitudes or behaviors (high or low EE status), but quite another to assume that contemporary attitudes are irrelevant as determinants of the behavior of others. It is also interesting to note that a recent report by Nuechterlein et al. (1986), involving preliminary data from a comparable sample of recent-onset, predominantly first-admission schizophrenic patients, failed to replicate the association between EE status of relatives and duration of illness.

Another line of research has investigated the nature of schizophrenic patients' somatic responses to high- and low-EE relatives when in direct face-to-face contact with one another. These data have been used to document that high- and low-EE relatives create distinctive environmental conditions that produce differential levels of emotional stimulation.

For example, it had been found that in high-EE families, but not low-EE families, verbal interchanges are paralleled by increasing psychophysiological arousal and reactivity (Sturgeon, Kuipers, Berkowitz, Turpin, & Leff, 1981; Tarrier, Vaughn, Lader, & Leff, 1979) in the patient and, in one study with disturbed teenagers hypothesized to be at risk for schizophrenia, in both parents and offspring (Valone et al., 1983). These data suggest that a negative affective climate in these families may enhance the likelihood of relapse by raising the level of arousal in these patients beyond the limits of their vulnerable postpsychotic coping mechanisms.

The role of intervention studies in clarifying the direction of effects

That the affective climate of the family may be causally related to relapse has been investigated within the framework of the Falloon et al. (1982) aftercare intervention study that contrasted a behavioral family management program with a comparable individual, patient-focused program in which all patients received regular maintenance antipsychotic medication. The direct interaction task used in the Miklowitz et al. (1983) study was repeated two times in the Falloon et al. (1982) study: before entry into the study, and after 3 months of intensive treatment. The parental data were coded by the AS system at both times. Pre- post comparisons (Doane, Falloon, Goldstein, & Mintz, 1985; Doane, Goldstein, Miklowitz, & Falloon, 1986) indicated that the family management program, on average, produced a greater reduction of negative affect in the family than did the individual-patient-focused intervention, and those families in which this reduction occurred were least likely to see their young adult schizophrenic offspring experience relapse by the 9-month follow-up point.

Similar findings were recently reported by Hogarty et al. (1986) using the original CFI method of EE assessment before and after 1 year of (a) family management, (b) social skills training for the patient, (c) a combination of the first two, or (d) regular maintenance drug therapy. All families in these studies were originally selected as being high-EE. The rate of change from high to low EE status was greatest in the family treatment groups (family alone or family and social skills) and lowest in the drug-only condition. However, regardless of the assigned treatment condition, when relatives did shift to a low EE status, the patient relapse rate was zero, whereas when that did not occur, the rate averaged 40%.

Although studies carried out to date suggest that relatives' affective attitudes toward a recently discharged schizophrenic patient may play some role in the subsequent course of the patient's disorder, there still are many unanswered questions in this area. First, though there is little evidence that high-EE attitudes are simply reactions to variations in the clinical state of the patient, many of the direct interaction studies have not carefully examined the more subtle aspects of how patients relate to their family members. Given that EE is measured when family members are going through a major crisis involving either the hospitalization or rehospitalization of a spouse or offspring, there may be attributes of the crisis or its history, as suggested by MacMillan et al. (1986), that can help us understand variations in these responses to the patient's disorder. It is likely that high-EE attitudes and negative affective behaviors toward patient-relatives have complex origins, as suggested by Leff and Vaughn (1985), and investigators should go beyond the convenient high–low EE typology in order to understand not only the natural history of a schizophrenic disorder but also the natural history of relatives' varying efforts to cope with the many difficult demands of a close relative with schizophrenia residing in or near their home. This literature will ultimately profit from a reinterpretation of the data within the framework of a vulnerability–stress model applied to the *relatives* of schizophrenics as well.

References

Asarnow, J. R., & Goldstein, M. J. (1986). Schizophrenia during adolescence and early adulthood: A developmental perspective on risk research. *Clinical Psychology Review, 6,* 211–35.

Bateson, G., Jackson, D., Haley, J., & Weakland, J. (1956). Toward a theory of schizophrenia. *Behavioral Science, 1,* 252–64.

Bowen, M. (1960). A family concept of schizophrenia. In D. D. Jackson (Ed.), *The etiology of schizophrenia* (pp. 346–72). New York: Basic Books.

Brown, G. W. (1959). Experiences of discharged chronic schizophrenic mental hospital patients in various types of living group. *Millbank Memorial Fund Quarterly, 37,* 105–31.

Brown, G. W. (1985). The discovery of expressed emotion: Induction or deduction? In J. Leff & C. Vaughn (Eds.), *Expressed emotion in families* (pp. 7–25). New York: Guilford Press.

Brown, G. W., Birley, J. L. T., & Wing, J. K. (1972). Influence of family life on the course of schizophrenic disorders: A replication. *British Journal of Psychiatry, 121,* 241–58.

Brown, G. W., Monck, E. M., Carstairs, G. M., & Wing, J. K. (1962). Influence of family life on the course of schizophrenic illness. *British Journal of Preventive and Social Medicine, 16,* 55–68.

Doane, J. A., Falloon, I. R. H., Goldstein, M. J., & Mintz, J. (1985). Parental affective style and the treatment of schizophrenia: Predicting course of illness and social functioning. *Archives of General Psychiatry, 42,* 34–42.

Doane, J. A., Goldstein, M. J., Miklowitz, D. J., & Falloon, I. R. H. (1986). The impact of individual and family treatment on the affective climate of families of schizophrenics. *British Journal of Psychiatry, 148,* 279–87.

Doane, J. A., West, K. L., Goldstein, M. J., Rodnick, E. H., & Jones, J. E. (1981). Parental communication deviance and affective style: Predictors of subsequent schizophrenia spectrum disorders in vulnerable adolescents. *Archives of General Psychiatry, 38,* 679–85.

Dulz, B., & Hand, I. (1986). Short-term relapse in young schizophrenics: Can it be predicted and affected by family (CFI), patient and treatment variables? An experimental study. In M. J. Goldstein, I. Hand, & K. Hahlweg (Eds.), *Treatment of schizophrenia: Family assessment and intervention* (pp. 54–75). Berlin: Springer-Verlag.

Falloon, I. R. H., Boyd, J. L., McGill, C. W., Razani, J., Moss, H. G., & Gilderman, A. (1982). Family management in the prevention of exacerbations of schizophrenia: A controlled study. *New England Journal of Medicine, 306,* 1437–40.

Garmezy, N., & Rodnick, E. H. (1959). Premorbid adjustment and performance in schizophrenia: Implications for interpreting heterogeneity in schizophrenia. *Journal of Nervous and Mental Disease, 129,* 450–66.

Goldstein, M. J. (1985a). Family factors that antedate the onset of schizophrenia and related disorders: The results of a fifteen year prospective longitudinal study. *Acta Psychiatrica Scandinavica, 71,* 7–18.

Goldstein, M. J. (1985b, April). *The UCLA family project.* Paper presented at an NIMH research conference: Risk Studies in Schizophrenia: Current Status and Future Directions, San Francisco.

Goldstein, M. J., Judd, L. L., Rodnick, E. H., Alkire, A. A., & Gould, E. (1968). A method for the study of social influence and coping patterns in the families of disturbed adolescents. *Journal of Nervous and Mental Disease, 147,* 233–51.

Goldstein, M. J., & Rodnick, E. H. (1975). The family's contribution to the etiology of schizophrenia: Current status. *Schizophrenia Bulletin, 14,* 48–63.

Hogarty, G. E. (1985). Expressed emotion and schizophrenic relapse: Implications from the Pittsburgh study. In M. Alpert (Ed.), *Controversies in schizophrenia* (pp. 354–65). New York: Guilford Press.

Hogarty, G. E., Anderson, C. M., Reiss, D. J., Kornblith, S. J., Greenwald, D. P., Javna, C. D., & Madonia, M. J. (1986). Family psychoeducation, social skills training, and maintenance chemotherapy in the aftercare treatment of schizophrenia. *Archives of General Psychiatry, 43,* 633–42.

Jacob, T. (1975). Family interaction in disturbed and normal families: A methodological and substantive review. *Psychological Review, 82,* 33–65.

Jenkins, J. H., Karno, M., de la Selva, A., Santana, F., Telles, C., Lopez, S., & Mintz, J. (1986). Expressed emotion, maintenance pharmacotherapy, and schizophrenic relapse among Mexican-Americans. *Psychopharmacology Bulletin, 22,* 621–7.

Kendler, K. S., & Gruenberg, A. M. (1984). An independent analysis of the Danish Adoption Study of Schizophrenia. VI: The relationship between psychiatric disorder as defined by DSM-III and the relatives and adoptees. *Archives of General Psychiatry, 41,* 555–64.

Laing, R. D., Philipson, H., & Lee, A. E. (1966). *Interpersonal perception: A theory and a method of research.* London: Tavistock Publications.

Leff, J., & Vaughn, C. (1985). *Expressed emotion in families.* New York: Guilford Press.

Lidz, T., Cornelison, A. R., Fleck, S., & Terry, D. (1957). The intrafamilial environment of schizophrenic patients. II: Marital schism and marital skew. *American Journal of Psychiatry, 114,* 241–8.

Liem, J. H. (1980). Family studies in schizophrenia: An update and a commentary. *Schizophrenia Bulletin, 6,* 429–59.

MacMillan, J. F., Gold, A., Crow, T. J., Johnson, A. L., & Johnstone, E. C. (1986). Expressed emotion and relapse. *British Journal of Psychiatry, 148,* 133–43.

Miklowitz, D. J. (1985). *Family interaction and illness outcome in bipolar and schizophrenic patients.* Unpublished doctoral dissertation, University of California, Los Angeles.

Miklowitz, D. J., Goldstein, M. J., & Falloon, I. R. H. (1983). Premorbid and symptomatic characteristics of schizophrenics from families with high and low levels of expressed emotion. *Journal of Abnormal Psychology, 92,* 359–67.

Miklowitz, D. J., Goldstein, M. J., Falloon, I. R. H., & Doane, J. A. (1984). Interactional correlates of expressed emotion in the families of schizophrenics. *British Journal of Psychiatry, 144,* 482–7.

Nuechterlein, K. H., Snyder, K. S., Dawson, M. E., Rappe, S., Gitlin, M., & Fogelson, D. (1986). Expressed emotion, and fixed-dose fluphenazine deconoate maintenance, and relapse in recent-onset schizophrenia. *Psychopharmacology Bulletin, 22,* 633–9.

Rodnick, E. H., & Garmezy, N. (1957). An experimental approach to the study of motivation in schizophrenia. In M. R. Jones (Ed.), *Nebraska symposium on motivation* (pp. 109–84). Lincoln: University of Nebraska Press.

Rodnick, E. H., Goldstein, M. J., Doane, J. A., & Lewis, J. M. (1981). Association between parent–child transactions and risk for schizophrenia: Implications for early intervention. In M. J. Goldstein (Ed.), *Preventive interventions in schizophrenia: Are we ready?* (pp. 156–72). Washington, DC: U.S. Government Printing Office.

Strachan, A. M., Leff, J. P., Goldstein, M. J., Doane, J. A., & Burtt, C. (1986). Emotional attitudes and direct communication in the families of schizophrenics: A cross-national replication. *British Journal of Psychiatry, 149,* 279–87.

Sturgeon, D., Kuipers, L., Berkowitz, R., Turpin, G., & Leff, J. (1981). Psychophysiological responses of schizophrenic patients to high and low expressed emotion relatives. *British Journal of Psychiatry, 138,* 40–5.

Tarrier, N., Vaughn, C., Lader, M. H., & Leff, J. P. (1979). Bodily reactions to people and events in schizophrenia. *Archives of General Psychiatry, 36,* 311–15.

Tienari, P., Sorri, A., Lahti, I., Naarala, M., Wahlberg, K., Moring, J., Pohjola, J., & Wynne, L. (1985, April). *Interaction of genetic and psychosocial factors in schizophrenia. The Finnish adoptive family study: A longitudinal combination of the adoptive family strategy and the risk research strategy.* Paper presented at the NIMH research conference: Risk Studies in Schizophrenia: Current Status and Future Directions, San Francisco.

Tienari, P., Sorri, A., Naarala, M., Lahti, I., Pohjola, J., Bostrom, C., & Wahlberg, K. (1983). The Finnish adoptive family study: Adopted-away offspring of schizophrenic mothers. In H. Stierlin, L. C. Wynne, & M. Wirsching (Eds.), *Psychosocial intervention in schizophrenia* (pp. 21–34). Berlin: Springer-Verlag.

Valone, K., Norton, J. P., Goldstein, M. J., & Doane, J. A. (1983). Parental expressed emotion and affective style in an adolescent sample at risk for schizophrenia spectrum disorders. *Journal of Abnormal Psychology, 92,* 399–407.

Vaughn, C. E., & Leff, J. P. (1976). The influence of family and social factors on the course of psychiatric illness: A comparison of schizophrenic and depressed neurotic patients. *British Journal of Psychiatry, 129,* 125–37.

Vaughn, C. E., Snyder, K. S., Jones, S., Freeman, W. B., & Falloon, I. R. H. (1984). Family factors in schizophrenic relapse: Replication in California of the British research on expressed emotion. *Archives of General Psychiatry, 41,* 1169–77.

Wechsler, D. (1981). *Manual for the Wechsler Adult Intelligence Scale.* New York: Psychological Corporation.

Wynne, L. C., & Singer, M. T. (1964). Thought disorder and family relations of schizophrenics. 4. *Archives of General Psychiatry, 12,* 201–12.

Wynne, L. C., Singer, M. T., Bartko, J. J., & Toohey, M. L. (1977). Schizophrenics and their families: Research on parental communication. In J. M. Tanner (Ed.), *Developments in psychiatric research* (pp. 254–86). London: Hodder & Stoughton.

Zubin, J., & Spring, B. J. (1977). Vulnerability: A new view of schizophrenia. *Journal of Abnormal Psychology, 86,* 103–26.

19 Long-range schizophrenia forecasting: many a slip twixt cup and lip

Daniel R. Hanson, Irving I. Gottesman, and Leonard L. Heston

Potholes in the road to prediction

The task of making predictions constantly challenges those of us who treat and study the mentally ill. On the clinical front, we are required to predict which patients will respond to various therapies, which patients will need hospitalization, which will kill themselves or harm others. Fortunately, experience, as quantified in empiric base rates, helps with these predictions if we maintain a clear head and go with the base rates rather than rely on clinical hunches. It is a fact that actuarial prediction is nearly always better than clinical judgment (Grove, 1986; Meehl, 1954). The clinician's task becomes one of evaluating the patient so as to decide which base rates apply. For many years we have admired the clear and critical thinking that Norman Garmezy (1968, 1974) has brought to our task; most often we agreed with his formulations and have every reason to believe that the processes of influence have been mutual.

The treatment of mental illness, though still leaving much to be desired, has made great strides, and scientists' efforts are turning toward new goals. In the last decade, much research in mental illness has focused, for the first time, on trying to predict mental illness in individuals not yet affected. Achieving the power of prediction may point the way to the eventual goal of designing rational interventions that will prevent future mental illness in those people identified to be at risk. Success will depend, in part, on the wisdom and endurance of scientists engaged in this brand of research. Success will also depend, in large part, on the nature of the illness. We have confidence in the former (including ourselves, but, of course, clinical opinion is most unreliable when our own egos are involved). We have major doubts about the predictable nature (and nurture) of some forms of mental illness. This chapter explores some of our questions about forecasting future schizophrenia. We shall follow the model of confrontation with reality, sentiment set aside, exemplified by our esteemed colleague Norman Garmezy (1968).

424

We take as a given that there are necessary but not sufficient genetic components to schizophrenia. These contributors are theorized to be specific factors that predispose a person to schizophrenia rather than to heart disease or to bipolar psychosis. We also believe that there are nonspecific inherited traits (e.g., IQ, personality factors) that may enhance or interfere with a person's ability to cope and thus alter the likelihood of breakdown; see Gottesman, Shields, and Hanson (1982, chapter 11) for further elaboration. We also assume that there are important environmental contributors to the development of schizophrenia that may either protect a predisposed individual or render one more vulnerable. Thus, we view the development of schizophrenia as multifactorially determined. If this assumption is true, predictability becomes immediately difficult, as Karl Popper concluded many years ago:

> The crucial point (about causation) is this: although we may assume that any actual succession of phenomena proceeds according to the laws of nature, it is important to realize that practically *no sequence of, say, three or more causally connected concrete events proceeds according to any single law of nature*. If the wind shakes a tree and Newton's apple falls to the ground, nobody will deny that these events can be described in terms of causal laws. But, there is no single law, such as that of gravity, nor even a single definite set of laws, to describe the actual or concrete succession of causally connected events; apart from gravity, we should have to consider the laws explaining wind pressure; jerking movements of the branch; the tension in the apple's stalk; the bruise suffered by the apple on impact; all of which is succeeded by chemical processes resulting from the bruise, etc. The idea that any concrete sequence or succession of events (apart from such examples as the movement of a pendulum or a solar system) can be described by any one law, or by any one definite set of laws, is simply mistaken. (Popper, 1961, p. 117)

Freud agreed: "The chain of causation can always be recognized with certainty if we follow the line of analysis, whereas to predict it along the line of synthesis is impossible" (1920/1955, p. 167). We do not want to disparage the noble hope of preventing mental illness. However, if the development of schizophrenia is due to multiple factors, like the bruising of the apple, and if predicting the onset of schizophrenia is like predicting if and when the apple will fall and be bruised, our task will be most difficult. By analogy, we shall have to be able to *predict* the apple's average ripening time, which is relatively easy because it is a function of the tree's genotype and conditions of rearing (and thus, in principle, knowable). Additionally, we can count on gravity as always being constant (more or less). It will be more difficult to predict other factors such as pollination, rainfall, temperature, wind, and storms, as well as the behavior of any raccoons in the area that feed on apples. Pollination and raccoons are not included in our list just for whimsy. They provide a counterpoint to factors such as temperature and rainfall that affect all apples on the tree. In addition, there are idiosyncratic factors that may affect only a single apple.

So far, no specific environmental contributor to schizophrenia has been identified, with the possible exception of drugs that are dopamine agonists. Perhaps specific factors exist, but after all these years of searching with negative results it seems reasonable to conclude that no single factor is extant in the more molar aspects of the environment, and investigations will have to turn to a more molecular perspective. Alternatively, the environmental contributors may be molar events, but may be different for different schizophrenic individuals. Stress may be the common denominator, but the idiosyncratic stressors may come from many different sources and may come at different times in development for different schizophrenics. Prenatal and birth complications, viral infections of the central nervous system (CNS), early deprivations, family communication deviance, school failure, accidental injury, illness, death among friends or family, "bad trips," and a vast range of other kinds of bad luck may have obvious effects on the development of a schizophrenic, but it will be impossible to prophesy many of the events in advance (let alone their effects).

The base rate blues

Thirty years ago, Meehl and Rosen (1955) set down some important advice for those of us interested in making predictions based on the results of psychological and medical tests. They made it clear that the effectiveness of any screening procedure is dependent, in large part, on the base rate of the trait in the population being studied. One of the basic principles exemplified by their work is that the rarer a condition is, the harder it will be to detect or predict it. Table 19.1 illustrates this phenomenon. The values in the table were computed using Bayes's theorem, as follows:

$$P_d = \frac{PSe}{PSe + Q(1 - Sp)}$$

where P_d is the probability of having the disease given a positive test score, P is the base rate of the disease in the population, Q equals 1 minus P, Se is the sensitivity of the test, and Sp is the specificity of the test. In this example, we have set the *sensitivity* at 90%. That is, if this test is given to a group of schizophrenics, 90% of them will be correctly identified by the test as having schizophrenia. We have set the *specificity* of the test to 95%, which is to say that if a group of normals are given the test, 95% of them will be viewed correctly as normal. Another way of saying this is that the false negative rate is only 10%, and the false positive rate is only 5%. These are unusually high values compared with those for most psychological tests, and even compared with most medical tests. Most real-life test results will not have such high specificity or sensitivity and will result in even more problematic results than in our illustration. It is extremely important to have a high specificity (that is, a low false positive rate) when trying to predict future schizophrenia. This is

Table 19.1. *Probabilities of having schizo-*
phrenia given a positive test for schizophre-
nia (P_d) for different population base rates
(P) with the test sensitivity of 90% and speci-
ficity of 95% held constant

P	P_d
.5	.947
.25	.875
.1	.667
.01	.153
.001	.0182

clearly a judgment value, but we believe that if the predictions lead to interventions, it would be exceedingly unwise to label normal people as potential
schizophrenics. The burden of worry imposed on these people could cause
considerable distress, and any attempt to intervene when these people would
ordinarily be normal would violate the first principle of medicine to do no
harm. In actuality, we think that a specificity of 95% is probably too low and
that any researcher engaged in developing prediction criteria for forecasting
schizophrenia in the general population should aim for a rate of false positives
near zero.

In our worked example in Table 19.1 we see that when the test is applied to
a population that is 50% schizophrenic, the test works well. Approximately
95% of the identified cases will be schizophrenic. However, as the base rate in
the test population decreases, the effectiveness of the test decreases dramatically. When studying children of schizophrenics, we expect about 10–15% of
them to eventually break down. Using a 10% base rate, a specificity of 95%,
and a sensitivity of 90%, the probability of accurately being detected as schizophrenic is only two-thirds. One-third of the people identified as having schizophrenia on the test will actually be normal. By the time we get to a population
where the base rate of schizophrenia is about 1% (as it is in the general
population) P_d drops to about 15%. That is, of all the people who are said to
be schizophrenic according to the screening test, only 15% of them will actually be schizophrenic, and the remaining 85% identified as schizophrenic will
not have the disorder. Thus, it is obvious that even with a test that has very
high specificity and sensitivity, the majority of the people said to have schizophrenia will not actually have it if the population being screened has a low
base rate of schizophrenia. This could make efforts at intervention appear
quite successful, because the vast majority of people identified to be at risk
and treated would have been free of schizophrenia with no intervention.

One way to circumvent this base rate problem is to use multiple indicators
(Ginsberg-Fellner et al., 1985). If the indicators are independent of each

other within the taxon, and if the prediction of future schizophrenia is based on "hitting" on, say, four indicators, then the drop-off in P_d will be much less severe. A description of the mathematics of using multiple indicators is beyond the scope of this chapter (Hanson, Gottesman, & Heston, 1976). It is sufficient to note that improvement in P_d is not a simple linear function of a number of indicators. For the time being, it is enough to ponder the difficulty and complexity of devising multiple independent valid indicators that have high sensitivity and especially high specificity and that pass the test of cross-validation.

As in the case of blues music, the theme of this song is a sad one for the listener, but it carries a basic truth. Simple Bayesian statistics point out all too clearly the difficulty in predicting rare events. The only exceptions to this rule occur when a phenomenon can be described by a single and straightforward application of one of the laws of thermodynamics, such as predicting solar eclipses. We are thankful that complex human behavior cannot be reduced to simple equations, but we have to acknowledge the immense difficulty of predicting rare and multifactorially determined traits.

Concepts from developmental biology

The use of the prefix "multi" in our multifactorial developmental view of schizophrenia may trigger synapses in our social science readers that will lead them to think of such methods as multiple regression analysis or factor analysis to try to capture the multiple determinants of schizophrenia. We want to point out that such methods appear woefully inadequate to us, for several reasons. First of all, when used for prediction, such methods make use of data already gathered, as, for example, when *already known* high school grades, SAT scores, IQ scores, and the like are used to predict college performance. This strategy follows what we current and former Minnesotans call "Meehl's law": The best predictor of future behavior is past behavior. However, this "law" does not take into consideration future developmental perturbations that may dramatically alter the course of development (Meehl, 1957). We see predicting future schizophrenia more like trying to predict which high school student will contract encephalitis, sustain brain damage, and thus be unable to go to college. Hopefully, the situation for schizophrenia is not going to be that difficult. Those scientists who try to develop prediction equations for schizophrenia will have to come to grips with *epigenetic* and *ontogenetic* developmental concepts. The prediction equations will have to have provisions for continual recalculation of the predictions based on changes in the trait-relevant environmental factors – if we can ever figure out what those environmental factors are for schizophrenia. The adjustments for time and developmental factors will have to continue well into the risk period (e.g., age 45 or 50 or more). It seems a bit presumptuous to try to predict a paraphrenia from data collected only in childhood; the situation is not analogous to the imminent predictability of Huntington's disease – a dominant gene on chromosome 4, very near to band p16.1.

Favism provides another instructive example of an illness in which the mode of inheritance and locus are known (X-linked, X,q28), the clinical features are rather straightforward (hemolytic anemia), the pathophysiology is understood (a deficiency of glucose-6-phosphate dehydrogenase (G-6-PD) in red blood cells), and the trait-relevant environmental stressors are clearly defined (eating the bean of the *Vicia faba* plant or inhaling its pollen). Certain other agents, such as sulfa drugs, primaquine (an antimalaria medicine), or naphthalene (used in mothballs), will also trigger the illness. Now suppose that a hematologist is in the same position that the schizophreneologist is in. That is, there is no way of detecting which children of parents with hemolytic anemia (some of whom have favism and some of whom have hemolytic anemia for other reasons) have inherited the G-6-PD deficiency gene. Further suppose that the hematologist does not know what the trait-relevant environmental factors are. Finally, suppose that one of the offspring who inherited the abnormal gene was, at the age of 35, driving past a field of fava beans, had a flat tire just there, inhaled the pollen while changing the tire, and developed hemolytic anemia. Would we expect the hematologist to predict the illness 10 or 20 years in advance?

A second problem with the rather standard social science way of thinking about multiple determinants/correlations/predictions is the reliance on linear models. We are familiar with the literature that suggests that linear models often are as good as, if not superior to, nonlinear models for some kinds of predictions (Dawes & Corrigan, 1974). But the phenomena predicted in these models often are quite different from phenomena encountered in biological development, where distinctly nonlinear models such as catastrophe theories (Kalbfleisa & Prentice, 1980) fit the data better and predict extreme deviations from linear trends. No linear model of growth rate, metabolic rate, diet, respiration, or other physiological property could predict the metamorphosis of a tadpole into a frog, or a caterpillar into a butterfly. These are not linear events. Some type of biological switch, sometimes in conjunction with environmental triggers (e.g., change in temperature or photoperiod), brings about the metamorphosis of one type of creature into a totally different bodily form. Likewise, neuropsychopathological disorders such as Huntington disease, bipolar psychosis (Lumry, Gottesman, & Tuason, 1982), and possibly schizophrenia may represent the turning on or turning off of developmental switches that send the normal course of development into an entirely abnormal direction.

We are clearly postulating a disease model of schizophrenia; we do not view it as quantitatively different from normal, but as qualitatively different. We are not reopening the debate of the last decade or two in developmental psychology over whether *normal* development proceeds continuously or in discrete stages; we view normal development as quantitative. However, when disease intervenes, the changes often are qualitative, and the premorbid course of development may bear no relationship to eventual outcomes. With a threshold model we can have our cake and eat it too (Gottesmen et al., 1982; McGue, Gottesman, & Rao, 1986).

This leads us to the concept of *effective genotype* (Gottesman, 1974; Hanson & Gottesman, 1979). The human genome contains some 2–4 million genes, but in most of the body only 3–6% are "turned on" at any one time. Many genes are expressed only in the brain (Sutcliffe, Kiel, Bloom, & Milner, 1987; Sutcliffe, Milner, Gottesfeld, & Reynolds, 1984), and in the CNS approximately 20% of these genes are active at any one time. During the course of development, different genes are turned off and on depending on the "genetic blueprint" and the organism's needs. The genes in effect at any one time are only a small fraction of the total genome. The most clear-cut example in humans is found in the hemoglobin system, where, early in development, embryonic hemoglobin is the predominant molecule synthesized. Later, fetal hemoglobin is produced, but after birth the production of fetal hemoglobin is switched off (with a few exceptions) in favor of the adult form. The turning on and off of lactase production during the time of suckling in mammals is another example. In tadpoles, the genes for tails are turned off during metamorphosis to frog; in caterpillars, the genes for wings lie dormant until they are switched on during pupation.

We propose that similar phenomena may occur during the development of schizophrenia. Monozygotic twins discordant for schizophrenia provide the clearest example in which two identical *total* genotypes develop into very different phenotypes, presumably because of different effective genotypes. In the affected individual, the schizophrenic genes are switched on (or some counterregulatory normal genes are switched off). The normal co-twin has a different effective genotype; the switches are set in the healthy position. We know from Fisher's work (1971) and the follow-up of her twins by I. I. Gottesman and A. Bertelsen (Gottesman & Bertelsen, 1989) that the normal co-twins carried the abnormal genotype, because the risk for schizophrenia in their adult offspring was about 10% and was not different from the risk in the affected twins' children. Somehow, the schizophrenic diathesis lay dormant in the normal co-twins, but was actualized in some of their offspring just as in their ill co-twins. This proposed switch process further complicates the task of predicting future schizophrenia in those individuals who are thought to be at risk for genetic or biological or environmental reasons.

The natural history of schizophrenia

Why does anyone believe that adult schizophrenia can be predicted in individuals who are still children? Answers to this question often start with references to the old masters, Kraepelin and E. Bleuler, who reported that somewhere between "more than half" (Bleuler, 1911/1950, p. 251) and a "considerable number" (Kraepelin, 1919, p. 236) of schizophrenics showed personality anomalies even in childhood. Manfred Bleuler's exhaustive life studies agreed that at least half of schizophrenics showed some form of personality anomaly long before the onset of psychosis (Bleuler, 1978). However, all three of these authors agreed that there was no (monolithic) premorbid personality "type" and that the range of observed premorbid personalities extended from totally normal in many people to schizoid, psychopathic, or obsessive-compulsive in others. E. Bleuler believed that these early anomalies often were the first signs of schizophrenia, and that belief, shared by many, provided the main foundation supporting current efforts to seek out predictors of future schizophrenia (Watt, Grubb, & Erlenmeyer-Kimling, 1982; Erlenmeyer-Kimling & Cornblatt, 1984).

The retrospective views of the development of schizophrenia have, however, failed to clearly delineate the natural history of schizophrenia because they have been incomplete or have been biased by knowledge of the outcome. A number of strategies have been developed to skirt these problems, including the so-called follow-up, follow-back, and high-risk methods. The follow-up method often makes use of records of deviant children, who are then reassessed in adulthood to see which, if any, have become schizophrenic. Because most schizophrenics are not sick enough in childhood to be seen by mental health workers, this method views a markedly unrepresentative sample and probably overestimates the frequency of conduct disorder (now "disruptive behavior disorders") in the premorbid picture. The follow-back method starts with adult schizophrenics and then searches through school records and other prospectively gathered data on these individuals. This method is less biased from a sampling point of view, but it suffers from lack of detail. The results of follow-up and follow-back research have been summarized extensively (Garmezy & Streitman, 1974; Nuechterlein, 1986; Offord & Cross, 1969; Watt, 1978) and will be commented on only briefly.

The overall conclusions of the follow-up and follow-back methods agree and expand the retrospective views that (a) some schizophrenics are abnormal from early years, whereas others are indistinguishable from normal, (b) the abnormalities cover the entire spectrum of childhood psychopathology, (c) only a minority of preschizophrenics are schizoid in the usual sense, (d) simple shyness alone does not foretell schizophrenia, (e) the childhood IQs of schizophrenics sometimes are lower than those of their siblings and correlate poorly with sibling IQs, and (f) males, more often than females, appear to have distinguishing premorbid abnormalities. Pointed criticism concerning the quality and validity of the diagnoses of schizophrenia that went into much of this literature would require a chapter to itself.

The convergence of opinion among retrospective, follow-up, and follow-back methods is reassuring. However, we fear that it may lead to a false sense of security. None of these data provide any evidence that premorbid abnormalities are in any way causally linked to schizophrenia. It is only an assumption that early abnormalities represent early signs of schizophrenia. This type of thinking follows a simple linear model of development (puppies become dogs) and may represent the logical fallacy of arguing that temporal relationships are due to causal relationships. When viewed from the perspective of a more complex nonlinear developmental model (caterpillars become butterflies, or at least moths), the simple linear model is found wanting. The linear model that suggests that early abnormalities grow into later abnormalities does not address the mystery of the large number of schizophrenics who are clinically normal up until quite near their breakdowns. A developmental model of schizophrenia must include these individuals too. The linear model predicts that normals should grow up to be normal, but obviously that is not the case for many schizophrenics. Something happened to profoundly deflect a normal canalization of development. It can be argued that if we really looked closely enough, say during psychoanalysis, at the so-called normals, we would find abnormalities. That may be the case, and it is one of the main goals of high-risk research. However, it is also possible that it might not be the case. No matter how closely we looked at caterpillars, we would never find wings, though with DNA sequencing techniques we might find the genes for wings.

Our second concern about the causal relationships, if any, between childhood abnormalities and adult schizophrenia centers on issues of specificity (Hanson & Gottesman, 1976). The premorbid picture is extremely heterogeneous. The pre-illness personalities and abnormalities found among people who later become schizophrenics also are found among people who develop many nonschizophrenic adult abnormalities, as well as among people who grow up to be normal. This clashes with our view that there are specific genetic factors that are necessary for the development of schizophrenia. The preponderance of behavioral genetic literature shows that, for example, if one twin is schizophrenic and the other twin develops a mental illness, the second twin's illness will almost always be schizophrenia or some variation of a schizophrenic spectrum. What is inherited is specific for schizophrenia and does not result in a general predisposition toward mental illness. Thus, we have to wonder if the heterogeneous and nonspecific premorbid abnormalities, when found, represent something other than the specific major diathesis for schizophrenia.

The task of determining whether or not childhood behavioral abnormalities are causally linked to adult schizophrenic outcome is a task for future research. At least four possibilities must be considered: (a) Childhood indicators might represent the earliest signs or effects of an already begun schizophrenia, as Bleuler thought. If such were the case, the early childhood abnormalities would indicate when the schizophrenic process began, but would not necessarily shed light on either the genetic or the environmental contributors toward the development of schizophrenia. (b) Childhood predictors of adult schizophrenia might identify potentiators (Meehl, 1973) or correlates of potentiators that lead to breakdown. Such potentiators might be parts of the predisposed individual's environment or general genetic background. For example, school failure by high-risk children might predict future breakdown. Such a school failure sign might be due to family pathology (or low IQ). Yet the school failure sign would be neither a consequence of a high-risk genotype nor, by iself, an early sign of schizophrenic behavior. Many other children who experienced school failure would grow up to be nonschizophrenic, and many schizophrenics would not have a history of failure in school. (c) Abnormal childhood characteristics might be indicators of a high-risk genotype. Such indicators might point the way toward specific neurobiological defects associated with the development of schizophrenia and might denote individuals with the potential for future schizophrenia. However, many of these individuals may never develop a full schizophrenic picture, and the course of their development may even take them back into a totally normal pattern of behavior. (d) The early childhood abnormalities seen in the history of some schizophrenics might have nothing to do with schizophrenia at all, but might represent their reaction or adaptation to chaotic environments. We know that some (a minority, to be sure) schizophrenics have schizophrenic parents or parents who are otherwise abnormal; see, for example, the Genain quadruplets (Rosenthal, 1963).

Most follow-up and follow-back studies have failed to assess the early environments of schizophrenics. Those authors who have (Bleuler, 1978; Ricks & Berry, 1970) have found high rates of abnormalities in the families of preschizophrenics. Manfred Bleuler estimated that about a third of his probands grew up in "horrible" conditions. Furthermore, the bulk of the evidence from ongoing high-risk studies shows that when significant abnormalities are reported in the children of schizophrenic parents, similar findings are also observed among the children of nonschizophrenic but psychotic parents (Lewin, 1984). This suggests that early behavioral abnormalities often may represent the generalized effects of living with disturbed parents and may not point directly to specific etiological determinants of mental illness. Manfred Bleuler (1984, p. 538) believed that "it is important to point out that schizoid personality development in the premorbid history of a schizophrenic is closely associated with disorganized childhood circumstances." From this point of view, the early childhood abnormalities of some schizophrenics may represent nonspecific environmental effects that would occur to virtually anyone living in a chaotic environment. If the schizophrenics had been reared in a less chaotic environment (e.g., had been adopted into normal homes), they might have grown up to be schizophrenic anyway, but could have had a very different premorbid course of development. Likewise, many deviant children living in disturbed homes may shed their behavioral problems when exposed to a normal environment and may grow up to be normal (Schulsinger, 1980).

Preliminary findings from our high-risk project

Our high-risk sample was composed of 33 children born to a schizophrenic mother or schizophrenic father or both. These children were compared to 36 children who each had one or both parents with some nonschizophrenic but major form of psychopathology, and they were also compared to two samples of children of normals, the parents in one sample being matched to the parents of the schizophrenics for social class, age of mother at the time the child was born, and parity. We made use of data collected through a larger study on the relationships between birth and pregnancy complications and childhood outcome. The full details of our sampling and our preliminary findings through a 7-year follow-up were presented in detail a decade ago (Hanson et al., 1976). In our original paper we argued that the key to high-risk research was not in looking for group differences between high-risk samples and control samples but in searching for specific individuals within the high-risk sample who were most likely to develop schizophrenia in adulthood. This strategy is important, because if only 10% or 15% of the high-risk children go on to develop schizophrenia, they may not be so deviant in childhood as to pull the mean for their sample a significant distance away from the mean for control groups. There may be significant findings in certain individuals who are destined to be schizophrenic, but the magnitudes of the differences may not be large enough, or the numbers of people in whom they occur may not be large enough, to create group differences. Thus, we set out to identify individual children who distinguished themselves as being particularly schizophrenia-prone as compared with the remainder of their own high-risk population and control groups. Our procedures were exploratory in nature and were offered as an example of the kind of analysis that needs to be done, but by no means do we claim that they were ideal. As we had hypothesized, we only rarely found significant group mean differences, and when we did find such differences they made no logical sense and were not more common than one would expect by chance. However, in our efforts to isolate specific individuals who might be at especially high risk for schizophrenia, we did find five individuals who were distinguished by having poor motor performance and large intraindividual variances on a multitude of psychological tests and who had behavioral problems ("schizoid"-like), as assessed by behavioral rating schedules. All five of these children came from the group of children with schizophrenic parents, giving us a "hit rate" of 17%. No such children were found in any of the three control samples. Brief case histories of these children were presented in our original publication to show that these were far from normal children at age 7.

We are now engaged in a follow-up study of the high-risk children and their controls, with the aid of funding from the John D. and Catherine T. MacArthur Foundation research network headed by Norman Garmezy. Our pilot follow-up efforts involve a search of public records concerning these children and also an interview with one parent of each child, almost always the parent who is not mentally ill. So far, we have follow-up data on four of the original five "special" children selected by our three indicators, along with data for many of the controls. We have been unable to locate the fifth child at this time, but we have not yet made "a full-court press" because the individuals doing the search and follow-up interviews are blind to the parents' diagnostic status and to the children's risk status. We do not want to put too much emphasis on following up our one remaining special child for fear of un-blinding the interviewers. All of our study children are now in their early twenties. The results of our preliminary follow-up have surprised us and, as one might guess, have informed the preceding discussion.

Of the four special high-risk children we have been able to follow, none has any evidence of major psychiatric disturbance currently. The reader is re-ferred to our original report (Hanson et al., 1976) for the case histories of the original five children who were positive on our indicators. These children are identified as cases A through E.

Case D has so far eluded our follow-up pursuits. Case A is currently mar-ried and has been steadily employed in a blue-collar manufacturing position for the last 4 years. However, the subject had a rather stormy period during adolescence. During grade school he received counseling and special educa-tion for learning problems and was eventually expelled for his conduct distur-bance. During his teen years he did abuse alcohol and marijuana, but now is abstinent. Between the ages of 11 and 18 he was frequently in trouble with the law for stealing. At the age of 11 he was placed in an adolescent treatment facility for 2 years, and at the age of 16 he was in a juvenile correction center for 1.5 years. He had also spent 10 days in the county jail for theft. Interest-ingly, the patient's father, who was one of our most severe schizophrenics, also had a history of poor school performance and failed the fourth and sixth grades; he was viewed as incorrigible and was expelled in the 10th grade. During his own school years the father engaged in numerous antisocial acts, including theft, breaking school windows, threatening teachers, and truancy. At the age of 15 the father was sent to a juvenile correctional facility for purse snatching and was later incarcerated for receiving stolen goods and received an additional term in jail for larceny. He, too, had a history of abusing drugs. Case B had no reported adolescent problems, graduated from high school, attended college for 3 years, and has been steadily employed for the last 1.5 years in a baggage handling job. Case C also had no additional childhood or adolescent problems, completed high school, and has been working steadily for the last 2 years as a skilled laborer in a manufacturing company. Case E's only problem was a DWI charge. The patient's mother, who was the infor-mant for the follow-up, and with whom the patient still lives, reports no other evidence of alcohol or drug problems and no psychiatric symptoms. The patient is working full-time as a carpenter and a house painter.

In spite of the difficult backgrounds that these children have experienced and in spite of their early psychopathology, they appear to be making ade-quate adjustments as young adults. Our follow-up plans include direct inter-views with the subjects, including structured interviews, which will undoubt-edly produce much more information. However, on this preliminary basis, these individuals, as well as most of the other members of our sample, are making decent adjustments. The only subject who has had any formal psychiatric diagnosis is the daughter of a schizophrenic; at the age of 16 she developed bulimia and depression, and at the age of 18 she took a minor overdose of aspirin. She has been charged twice for passing bad checks. She had been adopted shortly after birth and grew up in a stable home. Her early premorbid history was remarkable for the absence of any indicators of future problems. Her 4-year IQ was 105, and her 7-year IQ was 110. On all behavior rating profiles and behavioral summaries she was described as a normal child. At 4 years she was described as "normal, pleasant, sweet-tempered and willing." At 7 years she was described as a "middle to bright average in intellectual functioning . . . pleasant, and enjoys both interpersonal and task aspects of testing." Some mild tension was observed, and she was viewed as "a trifle self-doubting but responsive to encouragement." The only other bad outcome among these children of schizophrenics was the death of a 12-year-old girl who, while riding her bicycle, was run over by a car.

These results are preliminary and incomplete; yet they give us pause to wonder about the epigenetic development of psychopathology and the epigenetic development of normality. The children we believed to be most likely to develop severe psychopathology have grown up and are coping with life fairly well. One child at very high risk did have trouble; it was not schizophrenic in nature, but was associated with character disorder or antisocial personality traits. It may be that he acquired these traits from his schizophrenic father, who also had antisocial features, and we may have an example of "segregation" of two independently inherited genetic predispositions. The father separated from the mother when the patient was 3 years old, and the patient has had no contact with him since. The only other child of a schizophrenic who had significant psychiatric problems was described as quite normal in childhood and had the advantage of a stable adoptive home. The results remind us of the findings of Heston, Denney, and Pauley (1966), who followed up 47 adults who had been institutionalized as children. Many of those children had been subjected to significant psychosocial deprivation and had significant behavioral problems. However, by adulthood, the majority of those children "grew out" of their childhood problems. They concluded that "it appears that the human organism has the happy capacity of reversing the effects of childhood emotional trauma" (Heston et al., 1966, p. 1109).

In recent years, Garmezy and others have pointed out the need to study the "invulnerables." We agree that if we could discover and then teach certain qualities of living that would make a person immune to psychopathology it would be a tremendous advance in our field. However, we have to wonder if invulnerability is not simply normality; perhaps the human organism is endowed with a remarkable capacity to channel development in the direction of health. That is to say, invulnerability is not something extra that is added but something that will happen naturally as long as the perturbations to development (through environmental forces or inherited illness) are not too great. No one would suggest that the 50% of children of Huntington disease patients who grow up healthy possess the trait of invulnerability, except in the sense that they are "invulnerable" because they do not have the gene for Huntington disease. There is nothing special added to their normality to make them disease-free. The value and frequency of being normal are greatly underrated.

A follow-up of the Hathaway-Monachesi sample of 15,000 adolescent MMPIs

From 1948 to 1954, Starke R. Hathaway and Elio D. Monachesi assembled the largest collection of representative adolescent MMPIs that ever was or probably ever will be assembled. They succeeded in giving the MMPI to 15,300 ninth-grade students in the state of Minnesota, collected a vast amount of social behavioral and demographic information about these students, and followed-up a good number of them in the 12th grade with retest MMPIs (Gottesman, Hanson, Kroeker, & Briggs, 1987a). This data bank provides a unique opportunity to examine prospectively psychological test results that were gathered without any apparent sampling biases, as the entire public school population was well sampled. We began a pilot study to follow-up some of this cohort. We asked the question whether or not the MMPI could predict or detect future schizophrenia at age-15 testing. Our pilot research involved comparing our list of 15,000 adolescents with a list of all patients admitted to Minnesota state psychiatric hospitals and the criminal justice system over the period of time these adolescents were young adults in the early 1970s. We found a total of 183 individuals from the original Hathaway-Monachesi sample who had been in one of our state institutions for deviant behavior. One of us (D.H.) reviewed the charts for the psychiatric and alcoholic patients, tracked down the records from other hospitals where these patients had received psychiatric care, and assembled a case history for each patient. These histories were then submitted to the two other authors (I.G. and L.H.) for diagnosis of schizophrenia. To these 22 cases we added another 4 cases whose state hospital diagnoses indicated schizophrenia, but because the original charts had been lost or destroyed, we could not review them in detail. The mean MMPI for the 26 ninth-graders who developed schizophrenia were compared with those for their same-sex classmate controls as ninth-graders. The future schizophrenics as a group clearly appeared different in the ninth grade, as compared with their controls who were never (to our knowledge) institutionalized. The future schizophrenics' elevations on the schizophrenic and psychopathic deviate scales were above a T score of 70, and a full standard deviation higher than scores for controls, with interesting sex differences. These findings are in tune with the belief, as discussed earlier in this chapter, that symptoms of schizophrenia may be present at a relatively early age.

The real question, however, is whether the MMPI is predicting future

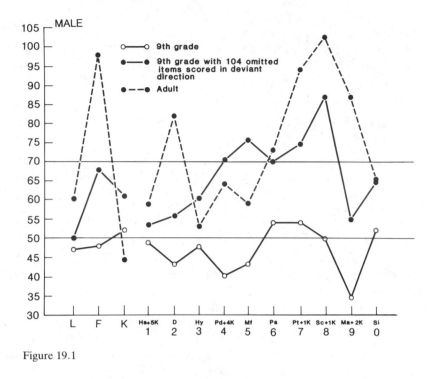

Figure 19.1

schizophrenia or is detecting schizophrenia that has already begun. One way of addressing this question is to look at the MMPIs of the early-onset cases versus the late-onset cases. Presumably, if the MMPI has the power to predict schizophrenia in the same way that the astronomer can predict eclipses next year or 10,000 years from now, the late-onset cases should be as predictable as the early-onset cases. We used age at first hospitalization as an objective estimate for age at onset and divided our schizophrenic sample into two on either side of the median. For the earlier-onset half of the sample, the mean age at first hospitalization was 19.8 years, or roughly 5 years after they had taken the MMPI in the ninth grade. The later-onset group had a mean age at first hospitalization of 27 years, which was more than a decade from the time they took the MMPI at age 15. We compared these two profiles with a population average for 14,000 of the 15-year-olds in the total Hathaway-Monachesi sample. It was clear that the early-onset patients appeared substantially more disturbed than did either the late-onset patients or the subjects in the normative sample. The early-onset patients were particularly noteworthy for their MMPI-associated schizoid characteristics of depression, anxiety, internalized anger, social alienation, and withdrawal (scales 2, 7, 4, and 0) as compared with the other groups. The late-onset patients would be quite difficult, if not impossible, to distinguish from their own controls based on their MMPIs.

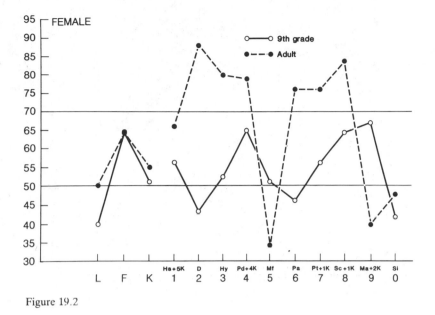

Figure 19.2

Our follow-up of these schizophrenics gave us the unique opportunity to study the prehospitalization MMPIs of the schizophrenics compared with their profiles after hospitalization and also provided a number of individual case histories that we found illustrative of our main points.

The first set of MMPI profiles (Figure 19.1) shows a remarkable transformation from complete normality at age 15, the lower profile, to textbook schizophrenia at age 22. Out of curiosity, we rescored the 104 items omitted at age 15 when we found that this boy had become hospitalized; the new profile was an eye-opener. Three further profiles generated during episodes of illness or remission never returned to the normal range or shape. He had two brothers hospitalized for mental illness. He reported being quiet and shy, with few friends, and uncomfortable around girls. Dropping out of school after the 11th grade (poor grades), he contracted rheumatic fever at age 20 and spent 6 months in bed. For 1.5 years after recovery he worked at home. He reported many symptoms of depression, visual hallucinations (flashing lights), and logorrhea and was admitted to a state hospital, at which time the most elevated profile was produced; treated with Stelazine and ECT, he was discharged after 18 weeks with a diagnosis of simple schizophrenia. He was rehospitalized within 4 months for a 65-week period, and then four more times, for a total period of 234 weeks in hospital. When last interviewed as an outpatient at age 33, he looked like a chronic residual patient.

The next set (Figure 19.2) shows a very common, prototypical sociopathic adolescent female profile at age 15, with a switch to textbook schizophrenia at

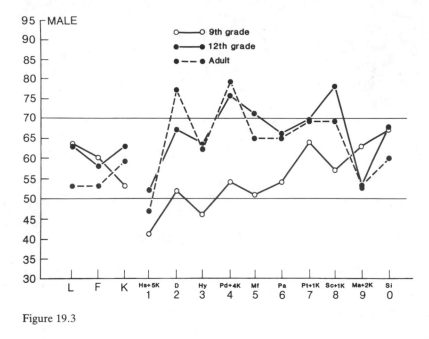

Figure 19.3

age 26 during the first week of her second hospitalization, which was a continuation of her first episode 7 weeks earlier. Her parents and two siblings had no
mental illness reported. The patient was an excellent student in high school,
but had a restricted social life (never dated, no parties; her parents were
orthodox Lutherans); she worked as a professional performing artist after
graduation. At age 26 she was abandoned by a boyfriend after refusing his
sexual overtures during their engagement; she soon lost her job and began
excessive alcohol consumption. She appeared to be living in a dream world.
She was hospitalized, but refused to eat or see visitors; she was transferred to
a state hospital, where she appeared oriented, with memory intact. She had
no delusions, hallucinations, or thought disorder, but was introverted, shy,
and perfectionistic; she improved gradually on Stelazine plus Thorazine and
was discharged after a total of 24 weeks in hospital, with a chart diagnosis of
schizoid personality.

The third set of profiles (Figure 19.3) represents part of our lucky yield,
wherein one of our future schizophrenics had been given the MMPI in the 9th
and 12th grades, as well as 4 months after graduation during the patient's first
hospitalization for paranoid schizophrenia; he had already been diagnosed as
schizophrenic during his senior year, thus accounting for the similarity of the
two elevated and schizophrenic-suggestive profiles in the figure. The boy's
history contains "proof" of virtually all theories about the etiology of schizophrenia. He was the product of a difficult birth, with instrument delivery and
lacerations. His mother was 16 years old, and she and his 38-year-old father

were divorced when he was 6 years old; he was reared by his maternal grand-mother from 6 months to 2.5 years of age, when she left. The maternal grandmother and a maternal aunt were known to be mentally ill. He said that since the third grade he had felt different from everyone else, and by the seventh grade (2 years before the first MMPI in the figure) he was having trouble reading and concentrating. His tested IQ was superior (127). He had few friends and no extracurricular activities. At age 17 he was referred by a counselor to outpatient care for numerous problems (hostility, disinterest in school, depression, feeling confused, insomnia, worried about life and the future). He believed that his bosses at his after-school job had sexual ideas about him, that his minister and stepfather were homosexuals, and that he had "girls galore" (actually he had never had a date). He was diagnosed as schizophrenic and put on Thorazine. One year later, a few months after threatening suicide with a gun, he slashed his wrists superficially and was hospitalized (Pd and D over 70); he had a clear sensorium and good memory, but he believed that the Russians were going to bomb the hospital for Christ-mas; he also saw Sputniks and hid in his closet. He was diagnosed as paranoid schizophrenic. By age 20 he had had two more episodes much like the first; he was treated with phenothiazines and showed no response to repeated ECT.

The onset of schizophrenia in the last case probably began as early as age 10 and thus was rather atypical for schizophrenia as a whole. Nonetheless, an effort to "forecast" schizophrenia from his ninth-grade test results would have been an exercise in futility; he was not being truthful, and although the slant of the profile was suspiciously psychoticlike, the elevation was not contribut-ing to the mean profile differences mentioned earlier that led to clear differ-ences from both controls and normals. The first two cases illustrate other instances of futility, wherein multifactorial (including stochastic) processes led to switches from lives involving pseudonormal and normal limits to schizophre-nias at ages 22 and 26, respectively. Clearly, the MMPI alone is not sufficient to detect the relevant endophenotype that may mark the genotype we are pursuing in high-risk studies.

We shall yet overcome, despite the blues music and lyrics we have played so far. We have never been more optimistic about the future of long-range schizo-phrenia forecasting. Our optimism is not due to histrionic features in our personalities but rather to our reading of the burgeoning human genetics and neurobiology literature. The pace of relevant discoveries and applications is breathtaking. We refer to the advances in brain imaging techniques (Early, Reiman, Raichle, & Spitznagel, 1987), to advances in restriction enzyme polymorphism mapping (Feder, Gurling, Darby, & Cavalli-Sforza, 1985; Gurling, 1985), to advances in neurotransmitter defects as biological markers (Bondy, Ackenheil, & Birzle, 1987), and to advances incorporating popula-tion genetics and genetic epidemiology (Gottesman, McGuffin, & Farmer, 1987b; McGue & Gottesman, 1989). We are confident that Norman Garmezy will have a very active "retirement," during which time he can take us to task for our oversights and optimism and share in our joy for any successes in long-range forecasting. Any such joy must be tempered by the awesome responsibility of using such information humanely.

References

Bleuler, E. (1950). *Dementia praecox or the group of schizophrenias* (J. Zinkin, Trans.). New York: International Universities Press. (Original work published 1911)

Bleuler, M. (1978). *The schizophrenic disorders: Long-term patient and family studies* (S. M. Clemens, Trans.). New Haven: Yale University Press.

Bleuler, M. (1984). Different forms of childhood stress and patterns of adult psychiatric outcome. In N. F. Watt, E. F. Anthony, L. C. Wynne, & J. E. Rolf (Eds.), *Children at risk for schizophrenia* (pp. 537–42). Cambridge University Press.

Bondy, B., Ackenheil, M., & Birzle, W. (1987). ^{3}H-spiperone binding sites in lymphocytes as possible vulnerability marker in schizophrenia. *Journal of Psychiatric Research, 21,* 521–9.

Dawes, R. M., & Corrigan, B. (1974). Linear models in decision making. *Psychological Bulletin, 81,* 95–106.

Early, T. S., Reiman, E. M., Raichle, M. E., & Spitznagel, E. L. (1987). Left globus pallidus abnormality in never medicated patients with schizophrenia. *Proceedings of the National Academy of Sciences USA, 21,* 521–9.

Erlenmeyer-Kimling, L., & Cornblatt, B. (1984). Biobehavioral risk factors in children of schizophrenic parents. *Journal of Autism and Developmental Disabilities, 14,* 357–74.

Feder, J., Gurling, N. M. D., Darby, J., & Cavalli-Sforza, L. L. (1985). DNA restriction fragment analysis of the propiomelanocontin gene in schizophrenia and bipolar disorders. *American Journal of Human Genetics, 37,* 289–94.

Fisher, M. (1971). Psychoses in the offspring of schizophrenic monozygotic twins and their normal co-twins. *British Journal of Psychiatry, 115,* 981–90.

Freud, S. (1955). The psychogenesis of a case of homosexuality in a woman. In *The complete psychological works of Sigmund Freud* (Vol. 18). London: Hogarth. (Original work published 1920)

Garmezy, N. (1968). Contributions of experimental psychology to understanding the origins of schizophrenia. In J. Romano (Ed.), *The origins of schizophrenia* (pp. 201–13). Amsterdam: Excerpta Medica.

Garmezy, N. (1974). Children at risk: The search for the antecedents of schizophrenia. Part II. *Schizophrenia Bulletin, 9,* 55–125.

Garmezy, N., & Streitman, S. (1974). Children at risk: The search for the antecedents of schizophrenia, Part I. *Schizophrenia Bulletin, 8,* 13–90.

Ginsberg-Fellner, F., Witt, M. E., Franklin, B. N., Yagihashi, S., Toguchi, Y., Dobersen, M. J., Rubinstein, P., & Notkins, A. L. (1985). Triad of markers for identifying children at high risk of developing insulin-dependent diabetes mellitus. *Journal of the American Medical Association, 254,* 1469–72.

Gottesman, I. I. (1974). Developmental genetics and ontogenetic psychology: Overdue detente and propositions from a matchmaker. In A. Pick (Ed.), *Minnesota symposium on child psychology* (pp. 55–80). Minneapolis: University of Minnesota Press.

Gottesman, I. I., & Bertelsen, A. (1989). Confirming unexpressed genotypes for schizophrenia: Risks in the offspring of Fischer's Danish identical and fraternal discordant pairs. *Archives of General Psychiatry, 46,* 867–72.

Gottesman, I. I., Hanson, D. R., Kroeker, T. A., & Briggs, P. (1987a). New MMPI normative data and power transformed T-score tables for the Hathaway-Monachesi Minnesota cohort of 14,019 fifteen-year-olds and 3,674 eighteen-year-olds. In R. P. Archer (Ed.), *Using the MMPI with adolescents* (pp. 241–97). Hillsdale, NJ: Erlbaum.

Gottesman, I. I., McGuffin, P., & Farmer, A. (1987b). Clinical genetics as clues to the "real" genetics of schizophrenia. *Schizophrenia Bulletin, 13,* 23–47.

Gottesman, I. I., Shields, J., & Hanson, D. R. (1982). *Schizophrenia: The epigenetic puzzle.* Cambridge University Press.

Grove, W. M. (1986). *Clinical inference from psychological tests: Last nails in the coffin.* Paper presented at the Minnesota Psychological Association annual meeting.

Gurling, H. (1985). Application of molecular biology to mental illness: Analysis of genomic DNA and brain RNA. *Psychiatric Developments, 3,* 257–73.

Hanson, D. R., & Gottesman, I. I. (1976). The genetics, if any, of infantile autism and childhood schizophrenia. *Journal of Autism and Childhood Schizophrenia, 6,* 209–34.

Hanson, D. R., & Gottesman, I. I. (1979). Genetic concepts for psychopathology. In H. van Pragg, M. N. Lader, O. J. Rafaelsen, & E. J. Sachar (Eds.), *Handbook of biological psychiatry* (pp. 273–301). New York: Marcel Dekker.

Hanson, D. R., Gottesman, I. I., & Heston, L. L. (1976). Some possible indicators of adult schizophrenia inferred from children of schizophrenics. *British Journal of Psychiatry, 129,* 142–54.

Heston, L. L., Denney, D. D., & Pauley, I. B. (1966). The adult adjustment of persons institutionalized as children. *British Journal of Psychiatry, 112,* 1103–10.

Kalbfleisa, J. D., & Prentice, R. L. (1980). *The statistical analysis of failure time data.* New York: Wiley.

Kraepelin, E. (1919). *Dementia praecox and paraphrenia.* Edinburgh: Livingstone.

Lewin, R. R. J. (1984). Stalking the schizophrenia marker: Evidence for a general vulnerability model of psychopathology. In N. F. Watt, E. J. Anthony, L. C. Wynne, & J. E. Rolf (Eds.), *Children at risk for schizophrenia* (pp. 545–50). Cambridge University Press.

Lumry, A., Gottesman, I. I., & Tuason, U. B. (1982). MMPI states dependency during the course of bipolar psychosis. *Psychiatry Research, 7,* 59–67.

McGue, M., & Gottesman, I. I. (1989). Genetic linkage in schizophrenia: Perspectives from genetic epidemiology. *Schizophrenia Bulletin, 15,* 281–92.

McGue, M., Gottesman, I. I., & Rao, D. C. (1986). The analysis of schizophrenia family data. *Behavior Genetics, 16,* 75–87.

Meehl, P. E. (1954). *Clinical versus statistical prediction: A theoretical analysis and a review of the evidence.* Minneapolis: University of Minnesota Press.

Meehl, P. E. (1957). When shall we use our heads instead of the formula. *Journal of Counseling Psychology, 4,* 268–72.

Meehl, P. E. (1973). Specific genetic etiology, psychodynamics, and therapeutic nihilism. In P. E. Meehl (Ed.), *Psychodiagnosis: Selected papers* (pp. 182–99). Minneapolis: University of Minnesota Press.

Meehl, P. E., & Rosen, A. (1955). Antecedent probability and the efficiency of psychometric signs, patterns, or cutting scores. *Psychological Bulletin, 52,* 194–216.

Nuechterlein, K. (1986). Childhood precursors of adult schizophrenia. *Journal of Child Psychology and Psychiatry, 27,* 133–44.

Offord, D. R., & Cross, L. A. (1969). Behavioral antecedents of adult schizophrenia. *Archives of General Psychiatry, 21,* 267–83.

Popper, K. (1961). *The poverty of historicism.* London: Routledge & Kegan Paul.

Ricks, D. F., & Berry, J. C. (1970). Family patterns that precede schizophrenia. In M. Roff & D. Ricks (Eds.), *Life history research in psychopathology* (pp. 31–50). Minneapolis: University of Minnesota Press.

Rosenthal, D. (1963). *The Genain quadruplets.* New York: Basic Books.

Schulsinger, H. (1980). Clinical outcome of ten years follow-up of children of schizophrenic mothers. In S. B. Selles, R. Crandall, M. Roff, J. Strauss, & W. Pollin (Eds.), *Human functioning in longitudinal perspective* (pp. 33–40). Baltimore: Williams & Wilkins.

Sutcliffe, J. G., Kiel, M., Bloom, F. E., & Milner, R. J. (1987). Gene activity in the CNS, a tool for understanding of brain function and dysfunction. In F. Vogel & K. Sperling (Eds.), *Human genetics* (pp. 474–83). Berlin: Springer-Verlag.

Sutcliffe, J. G., Milner, R. J., Gottesfeld, J. M., & Reynolds, W. (1984). Control of neuronal gene expression. *Science, 225,* 1308–15.

Watt, N. F. (1978). Patterns of childhood social development in adult schizophrenics. *Archives of General Psychiatry, 35,* 160–5.

Watt, N. F., Grubb, T. W., & Erlenmeyer-Kimling, L. (1982). Social, emotional, and intellectual behavior at school among children at high risk for schizophrenia. *Journal of Consulting and Clinical Psychology, 50,* 171–81.

20   Vulnerability factors in children at risk:
      anomalies in attentional functioning and
      social behavior

Keith H. Nuechterlein, Susan Phipps-Yonas,
Regina Driscoll, and Norman Garmezy

The challenge of understanding the origins, precursors, and core abnormalities of schizophrenic disorders has led a number of investigators to the so-
called high-risk method during the last three decades. To avoid confounding
the consequences of these disorders with their causes and precursors, investigators have focused on individuals who are not manifesting schizophrenic
disorders, but who are at increased risk for their development (Garmezy,
1974, 1978; Garmezy & Streitman, 1974). The most popular of these strategies has been the study of children born to a schizophrenic parent, whose risk
for schizophrenia is known to be substantially higher than the population base
rate. Estimates of the eventual incidence of schizophrenia among children of a
schizophrenic parent range from 3% to 15%, depending on the breadth of the
diagnostic criteria employed and other factors, an incidence 10 to 15 times the
base rate for comparable populations (Gottesman & Shields, 1982; Kendler,
Gruenberg, & Tsuang, 1985). In addition, considering the data from twin and
adoption studies, one can assume that some offspring of a schizophrenic
parent who do not develop schizophrenia nevertheless have an increased
genetic vulnerability to such disorders.

    The Minnesota High-Risk Studies, which were developed under the overall
direction of Norman Garmezy and are part of a larger research program
entitled Project Competence, have employed this research strategy in a series
of investigations focusing on potential vulnerability factors and prodromal
anomalies in schizophrenic disorders. This chapter integrates data from sev-

This research was supported by grants to Norman Garmezy and to Norman Garmezy and Keith
Nuechterlein from the Schizophrenia Research program of the Scottish Rite, Northern Masonic
Jurisdiction, U.S.A. Additional analyses of the peer nomination data were supported by a UCLA
Academic Senate grant to Keith Nuechterlein and by the Data Management Unit of the UCLA
Clinical Research Center for the Study of Schizophrenia (National Institute of Mental Health
research grant MH-30911). The authors thank Daniel Goldstein, Richard Rexiesen, John
Shabatura, and Mark Vangen for their help with data collection and Jim Mintz, Ph.D., and Sun
Hwang, M.S., M.P.H., for their consultation on data analyses.

eral studies in the final phase of the Minnesota High-Risk Studies. First, we shall present the overall subject recruitment strategy and the individual studies of attention and cognition that were completed during this phase. Following the individual study descriptions, we shall examine interrelationships between attentional and cognitive functioning, on the one hand, and social behavior, on the other, to determine the extent to which these two domains overlap among representative normal children, children at risk for schizophrenia, and hyperactive children during late childhood and early adolescence. Among children at risk for schizophrenia, these analyses are relevant to whether an attentional abnormality is a primary vulnerability indicator or part of a constellation of anomalies across several domains of functioning. The appearance of different associations between attentional and social functioning in hyperactive children, as compared with children of a schizophrenic parent, would help to differentiate further the characteristic patterns of behavior associated with childhood hyperactivity and vulnerability to schizophrenia.

The research samples

The Minnesota studies of children at high risk for schizophrenia and other psychopathology have involved predominantly cross-sectional assessments of high-risk samples in an attempt to delineate the most promising variables on which children vulnerable to schizophrenic disorders might be distinguished. Throughout this series of studies, comparison groups defined by nonschizophrenic maternal psychopathology and by childhood psychopathology have been included to shed light on the similarities and differences of any anomalies in these groups as compared with those found among the children of schizophrenic mothers. The children of schizophrenic mothers, as well as the children in the other groups selected for maternal psychopathology and for childhood psychopathology, have been referred to as "target" children within the Minnesota studies.

In addition to these target groups, the Minnesota studies have included both representative normal children and children matched with the target children on demographic variables and, most recently, also matched on peer evaluation level, to allow an examination of the possible roles of these factors in any differences on other variables between target children and representative normal peers. This reseach design is admittedly rather complex, but this complexity has allowed isolation of the specificity of abnormalities and has allowed potential confounding demographic factors to be ruled out as spurious sources of any abnormalities that characterize children at risk for schizophrenia.

The Minnesota project has included three distinct periods of sample recruitment. The initial sample of 356 children, including 31 children of schizophrenic mothers, was recruited in 1968–9 for the studies of peer and teacher ratings and of academic performance by Rolf (1972, 1976) and Rolf and Garmezy (1974). The second sample of 240 children, including 20 children born to schizophrenic mothers, was recruited in 1970–1 for the reaction time research of Marcus (1973), which has been summarized by Garmezy (1978) and Garmezy and Devine (1984).

A final sample of 183 individually assessed children, including 24 children of schizophrenic mothers, was recruited through review of psychiatric admissions during 1971–5 for research on vigilance by Nuechterlein (1983, 1984) and was expanded 1 year later, by the addition of more stratified normal comparison children and a group of antisocial delinquent children, to a total of 231 children for the cross-modal reaction time research of Phipps-Yonas (1984) and the incidental and intentional learning research of Driscoll (1984). In addition to the individually assessed children, peer evaluation data were collected on a much larger sample ($n = 1,029$) that comprised all same-sex children in the same classrooms as the children of schizophrenic mothers, the children of nonpsychotic but psychiatrically disordered mothers, and hyperative children. The sample used in the Nuechterlein, Phipps-Yonas, and Driscoll studies during the final phase of the high-risk research will be the focus of this chapter.

Children of schizophrenic mothers

Children who had schizophrenic biological mothers served as the group at heightened risk for schizophrenia. These children were identified on the basis of (a) screening of consecutive admissions of mothers at one large state hospital and another major public hospital that serve the Minneapolis area to identify women with hospital diagnoses of schizophrenia who had children in the 9- to 16-year-old age range, (b) diagnostic review in 1975–6 by three clinical psychologists (Norman Garmezy, Vernon Devine, and Keith Nuechterlein) who made independent ratings of symptoms and diagnoses, and (c) location of the children in the public school system to allow selection of normal comparison subjects at the public school sites. Patients with organic brain syndrome, alcoholism, or mental retardation were excluded. Patients for whom diagnostic agreement was not reached by at least two of the three judges were also excluded from the study sample, as were women whose children were not attending the public school system.

The initial diagnoses of schizophrenia were based on two sets of criteria: the research classification criteria developed by Kety, Rosenthal, Wender, Schulsinger, and their colleagues in the Danish adoption studies (Kety, Rosenthal, Wender, & Schulsinger, 1968; Kety, Rosenthal, Wender, Schulsinger, & Jacobsen, 1978; Rieder, Rosenthal, Wender, & Blumenthal, 1975) and DSM-II criteria. Diagnostic judges were required to make ratings of 48 psychiatric symptoms, using the Case Record Rating Scale (Strauss & Harder, 1975), as they reviewed all case records from the index and prior hospitalizations to aid in the determination of their diagnostic judgments. Of the 24 index schizophrenic mothers who were included in the initial study of this project phase by Nuechterlein (1983), unanimous first-choice diagnoses of schizophrenia were received by 21 women using the criteria for certain schizophrenia from the

Danish adoption studies, and by 22 women using DSM-II criteria. In the remaining cases, two judges assigned a first-choice diagnosis of schizophrenia, and the third judge listed schizophrenia as a possible diagnosis.

These patients were rediagnosed in 1981–2 using the Research Diagnostic Criteria (RDC) (Spitzer, Endicott, & Robins, 1978) to examine the impact of a narrower definition of schizophrenia on the group discriminations that had been achieved using the initial diagnoses. These diagnoses were based on independent review of the Case Record Rating Scale data and accompanying symptom descriptions by two clinical psychologists (William S. Edell and Keith Nuechterlein). This review indicated that the initial schizophrenic index group contained 13 patients who met RDC criteria for schizophrenia, 8 patients with RDC schizoaffective disorder, and 3 patients who had multiple RDC schizotypal features and met DSM-III criteria for schizotypal personality disorder. These alternative diagnoses were used to reanalyze the data from vigilance measures using an RDC schizophrenia definition (Nuechterlein, 1983).

The degree of psychiatric impairment was rated by the original three diagnostic judges on the 100-point Global Assessment Scale (GAS) (Endicott, Spitzer, Fleiss, & Cohen, 1976) and on a 7-point General Psychopathology Scale devised by John S. Strauss, M.D. The mean GAS scores (averaged across the three raters) in the schizophrenic sample ranged from 21.7 to 50.0, with a mean of 31.2, where low scores index low levels of functioning. In the psychiatric comparison mothers, mean GAS scores ranged from 36.7 to 75.0, with a mean of 55.7. (The GAS was modified slightly to exclude a single serious suicide attempt as a criterion for ratings in the 31–40 range, in order to decrease its dependence on a temporary suicidal state. This change tended to improve the scores of the psychiatric comparison mothers, as these women primarily displayed depressive symptoms and had in several cases entered a hospital because of a suicide attempt.) The General Psychopathology Scale was used to an even greater extent than the GAS to measure ongoing psychiatric impairment rather than the transient level of psychiatric impairment. The schizophrenic mothers had mean scores ranging from 6.7 (7 = Most severely ill) to 4.7 (5 = Markedly ill), with a mean of 5.5. The psychiatric comparison mothers ranged from 5.0 (Markedly ill) to 2.7 (Mildly disturbed), with a mean of 3.8, for these ratings of the usual level of psychiatric symptoms.

Children of nonschizophrenic, psychiatrically disordered mothers

The selection of a comparison group of psychiatrically disordered index mothers emphasized the exclusion of schizophrenia and of schizophrenia spectrum disorder as defined in the Danish adoption studies (Kety et al., 1968, 1978; Rosenthal, 1975). This strategy was designed to produce a group of children who would not be expected to be at increased risk for schizophrenia, despite having psychiatrically disordered biological mothers. These index mothers received no first-choice judgments of certain or possible schizophrenia or of schizoid or paranoid personality disorder in the Kety et al. (1968)

Table 20.1. *Sample selection summary for children born to mothers with schizophrenia or with nonpsychotic psychiatric disorders*

Reason for exclusion at initial chart review	n	Disposition of cases submitted to three clinical judges	n
No children	496	Moved to private school	10
Children too old	246	Moved out of city	1
Children too young	108	Children not locatable or not accessible	5
Residence outside city	129		
Residence not locatable	113	Children still too young at end of study	3
Children in private school	10		
Patient too old or too young	53	Diagnosis disagreement	3
Patient alcoholic	20	Diagnosis judged nonschizrenic psychosis	2
Patient has organic brain syndrome	5	Diagnosis judged organic brain syndrome	1
Patient has IQ < 70	4		
Chart not available	44	Insufficient information for diagnosis	1
Insufficient chart information	31	Refused participation	2
Total cases excluded	1,259	Included as index schizophrenic mother	24
		Included as index nonpsychotic, psychiatrically disordered mother	20
		Total cases judged	72

Source: Adapted from Nuechterlein (1983); copyright 1983 by the American Psychological Association; reprinted by permission.

system, nor any first-choice DSM-II judgments of schizophrenia. These mothers were recruited at the same hospitals, with the same exclusion criteria used for the schizophrenic mothers. Diagnostic reviews of these cases were intermingled with those for potential schizophrenic index mothers to avoid any global rating set that would favor a schizophrenic or nonschizophrenic diagnostic judgment. Most of the mothers included in this comparison sample showed primarily depressive symptoms, without accompanying psychotic symptoms, which in many cases met the criteria for major depressive disorder by RDC. However, because this sample was not wholly homogeneous with regard to depressive symptoms, we refer to these patients as nonpsychotic, psychiatrically disordered mothers. The sample selection process for the children of schizophrenic mothers and the children of nonpsychotic, psychiatrically disordered mothers is summarized in Table 20.1.

Hyperactive children

A sample of hyperactive children drawn from two child guidance clinics was recruited to provide a comparison group of children with demonstrated psychopathology, in order to evaluate the severity and nature of any anomalies found among the children of schizophrenic mothers. Because the Minnesota High-Risk Studies have focused on the possible role of attentional abnormalities as possible vulnerability indicators for schizophrenia, hyperactive children were selected in this final set of studies to allow an examination of the similarities and differences between their attentional difficulties and those that might characterize children vulnerable to schizophrenic disorders. Although hyperactive children show prominent attentional disturbances clinically, even to the extent that this diagnosis was renamed attention deficit disorder in DSM-III (American Psychiatric Association, 1980), these children apparently have no particular increased risk for adult schizophrenia (Borland & Heckman, 1976; Mendelson, Johnson, & Stewart, 1971; Stewart, de Blois, & Cummings, 1980; Weiss, Hechtman, Perlman, Hopkins, & Wener, 1979). Thus, comparison of attentional abnormalities in this group and those found among children of schizophrenic mothers should shed some light on any aspects of attentional functioning that are specifically relevant to vulnerability to schizophrenia.

The selection of the hyperactive group involved use of the results of a factor analysis of child outpatient symptoms (Nuechterlein, Soli, Garmezy, Devine, & Schaefer, 1981; Soli, Nuechterlein, Garmezy, Devine, & Schaefer, 1981) based on the Achenbach Symptom Checklist (Achenbach, 1966). The hyperactive children selected were required to have a high factor score on the Hyperactivity factor (>50% of total possible score) and low scores on the Delinquency and Rebelliousness factors (≤33% and 50% of total possible scores, respectively). This selection of children without predominant delinquent or rebellious patterns yielded a narrow-spectrum hyperactive group for the Nuechterlein (1983) vigilance study that was supplemented in subsequent studies by an antisocial delinquent group whose members were not hyperactive. The selected hyperactive children were also required to have clear Achenbach Symptom Checklist symptoms of "restless, hyperactive" and "can't concentrate, distractible, short attention span," in order to keep this group comparable to the "attention deficit disorder with hyperactivity" diagnosis in DSM-III.

Potential hyperactive subjects who were on psychoactive medication or who had clear neurological disorder, IQ < 75, or major psychiatric illness in a parent were excluded. Fourteen children who met all criteria were included in the initial vigilance study.

Matched and representatively stratified normal comparison children

The research design included two types of normal comparison groups to allow comparisons with a larger, representatively stratified normal sample and a "normal" sample whose members were individually matched to the children in each target group on sex, age, reading vocabulary and comprehension scores, socioeconomic status, and peer evaluation level. Peer evaluation level was used as an additional matching variable in the final series of studies in the Minnesota High-Risk Studies because it is among the best childhood predictors of global level of adult mental health (Cowan, Pederson, Babigian, Izzo, & Frost, 1973; Roff, 1970). Any deficits among the children of schizophrenic mothers that remained evident even in comparison with sociometrically matched peers would be expected to be more specific to vulnerability to schizophrenia than to poor adult mental health in general. A separate matched comparison sample was selected for each of the three target groups. These groups were formed by choosing the best match within the classroom of each target child.

The stratified normal comparison group was formed by representatively sampling the top, middle, and bottom thirds of a peer evaluation ranking completed in the classrooms of the target children. The peer evaluation procedure was a 27-role adaptation of the Rubenstein, Fisher, and Iker (1975) version of the Class Play (Bower, 1960). In this procedure, children were asked to nominate classmates for roles in a hypothetical class play. Nominations were noted on individual checklists for roles describing various social and academic behaviors, such as "Somebody who makes friends easily." A classroom ranking was created by averaging the rank orders of the numbers and the percentages of negatively toned nominations for social behavior roles. These two variables were chosen because of their predictive value for later psychiatric contact (Cowen et al., 1973). A representative group of 67 peers was chosen across the classrooms of the target children for the initial vigilance study.

Potential matched or stratified normal comparison subjects were screened through school records to exclude children with child guidance or psychiatric referrals, neurological disorders, or relevant physical handicaps. Subjects in all groups were required to have visual acuity of 20/30 or better, with corrective lenses if necessary. The background characteristics of subjects in the seven subject groups included in the initial vigilance study are shown in Table 20.2.

The vigilance study

The three studies of information processing in this final phase of the Minnesota High-Risk Studies were designed to examine further the implications of the finding of Marcus (1973) that children of schizophrenic mothers showed slower overall simple reaction times within an attentional paradigm originally employed by Rodnick and Shakow (1940) with schizophrenic patients. In order to delineate the nature of any attentional abnormality characterizing children at risk for schizophrenia, we sampled potentially different components of the wide range of phenomena included under the broad rubric

Table 20.2. *Background data for the initial subject groups*

Group	Sex M	Sex F	Age (years) M	Age (years) SD	Vocabulary score[a] M	SD	n	Comprehension score[a] M	SD	n	Socioeconomic status[b] M	SD	n
Children of schizophrenic mothers	14	10	13.1	1.8	45	31	22	49	29	22	4.9	1.2	23
Matched comparison children	14	10	12.8	1.5	47	28	22	50	30	22	4.3	1.5	23
Children of nonpsychotic, psychiatrically disordered mothers	11	9	13.0	1.5	44	24	16	45	29	16	4.6	2.1	19
Matched comparison children	11	9	12.8	1.5	47	27	16	48	27	16	4.3	1.9	19
Hyperactive children	14	0	12.8	1.5	38	20	13	40	25	13	4.4	1.1	13
Matched comparison group	14	0	13.0	1.9	42	23	13	32	25	13	4.9	1.4	13
Stratified normal comparison children	43	24	12.8	1.7	53	27	64	52	29	64	4.7	1.7	63

[a]Vocabulary and comprehension scores are percentiles on the Gates-MacGinitie Reading Achievement Test from school records; *n* values indicate the numbers of children for whom data were available.

[b]The highest known occupation of the head of household was evaluated on the 7-point Occupation scale from the Amherst modification of Hollingshead's Two-Factor Index of Social Position. A high score represents low socioeconomic status; *n* values indicate the numbers of children for whom this information was available.

Source: Adapted from Nuechterlein (1983); copyright 1983 by the American Psychological Association; reprinted by permission.

of "attention." The selection of components followed the distinctions proposed by Zubin (1975) among sustained attention, shift of attention, and selective attention. In this schema, sustained attention or vigilance refers to maintenance of a focus over time after selection of a focus is completed. A shift of attention refers to the efficiency with which an attentional focus can be moved between temporally successive stimuli. Finally, selective attention concerns the processes by which selection between simultaneous relevant and irrelevant stimuli is completed.

The research on sustained attention directed by Nuechterlein (1983, 1984) involved adaptations of the continuous performance test (CPT), a visual vigilance task that had been shown in previous studies to detect performance deficits among chronic schizophrenic patients and among remitted acute schizophrenic patients (Asarnow & MacCrimmon, 1978; Orzack & Kornetsky, 1966; Wohlberg & Kornetsky, 1973). At the time that this vigilance study was initiated, early data analyses from the New York State Psychiatric Institute High-Risk Project (Erlenmeyer-Kimling & Cornblatt, 1978; Rutschmann, Cornblatt, & Erlenmeyer-Kimling, 1977) also indicated that at least one new, atypical version of the CPT was able to detect early performance deficits among children of schizophrenic patients. On the other hand, Asarnow, Steffy, MacCrimmon, and Cleghorn (1977) were reporting that a CPT deficit was not found among children of schizophrenic patients using a more traditional CPT version, although they detected performance deficiencies on other information processing tasks. Thus, some CPT versions seemed to have promise for isolation of a potential vulnerability factor for schizophrenia, but further systematic investigation of this possibility under varying CPT conditions was clearly needed.

The term "continuous performance test" derives from the procedure originally developed by Rosvold, Mirsky, Sarason, Bransome, and Beck (1956) for examination of sustained alertness in neurologically impaired subjects. Its stimulus characteristics have not been standardized across studies in the literature; so it is most productive to think of this term as referring to a class of short, rapidly paced visual vigilance tasks rather than a single test. Typically, the subject is asked to monitor a series of randomly ordered individual stimuli (usually letters or numbers) as they are briefly presented with small interstimulus intervals and to indicate each time that a predesignated target stimulus appears. The target stimulus can be a stimulus on a single presentation (such as the letter X) or can involve a short-term memory component (such as each X that is immediately preceded by an A). An individual stimulus usually is presented for 40 to 200 ms, with interstimulus intervals of 1 to 1.5 s over a 5- to 15-min continuous vigilance period, with targets occurring relatively infrequently (10–25% of stimuli). Thus, continuous alertness and relatively rapid processing of each stimulus are required for optimal performance.

The CPT version developed by Rutschmann et al. (1977) and Erlenmeyer-Kimling and Cornblatt (1978) is distinctive in that it involves presentation of slides of playing cards at relatively long (600 ms) exposures and requires children to detect each time that two identical playing cards occur in succession. This version differs from most traditional CPT versions by employing a relative target rather than an absolute target (successive matching of the current stimulus to the memory of the preceding stimulus) and two stimulus dimensions (number and suit) rather than one. Because memory load within vigilance tasks has been found to be an important influence on the interrelationships of task performance for normal adults (Davies & Parasuraman, 1982; Parasuraman & Davies, 1977), performance on this CPT version with an unusually high memory load might not be comparable to that on more traditional CPT versions on which the earlier literature on schizophrenic performance deficits was based. Thus, direct comparison of results from the playing-card CPT with those from a more traditional CPT version was deemed important.

Manipulating specific stimulus and response characteristics within the CPT is also useful for identifying the nature of various possible CPT performance deficits, beyond the issue of the difference between the playing-card CPT and traditional CPT versions (Nuechterlein, 1983). Furthermore, prior research had not addressed whether or not any CPT deficit among children of schizophrenic mothers was also found among children of other psychiatrically disordered parents. Similarly, comparison of CPT deficits among children of schizophrenic parents and deficits found among hyperactive children was important to determine if distinctions among these abnormalities could be found. Finally, the role of motivational factors in any performance deficit among children of schizophrenic patients needed to be examined.

Thus, the vigilance research in the Minnesota High-Risk Studies focused on several issues. First, the investigation sought to follow up the reaction time performance deficit found by Marcus (1973), particularly to determine if this reaction time slowing might indicate that a deficit in vigilance level characterizes children at risk for schizophrenia, as indicated by the results of Erlenmeyer-Kimling and Cornblatt (1978) using a CPT with a high memory load. Second, we sought to relate the playing-card CPT of Erlenmeyer-Kimling and Cornblatt (1978) to a traditional CPT and to new CPT adaptations that systematically varied stimulus and response dimensions in order to determine what CPT conditions were associated with sensitivity to deficits among children of schizophrenic patients. Third, we examined whether or not any vigilance deficit in children of schizophrenic patients was also found in children of parents with nonschizophrenic psychiatric disorders or in hyperactive children. Finally, we explored the possible role of motivation in any vigilance performance deficit.

Procedures of the vigilance study

Nuechterlein (1983, 1984) administered six conditions of the CPT to each of the 183 children whose selection was described in the previous sections: (a) the playing-card CPT developed by Erlenmeyer-Kimling and Cornblatt (1978); (b) a traditional CPT with relatively brief stimulus exposures (40 or 50 ms, depending on the subject's age), clearly focused, single-digit stimuli, and a single-digit target, the numeral 5; (c) a newly developed degraded-stimulus CPT that places extra burden on stimulus encoding and feature extraction processes by means of blurring the single-digit stimuli and superimposing a random pattern of visual noise; (d) a repetition of the degraded-stimulus CPT with incentive feedback on correct target detections (hits); (e) a repetition of the degraded-stimulus CPT with incentive feedback on false alarms; (f) a newly developed response-reversal CPT that places extra burden on response selection and inhibition aspects of information processing by requiring a response to each single-digit stimulus except the former target.

The data from each of the CPT conditions, except for the traditional CPT condition, were transformed into signal detection theory indices of sensitivity and response criterion (Green & Swets, 1966; McNicol, 1972). The traditional, single-numeral-target CPT condition did not produce sufficient errors of omission (target misses) and errors of commission (false alarms) to allow reliable signal detection indices to be derived. It was analyzed using these traditional CPT scores. An advantage of signal detection theory analyses is that the sensitivity and response criterion dimensions of performance represent separate underlying processes that are not always apparent in the traditional raw CPT scores. Signal detection theory combines information from the errors of omission and errors of commission to derive sensitivity and response criterion indices. "Sensitivity" refers to the person's ability to discriminate the target stimuli from the nontarget stimuli, which can be measured by the index d'. "Response criterion" refers to the amount of perceptual evidence that a person demands before responding that a stimulus is a target, which can be measured by beta (β). An individual who has relatively many errors of omission but few errors of commission may have the same ability to discriminate the target from the nontarget stimuli as an individual who has relatively few errors of omission but many errors of commission. Signal detection theory analyses allow the former person to be described as cautious (high β) and the latter as liberal (low β) in response criterion, while indicating that the two people have the same sensitivity or signal/noise discrimination (d') level.

Results of the vigilance study

To examine the internal structure of the data, a principal components analysis with direct quartimin rotation was completed for the major dependent variables, using the subjects from the representatively stratified normal group. The variables included the d' level and β level from each of five conditions of the CPT with sufficient errors to allow signal detection theory analyses, 14 personality and motivational ratings, and a global index of negative peer appraisal. Five factors with eigenvalues greater than 1.5 accounted

Table 20.3. *Loadings on oblique factors derived from CPT, behavior rating, and peer evaluation variables*

Variable	Loading	Variable	Loading
Factor 1: Emotionality		*Factor 4: Fearful Inhibition*	
Emotional reactivity	.89	Fearfulness	.89
Activity level	.77	Self-confidence	−.73
Dependence	.74	Friendliness with examiner	−.55
Friendliness with examiner	.56	Free style communication	−.43
Free style of communica-		*d'* response reversal	.37
tion	.55	Passivity	.35
Self-confidence	−.52		
Negative peer evaluation	.45		
Emotionality after frustra-			
tion	.44		
Passivity	−.36		
Factor 2: d'		*Factor 5: β*	
d' degraded stimulus	.88	Ln β feedback on false	
d' feedback on hits	.85	alarms	.72
d' feedback on false alarms	.85	Ln β feedback on hits	.61
d' playing cards	.55	Ln β degraded stimulus	.61
d' response reversal	.44	Ln β response reversal	.59
Attention span (rated)	.34	Impulsivity	−.45
		d' response reversal	−.44
		Ln β playing cards	.42
Factor 3: Task Orientation			
Goal orientation	.83		
Cooperation	.77		
Agreeability	.71		
Emotionality after frustra-			
tion	.55		
Attention span (rated)	.45		
Passivity	.37		
Impulsivity	−.33		

Source: Nuechterlein (1983); copyright 1983 by the American Psychological Association; reprinted by permission.

for 59% of the total variance (Nuechterlein, 1983). As shown in Table 20.3, the *d'* level from each CPT version loaded on a single factor, and the β level from each version loaded on a separate factor, indicating that the two dimensions of sensitivity and response criterion shared variance across the five CPT conditions. The three other factors were derived from the personality and motivational ratings and reflected Emotionality, Task Orientation, and Fearful Inhibition.

Vigilance level in sustained attention tasks often is represented by the average *d'* level throughout the vigilance period in experimental psychology

Table 20.4. *Correlations among CPT conditions for errors of omission (target misses) and d' for* stratified normal children

	CPT condition				
CPT condition	Degraded stimulus	Hit feedback	False alarm feedback	Playing cards	Response reversal
Errors of omission (misses)					
Conventional numeral	.40**	.28*	.47**	.50**	.17
Degraded stimulus		.62**	.63**	.47**	.12
Hit feedback			.67**	.38**	.18
False alarm feedback				.46**	.22
Playing cards					.31*
d' level (signal/noise discrimination level)					
Degraded stimulus		.72**	.65**	.39**	.30*
Hit feedback			.75**	.39**	.26*
False alarm feedback				.42**	.20
Playing cards					.43**

*$p < .05$; **$p < .01$.
Note: $n = 67$ for all correlations except those involving the response reversal condition, for which $n = 65$.

(Parasuraman, 1984) and the total number of errors of omission in the clinical literature (Kornestsky, 1972). To illustrate further the relationships among the CPT conditions, Table 20.4 presents the correlations among all six CPT conditions for the traditional score, errors of omission (target misses), and for the signal/noise discrimination or sensitivity level, d', among the five CPT conditions allowing its reliable derivation. Again, the large, representative normal comparison group was used to examine task interrelationships. Errors of omission were moderately correlated across most CPT conditions, including the interrelationships between the conventional numeral CPT and the newer forms of the CPT. The d' levels were also moderately correlated across most conditions, with stronger associations among the three conditions using degraded stimuli than among the remaining versions. This evidence suggests that in addition to components of information processing that are specific to a given version, these CPT conditions tap a common dimension of vigilance level that cuts across the tasks among these 9- to 16-year-old children.

To examine the hypothesis that the group of children of schizophrenic mothers included an excessive number of children with poor signal/noise discrimination levels during vigilance, a cutoff point at the tenth percentile of the stratified normal comparison group was used. As shown in Table 20.5, 29% (7 of 24) of the children born to schizophrenic mothers had factor scores on the d' factor below this cutoff, whereas only 9% (6 of 65) of the stratified normal children had signal/noise discrimination levels in this low range. Neither the

Table 20.5. *Percentages and frequencies of children obtaining extremely low factor scores on CPT d' (signal/noise discrimination) or CPT (response caution)*

Group	n	Low d' %	f	Low β %	f
Stratified normal children	65	9	6	8	5
Children of all schizophrenic mothers[a]	24	29	7**	4	1
Children of RDC schizophrenic mothers	13	31	4*	8	1
Children of RDC schizoaffective mothers	8	25	2	0	0
Children of DSM-III schizotypal personality disorder mothers	3	33	1	0	0
Matched comparison children	24	8	2	4	1
Children of nonpsychotic, psychiatrically disordered mothers	20	10	2	0	0
Matched comparison children	20	10	2	5	1
Hyperactive children	14	14	2	29	4*
Matched comparison children	14	0	0	7	1

[a]Diagnoses based on the schizophrenia criteria of Kety et al. (1968).
Note: *$p = .05$, compared with the frequency for the stratified normal group; **$p = .03$, compared with the frequency for the stratified normal group; and $p = .07$, compared with the matched group.
Source: Adapted from Nuechterlein (1983); copyright 1983 by the American Psychological Association; reprinted by permission.

children of the nonpsychotic, psychiatrically disordered mothers nor the hyperactive children showed a similar significant excess of low d' factor scores. On the other hand, the hyperactive group included an excessive number of children with scores on the β factor that fell below the tenth percentile of the stratified normal group, whereas children of schizophrenic mothers did not show this pattern.

Analyses of group means, rather than the frequency of extreme scorers, showed basically parallel results (Nuechterlein, 1983). Analyses were adjusted for sex to eliminate any effects of different male/female composition across groups. Children of schizophrenic mothers had a mean d' factor score of $-.52$, adjusted for sex, which was significantly and approximately one-half standard deviation lower than that of $-.01$ for stratified normal children. On the other hand, hyperactive children had significantly lower mean β factor scores than did stratified normal children, children of schizophrenic mothers, or children of nonpsychotic, psychiatrically disordered mothers (adjusted means of $-.67$, $-.01$, $.03$, and $-.10$, respectively).

Parallel analyses contrasted the children of schizophrenic mothers, children of nonpsychotic, psychiatrically disordered mothers, and hyperactive children with their individually matched normal comparison children (Nuechterlein, 1983). The results were essentially the same as those just described, indicating

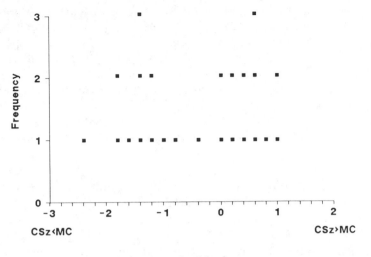

Figure 20.1. Distribution difference scores formed by subtracting CPT *d'* factor scores of individually matched normal comparison children from those of children of schizophrenic mothers. A negative score indicates that the child of the schizophrenic mother showed poorer signal/noise discrimination than did the matched normal child.

that the differences could not be explained by the matching variables of sex, age, reading vocabulary or comprehension level, socioeconomic status, or peer evaluation level.

To examine further the distribution of *d'* factor score deficits among children of schizophrenic mothers, we recently plotted the difference scores formed by subtracting the *d'* factor score of the individually matched normal comparison child from that of each child of a schizophrenic mother. This difference score would help to control for any effects of the matching variables on *d'* scores and would be negative if the child of a schizophrenic mother showed poorer CPT signal/noise discrimination than did the matched comparison child. Because the factor analysis of the dependent variables was completed with the representatively stratified normal children, the *d'* factor scores had a mean of zero and a standard deviation of 1.00 among this group. Thus, subtracting the *d'* factor score of the matched comparison child from that for each child of a schizophrenic mother produced a *d'* deficit index scaled in terms of the standard deviation for the representatively stratified normal group. The distribution of these difference scores (Figure 20.1) is of interest not only because it visually illustrates the deficits among children of schizophrenic mothers but also because it looks bimodal. Note the presence of an excess of difference scores below −1.0, as compared with above 1.0, which represents an excess of instances in which the child of a schizophrenic mother had a *d'* factor score substantially lower than that of the matched comparison child.

This distribution provides no direct evidence of genetic transmission of the CPT d' deficit, but the tendency toward bimodality is intriguing because vulnerability factors influenced by single major genes might be expected to have a bimodal distribution among children of schizophrenic mothers. Thus, although the seeming bimodality of this index could arise from either group, a clear theoretical explanation of bimodality is available only for the children of schizophrenic mothers. Further research with larger samples will be required to determine if this suggestion of bimodality can be confirmed, as the sample reported here was too small for such a determination, and the appearance of bimodality was much clearer in these difference scores than in the raw factor scores.[1]

Analyses were completed to determine if the children in subject pairs in which the child of a schizophrenic mother showed a deficit in d' factor score relative to the matched comparison child (the lower subgroup in Figure 20.1) differed from the remaining children on any of the matching variables. The 12 children of schizophrenic mothers with d' factor scores more than 0.2 smaller than those of their matched controls were contrasted with the remaining 12 children of schizophrenic mothers. No significant differences were found. A mild tendency for the offspring of schizophrenic mothers with d' factor scores lower than those of their matched controls to be younger than the remaining offspring of schizophrenic mothers was observed ($M = 12.6$ vs. 13.5 years, respectively), but this difference was not statistically significant ($p > .20$). Thus, the distribution of differences in d' factor scores does not appear to be accounted for by these background variables.

Analyses of individual CPT conditions indicated that the d' score from the degraded stimulus CPT condition could identify the excessively large subgroup of children of schizophrenic mothers with poor performance just as effectively as the d' factor score that summarized performance across five CPT conditions (Nuechterlein, 1983). A hit rate lower than the tenth percentile of the stratified normal sample (a high number of errors of omission) on the degraded-stimulus CPT condition also characterized a disproportionately large subgroup of the children of schizophrenic mothers (29%, or 7 of 24) compared with the stratified normal children (9%, or 6 of 67) ($p = .02$, Fisher's exact test). As in the Asarnow et al. (1977) results, the hit rate of conventional numeral CPT did not significantly differentiate children of schizophrenic mothers from normal comparison children. Based on the pattern of results across all available studies, it thus appears that the conventional CPT with a clearly focused, single-numeral or single-letter target stimulus is less sensitive to deficits in children at risk for schizophrenia than are CPT versions that involve higher demands on processing capacity (Nuechterlein & Dawson, 1984).

---

[1] We thank Jim Mintz of the UCLA Clinical Research Center for the Study of Schizophrenia for helping to rule out various potential statistical artifacts that might produce a bimodal distribution.

The results summarized thus far indicate that children born to schizophrenic mothers, particularly a subgroup, show lowered signal/noise discrimination (sensitivity) in more demanding versions of the CPT. Children of mothers with disorders outside the schizophrenia spectrum do not show this deficit. Hyperactive children are distinguished by a low response criterion level that is consistent with an impulsive cognitive style. Although in this first study, hyperactive children did not show impaired signal/noise discrimination levels, a subsequent study by O'Dougherty, Nuechterlein, and Drew (1984) demonstrated that younger hyperactive children selected on the basis of the hyperactivity index from the revised Conners Teacher Rating Scale (Goyette, Conners, & Ulrich, 1978) did show such impairments, as well as lowered response criterion cutoff levels. Thus, the distinctive feature of hyperactive children appears to be the lower response criterion levels, rather than necessarily the absence of signal/noise discrimination deficits.

Finally, this vigilance study included three lines of evidence that argue against any simple motivational explanation for the CPT signal/noise discrimination deficits of children at risk for schizophrenia. First, the principal components analysis produced a Task Orientation factor that represented a dimension of directed motivation based on experimenter ratings. Children of schizophrenic mothers did not show lower factor scores than did normal comparison subjects on this dimension. Second, unless the unmotivated subject should respond in a completely random fashion, motivational deficiencies would be expected to be reflected in heightened response criterion levels, not in lowered perceptual sensitivity (Swets & Sewall, 1963). Yet children at risk for schizophrenia showed normal response criterion levels. Third, children of schizophrenic mothers did not show a differential improvement in d' with incentive feedback during the degraded-stimulus CPT, which would be expected if these children were not as optimally motivated as the normal control children in the condition without feedback. These lines of evidence indicate that the CPT signal/noise discrimination deficit among children at risk for schizophrenia does not seem attributable to observable or transient motivational deficiencies.

The cross-modal reaction time study

Reaction time (RT) studies have long been popular among schizophrenia researchers; see the review by Nuechterlein (1977). The consistency of the differences in schizophrenic and normal responses within RT tasks, the relationship between RT performance and adaptive potential, and the suitability of the RT measure across developmental stages made the paradigm an obvious choice for risk researchers. In addition, as noted earlier, a study carried out in an earlier phase of the Minnesota High-Risk Studies by Marcus (1973) demonstrated significant deficiencies in the overall RT performances of children born to schizophrenic mothers. The study of cross-modal RTs directed by Phipps-Yonas (1984) was undertaken for the purpose of replicating and extending those findings. In addition to determining if the overall slowing of RTs among children of schizophrenic mothers that occurred in the Marcus (1973) study could be replicated, Phipps-Yonas used visual and auditory stimuli in cross-modal and ipsimodal sequences as the imperative stimuli to determine if high-risk children demonstrated the same difficulty in shifting modalities that had been found among schizophrenic patients (Sutton, Hakerem, Zubin, & Portnoy, 1961; Sutton & Zubin, 1965). She also examined the ways in which response latencies were affected by information regarding the modality of an anticipated stimulus and by correct or incorrect "guessing" of the next stimulus modality by the subject.

Subjects for the RT study

All of the target children studied by Nuechterlein in the vigilance research were included in this investigation in the following academic year, with the exception of two children of schizophrenic mothers, both of whom were adolescents who had dropped out of school. One was facing criminal charges, and the other, pregnant at age 14, had run off, according to her father, with a "gypsy." An additional target group not examined by Nuechterlein (1983) involved antisocial delinquent children.

Male antisocial delinquent children were selected based on Achenbach Symptom Checklist factor scores (Soli et al., 1981) that were elevated for Delinquency (at least three symptoms present) or Rebelliousness (at least three symptoms present), but not for Hyperactivity (neither "Restless, hyperactive" nor "Can't concentrate, distractible, short attention span" present). Female antisocial delinquent children were chosen based on elevations on the female factors of Delinquency and Interpersonal Aggression (at least three symptoms on one of these factors) and again the absence of the two core hyperactivity symptoms. Four antisocial delinquent children were recruited at one of the child guidance clinics from which the hyperactive sample was drawn. These were joined by 12 others who were selected from two special schools within the public school system for children with behavioral problems. The principals at those institutions were asked to describe their 67 students. Audiotapes of these interviews were rated independently by three project members using the Achenbach Symptom Checklist. The judgments were averaged for case selection purposes. Thus, the additional target group consisted of 16 children classified as antisocial delinquent, but *not* hyperactive. Because of the special status of the educational placement of most of the antisocial delinquent subjects, it was not appropriate to use matched controls from their classrooms, and consequently there was no matched control group for this sample. Similarly, the peer evaluation procedure was not completed, because these children were not attending classrooms that contained a representative sampling of same-age peers.

The number of stratified comparison children was also increased. Several of the original group of 67 students had moved out of the state and needed to be replaced. Others were recruited in such a way as to maintain age and sex distributions similar to those for the 131 target and matched control children. The stratified normal group for this study consisted of 33 children with composite peer evaluation ranking in the top third for the classroom, 34 children in the middle third, and 33 children in the bottom third.

The mean age of the subjects at the time of the cross-modal RT assessment was 13 years, 7 months, which was approximately 1 year older than at the vigilance assessment administered by Nuechterlein.

RT procedures

Most of the RT experimental sessions were conducted at the subjects' schools in quiet, well-lit rooms. During the task, the subject wore headphones that played white noise as well as the auditory stimulus. A white flash displayed on a large board directly in front of the subject constituted the visual stimulus.

Five experimental conditions were presented. In each condition, a light off to the side of the central panel lit up as the signal to press the response button positioned in front of the subject. The latency of the button press was recorded, without the subject's awareness, as an unobtrusive index of readiness to begin or general motivation. The imperative stimulus occurred, 2, 4, or 7 s after the button was pressed, in a quasi-random sequence. The time that the subject took to release the button in response to the stimulus constituted the dependent variable. Nine percent of all of the trials were catch trials (i.e., no imperative stimulus was presented).

The order of the first two conditions was reversed for half of the subjects. Each entailed 33 trials in which the imperative stimulus was always a light in the center panel or a tone on the headphones. The third condition, modeled after the Sutton and Zubin procedure, involved 66 trials with the visual and auditory imperative stimuli intermixed randomly. Prior to commencing the fourth condition, the side lights that alerted the subject to press the response button were labeled "light" and "tone," and only one of these panels lit up to begin each trial in the conditions that followed. For the first 20 trials, the modality information (i.e., light versus tone) provided by this cue was correct. For the second 20 trials, the subject was informed that the modality cue would be wrong "once in a while," as indeed it was 20% of the time. The experimenter indicated that the signal would be "sometimes right, sometimes wrong" during the third set of 20 trials, for which the cue was accurate for 50% of trials. In the final 32-trial condition, the subject was instructed to predict the modality of the next imperative stimulus by pressing either the light or tone panel. Trials following these "guesses" were adjusted to make the guess accurate for a random 50% of trials.

The median response latencies and the intrasubject standard deviations were the basic dependent variables. Anticipatory responses and other extraneous behaviors were also scored. After the experimental task was completed, each subject was engaged in a 5- to 10-min semistructured interview that focused on the subject's feelings regarding the task, on any cognitive strategies that had been employed, on attributions regarding success or failure, and on the perceived level of achievement. Each subject was also rated by the experimenter on general level of effort and cooperation.

RT results

A series of two-, three-, and four-way analyses of variance constituted the primary data analyses. Because the multiple experimental groups differed in size and composition, several separate comparisons were necessary. Each target group was compared with its matched control group on each dependent variable. Differences between target groups and the stratified comparison group and differences among target groups were examined through a second series of analyses of variance. Final sets of contrasts were completed between the stratified normal subjects at high, medium, and low peer rankings.

A principal components analysis with direct quartimin rotation was employed to examine the internal structure of the data and to obtain summary scores. Five factors with eigenvalues greater than 1.0 accounted for 51% of the variance. The first of these was a strong and obvious overall speed factor with loadings from the major median RT variables that was labeled RT Level and Variability. The second factor represented no interpretable construct. The final three factors were labeled Interest and Motivation, Behavioral Impulsivity, and Starting Speed. Cutoff points on each factor below and above which 10% of the stratified control subjects fell were selected to examine differential rates of deviant scorers across groups. The Mahalanobis distances between subjects on the combination of all factors were also examined as an index of the deviance of each subject from the overall mean for the stratified normal group.

A second, rationally derived approach to identifying atypical children involved examining nine variables that cut across all competence areas. These included peer evaluation ranking, two reading achievement test scores, median RTs, intrasubject-RT variability measures, the motivation and cooperation rating, and two summary scores (Impulsivity and Atypical Experimental Behaviors). A negative cutting score for each variable was set at the value below which 20% of the 159 normal comparison subjects scored; a positive cutting score for six of the variables was set at a point above which 12% of this group fell. These cutoff points were used, rather than 10% and 90th percentile points, because too many normal control subjects had tied scores at the 10th and 90th percentile points of the distributions of these variables. The combination of a negative hit on five or more of the nine variables and an absence of any positive hits was taken as an indication of general deviance. Similarly, a positive hit on two or more of six variables for which such was possible was assessed as evidence of general superiority of functioning.

A number of interesting findings concerning the experimental manipulations are consistent with results from other RT studies of children. As expected, the males had faster and more consistent RTs than the females, and the older children outperformed the younger subjects.

Peer evaluation ranking also showed strong relationships to both overall RT and consistency of RT over trials in the stratified normal group. Although none of the 33 children in the top third of the peer nomination ranking were classified as generally deviant, 30% of their low-ranked peers were so identified. It was also noteworthy that approximately one-third of the subjects in the top third of the peer evaluation ranking had superior scores on two or more of the general competence variables, whereas that was true for only 2 of the 33 low-ranked stratified normal children.

Significant performance abnormalities in the target groups, however, were rather rare. The 22 children of schizophrenic mothers could not be distinguished from their matched controls and were remarkably similar to the stratified normal group. No statistically significant mean differences were found between children of schizophrenic mothers and the normal comparison children in the speed of their reactions to the imperative stimuli, the variability of their performance, or other extraneous behaviors. All efforts to identify a special subset of deviant children within this high-risk group also failed for this variable set.

The RT performances of the 20 children of mothers with nonschizophrenic psychiatric disorders also appeared to be quite normal. These children could not be differentiated statistically from their matched controls or from the stratified controls on the RT variables.

The response latencies of the 14 hyperactive boys were neither slower nor more variable than those of the matched comparison subjects during the first three conditions of this study. However, their RT performances did fall off and became significantly inferior to those of normal comparison subjects in the last two conditions, possibly reflecting decreasing ability or motivation to maintain performance over the session.

The 16 antisocial delinquent subjects performed poorly across all of the conditions in terms of both the speed and variability of their RTs. This group also contained the highest proportion of generally deviant subjects in the analysis of deviant scores on empirical factors, as well as in the analysis of the rationally derived core variables.

In summary, the antisocial delinquent group showed the most deviant RT performances of the four target groups, followed by the deviance of hyperactive children, which was restricted to the last two of five RT conditions. Deviant performance that might be associated with vulnerability to schizophrenic disorder was not evident within this cross-modal RT study.

The intentional and incidental learning study

This study, directed by Driscoll (1980, 1984), examined aspects of selective attention as manifested in incidental and intentional learning. "Selective attention" refers to the processes by which an individual ignores irrelevant stimuli and focuses on task-relevant variables. Selective attention has frequently been reported to be deficient in patients with schizophrenic disorders (McGhie & Chapman, 1961). The ability to ignore irrelevant stimuli has also been of interest to developmental psychologists, who often have used incidental–intentional learning paradigms to study the development of strategies of selective attention (Druker & Hagen, 1969; Hagen & Sabo, 1967; Maccoby & Hagen, 1965).

Developmental studies have shown that children have greater ability with increasing age to learn material to which their attention is directed by experimental instructions; this constitutes their capacity for *intentional learning*. *Incidental learning* is defined as learning that takes place in the absence of a "set" to learn (Postman, 1964). When children are exposed to an array of material, only some of which is essential to the assigned learning task, the degree to which they acquire the extraneous material constitutes their level of incidental learning.

A number of studies (Sabo & Hagen, 1973) have reported that incidental learning declines at approximately 12 or 13 years of age, which has been viewed as evidence for the hypothesis that children's ability to attend selectively and to screen out irrelevant material shows a developmental course in childhood. However, other studies (Deichmann, Speltz, & Kausler, 1971; Hale & Piper, 1973; Hawkins, 1973) have not found a decline in incidental learning after the latency age years. That discrepancy prompted a closer examination of the incidental learning phenomenon.

The definition of incidental learning as the absence of a set to learn presents problems, because it is difficult to infer the absence of a mental phenomenon. Driscoll (1980) noted that the incidental stimuli used in the learning tasks in developmental studies differed in whether they were intrinsic or extrinsic to the experimentally defined learning task, a distinction made by Postman (1964). When features of the learning material are integral to the material but are not required for the intentional learning task (e.g., the colors of geometric shapes when the discrimination of shapes is central), these features are considered incidental but *intrinsic* components of the experimentally defined learning task. When, on the other hand, the incidental features have no direct relation to the learning task, these peripheral items are defined as *extrinsic* components. Driscoll noted that studies that show a decline in incidental learning at age 13 usually involved the learning of material that was extrinsic to the central task, whereas those studies that showed incidental learning to parallel intentional learning and to increase steadily throughout childhood usually involved tasks whose incidental stimuli were intrinsic to the central task. Driscoll hypothesized that the ability to eliminate learning of extrinsic incidental features of a learning task demonstrated the increasing ability of the child to focus attention on task-relevant variables, whereas the ability to note the incidental but intrinsic features of stimuli in a learning task reflected the child's increasing ability to scan, discriminate, and retain learned material along multiple dimensions. Thus, extrinsic incidental learning constitutes inefficient learning, but intrinsic incidental learning constitutes more complex learning ability.

Subjects for the intentional and incidental learning study

The children who participated in this phase of the research were essentially the same ones who were examined in the cross-modal RT study, with minor exceptions. One hyperactive child and two stratified normal comparison children were not available for this testing session, thereby reducing these sample sizes to 13 and 98, respectively. Children were examined individually by Driscoll at their schools within the same school year as they were seen by Phipps-Yonas.

Intentional and incidental learning procedures

Driscoll devised tasks to compare the extrinsic and intrinsic incidental learning characteristics of high-risk children. In order to influence what was learned, Driscoll manipulated the learning set and task demands in the learning situation, as well as the intrinsic-versus-extrinsic nature of the incidental material. In the first task, the children were presented in each trial with three pictures of common objects, one of which was enclosed in a black box. They were instructed to remember the item in the black box for later recall. At no time did the task require that the other items be scanned or retained for successful completion of the intentional learning. The other two items, therefore, remained peripheral or extrinsic to the task. The children were later tested for recall and recognition of all of the items.

In the second task, the children were again presented with an array of pictures of three common objects, but without demarcation of an item with a black box. In each of five trials with a given set of pictures, the subjects were required to "figure out" which item was to be recalled later by responding to one and receiving feedback about the correctness of that response. Thus, this second task required that all of the items be scanned and that a discrimination be made between correct and incorrect items. In this way, all features of the pictures became intrinsic components of the task, either perceptually or cognitively. In addition, in the second task, auditory distraction was added. The children listened to a list of words being read through headphones while performing the central task. This auditory distraction allowed examination of extrinsic incidental learning, learning of the auditorily presented words, within the context of the intrinsic incidental learning task.

Results of the intentional and incidental learning study

An examination of the relationships of the background variables of sex, parental social class, and academic achievement test scores to the major learning variables in the study was completed. No significant sex differences were discernible, although social class was related to three measures of intentional learning. Percentile scores on the Vocabulary and Comprehension tests of the Gates-MacGinitie Reading Achievement Test were significantly associated with measures of intentional and intrinsic incidental learning, but were not related to measures of extrinsic incidental learning. Considering the known relationship between achievement test scores and intelligence, the correlations with achievement test scores suggest that intentional and intrinsic incidental learning measures may be related to intelligence, whereas extrinsic incidental learning may not.

The major predictions were that (a) extrinsic incidental learning would fail to rise after grade seven, (b) intrinsic incidental learning would continue to rise after grade seven, (c) intrinsic incidental learning would be greater than extrinsic incidental learning, and (d) children of schizophrenic mothers would demonstrate extrinsic incidental learning that would continue to rise after grade seven, indicating an inability to selectively attend to relevant stimuli.

The results did not support most of these major hypotheses. Although intrinsic incidental learning was significantly higher than extrinsic incidental learning, neither type of incidental learning showed significant changes with age. Given that the usual developmental changes in incidental learning were not present among the normal children under the conditions of this study, it was not surprising that the offspring of schizophrenic mothers did not show the predicted continued rise in extrinsic incidental learning after grade seven. The more general prediction that the children of schizophrenic mothers would show more extrinsic incidental learning than normal comparison children was not borne out by the results for either visual or auditory stimuli, nor was the intentional learning of the children of schizophrenic mothers impaired. These high-risk children showed remarkably high rates of intentional learning that did not differ from those for their matched normal comparison group or the stratified comparison group.

One prediction that did receive support concerned the performances of the children of schizophrenic mothers under the auditory distraction condition. A decrement in intentional learning had been predicted for all groups in this condition relative to the first condition, with the children of schizophrenic mothers and the hyperactive children predicted to show differentially greater loss. The results indicated that only the children of schizophrenic mothers showed significantly poorer central recall in the second task than in the first, possibly suggesting a subtle deficit associated with auditory distractibility. The decreased central recall under auditory distraction conditions among children of schizophrenic mothers occurred in spite of ratings indicating good cooperativeness during the tasks.

Performance impairment under conditions of auditory distraction has been shown to be a characteristic of adult schizophrenia (Lawson, McGhie, & Chapman, 1967; McGhie, Chapman, & Lawson, 1965; Oltmanns, 1978; Oltmanns & Neale, 1975). Furthermore, Harvey, Winters, Weintraub, and Neale (1981) found that children of schizophrenic patients were particularly affected by the interference of auditory distraction during recall of items that demanded effortful rehearsal for later recall. Thus, the significant impact of auditory distraction on intentional learning among children of schizophrenic mothers in Driscoll's research, although a subtle effect, is consistent with other results and is noteworthy.

As expected, the children of nonpsychotic, psychiatrically disordered mothers typically did not differ significantly on the learning measures from their matched comparison group or the stratified normal group.

The hyperactive children were characterized by inconsistency and unpredictability on the learning measures. The hyperactive children showed significantly poorer learning than did their matched comparison group on intentional and incidental learning for some of the test measures, but not for others. This subject group, more than any other, showed evidence of inability to focus on the central task. The hyperactive children also displayed more recognition of incidental material at the expense of intentional learning than did any other group. Although they did not show more extrinsic incidental learning of visual stimuli, the hyperactive children did recall significantly more extrinsic auditory material than any of the other groups, suggesting a failure to ignore irrelevant stimuli.

The antisocial delinquent children showed the least adequate learning and the most deviant patterns of adaptation. Their ratings of cooperativeness during the experimental session were the lowest of any group. Thus, a low motivation level is likely to have played a significant role in the poor performance of this group.

To reduce the variable set in order to examine differential rates of deviant scorers, a principal components analysis with direct quartimin rotation for simple loadings was completed for the 15 major variables of this study using the 98 stratified normal comparison subjects. Four factors with eigenvalues greater than 1.00 were derived, accounting for 65% of the total variance. These factors were identifiable as Intentional Learning, Incidental Learning, Triad Recognition, and Auditory Incidental Learning.

The distributions of factor scores for the target groups and the stratified normal group were compared to determine if disproportionate numbers of target children could be identified below the 10th percentile of the normal distribution of factor scores for the stratified normal children. Only the antisocial delinquent group showed a frequency of low-scoring subjects that was significantly higher than that in the stratified normal sample. Forty-four percent of these subjects had very low scores on the Intentional Learning factor, compared with only 11% of the stratified normal subjects.

In summary, the intentional learning and incidental learning of children born to schizophrenic mothers were generally not deviant in this study. They performed as well as matched and stratified normal groups on learning measures that may be related to intelligence. Their cooperation during the experimental session was excellent, indicating good motivation and social appropriateness. With the singular exception of significant sensitivity to auditory distraction, the children of schizophrenic mothers appeared to be a socially and intellectually competent group in this study of selective attention during simple learning tasks.

Relationships between information processing and social behavior

In recent analyses, we examined whether or not the major dimensions of information processing performance assessed in the studies of vigilance, cross-modal RT, and intentional and incidental learning were related to dimensions of social and academic behavior evident to the children's peers. In particular, we focused on whether or not the CPT signal/noise discrimination (d') deficit within a subgroup of children born to schizophrenic mothers was associated with any concurrent deviant social behavior. If so, it would raise the question of whether this abnormality in vigilance level was part of a broader pattern of deviance, or conceivably even secondary to already deviant social behavior, as opposed to a primary abnormality that preceded social deviance.

In addition to this specific issue, we examined relationships between peer-rated social and academic behaviors and the major information processing performance dimensions among the stratified normal comparison children to provide a broader context for an understanding of the performance dimensions within the normal behavioral range. We then also determined whether parallel or distinctive interrelationships between social behavior and information processing performance characterized the children of schizophrenic mothers. Similarly, we evaluated the social behavior correlates of information processing within the hyperactive sample to see if any distinctive relationships might shed additional light on the abnormalities found in this disorder.

To reduce the peer nomination data to a few summary dimensions, we completed a principal components analysis of the 27 Class Play roles, using data from 1,029 children in 68 public school classrooms attended by target children. Five factors with eigenvalues greater than 1.0 were found to account for 67% of the variance. The rotated orthogonal factors are clearly interpretable as Conventional Achievement, Aggression, Oversensitivity and Social Isolation, Poor Comprehension, and Sociability.

Table 20.6. *Peer evaluation factor scores of low-CPT-d' subgroup and other children of schizo-phrenic mothers*

	CPT d' level		
Peer evaluation factor	Low ($n = 7$)	Not low ($n = 17$)	t
Conventional Achievement	−.28	.22	−1.41
Aggression	.02	.01	0.03
Oversensitivity and Social Isolation	.49	−.05	1.06
Poor Comprehension	−.07	−.05	−0.06
Sociability	−.01	−.46	1.70

Note: For $p < .05$, $t(22) = 2.07$. The peer evaluation factor scores have a mean of zero and a standard deviation of 1.00 for the total sample of 1,029 schoolchildren.

Social behavior of the subgroup with low CPT d'

The possibility that the impaired signal/noise discrimination of a subgroup of children born to schizophrenic mothers was associated with concurrent abnormalities in social behavior was assessed by contrasting the low-CPT-d' subgroup with the remaining offspring of schizophrenic mothers. As can be seen in Table 20.6, the subgroup with low CPT d' was not distinguishable from the remaining children of schizophrenic mothers on the five factor scores from the peer nomination procedure. The peer ratings of the subgroup with low CPT signal/noise discrimination generally were close to the mean for the entire sample of 1,029 children, which was zero for these factor scores (*SD* = 1.00). The peer evaluation factor on which the low-d' subgroup showed the largest deviation from the mean for the entire sample was Oversensitivity and Social Isolation, but this difference between the low-d' children and the remaining offspring of schizophrenic mothers did not approach statistical significance. Thus, these analyses indicate that the children of schizophrenic mothers with impaired signal/noise discrimination during vigilance did not have major concurrent anomalies in social behavior, thereby arguing against the CPT abnormality being secondary to abnormal social functioning.

Associations between information processing and social behavior among normal children

To examine the association of information processing performance with peer evaluation within the "normal" range, we computed product-moment correlations within the stratified normal group between four major information processing factors from the three studies just described and the five peer nomination factors. Six of these 20 correlations were found to be significant at the .05 level or better, which was substantially more than the 1 in

Table 20.7. *Stratified normal children: correlations between information processing factor scores and peer evaluation factor scores*

| | Information processing factor | | | |
Peer evaluation factor	CPT d'	RT Level and Variability	Intentional Learning	Incidental Learning
Conventional Achievement	.20	−.08	−.10	.31*
Aggression	.13	.16	−.05	−.13
Oversensitivity and Social Isolation	−.28*	.37**	−.35**	−.17
Poor Comprehension	.16	.14	−.30*	−.01
Sociability	.38**	−.10	−.03	.13

*$p < .05$; **$p < .01$.
Note: These correlations use stratified normal subjects who participated in the initial vigilance study to maximize sample comparability across performance dimensions; $n = 64$ for CPT d' factor; $n = 59$ for RT factor; $n = 58$ for the two learning factors.

20 that might be expected by chance. As shown in Table 20.7, the most consistent significant correlate of information processing performance was the Oversensitivity and Social Isolation factor. High scores on this factor were associated in the stratified normal group with significantly lower CPT d', higher simple RT medians and intrasubject variability, and lower intentional learning. These three information processing factors had been found in previous analyses to be moderately intercorrelated, a pattern that we have suggested may reflect a common relationship to intensity of focused attention (Nuechterlein, Phipps-Yonas, Driscoll, & Garmezy, 1982). The Oversensitivity and Social Isolation factor indicates peer nominations for roles such as "Somebody who is often left out" and "A person who is often frightened and doesn't like to take chances." Thus, among the normal comparison children, overly sensitive, easily frightened children who were isolated socially were likely to show poorer performances across three different sets of tasks that involved demands for intensive, focused attention. Also fitting this general pattern was the association between low scores on the Sociability factor (a factor typified by "Somebody who makes friends easily") and low CPT d' scores, but that relationship did not generalize to the RT Level and Variability and the Intentional Learning performance dimensions.

The relationship between high peer-perceived Poor Comprehension (e.g., "Somebody who does not understand schoolwork") and low Intentional Learning factor scores appears meaningful and is consistent with the evidence of an association between intentional learning and reading achievement test scores that was mentioned earlier. Finally, we shall not interpret the association of peer-perceived Conventional Achievement and Incidental Learning, because an examination of the scatterplot revealed that the significant correlation was due to one extreme outlier.

Table 20.8. *Children of schizophrenic mothers: correlations between information processing factor scores and peer evaluation factor scores*

	Information processing factor			
Peer evaluation factor	CPT d'	RT Level and Variability	Intentional Learning	Incidental Learning
Conventional Achievement	.33	−.13	.17	.35
Aggression	.07	.02	.03	−.19
Oversensitivity and Social Isolation	−.18	.20	−.30	−.07
Poor Comprehension	.15	.31	−.20	−.16
Sociability	−.27	.14	−.26	−.47*

*$p < .05$
Note: $n = 24$ for CPT d' factor; $n = 22$ for RT and learning factors.

Associations between information processing and social behavior among children of schizophrenic mothers and among hyperactive children

We examined the same correlation matrix among children born to schizophrenic mothers to determine if similar relationships were present between the major dimensions of information processing performance and peer-rated social and academic behavior. As shown in Table 20.8, only 1 of 20 correlations was found to be statistically significant at the $p < .05$ level, which may indicate that even that correlation was due to chance. This significant correlation suggests an association between low Sociability ratings and high Incidental Learning performance, a relationship that did not appear among the stratified normal children.

The correlations that were significant among the stratified normal children generally were slightly weaker, although not significantly so, among the offspring of schizophrenic mothers. In particular, the CPT d' factor score, which was found to be significantly lower among children of schizophrenic mothers, had no significant peer-rated social behavior correlates within these children. This analysis supplements the examination of the low-CPT-d' subgroup noted earlier, in this case treating the CPT d' factor as a continuous rather than dichotomous variable to evaluate social behavior correlates. It is noteworthy that the tendency toward a negative correlation (-0.27) of CPT d' and Sociability among children of schizophrenic mothers was significantly different from the positive correlation between these variables in the stratified normal group (0.38) and in the hyperactive group (0.42) ($p < .05$ by Fisher r-to-Z transformation). Thus, among children of schizophrenic mothers, the usual positive relationship between low CPT d' level and lack of extensive friendships was apparently disrupted. One might speculate that this change in the correlates of the CPT d' factor among children of schizophrenic mothers could be related to additional influences on CPT d' levels in a sample in which vulnerability factors for schizophrenia were more prevalent than in the general population. Thus, if the CPT d' level is affected by vulnerability to schizophrenia, as well as other determinants, the CPT d' level within offspring of schizophrenic patients may reflect the influence of vulnerability to schizophrenia to a greater extent than it does in the general population.

Within the hyperactive sample, examination of peer nomination correlates of information processing focused on the CPT β factor, which had indicated that the hyperactive children had a less cautious response style than did normal children or either of the two groups of children with psychiatrically disordered mothers. Within the sample of 14 hyperactive children, low scores on response caution (low CPT β factor scores) were significantly associated with high scores on the peer nomination factors of Aggression ($r = -.55, p < .05$) and of Oversensitivity and Social Isolation ($r = -.62, p < .05$). Examination of the correlations for individual peer nomination roles suggested that the social isolation items rather than the oversensitivity items were responsible for the association with the second factor. Specifically, within the hyperactive sample, the CPT β factor correlated $-.70$ ($p < .01$) with the number of nominations for "Somebody who is often left out" and $-.50$ ($p < .07$) with the number for "A person who has a hard time joining groups." The Aggression item with the strongest correlation with the CPT β factor score ($r = -.70, p < .01$) was "A person who fights and argues more often than others." Thus, the hyperactive children who had the highest levels of aggressive behavior and who were socially isolated showed the greatest lack of caution in their responses during the CPT conditions. One possible hypothesis from these data is that the low CPT response caution and the aggressive behavior stemmed from a common trait of impulsivity that was particularly extreme in some of the hyperactive children, leading them to be isolated by their peers. Such an association of low CPT β factor scores to high Aggression and to high Oversensitivity and Social Isolation scores did not occur in either the stratified normal sample or the sample of children of schizophrenic mothers, where these correlations were not significantly different from zero (all $-.05$ to $.08$). These correlations may, therefore, reveal a distinctive pattern within hyperactive children that should be examined further within larger samples.

Summary

This final phase of the Minnesota High-Risk Studies examined attention, cognition, and social behavior of 9- to 17-year-old offspring of schizophrenic mothers, offspring of nonpsychotic, psychiatrically disordered mothers, hyperactive children, antisocial delinquent children, and matched and representatively stratified normal children. A study of vigilance performance showed an impairment in children at risk for schizophrenia in signal/noise discrimination level during high-processing-load versions of the CPT. This

CPT signal/noise discrimination deficit appeared particularly to characterize a subgroup of the offspring of schizophrenic mothers. Hyperactive children were distinguished by their low scores on another dimension of vigilance performance that indicated willingness to respond to stimuli as relevant even when the perceptual evidence for their relevance was meager. The signal/noise discrimination deficit during vigilance among children of schizophrenic mothers could not be accounted for by any simple motivational explanation. Based on research summarized here and other recent findings (Cornblatt & Erlenmeyer-Kimling, 1985; Nuechterlein, 1985; Nuechterlein, Edell, Norris, & Dawson, 1986; Rutschmann, Cornblatt, & Erlenmeyer-Kimling, 1986), a signal/noise discrimination deficit during high-processing-load CPT versions appears to be a possible indicator of vulnerability to schizophrenia.

Studies of cross-modal RT and of intentional and incidental learning did not reveal performance deficits among the children of schizophrenic mothers, with the exception of a significant decrement in intentional learning across task conditions that may indicate a sensitivity of intentional learning to auditory distraction that did not characterize the other groups. Thus, the performance deficit among such children at risk for schizophrenia was not generalized to all cognitive tasks. Antisocial delinquent children showed the greater impairment in RT and learning performance. The low cooperation ratings received by the antisocial delinquent group suggested that poor motivation may have played an important role in their performance. In the intentional and incidental learning study, the hyperactive children recalled more irrelevant auditory information that was extrinsic to the central visual learning task than did any of the other groups. The hyperactive children were characterized by recognition of incidental material at the expense of intentional learning, suggesting a deficit in selective attention to relevant stimulus dimensions.

Our recent examination of the peer nomination data in relationship to the attentional and cognitive performance data led to several conclusions. First, among representative normal children, low CPT signal/noise discrimination level, slow simple RT, and poor intentional learning were significantly related to high peer-perceived emotional oversensitivity and social isolation. Low intentional learning performance on visual learning tasks was also significantly related to lack of comprehension in the classroom, as perceived by peers. Second, the CPT signal/noise discrimination deficit among a subgroup of children at risk for schizophrenia was not accompanied by significant deviance on any of five dimensions of concurrent social behavior and was therefore not likely to have been secondary to abnormalities in this domain of functioning. Specifically, the usual relationship between low CPT signal/noise discrimination level and low sociability was significantly altered and was not present among these children of schizophrenic mothers. Finally, among hyperactive children, but not representative normal children or children of schizophrenic mothers, low levels of cautiousness in responding to stimuli during the CPT conditions were associated with high peer-rated aggressiveness and social isolation. Thus, in addition to the finding that hyperactive children, in general, showed abnormally low criterion settings for responding during the CPT, the lowered CPT response caution had a distinctive relationship to these additional social difficulties within hyperactivity.

References

Achenbach, T. M. (1966). The classification of children's psychiatric symptoms: A factor analytic study. *Psychological Monographs, 80*(7, Whole No. 615).

American Psychiatric Association (1980). *Diagnostic and statistical manual of mental disorders* (3rd ed.). Washington, DC: Author.

Asarnow, R. F., & MacCrimmon, D. J. (1978). Residual performance deficit in clinically remitted schizophrenics: A marker of schizophrenia? *Journal of Abnormal Psychology, 87,* 597–608.

Asarnow, R. F., Steffy, R. A., MacCrimmon, D. J., & Cleghorn, J. M. (1977). An attentional assessment of foster children at risk for schizophrenia. *Journal of Abnormal Psychology, 86,* 267–75.

Borland, B. L., & Heckman, H. K. (1976). Hyperactive boys and their brothers: A 25-year follow-up study. *Archives of General Psychiatry, 33,* 669–75.

Bower, E. M. (1960). *Early identification of emotionally handicapped children in school.* Springfield, IL: Charles C Thomas.

Cornblatt, B. A., & Erlenmeyer-Kimling, L. (1985). Global attentional deviance as a marker of risk for schizophrenia: Specificity and predictive validity. *Journal of Abnormal Psychology, 94,* 470–86.

Cowen, E. L., Pederson, A., Babigian, H., Izzo, L. D., & Frost, M. A. (1973). Long-term follow-up of early detected vulnerable children. *Journal of Consulting and Clinical Psychology, 41,* 438–46.

Davies, D. R., & Parasuraman, R. (1982). *The psychology of vigilance.* London: Academic Press.

Deichmann, J. W., Speltz, M. B., & Kausler, D. H. (1971). Developmental trends in the intentional and incidental learning components of a verbal discrimination task. *Journal of Experimental Child Psychology, 11,* 21–34.

Driscoll, R. M. (1980). *Incidental and intentional learning as measures of selective attention in children vulnerable to psychopathology.* Unpublished doctoral dissertation, University of Minnesota.

Driscoll, R. M. (1984). Intentional and incidental learning in children vulnerable to psychopathology. In N. F. Watt, E. J. Anthony, L. C. Wynne, & J. E. Rolf (Eds.), *Children at risk for schizophrenia: A longitudinal perspective* (pp. 320–6). Cambridge University Press.

Druker, J. F., and Hagen, J. W. (1969). Developmental trends in the processing of task relevant and task irrelevant information. *Child Development, 40,* 371–82.

Endicott, J., Spitzer, R. L., Fleiss, J. L., & Cohen, J. (1976). The Global Assessment Scale: A procedure for measuring overall severity of psychiatric disturbance. *Archives of General Psychiatry, 33,* 766–71.

Erlenmeyer-Kimling, L., & Cornblatt, B. (1978). Attentional measures in a study of children at high-risk for schizophrenia. *Journal of Psychiatric Research, 14,* 93–8.

Garmezy, N. (1974). Children at risk: The search for the antecedents of schizophrenia. Part II: Ongoing research programs, issues, and intervention. *Schizophrenia Bulletin, 1*(Experimental Issue No. 9), 55–125.

Garmezy, N. (1978). Attentional processes in adult schizophrenia and in children at risk. *Journal of Psychiatric Research, 14,* 3–34.

Garmezy, N., & Devine, V. (1984). Project Competence: The Minnesota studies of children vulnerable to psychopathology. In N. F. Watt, E. J. Anthony, L. C. Wynne, & J. E. Rolf (Eds.), *Children at risk for schizophrenia: A longitudinal perspective* (pp. 289–303). Cambridge University Press.

Garmezy, N., & Streitman, S. (1974). Children at risk: The search for the antecedents of schizophrenia. Part I: Conceptual models and research methods. *Schizophrenia Bulletin, 1*(Experimental Issue No. 8), 14–90.

Gottesman, I. I., & Shields, J. (1982). *Schizophrenia: The epigenetic puzzle.* Cambridge University Press.

Goyette, C. H., Conners, C. K., & Ulrich, R. F. (1978). Normative data on revised Conners parent and teacher rating scales. *Journal of Abnormal Child Psychology, 6,* 221–36.

Green, D. M., & Swets, J. A. (1966). *Signal detection theory and psychophysics.* New York: Wiley.

Hagen, J. W., & Sabo, R. A. (1967). A developmental study of selective attention. *Merrill-Palmer Quarterly, 13,* 159–72.

Hale, G. A., & Piper, R. A. (1973). Developmental trends in children's incidental learning: Some critical stimulus differences. *Developmental Psychology, 8,* 327–35.

Harvey, P., Winters, K., Weintraub, S., & Neale, J. M. (1981). Distractibility in children vulnerable to psychopathology. *Journal of Abnormal Psychology, 90,* 298–304.

Hawkins, R. P. (1973). Learning of peripheral content in films: A developmental study. *Child Development, 44,* 214–17.

Kendler, K. S., Gruenberg, A. M., & Tsuang, M. T. (1985). Psychiatric illness in first-degree relatives of schizophrenic and surgical control patients: A family study using DSM-III criteria. *Archives of General Psychiatry, 42,* 770–9.

Kety, S. S., Rosenthal, D., Wender, P. H., & Schulsinger, F. (1968). The types and prevalence of mental illness in the biological and adoptive families of adopted schizophrenics. In D. Rosenthal & S. S. Kety (Eds.), *The transmission of schizophrenia* (pp. 345–62). Oxford: Pergamon.

Kety, S. S., Rosenthal, D., Wender, P. H., Schulsinger, F., & Jacobsen, B. (1978). The biologic and adoptive families of adoptive individuals who became schizophrenic: Prevalence of mental illness and other characteristics. In L. C. Wynne, R. L. Cromwell, & S. Matthysse (Eds.), *The nature of schizophrenia: New approaches to research and treatment* (pp. 25–37). New York: Wiley.

Kornetsky, C. (1972). The use of a simple test of attention as a measure of drug effects in schizophrenic patients. *Psychopharmacologia, 24,* 99–106.

Lawson, J. S., McGhie, A., & Chapman, J. (1967). Distractibility in schizophrenia and organic cerebral disease. *British Journal of Psychiatry, 113,* 527–35.

Maccoby, E. E., and Hagen, J. W. (1965). Effects of distraction upon central versus incidental recall: Developmental trends. *Journal of Experimental Child Psychology, 2,* 280–9.

McGhie, A., and Chapman, J. (1961). Disorders of attention and perception in early schizophrenia. *British Journal of Medical Psychology, 34,* 103–16.

McGhie, A., Chapman, J., and Lawson, J. S. (1965). The effect of distraction on schizophrenic performance. 1. Perception and immediate memory. *British Journal of Psychiatry, 111,* 383–90.

McNicol, D. (1972). *A primer of signal detection theory.* London: Allen & Unwin.

Marcus, L. M. (1973). Studies of attention in children vulnerable to psychopathology. *Dissertation Abstracts International, 33,* 5023B. (University Microfilms No. 73-10, 606)

Mendelson, W., Johnson, N., & Stewart, M. (1971). Hyperactive children as teenagers: A follow-up study. *Journal of Nervous and Mental Disease, 153,* 272–9.

Nuechterlein, K. H. (1977). Reaction time and attention in schizophrenia: A critical evaluation of the data and theories. *Schizophrenia Bulletin, 3,* 373–428.

Nuechterlein, K. H. (1983). Signal detection in vigilance tasks and behavioral attributes among offspring of schizophrenic mothers and among hyperactive children. *Journal of Abnormal Psychology, 92,* 4–28.

Nuechterlein, K. H. (1984). Sustained attention among children vulnerable to adult schizophrenia and among hyperactive children. In N. F. Watt, E. J. Anthony, L. C. Wynne, & J. E. Rolf (Eds.), *Children at risk for schizophrenia: A longitudinal perspective* (pp. 304–11). Cambridge University Press.

Nuechterlein, K. H. (1985). Converging evidence for vigilance deficit as a vulnerability indicator for schizophrenic disorders. In M. Alpert (Ed.), *Controversies in schizophrenia: Changes and constancies* (pp. 175–98). New York: Guilford Press.

Nuechterlein, K. H., & Dawson, M. E. (1984). Information processing and attentional functioning in the developmental course of schizophrenic disorders. *Schizophrenia Bulletin, 10,* 160–203.

Nuechterlein, K. H., Edell, W. S., Norris, M., & Dawson, M. E. (1986). Attentional vulnerability indicators, thought disorder, and negative symptoms. *Schizophrenia Bulletin, 12,* 408–26.

Nuechterlein, K. H., Phipps-Yonas, S., Driscoll, R. M., & Garmezy, N. (1982). The role of different components of attention in children vulnerable to schizophrenia. In M. J. Goldstein (Ed.), *Preventive intervention in schizophrenia: Are we ready?* (DHHS Publication No. ADM 82-1111, pp. 54–77). Washington, DC: U.S. Government Printing Office.

Nuechterlein, K. H., Soli, S. D., Garmezy, N., Devine, V. T., & Schaefer, S. M. (1981). A classification system for research in childhood psychopathology. Part II: Validation research examining converging descriptions from the parent and the child. *Progress in Experimental Personality Research, 10,* 163–202.

O'Doughtery, M., Nuechterlein, K. H., & Drew, B. (1984). Hyperactive and hypoxic children: Signal detection, sustained attention, and behavior. *Journal of Abnormal Psychology, 93,* 178–91.

Oltmanns, T. F. (1978). Selective attention in schizophrenic and manic psychosis: The effect of distraction on information processing. *Journal of Abnormal Psychology, 87,* 212–25.

Oltmanns, T. F., & Neale, J. M. (1975). Schizophrenic performance when distractors are present: Attentional deficit or differential task difficulty? *Journal of Abnormal Psychology, 84*(3), 205–9.

Orzack, M. H., & Kornetsky, C. (1966). Attention dysfunction in chronic schizophrenia. *Archives of General Psychiatry, 14,* 323–6.

Parasuraman, R. (1984). The psychobiology of sustained attention. In J. S. Warm (Ed.), *Sustained attention in human performance* (pp. 61–101). New York: Wiley.

Parasuraman, R., & Davies, D. R. (1977). A taxonomic analysis of vigilance performance. In R. R. Mackie (Ed.), *Vigilance: Theory, operational performance, and physiological correlates* (pp. 559–74). New York: Plenum.

Phipps-Yonas, S. (1984). Visual and auditory reaction time in children vulnerable to psychopathology. In N. F. Watt, E. J. Anthony, L. C. Wynne, & J. E. Rolf (Eds.), *Children at risk for schizophrenia: A longitudinal perspective* (pp. 312–19). Cambridge University Press.

Postman, L. (1964). Short-term memory and incidental learning. In A. W. Melton (Ed.), *Categories of human learning* (pp. 145–201). New York: Academic Press.

Rieder, R. O., Rosenthal, D., Wender, P., & Blumenthal, H. (1975). The offspring of schizophrenics: Fetal and neonatal deaths. *Archives of General Psychiatry, 32,* 200–11.

Rodnick, E., & Shakow, D. (1940). Set in the schizophrenic as measured by a composite reaction time index. *American Journal of Psychiatry, 97,* 214–25.

Roff, M. (1970). Some life history factors in relation to various types of adult maladjustment. In M. Roff & D. F. Ricks (Eds.), *Life history research in psychopathology* (pp. 265–87). Minneapolis: University of Minnesota Press.

Rolf, J. E. (1972). The social and academic competence of children vulnerable to schizophrenia and other behavior pathologies. *Journal of Abnormal Psychology, 80,* 225–43.

Rolf, J. E. (1976). Peer status and the directionality of symptomatic behavior: Prime social competence predictors of outcome for vulnerable children. *American Journal of Orthopsychiatry, 46,* 74–87.

Rolf, J. E., & Garmezy, N. (1974). The school performance of children vulnerable to behavior pathology. In D. F. Ricks, A. Thomas, & M. Roff (Eds.), *Life history research in psychopathology* (Vol. 3, pp. 87–107). Minneapolis: University of Minnesota Press.

Rosenthal, D. (1975). Discussion: The concept of subschizophrenic disorders. In R. R. Fieve, D. Rosenthal, & H. Brill (Eds.), *Genetic research in psychiatry* (pp. 199–208). Baltimore: Johns Hopkins University Press.

Rosvold, H. E., Mirsky, A., Sarason, I., Bransome, E. D., Jr., & Beck, L. H. (1956). A continuous performance test of brain damage. *Journal of Consulting Psychology, 20,* 343–50.

Rubenstein, G., Fisher, L., & Iker, H. (1975). Peer observation of student behavior in elementary school classrooms. *Developmental Psychology, 11,* 867–8.

Rutschmann, J., Cornblatt, B., & Erlenmeyer-Kimling, L. (1977). Sustained attention in children at risk for schizophrenia: Report on a continuous performance test. *Archives of General Psychiatry, 34,* 571–5.

Rutschmann, J., Cornblatt, B., & Erlenmeyer-Kimling, L. (1986). Sustained attention in children at risk for schizophrenia: Findings with two visual continuous performance tests in a new sample. *Journal of Abnormal Child Psychology, 14,* 365–85.

Sabo, R., & Hagen, J. W. (1973). Color cues and rehearsal in short-term memory. *Child Development, 44,* 77–82.

Soli, S. D., Nuechterlein, K. H., Garmezy, N., Devine, V. T., & Schaefer, S. M. (1981). A classification system for research in childhood psychopathology. Part I: An empirical approach using factor and cluster analyses and conjunctive decision rules. *Progress in Experimental Personality Research, 10,* 115–61.

Spitzer, R. L., Endicott, J., & Robins, E. (1978). *Research diagnostic criteria (RDC) for a selected group of functional disorders* (3rd ed.). New York: Biometric Research.

Stewart, M. A., de Blois, C. S., & Cummings, C. (1980). Psychiatric disorder in the parents of hyperactive boys and those with conduct disorder. *Journal of Child Psychology and Psychiatry, 21,* 283–92.

Strauss, J. S., & Harder, D. W. (1975). *The case record rating scale: A method of rating symptom and social function data from case records.* Unpublished manuscript.

Sutton, S., Hakerem, G., Zubin, J., & Portnoy, M. (1961). The effects of shift of sensory modality on serial reaction time: A comparison of schizophrenics and normals. *American Journal of Psychology, 74,* 224–32.

Sutton, S., & Zubin, J. (1965). Effects of sequence on reaction time in schizophrenia. In A. F. Welford & J. E. Buren (Eds.), *Behavior, aging, and the nervous system.* Springfield, IL: Charles C Thomas.

Swets, J. A., & Sewall, S. T. (1963). Invariance of signal detectability over stages of practice and levels of motivation. *Journal of Experimental Psychology, 66,* 120–6.

Weiss, G., Hechtman, L., Perlman, T., Hopkins, J., & Wener, A. (1979). Hyperactives as young adults: A controlled perspective ten-year follow-up of 75 children. *Archives of General Psychiatry, 36,* 675–81.

Wohlberg, G. W., & Kornetsky, C. (1973). Sustained attention in remitted schizophrenics. *Archives of General Psychiatry, 28,* 533–7.

Zubin, J. (1975). Problem of attention in schizophrenia. In M. L. Kietzman, S. Sutton, & J. Zubin (Eds.), *Experimental approaches to psychopathology* (pp. 139–66). New York: Academic Press.

21 Schizophrenia: a new model for its transmission and its variations

Philip S. Holzman

A cure for schizophrenia, one of the most severe mental diseases, must await an understanding of its origins and pathogenesis, and the search for the origins of schizophrenia has been slowed by several difficulties; not the least of which has been that definition of the disorder has relied exclusively on description of symptoms and the observed course of the disorder. We lack a valid identifying criterion for schizophrenia that would signal its presence. Kraepelin and Bleuler had no such criterion to offer, and therefore they relied on careful description of symptoms. This has resulted in continuing ambiguities and disputes, such as whether or not schizophrenia and manic-depressive illness are distinct syndromes or diseases. Although it is clear that neither disorder is homogeneous, it is not clear that they are distinct from each other, at least from the vantage point of symptoms alone. Resolution of these uncertainties will depend on finding valid markers for a given disorder, that is, indicators of the presence of the disease that may be behavioral, anatomical, or biochemical and are not necessarily coincident or identical with the current defining symptoms of the disease. These markers should help us to advance beyond our current inadequate understanding of the causes of the schizophrenias, to use a term that recognizes the heterogeneity of the condition. I shall describe to you one such marker – a disorder of smooth pursuit eye movements – that has more than mere promise of being such an aid in untangling the mysteries of schizophrenia. This eye movement dysfunction can serve to guide us through the labyrinth of schizophrenic disorganization as Ariadne's thread guided Theseus on his mission to slay the Minotaur.

I shall try to show that smooth pursuit eye movement dysfunction can serve as a genetic indicator of schizophrenia, that indeed it is specific for schizophrenia, that it is not an artifact of conditions that usually plague objective studies of schizophrenia, and that it not only can serve as such an indicator but also

The investigations discussed here were supported by grants MH-31340 and MH-31154 from the U.S. Public Health Service and by a grant from the Schizophrenia Research Program of the Scottish Rite, Northern Masonic Jurisdiction, U.S.A.

has the potential for revealing which areas of the central nervous system may be implicated. It thereby supports the theory of distinctions between the schizophrenias and the major affective disorders.

This strategy is a bit different from the usual approaches to the study of how schizophrenia is transmitted. The usual approaches to the transmission of schizophrenia have focused on counting the numbers of schizophrenic people in families and the extent of concordance in twin samples. These studies have uniformly failed to yield results that would be consistent with schizophrenia being transmitted as a Mendelian trait. The incidence of schizophrenia among first-degree relatives of schizophrenics is between 3.2% and 15%; among the offspring of schizophrenic persons the expected rates would be 25% or 50% for a recessive or dominant gene. The concordance in monozygotic twins is about 45%; the expected concordance rate would be 100% for complete genetic determination. The figures obtained are therefore far too low to represent a Mendelian pattern of transmission.

Two attempts to explain these data in Mendelian terms have not been promising enough to spawn a vigorous research thrust. The first was to invoke the concept of penetrance. As Matthysse and Kety (1986) remarked, "the explanation in terms of partial penetrance is a 'confession of ignorance'; it is a sure sign that the list of causal factors is incomplete." The second attempt was to assume that what was genetically transmitted was not clinical schizophrenia, but a *vulnerability* to schizophrenia. The concept of vulnerability has been helpful insofar as it has recognized the complexity of transmission. Yet, as Matthysse and Kety (1986) commented, vulnerability is not an entity. It is a hypothetical construct. The task, therefore, is to discover the actual traits that are transmitted and that truly predispose a person to schizophrenia. The strategy suggested by this criticism of the vulnerability construct is the one that I shall describe. It focuses on an observable component of schizophrenia, a disorder of smooth pursuit eye movements, that nevertheless is not a symptom of the clinical disorder, but that seems to segregate in a Mendelian pattern in schizophrenia, but not in manic-depressive illness. I shall describe this disorder by first tracing the history of this discovery. Then I shall show its promise as a biological marker and as a clue to pathogenesis.

In 1973 we reported that a large proportion of schizophrenic patients showed smooth pursuit eye movement dysfunctions (Holzman, Proctor, & Hughes, 1973). That report was followed by a replication (Holzman et al., 1974), employing a much larger sample, that included evidence that about 40% of the first-degree relatives of schizophrenic patients showed the same kinds of eye movement dysfunctions, although the relatives themselves were not clinically ill. These studies raised a number of questions that required answers before one could place any confidence in the basic finding. For example, one needed to know whether these results were attributable to drug treatment, to inattention, or to improper instrumentation and whether or not they were specific for schizophrenia. But if these possible artifacts could be eliminated, smooth pursuit eye movement dysfunctions could represent a central nervous system dysfunction that would provide leads to pathogenesis and to family transmission.

At this point I shall digress to describe briefly the nature of the eye movements under discussion. There are two types of eye movements involved in this phenomenon. The first is the saccadic or rapid eye movement that occurs thousands of times each day. These movements serve to fix the eye on a target. A second type of eye movement is the tracking or pursuit movement that follows the target once caught by the saccade. These pursuit movements act to keep the target on the retina. In normal pursuit, these two control systems are coordinated. The eye movement dysfunctions in schizophrenia occur in the course of tracking movements when saccadic eye movements interrupt those tracking movements. In many psychotic patients and their relatives there is a complete replacement of tracking by a large saccade or, more usually, by small, frequent interruptions of pursuit movements by rapid eye movements.

Our two reports actually constituted a rediscovery of a finding reported in 1908 by Diefendorf and Dodge. Diefendorf and Dodge (1908) took motion pictures of eye movements, and their photographs yielded superb records that are unsurpassed even today. They claimed two results: The first was that only schizophrenics showed disordered pursuit movements; manic-depressive patients did not. The second was that the eye movement dysfunctions involved only smooth pursuit movements. The rapid or saccadic movements were unimpaired. Because saccadic movements were normal, and all patients showed obvious attempts to follow the target, Diefendorf and Dodge concluded that the eye movement dysfunction was genuine and was not a reflection of inattention. Indeed, they believed that the eye movement dysfunction represented a fundamental constituent of the schizophrenic process. Recall that their studies were completed decades before the introduction of the phenothiazines, and so, at least in Diefendorf and Dodge's study, the eye movement dysfunctions were not due to those drugs.

In 1934, Couch and Fox attempted to repeat that study. They, too, found pursuit disturbances in schizophrenic patients, but they found that large numbers of manic-depressives showed similar eye movement dysfunctions. When Couch and Fox (1934) retested their patients, they noticed that many patients who initially had shown pursuit impairment showed improved eye movements after they had recovered from their acute psychotic episodes. Couch and Fox interpreted their results as suggesting that pursuit eye movement impairments in psychotic patients were essentially indicators of inattention or poor motivation. It is of great interest, however, that a large number of their patients were receiving sodium amytal to calm their excitement, and on recovery from their acute psychotic disturbances, drug treatment was discontinued. It is now known that barbiturates disrupt pursuit movements by inducing nystagmus. Therefore, the eye movement disturbances Couch and Fox noticed in their patients can be attributed to the effects of barbiturate drug treatment, and the improvement may very well have reflected the cessation of such treatment.

The basic finding from our laboratory was that 50% to 86% of schizophrenic patients had pursuit movement dysfunctions. This association has been replicated many times in other laboratories. The percentages have varied with the samples tested: Long-term chronic schizophrenic patients from state hospital facilities have shown the highest prevalence of pursuit dysfunctions; schizophrenic patients in private, active treatment centers have shown lower prevalences. There are several possible sources of error, and we systematically investigated each of them.

The first possible source concerns the effects of the therapeutic drugs administered to psychiatric patients. This set of drugs arouses suspicion because they disrupt motor functioning in one way or another. These include the neuroleptics, the tricyclics, monoamine oxidase (MAO) inhibitors, and lithium carbonate. Several factors, however, suggest that the neuroleptic drugs cannot be inducing the pursuit dysfunction. First, Diefendorf and Dodge's study predated the introduction of the phenothiazines by almost 45 years. Another factor concerns the set of single-dose studies that we conducted using normal persons (Holzman, Levy, Uhlenhuth, Proctor, & Freedman, 1975; Levy, Lipton, & Holzman, 1981). Single doses of chlorpromazine, diazepam, secobarbital, alcohol, and chloral hydrate all produced considerable drowsiness and somnolence in the subjects, but only secobarbital, alcohol, and chloral hydrate disrupted pursuit movements. These effects clearly were temporary and dose-related. Thus, central nervous system depressants interfere with pursuit movements; neuroleptic drugs do not.

In our 1974 study (Holzman et al., 1974) we reported that 17 patients whose conditions were diagnosed as schizophrenic by DSM-II criteria were reclassified as nonschizophrenic by stricter criteria; 16 of those 17 had been receiving phenothiazines for several months, and 15 of those 16 showed normal pursuit movements. Thus, continued neuroleptic treatment does not necessarily produce impairments in smooth pursuit movements. Nor does the withdrawal of neuroleptics from schizophrenic patients with impaired eye movements result in improved pursuit movements.

Yet another line of evidence fails to implicate neuroleptic drugs. The large numbers of unaffected relatives of schizophrenic patients who have shown poor pursuit movements have not been hospitalized or treated for mental illness. It is thus possible for a person to have disrupted pursuit movements without ever having been ill or been treated. Levy et al. (1985), however, showed that treatment with lithium carbonate could induce impairments in smooth pursuit movements.

We also examined the effects of recording method, scoring technique, and target characteristics, and we were able to conclude that none of these could account for the appearance of pursuit dysfunctions in psychotic patients.

The role of attention is more complicated. All investigations of psychotic patients have raised questions about the patients' motivation and attention to the task. Indeed, both Kraepelin (1919) and Bleuler (1911/1950) postulated an underlying disorder of attention in schizophrenia. The German language distinguishes two qualities of attention: *Auffassung,* the grasping and comprehending of information, and *Aufmerksamkeit,* the active directed attending to an object. Kraepelin believed that the former was unimpaired, whereas the latter was almost always impaired, in schizophrenic conditions. Surely Kraepelin's remarks are confirmable by all clinicians; schizophrenic patients are notoriously inattentive. It is therefore of considerable importance to determine if these patients have impaired pursuit movements because they are not paying attention to the moving stimulus, in which case the findings of impaired pursuit movements are trivial and merely reflect the characteristic negligence and weakened motivation of psychotic patients. For several reasons, however, we believe that faulty voluntary attention – in the form of inattention or distraction – cannot be held responsible for the pursuit disruptions.

First, attempts to sharpen and enhance patients' attention to the moving stimulus resulted in no improvements in their tracking integrity (Holzman et al., 1974). Three other studies (May, 1979; Pivik, 1979; Shagass, Amadeo, & Overton, 1974), using different techniques, reported that alerting subjects and rewarding subjects failed to change performance.

Second, manipulation of the stimulus (by placing arabic numbers on it and requiring the subjects to read the numbers, by intermittently changing their appearances on the target, or by changing the color of the target) did significantly improve the tracking (Holzman, Levy, & Proctor, 1976; Shagass, Roemer, & Amadeo, 1976). Yet the improvement was never enough to erase the differences between normal subjects and schizophrenic patients. The most obvious improvements occurred in square-wave tracking, in which smooth pursuit was almost completely replaced by a large saccadic shift. Only slight improvements, however, occurred in the poor tracking that was characterized by frequent small saccadic intrusions.

In several publications we have remarked that it is unparsimonious to attribute eye movement dysfunctions to deficient voluntary attention simply because tracking errors are reduced by manipulating the target, that is, by making it more interesting, as in the case of putting arabic numerals on it. It is noteworthy that in these studies, the subjects were always unaware that they were tracking poorly or that their tracking improved with the dominant cognitive task, suggesting that conscious motivational variables were not sufficient to explain the occurrence of abnormal pursuit movements. Moreover, number reading and color changes led to improvements regarding the eye tracking disruptions that were induced by alcohol, secobarbital, and chloral hydrate in normal subjects, thus providing further evidence that these shifts were not necessarily linked to poor motivation and inattention.

Yet another perspective on attentional correlates of disrupted pursuit movements was provided by attempts to *interfere* with eye tracking performance in normal subjects. Brezinova and Kendall (1977) studied the effects of stress, distraction, and fatigue in normal subjects with normal tracking. They found that smooth pursuit movements deteriorated only during the most difficult of their interfering tasks, which was to subtract 13s from 200 serially while following the target with their eyes for 60 min. Brezinova and Kendall (1977) judged that the disturbances in eye tracking produced by these manipulations were indistinguishable from those observed in schizophrenic patients, and they therefore concluded that impaired voluntary attention accounted for the deviant pursuit movements in schizophrenics. In our laboratory we repeated that experiment, and we found that during distraction of normal subjects, pursuit movements were characterized by large-amplitude saccades, in a setting of otherwise intact pursuit movements. In contrast, schizophrenic patients showed persistent disruption of their pursuit movements. With minimal training, naive raters, blind to the subjects' identities and diagnostic categories, were able to distinguish between the normal tracking and distracted tracking of normal subjects, and they distinguished both of these from the impaired tracking of schizophrenics (Lipton, Frost, & Holzman, 1980a). Thus, although distraction and simple inattentiveness produced tracking disruptions, those disruptions were easily distinguished from the tracking abnormalities among psychotic patients. Thus, different processes accounted for tracking disorders in psychotic patients and in normal subjects who were distracted.

Studies of saccadic latency have shown that schizophrenic patients with abnormal pursuit movements are highly accurate in their saccadic eye movements, which require more intense attentional involvement than do pursuit movements (Iacono, Tuason, & Johnson, 1981; Levin, Holzman, Rothenberg, & Lipton, 1981a). That is, when required to follow a target that moved in discrete steps – a task repeated many times – the saccadic eye movements of schizophrenic patients found the target accurately, and the latency of their saccadic movements was quite normal – and so was the relationship between speed of eye movement and amplitude of excursion. That task, which in our laboratory took 20 min, required more intense attentional involvement than did the 2 min of pursuit trials.

Finally, correlations between tracking integrity and several measures of voluntary attention, such as reaction time, short-term memory, and size estimation, have shown only zero-order correlations (Spohn, 1981).

It is therefore reasonable to dismiss the reports of eye movement dysfunctions in psychoses as reflecting merely artifacts due to drug effects, recording and scoring errors, special characteristics of targets, or inattention. The particular stage of the illness does not seem to be a factor, nor does the subtype of illness, age, sex, or premorbid adjustment. There is, however, a significant tendency for a higher prevalence of eye tracking dysfunctions among patients with long-term chronic schizophrenic psychoses than among patients whose conditions are of more recent onset.

I return now to the genetic story. Our 1974 study (Holzman et al., 1974) showed that schizophrenic patients and their first-degree relatives accounted for over 80% of abnormal pursuit movements in a sample of over 200 subjects. About 45% of the family members of schizophrenics manifested qualitative disruptions of pursuit movements, in contrast to about 10% of the first-degree relatives of nonschizophrenic psychiatric patients. In addition, we reported that abnormal pursuit movements in a schizophrenic proband tended to be associated with poor tracking in at least one of the two clinically unaffected parents. These data raise the question whether or not eye movement dysfunctions associated with psychosis are genetically transmitted and, if so, whether or not they indicate an inherited predisposition to psychosis.

An early probe of that question made use of studies of twins as the method of investigation. The search was to see if there were high concordance rates in monozygotic (MZ) twins and half that concordance in dizygotic (DZ) twins for eye tracking dysfunctions. We were able to locate sets of MZ and DZ twins who were clinically discordant for schizophrenia. Professor Einar Kringlen of the University of Oslo had identified and studied these twins, and in a landmark study of a national sample of twins he had determined that the clinical concordance for schizophrenia was 25% for MZ twins and 9% for DZ twins, using a set of strict criteria for schizophrenia (Kringlen, 1967). This sample of Norwegian twins provided us with the sets of MZ and DZ twins discordant for schizophrenia. Professor Kringlen joined us in that study and continues to be an active collaborator.

If we were to find that among these clinically discordant twins, the eye tracking dysfunctions showed a 2 : 1 ratio of concordance, we would have encouraging, but not yet conclusive, evidence of a trait marker for schizophrenia. That is, we would have some evidence for a stable trait that was associated with schizophrenia but was not a symptom of the disorder itself. An example of such a trait marker is the presence of hemoglobin X for sickle cell anemia. Such a trait should be present in those who are predisposed to schizophrenia – or to another psychosis – and the trait should be present whether or not those susceptible people are clinically ill.

In our first twin study (Holzman et al., 1977), the actual clinical concordance was 18% for MZ sets (2 of 11 sets were, on reexamination, concordant) and zero for the DZ sets (none of 15 sets). The incidence of eye movement dysfunctions among the 26 probands with diagnoses of schizophrenia was 69%; it was 54% among their 24 discordant co-twins. These rates were consistent with previous results reported for non-twin schizophrenics and their first-degree relatives. The actual qualitative concordance for eye movement dysfunctions, however, was 5 of 7 in the MZ sets (71%) and 7 of 13 in the DZ sets (54%). Those pairs in which there was a concordance for *unimpaired* eye tracking were not counted, because 92% of the general population are concordant for unimpaired eye tracking.

The age-corrected product moment correlation for a quantitative score of tracking integrity was .71 for MZ pairs and .22 for DZ pairs. Thus, there was a significant tendency for the quality of tracking – whether normal or deviant – to be alike among MZ pairs, but not as strongly alike among DZ pairs. Because 86% of the MZ pairs concordant for bad tracking were clinically discordant, the eye movement dysfunction reflected neither the consequences of having a schizophrenic illness nor the effects of having been treated for the psychosis.

The small sizes of the twin sample limited the statistical power of those concordance estimates. Furthermore, the mean age for the sample was 55 years, and because pursuit integrity tends to degrade with age, the high concordance for abnormal pursuit among the MZ pairs could reflect a tendency for such twins to age in similar ways. A second twin study (Holzman, Kringlen, Levy, & Haberman, 1980) sought to clarify those issues using 10 MZ and 15 DZ pairs. Their mean age was 31; 40% of the MZ pairs and none of the DZ pairs were concordant for psychosis. The proband-wise concordance for eye tracking dysfunctions, however, was 100% and 33% for MZ and DZ pairs, respectively, and the age-corrected product moment correlations for quantitative eye tracking scores were .77 and .39 for the MZ and DZ sets.

These two studies showed statistically that regardless of age, MZ twin pairs showed greater eye tracking similarity than did DZ pairs, and these concordance rates were about 80% of the theoretically predicted values for a trait under polygenic control. These studies suggest that there is a significant genetic contribution to eye tracking efficiency. The studies, however, did not unequivocally rule out nongenetic mechanisms that may be responsible for both psychosis and eye tracking dysfunctions, such as viral, toxic, and prenatal influences. Nor did these studies address the relationship between eye tracking dysfunctions and schizophrenia, because we did not employ comparison groups consisting of twins with other psychoses.

More extensive data on the prevalence of eye tracking dysfunctions in family members of schizophrenic and nonschizophrenic psychotic patients will be required before our understanding of the significance of eye tracking dysfunction as a trait indicator of schizophrenia is complete. As already mentioned, in our early studies (Holzman et al., 1974) we found that tracking dysfunctions were more strongly associated with schizophrenia than with any other psychiatric condition. Nonschizophrenic psychotic patients accounted for about 22% of the eye tracking dysfunctions, and only 8% of normal subjects showed pursuit disturbances. Charles Shagass and his colleagues, however, reported that significant numbers of patients with major affective disorders also showed pursuit disruptions (Shagass et al., 1974). In 1980 our laboratory reported that of 32 patients meeting the criteria for schizophrenia and major affective disorder, 50% of both groups showed pursuit abnormalities (Lipton, Levin, & Holzman, 1980b). Pursuit disruption is also found in many central nervous system disorders. It is well known, for example, that eye tracking dysfunctions are associated with a variety of neurological syndromes, such as Parkinson's disease, multiple sclerosis, and those following hemispheric and brain-stem lesions. But no obvious central nervous system diseases have been reported in association with functionally psychotic patients or in their family members who show eye tracking disorders.

Although in central nervous system diseases eye tracking dysfunction is an *outcome* or a reflection of those diseases, in psychosis it is unclear whether pursuit impairment is a trait variable or reflects a state-related impairment. There is evidence of high stability over a 2-year period in a clinically normal population (Iacono & Lykken, 1981), and the high incidence of eye tracking dysfunctions in the unaffected relatives of schizophrenic patients argues for trait status for these tracking disorders. But the question of their trait or state status in psychosis is nevertheless unclear.

This question may be partially resolved by noting that in many instances, lithium carbonate, a common treatment for bipolar affective disorder, produces eye tracking dysfunctions. Iacono, Pelequin, Lumry, Valentine, and Tuason (1982) reported that among bipolar patients receiving lithium, there was greater mean tracking error than among those not receiving lithium. Levy et al. (1985) systematically observed bipolar patients on and off lithium and reported that lithium disrupted pursuit in a significant number of patients, including outpatients and patients in remission. A trait status of these dysfunctions for schizophrenia is suggested by their high frequency among chronic schizophrenics and among almost 40% of their first-degree relatives. The increased prevalence of these tracking disorders in patients with major affective disorders can at least partially be attributed to the effects of lithium. In such patients, therefore, the appearance of eye tracking dysfunctions may be state-related, an epiphenomenon of the treatment. It remains for family pedigree studies to provide stronger data to support a trait status for the eye movement dysfunctions in schizophrenia.

In our 1974 study (Holzman et al., 1974), about 45% of first-degree relatives of schizophrenics also showed eye movement dysfunctions that were indistinguishable from those shown by the schizophrenic patients. In contrast, only 10% of the relatives of nonschizophrenics showed similar dysfunctions. In a more systematic study of family members, we reported that smooth pursuit eye movement dysfunctions occurred in 34% of the parents (or 55% of parental pairs) of schizophrenic patients, compared with only 10% of the parents (or 17% of parental pairs) of manic-depressive patients (Holzman, Solomon, Levin, & Waternaux, 1984). Parental eye movement dysfunctions were significantly related to whether or not the patient was schizophrenic, but not to whether or not the patient's eye movement performance was disrupted. Levy et al. (1983) also showed that of 47 first-degree relatives of 21 patients with bipolar affective illness, only 13% showed abnormal pursuit movements, a figure that is not significantly different from the normal population incidence. When they excluded those relatives who themselves had been hospitalized and treated for affective disorders, or who were currently receiving lithium, only 2% of the sample showed impaired pursuit. There is, therefore, strong evidence that these eye movement dysfunctions are associated with schizophrenia and tend to occur within families in which there is a member with clinically diagnosed schizophrenia.

At this point I shall turn to the neuroophthalmology of the eye movement dysfunction. Our studies of attention convinced us that we were observing a phenomenon regulated within the central nervous system and relatively unaffected by voluntary attention and motivation. We therefore believed that we could investigate the source of the dysfunction within the brain.

Lipton et al. (1980b) reported that every patient with impaired horizontal pursuit movements had impaired vertical pursuit movements. It is known that vertical and horizontal movements are regulated separately at the level of the brain stem, but are associated at the higher centers. We concluded that the congruence was attributable to a single process that was common to both vertical and horizontal tracking. This common disorder probably was localizable higher in the central nervous system than the brain stem. In this same study, 44 of 46 subjects showed normal oculocephalic reflexes, that is, pursuit eye movements that had been generated by head movements. This was true whether or not smooth pursuit movement was disrupted when, with the head held still, the subject followed a moving target. The oculocephalic reflex requires an intact brain stem and vestibular mechanisms; smooth pursuit movement that is generated by consciously following a moving target requires an intact cortex as well. We therefore suggested a cortical locus for the eye movement dysfunctions that are associated with schizophrenia. We later confirmed this and showed, in addition, that compensatory eye movements made when refixating a target with both head and eyes – a brain-stem and vestibular process called the vestibular ocular reflex – were entirely normal (Levin, Jones, Stark, Merrin, & Holzman, 1982a). Furthermore, when these same patients tracked a target with head and eyes – a cortical process – their eye movements were impaired. Add to this evidence Levy's finding of normal vestibularly induced nystagmus in schizophrenic patients (Levy, Holzman, & Proctor, 1978) and the picture becomes clearer: The vestibular system and the brain stem seem to be functioning normally.

A further test by Latham, Holzman, Manschreck, and Tole (1981) examined schizophrenic patients on optokinetic nystagmus that was generated in two ways: full-field stimulus, which is presumed to implicate subcortical centers and pathways, and partial-field stimulus, which is essentially smooth pursuit movement with refixation saccades that implicates cortical centers primarily. Pursuit was entirely normal in the full-field condition, that is, when no contours were visible to the patients. But all patients who showed smooth pursuit impairments showed similar impairments on the smooth pursuit leg of the partial-field optokinetic nystagmus. Because full-field optokinetic nystagmus is regulated in the paramedian pontine reticular formation in the brain stem and partial-field optokinetic nystagmus is essentially cortical in its pathways, we became convinced by this additional evidence that the pursuit abnormalities seen in schizophrenic patients represented cortical dysfunctions.

All of these studies demonstrated that the eyes of schizophrenics could be made to move smoothly by vestibular and brain-stem stimulation. These centers and the extraocular muscles were therefore intact. Thus, the motor system of eye movement control was intact. This system includes the vestibular nuclear projections and the vestibulocerebellum, which receives ascending vestibular fibers. However, when pursuit movements of schizophrenics were stimulated by visual targets (as in partial-field optokinetic nystagmus and in following a moving target), impairments were noteworthy.

One further bit of evidence for a cortical location of pursuit dysfunctions: Levin et al. (1981a,b) and Iacono et al. (1981) reported that saccadic latencies were normal in schizophrenics whether or not those patients showed impaired pursuit movements. Levin et al. (1982b) showed that the dynamic characteristics of those saccades – that is, the covariation of amplitude and speed of amplitude and duration of saccades – were normal. These data make it unlikely that the tracking dysfunctions are localized at the horizontal gaze center in the paramedian pontine reticular formation, because the subcortical control centers of saccadic eye movements and of horizontal pursuit movements meet at the paramedian pontine reticular formation. The work of Bizzi and Schiller (1970) at the Massachusetts Institute of Technology suggests that it is unlikely that saccades are generated in the frontal cortex.

We can conclude the following: Eye tracking dysfunctions in schizophrenia are not related to brain-stem dysfunction, nor are they related to generalized oculomotor dysfunction, to inability to generate slow pursuit eye movements, or to generalized slowing of all motor systems. A cortical locus for the dysfunction is therefore suggested.

What is the nature of the impairment? The 1908 study by Diefendorf and Dodge used photographs of eye movements. Those reproductions were astonishingly accurate, and even today they have not been equaled. In examining their photographs, Diefendorf and Dodge emphasized that the pursuit eye movements of schizophrenic patients were interrupted by saccades, in a pattern they called "stepping." In a study by Levin et al. (1982a) from our laboratory, in cooperation with Professor Lawrence Stark at the University of California, Berkeley, we were able to determine, using a high-resolution reflected infrared light technique, that Diefendorf and Dodge had been correct: Schizophrenic patients with irregular pursuit movements show high incidences of saccadic intrusions and of saccadic smooth pursuit tracking (Levin et al., 1982a). In saccadic smooth pursuit tracking, these are generally compensatory eye movements that correct for low-gain pursuit, which causes the eye to fall behind the target and produces retinal slip. The substitutions of saccades for slow pursuit thus aid the eye in refoveating the target. In saccadic intrusions, however, rapid eye movements intrude into the pursuit movements. These intrusions are not necessarily corrective saccades; they consist of intrusions called "square-wave jerks," but anticipatory as well as retrogressive saccades and double saccadic pulses are also seen, and these are only rarely observed in normals. Both saccadic intrusions and saccadic smooth pursuit tracking are found in some neurological conditions, such as Parkinson's disease, amblyopia, and congenital achromatopia. They are also found, but at reduced frequency, in normal subjects.

It is of special interest that Levin et al. (1982a) observed the same saccadic intrusions and saccadic smooth pursuit tracking, not only when schizophrenic subjects followed a target with head restrained but also in head-eye pursuit, in visual fixation, and in vergence eye movements. But these movements were not present when the eyes were made to move by vestibular control, as in head oscillations.

The relationships of eye tracking dysfunctions to the symptoms of schizophrenia are not clear. Nor are there any obvious relationships between the eye movement disorders that are found in schizophrenic patients and those seen with structural brain damage. It has been reported by Weinberger, however, that schizophrenic patients with enlarged ventricles, as visualized on CT images, show a particularly high incidence of eye movement dysfunctions (Weinberger & Wyatt, 1982). Similar eye movement dysfunctions have been reported in patients with Alzheimer-type dementia. The dysfunction that manifests itself as saccadic intrusions and saccadic tracking seems to be essentially a disinhibitory phenomenon. As outlined earlier, in executing a pursuit movement, the control over saccades and smooth tracking must be coordinated. After it has placed the target on the fovea, the saccadic system must be turned off while the pursuit system is turned on to match eye velocity with that of the target. Only when there is retinal slippage should the saccadic system be brought in as a corrective and then turned off again. The unusually high frequency of these saccadic intrusions and the absence of corrective functions suggest a process in which the saccadic system is disinhibited. These processes point to an impaired capacity to center attention on a target in the face of an intention to perform that task. The tracking impairments thus point to nonmotivational, nonvoluntary processes in attention that involve higher cortical functions. A similar conclusion concerning the role of disinhibition has been reached from consideration of the thought disorders characteristic of psychosis and the particular types of thought disorders that occur in schizophrenia (Holzman, 1978).

My colleague, Smadar Levin, has argued for a role for frontal lobe dysfunctions in the eye movement impairments (Levin, 1984a,b). She has noted the direct inhibitory function of the frontal eye fields on the superior colliculus, or their inhibitory function mediated by other eye movement centers, such as the substantia nigra pars reticulata. It is noteworthy that the frontal eye fields project to the caudate nucleus, which in turn projects to the substantia nigra pars reticulata. These cells send inhibitory gamma-aminobutyric acid (GABA) projections to the superior colliculus. These inhibitory GABA neurons exert a tonic restraining effect on saccadic movements. At the National Institutes of Health, Hikosaka and Wurtz (1981, 1983) showed that the effect of the substantia nigra was blocked by intracellular injection of a GABA antagonist (bicuculline) in the superior colliculus of an alert monkey. The GABA agonist produced increased saccadic latencies and a diminished frequency of saccades. The GABA antagonist significantly increased the number and frequency of saccades, with accompanying difficulty on the part of the monkey in suppressing saccades, resulting in inability to maintain fixation.

These are tempting leads. They point to the role of the substantia nigra and GABA in saccadic inhibition, and indirectly they point to the frontal eye fields, which may be involved in the control of those systems.

At this juncture, I once again pick up the thread of family transmission. My colleagues and I believe that we have evidence that the pursuit dysfunctions are transmitted within the families of schizophrenics, but not within the families of patients with major affective disorders. What model of transmission is consistent with our data?

I must point out that there is an apparent paradox in these data. A number of schizophrenic patients with unimpaired pursuit movements have parents with eye tracking abnormalities. In our two twin studies there were five sets of DZ twins in which the clinically affected twin had good tracking, but the unaffected co-twin had impaired tracking. How to account for these data?

Dr. Steven Matthysse, Dr. Kenneth Lange, and I have suggested a model (Matthysse, Holzman, & Lange, 1986) to account for these paradoxes. The Matthysse model postulates a latent trait that is transmitted in quasi-Mendelian fashion. That is, although the presence of the latent trait is determined by a single major locus, the latent trait can occur without the allele that is responsible for it – as a phenocopy – and the allele can be present without the trait – as in partial penetrance. The model further proposes that the central nervous system disease process that is the outcome of the latent trait produces clinical schizophrenia and bad eye tracking. It accomplishes this because it can invade one or more regions of the brain separately or together; the symptoms that arise reflect the brain regions invaded.

The model assumes that the smooth pursuit system is more likely to be invaded than the system that is involved in schizophrenic psychosis – whatever that system is. The model also assumes that this disease process is at least partially genetically determined. This situation resembles that of type I diabetes: The deficiency of insulin is transmitted by a gene. Those who have this gene are susceptible to the disease, but the disease is not inevitable. Triggering events like viral invasions or chemical injuries are evidently necessary. And some experiences can be protective; a recent Scandinavian study indicated that being breast-fed longer than 3 months may be such a protective factor. According to the model, schizophrenia with good eye tracking occurs when the disease invades the less probable area and spares the more probable one. First-degree relatives will also be at risk for having the same disease process, and that process will cause eye movement dysfunctions with high probability, and schizophrenia with low probability.

The disease process is, of course, hypothetical, and we therefore call it a *latent* trait. Unlike schizophrenia and eye tracking dysfunctions, the trait is not observed, although in principle it is capable of being observed. We presume that when the necessary tools for observing it become available, it will be found. We have chosen a single-gene model because it is the simplest, and Matthysse has constructed an equation for testing its fit to our data. The equation includes the following variables: (a) the probability of the latent trait giving rise to good and bad tracking; (b) the probability of the latent trait giving rise to schizophrenia in the general population; (c) the probability of the occurrence of phenocopies and the penetrance of the latent trait in heterozygotes and homozygotes. The equation is then employed to search for the probability of any family member having the latent trait. If an individual has the latent trait, the likelihood of having schizophrenia or eye movement dysfunction or both can be computed. The mathematics are those of maximum likelihood estimates. When this is accomplished, one can test, as Matthysse has done, whether the eye movement dysfunctions in schizophrenia or in manic–depressive illness are independent expressions of the latent disease process or are epiphenomena, that is, an outcome of having the disease itself.

The results of the mathematical test are that for schizophrenia the data fit the latent trait model, but for manic–depressive illness the data are more easily explained as epiphenomena. That is, in manic–depressive illness, poor eye tracking is an outcome of the disease; in schizophrenia, it is an outcome of family transmission. In schizophrenia, the latent trait can lead to schizophrenia or bad eye tracking or both, but eye tracking dysfunctions are about 6 times more likely to occur than schizophrenia. The incidence of the latent trait in the general population is calculated to be about 4.4%; 83.6% of schizophrenics have it, and so do 36.1% of bad trackers (that is, 8.2 times more likely than in the general population). The probability of having the latent trait is thus 19 times greater among schizophrenics and 8.2 times greater among those with bad tracking than in the general population. But the latent trait can be present without the gene, as in a phenocopy, although almost all of those who carry the latent trait have the gene that the model postulates. A recent study of offspring of discordant twins confirmed these parameters (Holzman et al., 1988).

The study of people who have an underlying disease process without the obvious symptoms of the disease is an extremely valuable undertaking, because they are free of the biological, social, and psychological complications of the disease. The picture of schizophrenia that emerges from this work is not unique in the annals of medicine. A similar model of transmission is provided by neurofibromatosis (von Recklinghausen's disease), the gene for which is an autosomal dominant, but with variable expressivity. Thus, the full syndrome occurs much more rarely than do one or two indicators of it: Tumors of the peripheral nerve endings, hydrocephaly, subnormal intelligence, café au lait spots, and areas of depigmentation are all manifestations of the disease. As in schizophrenia, it is not unusual, therefore, that a family history of neurofibromatosis may be well hidden or apparently absent in the case of a proband with the full syndrome. Furthermore, family members with the disease may be overlooked because they manifest only the mildest of symptoms.

I emphasize that these are heuristic positions, and we are prepared to modify them on the basis of data. Our work has tested the quasi-Mendelian latent structure model only once (Holzman et al., 1988). Nevertheless, the maximum likelihood method has given a reasonable mapping of the transmission of schizophrenia and of smooth pursuit eye movement dysfunctions, and it clearly differentiates schizophrenia from manic–depressive illness with respect to the basic underlying disease processes, even though both are associated with the appearance of eye movement dysfunctions. Because of this method, we are prepared now to study people who appear to be psychiatrically normal but who have high or low probabilities for possessing the latent trait for schizophrenia. We hope that the possibility of such investigations, employing the newer brain mapping techniques such as magnetic resonance imaging and positron emission tomography, as well as molecular genetic techniques, will lead to further advances in our understanding of the nature of schizophrenia.

References

Bizzi, E., & Schiller, P. H. (1970). Single unit activity in the frontal eye fields of unanesthetized monkeys during eye and head movement. *Experimental Brain Research, 10,* 151–8.

Bleuler, E. (1950). *Dementia praecox, or the group of schizophrenias* (H. Zinkin, trans.). New York: International Universities Press. (Original work published 1911)

Brezinova, V., & Kendall, R. S. (1977). Smooth pursuit eye movements of schizophrenics and normal people under stress. *British Journal of Psychiatry, 130,* 59–63.

Couch, F. H., & Fox, J. C. (1934). Photographic study of ocular movements in mental disease. *Archives of Neurology and Psychiatry, 34,* 556–78.

Diefendorf, A. R., & Dodge, R. (1908). An experimental study of the ocular reactions of the insane from photographic records. *Brain, 31,* 451–89.

Erlenmeyer-Kimling, L., Cornblatt, B., & Golden, R. R. (1983). Early indicators of vulnerability to schizophrenia in children at high genetic risk. In S. B. Guze, F. J. Earls, & J. E. Barrett (Eds.), *Childhood psychopathology and development* (pp. 247–64). New York: Raven Press.

Hikosaka, O., & Wurtz, R. H. (1981). The role of substantia nigra in the initiation of saccadic eye movements. In A. F. Fuchs & W. Becker (Eds.), *Progress in oculomotor research* (pp. 145–52). New York: Elsevier.

Hikosaka, O., & Wurtz, R. H. (1983). Visual and oculomotor functions of monkey substantia nigra pars reticulata. IV. Relation of substantia nigra to superior colliculus. *Journal of Neurophysiology, 49,* 1285.

Holzman, P. S. (1978). Cognitive impairment and cognitive stability: Towards a theory of thought disorder. In G. Serban (Ed.), *Cognitive defects in mental illness* (pp. 361–76). New York: Brunner/Mazel.

Holzman, P. S., Kringlen, E., Levy, D. L., & Haberman, S. (1980) Deviant eye tracking in twins discordant for psychosis: A replication. *Archives of General Psychiatry, 37,* 627–31.

Holzman, P. S., Kringlen, E., Levy, D. L., Proctor, L. R., Haberman, S., & Yasillo, N. J. (1977). Abnormal pursuit eye movements in schizophrenia: Evidence for a genetic marker. *Archives of General Psychiatry, 34,* 802–5.

Holzman, P. S., Kringlen, E., Matthysse, S., Flanagan, S. D., Lipton, R. B., Cramer, G., Levin, S., Lange, K., & Levy, D. L. (1988). A single dominant gene can account for eye tracking dysfunctions and schizophrenia in offspring of discordant twins. *Archives of General Psychiatry, 45,* 641–7.

Holzman, P. S., Levy, D. L., & Proctor, L. R. (1976). Smooth pursuit eye movements, attention and schizophrenia. *Archives of General Psychiatry, 33,* 1415–20.

Holzman, P. S., Levy, D. L., Uhlenhuth, L. R., Proctor, L. R., & Freedman, D. X. (1975). Smooth-pursuit eye movements and diazepam, CPZ, and secobarbital. *Psychopharma-cologia, 44,* 111–15.

Holzman, P. S., Proctor, L. R., & Hughes, D. W. (1973). Eye-tracking patterns in schizophrenia. *Science, 181,* 179–80.

Holzman, P. S., Proctor, L. R., Levy, D. L., Yasillo, N. J., Meltzer, H. Y., & Hurt, S. W. (1974). Eye tracking dysfunctions and schizophrenic patients and their relatives. *Archives of General Psychiatry, 31,* 143–51.

Holzman, P. S., Solomon, C. M., Levin, S., & Waternaux, C. S. (1984). Pursuit eye movement dysfunctions in schizophrenia: Family evidence for specificity. *Archives of General Psychiatry, 41,* 136–9.

Iacono, W. G., & Lykken, D. T. (1981). 2 year retest stability of eye tracking performance and comparison of electrooculographic and infra-red recording techniques: Evidence of EEG in the electro-oculogram. *Psychophysiology, 18,* 49–55.

Iacono, W. G., Pelequin, L. J., Lumry, A. E., Valentine, R. H., & Tuason, V. B. (1982). Eye tracking in patients with unipolar and bipolar affective disorders in remission. *Journal of Abnormal Psychology, 91,* 35–44.

Iacono, W. G., Tuason, V. B., & Johnson, R. A. (1981). Dissociation of smooth pursuit and saccadic eye tracking in remitted schizophrenics. *Archives of General Psychiatry, 38,* 991–6.

Kraepelin, E. (1919). *Dementia praecox and paraphrenia* (R. M. Barclay, trans.). Chicago Medical Book.

Kringlen, E. (1967). Heredity and environment in the functional psychoses. *Universitetsforlaget* (Norwegian Monographs on Medical Science).

Latham, C., Holzman, P. S., Manschrek, T., & Tole, J. (1981). Optokinetic nystagmus and pursuit eye movements in schizophrenia. *Archives of General Psychiatry, 38,* 997–1003.

Levin, S. (1984a). Frontal lobe dysfunctions in schizophrenia. II. Impairments of psychological and brain functions. *Journal of Psychiatric Research, 18,* 57–72.

Levin, S. (1984b). Frontal lobe dysfunctions in schizophrenia. I. Eye movement impairments. *Journal of Psychiatric Research, 18,* 27–55.

Levin, S., Holzman, P. S., Rothenberg, S. J., & Lipton, R. B. (1981a). Saccadic eye movements in psychotic patients. *Psychiatry Research, 5,* 47–58.

Levin, S., Jones, A., Stark, L., Merrin, E. L., & Holzman, P. S. (1982a). Identification of abnormal patterns in eye movements of schizophrenic patients. *Archives of General Psychiatry, 39,* 1125–30.

Levin, S., Jones, A., Stark, L., Merrin, E. L., & Holzman, P. S. (1982b). Saccadic eye movements of schizophrenic patients measured by reflected light technique. *Biological Psychiatry, 17,* 1277–87.

Levin, S., Lipton, R. B., & Holzman, P. S. (1981b). Pursuit eye movements in psychopathology: Effects of target characteristics. *Biological Psychiatry, 16,* 255–67.

Levy, D. L., Dorus, E., Shaughnessy, R., Yasillo, N. J., Pandey, G. N., Janicak, P. G., Gibbons,

R. D., Gaviria, M., & Davis, J. M. (1985). Pharmacologic evidence for specificity of pursuit dysfunction to schizophrenia: Lithium carbonate associated abnormal pursuit. *Archives of General Psychiatry, 42,* 335–41.

Levy, D. L., Holtzman, P. S., & Proctor, L. R. (1978). Vestibular responses in schizophrenia. *Archives of General Psychiatry, 35,* 972–81.

Levy, D. L., Lipton, R. B., & Holzman, P. S. (1981). Smooth pursuit eye movements: Effects of alcohol and chloral hydrate. *Journal of Psychiatric Research, 16,* 1–11.

Levy, D. L., Yasillo, N. J., Dorus, E., Shaughnessy, R., Gibbons, R. D., Peterson, J., Janicak, P. G., Gaviria, M., & Davis, J. M. (1983). Relatives of unipolar and bipolar patients have normal pursuit. *Psychiatry Research, 10,* 285–93.

Lipton, R. B., Frost, L. A., & Holzman, P. S. (1980a). Smooth pursuit eye movements, schizophrenia, and distraction. *Perceptual and Motor Skills, 50,* 159–67.

Lipton, R. B., Levin, S., & Holzman, P. S. (1980b). Horizontal and vertical pursuit movements, the oculocephalic reflex, and the functional psychoses. *Psychiatry Research, 3,* 193–203.

Matthysse, S., Holzman, P. S., & Lange, K. (1986) The genetic transmission of schizophrenia: Application of Mendelian latent structure analysis to eye tracking dysfunctions in schizophrenia and affective disorder. *Journal of Psychiatric Research, 20*(1), 57–65.

Matthysse, S., & Kety, S. S. (1986). The genetics of psychiatric disorders. In P. A. Berger & H. K. H. Brodie (Eds.), *American handbook of psychiatry* (pp. 160–9). New York: Basic Books.

May, H. J. (1979) Oculomotor pursuit in schizophrenia. *Archives of General Psychiatry, 36,* 827.

Pivik, R. T. (1979). Smooth pursuit eye movements and attention in psychiatric patients. *Biological Psychiatry, 14,* 859–79.

Shagass, C., Amadeo, M., & Overton, D. A. (1974). Eye-tracking performance in psychiatric patients. *Biological Psychiatry, 9,* 245–60.

Shagass, C., Roemer, R. A., & Amadeo, M. (1976). Eye tracking performance and engagement of attention. *Archives of General Psychiatry, 33,* 121–5.

Spohn, H. D. (1981). *Correlates of eye tracking in schizophrenic patients.* Paper presented at an eye tracking methodology conference, Boston.

Weinberger, D. R., & Wyatt, R. J. (1982). Cerebral ventricular size: A biological marker for subtyping chronic schizophrenia. In E. Usdin & J. Handin (Eds.), *Biological markers in psychiatry and neurology* (pp. 505–12). New York: Pergamon Press.

22   Premorbid competence and the courses and outcomes of psychiatric disorders

Marion Glick and Edward Zigler

Research findings in psychopathology teach us that knowledge about human strengths and adaptive capacities is as important as knowledge about vulnerabilities for an adequate prediction of outcome. This emphasis on positive attributes and competence has been a hallmark of Norman Garmezy's research and has been the theme that has connected his earlier work on adult schizophrenia (Garmezy, 1970; Garmezy & Rodnick, 1959) to later studies of coping and stress resistance in groups of children at high risk for psychiatric disorders (Garmezy, 1971, 1983; Garmezy, Masten, Nordstrom, & Ferrarese, 1979; Garmezy, Masten, & Tellegen, 1984; Masten & Garmezy, 1985).

In our work on the developmental approach to psychopathology, we share that concern with competence. In viewing a patient's premorbid competence as a broad, though imperfect, benchmark of maturity level, our assumption is that the premorbid competence construct does not merely designate subtypes (i.e., process vs. reactive) within schizophrenic disorders but is broadly applicable to patients in many diagnostic groups. Thus, this work shares with Garmezy's research the assumption that the study of competence not only pertains to specific disorders but also has broad applicability.

A major contribution of research on competence and developmental approaches to psychopathology is that it has provided means for bridging the gap between studies of adaptive behavior and psychopathology (Garmezy et al., 1984). Increased knowledge about adaptive functioning furthers an understanding of psychopathology, just as greater knowledge about malfunctioning provides essential information about the nature of adaptive processes (Cicchetti, 1984; Rutter & Garmezy, 1983; Sroufe & Rutter, 1984; Zigler & Glick, 1986). A framework that incorporates the study of normal development and adaptive functioning seems essential for an understanding of psychopathology. A central aspect of psychopathology is that individuals move between

Preparation for this chapter was supported by research grant HD-03008 from the National Institute of Child Health and Human Development.

497

pathological and nonpathological (premorbid and postmorbid) forms of functioning. Furthermore, even in the midst of pathology, patients display adaptive mechanisms.

An area of concern in our work has been the relationship between premorbid competence and outcome for patients with a variety of psychiatric diagnoses. Inherent in the developmental interpretation of premorbid competence is a broad view of outcome that encompasses (a) whether or not the individual becomes mentally ill, (b) the age at which the illness becomes manifest, and (c) the outcome of the disorder following initial treatment and/or institutionalization. The major portion of this chapter presents our developmental view and examines relationships between premorbid competence and both the age of initial hospitalization and the outcome following initial institutionalization for patients in different diagnostic groups.

A secondary concern in this chapter involves the relationships among symptom expression, premorbid competence, and prognosis. In our research, different modes of symptom expression have been found to be associated with different levels of premorbid competence and with outcome, broadly conceptualized. These different modes of symptom expression, presumed to reflect differences in adult developmental levels, closely resemble the internalizing–externalizing dimension in childhood symptoms that Garmezy and other workers have found to be associated with competence in childhood and with prognosis for adult adjustment (Achenbach & Edelbrock, 1978; Cicchetti & Pogge-Hesse, 1982; Garmezy & Streitman, 1974; Kohlberg, LaCrosse, & Ricks, 1972; Robins, 1966; Rolf & Garmezy, 1974; Rutter & Garmezy, 1983; Sroufe & Rutter, 1984). Thus, the research to be reviewed here accords with the emphasis in Garmezy's work because it considers competence and adaptive functioning even in the midst of pathology and because it emphasizes the continuity between pathological and nonpathological behaviors. Such continuity is provided by the individual's underlying developmental level.

Premorbid competence and developmental level

The developmental approach to adult psychopathology presumes a process of growth underlying psychological functioning. Individuals can be viewed as functioning at different levels along this underlying developmental continuum. Equally fundamental to this approach is the assumption that an individual's developmental level continues to influence behavior after the patient has been designated "pathological," just as it did prior to this designation during the patient's premorbid period. In becoming symptomatic, an individual is not presumed to change habitual modes of responding. Rather, for each maturity level, there are assumed to exist effective patterns of adaptation, as well as pathological deviations from these patterns. Thus, both the normal and pathological aspects of an individual's functioning can be seen as reflecting the maturity level attained.

Premorbid competence has been a central construct in the developmental approach to adult psychopathology since the inception of the work concerning this formulation (Zigler & Phillips, 1960). The view of development underlying the approach derives primarily from Werner's organismic developmental theory (Werner, 1948; Werner & Kaplan, 1963), although other developmental theorists (Lewin, 1936; Piaget, 1951; Rapaport, 1951) have also influenced this work. Organismic developmental theory presupposes an inherent relationship between developmental level and coping effectiveness. At lower developmental levels, response systems are presumed to be globally organized, with few mediating structures (Werner, 1948; Werner & Kaplan, 1963). At these levels, therefore, functioning is more reactive and stimulus-bound, compelled by external forces and internal need states. In the course of development through greater differentiation and hierarchical integration, an individual becomes increasingly able to separate immediate internal reactions from an organized view of the external situation. Thus, a person becomes ever more able to plan, to control and respond selectively to internal and external forces, and to initiate interactions with the environment. Gratification can be delayed, and goals envisioned, and it becomes possible to employ substitutive means and alternative ends in order to achieve these goals. Flexibility and adaptive capacities, therefore, increase as a function of development.

Within the developmental approach to psychopathology, an individual's developmental level is seen as representing no less than the total information processing system utilized by the individual in mediating all behaviors. This developmental level construct is thus quite broad, presumed to be applicable to cognitive, social, and emotional realms of functioning. A problem, particularly in regard to adult behavior, has been how to gauge developmental level when the construct is broadly defined. Zigler and Glick (1986) have discussed some of the difficulties in implementing the developmental level construct as it relates to adult behavior and have considered important recent advances in the area, especially those of Loevinger (Hauser, 1976; Loevinger, 1976) and Vaillant (1971, 1974). At the outset of the work on the developmental approach to psychopathology, such gauges of developmental level were not available. Furthermore, the findings of Loevinger and Vaillant, though they clearly have emphasized adaptive functioning, have to date seldom been applied to the study of disordered groups (Noam et al., 1984).

Zigler and Phillips (1960, 1961b) believed that the developmental level construct was too broad and contained too many facets to permit a direct, simple, and practical single measure. Given the inherent relationship between developmental level and coping effectiveness, they chose to measure, instead, the individual's premorbid social competence, which was conceptualized as a broad, though imperfect, benchmark of maturity level. The premorbid competence measure and the rationale underlying the selection of the variables employed as indices of premorbid competence have been described at length (Zigler & Glick, 1986; Zigler & Levine, 1981b). Briefly, the measure examines a patient's placement on six variables thought to be indicative of the patient's cognitive, interpersonal, and social functioning. These variables are age, education, occupation, employment history, marital status, and intelligence. (In actual research practice, the intelligence variable often has been omitted because of unavailability of IQ scores.) Zigler and Phillips (1960) recognized that each of these variables had a considerable margin of error and that none taken in isolation would be a particularly good indicator of developmental level. The hope was that the general pattern of scores, as reflected in the mean for the six variables, would provide a broadly derived, reliable gauge of an elusive construct: an adult individual's underlying developmental level. Scoring, which is based on examination of psychiatric case records, has been found to be highly reliable. As Strauss and Harder (1981) noted, if adequate reliability can be demonstrated, case record analysis represents a valuable tool for clinical research.

The premorbid competence measure has been found to be positively correlated with Rorschach developmental level scores (Lerner, 1968) and with maturity in moral reasoning, as assessed by Kohlberg's test (Quinlan, Rogers, & Kegan, 1980). The heuristic value of the scale has been firmly established by the findings that premorbid competence is significantly related to each of the following major variables in psychopathology: diagnosis, symptoms, defenses employed, prognosis and psychiatric outcome, the essential–reactive distinction in alcoholism, the paranoid–nonparanoid distinction in schizophrenia, the magnitude of an individual's self-image disparity, and humor responses. This research has been reviewed and summarized by Zigler and Glick (1986) and Zigler and Levine (1981a).

Premorbid competence and prognosis

Developmental theory has generated the broad expectation that individuals at higher developmental levels should display less debilitating courses of their disorders and more favorable psychiatric outcomes than should persons with similar disorders who function at lower developmental levels. However, the developmental view does not imply that vulnerability to disorder is reducible to developmental level. In fact, higher developmental levels of functioning may create certain kinds of problems that developmentally less mature individuals will be less likely to experience. Such problems associated with higher developmental status include internal dilemmas resulting from greater internalization of societal standards and consequently heightened guilt. Inasmuch as self-castigation and self-blame are prominent aspects of depression (Abramson & Sackeim, 1977; Kovacs & Beck, 1978), findings that affective disorder diagnoses and symptoms reflecting depression and turning against the self are more frequent in high-competence individuals than in low-competence individuals (Glick, Zigler, & Zigler, 1985; Lewine, Watt, Prentky, & Fryer, 1980; Zigler & Phillips, 1960, 1961a) point to this downside aspect of higher developmental status. The consistent evidence that real–ideal self-image disparity increases as a function of developmental level accords with the view that greater internalization of societal standards characterizes higher developmental functioning (Achenbach & Zigler, 1963; Glick & Zigler, 1985; Mylet, Styfco, & Zigler, 1979). Despite these problems that may particularly accrue to higher developmental levels of functioning, the increased differentiation and hierarchical integration that accompany development inherently allow for greater adaptability and coping effectiveness. With greater adaptive resources at their disposal, high-developmental-level individuals should less frequently succumb to life's stresses, and if they break down, such individuals should be able to cope more actively and determinedly with the problems related to their disorders. This would suggest that such individuals should less frequently become psychologically disordered, should manifest such disorders later in life, and should display more favorable psychiatric outcomes than should individuals who function at developmentally lower levels.

Given the intrinsic interconnection between developmental level and coping effectiveness, the developmental formulation takes a broader view of prognosis than the more typical concern with outcome following the appearance of definable and debilitating forms of psychopathology. Within the developmental approach to psychopathology, prognosis is defined by three related measures, each of which retains a considerable degree of independence: (a) whether or not the individual becomes mentally ill, (b) the age at which this illness becomes manifest, and (c) the outcome of the illness after initial treatment and/or institutionalization.

Premorbid competence and psychiatric outcomes in schizophrenic and nonschizophrenic patients

The premorbid social competence construct had its origin in efforts to bifurcate the schizophrenic syndrome into process (poor premorbid history) and reactive (good premorbid history) subtypes, presumed to be dichotomous with regard to etiology, the course of the disorder, and outcome. The classic definitions of process and reactive schizophrenia have previously been summarized (Garmezy & Rodnick, 1959; Higgins, 1964; Zigler & Phillips, 1962). Although a positive relationship between premorbid social competence and outcome frequently has been reported for schizophrenic patients (Garmezy, 1970; Knight, Roff, Barnett, & Moss, 1979; Stoffelmayr, Dillavou, & Hunter, 1983; Strauss & Carpenter, 1977), the reasons for this relationship remain controversial. One view is that the process–reactive distinction designates subtypes specific to schizophrenic disorder. Within this view, the process form is presumed to mirror an organic cause, whereas the reactive type is conceptualized as psychogenic in origin, involving substantial precipitating stress. Consistent with this position, Rosen, Klein, Levenstein, and Shahinian (1969) reported a relationship between premorbid competence and outcome for a heterogeneous group of patients and for a schizophrenic subgroup, but found no such relationship for nonschizophrenic patients examined separately. However, that study examined a relatively small and disproportionately female group of nonschizophrenic patients, and the findings obtained were not robust (Zigler, Glick, & Marsh, 1979).

In contrast to this position, the developmental approach to psychopathology views premorbid competence as an approximate indicator of maturity level. This interpretation generates the expectation that the premorbid competence–outcome relationship is not unique to schizophrenia but should also be found with various nonschizophrenic diagnostic groups (Garmezy, 1970; Zigler et al., 1979; Zigler & Phillips, 1961b). We have examined relationships between premorbid competence and hospitalization measures of psychiatric outcome in male and female patients with various diagnoses: schizophrenia, affective disorder, neurotic disorder, and personality disorder (Glick & Zigler, 1986; Marsh, Glick, & Zigler, 1981; Zigler et al., 1979; Zigler & Phillips, 1961b). In all these investigations, higher-competence patients were found to have been hospitalized for shorter periods of time, both on initial hospitalization and during rehospitalizations. This positive relationship between higher premorbid competence and more favorable outcome has been found in females (Glick & Zigler, 1986) as well as males (Zigler et al., 1979) and in samples composed entirely of nonschizophrenic patients (Glick & Zigler, 1986). Other studies have provided additional evidence that premorbid competence is related to outcome in a variety of nonschizophrenic groups. This research supplements our own in that it encompasses outcome criteria other than hospitalization measures and includes studies with prospective as well as retrospective designs. Strauss, Kokes, Carpenter, and Ritzler (1978), in a prospective study, found that for both schizophrenic and nonschizophrenic samples the variables of premorbid employment and social relations (the major dimensions of premorbid competence) provided the best prediction of outcome criteria that included the following measures: social relations, employment, symptom severity, duration of hospitalization, and total outcome. Prentky, Lewine, Watt, and Fryer (1980) found that of the many predictor variables they examined, premorbid competence (as assessed by the Zigler-Phillips index) was the most potent predictor of length of hospitalization. Their sample was composed of patients with diagnoses of schizophrenia, personality disorder, neurotic disorder, and depressive psychosis. The majority of the patients examined were nonschizophrenic, and almost half were nonpsychotic. A relationship between social competence, as assessed by a modified version of the Zigler-Phillips scale, and outcome was likewise noted by Finney and Moos (1979) for alcoholic patients participating in a variety of inpatient and outpatient treatment programs. Other investigators also reported significant relationships between premorbid competence variables and outcome in groups of patients with varying diagnoses, but containing sizable numbers of nonschizophrenic patients; see Garmezy et al. (1979) for a review of the research. Moreover, variables associated with social competence were found to be related to improvement in outpatient psychotherapy in studies in which many patients were neither schizophrenic nor psychotic (Luborsky, Chandler, Auerbach, Cohen, & Bachrach, 1971).

The relationship between social competence variables and favorable life outcomes may even pertain to nonpatient groups and extend to individuals at the opposite end of the adjustment spectrum from schizophrenic patients. In his 35-year prospective study of Harvard sophomores originally selected on the basis of superior adjustment, Vaillant (1974, 1978) found that marital stability and satisfaction and career adjustment were highly related to broad indices of adult life adjustment. Conversely, those individuals with evidence of psychopathological problems were significantly less likely to display good marital or work adjustment. Vaillant (1976) also found evidence that indices of marital and work adjustment were related to indicators of ego development, including maturity of defenses. Vaillant's conclusion that it was the "men's successes . . . not their symptoms or their failures [that] predicted subsequent mental health" (1976, p. 20) accorded with that of Kohlberg et al. (1972). Based on their review of research concerning the adult adjustment of children originally treated in child guidance clinics, Kohlberg et al. (1972) concluded that "the best predictors of absence of adult mental illness and maladjustment are the presence of various forms of competence and ego maturity rather than the *absence* of problems and symptoms as such" (p. 1274). These conclusions underscore both the positive emphasis of the developmental approach and the efficacy of such an emphasis.

Age at first hospitalization for schizophrenic and nonschizophrenic psychiatric patients

In the literature dealing with psychopathology, studies of prognosis usually are confined to the course of a disorder following its onset, typically defined by when the individual comes into contact with a provider of mental health services. An important feature of textbook descriptions of the courses of various mental disorders is the age of the patient at initial onset. Evidence has now been presented that age of first treatment and outcome are related, with a later first psychiatric treatment being associated with a better outcome (Möller, von Zerssen, Werner-Eilert, & Wüschner-Stockheim, 1982; Rosen, Klein, & Gittleman-Klein, 1971). Developmental thinking incorporates both these variables as aspects of a broader definition of prognosis. In addition to displaying better prognoses after initial treatment, the developmental formulation generates the expectation that individuals at higher developmental levels will be less likely to succumb to psychological disorders, and if they do, such individuals will be older at the time their disorders become manifest than will individuals at lower developmental levels. In regard to the likelihood of disorder, Zigler and Phillips (1961a) found that as a group, hospitalized psychiatric patients displayed lower premorbid competence than did the general population. With respect to the age at which a disorder becomes sufficiently manifest to require treatment, the hypothesis that higher-competence individuals will be first hospitalized at an older age has now been examined in male and female patients with schizophrenic diagnoses (Zigler & Levine, 1981a) and diagnoses of affective disorder, neurosis, and personality disorder (Glick et al., 1985). Higher competence was found to be associated with an older age at first hospitalization for all diagnostic groups examined by Glick et al. (1985) and for most schizophrenic subsamples examined by Zigler and Levine (1981a).[1]

Premorbid competence, symptom expression, and prognosis

The developmental approach to psychopathology does not view symptoms solely as indices of some pathological state. Rather, specific symptom patterns are presumed to reflect underlying developmental levels. Two developmental categorizations of symptoms have been employed frequently in our research: (a) categorization as indicative of three general role orientations reflecting an individual's implicit assumptions about the self in relation to others; (b) categorization in terms of the relative dominance of expression in thought versus action.

The three role orientations, with examples of symptoms composing each, are (a) self-deprivation and turning against the self (e.g., suicide attempt, suicidal ideas, self-deprecation, depression), (b) self-indulgence and turning against others (e.g., drinking, assaultive behavior, threatening assault, disturbed or destructive behavior), (c) avoidance of others (e.g., withdrawal, suspiciousness, bizarre ideas and delusions).

These symptom clusters were first empirically isolated and conceptually ordered by Phillips and Rabinovitch (1958). Originally they were conceptualized as representing three steps along a developmental continuum. Turning against the self was conceptualized as representing the highest level, because that role orientation implied the internalization of societal standards, with consequent social guilt. Such internalization was presumed to characterize developmentally higher functioning (Achenbach & Zigler, 1963; Bybee, 1986). Turning against others was originally conceptualized as representing an intermediate level, and avoidance of others was viewed as representing the

---

[1] The major exception to this general pattern of findings was the absence of a significant relationship between premorbid competence and age at first hospitalization among male nonparanoid schizophrenic patients in a Veterans Administration (VA) hospital (Zigler & Levine, 1981a). The frequent noncomparability of findings between VA hospital patients and state hospital patients has been discussed by Zigler, Levine, and Zigler (1976).

lowest developmental form (Phillips & Rabinovitch, 1958). However, subsequent research findings have been more consistent with a two-stage model (turning against the self indicating higher functioning than both turning against others and avoidance of others) than with a three-stage model (each role orientation representing a step along a developmental continuum) (Quinlan et al., 1980; Zigler & Phillips, 1960, 1962). At present, then, role orientation is conceptualized in terms of the two-stage model.

The categorization of symptoms as involving expression in thought versus action derives from the fundamental assumption in developmental theory that developmentally earlier behavior is marked by immediate, direct, and unmodulated responses to external stimuli and internal need states, whereas developmentally higher functioning is characterized by the appearance of indirect verbal behavior patterns that are ideational, conceptual, and symbolic. Developmental theorists of both the psychoanalytic persuasion (Freud, 1952; Hartmann, 1952; Rapaport, 1951) and the nonpsychoanalytic persuasion (Lewin, 1936; Piaget, 1951; Werner, 1948) view this shift in emphasis from action to thought as a central expression of the developmental sequence. Symptoms involving expression in thought include, for example, suspiciousness, delusions, suicidal ideas, and threats of assault, whereas symptoms in the action category include assaultive behavior, acts of robbery, irresponsible behavior, and suicidal attempts.

The assumption that symptoms indicative of turning against the self and symptoms involving expression in thought rather than action reflect developmentally higher functioning is supported by findings that symptoms in these two categories are more frequently displayed by high-premorbid-competence individuals, whereas lower-competence individuals more frequently display symptoms involving expression in action and symptoms indicative of the role orientations of turning against others and avoidance of others (Mylet et al., 1979; Phillips & Zigler, 1961; Raskin & Golob, 1966; Zigler & Phillips, 1960, 1962). Because developmentally higher functioning is presumed generally to result in more favorable prognoses, patients manifesting symptoms in the turning-against-the-self category and the thought category would be expected both to be older at first hospital admission and to display better outcomes following institutionalization. By contrast, individuals whose symptoms predominantly reflect expression in action and the role orientations of turning against others and avoidance of others would be expected to be younger at first hospitalization and to display poorer outcomes following hospital treatment. The role orientation of turning against the self has been found to be related to an older age at first hospitalization (Glick et al., 1985) and to shorter initial hospitalization (Phillips & Zigler, 1964). A predominance of thought symptoms as compared with action symptoms has also been found to be related to an older age at first hospitalization (Glick et al., 1985), but no simple relationship has appeared between the thought–action dimension and the length of initial hospitalization (Phillips & Zigler, 1964). However, Phillips and Zigler (1964) did discover an interaction effect that primarily reflected the tendency within the thought symptom category for low-competence patients to have longer initial hospitalizations than high-competence patients within that symptom category.

A major distinction in research on child psychopathology has been between internalizing behavior problems involving emotional disorders and externalizing behavior problems involving conduct disorders (Achenbach, 1966; Achenbach & Edelbrock, 1978; Rutter & Garmezy, 1983). The internalizing category, which includes such problems as phobias, refusal to eat, obsessions, and depression (Achenbach, 1966), can be conceptualized as reflecting both expression in thought (Katz, Zigler, & Zalk, 1975) and turning against the self. By contrast, externalizing behavior problems, which include a variety of antisocial acting-out behaviors, reflect both turning against others and symptom expression in direct action (Katz et al., 1975). Katz et al. (1975) presented evidence for the developmentally higher status of internalizing symptoms as compared with externalizing symptoms in childhood, and Kohlberg et al. (1972) held a similar view. The findings that children displaying lower social competence more frequently manifest externalizing symptoms than internalizing symptoms (Achenbach & Edelbrock, 1981; Rolf & Garmezy, 1974) and that externalizing symptoms in childhood are more likely than internalizing symptoms to be associated with adult maladjustment (Garmezy & Streitman, 1974; Kohlberg et al., 1972; Robins, 1966; Rutter & Garmezy, 1983; Sroufe & Rutter, 1984) parallel our own results described earlier.

Summary of the research and directions for further study

The research reviewed provides considerable support for the view that developmental differences in adult psychiatric patients are associated with prognosis, broadly defined as including age at initial hospitalization and outcome following hospital treatment. Premorbid competence as an indicator of developmental level has been found to be associated with both these aspects of prognosis in male and female patients in a variety of diagnostic groups. Developmental orderings of symptoms have likewise been found to be related to age at first hospitalization for male and female patients in various diagnostic groups. Some relationships have also been discovered between these symptom orderings and outcome following hospitalization. In cutting across disorders, and pertaining equally to healthy and pathological functioning, the developmental level construct and the concept of competence provide a unitary framework within which continuities can be discerned between discrete syndromes (e.g., schizophrenia and affective disorder) and more generally between adaptive and maladaptive functioning.

The prediction of outcome, along with an understanding of treatment effectiveness,[2] is of primary concern in psychopathology research (Cromwell & Pithers, 1981). What current dysfunctions presage for future life adjustment is certainly an overriding issue for patients, their families, the clinicians who counsel them, and those who are responsible for practical administrative decisions. The research reviewed in this chapter points to the contribution that knowledge about adaptive and nonpsychopathological aspects of functioning makes in the prediction of so central a variable as psychiatric outcome. As Garmezy et al. (1984) noted, the neglect of such "adaptive and resilient . . . attributes . . . may have caused our predictions of disorder to go awry" (p. 109).

Despite the positive relationships that have been discovered among premorbid competence, developmental orderings of symptoms, and prognosis in adult psychopathology, and even though somewhat similar relationships have been observed in longitudinal studies of children, adolescents, and nondisturbed adults (Garmezy et al., 1984; Garmezy & Streitman, 1974; Kohlberg et al., 1972; Vaillant, 1974, 1978), much remains unclear about the processes that underlie competent functioning and contribute to the predictive efficacy of premorbid competence measures.

In the area of adult psychopathology, a number of issues require clarification. One question is why female schizophrenic patients so consistently show higher premorbid competence scores than males (Farina, Garmezy, & Barry, 1963; Farina, Garmezy, Zalusky, & Becker, 1962; Klorman, Strauss, & Kokes, 1977; Lewine, 1981; Zigler & Glick, 1986; Zigler & Levine, 1983). Further, it is unclear whether or not female patients with other psychiatric diagnoses (e.g., affective disorder, personality disorder) also showed better premorbid adjustment than did their male counterparts (Glick et al., 1985; Lewine et al., 1980; Phillips & Zigler, 1964). The data concerning gender differences in premorbid competence have been reviewed and discussed elsewhere (Klorman et al., 1977; Zigler & Glick, 1986). Here, therefore, we only note the importance of this issue and the need for research clarification.

A second issue is that little is understood about what variables mediate the relationship between premorbid competence scores and outcome. As Held and Cromwell (1968) suggested, the global construct of premorbid competence must be replaced by a more specific understanding of the component variables in premorbid competence measures. Factor analyses of the Zigler-Phillips scale (Zigler & Glick, 1986; Zigler & Levine, 1981b) suggest that this measure reflects at least two dimensions: a factor involving instrumental role functioning and the striving for personal advancement (the education and occupation variables) and a factor of social participation (the marital status variable, most frequently paired with age). In regard to the possibility raised by some workers (Nuttall & Solomon, 1965, 1970; Raskin & Golob, 1966;

---

[2] Some treatment implications of the developmental approach to psychopathology were considered by Zigler and Glick (1986), although these have not yet been addressed in research.

Turner & Zabo, 1968; Zigler & Child, 1973) that the predictive efficacy of the premorbid competence scale derives solely from its overlap with socioeconomic status, the factor analytic results suggest that the premorbid competence measure, though including a factor of social class (the education and occupation variables), is broader than socioeconomic status.

A question that has been raised in regard to childhood competence (Garmezy et al., 1979, 1984) and in regard to premorbid competence in adult psychopathology (Zigler & Glick, 1986) is what personality characteristics underlie those attainments that we employ as indicators of coping effectiveness and developmentally higher functioning.

One personality variable considered in our work is the magnitude of an individual's real–ideal self-image disparity. In contrast to psychodynamic formulations, which view increased self-image disparity as a sign of maladjustment (Rogers & Dymond, 1954; Scott, 1958), the developmental position interprets increased real–ideal self-image disparity as a natural concomitant of normal growth and development. A sizable body of data now accords with this developmental view; see Glick and Zigler (1985) for a review of the research and an extended treatment of the rationale underlying the developmental approach to self-image disparity. Higher-premorbid-competence patients exhibit greater real–ideal self-image disparity than do low-competence patients (Achenbach & Zigler, 1963; Mylet et al., 1979). These findings, together with evidence reviewed earlier in the chapter concerning the greater frequency of symptoms indicative of turning against the self in high-developmental-level individuals, suggest a greater incorporation of societal values and consequent social guilt in high-competence patients than in low-competence patients. A pathological solution to life's problems and the institutionalization to which such a solution leads should thus be less acceptable to the high than to the low-premorbid-competence patient. This unacceptability of a pathological solution should result in an improved prognosis.

The contributions of the self-image to competent functioning in childhood and adolescence have been considered by many workers (Garmezy, 1983; Garmezy et al., 1979, 1984; Sundberg, Snowden, & Reynolds, 1978; Zigler & Trickett, 1978), although the emphasis frequently has been on self-esteem rather than on the motivation provided by greater incorporation of societal values. One factor found by Garmezy et al. (1984) to be associated with childhood competence was composed of items concerning both self-esteem and the child's levels of aspiration and achievement motivation. The loading of these items on a single factor suggests a possible relationship between self-esteem (a favorable real self-image) and the presence of internal standards and aspirations (a positive ideal self-image) in healthy functioning. A recent expansion of the developmental interpretation of self-image disparity (Glick & Zigler, 1985) also considered the integration of real and ideal views of the self as indicative of developmentally higher and adaptive functioning.

A number of other personality characteristics frequently have been suggested as factors underlying competence: (a) an internal locus of control or a sense of effectance versus learned helplessness (Baumrind, 1975; Garmezy, 1983; Garmezy et al., 1979; Sundberg et al., 1978; White, 1959; Zigler & Trickett, 1978), (b) impulse control and the ability to delay gratification (Garmezy et al., 1979, 1984; Sundberg et al., 1978), (c) formal cognitive ability and cognitive complexity (Phillips, 1968; Sundberg et al., 1978; Zigler & Trickett, 1978), (d) social cognition and social skills (Garmezy, 1983; Garmezy et al., 1984; Selman & Demorest, 1984), and (e) a sense of social or moral responsibility (Baumrind, 1975; Phillips, 1968).

These variables have most frequently been considered in relation to childhood competence. Each can be interpreted developmentally, and measures have been developed to assess most of these variables in adulthood. Certainly that is the case with self-image and locus of control. Cognitive complexity and social cognition are among the dimensions assessed by Loevinger's test (Loevinger & Wessler, 1970). Relationships have been discovered between level of moral reasoning and premorbid competence in adult psychiatric patients (Quinlan et al., 1980), and the symptom categories employed in our developmental work (e.g., turning against the self versus turning against others, and expression in thought versus action) both tap the dimension of reflectivity versus impulsivity and mirror the distinction in childhood symptomatology between internalizing and externalizing modes of expression.

Closer examination of relationships among these measures and between each measure and premorbid competence in adult psychopathology should enlarge and increase the precision of our understanding of prognosis. Research in this direction should also help to bridge the gap between studies of stress resistance and competence in childhood and adult psychopathology. Garmezy et al. (1979) commented as follows:

If one looks toward research in psychopathology for insights into the nature of competence, the gaze is distracted by two factors: the narrowness of the demographic criteria used and the power of such demography to predict resistance to stress and recovery from the stigma of being a mental patient. Educational achievement, friendships, sexual attachments, and employment history record the statistics of one's adaptation. They share the uncommon virtues of being readily measurable and of bearing some degree of predictive validity. But are there not other manifestations of competence that might have equivalent or perhaps even greater power to provide a perspective into the adult futures of children? (p. 36)

Bridging the gap is essential, because a central task for developmental psychopathology is to understand from an organizational perspective the continuities and discontinuities between childhood and adult adaptation and maladaptation (Cicchetti, 1984; Masten & Garmezy, 1985; Rutter & Garmezy, 1983; Sroufe & Rutter, 1984).

References

Abramson, L., & Sackeim, H. A. (1977). A paradox in depression: Uncontrollability and self-blame. *Psychological Bulletin, 84,* 838–51.

Achenbach, T. (1966). The classification of children's psychiatric symptoms: A factor-analytic study. *Psychological Monographs, 80*(6, Whole No. 615).

Achenbach, T., & Edelbrock, C. (1978). The classification of child psychopathology: A review and analysis of empirical efforts. *Psychological Bulletin, 85,* 1275–301.

Achenbach, T., & Edelbrock, C. (1981). Behavior problems and competencies reported by parents of normal and disturbed children aged four through sixteen. *Monographs of the Society for Research in Child Development, 46*(Serial No. 188).

Achenbach, T., & Zigler, E. (1963). Social competence and self-image disparity in psychiatric and nonpsychiatric patients. *Journal of Abnormal and Social Psychology, 67,* 197–205.

Baumrind, D. (1975). The contributions of the family to the development of competence in children. *Schizophrenia Bulletin, 14,* 12–37.

Bybee, J. (1986). *The self-image and guilt: Relationships to gender, developmental level and classroom behavior.* Unpublished doctoral dissertation, Yale University.

Cicchetti, D. (1984). The emergence of child psychopathology. *Child Development, 55,* 1–7.

Cicchetti, D., & Pogge-Hesse, P. (1982). Possible contributions of the study of organic retardates to developmental theory. In E. Zigler & D. Balla (Eds.), *Mental retardation: The developmental difference controversy* (pp. 227–318). Hillsdale, NJ: Erlbaum.

Cromwell, R. L., & Pithers, W. D. (1981). Schizophrenic/paranoid psychoses: Determining diagnostic divisions. *Schizophrenia Bulletin, 7,* 674–88.

Farina, A., Garmezy, N., & Barry, H., III (1963). Relationship of marital status to incidence and prognosis in schizophrenia. *Journal of Abnormal and Social Psychology, 67,* 624–30.

Farina, A., Garmezy, N., Zalusky, M., & Becker, J. (1962). Premorbid behavior and prognosis in female schizophrenic patients. *Journal of Consulting Psychology, 26,* 56–60.

Finney, J., & Moos, R. (1979). Treatment and outcome for empirical subtypes of alcoholic patients. *Journal of Consulting and Clinical Psychology, 47,* 25–38.

Freud, A. (1952). The mutual influences in the development of ego and id: Introduction to the discussion. *Psychoanalytic Study of the Child, 7,* 42–50.

Garmezy, N. (1970). Process and reactive schizophrenia: Some conceptions and issues. *Schizophrenia Bulletin, 2,* 30–74.

Garmezy, N. (1971). Models of etiology for the study of children who are at risk for schizophrenia. In M. Roff, L. Robins, & M. Pollack (Eds.), *Life history research in psychopathology* (Vol. 2, pp. 9–34). Minneapolis: University of Minnesota Press.

Garmezy, N. (1983). Stressors of childhood. In N. Garmezy & M. Rutter (Eds.), *Stress, coping and development in children* (pp. 43–84). New York: McGraw-Hill.

Garmezy, N., Masten, A., Nordstrom, L., & Ferrarese, M. (1979). The nature of competence in normal and deviant children. In M. W. Kent & J. E. Rolf (Eds.), *The primary prevention of psychopathology: Promoting social competence and coping in children* (Vol. 3, pp. 23–43). Hanover, NH: University Press of New England.

Garmezy, N., Masten, A., & Tellegen, A. (1984). The study of stress and competence in children: A building block for developmental psychopathology. *Child Development, 55,* 97–111.

Garmezy, N., & Rodnick, E. H. (1959). Premorbid adjustment and performance in schizophrenia: Implications for interpreting heterogeneity in schizophrenia. *Journal of Nervous and Mental Disease, 129,* 450–66.

Garmezy, N., & Streitman, S. (1974). Children at risk: The search for antecedents of schizophrenia. Part I. Conceptual models and research methods. *Schizophrenia Bulletin, 8,* 14–90.

Glick, M., & Zigler, E. (1985). Self-image: A cognitive-developmental approach. In R. L. Leahy (Ed.), *The development of the self* (pp. 1–53). New York: Academic Press.

Glick, M., & Zigler, E. (1986). Premorbid social competence and psychiatric outcome in male and female nonschizophrenic patients. *Journal of Consulting and Clinical Psychology*, *54*, 402–3.

Glick, M., Zigler, E., & Zigler, B. (1985). Developmental correlates of age at first hospitalization in nonschizophrenic psychiatric patients. *Journal of Nervous and Mental Disease, 173*, 677–84.

Hartmann, H. (1952). Mutual influences in the development of ego and id. *Psychoanalytic Study of the Child, 7*, 9–30.

Hauser, S. T. (1976). Loevinger's model and measure of ego development: A critical review. *Psychological Bulletin, 83*, 928–55.

Held, J., & Cromwell, R. (1968). Premorbid adjustment in schizophrenia: The evaluation of a method and some general comments. *Journal of Nervous and Mental Disease, 146*, 264–72.

Higgins, J. (1964). The concept of process-reactive schizophrenia: Criteria and related research. *Journal of Nervous and Mental Disease, 138*, 9–25.

Katz, P., Zigler, E., & Zalk, S. (1975). Children's self-image disparity: The effects of age, maladjustment, and action–thought orientation. *Developmental Psychology, 11*, 546–50.

Klorman, R., Strauss, J. S., & Kokes, R. F. (1977). Premorbid adjustment in schizophrenia. III: The relationship of demographic and diagnostic factors to measures of premorbid adjustment in schizophrenia. *Schizophrenia Bulletin, 3*, 214–25.

Knight, R. A., Roff, J. D., Barnett, J., & Moss, J. L. (1979). Concurrent and predictive validity of thought disorder and affectivity: A 22 year follow-up of acute schizophrenics. *Journal of Abnormal Psychology, 88*, 1–12.

Kohlberg, L., LaCrosse, J., & Ricks, D. (1972). The predictability of adult mental health from childhood behavior. In B. Wolman (Ed.), *Manual of child psychopathology* (pp. 1217–84). New York: McGraw-Hill.

Kovacs, M., & Beck, A. T. (1978). Maladaptive cognitive structures in depression. *American Journal of Psychiatry, 135*, 525–33.

Lerner, P. M. (1968). Correlation of social competence and level of cognitive perceptual functioning in male schizophrenics. *Journal of Nervous and Mental Disease, 146*, 412–16.

Lewin, K. (1936). *Dynamic theory of personality*. New York: McGraw-Hill.

Lewine, R. R. J. (1981). Sex differences in schizophrenia: Timing or subtypes? *Psychological Bulletin, 90*, 432–44.

Lewine, R. R. J., Watt, N. F., Prentky, R. A., & Fryer, J. H. (1980). Childhood social competence in functionally disordered psychiatric patients and in normals. *Journal of Abnormal Psychology, 89*, 132–8.

Loevinger, J. (1976). *Ego development*. San Francisco: Jossey-Bass.

Loevinger, J., & Wessler, R. (1970). *Measuring ego development* (Vol. 1). San Francisco: Jossey-Bass.

Luborsky, L., Chandler, M., Auerbach, A., Cohen, J., & Bachrach, H. (1971). Factors influencing the outcome of psychotherapy: A review of quantitative research. *Psychological Bulletin, 75*, 145–85.

Marsh, A., Glick, M., & Zigler, E. (1981). Premorbid social competence and the revolving door phenomenon in psychiatric hospitalization. *Journal of Nervous and Mental Disease, 169*, 315–19.

Masten, A., & Garmezy, N. (1985). Risk, vulnerability and protective factors in developmental psychopathology. In B. B. Lahey & A. E. Kazdin (Eds.), *Advances in clinical child psychology* (Vol. 8, pp. 1–52). New York: Plenum Press.

Möller, H. J., von Zerssen, D., Werner-Eilert, K., & Wüschner-Stockheim, M. (1982). Outcome in schizophrenic and similar paranoid psychoses. *Schizophrenia Bulletin, 8*, 99–108.

Mylet, M., Styfco, S., & Zigler, E. (1979). The interrelationship between self-image disparity and social competence, defensive style, and adjustment status. *Journal of Nervous and Mental Disease, 167*, 553–60.

Noam, G., Hauser, S., Santostefano, S., Garrison, W., Jacobson, A., Powers, S., & Mead, M.

(1984). Ego development and psychopathology: A study of hospitalized adolescents. *Child Development, 55,* 184–94.

Nuttall, R. L., & Solomon, L. F. (1965). Factorial structure and prognostic significance of premorbid adjustment in schizophrenia. *Journal of Consulting Psychology, 29,* 362–72.

Nuttall, R. L., & Solomon, L. F. (1970). Prognosis in schizophrenia: The role of premorbid, social class, and demographic factors. *Behavioral Science, 15,* 255–64.

Phillips, L. (1968). *Human adaptation and its failures.* New York: Academic Press.

Phillips, L., & Rabinovitch, M. (1958). Social role and patterns of symptomatic behavior. *Journal of Abnormal and Social Psychology, 57,* 181–6.

Phillips, L., & Zigler, E. (1961). Social competence: The action–thought parameter and vicariousness in normal and pathological behavior. *Journal of Abnormal and Social Psychology, 63,* 137–46.

Phillips, L., & Zigler, E. (1964). Role orientation, the action–thought dimension and outcome in psychiatric disorder. *Journal of Abnormal and Social Psychology, 68,* 381–9.

Piaget, J. (1951). Principal factors in determining evolution from childhood to adult life. In D. Rapaport (Ed.), *Organization and pathology of thought* (pp. 154–75). New York: Columbia University Press.

Prentky, R. A., Lewine, R. R. J., Watt, N., & Fryer, J. H. (1980). A longitudinal study of psychiatric outcome: Developmental variables vs. psychiatric symptoms. *Schizophrenia Bulletin, 6,* 139–48.

Quinlan, D. M., Rogers, L. R., & Kegan, R. G. (1980, April). *Developmental dimensions of psychopathology.* Paper presented at a meeting of the Eastern Psychological Association, Hartford, CT.

Rapaport, D. (1951). Toward a theory of thinking. In D. Rapaport (Ed.), *Organization and pathology of thought* (pp. 689–730). New York: Columbia University Press.

Raskin, A., & Golob, R. (1966). Occurrence of sex and social class differences in premorbid competence, symptom and outcome measures in acute schizophrenia. *Psychological Reports, 18,* 11–22.

Robins, L. (1966). *Deviant children grown up.* Baltimore: Williams & Wilkins.

Rogers, C. R., & Dymond, R. F. (Eds.). (1954). *Psychotherapy and personality change.* University of Chicago Press.

Rolf, J., & Garmezy, N. (1974). The school performance of children vulnerable to behavior pathology. In D. F. Ricks, A. Thomas, & M. Roff (Eds.), *Life history research in psychopathology* (Vol. 3, pp. 87–107). Minneapolis: University of Minnesota Press.

Rosen, B., Klein, D., & Gittelman-Klein, R. (1971). The prediction of rehospitalization: The relationship between age of first psychiatric treatment contact, marital status and premorbid asocial adjustment. *Journal of Nervous and Mental Disease, 152,* 17–22.

Rosen, B., Klein, D., Levenstein, S., & Shahinian, S. (1969). Social competence and posthospital outcome among schizophrenic and nonschizophrenic psychiatric patients. *Journal of Abnormal Psychology, 74,* 401–4.

Rutter, M., & Garmezy, N. (1983). Developmental psychopathology. In M. Hetherington (Ed.), *Manual of child psychology* (Vol. 4, pp. 775–911). New York: Wiley.

Scott, W. (1958). Research definitions of mental health and mental illness. *Psychological Bulletin, 55,* 1–45.

Selman, R. L., & Demorest, A. P. (1984). Observing troubled children's interpersonal negotiation strategies: Implications of and for a developmental model. *Child Development, 55,* 288–304.

Sroufe, L. A., & Rutter, M. (1984). The domain of developmental psychopathology. *Child Development, 55,* 17–29.

Stoffelmayr, B., Dillavou, D., & Hunter, J. (1983). Premorbid functioning and outcome in schizophrenia: A cumulative analysis. *Journal of Consulting and Clinical Psychology, 51,* 338–52.

Strauss, J. S., & Carpenter, W. T., Jr. (1977). Prediction of outcome in schizophrenia. III: Five year outcome and its predictors. *Archives of General Psychiatry, 34,* 159–63.

Strauss, J. S., & Harder, D. W. (1981). The case record rating scale: A method for rating symptom and social function data from case records. *Psychiatry Research, 4,* 333–45.

Strauss, J. S., Kokes, R. F., Carpenter, W. T., Jr., & Ritzler, B. A. (1978). The course of schizophrenia as a developmental process. In L. C. Wynne, R. L. Cromwell, & S. Matthysse (Eds.), *The nature of schizophrenia: New approaches to research and treatment* (pp. 617–30). New York: Wiley.

Sundberg, N. D., Snowden, L. R., & Reynolds, W. M. (1978). Toward assessment of personal competence and incompetence in life situations. *Annual Review of Psychology, 29,* 179–221.

Turner, R. J., & Zabo, L. J. (1968). Social competence and schizophrenic outcome: An investigation and critique. *Journal of Health and Social Behavior, 9,* 41–51.

Vaillant, G. E. (1971). Theoretical hierarchy of adaptive ego mechanisms. *Archives of General Psychiatry, 24,* 107–18.

Vaillant, G. E. (1974). Natural history of male psychological health. II: Some antecedents of healthy adult adjustment. *Archives of General Psychiatry, 31,* 15–22.

Vaillant, G. E. (1976). Natural history of male psychological health. V: The relationship of choice of ego mechanisms of defense to adult adjustment. *Archives of General Psychiatry, 33,* 535–45.

Vaillant, G. E. (1978). Natural history of male psychological health. VI: Correlates of successful marriage and fatherhood. *American Journal of Psychiatry, 135,* 653–9.

Werner, H. (1948). *Comparative psychology of mental development.* New York: Follett.

Werner, H., & Kaplan, B. (1963). *Symbol formation: An organismic-developmental approach to language and the expression of thought.* New York: Wiley.

White, R. W. (1959). Motivation reconsidered: The concept of competence. *Psychological Review, 66,* 297–333.

Zigler, E., & Child, I. L. (Eds.). (1973). *Socialization and personality development.* Reading, MA: Addison-Wesley.

Zigler, E., & Glick, M. (1986). *A developmental approach to adult psychopathology.* New York: Wiley.

Zigler, E., Glick, M., & Marsh, A. (1979). Premorbid social competence and outcome among schizophrenic and nonschizophrenic patients. *Journal of Nervous and Mental Disease, 167,* 478–83.

Zigler, E., & Levine, J. (1981a). Age of first hospitalization of male and female paranoid and nonparanoid schizophrenics: A developmental approach. *Journal of Abnormal Psychology, 90,* 458–67.

Zigler, E., & Levine, J. (1981b). Premorbid competence in schizophrenia: What is being measured? *Journal of Consulting and Clinical Psychology, 49,* 96–105.

Zigler, E., & Levine, J. (1983). *Gender differences and symptomatology in schizophrenia.* Unpublished manuscript.

Zigler, E., Levine, J., & Zigler, B. (1976). The relation between premorbid competence and paranoid–nonparanoid status in schizophrenia: A methodological and theoretical critique. *Psychological Bulletin, 83,* 303–13.

Zigler, E., & Phillips, L. (1960). Social effectiveness and symptomatic behaviors. *Journal of Abnormal and Social Psychology, 61,* 231–8.

Zigler, E., & Phillips, L. (1961a). Case history data and psychiatric diagnosis. *Journal of Consulting Psychology, 25,* 258.

Zigler, E., & Phillips, L. (1961b). Social competence and outcome in psychiatric disorder. *Journal of Abnormal and Social Psychology, 63,* 264–71.

Zigler, E., & Phillips, L. (1962). Social competence and the process-reactive distinction in psychopathology. *Journal of Abnormal and Social Psychology, 65,* 215–22.

Zigler, E., & Trickett, P. (1978). IQ, social competence and evaluation of early childhood intervention programs. *American Psychologist, 33,* 789–98.

23 Relationships between adult development and the course of mental disorder

John S. Strauss and Courtenay M. Harding

Are adult development and the course of mental disorder related to each other in major ways, or are they mutually irrelevant? Polar opposite views have dominated this issue. From the beginning of modern psychiatry in the nineteenth century, two major theories of the course of mental disorders, the psychoanalytic and the natural history theories, have upheld opposite extremes. The natural history view has suggested that any mental disorder, like any other type of disease, has a natural history, so that developmental considerations are essentially irrelevant to course. In fact, this model states that a disorder or disease process is defined by its course, and that course is what establishes the disease as a diagnostic entity. Thus, for example, in describing dementia praecox – later called the group of schizophrenias by Bleuler (1911/1950) – Kraepelin brought together three rather different syndromes under one diagnostic entity because he believed that they each had a deteriorating course and outcome (Kraepelin, 1902).

In contrast to that approach, the psychoanalytic orientation has suggested that the course of a mental disorder is intimately tied to psychological developmental mechanisms. In this view, the course of a psychosis, for example, has been perceived as the result of the degree to which id, ego, and superego pressures and mechanisms can be reconciled, which in turn is a function of their developmentally influenced strengths and patterns of functioning (Freud, 1924).

In this chapter we shall review briefly some recent major trends in understanding the course of mental disorders and adult aspects of development suggesting that these two domains are neither identical nor totally unrelated. Rather, they appear to reflect two separable processes, processes whose interactions are of major importance for intervention and theory.

The natural history model has lent itself particularly to systematic research.

This report was funded in part by National Institute of Mental Health grants MH-00340 and MH-34365 and by the Schizophrenia Research Program of the Scottish Rite, Northern Masonic Jurisdiction, U.S.A.

514

Because empirical data provide the best foundation for reassessing the polarities related to development and course, we shall trace the available evidence on this issue by starting with the progression of findings that have demonstrated a need to modify the natural history model for the course of mental disorders. Some aspects of the evolution of thinking about development as it relates to evolution in adulthood will then be described to suggest how the two opposite polarities in reality may need to be integrated.

Progress in understanding the course of mental disorders

The natural history model of mental disorders has the research advantage of making it possible to study a group of patients who have been reliably diagnosed and then analyze data from reliably assessed outcomes. In regard to the archetypal example of the natural history model, schizophrenia, it has been possible for investigators to utilize that model and demonstrate several facts about the course and outcome of schizophrenic disorders. First, it has been shown that, in contrast to the central hypothesis of the natural history model, diagnosis is not prognosis (Harding, Brooks, Ashikaga, Strauss, & Breier, 1987; Strauss & Carpenter, 1974b; Vaillant, 1978). It is not possible, in either the short or long term, to define a diagnostic group of patients by a cross-sectional symptom picture that predicts homogeneous outcome (Strauss & Carpenter, 1974a; Bleuler, 1974; Ciompi, 1980; Harding et al., 1987). Although diagnosis is of some importance prognostically – schizophrenic disorders, on the average, have a somewhat poorer prognosis than affective disorders (Tsuang, Woolson, & Fleming, 1979) – there is a wide range of outcome heterogeneity in schizophrenia as in other mental disorders.

In pursuing the natural history model further, studies of variables other than diagnosis as predictors of outcome have shown that there is a range of predictors and outcome characteristics that are important. Outcome itself is not a single entity that can be validly conceptualized as "good" or "bad" with great accuracy. Rather, several relatively independent aspects of outcome functioning exist. These include symptom type and severity, need for hospitalization, social relations functioning, and work functioning (Harding et al., 1987; Strauss & Carpenter, 1972). The characteristics other than diagnosis that predict outcome are approximately equal in prognostic importance to diagnosis itself (Strauss & Carpenter, 1977). They include premorbid social relations functioning, premorbid work functioning, and previous duration of illness. Studies of the relationships among predictors and outcome characteristics have demonstrated that there is a tendency for each of the prognostic characteristics to be the best predictor of its corresponding outcome variable. Thus, for example, premorbid work functioning tends to be the best predictor of work functioning at follow-up. At the same time, in each of these domains (work, social relationships, and symptom severity) there are cross-predictions as well (Strauss & Carpenter, 1972, 1974b, 1977).

The correlation matrix for the various predictor and outcome characteristics involves complex relationships. Based on the findings noted earlier, these relationships have been conceptualized as representing open-linked systems (Strauss & Carpenter, 1974b). For example, social relations functioning has a continuity over time that is probably generated by factors relatively specific to that system. At the same time, social relations functioning influences and is influenced by the functioning of the other systems. Thus, prediction and outcome studies have shown that the natural history model must be broadened to include interactions among various aspects of social functioning and hence a broad range of human behaviors.

Another direction that research on the natural history model has taken has been to incorporate environmental characteristics to explore ways in which they influence the "natural history." Considerable research suggests that stressful life events and family environment have an impact on the course of schizophrenia as well as other kinds of mental disorders (Brown & Birley, 1968; Day, 1981; Brown, Birley, & Wing, 1972; Vaughn & Leff, 1976). The importance of environment in understanding course is also supported by the inclusion of work functioning and social relations functioning in the prediction–outcome equation. Environmental factors in those areas, such as the availability of work and friends or the flexibility of social and occupational systems, are likely to play major roles in how these domains influence the course of disorder.

Finally, more recent empirical studies have suggested that beyond the open-linked systems and the impact of the environment, the person with a mental disorder is not entirely a victim of the disorder, but takes an active role to influence its course (Strauss, Harding, Hafez, & Lieberman, 1987). Patients with schizophrenia have reported in considerable detail the ways in which they have attempted to control, apparently with some success, even the most severe of their symptoms, such as delusions and hallucinations (Breier & Strauss, 1983). Patients also take an active role that is likely to impact on course through their collaboration or refusal to collaborate in treatment and through their selection of situations and settings that are stressful, challenging, and/or supportive.

Thus, recent research has shown that there are many ingredients affecting the course of a mental disorder such as schizophrenia. Many of these characteristics are not exclusively illness-centered, but involve the more general psychological and behavioral styles and skills by which people deal with various personal and social situations. Almost certainly these characteristics evolve at least partially under developmental influences, rather than reflecting processes related only to the endogenous characteristics of a disease.

Evolution of views regarding adult development

As with early concepts concerning the course of mental disorder, early views of development often tended toward defining rigid patterns and progressions. Emulating the biological sciences before them, investigators conceptualized development as an orderly, stepwise, and in most cases hierarchical advancement of the person interacting with the immediate environment (Erikson, 1950; Gesell & Ilg, 1946; Kohlberg, 1969; Piaget, 1947). Stages of development were viewed as closely linked to specific ages.

But more recent research has revealed many hidden complexities where previous views often had suggested the existence of simple linear sequences. Even the physical growth of an infant has been shown to have regressions, spurts, and restructurings (Lampl & Emde, 1983), rather than the neat and continuous course posited by many investigators (e.g., Tanner, 1978). Complexities and discontinuities with wide individual variations have shown up in studies of mental growth as well as physical growth (Emde, Gaensbauer, & Harmon, 1976; Fischer & Corrigan, 1981; McCall, 1979; White, 1970). Gardner (1983) has written of six types of intelligence, and Kaye (1983), Dunn and Kendrick (1983), and others have described the intense impact on growth that is produced by individual–environment interaction (Anastasi, 1958; Bell, 1968; Bronfenbrenner, 1977).

The role of the early strategies in obscuring these diverse factors and the impact of subsequent methodologic advances in demonstrating diversity have been major influences. Various authors have described methodologic problems relating to the impact on findings of task familiarity and experimenter effects (Donaldson, 1978; Rosenthal, 1966), cultural relativity (Brunner, 1983), and decreasing the gap in temporal measurements (Lampl & Emde, 1983).

For adult development, recent findings suggest that the relationships among various relevant factors are far less well understood and far more complex than had originally been imagined. Neugarten (1968), who has extensively pursued a "life cycle" paradigm with attention to specific subgroups, has found no generalizable framework. She has suggested that Jung (1933), Bühler (1933, 1935, 1962), Fromm (1941), Maslow (1954), Peck (1956), and White (1963) have all made significant contributions, but that as yet there is no theory that integrates an understanding of normal adult development. Vaillant has contended that Erikson's concept of the "eight stages of man" (1950) has been the only formal "attempt" at describing adult development. Indeed, Erikson's model has provided the primary basis for Gould (1972), Levinson, Darrow, Klein, Levinson, and McKee (1979), Neugarten (1979), and Vaillant (1977). However, empirical evidence for any of the definitions or orientations is modest. Vaillant and Milofsky (1980) have suggested that there is no model that "commands a consensus" (p. 1348), and Kaplan has referred to current conceptions as only "persuasive definitions" (1980, p. 187).

More recent research suggests that many aspects of adult development may not be tied specifically to age (Neugarten, 1979) and that life cycles may not always proceed in the same sequence (Hirschhorn, 1977). Many discontinuities in adult development have been revealed, such as the acquisition of new family roles when the grown child cares for the parent.

Other complexities of development demonstrated by more recent research include the ways in which various capacities may shift in opposite directions. For example, fluid intelligence can decrease while crystallized intelligence increases (Horn & Donaldson, 1980). In addition, studies have found diversity of aging patterns (Comfort, 1976; Neugarten, 1979), differential impacts of social environments on personality (Elder, 1974), differential impacts of different kinds of work and intellectual functioning (Kohn & Schooler, 1981), birth order effects (Schaie, 1973), and major differences associated with gender (Miller, 1976).

Thus, current thinking about adult development suggests some significant differences from the stereotyped patterns that were originally posited. Different pathways and factors may be especially influential in relation to gender and life history. Plasticity, resilience, discontinuity, regression, advancement, and compensation appear repeatedly across all ages.

Possible relationships between the courses of mental disorders and adult development

There is every reason to believe that people with mental disorders are undergoing developmental progressions and vicissitudes; these people too have developmental processes. The question is how the developmental processes in persons with mental disorders relate to the complex processes involved in the course of disorder itself.

The finding that various social functions were related to the course of schizophrenia first led us to suggest that course might in some way be viewed as a developmental process (Strauss, Kokes, Carpenter, & Ritzler, 1978). This conceptualization has been supported by studies revealing the impact on the course of disorder of environmental factors and the patient's active efforts, all of which have direct relevance to developmental issues as well. Connections between adult development and the course of disorder are further indicated by recent studies of long-term course in schizophrenia (Bleuler, 1974; Ciompi & Müller, 1976; Huber, Gross, Schüttler, & Linz, 1980; Tsuang et al., 1979; Harding et al., 1987). Some of the findings of late-life improvement and recovery have been interpreted as suggesting a possible relationship of developmental phases – whether biological, psychological, social, or some combination – to certain instances of improvement and even recovery.

Two examples illustrate more specifically the kinds of interactions between development and course of disorder that may occur. Cohen et al. (1959) suggested that the psychodynamic meaning of a particular family situation in adulthood, as influenced by child–family constellations, may be an important component in the etiology of mania. We have indicated that the meaning of such family situations and backgrounds may also be related to the course of manic disorders and may interact with pharmacologic interventions to influence recovery and exacerbations (Lieberman & Strauss, 1984).

In another example of adult development/course interaction, a study by Cutler and Strauss (submitted for publication) has suggested that developmental issues may be important in the way that personal successes and failures influence the course of mental disorders. For some of the patients assessed, the realistic implications of their successes that pushed those patients into roles of overwhelming responsibility appeared to be crucial in impeding recovery and promoting relapse. In other instances there were indications that fear about being more successful than one's parent had a toxic effect on potential success.

Based on the considerations cited earlier, the most valid approach for conceptualizing the relationship between adult development and the course of mental disorder may be to see them as separable processes with important interactions. In order to move beyond that general notion, the data can be viewed more specifically in two categories: the elements and the sequences of these systems.

Elements

We noted earlier that certain elements of the individual person are best conceptualized in a developmental framework and can have an impact on the course of mental disorder. These characteristics include such factors as a person's social skills, goals, and preferences regarding place and type of residence. They involve specific phenomena such as the tendency to withdraw, ways of dealing with disappointment, risk taking, modes of seeking support from other people, and passivity, as well as the changes these characteristics undergo over time (Strauss, Rakfeldt, & Harding, 1989).

Such characteristics have many ways of influencing the course of disorder. The tendency to withdraw from challenge, for example, or the desire for interpersonal intimacy, as these vary over developmental phases, may be crucial in determining whether or not a person has the "social supports" necessary to succeed in managing after being discharged from a psychiatric hospital (Breier & Strauss, 1984). The likelihood of dealing successfully with stressful life events is also influenced strongly by the social contacts one has in terms of their number and quality and how they are perceived (Henderson, 1981). Tendencies to "integrate" rather than "seal over" may be influenced by one's personality type and developmental state during the course of disorder (McGlashan, Levy, & Carpenter, 1976).

Sequences

From a temporal perspective, there may be sequences or phases in the evolution of disorder and in development that may interact in important ways. For example, a hospitalized young adult attempting to recover from a psychotic episode who becomes romantically involved with another patient constitutes an important example of the way in which the course of a disorder and one's developmental phase can influence each other. In such an instance, the patient's needs and vulnerabilities related to the disorder and the developmental issue about how to proceed with an intense relationship may impact on each other to influence recovery or recurrence of psychosis and developmental progression.

As another example of interaction between developmental phase and course of disorder, one young adult seen in an intensive follow-up study (Strauss, Hafez, Lieberman, & Harding, 1985) had become psychotic three times, each episode having followed an attempt to return to college. This subject said in the follow-up interview that occurred after his third psychotic break, "I guess I won't ever try to go to college again." Another example may be represented by the findings of improvement or recovery late in the course of disorder for some patients with schizophrenia. Some of these improvements may be attributable to shifts in developmental demands in later life.

It is extremely important to explore further the interface between sequences in development and in psychopathology. Until recently, the possibility that there even existed complex sequences in the course of a psychiatric disorder had generally been deemphasized by the natural history model. That theory, reflected in reports and research, often implied a straight-line course, whether the direction was toward deterioration or improvement. In contrast, clinicians know too well that vicissitudes in the course of a disorder are extremely common, but there has not been a conceptual model or a research base for dealing with these experiences.

Recently, in the intensive follow-up study mentioned earlier in which patients were interviewed repeatedly on a bimonthly basis (Strauss et al., 1985), it was shown that whether considering symptom severity, work function, or social relations, the course of a mental disorder appears never to be linear. Rather, there are major shifts in levels of functioning in each of these areas, often somewhat independent of each other. This complex evolution in the course of disorder and in functioning over time is impressive in the range of variations that occur. Based on these findings and further analysis of the courses observed, we postulated that there exist identifiable regularities in the evolution of disorder and functioning that may reflect underlying psychological, biological, and social processes.

Longitudinal principles at three levels were described. At the most minute level, sequences of individual–environment interactions were noted that reflected both positive (amplifying) and negative (limiting) feedback loops, as well as cumulative impacts. For example, a positive feedback loop occurred for a person who, becoming more depressed, also became more inattentive, then functioned more poorly at work, then became more depressed, then became even more inattentive.

At a second, more macroscopic level, "phases" were described. One example of such a phase is "woodshedding." In this phase there appears to be no gross change in functioning or symptoms, but at more subtle levels the patients make small increments of progress that seem to prepare them for the sudden changes that follow (Sparrow, 1985). At the broadest level, patients have described patterns in which they "sink as low" as they can go and then begin to improve suddenly and rapidly.

Sequences and phases of adult development have been described in more detail than has been accomplished for the course of disorder. Erikson's stages of adult development (1950) and Levinson's "seasons of a man's life" (Levinson et al., 1979) are examples. In these stages there appear to be certain clusters of goals, capacities, options, and vulnerabilities. These characteristics involve many of the same personal factors apparently influencing the course of mental disorder that we enumerated earlier. Considering the probability of complex patterns in the course of disorder and in the evolution of adult development, it seems highly likely that the interactions between course and development are influenced by such sequences and phases in both systems.

Clearly these are complex issues. We are dealing with two complicated systems, each of which is still only poorly understood. Perhaps there are some discoverable critical periods or phase sequences. Or, it may be, as Harding (1986) has suggested, that different phases or the timing of shifts may be out of synchrony with each other. Using Piaget's concepts of vertical and horizontal decalage, it may be possible to begin labeling and studying such dissynchronies.

Implications

There are major implications for research and treatment in viewing adult development and course of mental disorder as two interacting systems. First, such a view suggests that attempting to consider the course of mental disorders without noting the person's developmental situation is inadequate. Furthermore, both the stage of disorder and the developmental trajectory of the person will influence strongly the person's interactions with the environment. Thus, for treatment or research purposes, it is essential to evaluate from a longitudinal perspective where that person and the disorder are in their course and where that trajectory is likely to lead subsequently. Careful evaluation of the characteristics of the disorder, the characteristics of the personal, social, and occupational functioning of the person, and the interactions of these variables over their likely evolutions is a crucial part of such a perspective.

Given the history of excessive anecdotes and theorizing in the fields of psychopathology and development, we shall not at this time cite more examples or attempt to develop further a conceptual superstructure. It may be more useful merely to suggest a focus for an empirically based strategy to pursue these issues so that the interactions and the processes they suggest can be understood more completely. Because a wide range of characteristics and their evolutions and interactions over time are at issue, and all of these are incompletely known, it may be best at this time to focus on the individual person. Whether in research or clinical practice, it may be most important now to begin defining in more detail repeated patterns that might be specific for a given individual. Often this is already carried out clinically, although in relatively unsystematic ways. But defining such patterns has rarely been undertaken in research. Research findings should provide the knowledge that will be essential for improvements in understanding and treatment. Elsewhere we and others (Harding, 1986; Runyan, 1983; Strauss & Hafez, 1981; Strauss, Hafez, Harding, & Lieberman, submitted for publication) have suggested in more detail ways for conducting such research on complex clinical phenomena.

It is not yet possible to predict the course of disorder for a given person or even for a particular diagnostic group. It is possible, however, to provide a perspective for considering the evolution of a mental disorder and of the person who has it. This perspective, including attention to both psychopathologic and developmental issues, is not as simple as one might like. It can, however, teach us what occurs with real patients.

References

Anastasi, A. (1958). Heredity, environment, and the question, How? *Psychological Review, 65,* 197–208.

Bell, R. Q. (1968). A reinterpretation of the direction of effects in studies of socialization. *Psychological Review, 75*(2), 81–95.

Bleuler, E. (1950). Dementia praecox oder die Gruppe der Schizophrenien. In C. Aschaffenburg (Ed.), *Handbuch der psychiatrie* (J. Zinkin, Trans.). New York: International Universities Press. (Original work published 1911)

Bleuler, M. (1974). The long-term course of the schizophrenic psychoses. *Psychological Medicine, 4,* 244–54.

Breier, A., & Strauss, J. S. (1983). Self-control of psychotic disorders. *Archives of General Psychiatry, 40,* 1141–5.

Breier, A., & Strauss, J. S. (1984). Social relationships in the recovery from psychotic disorder. *American Journal of Psychiatry, 141*(8), 949–55.

Bronfenbrenner, U. (1977, July). Toward an experimental ecology of human development. *American Psychologist,* pp. 513–31.

Brown, G. W., & Birley, J. L. T. (1968). Crises and life changes and the onset of schizophrenia. *Journal of Health and Social Behavior, 9,* 203–14.

Brown, G. W., Birley, J. L. T., & Wing, J. K. (1972). Influence of family life on the course of schizophrenic disorders: A replication. *British Journal of Psychiatry, 121,* 241–58.

Brunner, J. (1983). State of the child. *New York Review of Books, 30*(16), 84–9.

Bühler, C. (1933). *Der menschliche Lebenslauf als psychologisches Problem.* Leipzig: S. Hitzel.

Bühler, C. (1935). The curve of life as studied in bibliographies. *Journal of Applied Psychology, 19,* 405–9.

Bühler, C. (1962). Genetic aspects of the self. *Annals of the New York Academy of Sciences, 96,* 730–64.

Ciompi, L. (1980). The natural history of schizophrenia in the long term. *British Journal of Psychiatry, 136,* 413–20.

Ciompi, L., & Müller, C. (1976). *Lebensweg und alter Schizophrenen. Eine katamnestic Lonzeitstudies bis ins Senum.* Berlin: Springer.

Cohen, M. B., Baker, G., Cohen, R. A., Fromm-Reichmann, F., and Weigert, E. V. (1959). An intensive study of twelve cases of manic-depressive psychosis. Psychiatry, *17,* 103–37.

Comfort, A. (1976). *A good age.* New York: Crown.

Cutler, J., & Strauss, J. S. (submitted for publication). The relationship of success and failure to the course of psychiatric disorder.

Day, R. (1981). Life events and schizophrenia: The "triggering" hypothesis. *Acta Psychiatrica Scandinavica, 64,* 97–122.

Donaldson, M. (1978). *Children's minds.* New York: Norton.

Dunn, J., & Kendrick, C. (1983). *Siblings: Love, envy, and understanding.* Cambridge, MA: Harvard University Press.

Elder, G. H., Jr. (1974). *Children of the Great Depression.* University of Chicago Press.

Emde, R. N., Gaensbauer, T., & Harmon, R. (1976). Emotional expression in infancy: A biobehavioral study. *Psychological Issues, 1*(37).

Erikson, E. (1950). *Childhood and society.* New York: Norton.

Fischer, K. W., & Corrigan, R. (1981). A skill approach to language development. In R. Stark (Ed.), *Language behavior in infancy and early childhood* (pp. 245–73). Amsterdam: Elsevier.

Freud, S. (1924). Neurosis and psychosis. In *The standard edition of the complete psychological works of Sigmund Freud* (Vol. 19, pp. 173–9). London: Hogarth Press.

Fromm, E. (1941). *Escape from freedom.* New York: Holt, Rinehart & Winston.

Gardner, H. (1983). *Frames of mind: The theory of multiple intelligence.* New York: Basic Books.

Gesell, A., & Ilg, F. (1946). *The child from five to ten.* New York: Harper.

Gould, R. (1972). The phases of adult life: A study in developmental psychology. *American Journal of Psychiatry, 129,* 521–31.

Harding, C. M. (1986). Speculations on the measurement of recovery from severe psychiatric disorder and the human condition. *Psychiatric Journal of the University of Ottawa, 11*(4), 199–204.

Harding, C. M., Brooks, G. W., Ashikaga, T., Strauss, J. S., & Breier, A. (1987). The Vermont longitudinal study of persons with severe mental illness. II: Long-term outcome of subjects who retrospectively met DSM-III criteria for schizophrenia. *American Journal of Psychiatry, 144*(6), 727–35.

Henderson, S. (1981). Social relationships, adversity and neurosis: An analysis of prospective observations. *British Journal of Psychiatry, 138,* 391–8.

Hirschhorn, L. (1977). Social policy and the life cycle: A developmental perspective. *Social Science Review, 51,* 434–50.

Horn, J. L., & Donaldson, G. (1980). Cognitive development in adulthood. In O. G. Brim & J. Kagan (Eds.), *Constancy and change in human development* (pp. 445–529). Cambridge, MA: Harvard University Press.

Huber, G., Gross, G., Schuttler, R., & Linz, M. (1980). Longitudinal studies of schizophrenic patients. *Schizophrenia Bulletin, 6*(4), 592–605.

Jung, C. G. (1933). *Modern man in search of a soul.* New York: Harcourt, Brace & World.

Kaplan, B. (1980). *The past as prologue, prelude, and pretext.* Paper presented at a symposium on developmental psychology: History of Philosophy and Philosophy of History, Montreal.

Kaye, K. (1983). *The mental and social life of babies: How parents create persons.* University of Chicago Press.

Kohlberg, L. (1969). Stage and sequence: The cognitive-development approach to socialization. In D. A. Goslon (Ed.), *Handbook of socialization theory and research* (pp. 347–480). Chicago: Rand-McNally.

Kohn, M. L., & Schooler, C. (1981). Job conditions and intellectual flexibility: A longitudinal assessment of their reciprocal effects. In E. F. Borgatta & D. J. Jackson (Eds.), *Factor analysis and measurement in sociological research: A multi-dimensional perspective* (pp. 281–313). Beverly Hills: Sage.

Kraepelin, E. (1902). Dementia praecox. In *Clinical psychiatry: A textbook for students and physicians* (6th ed., A. R. Diefendorf, Trans.). New York: Macmillan.

Lampl, M., & Emde, R. N. (1983). Episodic growth in infancy: A preliminary report on length, head circumference, and behavior. In K. W. Fischer (Ed.), *Levels and transitions in children's development* (pp. 21–36). San Francisco: Jossey-Bass.

Levinson, D. J., Darrow, C., Klein, E. B., Levinson, M. H., & McKee, B. (1979). *Seasons of a man's life*. New York: Knopf.

Lieberman, P. B., & Strauss, J. S. (1984). The recurrence of mania: Evnironmental factors and medical treatment. *American Journal of Psychiatry, 141*(1), 77–80.

McCall, R. B. (1979). Qualitative transitions in behavioral development in the first two years of life. In M. H. Bornstein & W. Kessen (Eds.), *Psychological development from infancy: Image to intention* (pp. 183–224). Hillsdale, NJ: Erlbaum.

McGlashan, T. H., Levy, S. T., & Carpenter, W. T. (1976). Integration and sealing over: Clinically distinct recovery styles from schizophrenia. *Archives of General Psychiatry, 32,* 1269–72.

Maslow, A. H. (1954). *Motivation and personality*. New York: Harper & Row.

Miller, J. B. (1976). *Toward a new psychology of women*. Boston: Beacon Press.

Neugarten, B. L. (Ed.). (1968). *Middle age and aging: A reader in social psychology*. University of Chicago Press.

Neugarten, B. L. (Ed.). (1979). Time, age, and the life cycle. *American Journal of Psychiatry, 136*(7), 887–94.

Peck, R. (1956). Psychological developments in the second half of life. In J. E. Anderson (Ed.), *Psychological aspects of aging* (pp. 44–9). Washington, DC: American Psychological Association.

Piaget, J. (1947). *Le jugement et le raisonnement chez l'enfant*. Neuchatel: Delachaux & Niestle.

Rosenthal, R. (1966). *Experimenter effects in behavioral research*. New York: Appleton-Century-Crofts.

Runyan, W. M. (1983). Idiographic goals and methods in the study of lives. *Journal of Personality, 41,* 413–37.

Schaie, K. W. (1973). Methodological problems in descriptive developmental research on adulthood. In J. R. Nesselroade & H. W. Reese (Eds.), *Life-span developmental psychology: Methodological issues* (pp. 253–80). New York: Academic Press.

Sparrow, J. (1985). *Woodshedding: A phase in recovery from psychosis*. Unpublished doctoral dissertation, Yale University School of Medicine.

Strauss, J. S., & Carpenter, W. T. (1972). Prediction of outcome in schizophrenia. I: Characteristics of outcome. *Archives of General Psychiatry, 27,* 739–46.

Strauss, J. S., & Carpenter, W. T. (1974a). Characteristic symptoms and outcome in schizophrenia. *Archives of General Psychiatry, 30,* 429–34.

Strauss, J. S., & Carpenter, W. T. (1974b). Prediction of outcome in schizophrenia. II: Relationships between predictor and outcome variables. *Archives of General Psychiatry, 31,* 37–42.

Strauss, J. S., & Carpenter, W. T. (1977). Prediction of outcome in schizophrenia. III: Five-year outcome and its predictors. *Archives of General Psychiatry, 34,* 159–63.

Strauss, J. S., & Hafez, H. (1981). Clinical questions and "real" research. *American Journal of Psychiatry, 138*(12), 1592–7.

Strauss, J. S., Hafez, H., Harding, C. M., & Lieberman, P. (submitted for publication). Clinical questions and real research. II: Systematic exploratory research.

Strauss, J. S., Hafez, H., Lieberman, P., & Harding, C. M. (1985). The course of psychiatric disorder. III: Longitudinal principles. *American Journal of Psychiatry, 142*(3), 289–96.

Strauss, J. S., Harding, C. M., Hafez, H., & Lieberman, P. (1987). The role of the patient in recovery from psychosis. In J. Strauss, W. Boker, & H. Brenner (Eds.), *Psychosocial management of schizophrenia* (pp. 160–6). Toronto: Huber.

Strauss, J. S., Kokes, R. F., Carpenter, W. T., & Ritzler, B. A. (1978). The course of schizophrenia as a developmental process. In L. C. Wynne, R. L. Cromwell, & S. Matthysse (Eds.), *Nature of schizophrenia: New findings and future strategies* (pp. 617–30). New York: Wiley.

Strauss, J. S., Rakfeldt, J. R., & Harding, C. M. (1989). Psychological and social aspects of negative symptoms. *British Journal of Psychiatry, 155,* Suppl. 7, 128–32.

Tanner, J. M. (1978). *Fetus into man: Physical growth from conception to maturity.* Cambridge, MA: Harvard University Press.

Tsuang, M., Woolson, R., & Fleming, J. (1979). Long-term outcome of major psychoses. I: Schizophrenia and affective disorders compared with psychiatrically symptom-free surgical conditions. *Archives of General Psychiatry, 36,* 1295–301.

Vaillant, G. (1977). *Adaptation to life.* Boston: Little, Brown.

Vaillant, G. (1978). A 10-year follow-up of remitting schizophrenics. *Schizophrenia Bulletin, 4*(11), 78–85.

Vaillant, G. E., & Milofsky, E. (1980). Natural history of male psychological health. IX: Empirical evidence for Erikson's model of the life cycle. *American Journal of Psychiatry, 137*(11), 1348–59.

Vaughn, C. E., & Leff, J. P. (1976). The influence of family and social factors on the course of psychiatric illness: A comparison of schizophrenic and depressed neurotic patients. *British Journal of Psychiatry, 129,* 125–37.

White, R. W. (1963). *The study of lives.* New York: Atherton.

White, S. H. (1970). Some general outlines of the matrix of developmental changes between five and seven years. *Bulletin of the Ortin Society, 20,* 41–57.

A closing note: Reflections on the future

Norman Garmezy

The diversity and richness of the contributions to this volume bespeak a bright future for the study of risk and protective factors in the development of various types of psychopathology. Here are to be found excellent chapters devoted to (a) a range of disorders, including schizophrenia, depression, organic pathology, bulimia, and AIDS, as seen from (b) a varied set of disciplines that include clinical and developmental psychology, epidemiology, neuropsychology, genetics, psychiatry, and pediatric neurology, evaluated (c) by a set of varied investigative modes, including case studies, personality and diagnostic assessments, cross-sectional and longitudinal research methods, and experimental laboratory studies.

How, then, to reflect on the future of a field capable of embracing such heterogeneity? To suggest the content of a future scientific agenda for such an emergent discipline would be presumptuous, but at age 71 that may be permitted, or at least forgivable. A dedication to the view that developmental psychopathology is a wave of the future may be the needed cachet for writing this closing statement.

In any case, if editors command, one has to listen. And these editors – Jon Rolf, Ann Masten, Dante Cicchetti, Keith Nuechterlein, and Sheldon Weintraub – are very special people in my life-span development. Once they were former graduate students, later they were research colleagues, and always they have been valued friends. They have invited me to try my hand at a closing commentary. "Something of a look to the future," one said, which reminded me of some powerful lines by William Wordsworth:

> Enough, if something from our hands have
>   power
> To live and act, and serve the future hour.

The hands and heads of 55 authors, powerful indeed, have fashioned this important look at the emergent field of developmental psychopathology – a field that, as editor Cicchetti has indicated, has powerful links to an illustrious

527

past illumined by the likes of Piaget, Werner, Weiss, the Freuds, James, Darwin, Jackson, Goldstein, Shakow, Bowlby, and Meyer, that enjoys a rich present, revealed by the contributors to this volume and by numerous others, and that looks to future enrichment of our knowledge of the etiology, assessment, classification, and treatment of the organic, emotional, social, and cognitive disorders of infancy, childhood, and adolescence.

Over the decade ahead, our growing knowledge of risk and protective factors and the mechanisms and processes that underlie their expression undoubtedly will play an important role in a maturing science of developmental psychopathology.

To suggest the content of the future scientific agenda, however, given the current diversity of content that marks the field, as witness this volume, is a difficult venture. If I suggest some likely directions for the future, these stem from a view framed by the past 28 years of Minnesota-based research, initially with children presumed to be vulnerable to psychopathology, and more recently with more fortunate children whose lives are marked by resistance to disordered behavior and by resilience and retained competence, despite the presence of highly stressful and disadvantaging circumstances.

Now, with all consumer warnings set out, here is my catalogue of a number of research areas that may warrant extended study in the field of developmental psychopathology, focused on the search for risk and protective factors and mechanisms (Garmezy, 1988).

1. There is a need for competing models of the development of psychopathology that can serve as the basis for definitive empirical tests of their comparative power. Two decades ago, Zubin (1969), in outlining specific scientific models for psychopathology in the 1970s, listed the developmental model as one of six then current that he thought worthy of definitive investigation (the others were the ecological, learning, genetic, internal environment, and neurophysiological models). It is interesting to reconsider Zubin's insightfulness and circumspection with regard to the characteristics of the developmental model:

The developmental model of aetiology is built on the assumption that mental disease develops as a result of some specific deprivation or interference during a critical period of development, when the resulting deficit is crucial.

Identification of the critical periods of development is still moot, with research covering the entire ontogenetic range: foetal and neonatal periods, childhood, adolescence, adulthood, middle age, and old age. Moreover, the values of the variables that may affect behavior at the critical junctures are still to be specified. At present, such obvious factors as toxemia during the gestation period, restricted early experience, limited peer interaction during early childhood, deviant friendship patterns during adolescence, poor psychosexual adjustment patterns, poor vocational adjustment patterns, unsatisfactory role development in family, vocation, and society, and social isolation in old age can be tabulated as important *potential* causal agents. . . .

Since the developmental model represents the unfolding of the individual, it seems that in this model the nexus between personality and psychopathology might be found. In tracing back toward this nexus, we are really entering into the anamnesis or history of the individual, and this aspect of the investigation of psychopathology is one of those most urgently in need of further research and instrumentation, as is prospective research in this area. . . .

The deviant behavioral responses elicited by developmental factors are difficult to separate from the deviations in the factors themselves. For example, how much of the child's withdrawing behavior is a natural consequence of the type of friendship patterns he is exposed to, and how much of it is endogenous. Here again, we must have independent measures of parameters of the environment that are still unidentified. . . .

Finally it should be pointed out that certain kinds of developmental models may be considered as special cases of the ecological model. In a model, for example, that postulates weak family structure – e.g., broken homes – as crucial for the development of psychopathology, what is really being suggested is that childhood is an optimal period for *transmitting* certain effects from the socio-cultural environment to the individual. Such a conceptualization may lead one to consider the role of learning in relation to psychopathology. (pp. 289–91)

Zubin, one of the most distinguished experimental psychopathologists of this century, had anticipated a whole set of requirements for sound model building and tests of the efficacy of its formulations: (a) the extension of research studies that would encourage attention to the use of follow-back, follow-up, and longitudinal study methods to collect data to test the predictive power of the model; (b) a broad attention to research designs that would include detailed naturalistic observations, case studies, and experimental laboratory studies; (c) a "life-span developmental" view of the growth and adaptation of the human organism. But perhaps most important of all, by perceiving the linkage of development to learning, genetics, ecology, and the biology of the organism, Zubin provided an early glimpse of the integrative power of the developmental model.

Within one year of Zubin's presentation, a major volume edited by Goulet and Baltes (1970) provided the opening shot of a life-span developmental psychology heard 'round the world. Now, with the passage of two decades, the linkage of psychopathology and life-span developmental study is under way, with benefits to be derived from an integration of the two domains.

But the formulations of requisite variables, influencing age contexts, the long-term consequences of identified risk and protective factors, tests of specific hypotheses generated by the model, and comparisons of the efficacy of competing models should be part of the research agenda; that there will be competition among models is neither to be decried nor discouraged. The power of a model lies in its predictive validity, not in the expostulatory power of the model's creator.

Graduate students over the years who have taken my introductory course in psychopathology will recall my continued citation of philosopher of science Abraham Kaplan's view of the competitive role played by models: "The dangers are not in working with models, but in working with too few, and those too much alike, and above all, in belittling any efforts to work with anything else" (Kaplan, 1964, p. 293).

2. There is a need for studies of the physical, cognitive, social, and emotional developments among groups of normal children, children at risk for specific disorders (e.g., antisocial disorder, affective disorders, and schizophrenia) and children already manifestly disturbed. It is particularly important that we include these groups within the same programmatic studies of risk and protective factors, rather than seeking to piece together independent normative and pathological studies to generate inferences of similarities and differences that presumably exist among these groups.

3. Rutter's view that the significant studies to be done in risk research are those that seek to discover the mechanisms and processes that underlie the operation of risk and protective factors is a critically important point. In addition to a suggested method for doing so provided by Rutter in his chapter on psychosocial resilience and protective mechanisms (chapter 9, this volume), his call for the search for underlying processes deserves attention, as do the means for accomplishing this feat. How to generate the needed information from which to infer process is the critical issue. Two examples, social class and intelligence, suggest that an attempt at decomposition or disaggregation of identifiable risk and protective factors may be one avenue into identifying relevant mechanisms. Two examples will suffice.

Social class is the great cutting variable of sociology. Numerous epidemiological studies have identified low social class status as a predisposing risk factor in several mental disorders. By contrast, high social status appears to operate as a protective factor to inhibit the expression of seriously disordered behavior. The broader issue is not the status element per se, but rather the underlying processes implicated in living under conditions of disadvantage. For Block (1971), this requires a "psychologizing" of the social class variable. To do so, questions must be asked: What are the constituent components of low social class status (e.g., overcrowding, inadequate nutrition, poor health care, the absence of positive role models, the compounding of anxieties) that relate to actualized risk or escape from risk? The analysis and linkage of the components of lower socioeconomic status may provide insights into the underlying processes inherent in positive and negative social class variants that can heighten or inhibit dispositional factors operative in disordered behavior. To this may well be added the necessary analysis of cultural variants that are so characteristic of a pluralistic America.

Intelligence, too, can be decomposed to suggest processes that may operate to facilitate protection against the adverse effects of severe stress. Pellegrini, Masten, Garmezy, and Ferrarese (1987) have reported a "social comprehension" factor that relates to competence under stress. Strongly correlated with IQ, this composited measure contributes significantly to both social and academic competence, strong mediators of the quality of engagement of the child in the world of school and peers. Although data are not available as to a potential relationship between social comprehension and Sternberg's conception of "practical intelligence" (Sternberg, 1986), this may be a direction that can unlock specific processes that affect solutions to problems induced by exposure to powerful stressors. A focus in research aimed at elaborating those components of intelligence that are instrumental for the child in meeting and overcoming stress is essential to help in predicting adaptive behavior under stress.

4. There is a great need to track the psychophysiological and neuropsychological processes involved in attributes such as attentional functioning on which the development and acquisition of multiple types of competencies depend and that provide a protective screen against various types of stressors. Some research of this type has had a demonstrable payoff in studies of children at risk for schizophrenia; extension to other mental and behavioral disorders of childhood seems warranted.

5. It is critical that studies of the biology of risk and protective factors proceed apace with psychological investigations. Important in this domain is the study of the biology of temperament and its phenotypic transformations over time, a systematic effort to piece together genetic contributions in the formation of personality traits, including predispositions toward risk for a variety of disordered behaviors, as adduced from patterns of familial inheritance, family pedigree analysis, adoption and twin studies, and so forth.

6. Necessary to advances in risk research is the mapping of significant events in lives through time, particularly those that appear to be in temporal proximity to, and correlated with, so-called turnarounds, as reflected in striking changes in adaptational trajectories over time.

7. The usual image of longitudinal studies is that of a long-term commitment that requires years of investigation before ultimate outcomes are observed. However, a case can be made for short-term longitudinal studies to study changes in life-span developmental trajectories. The context for such studies can be the occurrence of specific stressful major life events that disrupt an individual's pattern of positive or negative adaptation. For example, the Minnesota studies have suggested that competent children who are positively and actively "engaged" in classroom and peer activities under low stress have counterparts who, under high stress, disengage themselves from these positive activities. By contrast, low-competence children who tend to be disruptive at low stress levels have counterparts who tend to be more disruptive under conditions of high stress (Masten et al., 1988). This has led us to hypothesize that loss of adaptive functioning, though it may be an indicator of the consequences of stress, may not be an indicator of one's ability to overcome stress. Equally important may be the rapidity with which competence functions show recovery to an earlier prestress basal level. This type of study has not been performed, but systematic exploration of speed of recovery may reveal the distinguishing characteristics of children and adolescents whose multiform

competencies (e.g., cognitive, social, emotional) stand in contrast to those of others marked by a heavier weighing of risk components and a lesser ability to recover from strong negative life events.

8. The term "coping" is a prominent construct in considering the efficacy of an individual's response to stress. Certainly there is no shortage of volumes devoted to the topic (Field, McCabe, & Schneiderman, 1985; Garmezy & Rutter, 1983; Lazarus & Folkman, 1984; Levine & Ursin, 1980; Moos, 1977, 1986; Murphy & Moriarty, 1976). But coping as a construct leaves much to be desired. Its limitation resides in the quality of the instruments for measuring coping, their lack of sound psychometric properties, the failure to develop adequate standardization data, and the questionable assumption of transsituational generalizations that can be drawn from test responses to hypothetical or even actual situations. The problem of response generalization is particularly interesting. One would expect resilient persons to have a broader repertoire of response solutions in stressful situations (other than extraordinary traumas). Data from Pellegrini et al. (1987) on the social problem-solving capabilities of competent children under stress are supportive of this contention. Transsituational stress responsiveness among children of varied competencies remains an area lacking an empirical base. Thus, though coping is a construct of potential significance, its systematic exploration has yet to appear in our literature. There is a critical need to render the coping construct operational, to create a major instrument marked by rigorous standardization, adequate psychometric properties, and strong evidence of the instrument's reliability and validity. That would be a basic step forward in the creation of a coping measure with which to study individual reactivity to truly stressful situations.

There are undoubtedly many other areas that the various authors of this volume would cite as future directions for research. Such market lists are valuable starting points for moving forward in our investigations of risk and protective factors. The dedication of numerous researchers, including those represented in this volume, provides a favorable prognosis for the future. Developmental psychopathology and the study of reactivity to disadvantaging statuses and circumstances appear to be in good hands.

Finally, an effort to express my deep appreciation to the many people who have played important roles in my professional and personal life: To the editors of Cambridge University Press, Susan Milmoe and Helen Wheeler, I offer my deep appreciation for the volume itself and the splendid cocktail party and dinner held at SRCD's biennial meeting in 1987. A "thank you," also, to the many authors and to the editors of this volume, who have been colleagues and partners over an exciting four decades of research. To all of them goes my gratitude for making the past such an exciting scientific venture.

I have had the good fortune to have been affiliated with two supportive university departments of psychology, first at Duke University for 10 years and then at the University of Minnesota for 28 additional years. To my many colleagues and students in those settings I express my gratitude for having helped to make the academy the splendid world it is. Four mentors have played important roles in providing assistance, insight, and understanding: David Shakow, Eliot Rodnick, Michael Rutter, and I. E. Farber. To my former and current graduate students goes my deep appreciation for the collaborations we have enjoyed and for their reversal of the teacher–student role on numerous occasions.

How can one fully express appreciation to faculty colleagues who shared in three separate research adventures: Eliot Rodnick in the Duke studies of motivational factors in schizophrenia deficits; Vernon Devine in the Minnesota studies of children vulnerable to psychopathology; and, currently, Ann Masten and Auke Tellegen in our studies of stress-resistant children. In each of these research programs there were many doctoral student colleagues whose individual dissertations brought understanding and growth to our efforts.

Perhaps most important of all, there is one who has provided a lifetime of support and encouragement. She is known to all as Edie Garmezy, my lifelong companion, whose love has been truly longitudinal in scope and evident over all those risk elements that inhered in military service during World War II, in graduate school, in the early and later years of an academic career, and into this initial year of retirement. Thanks, too, to some special people known as Kathy, Andy, Pat, Larry, Lisa, Grant, Alex, Adam, and Benjamin Garmezy – all part of a wonderful lifetime of joy and zest in family, in friendships, in teaching, and in research.

References

Block, J. (1971). *Lives through time.* Berkeley, CA: Bancroft.

Field, T. M., McCabe, P. M., & Schneiderman, N. (Eds.). (1985). *Stress and coping.* Hillsdale, NJ: Erlbaum.

Garmezy, N. (1988). Longitudinal strategies, causal reasoning and risk research: A commentary. In M. Rutter (Ed.), *Studies of psychosocial risk: The power of longitudinal data* (pp. 29–44). Cambridge University Press.

Garmezy, N., & Rutter, M. (Eds.). (1983). *Stress, coping and development in children.* New York: McGraw-Hill.

Goulet, L. R., & Baltes, P. B. (Eds.). (1970). *Life-span developmental psychology: Research and theory.* New York: Academic Press.

Kaplan, A. (1964). *The conduct of inquiry.* San Francisco: Chandler Publishing Co.

Lazarus, R. S., & Folkman, S. (1984). *Stress, appraisal, and coping.* New York: Springer.

Levine, S., & Ursin, H. (Eds.). (1980). *Coping and health.* New York: Plenum Press.

Masten, A. S., Garmezy, N., Tellegen, A., Pellegrini, D. S., Larkin, K., & Larsen, A. (1988). Competence and stress in school children: The moderating effects of individual and family qualities. *Journal of Child Psychology and Psychiatry, 29,* 745–64.

Moos, R. H. (Ed.). (1977). *Coping with physical illness.* New York: Plenum Press.

Moos, R. H. (Ed.). (1986). *Coping with life crises.* New York: Plenum Press.

Murphy, L. B., & Moriarty, A. E. (1976). *Vulnerability, coping, and growth.* New Haven: Yale University Press.

Pellegrini, D. S., Masten, A. S., Garmezy, N., & Ferrarese, M. J. (1987). Correlates of social and academic competence in middle childhood. *Journal of Child Psychology and Psychiatry, 28,* 699–713.

Sternberg, R. J. (1986). Introduction: The nature and scope of practical intelligence. In R. J. Sternberg & R. K. Wagner (Eds.), *Practical intelligence* (pp. 1–10). Cambridge University Press.

Zubin, J. (1969). The biometric approach to psychopathology – revisited. In J. Zubin & C. Shagass (Eds.), *Neurobiological aspects of psychopathology* (pp. 281–309). New York: Grune & Stratton.

Author index

535

Subject index